THE PRACTICE OF
MARKETING
RESEARCH

THE PRACTICE OF
MARKETING
RESEARCH

James E. Nelson
The University of Colorado at Denver

KENT PUBLISHING COMPANY

A Division of Wadsworth, Inc.

BOSTON, MASSACHUSETTS

Senior Editor: David S. McEttrick
Production Editor: Nancy J. Crow
Interior and Cover Designer: Catherine L. Dorin
Production Coordinator: Linda Card

Kent Publishing Company
A Division of Wadsworth, Inc.

Printed in the United States of America

1 2 3 4 5 6 7 8 9 — 85 84 83 82

Library of Congress Cataloging in Publication Data

Nelson, James E. (James Earle), 1943–
  The practice of marketing research.

  Includes bibliographies and index.
  1. Marketing research. I. Title.
HF5415.2.N39   658.8′3   81–20742
ISBN 0–534–01068–7   AACR2

Preface

This text provides an up to date introduction to the uses and techniques of marketing research. It represents a mainstream approach to the topic, with a strong emphasis on practical aspects.

APPROACH

The text's organization reflects the research process. Part I introduces the role of marketing research and overviews the entire process. Parts II–VI focus on each stage within the process—defining the research problem, asking and evaluating research questions, sampling, analyzing data and communicating research results. Some instructors may prefer to cover Part IV (Sampling) before Part II (Asking and Evaluating Research Questions), reasoning that researchers must know sampling details before drafting questions. Others will prefer the sequence above, reasoning that researchers must know which questions they will ask before estimating sample size. Either sequence works; both reflect research practice.

ORGANIZATION

   Each chapter contains numerous examples that clarify concepts and illustrate practice. All chapters contain a listing of "key terms" and substantive discussion questions. Chapters 12–19 also include short problems on sampling and data analysis. The text also contains twenty cases of varying length and complexity, covering a variety of research problems in both the private and public sectors. A companion student guide/research manual, *Exercises in Marketing Research*, also written by the author, provides additional skill development and field-work material for use in courses with a "hands on" orientation.

HIGHLIGHTS

A few other points deserve special mention. The entire manuscript was class-tested not once, but twice, guaranteeing fewer errors and better clarity of presentation—particularly in the statistical chapters. Chapter 4 (Secondary Data) includes unique and helpful "Search Processes" for finding and using relevant data from government, trade, and academic sources, rather than simply cataloguing them. Chapter 12 includes a brief, convenient review of basic statistics, serving as a short "refresher course" for readers whose statistical skills are rusty. Chapters 15–19 (Analyzing Data) discuss techniques using an organization by research purpose and measurement level, so students can more easily identify and apply the proper technique—and better understanding of the relationship between measurement level and data analysis.

ACKNOWLEDG-MENTS

Appearances to the contrary, no one writes a book alone. Three typists capably and cheerfully typed the manuscript, several times, at odd hours: Charlene Duncan, Shirley Lukkason, and Sheila Whitesitt. Many colleagues contributed through their work as summarized in marketing and research related journals, texts, and other publications. Several others contributed by providing cases and Chapter 21. Ten provided insightful and incisive reviews of the manuscript: Leland L. Beik (Pennsylvania State University), Mary C. Gilly (Southern Methodist University), Michael J. Houston (University of Wisconsin, Madison), Roger Kerin (Southern Methodist University), Richard J. Lutz (University of California, Los Angeles), J. Barry Mason (University of Alabama), Kenneth C. Schneider (Saint Cloud State University), and Bruce L. Stern (Portland State University). My editor, Dave McEttrick, helped greatly to organize the book. To these people and the many others who over the years clarified my thinking about marketing research, my appreciation. And to those I have failed despite numerous footnotes to give credit where credit is due, my apologies.

I am grateful to the Literary Executor of the late Sir Ronald A. Fisher, F.R.S., to Dr. Frank Yates, F.R.S., and to Longman Group Ltd., London, for permission to reprint Tables III, IV, and V from their book *Statistical Tables for Biological, Agricultural and Medical Research* (6th ed., 1974). I also want to thank the marketing faculty at the University of Minnesota for their understanding and support for two years. In particular, I want to thank Bill Rudelius and Dick Cardozo for two conversations that took place very early in the writing. Finally, I want to thank my family, Cody and Ian, for a conversation that never took place.

James E. Nelson
Denver, Colorado

Contents

PART III

Asking and Evaluating Research Questions   173

CHAPTER 7

Questions of Fact: Behavior and Socioeconomic Characteristics   175

CHAPTER 8

Questions of Psychological Characteristics: Qualitative Data   199

CHAPTER 9

Questions of Psychological Characteristics: Quantitative Data   215

PART VI
Communicating Results and Research Ethics 571

CHAPTER 20
Interpreting and Reporting Research Results 573

CHAPTER 21
Ethics and Marketing Research 591

Cases for Part VI 618

Appendix Tables 637

Glossary 645

Index 657

THE PRACTICE OF
MARKETING
RESEARCH

Introduction to Marketing Research

Introducing Marketing Research

Marketing research is:

Johnson's Wax completing over fifty studies of consumers, advertisements, and product formulas over three years before introducing Agree Shampoo in 1978. Study results described consumers' hair care practices, their concern for the "greasies," and their favorable reaction to the shampoo itself.[1]

Two researchers investigating prices of products sold to the U.S. Air Force, those sold under sole-source conditions and those sold under competitive conditions. Results showed that competitive conditions reduced prices between 10.8 and 17.5%.[2]

Jewel Food Companies in Chicago recording license numbers of cars parked in the lots of its stores. Using license numbers to identify shoppers and using shoppers' addresses in a U.S. Census Bureau computer program, researchers were able to describe each store's market in terms of its geographic area and socioeconomic characteristics.[3]

---

[1] *Marketing News* (January 12, 1979), pp. 14–15.

[2] David N. Burt and Joseph E. Boyett, Jr., "Reduction in Selling Price after the Introduction of Competition," *Journal of Marketing Research* 16 (May 1979): 275.

[3] David J. Blum, *Wall Street Journal* (March 26, 1980), p. 42.

Lone Star Brewery measuring reactions of beer drinkers to phrases, music, and actors before producing a television commercial. After the commercial appeared, consumers actually called stations with requests to rerun it and bought Lone Star Beer at a rate that reversed a ten-year sales decline.[4]

We deduce from these examples that marketing research is research on any aspect of marketing. More rigorously, we define **marketing research** as the systematic, impartial, and complete design, execution, and reporting of investigations to help solve product, price, distribution, and promotion problems.

Let us examine key words in the definition more closely. Marketing research is systematic, impartial, and complete. *Systematic* means that marketing research studies use detailed designs to guide activities from beginning to end. *Impartial* means that studies proceed objectively. *Complete* means that studies continue until problems are solved. Together, systematic, impartial, and complete mean that marketing research studies proceed scientifically, in just the same way as research studies in physics, chemistry, and other physical sciences.[5] Finally, marketing research helps *solve problems;* it exists only when specific problems in marketing management exist. We consider the nature of these problems as marketing management decisions in our next section.

Marketing Research Serves Marketing Management

Marketing research provides information useful in making marketing management decisions.

MARKETING MANAGEMENT DECISIONS

Problems connected with marketing goals, strategies, tactics, and actions require marketing management decisions. **Marketing goals** describe measurable end states or standards of performance that marketing organizational units try to attain by an identified time. Examples of such goals follow:

- Maintain a 10 percent market share in the Western region during 1982.
- Reduce selling costs 5 percent compared to the fourth quarter of 1981.

---

[4]Thomas E. Turicchi, *Marketing News* (September 1, 1976), p. 10.

[5]For an expanded discussion on the scientific method and marketing research, see Harper W. Boyd, Jr., Ralph Westfall, and Stanley F. Stasch, *Marketing Research: Text and Cases* 4th ed. (Homewood, Ill.: Richard D. Irwin, 1977), Chap. 2.

- Increase consumer brand awareness to 40 percent by the end of the second quarter.
- Attain distribution in 75 percent of all retail food outlets in Wisconsin by the end of 1982.

We can see that marketing goals apply to sales, marketing costs, consumers, and other aspects of marketing. Realistic marketing goals depend on marketing research information; so do accurate estimates of organizational performance on these goals.

Marketing strategies are determined after goals are set. **Marketing strategies** describe long-term commitments of the firm's resources to meet marketing goals. They indicate the means by which ends will be achieved. For example, a firm might describe its product strategy as sales maintenance through product line extension. Accordingly, the firm would remain in existing markets and add new and improved models of existing products. Another firm might have its product strategy as sales growth through product differentiation in related markets. To implement this strategy, the firm would spend more money on research and development and produce new products from related technologies. Other firms might follow still different product strategies.[6] Of course, all these firms would also employ strategies covering other aspects of marketing—pricing, distribution, and promotion. All firms benefit from marketing research information, which they need to select, execute, and evaluate their strategies.

Marketing tactics follow marketing strategies. **Marketing tactics** describe shortrun plans and policies consistent with marketing goals and strategies. They give more specific direction to marketing managers. For example, promotion tactics might state that a firm should:

1. advertise only in magazines and on network television;
2. assign sales personnel only to territories showing a minimum market potential of $400,000; and
3. employ couponing only during one quarter of the year.

Again, other tactics would apply to other aspects of marketing. And, again, all marketing tactics benefit from marketing research in their selection, execution, and evaluation.

Finally, marketing management decisions also address marketing actions. **Marketing actions** consist of specific things done to implement the marketing goals, strategies, and tactics. With reference to our first promotion tactic in the preceding list, a manager might take such marketing actions as these:

---

[6]George S. Day, "A Strategic Perspective on Product Planning," *Journal of Contemporary Business* (Spring 1975), pp. 1–34.

1. advertise only in *Better Homes and Gardens* and *Newsweek;*

2. place only half-page advertisements; and

3. advertise product reliability as the product's primary advantage.

These and other marketing actions undertaken for any aspect of marketing always benefit from marketing research information.

Figure 1.1 summarizes the foregoing description of marketing management. Marketing research information applies at all points in the diagram.

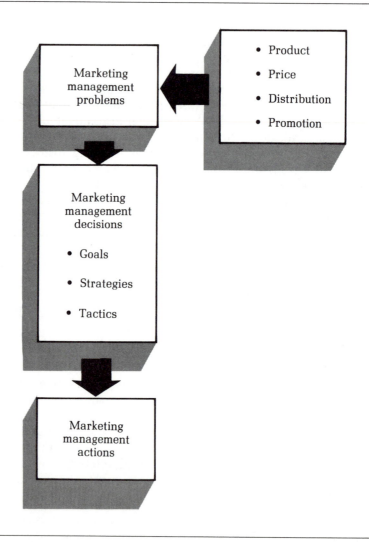

FIGURE 1.1
The nature of marketing management

Another way of describing the nature of marketing management (and, thus, the nature of marketing research information) is in terms of marketing management functions. Marketing management functions separate into four categories: planning, organizing, leading, and controlling.[7] Planning consists of present-day activities that specify both future activities and future performance. Resulting plans may apply to next week, next quarter, next year, the next five years, or even to the next twenty years. To prepare such plans requires marketing research information and marketing research analysis.

The organizing function in marketing management consists of analyses of and decisions about tasks that people perform in the firm. For example, one firm may divide marketing responsibilities by product lines, allowing each manager to operate much like a president of a one-product firm. Another may divide responsibilities by customer class, allowing each manager to make decisions for all products sold to accounts in his or her class. Yet another may assign responsibilities by marketing function, giving all advertising decisions to one manager, all pricing decisions to another, and so on. Organizing analyses and decisions occur infrequently in most firms. When they do, marketing research assists by collecting information on organizational structure and organizational effectiveness in similar firms.

The leading function in marketing management involves getting organizational tasks accomplished through others. Leading activities include establishing reward systems that motivate and encourage all marketing personnel. They include giving direction and guidance to subordinates. Most important, they include numerous implementing decisions that operationalize marketing strategies and tactics. Marketing research provides information useful in selecting rewards systems, determining the nature that direction and guidance should take for each subordinate, and making operational decisions.

The controlling function in marketing management detects differences between planned and actual performance. Most control activities in the firm regularly produce performance information as monthly sales figures, quarterly market share estimates, and the like. However, these regularly appearing reports exemplify not marketing research but a marketing information system (MKIS), a topic we shall take up later in the chapter. Other ad hoc control activities exist as marketing research studies; these, too, estimate results of marketing strategies, tactics, and actions but on a nonrecurring basis.

We can see that planning, organizing, leading, and controlling really describe rather universal management functions. For example, a financial manager may plan the firm's capital requirements for the next budget period; a research and development manager may organize a technical development team for a new production process; a production manager may direct foremen to schedule overtime; and a personnel manager may

---

[7]James A. F. Stoner, *Management* (Englewood Cliffs, N.J.: Prentice-Hall, 1978), pp. 17–19.

control for equitable hiring practices. Only when these universal management functions apply to marketing problems—those associated with products, prices, distribution, or promotion—do we have marketing management.

Our model of the nature of marketing management appears more completely in Figure 1.2.

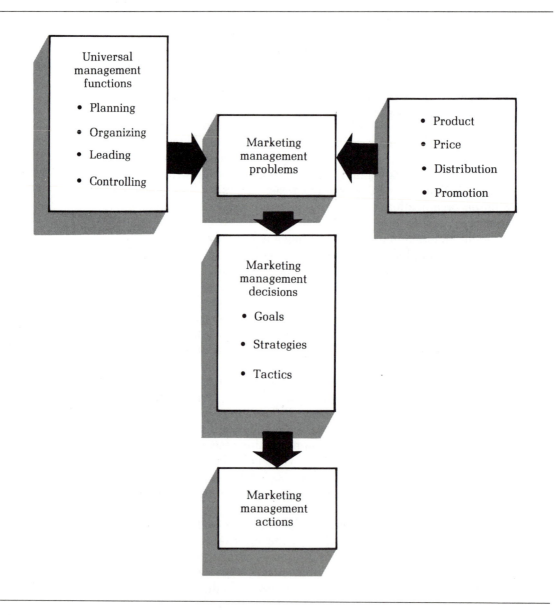

FIGURE 1.2
The nature of marketing management (expanded)

All marketing management problems, decisions, and actions take place in three rich environments—an internal marketing environment, an internal organization environment, and an external organization environment. Although we will go into them more completely in Chapter 3, we learn a little about the three environments now so we can use them in our consideration of the nature of marketing research information. **MARKETING MANAGEMENT ENVIRONMENTS**

An **internal marketing environment** encompasses whatever occurs inside the marketing organizational unit. It is the milieu that contains decisions, strategies, actions, budgets, personnel, histories, philosophies, and other concepts that apply to products, prices, distribution, and promotion. This internal marketing environment must absorb the many consequences of a marketing action. Estimates of such consequences (either before or during the action) and analyses after the action often require marketing research information.

An **internal organization environment** encompasses the other (nonmarketing) phenomena inside the firm. Its much larger boundaries surround such things as corporate objectives, corporate strategies, and management practices and performance in other specialized areas of the firm: finance, research and development, production, and personnel. This environment, too, would feel the impact of a marketing action; estimates of the impact improve with marketing research information.

An **external organization environment** encompasses conditions outside the firm. It includes such factors as competitors, consumer segments, suppliers, technology, economic conditions, and governments. Here, marketing management interest often lies less with estimating the impact of marketing actions on these factors than with just the opposite—that is, the environmental factors decidedly influence the success or failure of all marketing actions. Thus, before making decisions, marketing managers need to understand the external organization environment completely; they rely heavily on marketing research information.

Another way, then, of describing the nature of marketing management (and of marketing research information) is in terms of these three environments. We add to our model one more time, as shown in Figure 1.3.

Marketing research helps solve problems in marketing management. What problems? The problems pertain to products, prices, distribution channels, and promotion and require managers to plan, organize, lead, and control. In particular, the problems relate to marketing goals, strategies, tactics, and actions. The marketing problems occur inside the marketing organizational unit, inside the organization itself, and inside an external environment. Marketing research helps solve these problems by comparing alternate solutions and recommending courses of action. It also helps solve these problems by assessing the effects of previously implemented solutions. **SUMMARY**

One final point: throughout this discussion we have assumed that

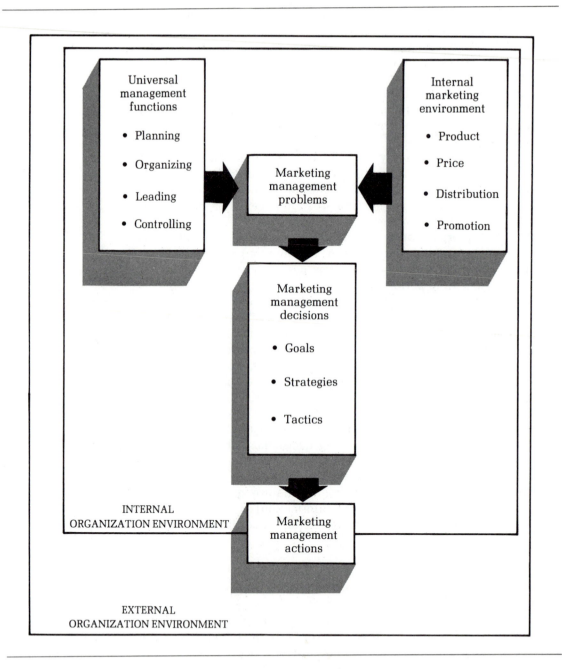

FIGURE 1.3
The nature of marketing management and marketing research information

managers and researchers face well-defined problems. However, quite often they face much less definite situations and they need *exploratory* marketing research. Such research helps to identify and understand the problem, to determine alternate solutions, or to do both. Thus, a more complete description of marketing research information is that it helps either to identify or to solve marketing management problems.

How Marketing Research Is Performed

To understand marketing research further, we consider it now in terms of three other elements: the performers, the activities, and the costs. We shall see that marketing research consists of numerous organizations and many individuals performing a wide variety of activities at considerable cost.

Marketing research performers exist either inside or outside the firm that is facing the marketing management problem. We identify the former as researchers inside the firm and the latter as researchers outside the firm. Outside researchers work for independent research suppliers. Such suppliers divide further into general and specialized categories.

MARKETING RESEARCH PERFORMERS

General research suppliers will both design and execute custom research for all kinds of clients. For example, Burke International Research Corporation, one general research supplier, works with clients whose interests include corporate image, prepackaged baked goods, men's underwear, oil containers, life insurance, microwave cooking, electronic ovens, and nuclear power plants, among others. Burke will undertake almost any marketing research activity—from conducting a survey on advertising effectiveness to executing a test market to simulating sales for a new product.

In contrast, **specialized research suppliers** perform narrower research on selected aspects of marketing—products, advertisements, retailers and wholesalers, and consumers, for example—all as they apply to only one or a few industries. Some other specialized research suppliers perform only selected marketing research activities, most often in data collection or data analysis. For example, Advanced Data Analysis will take a customer's completed questionnaires, process them, perform a variety of analyses, and then transmit results to computer terminals in the customer's office.

Table 1.1 lists the twenty-three largest outside suppliers. We will discuss several of these in more detail in Chapter 4.

Researchers inside the firm usually work for a separate marketing research department.[8] Their firms reflect diverse goals and orientations:

---

[8]This statement and the rest of this paragraph summarize some research by Dik Warren Twedt, ed., *1978 Survey of Marketing Research* (Chicago: American Marketing Association, 1978), pp. 9–25.

TABLE 1.1
Top Twenty-three Research Suppliers Based on 1979 Research Revenues

Supplier	1979 Research Revenues ($ Millions)
A. C. Nielsen Company	302.1
IMS International	88.8
SAMI	54.4
Arbitron	44.1
Burke International Research Corporation	42.6
Market Facts	19.3
Westat Inc.	14.4
Audits & Surveys	14.0
Marketing and Research Counselors	13.1
ASI Market Research	12.3
Chilton Research	12.0
Yankelovich, Skelly, & White	11.8
Ehrhart-Babic Associates	10.4
National Family Opinion	10.0
NPD Research	9.7
Data Development Corporation	9.6
Louis Harris & Associates	9.3
National Analysts	8.7
Opinion Research Corporation	8.2
Elrich & Lavidge	7.1
Walker Research	7.0
Starch INRA Hooper	5.5
Decisions Center	5.1
Total	$719.5

Source: Reprinted from the May 19, 1980 issue of *Advertising Age.* © 1980 by Crain Communications, Inc., p. 3.

consumer product manufacturers, industrial product manufacturers, advertising agencies, publishers, broadcasters, retailers, wholesalers, financial services, and other profit and nonprofit organizations. Researchers in these firms occupy staff positions, reporting most often to a sales or marketing manager or to a top corporate manager. Like researchers outside the firm, they undertake research only when decision makers in the firm agree to fund marketing research activities from usually limited budgets.

Researchers inside the firm often find much of their time spent with researchers outside the firm; that is, many firms staff rather small marketing research departments, whose purpose is to design research studies and

EXHIBIT 1.1
Characteristics of Successful Researchers

Gestalt Thinking:	the ability to question and to see the present marketing problem as a whole before becoming wrapped up in details. This means seeing the present problem as part of earlier problems and as part of the three environments (see page 9), as the environments continually change.
Creative Thinking:	the ability to think innovative thoughts. This leads to applying old research methods to new problems, keeping abreast of and trying new methods, and even originating new methods.
Customer Understanding:	the awareness of how buyers make their purchase decisions. This includes knowledge of what, where, how, when, and why customers buy. It also includes knowledge of what, where, how, when, and why the firm sells.
Statistical Skills:	the ability to apply simple and complex analyses to research data and produce meaningful findings. This skill also involves the ability to question and direct more expert statisticians in producing similar ends.
Communication Skills:	the ability to interview executives and others; to write cogent, complete, and managerially relevant research proposals and reports; and to present effective oral proposals and reports.

Source: Based on Emanual Demby, "Success in Marketing Research," *Marketing News* (January 28, 1977), pp. 4 ff.

to contract with outside research suppliers for their execution. These firms make this choice for several reasons: it costs less to contract for marketing research then it does to maintain the capability in-house; outside suppliers often provide more objective research; and outside suppliers often specialize in highly technical areas. However, many other firms maintain large marketing research departments, which sometimes contract with outside suppliers and sometimes perform their own research.

Performer Characteristics. Researchers inside and outside the firm should possess certain characteristics to be successful. We identify five general characteristics in Exhibit 1.1; researchers working on specific research projects should possess other characteristics as well.[9]

Careers in Marketing Research. What's it like to work as a marketing researcher? Generally interesting, challenging, rewarding, busy, and technical. In one researcher's opinion:

---

[9]For some specific characteristics needed by new product researchers, see C. Merle Crawford, "Marketing Research and the New Product Failure Rate," *Journal of Marketing* 41 (April 1977): 57.

Marketing research demands a mind that can shift gears constantly and be satisfied with a day that sees six new projects begun but none of the six that had to be worked on that day ever even touched.[10]

Our general description of working as a marketing researcher differs little from a job description for a sales representative, a brand manager, an advertising copywriter, a retail buyer, or any other marketing position. All marketing jobs tend to be fast paced and dynamic. The marketing research job is, however, "technical," which many other marketing jobs are not. Our understanding of careers in marketing research will benefit from the more explicit descriptions to be found in Exhibit 1.2.

With a bachelor's degree, a person would be likely to start work as a junior analyst. With a master's degree, a person would probably start as an analyst or statistician. With either degree, stronger candidates for either of the analyst positions are those who have completed a variety of college courses in marketing, other business areas, statistics, psychology, social psychology, and economics.[11] They also have taken at least one computer course. Stronger candidates for the statistician positions usually possess narrower academic backgrounds, emphasizing course work in applied statistics and computer-assisted data analysis.

Compensation accompanying job titles described in Exhibit 1.2 depends on the type of firm, size of the research department, company revenues, and the researcher's experience, responsibilities, and performance.[12] Thus, we may make only rough estimates of the average compensation paid in 1982 to all researchers occupying jobs identified in Exhibit 1.2; in Table 1.2 we can see average compensation paid to researchers. Of course, salaries for persons just entering these jobs would usually be lower.

MARKETING RESEARCH ACTIVITIES In the preceding section, we saw what performers of marketing research do and roughly what they are paid. Here we look specifically at the breadth, or variety, of marketing research activities.[13] Twedt divides all marketing research activities into five major areas: business economics and corporate research, corporate responsibility research, advertising research, product research, and sales and market research. Within each area, he identifies a number of more specific activities. We can see in Table 1.3 Twedt's survey results for 798 U.S. firms.

---

[10]Neil Holbert, *Careers in Marketing* (Chicago: American Marketing Association, 1976), p. 21.

[11]Al Blankenship, "What Marketing Research Managers Want in Trainees," *Journal of Advertising Research* 15 (February 1975): 7–14.

[12]Twedt, *1978 Survey*, pp. 45–65.

[13]This section draws from Twedt, *1978 Survey*, pp. 40–44.

EXHIBIT 1.2
Selected Marketing Research Job Titles and Descriptions

Research director:	This person manages and takes responsibility for the entire research function in the firm. A research director initiates independent projects and accepts assignments from marketing decision makers. A research director directly or indirectly supervises all personnel in the research department.
Assistant research director:	This person is a senior staff member who exercises responsibility as the second in command. The assistant research director makes decisions in areas assigned by the research director.
Senior analyst:	Sometimes called a project director, this person works with marketing decision makers in defining the marketing problem, selecting types of data sources, designing data collection forms, designing sampling and data collection procedures, analyzing data, interpreting data, and reporting results. The senior analyst works with a minimum of supervision and holds primary responsibility for meeting budget and timing constraints.
Analyst:	This person assists the senior analyst but may take primary responsibility for certain parts of a research project. An analyst may draft the data collection form, pretest, and revise it to final form for approval by the senior analyst. An analyst may undertake initial analysis and interpretation of data.
Junior analyst:	This person assists superior analysts as directed. A junior analyst performs routine assignments such as editing and coding questionnaires, performing statistical calculations, and conducting library research, all under close supervision.
Statistician:	This person is a consultant on the theory and application of statistical techniques to research projects during the design and execution of the research. Areas of expertise include sampling, data analysis, and computer programs.
Librarian:	This person builds and maintains a library of clippings, research articles, reports, books, and other materials to support the research department.
Clerical supervisor:	This person supervises clerical help who code and process research data.
Field work director:	This person hires, trains, and supervises telephone and personal interviewers. The director may also check or validate a sample of each interviewer's work for accuracy.

Source: Adapted from Dik Warren Twedt, ed., *1978 Survey of Marketing Research* (Chicago: American Marketing Association, 1978), appendix.

TABLE 1.2
Average Compensation Estimates by Marketing Research Job Title for 1982

Job Title	Compensation Estimate ($ 000)
Research director	50.1
Assistant research director	43.5
Senior analyst	33.9
Analyst	25.5
Junior analyst	16.8
Statistician	31.6
Librarian	16.7
Clerical supervisor	19.8
Field work director	21.0

Source: Extrapolated from Dik Warren Twedt, ed., *1978 Survey of Marketing Research* (Chicago: American Marketing Association, 1978), p. 57.

Over 90 percent of the firms Twedt surveyed perform research to measure market potentials, market shares, and market characteristics. Nearly 75 percent use research to test existing products, establish sales quotas and territories, locate plants and warehouses, and assist a management information system. About 50 percent conduct research on advertising copy, consumer motivations, foreign markets, and the legal environment of advertising and promotion activities. A like percentage carry out research using test markets and consumer panels.

As we might expect, some types of firms perform certain activities in Table 1.3 more frequently than other firms do. For example, manufacturers of consumer products much more frequently conduct advertising research than do manufacturers of industrial products. Advertising agencies less frequently perform sales analyses than do suppliers of financial services (banks, savings and loan associations, insurance underwriters, etc.). Still, in the majority of activities, percentages vary only moderately across all types of firms.

MARKETING RESEARCH COSTS

All these activities incur significant costs. Already we have seen in Table 1.1 that the twenty-three largest outside suppliers of marketing research charged their clients nearly three-quarters of a billion dollars in 1979. (Undoubtedly, they produced research benefits greatly exceeding this amount.) To estimate the entire cost of marketing research in our economy, we must add in these other costs as well:

1. research conducted by approximately 350 smaller outside suppliers;

2. research conducted by nonprofit research suppliers;

TABLE 1.3
Marketing Research Activities and Percentage of Firms Performing (n = 798)

MARKETING RESEARCH ACTIVITIES	FIRMS PERFORMING (%)
Business Economics and Corporate Research	
Short range forecasting (up to 1 year)	85
Long range forecasting (over 1 year)	82
Studies of business trends	86
Pricing studies	81
Plant and warehouse location studies	71
Acquisition studies	69
Export and international studies	51
MIS (Management Information System)	72
Operations research	60
Internal company employees	65
Corporate Responsibility Research	
Consumers "Right to Know" studies	26
Ecological impact studies	33
Studies of legal constraints on advertising and promotion	51
Social values and policies studies	40
Advertising Research	
Motivation research	48
Copy research	49
Media research	61
Studies of effectiveness	67
Product Research	
New product acceptance and potential	84
Competitive product studies	85
Testing of existing products	75
Packaging research design or physical characteristics	60
Sales and Market Research	
Measurement of market potentials	93
Market share analysis	92
Determination of market characteristics	93
Sales analysis	89
Establishment of sales quotas, territories	75
Distribution channel studies	69
Test markets, store audits	54
Consumer panel operations	50
Sales compensation studies	60
Promotional studies of premiums, coupons, sampling, deals, etc.	52

Source: Dik Warren Twedt, ed., *1978 Survey of Marketing Research* (Chicago: American Marketing Association, 1978), p. 40. Reprinted by permission.

3. research conducted by marketing research departments of manufac-
    turers, advertising agencies, publishers, and other firms; and

4. research conducted by agencies of the federal, state, and local
    governments.[14]

These expenditures plus those in Table 1.1 easily exceeded $1.0 billion in
1979. They likely will exceed $1.5 billion in 1982.[15]

Marketing Research and Marketing Information Systems

One function of marketing research, we said, is to help solve specific marketing management problems. Yet, even in the absence of such problems,
something looking suspiciously like marketing research data also flows to
decision makers. For example, a decision maker at General Mills receives
reports of regional market shares for breakfast cereals, shipments from
company warehouses, competitive advertising activity, and a host of other
data (on weekly, monthly, or quarterly bases)—whether or not a problem
exists. While the data may solve a specific marketing management problem, this was not the primary purpose in their collection. Rather, these
data are collected for awareness (to indicate the existence of potential or
previously unrecognized marketing problems) or for proof (to show that
solutions already implemented have worked). Most of the data are collected for some purpose other than the solution of marketing management
problems.

In short, such data represent not the product of marketing research
but of a **marketing information system (MKIS).** An MKIS collects, structures, and transmits marketing data to decision makers on a regular,
orderly basis. It contrasts with marketing research, which operates similarly but on a sporadic basis. Further, an MKIS usually requires that
decision makers manipulate its data to produce more meaningful information, using procedures contained in the MKIS. For example, one decision maker may desire to break monthly sales data down by territory, customer class, salesperson. Another may want sales broken down by
product, region, and week. Simple MKIS computer commands accomplish
this function. Finally, an MKIS often allows decision makers to forecast
future data values and to examine values for meaningful differences,
again using procedures in the MKIS.

Thus, an MKIS complements marketing research in the firm. The

---

[14]Jack Honomichl, *Advertising Age* (May 19, 1980), p. 3. Honomichl also identifies the eight
largest research firms in categories (2), (3), and (4) and their research expenditures for 1979
in *Advertising Age* (June 16, 1980), p. 60.

[15]Another way of looking at marketing research costs is in terms of percentages of sales.
See Twedt, *1978 Survey*, pp. 31–38.

EXHIBIT 1.3
Marketing Research and Marketing Information Systems

	Marketing Research	*Marketing Information System (MKIS)*
Primary Emphasis:	Solve a specific problem	Recognize problems, monitor solutions
Secondary Emphasis:	Recognize a specific problem, monitor a solution	Solve numerous problems
Incidence:	Ad hoc, sporadic	General, periodic

relationship may be evolutionary—in which case marketing research precedes the development of an MKIS and provides information useful in its design and implementation. Or, the relationship may be sequential—an MKIS helps recognize a problem, marketing research produces a solution, and the MKIS evaluates its effectiveness. Or, the relationship may be nonexistent—marketing research identifies a problem, investigates solutions, and evaluates effectiveness totally apart from MKIS operations. All three relationships exist in our economy and even in a single firm.

We can see a summary of the differences between marketing research and an MKIS in Exhibit 1.3. Apart from a brief discussion of MKIS data in Chapter 4, further exposition of an MKIS is left to other sources.[16]

Chapter Summary

Marketing research helps determine marketing management decisions. It reduces, not eliminates, uncertainty connected with decisions by describing the various marketing and organization environments. Such information only helps; the decision maker always retains the option of making decisions without prior research. Such decisions save the time and other resources consumed by marketing research but incur more risk.

Marketing researchers work either inside or outside of the decision maker's firm. Both kinds of researchers need to see the marketing problem in an encompassing fashion, think creatively, understand the firm's customers, possess statistical skills, and communicate well. They need college-level training in marketing, other business areas, statistics, psychology, social psychology, economics, and computers. They work for the decision maker, who funds and uses the results of their efforts.

Marketing research operates in the general areas of business econom-

---

[16]For example, see William R. King, *Marketing Management Information Systems* (New York: Mason/Charter Publishers, 1977).

ics and the corporation as a whole. It operates further in such specific corporate areas as advertising, products, sales, and markets. Likewise, so do marketing information systems. However, MKIS activities tend to focus on no specific problem because they provide data in a recurring fashion.

Chapter Review

KEY TERMS

Marketing research

Marketing strategies

Marketing management functions

Internal organization environment

Gestalt thinking

Senior analyst

MKIS

DISCUSSION QUESTIONS

1. A nonprofit organization such as a university has no need of marketing research. Discuss.

2. Marketing research reduces the guesswork associated with marketing decisions. Discuss.

3. Give an example that shows how the nature of marketing management and marketing research information relate.

4. Identify some reasons why a marketing manager might not perform marketing research to help solve a problem.

5. Successful marketing researchers are made not born. How?

6. What do marketing researchers do?

7. Compare and contrast marketing research with marketing information systems.

Additional Readings

Kotler, Philip. *Marketing Management: Analysis, Planning and Control*, 4th ed. Englewood Cliffs, N.J.: Prentice-Hall, 1980.

This is a widely adopted, standard treatment of marketing management. The book covers everything from the analysis of market opportunities through implementing marketing strategies and controlling market operations. Readable, practical, and widely quoted.

Ritchie, J. R. Brent. "Roles of Research in the Management Process." *MSU Business Topics* (Summer 1976), pp. 13–22.

This article provides an encompassing view of research as it applies to management decision making. All decision-related research divides into five categories: operational research, managerial research, policy research, action research, and evaluation research. These research types apply to management decisions not only in marketing but in finance, production, control, personnel, and coordination. They typically produce different information as research outputs.

Smith, Stewart A. "Research and Pseudo-Research in Marketing." *Harvard Business Review* (March–April, 1974), pp. 73–76.

> Pseudoresearch is the counterpart in appearances to the view of marketing research presented in this chapter. Instead of solving marketing problems, pseudoresearch serves as "window dressing" to justify decisions already made, to impress decision makers with its sophistication, or to bolster decision makers' and researchers' egos. According to Smith, much marketing research is more properly called pseudoresearch.

CHAPTER 2

The Process, the Design, and the Proposal

How the Marketing Research Process Works

Now that we know a few things about marketing research we can begin a more detailed study. It's useful here to look at a **marketing research process** that describes general steps or phases common to all marketing research studies. Figure 2.1 illustrates. Each of the eight steps in the marketing research process is discussed briefly in the paragraphs that follow. Later in this book, whole chapters are devoted to their explanation. For now, we should look at the entire process in search of the underlying logic.

Obviously, marketing research must commence with a definition of the problem that needs solving. Just as obviously, reporting the research and subsequent evaluation of the entire process must be last. In between, we must identify data sources—that is, specify from whom or what we will collect data; then we select data collection methods and design the sample; next we design forms for data collection. At this point we collect data. Analyzing and interpreting data must occur next; then the report is prepared. Let us briefly consider each step.

Part of defining the marketing problem means understanding the circumstances that led the decision maker to request research. We want to be sure the proposed research focuses on the problem and not on the problem's symptoms. The decision maker, past research, and experts inside and outside the firm all provide information useful in defining the problem. This information greatly narrows the research task: a problem well defined is half solved.

DEFINING THE MARKETING PROBLEM

23

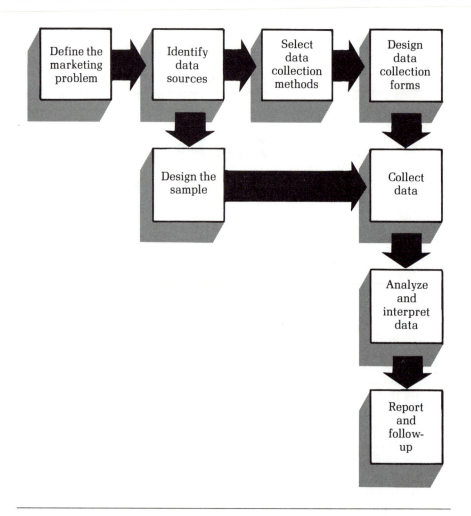

FIGURE 2.1
The marketing research process

Another part of defining the problem means understanding the problem's potential solutions. There are two general rules:

- The problem must have more than one potential solution.
- Solutions must be assessable in terms of previously specified performance parameters.

The rules are easily explained. The first implies that if a problem has one and only one potential solution, conducting marketing research only wastes resources: the decision maker will make the same decision with or without research. The second implies that performance variables the decision maker will use to evaluate potential solutions should guide the research; for example, sales, market share, brand awareness, and customer satisfaction, are just some among a host of criteria. Knowledge of which performance variables the decision maker considers important allows the researcher to design research that is relevant and specific.

Defining the marketing problem is the most important step in the entire research process. If the problem is improperly defined, conducting the best marketing research in the world will not help. We will simply get a terrific answer to the wrong problem. If the problem is loosely defined, too much time, money, and energy will be expended in the research process. Thus, adequate and precise problem definition is a major responsibility for both researcher and decision maker. We discuss problem definition in detail in Chapter 3.

A data source is simply something or someone who supplies necessary data or information. Data sources are of two types: secondary and primary. **Secondary data sources** are repositories of data originally collected for some other purpose than to solve the marketing problem at hand. Examples are the U.S. Census, company records, an article in the *Journal of Marketing*, and this text; all contain data that might be used to solve a particular marketing problem even though that use was not the specific purpose for their collection.

IDENTIFYING DATA SOURCES

Primary data sources are just the opposite. **Primary data sources** are people, things, or organizations from which researchers collect new data specifically to solve the present marketing problem. Some possible primary data sources are consumers, retailers, wholesalers, manufacturers, competitors, and various government units.

It often is not clear which data sources we should use to solve a given marketing problem. Consider a wholesaler interested in expanding its sales territory to include either Georgia or Tennessee. The decision maker specifies a single performance parameter—unit sales. We might proceed by using consumers as a data source, conducting surveys in the two states and estimating unit sales from their responses. Or we might reference the *Census of Wholesale Trade* to find industry sales for the two states and estimate unit sales by applying an expected percentage calculated from company records. Or, we might survey retailers in the two states to yield still different sales estimates. In sum, then, the possible data sources for this and most other marketing research studies are many and diverse; it is up to the market researcher to determine which are more appropriate.

Once sources are determined, we must consider how to go about collecting data. For secondary data, the data collection method is quite simple: we search and record. The search should be exhaustive (complete). It may be frustrated by source delay and, occasionally, by refusal. It almost always will prove worthwhile to examine each source's methodology and findings in a critical manner. We shall look more closely at the search for secondary data in Chapter 4.

SELECTING DATA COLLECTION METHODS

Selecting a data collection method for primary data is less simple because there are more possibilities. There are five basic methods from which to choose: experiments, surveys, observations, simulations, and the qualitative techniques.

Experiments are situations that are partly real, partly artificial, in which influencing variables on the marketing problem are either varied or controlled. For example, consumers might bake, taste, and evaluate different cake mixes in a laboratory. A survey is the systematic questioning of members of the population of interest. Mail questionnaires, telephone surveys, and personal interviews are all well known examples of surveys. The observation data collection method, on the other hand, uses no verbal communications to collect data; we merely observe and record what we see. Simulations use either simple or complex models to generate data: a breakeven diagram is an example of a simple model; a complex model would be a computer program that predicts a firm's competitive market share based on its advertising and pricing decisions. Finally, qualitative techniques are heavily psychological in origin. Their primary function is to get beneath consumers' superficial responses and uncover true reactions to sensitive research questions. We defer more complete study of these five data collection methods until Chapters 5, 6, and 8.

DESIGNING DATA COLLECTION FORMS

After determining data collection methods, we must design data collection forms. Sometimes this step in the marketing research process takes little time, as when we collect data only from secondary sources. More often, however, this step takes a very large amount of time. Consider a mail survey questionnaire for a study of 1000 Los Angeles housewives' shopping habits. Let's say we want to measure the respondents' image of three large discount store chains, their idea of what features are important in store selection, and their knowledge of store advertising messages (print and broadcast media). It would be a lengthy process, indeed, to: (1) identify consumers' relevant store image and selection criteria, (2) combine these criteria with a selected set of advertising knowledge questions, (3) pretest, (4) revise, and finally (5) construct the final questionnaire.

Considerations in this process include consumer understanding and reaction to the questionnaire, data analysis and computer processing requirements, and even printing and postage costs. Chapters 7, 8, 9, 10, and 11 provide details on designing data collection forms.

DESIGNING THE SAMPLE

While we decide on data collection methods and forms, we should also design the sample. To sample is simply to select some units of the population of interest for measurement. The term *population of interest* doesn't necessarily mean people. It also applies to retail stores, products, advertisements, prices—to any set of data sources that will supply measurements on variables of interest in our research.

Designing the sample involves two major items: sampling methods and sample size. A detailed sampling plan accounts for both these items.

Considerations in its preparation include: the availability of a list of members of the population of interest, the procedure by which we will generalize sample results to the entire population, and our resource constraints. By and large, we'll use one or more probability sampling methods; choices include simple random, stratified random, systematic, and cluster sampling. Each has unique procedures for drawing the sample and for calculating various statistics. Each also has largely unique conditions for its use. We will examine these topics, along with sample size determination, in Chapters 12, 13, and 14.

Data collection, the next step in the marketing research process, involves decisions of who will assemble the data, where, when, and how. Only for the simplest marketing research studies will these decisions be easy; that is, only when the researcher alone collects all the data is it possible to avoid the managerial problems that otherwise typify this step. Even then the researcher will have to ask questions that cannot be answered mechanically.

COLLECTING DATA

 Consider a simple sales territory expansion problem that a researcher will solve by herself using secondary data. She identifies data sources and begins to search and record. However, very early in data collection she finds that she must adjust some data because they are not in a proper form. For example, data might not be up to date or not apply to the exact geographic area in her study. She might also find that different secondary data sources report different data values for the same variable. Therefore, she will need a decision procedure that allows her to adjust and assemble the data exactly as she needs it. Almost always there will be regular instances of such judgment required even when she is the sole researcher in the project.

 Major considerations arise when others assist the researcher, that is, when one becomes a manager in addition to being the researcher. Issues such as organizing, staffing, training, compensating, and controlling a research team are complicated matters. Moreover, some of those assisting the researcher are not members of the research team; they are actually workers for other departments or even other firms. Getting the research job done through all these people will require polished management skills. We explore these skills in more detail in Chapters 5 and 6.

Analyzing data means the manipulation of numbers, words, or other symbols to facilitate data interpretation. Interpreting data means the attachment of meaning to numbers, words, or other symbols. While the two processes, analyzing and interpreting, look much the same and usually go hand in hand, the distinction is important.

ANALYZING AND INTERPRETING DATA

 Analyzing data involves a large number of rather structured techniques and statistics. Each reflects one of seven purposes: characterizing what is typical, showing variability, presenting the distribution, describing relationships, estimating and forecasting, describing differences between groups and variables, and showing causality.[1] Most of us probably remember some specific analytical techniques and statistics (*t*-tests, means, medians, correlation coefficients, etc.) from statistics course work that have these purposes in mind. We shall look at many of these in Chapters 15 through 19 along with some new analytical tools.

In contrast, interpreting data involves less structure, more intuition, and an equal amount of researcher effort. The last comment often surprises beginning students in marketing research who feel that most data should be self-interpreting; that is, they feel that most data should "speak for themselves" and clearly indicate direction to a logical decision maker. Such is seldom the case. Rather, data almost always require effort to extract their meanings; a primary task of marketing research is to provide meanings that most assist the decision maker. We shall examine data interpretation in Chapter 20.

MAKING THE REPORT AND FOLLOWING UP

Both oral and written reports summarize the marketing research study for decision makers. Formats for these reports vary depending on the company, intended audience, and type and complexity of the completed research. In all situations, however, there are some common concerns: sections in the report should describe methods used, cover findings and recommendations, and indicate limitations. The entire report should be accurate, complete, clear, brief, interesting, free of jargon, free of grammatical errors, and explicit about the managerial implications of the research. No small task, indeed!

After preparing the report to communicate research results, the researcher still has one more obligation—an evaluation or follow-up of the entire process. Of particular interest are things that might have been done differently to improve the study; recommendations that were not implemented by the decision maker, and why; the anticipated research benefits compared to actual research costs; and finally, future research needs and implications. This follow-up phase is necessary because we ought to learn from what we have done. We should develop long-term instead of short-term relationships with decision makers. These topics also appear in Chapter 20.

INTEGRITY OF THE MARKETING RESEARCH PROCESS

We have briefly discussed eight steps in the marketing research process: define the marketing problem, identify data sources, select data collection methods, design data collection forms, design the sample, collect data, analyze and interpret data, and report results and evaluate the entire process. The process is universal. These steps or others similarly titled will be found in any marketing research study and in most marketing research

---

[1]This identification largely follows that of Claire Selltiz et al., *Research Methods in Social Relations*, rev. ed. (New York: Holt, Rinehart, and Winston, 1966) Chap. 11.

texts.[2] Each source may show a different number of steps, but this is unimportant; what is important is understanding that there is a sequence for the research steps—each is interdependent with both preceding and subsequent steps.

To see this, consider that when we define the problem, we must specify what variables influence the problem. This specification partly determines the identity of data sources, design of the sample, and design of the data collection form, which, in turn, partly determines how the data can be analyzed. Form of the analysis dramatically influences our ability to make conclusions and recommendations in the research report. Moreover, consider that requirements of later decisions in the process influence earlier decisions. For example, certain analytical techniques make their own requirements: data must be collected in a particular fashion, samples must exceed a minimum size, and problem definitions must be in a certain form. Different data collection methods require their own question and response formats on the data collection form. Different sample designs require different identifications of data sources. The interdependency of the steps will surface repeatedly throughout our more detailed study of marketing research.

One final point: it is reasonable to assume that once a marketing problem is defined, marketing research always follows. Such is not the usual case at all. Decision makers constantly recognize marketing problems and constantly make decisions without conducting any intermediate marketing research. They regularly compare costs and benefits of proposed marketing research and proceed with research only when the latter outweigh the former.

Choosing a Marketing Research Design

A **marketing research design** consists of the set of plans for carrying out a specific marketing research project. We apply the general marketing research process we have just discussed to devise a set of plans to collect data to help solve a specific marketing problem.

Such research designs are as varied as the problems they mean to solve. One research design may plan to use only primary data while another may plan to use only secondary data while still another may plan for both. One design may call for collecting data only with a survey; another may plan to use an experiment, observation, simulation, qualitative technique, or some combination of these methods. One may require either a probability or a nonprobability sampling method while another may call for a census. Some designs will specify only two analytical techniques while others may use ten. Depending on complexity, one research design can occupy a centimeter of file space, while another may need a meter.

---

[2]See, for example, Harper W. Boyd, Jr., Ralph Westfall, and Stanley F. Stasch, *Marketing Research,* 4th ed. (Homewood, Ill.: Richard D. Irwin, 1977), pp. 205–12.

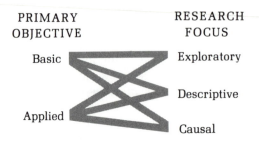

FIGURE 2.2
Research designs classified by primary objective and research focus

RESEARCH
DESIGN
CLASSIFICATION

Because of this variety in research designs, we will find it helpful to classify them according to primary objective and research focus. As Figure 2.2 shows, this classification yields six possible research designs:

- basic exploratory,
- basic descriptive,
- basic causal,
- applied exploratory,
- applied descriptive, and
- applied causal.[3]

A **basic research** design is planned when research will have the primary objective of extending theoretical knowledge about marketing. For example, basic research may identify how different consumers mentally process advertising messages that range in content from very simple to very complex. The practical value of basic research is always uncertain at the time of research design. By contrast, **applied research** has the objective of helping marketing decision makers achieve specific organizational goals. The practical value of applied research is always closely examined while planning a research design.

However, the division between basic and applied research is not as sharp as Figure 2.2 indicates: a particular research design may be partly basic and partly applied. The test, in our classification, is whether the project's primary research objective is basic or applied. We should also note that findings produced by the execution of a strictly basic research design

---

[3]There are at least seven other bases for classifying research designs. See C. William Emory, *Business Research Methods* (Homewood, Ill.: Richard D. Irwin, 1976), pp. 78–83 for a discussion.

may eventually have applied implications, and vice versa. In this book, note that the emphasis is on applied research designs.

Both basic or applied research designs may be exploratory, descriptive, or causal, depending on research focus—that is, depending on the type of findings the research is designed to produce. An **exploratory research** design often produces findings as hypotheses (to be later tested by descriptive or causal research). Or it may produce findings that allow the decision maker to understand the marketing problem more fully: for example, an applied exploratory research project might conclude that sales force motivation, retail inventory control, and shelf life are probably responsible for low sales of a particular product, while price and poor advertising policies are probably not. It would remain for future research to determine both what caused these problems and what could be done to solve them.

A **descriptive research** design produces findings that explain consumers, organizations, objects, concepts, or events. Descriptive findings take a wide variety of forms—such as statements of what is typical, how variables vary, how variables are related, how groups are similar and different, and what future variable values can be expected. To return to our example above concerning low sales of a particular product, a descriptive research project might be designed to report average levels of motivation for excellent, average, and inferior salespersons. Or it might be designed to report the relationship between store size and the number of stockouts, and prediction of average, minimum, and maximum shelf lives for the product under various temperature and humidity conditions.

A **causal research** design yields findings showing that a change in one variable produces a change in another. Continuing with our example, a causal research project might find that a salary increase of 5 percent reduces sales force turnover by about 50 percent. Or it might find that adding a preservative increases shelf life from about two months to six. Causal research designs almost always consist of laboratory or field experiments.[4]

This book emphasizes descriptive research designs.

Regardless of its classification, the design of any research project entails decisions relating to each stage of the marketing research process. Such decisions address the sorts of issues shown in Exhibit 2.1. The apparent complexity and diversity of research design issues may seem somewhat daunting, but by the end of this book we will have become familiar with all of them.

RESEARCH DESIGN ISSUES

---

[4]An increasingly popular alternative approach is causal modeling, with which one can infer causality from associative data. For an introduction to the topic, see H. M. Blalock, Jr., ed., *Causal Models in the Social Sciences* (Chicago: Aldine Atherton, 1971). See also Richard P. Bagozzi, *Causal Models in Marketing* (New York: John Wiley & Sons, 1980) for a more complete treatment.

EXHIBIT 2.1
Design Issues in the Marketing Research Process

Stage in the Marketing Research Process	Typical Marketing Research Design Issues
Define the Marketing Problem	What are the research objectives?
	What is the problem background, the problem environment?
	What variables influence the problem?
	What options does the decision maker have as potential solutions to the problem?
Identify Data Sources	What variables may be measured from what primary and secondary data sources?
	How do the several sources compare in terms of data relevancy, accuracy, and collection cost?
Identify Data Collection Methods	What are the relative strengths and weaknesses of experimental, survey, observation, simulation, and qualitative designs in solving the marketing problem?
	What errors attend these data collection methods in solving the marketing problem?
Design Data Collection Forms	What questions of behavior, socioeconomic characteristics, and psychological characteristics must be asked?
	How should such questions be worded?
	In what form will data sources make their responses?
	What sequence of questions will be asked?
	What validity and reliability attend this measurement process?
	What levels of measurement do questions represent?
Design the Sample	Should probability or nonprobability sampling methods be used?
	What sampling frame should be used?
	How large a sample is needed?
	How much error attends the sampling process?
Collect Data	How shall the research team be organized?
	Who will participate as members of the research team?
	How shall researchers be trained?
	How shall researchers be compensated?
	How much error attends the data collection process?
Analyze and Interpret Data	What analytical techniques will be used?
	What computer programs are available?
	How shall data editing and data coding proceed?
	What kinds of final report tables result?
Report and Follow-up	What oral and written reports are needed?
	Who will listen to and read them?

Research designs commonly consider two other issues beyond those listed in Exhibit 2.1: when will the research be completed and how much will it cost? Obviously, these are important considerations, especially for the decision maker who pays for the execution of each research design.

The researcher usually prepares, or at least considers alternate research designs—comparing strengths and weaknesses—before choosing one as a recommendation to the decision maker. He or she must anticipate the question of an alternate design and be able to justify one design as superior to others. There are several justification bases: result relevancy, accuracy, timeliness, and management actionability—in addition to his or her own capabilities and experiences as a researcher. We examine all but the experiential justification later in this chapter.

Researchers develop many research designs quite easily as replications or slight modifications of past research. However, they still stay alert for shortcomings in the old research design, environmental changes, and advances in marketing research—all of which call for changes. Unique or first-time research designs deserve more comment. For these, development occurs as translation of the marketing management problem into a marketing research problem. This process requires much contact between decision maker and researcher and the researcher's possession of certain characteristics regarding dealing with people and use of earlier research.

DEVELOPMENT OF RESEARCH DESIGNS

Both decision maker and researcher should be jointly involved in defining the marketing research problem and in determining the form of the final report—the first and last steps in the marketing research process. Decision makers generally have more interest in these two steps and the expertise to provide valuable input. They have less to say about intervening steps in the process—design decisions on information sources, data collection methods, forms, sampling, data collection activities, and analysis. These are the researcher's primary responsibilities (along with the first and last steps).

Throughout the design decision process, the researcher must be able to work effectively with people. He or she will frequently contact other researchers and those in other departments and organizations, few of whom will share the same level of interest in the project. Tact, an inquiring nature, creativity tempered with experience, an ability to anticipate research results, and perseverance will all be required. Needed, too, will be liberal doses of logic and common sense.

The researcher should also be capable of learning from summaries of earlier research. Such summaries are especially useful because they provide timing and cost details that may apply to the present design. Notice what is really being discussed here is the need for some informal yet rigorous preliminary research in developing a research design. The more care and detail the researcher includes, the easier the design will be to execute.

Finally, as a last comment on developing a research design, recall an earlier conclusion relating to the marketing research process: each decision made in one step of the process dramatically influences those which follow. The same holds true for each issue in research design.

EVALUATION OF RESEARCH DESIGNS

To complete the development of a research design, both researcher and decision maker evaluate it against this question: will the design solve the marketing problem at a reasonable cost? A **technical evaluation** of the research design assesses whether or not proposed research will solve the marketing problem. A **cost-benefit evaluation** of the research design examines whether estimates of research costs seem reasonable when viewed against research benefits. Let us examine these two types of evaluation more closely.

Technical Evaluation. Criteria for a technical evaluation are the design's showing evidence that results will be relevant, accurate, timely, and actionable.

Research Relevancy. A first technical evaluation area pertains to research relevancy: Does the research apply to the causes of the marketing problem? And does the decision maker perceive the research design as a good one? For example, the decision maker might see the proposed research as irrelevant because the researcher does not understand the decision maker's view of potential causes of the problem. Consider a request for research to answer this question: "What can be done to reduce salesforce turnover in Territory X?" We should readily see that this request is more a symptom statement than a problem statement. Suppose the entire situation is diagrammed as in Exhibit 2.2.

Exhibit 2.2 is easy to interpret. In asking "what can be done to reduce salesforce turnover," the decision maker focused on a problem symptom and neglected to look for its cause. The researcher and decision maker viewed different factors as likely causes of the symptom. Each included only one actual cause, and the two share only one likely cause. Final research recommendations appear to solve only part of the problem and then only if the decision maker accepts the recommendation to increase advertising (which is not likely because inadequate advertising support was not one of the decision maker's likely causes). In other words, research results appear irrelevant to the decision maker because researcher and decision maker had two different views of the problem.

Research results can also appear irrelevant if the researcher does not understand the decision maker's objectives, potential options to solve the problem, and reasons for requesting the study. Continuing our example, suppose the decision maker's objective is to correct the problem in six months or less. In this case the final recommendation to improve sales-

EXHIBIT 2.2
Marketing Research Problem Schematic

Unknown Actual Problem Causes	Problem Symptoms	Likely Problem Causes as Viewed By:		Final Research Recommendations
		Decision Maker	Researcher	
Inadequate advertising support	High salesforce turnover	Inferior product design	Inadequate advertising support	Increase advertising
Inferior product design	Low morale	Poor salesforce selection	Poor salesforce selection	Improve salesforce selection
	Low average order size	Late deliveries	Poor salesforce training	Cut prices 5 percent
		Lack of selling incentives	High prices	
			Ineffective sales territory allocation	

force selection will seem largely irrelevant because of its delayed effect. Suppose further that a price cut in Territory X is impossible because of legal and company policy restrictions. Again results will be seen as irrelevant, now because the researcher did not understand the decision maker's potential options. Finally, suppose that the researcher did not have the full picture—that the reason for the original request was to improve Territory X's performance relative to that of Territory Y, a superior territory. Consequently, the decision maker will feel that this research (which fails to compare the two territories) is almost totally irrelevant.

Research Accuracy. A second technical consideration is the extent to which a research design leads to results free of error. The concept is research accuracy—the absence of both stable and random departures from usually unknown "true" data values. Stable departures from truth are repeatable errors, like measuring your weight with a bathroom scale that always reads five pounds light. Random departures are nonrepeatable errors, like measuring your height with a rubber band yardstick. Apart from measurement, both types of error also concern researchers in sampling and data analysis activities.

Stable and random errors attend any sampling process. For example, researchers may err in defining their populations of interest. Or, they might use an outdated list from which to select sample members. Or, more basically, consider that any sample researchers take inherently produces sampling errors because the sample includes responses from only part of the total population.

Stable and random errors also attend any data analysis process. To illustrate—coders, as they assign numbers to responses, may make perceptual and mechanical errors. Keypunchers, as they transfer data from collection forms to computer cards, may make similar mistakes. Researchers may use an improper data analysis method, misinterpret results, or report incorrect data. All lead to departures from truth.

We conclude then that researchers cannot conduct perfectly accurate marketing research. Quite so. Accuracy, like relevancy, is always a matter of degree and never an either–or consideration. Researchers do want their research designs and executions to be as accurate as possible, given available resources; and it is a goal of this book to provide concepts and methods that reduce all errors. Beyond this, there is something else to consider on the subject of research accuracy: Certain aspects of a research design may be intentionally more or less accurate than others. That is, researchers desire to minimize total error in research design rather than to focus narrowly on error in just one design aspect. For example, they may knowingly allow more sampling error in order to save resources to lower data collection error. Other error tradeoffs are also possible.[5]

Research Timing.   A third technical consideration is research timing. Stated simply, the most relevant and accurate research results in the world may seem worthless if they arrive too late to help make a decision. Timing of research results is especially critical for seasonal marketing decisions. A missed deadline of only one week may have the impact of a one year's delay. A missed deadline also gives more time for competitors to act, raising the possibility of the firm's losing those benefits that normally accrue to the industry innovator. Timing of research results may even mean the difference between the organization's healthy survival or its early demise.

Consequently, the importance of setting realistic completion estimates in marketing research is hard to overstate. Even more important is meeting the deadlines. For most research designs, it is usually sufficient to estimate completion dates of major research design stages; one should allow some reasonable amount of slack time to cover unforseeables and be prepared to negotiate with the decision maker. A final, rather rigid time frame for design execution will result.[6] (With increased resources, researchers can sometimes complete the design ahead of schedule.)

Research Actionability.   A last technical consideration is the potential of planned research to yield results that the decision maker will be

---

[5]An error framework that is different but encompasses the idea of error trade-off can be found in Donald S. Tull and Del I. Hawkins, *Marketing Research: Meaning, Measurement, and Method* (New York: Macmillian, 1976), pp. 122–27.

[6]More complex designs may benefit from graphic representation in a PERT or GERT analytical framework. These techniques provide explicit estimates of completion dates based on optimistic, pessimistic, and realistic assumptions. A good review of PERT is in Tull and Hawkins, *Marketing Research*, pp. 107–12. GERT differs from PERT in allowing probabilistic branching and repeated activities; a good introduction is A. Coskun Samli and Carl Bellas, "The Use of GERT in the Planning and Control of Marketing Research," *Journal of Marketing Research* 8 (August 1971): 335–39.

willing and able to put into action, research actionability. Partly this consideration is a function of the first three—that is, research designs will be evaluated as more actionable if results promise to be relevant, accurate, and properly timed.

However, actionability also requires that the researcher be oriented to the decision maker's point of view while maintaining objectivity throughout the entire research process. Researchers find this difficult to do, especially because they often work on projects for several different decision makers at the same time.

Actionability also requires conscious effort to close a natural communications gap between each decision maker and the researcher:

> There is a major communications gap between marketing research management and product or marketing management. All too often the researcher is deemed an academic, unrealistic technician and not a marketing strategist. He is not involved in strategic thinking, and he is not brought into the strategic picture seen by top management before the decisions are made.

> As a result, the researcher withdraws and views marketing management as pragmatic, opportunistic, and perhaps not very bright. His defensive reaction forces him into becoming increasingly academic, increasingly technically oriented, and therefore misses the boat when it comes to the real issue of getting involved with the decision process and a correct decision.[7]

Clearly, it is in both parties' best interests that this gap be closed.

Cost-Benefit Evaluation.   Along with a technical evaluation of a research design, researcher and decision maker also perform a cost-benefit evaluation. They do so using one or more of four methods: judgmental, simple savings, present value, and Bayesian. We discuss the first three here but save the fourth for Chapter 14, because of its sophistication and additional application to determining sample size.

Judgmental Method.   In the judgmental method, the decision maker, alone or with the help of others, subjectively weighs research benefits against research costs and reaches a conclusion. Such a process is difficult to describe (can we really describe why we do anything?), but is partly based on the decision maker's experience, memory, attitudes toward risk, intuition, intelligence, perceptual skills, peer group orientation, organizational climate, and competitive situation. The process is largely intuitive, internal, and personal.

---

[7]This statement is attributed to an unknown marketing practitioner by C. Merle Crawford in "Marketing Research and the New Product Failure Rate," *Journal of Marketing* 41 (April 1977): 56.

Such is undoubtedly the way most decisions to proceed with marketing research are made. Making an overall evaluation, we might conclude that this judgmental decision making procedure is largely adequate. Individuals generally make good decisions, and both they and their organizations generally prosper and grow.

However, some shortcomings are inherent in the method and we should identify them. The judgmental method is extremely difficult to communicate. Conclusions, after all, are intuitive and personal, which makes it difficult to explain to others why we decided as we did. Because of this, the judgmental method is also difficult to teach and learn. Moreover, because the method lacks structure, decisions vary. Different decision makers reach different decisions when faced with the same marketing problem and the same research design. Even one decision maker might decide differently when faced with identical problems and identical research designs on two different occasions.

To counter these shortcomings of the judgmental method, the next two methods of cost-benefit evaluation use procedures that are more rigid and open.[8] They do lead to precise answers to this question of whether or not to conduct research, but these methods are actually only refinements to the judgmental method. We intend them as complements—not substitutes—for experienced judgment.

The Simple Savings Method. The simple savings method begins by assuming that a decision maker can make a reasonable estimate of the costs of a decision mistake. For example, let us suppose the marketing problem concerns which one of three new products a firm should introduce in a market and that choosing the wrong one would cost the firm an estimated $100,000. Making the decision on an eyes-closed, random basis implies the estimated cost of a mistake to be $0.33 \times \$100,000$, or $33,000. Suppose, however, that good decision making based on presently known information is estimated to reduce this mistake probability to 0.20. Now the estimated cost of a mistake is only $0.20 \times \$100,000$, or $20,000. If marketing research is conducted, suppose the estimated likelihood of an error drops to 0.10. Thus, the estimated cost of error, given marketing research, reduces to $10,000. In this situation, the most a decision maker should pay for marketing research is $20,000 - \$10,000$, or $10,000.

We often feel somewhat uncomfortable with the simple savings method, largely because of subjective elements. Indeed, estimates of both mistake likelihood and costs are subjective. But notice these are the only elements of subjectivity and that they are completely out in the open for question and discussion. Different decision makers may prefer different estimates; this method at least focuses on the bases for these differences.

---

[8]The following discussion is based on James H. Myers and A. Coskun Samli, "Management Control of Marketing Research," *Journal of Marketing Research* 6 (August 1969): 268–71.

Also, decision makers can easily perform a sensitivity analysis by varying the estimates of both error likelihoods and costs and seeing at which point decisions change. It may be, for example, that all proposed research is too expensive under even the most varied estimates of mistake costs.

The Present Value Method.   The present value method begins by considering the marketing research decision as an investment. In an introductory finance course, we learned how to define the net present value (NPV); the NPV of a decision to conduct marketing research is the sum of research returns minus research costs discounted over the life of the decision. Research returns can be described as the estimated difference between the decision maker's return with and without research. In symbols:

$$NPV = \sum_{t=1}^{N} \frac{R_t - C_t}{(1 + k)^t}$$

where N is the estimated life of the decision, R_t is the expected research return for the time period t, C_t is the expected cost of marketing research for period t, and k is the organization's internal rate of return. If NPV is positive, a decision to conduct proposed research is appropriate—assuming there is no other more profitable use of organizational resources.

Let us again use our example of the introduction of one of three new products. Suppose estimated research returns and costs for the most profitable product are as in Table 2.1, and the firm uses a 20 percent internal rate of return. As you can see, the firm loses money during year 1 because research returns are 0 while costs are substantial. However, by year 3 the research design is quite profitable; the NPV has become $197,700 over a six-year life.

All well and good, we may say; but there still seem elements of subjectivity in estimating returns, costs, and the internal rate of return. It is

TABLE 2.1
Calculations Illustrating the Present Value Method

Year (t)	Marketing Research Returns ($)	Marketing Research Costs ($)	$R_t - C_t$ ($)	$(1 + k)^t$	$\frac{R_t - C_t}{(1 + k)^t}$ ($)
1	0	50,000	− 50,000	1.20	− 41,700
2	50,000	30,000	20,000	1.44	13,900
3	150,000	10,000	140,000	1.73	81,000
4	200,000	10,000	190,000	2.07	91,600
5	100,000	10,000	90,000	2.49	36,200
6	50,000	0	50,000	2.99	16,700
					NPV = $197,700

true that different estimates lead to different decisions. In fact, our evaluative comments on the simple savings method also apply here and should be noted. The present value method's primary advantage is that it makes more explicit the estimates of future returns and research costs associated with a research decision. Its primary shortcoming is the problem of accurately estimating the differential return attributable to marketing research.

RESEARCH DESIGN SUMMARY   A marketing research design applies the marketing research process to a specific marketing problem. The application requires close contact between researcher and decision maker—and considerable effort. The application produces a complex set of plans for carrying out the marketing research project. Before undertaking the project, both researcher and decision maker should be satisfied that the design will solve the marketing problem at reasonable cost. Decision makers largely make this evaluation from studying the research proposal, the preparation of which is our last topic for the chapter.

Writing a Marketing Research Proposal

When satisfied with a research design, the researcher summarizes it as a **research proposal.** This is a short (usually 1- to 10-page) document submitted to the decision maker as an overview of the intended research. See Box 2.1 for an example.

A research proposal has three functions: descriptive, quasi-contractual, and selling. As a descriptive device, the proposal briefly deals with each aspect of research design, from problem definition to the final report. It describes every major decision in black and white—so that researcher and decision maker can know whether they agree or disagree. The proposal functions almost as a contract between the two parties, to prevent misunderstandings and unpleasant "surprises" at project completion. The proposal also sells, because it presents the research design in a favorable light with the hope that the decision maker will fund it.

RESEARCH PROPOSAL CONTENT   The research proposal has the preceding three functions whether written for a decision maker outside the researcher's firm or inside it. However, proposals for decision makers outside the firm often contain more detail and nearly always contain additional topics: sections that assure confidentiality, indicate the nature of progress and final reports, describe payment procedures, present the qualifications of principal researchers, and state disposition procedures to be used for completed research materials.[9]

---

[9]David J. Luck et al., *Marketing Research*, 5th ed. (Englewood Cliffs, N.J.: Prentice-Hall, 1978), p. 128.

Box 2.1

Hanlon Automobile Dealer Image Study

Research Problem

Compared to a similar six-month period last year, the Hanlon automobile dealership has experienced an unexplained five percent sales decline. This has occurred while new car registration for the two-county market area increased at an annual rate of two percent. Management is aware of no major internal changes that could account for the problem. However, the competing Battaglia dealership changed ownership nine months ago and its new management seems more aggressive than the former one.

Research Objectives

The overall objective of this research is to compare consumer perceptions of the Hanlon and Battaglia dealerships. Three specific objectives guide the research:

1. Determine the relative importance of selected choice criteria consumers use in selecting an automobile dealer.

2. Measure consumer image of the Hanlon and Battaglia dealerships and an ''ideal'' dealership on these choice citeria.

3. Determine choice criteria importance and dealer image for different consumer segments.

Examples of choice criteria include price, service, salesperson honesty, inventory selection, and advertising. Consumer segments will be identified by age, income, occupation, and the dealer from which they bought their last new car.

Research Method

Research will be conducted in three stages. Stage one research will consist of interviews with a small number of recent new car purchasers to identify choice criteria used to select a car dealer. These criteria will be compared to those identified by Hanlon sales personnel. Stage one research will conclude with the development of a personal interview questionnaire for use in stage two.

Interviewers in stage two will administer the form to a random sample of 400 residents age 16 and over in the market area. At least 75 recent purchasers of a new car will be included

Choice Criteria	Entire Sample	Average Importance [a] of Choice Criteria to:	
		Recent Hanlon Customers	Recent Battaglia Customers
Price			
Service			
Salesperson honesty			
Inventory selection			
Advertising			
(Other Criteria as developed in stage one research)			

[a]Based on a 5-point scale (1 is low importance)

in the sample. Interviews should last no longer than thirty minutes. Respondents will remain anonymous and not be told the client's identity. Brief progress reports will be provided at the completion of stages one and two.

Stage three will consist of the analysis and reporting of results. Included will be a table, as above, showing the relative importance of choice criteria for the entire sample—for recent Hanlon customers and for recent Battaglia customers. Dealer image profiles will also be made; these will compare the three customer groups' attitudes toward the Hanlon, Battaglia, and an "ideal" dealership, with respect to the above choice criteria. Hanlon management will receive an interpretation of results and appropriate action-oriented recommendations. An oral report and five copies of a written report will be provided at the end of stage three.

Research Personnel

Interviewers will be briefed before beginning stage two.

The field supervisor and senior analyst

directing this research share twelve years' experience on similar studies. Descriptions of this work and a list of references is available on request.

Timing and Costs

Stage one research will be completed within two weeks of acceptance of this proposal.

Stage two research will be completed within six weeks of the completion of stage one.

Stage three research will be completed two weeks after the completion of stage two.

Cost of the study is $8500, payable on the following schedule:

$4000 at completion of stage two.

$4500 at completion of stage three.

Research Materials

All materials necessary and incidental to the execution of research described by this proposal are the property of the marketing research agency.

Such topics are usually adequately covered for inside proposals by previous experience, frequent oral communication opportunities, and company policy. Outside proposals, therefore, tend to stand more on their own because these topics are all spelled out.

Earlier we identified the content of a research proposal as a complete summary of major aspects of the research design. The decision maker expects to see sections in the proposal on problem definition, information sources, data collection methods and forms, sampling, data collection operations, data analysis, and reporting. And, as noted earlier, the decision maker gives special interest to summaries of the first and last aspects.

The decision maker's interest in the last aspect, reporting the research, centers, as we have seen, on research relevancy. The decision maker often wants to see the form of selected tables in the final report. That is, the researcher should anticipate types of research results and construct "dummy" tables showing intended summaries of important variables. Such a table would be titled and show column headings, but of course it would contain blanks for later insertion of actual results.

Also found in the proposal are estimates of timing and costs. The proposal should show estimated completion dates for significant aspects of the research design. These are usually stated in terms of the decision maker's date of proposal approval rather than actual calendar date. The proposal should clearly show the total cost of the research design but usually avoid cost breakdowns for specific research activities. Such practice keeps the proposal at a reasonable length as well as limits the possibility of the decision maker becoming excessively concerned with cost estimating procedures.

Just as important as a concern for content of the research proposal is a concern for form. Because research designs are complex and because decision makers often lack formal marketing research training, proposals sometimes confuse rather than clarify. To make the research proposal clear, write simply. Avoid jargon and narrow technical discussions. Include a summary of the proposal's major points as an introduction; peripheral material, if any, should appear in an appendix or technical note. Be brief. Emphasize topics relevant to the decision maker. Try to have a draft of the research proposal read by a competent reviewer to identify clarity problems.

RESEARCH PROPOSAL FORM

The form of the proposal depends partly on personal perferences of the decision maker. Some like the absence of detail while others prefer more. According to one researcher, most decision makers feel that "proposals are too long, too detailed, and too redundant."[10] Early in the discussion with the decision maker the researcher should also be able to gauge preferences and expectations on detail. The researcher should also be able to gauge the decision maker's preference on style. There is room for individuality in marketing research and creativity in research design; the proposal may make the difference between acceptance and rejection. However, the researcher must resist temptations to turn the proposal and other research reports into best sellers. Her or his primary concerns will be completeness and clarity—at the expense of style, if necessary.

Preparation of a marketing research proposal costs a lot of money—an estimate of $1000 to $2000 for the typical proposal seems reasonable, with more complex proposals costing on the order of $10,000.[11] Thus, offers to develop proposals and invitations for their submission should not be made lightly.

SUBMITTING A RESEARCH PROPOSAL

Decision makers outside the researcher's firm often use a competitive bidding process to select a research supplier. Choice is based on the submitted proposals. In addition to technical and economic considerations, then, the proposal will be judged on its completeness, comprehensibility, and interest level; these all will be seen as strong evidence of ability to

---

[10]Six Consultants Counsel Clients on How to Improve the Marketing Research They Buy," *Marketing News* (January 28, 1977), p. 13.

[11]Ibid.

produce quality research. Furthermore, outside decision makers often seek opinions of others, references cited by the researcher, regarding the quality of research the researcher has produced in the past.

Chapter Summary

The marketing research process runs like a thread through both research designs and research proposals. Each step in the process interrelates with others, and each requires careful planning.

Research designs apply the marketing research process to solve a particular marketing research problem. Research designs can have either exploratory, descriptive, or causal focuses—with either basic or applied primary objectives. The researcher must consider numerous specific issues: problem definition, data sources, data collection methods, forms, sampling, data collection operations, data analysis and interpretation, and reporting. Always this design is influenced by research cost, research timing, previous research, the decision maker, and relevant others.

The research proposal summarizes the research design. This short document is largely the basis for a decision to conduct marketing research or to make the marketing decision without research.

Whether or not proposed research will solve the problem is assessed by research relevancy, accuracy, timing, and actionability considerations. Relevancy is determined by the researcher's ability to understand the decision maker's problem and by measurement validity. Accuracy in marketing research is largely the absence of sampling and measurement process error. Timing of research results is often crucial to solving the marketing problem, especially for seasonal products, competitive industries, and weak firms. Actionability requires relevancy, accuracy, and timing, but, more completely, the researcher's objective orientation to the decision maker's situation throughout the entire research process.

A cost-benefit evaluation generally balances research costs against benefits and includes estimates of research accuracy. All such evaluations are subjective but are, at least, apparent and discussable in the simple savings and present value methods.

Chapter Review

KEY TERMS

Marketing research process	Marketing research proposal
Sampling	Data interpretation
Secondary data source	Research relevancy
Primary data source	Research accuracy
Applied marketing research	Research actionability
Exploratory marketing research	Marketing research design
Descriptive marketing research	

1. Can primary data ever become secondary data? Can secondary data ever become primary data?

2. What information sources might be used by:

   a) a manufacturer of shoes interested in selecting a few retailers in several large cities to carry its products?

   b) an advertising agency wanting to select a better advertisement theme from three possible approaches?

   c) a corner bar faced with a relocation decision?

   d) a retailer wondering whether or not to carry a new product?

3. Identify two populations of interest for which identifying or listing population members would be (a) easy, (b) difficult, (c) impossible.

4. Illustrate how each step in the marketing research process depends on previous steps.

5. How can exploratory research designs possibly be applied marketing research?

6. Why does there need to be a marketing research proposal for in-house research, that is, for research conducted by one agent for another inside a single organization?

7. What conditions limit a researcher's capability to estimate research benefits and costs?

8. Consider the following research returns and costs. Using an internal rate of return of ten percent, should research proceed? Suppose the internal rate of return was twenty percent instead, should research proceed? What do your answers imply about using the present value method in deciding whether to proceed or not with marketing research?

Year	Research Returns ($)	Research Costs ($)
1	20,000	70,000
2	20,000	10,000
3	40,000	10,000
4	40,000	10,000

Additional Readings

Emory, C. William. *Business Research Methods.* Homewood, Ill.: Richard D. Irwin, 1976.

   Chapters 3 and 4 provide a lucid alternative treatment of the research process and research designs.

Ferber, Robert, ed., *Handbook of Marketing Research.* New York: McGraw-Hill, 1974.

   No other single source covers marketing research as authoritatively and completely as this one. Chapters in the Handbook add detail to nearly every topic in this book, research design among them. Skim through chapters in Section II, Parts A through E, for items that catch your interest.

Gandz, Jeffrey, and Whipple, Thomas W. "Making Marketing Research Accountable," *Journal of Marketing Research* 14 (May 1977): 202–08.

Simulation and marketing management analyses are used in making a decision on whether or not to conduct marketing research.

Hulbert, James, and Lehmann, Donald R. "Assessing the Importance of the Sources of Error in Structural Survey Data." In *Control of Error in Market Research Data,* edited by John U. Farley and John A. Howard. Lexington, Mass.: Lexington Books, D. C. Heath, 1975. Also see Pessemier, E. A. "Data Quality in Marketing Information Systems," in Farley and Howard, ed. *Control of Error.*

Both of these chapters take up different ways of conceptualizing research error.

But now let's consider a more realistic example: suppose that no marketing action changes yet many performance parameters fluctuate. Or, consider that several marketing actions, all acting and interacting at once, each partly cause changes to any one performance parameter. Or, realize that a dynamic environment, which often includes unknown changes in competitors' marketing actions, shows a potential at least equal to marketing actions taken by our own firm for influencing performance parameters. No wonder the process of defining the marketing problem is creative, complex, and time consuming.

Problem Awareness

A decision maker encounters many performance discrepancies every day. Only when certain discrepancies exceed some threshold level, however, do we say that the decision maker is aware of a specific problem. Other remaining discrepancies continue to be tolerated.

DETERMINATION OF THE THRESHOLD LEVEL

Several rather general factors affect threshold level. Most important are the situational dynamics underlying the performance parameter. Picture a performance discrepancy as the location of a small ball, jarred slightly, from an equilibrium point (A) in the five situations shown in Figure 3.2. Threshold levels appear in each situation as dashed lines on either side of the ball. Quite obviously the decision maker is setting tighter threshold levels in the situations at the right. Failure to do so, as at the left, would mean that the situation of aberrant performance can become quite extreme before the decision maker becomes aware of the problem.

Personal characteristics of the decision maker, such as experience, personality, and risk style, also affect threshold levels. So do time pressures and the availability of organizational resources. Further, the amount of stable and random error present in observed values for performance parameters also affects threshold levels.

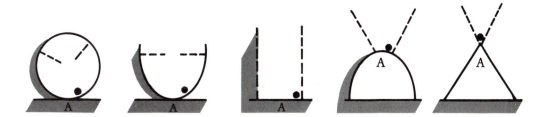

FIGURE 3.2
Performance parameter situational dynamics

TABLE 3.1
Regional Operating Results

	Mixers	Blenders
Advertising Costs		
North	$33,000	$30,000
South	$28,000	$13,000
Prices		
North	$10	$30
South	$9	$25
Units Sold		
North	10,000	7,000
South	6,000	3,000

SEGMENT CONTRIBUTION, PERFORMANCE VARIANCE ANALYSES

On a less general level, we introduce two techniques that help make the decision maker aware of a problem when analyzing certain performance data. The techniques are called **segment contribution analysis**[2] and **performance variance analysis.**[3] Both apply when performance discrepancy data appear in terms of unit sales, revenues, or profits. An example illustrates.

Segment Contribution Analysis. Consider a sales region for an appliance manufacturer whose performance is below historical expectations. To be more precise, suppose the region currently contributes 9.4 percent of its sales to profits and uncontrollable fixed expenses while last year it contributed 10.3 percent. Salesforce members sell two products, mixers and blenders, in the region's two territories, North and South. They receive a 10 percent commission on sales revenue as compensation. Current average prices, advertising costs, and unit sales by product and territory appear in Table 3.1. Standard manufacturing costs are $6 each for mixers and $10 each for blenders.

To proceed, we need these two basic accounting concepts:

- **Controllable variable costs**—expenses that vary predictably with some measure of activity during a given time period and originate in the organizational unit under consideration.

- **Controllable fixed costs**—expenses that stay stable regardless of level of activity during a given time period and originate in the organizational unit under consideration.

---

[2]Patrick M. Dunne and Harry I. Wolk, "Marketing Cost Analysis: A Modularized Contribution Approach," *Journal of Marketing* 41 (July 1977): 83–94.

[3]James M. Hulbert and Norman E. Toy, "A Strategic Framework for Marketing Control," *Journal of Marketing* 41 (April 1977): 12–20.

Some common examples of controllable variable costs are salesforce com-missions, a cents-off coupon included with a product, and a purchase price rebate. Some common examples of controllable fixed costs are sales-force salaries, advertising expenditures, and marketing research costs.

Both definitions state that these costs are controllable, that they orig-inate in the organizational unit under consideration. This means that the region incurs these costs solely because it exists; it would not incur them if it were eliminated.

Now look at Table 3.2, the regional contribution statement that made the firm's sales manager aware of the problem. Notice that it differs from a regional income statement; that is, no allocated or uncontrollable expenses show—for example, headquarter's interest and salary expenses—because they originate outside the organizational unit under consideration. Nor does the actual cost of goods sold show. Rather, stan-dard manufacturing costs appear because the region again should not be penalized or rewarded for performance based on outside actions. It is, in short, a regional contribution statement and not a regional income state-ment. Except for region operating costs, we should be able to derive all values shown in the statement for the current period from the data in Table 3.1.

Table 3.2 clearly indicates cause for concern. Despite an almost 10 percent increase in sales revenue, region contribution remains near con-stant for the two time periods. What marketing actions are likely to have caused this? To answer the question requires that region performance be analyzed by segment—in this case, products and territories. Such an anal-ysis is called a segment contribution analysis. A segment contribution analysis simply breaks down revenue, controllable fixed costs, and con-trollable variable costs by each segment. See Table 3.3.

TABLE 3.2
Regional Contribution Statement

	Current Period	Last Period
Revenue	$439,000	$400,000
Less:		
Standard Manufacturing Costs	196,000	184,000
Sales Commissions	43,900	40,000
Region Total Variable Cost	239,900	224,000
Region Contribution Margin	199,100	176,000
Less:		
Region Advertising Costs	104,000	90,000
Region Operating Costs	54,000	45,000
	158,000	135,000
Region Net Contribution to Profit and Overhead	41,100	41,000

TABLE 3.3
Segment Contribution Analysis

	Mixers		Blenders		Total	
	$	%	$	%	$	%
North						
Revenue	100,000	100.0	210,000	100.0	310,000	100.0
Less:						
Standard Manufacturing						
Costs	60,000	60.0	70,000	33.3	130,000	41.9
Sales Commissions	10,000	10.0	21,000	10.0	31,000	10.0
Total Variable Cost	70,000	70.0	91,000	43.3	161,000	51.9
Contribution Margin	30,000	30.0	119,000	56.7	149,000	48.1
Less Advertising Costs	33,000	33.0	30,000	14.3	63,000	20.3
Net Contribution (Loss)	(3,000)	(3.0)	89,000	42.4	86,000	27.7
South						
Revenue	54,000	100.0	75,000	100.0	129,000	100.0
Less:						
Standard Manufacturing						
Costs	36,000	66.7	30,000	40.0	66,000	51.2
Sales Commissions	5,400	10.0	7,500	10.0	12,900	10.0
Total Variable Cost	41,400	76.7	37,500	50.0	78,900	61.2
Contribution Margin	12,600	23.3	37,500	50.0	50,100	38.8
Less Advertising Costs	28,000	51.8	13,000	17.3	41,000	31.7
Net Contribution (Loss)	(15,400)	(28.5)	24,500	32.7	9,100	7.1
Total Revenue	154,000	100.0	285,000	100.0	439,000	100.0
Less:						
Standard Manufacturing						
Costs	96,000	62.3	100,000	35.1	196,000	44.6
Sales Commissions	15,400	10.0	28,500	10.0	43,900	10.0
Total Variable Cost	111,400	72.3	128,500	45.1	239,900	54.6
Contribution Margin	42,600	27.7	156,500	54.9	199,100	45.4
Less Advertising Costs	61,000	39.6	43,000	15.1	104,000	23.7
Net Contribution (Loss)	(18,400)	(11.9)	113,500	39.8	95,100	21.7

A hasty glance at Table 3.3 allows us to conclude that contribution deficiencies come from the mixers. Deeper examination yields more subtle conclusions:

1. Problems with the mixers seem to come from excessive advertising, especially in the South.

2. Contribution performance in the North betters that in the South both on an absolute dollar basis and on percentages.

However, these conclusions and others based on Table 3.3 come from some assumptions about what is "right" for the products and territories. For example, someone else might conclude that deficiencies come primarily from blenders in the North—perhaps blenders in the North should have contributed $120,000 on revenues of $360,000! Thus, we must continue our example with a performance variance analysis for a heightened awareness of the problem.

Performance Variance Analysis. We need a third basic accounting concept, **performance variance.** Marketing performance variances are the differences between planned and actual values for revenue, market, and cost-related performance parameters. We apply the concept to mixers in the South; the results appear in Table 3.4. Now advertising seems to be less the culprit than we thought earlier. Its unfavorable variance of $-\$6,000$ is only slightly more than the $-\$5,250$ produced by revenues, the market, and costs.

The effect of these last three performance parameters can be expressed more meaningfully as price and cost, market size, and market share variances. We need four symbols:

- S—share of total market
- M—total market sales in units
- Q—firm's quantity sold in units
- C—contribution per unit

and two subscripts:

- a—actual values
- p—planned values.

We express the **price and cost variance** by $(C_a - C_p)Q_a$. That is, the price and cost variance is simply the difference between actual and planned contribution per unit multiplied by the number of units actually sold. For our data we have the price and cost variance equal to

$$(\$2.10 - \$2.55)6,000 = -\$2,700$$

Thus, price and cost differences from planned values produce over half of the $-\$5,250$ variance.

We define the market size variance as the difference between actual and planned market size times planned market share times planned contribution per unit. In symbols, the **market size variance** is given by $(M_a - M_p)(S_p)C_p$. For our data, its value is

$$(180,000 - 200,000)(0.035)\$2.25 = -\$1,785$$

TABLE 3.4
Operating Results for Mixers in the South

Performance Parameter	Planned Performance	Actual Performance	Performance Variance
Revenues			
Unit Sales	7,000	6,000	(1,000)[a]
Unit Price	$9.50	$9.00	($.50)
Revenues	$66,500	$54,000	($12,500)
Market			
Total Market Unit Sales	200,000	180,000	(20,000)
Share of Market	3.50%	3.33%	(0.17%)
Cost per Unit			
Standard			
Manufacturing Costs	$6.00	$6.00	0
Sales Commissions	$0.95	$0.90	$0.05
Unit Contribution	$2.55	$2.10	($0.45)
Total Contribution	$17,850	$12,600	($5,250)
Advertising Costs	$22,000	$28,000	($6,000)

[a]Unfavorable values appear in parentheses.

The market share variance is defined as the difference between actual and planned market shares times the actual market size times the planned contribution per unit. In symbols, the **market share variance** is $(S_a - S_p)(M_a)C_p$, which, when applied to our data, yields $-$765. We now examine these variances in Table 3.5. We can see that the firm originally planned a loss of $4,150 for mixers in the South. Unfortunately, this increased to $15,400. Of the $11,250 increase, $6,000, or 53.3 percent, came from excess advertising costs. Unplanned price and cost, market size, and market share differences accounted for 24.0 percent, 15.9 percent, and 6.8 percent, respectively.

Now suppose variances for both products in both territories are as summarized in Table 3.6. Interpreting these variances, a researcher might

TABLE 3.5
Variance Summary for Mixers in the South

Planned Profit Contribution		($4,150)[a]
Advertising Variance	($6,000)	
Price and Cost Variance	($2,700)	
Market Size Variance	($1,785)	
Market Share Variance	($765)	
Total Variance		($11,250)
Net Contribution		($15,400)

[a]Unfavorable values appear in parentheses.

TABLE 3.6
Variance Summary

	Mixers—North	Mixers—South	Blenders—North	Blenders—South	Total
			Product—Territory		
Planned Profit Contribution	($3,000)[a]	($4,150)	$80,000	$31,000	$103,850
Advertising Variance	($4,000)	($6,000)	($8,000)	($1,000)	($19,000)
Price and Cost Variance	2,800	(2,700)	6,500	(3,800)	2,800
Market Size Variance	2,100	(1,785)	7,200	(2,200)	5,315
Market Share Variance	(900)	(765)	3,300	500	2,135
Total Variance per product in each territory	0	(11,250)	9,000	(6,500)	(8,750)
Net Contribution	($3,000)	($15,400)	$89,000	$24,500	$95,100

[a]Unfavorable values appear in parentheses.

begin to define the marketing problem by obtaining answers to these questions:

1. What caused excessive advertising costs for both products in both territories? What can be done to correct this?

2. Why does the North equal or exceed its planned performance for both products? Why does the South fall short of its? What marketing actions might remedy these variances?

3. Why are market shares below plan for mixers and above plan for blenders? What factors more strongly influence market share?

4. Were plans themselves poorly made or poorly executed?[4]

Answering these questions and undoubtedly raising others would require interviews and observations—principal activities in defining the problem.

Summary of the Awareness-Raising Techniques.   Segment contribution analysis and performance variance analysis sharply focus problem awareness activities. However, although they do thus conserve research resources, they also confine the decision maker's view of the problem to only a few, accounting-related performance parameters. They should be used with a situation analysis—our next step in the problem definition process—so that the decision maker won't miss or dismiss other important information before making a request for research.

[4]This question can be partly answered with some after-the-fact information on what planned values should have been, had they been based on more realistic forecasts. See Hulbert and Toy, "Strategic Framework."

TABLE 3.7
Questions Measuring the Organization's External Environment

Competitive Environment
Who competes?
What marketing strategies do competitors use?
What market shares do competitors achieve?
What are competitors' strengths and weaknesses?
What future marketing strategies might competitors use?
What other firms may compete in the future?

Customer Segments
Who buys in socioeconomic and psychological characteristic terms?
How much do segments buy?
How often do segments buy?
Where do segments buy?
When do segments buy?
What things do segments consider important when they buy?
On what factors do segments compare competing products before they buy?
What information sources do segments use?
What do segments do with the product after they buy?
What changes in the buying process are expected?
How do competitors' segments differ?

Supplier Environment
Who supplies raw materials and component parts?
What has been the history of the supplying relationship?
What will likely happen to this relationship in the future?
Who else might supply?
Which suppliers do competitors use?

Technological Environment
What product features and production process are patented?
How else does the firm control the relevant technology?
Is the firm a technological leader or follower?
What technological breakthroughs are expected? How soon?

Economic Environment
What is the short term GNP forecast?
What taxes, tariffs, and import quotas apply?
What is the shape and slope of the demand curve?

Legal and Political Environment
What federal, state, and local laws affect marketing decisions?
What regulatory policies and trade practice rules affect marketing decisions?
What is the firm's political visibility and vulnerability?

Situation Analysis

At this stage in the problem definition process, the researcher enters. Her or his task is to understand the marketing problem by investigating both the circumstances surrounding the research request and the problem's potential solutions.

Research requests do not appear in isolation but rather emerge from a rich network of surrounding circumstances. Understanding these circumstances is possible when the researcher knows both the organization's external environment and the decision maker's internal environment.

CIRCUMSTANCES SURROUNDING THE RESEARCH REQUEST

External Environment. The organization's external environment consists of forces outside the firm that influence performance parameters. In an introductory marketing course, we study such forces as competitors, customer (wholesalers, retailers, and consumers) segments, suppliers, technology, economic conditions, laws, and politics. The sorts of questions a researcher asks to achieve an understanding of these forces appear in Table 3.7.

Some questions in Table 3.7 will be more relevant than others in defining the marketing problem for a specific study. Furthermore, we should realize that the table does not represent a complete list of questions measuring the organization's external environment. Feel free to add others.

Internal Environment. Questions about the decision maker's internal environment complement those of the organization's external environment. Some questions about the internal organization environment apply either to the organization as a whole or to specific nonmarketing functional areas in the firm—production, finance, research and development, personnel, and others. Typical questions appear in Table 3.8.

Other questions relate to another aspect of the internal environment, the decision maker's internal marketing environment. They appear in Table 3.9. Again, we make no claims that the questions in Tables 3.8 and 3.9 represent all possible areas of inquiry in understanding the decision maker's internal environment.

Answers to questions in all three tables help to understand the decision maker's reasons for requesting marketing research. They set the stage for the definition of the marketing problem. Answers must be understood from both the researcher's viewpoint and the decision maker's viewpoint. Before marketing research advances at all, these answers should match almost completely.

The researcher should pay particular attention to answers whenever they relate to the decision maker's objectives. Always the decision maker will be organizationally and personally committed to accomplishing cer-

TABLE 3.8
Questions Measuring the Internal Organization Environment

What are the firm's long-term objectives and short-term goals?

What major strategies guide the firm?

What has been the firm's recent performance?

What are the firm's strengths in terms of capital, plant and equipment, personnel, location, time, technology, and other resources?

What factors limit performance?

What is the basic cost, volume, and profit structure of the firm?

What are the levels of sales, profits, and cash?

What are the missions, relationships, and authorities among organizational units?

What short-term changes may occur in the internal organizational environment?

tain objectives. Once a researcher understands the nature of these objectives, he or she can design research to help accomplish them. The researcher will find answers as existing statements of goals, strategies, and policies. To find other answers may require some modest preliminary research, and some may require more formal exploratory research. In general, to find answers always requires diligent interviewing, observing, and analyzing.

Interviewing begins quite clearly and most importantly with the decision maker. The researcher must understand the decision maker's view of the problem, along the lines of factors noted in Tables 3.7, 3.8, and 3.9. The researcher should conduct other interviews with people in the organization having additional insight on the problem, people either in marketing or in other functional areas. Still other interviews, with people outside the organization (consumers, wholesalers and retailers, suppliers, and regulatory agencies, for example), shed further light on the problem. Interviews may be conducted individually or on a group basis; they may be structured or unstructured in organization.

Diligent observation occurs as part of the interview process but is even more important in the collection of secondary data. Examples of frequently relevant internal secondary data include routine and special reports, earlier marketing research results, and other company documents and records. Some useful external secondary data include academic publications, trade association reports, commercially prepared industry studies, U.S. Census and other government agency publications, and case studies.

Diligent analysis requires the researcher to sift through interview and observation data to distinguish the more relevant from the less. The researcher must be flexible; creative; and competent to base the analysis on knowledge of human behavior in consumption and organizational settings, as well as on knowledge of marketing theory and practice, and on knowledge of the operation of the firm. To provide this knowledge goes

TABLE 3.9
Questions Measuring the Internal Marketing Environment

Product

What product lines and products does the firm make and sell?

What are sales, profits, and market shares by product lines and products?

What are growth rates and cash flows by product lines and products?

What relative advantages do product lines and products possess?

How are product lines and products positioned in the market?

How well do product lines and products complement each other in terms of product features, market segments, brand names, production processes, distribution channels, and salesforce?

What product lines or products in the firm compete with each other?

What new product lines and products will soon be introduced?

Price

What basic pricing strategies does the firm pursue?

What price lines exist among models in a product line?

What are costs and prices at various production levels?

How are prompt payment, seasonal, quantity, and trade discounts structured?

What freedom does the firm have to change prices?

How quickly can a pricing decision be made?

When was the last time prices were changed?

Distribution

What channels of distribution does the firm use?

What alternative channels might it use?

What are typical margins in the channels?

What services do channel members provide?

How well do channel members provide these services?

How many middlemen are used in a typical market area?

What criteria apply in selecting new middlemen?

How much power does the firm exercise in the channel?

Promotion

What is the size of the promotion budget by product line, territory, channel, and time period?

How is the promotion budget determined?

How is the promotion budget allocated between advertising, personal selling, and sales promotion activities?

What advertising appeals does the firm use?

How does the firm measure advertising effectiveness?

How large is the salesforce?

What are the capabilities of the salesforce?

What sales promotion activities does the firm use?

What promotion changes are expected?

beyond the scope of a text in marketing research. Other course work—in business administration and related fields—and professional experience share this burden.

POTENTIAL SOLUTIONS   The other half of understanding the marketing problem means investigating potential solutions. To understand potential solutions, the reseacher must identify them, estimate their performance consequences, and learn the decision maker's solution preferences.

Solution Identification.   A fully identified solution describes marketing actions to be taken as part of the solution, examines risk factors, and forecasts timing. We discuss each in turn.

A marketing problem solution must describe actions it would take to solve the problem and identify who inside and outside the organization would be the agents. The researcher must provide sufficient detail to allow the agents to understand what each action entails. The description should also include cost estimates for major actions.

A marketing problem solution must also examine risk. An examination of risk addresses both the consequences of a mistake and the chance of making one. The researcher should also recognize and report that some consequences may be more immediate and that some may be more easily reversed than others. The researcher should estimate the ability of the organization to tolerate any and all such consequences.

A marketing problem solution also forecasts timing. The researcher should forecast dates for the execution of major actions along with estimates of when benefits will begin to be felt. Forecasts of timing are especially important for firms with limited resources and those competing in seasonal industries.

Estimating the Performance Consequences.[5]   Statements of performance consequences estimate the degree to which a potential marketing action will solve the problem. To make these statements requires the researcher to identify performance parameters on which the degree will be measured. Researchers and decision makers must be sure proposed research addresses all relevant performance parameters. More than this, researchers and decision makers must establish critical values of all performance parameters before conducting descriptive and causal marketing research. For example, it is not enough to state that a proposed marketing action must favorably affect brand awareness, distribution, and shipping costs. Rather, the issue is the extent to which the proposed action must change organizational performance on these parameters. Research with

---

[5]This section borrows heavily from David J. Luck et al., *Marketing Research*, 5th ed. (Englewood Cliffs, N.J.: Prentice-Hall, 1978), pp. 82–83.

identified performance parameters but without specified critical values produces findings comparable to a 7:00 A.M. weather forecast that says today will be warm but fails to predict exact temperature—you have some research results but still don't know what to wear!

Thus, after agreeing with the decision maker on performance parameters and their critical values, the researcher must estimate the degree to which potential marketing actions satisfy them. Of course, the researcher does this much more easily upon completing the research. However, some estimation must occur here to narrow the scope of the research. Part of this estimation looks at the fit between potential actions and the environments discussed earlier. For example, even though an action may be technically "correct," it may be largely incompatible with the organization's resources and goals. A larger part of this estimation focuses on the technical correctness of potential actions based on an understanding of marketing theory and practice. For example, a proposed marketing action to lower price must be based on such considerations as price elasticity of demand, cost and price structure of the firm, and customary prices in the industry.

An equally large part of this estimation focuses on acceptance of the proposed action by people involved in or affected by the decision.[6] That is, a marketing action may be technically correct but unpopular to the extent that it is poorly executed. A less technically correct action might be better accepted and, therefore, more effective in terms of performance consequences.

Discovering Decision Maker Solution Preferences. As a last aspect of understanding potential solutions, the researcher must learn the decision maker's solution preferences. An initial consideration is the decision maker's decision freedom, a term that refers to the latitude permitted the decision maker within responsibilities assigned by the organization. Simply stated, a potential solution must be one the decision maker is free to implement.

Equally important, the researcher must learn how the decision maker deals with risk because "risk preferences can have a considerable effect on the kind of information desired and, therefore, on the research conducted."[7] To illustrate, picture two decision makers, one a risk taker and the other a risk avoider, both about to make a new product introduction decision. While both will request much the same research information, some differences will exist. For example, the risk taker will be quite inter-

---

[6]See N. R. F. Maier, "Psychology in Industrial Organizations," 4th ed. (Boston: Houghton Mifflin, 1973), pp. 130–35 for a more complete discussion of acceptance and decision making.

[7]Donald S. Tull and Del I. Hawkins, Marketing Research: Meaning, Measurement, and Method (New York: Macmillan, 1976), p. 50.

ested in research on marketing actions consistent with a favorable consumer response. To satisfy this interest, part of the research may address selection of the most effective advertising appeals, the best way to distribute free samples, and whether to use wholesalers or to sell directly to retailers. The risk avoider, on the other hand, will be more interested in minimizing the impact of an unfavorable consumer response. Part of this research may instead address methods of minimizing fixed costs, estimating consumer reaction to high prices, and determining whether to make or buy certain component parts of the product.

Stating the Problem

When satisfied that additional effort will likely produce little additional insight, the researcher considers the problem situation understood. Now comes the time to refine what usually is a mass of information into a succinct **problem statement,** or summary of the marketing problem. While usually only a few paragraphs long, the statement reflects an understanding of all topics we have discussed to this point in the chapter.

A problem statement begins with a simple exposition of the problem in terms of key symptoms or performance consequences. It identifies key marketing actions taken in the past and aspects of the organization's external and internal environments that both influence and constrain key symptoms. It identifies potential marketing actions that should solve the problem along with their estimated performance consequences. Taken together, these features of a problem statement set the stage for research objectives.

A problem statement ends with **research objectives** that state what proposed research intends to accomplish. At a general level, research objectives describe whether the research intends to produce exploratory, descriptive, or causal research findings to solve either basic or applied marketing problems. At a specific level, research objectives illustrate benefits that follow from the research. As examples, consider these:

- Estimate dealer reactions to a 10 percent price increase on mixers.
- Improve forecast accuracy for sales of mixers and blenders sold in the South.

Such objectives guide the conduct of research and serve as standards to control and evaluate research effectiveness. They help to organize proposals, progress reports, and final reports. Most important, research objectives provide a basis to construct research hypotheses, which we take up in the next section.

The problem statement should contain no differences between researcher and decision maker on aspects of problem definition Diligent interviewing, observing, and analyzing coupled with frequent meetings between the two parties help to achieve this harmony. Beyond these practices, some additional advice helps the researcher construct good problem statements:[8]

1. Formulate several different problem statements.

2. Criticize these different statements to examine critically their underlying assumptions, implications, and possible consequences.

3. Develop an integrated or synthesized problem statement by emphasizing the strengths of each different problem statement while minimizing their individual weaknesses.

4. Include persons in activities (1), (2), and (3) who are experiencing the problem, who have the expertise to define problems in various substantive domains, whose commitment to the problem definition and resulting marketing actions will be necessary for those actions to be implemented successfully, and who are expected to be affected by the outcomes of any marketing action to solve or manage the problem.

The more the researcher follows this advice, the more likely it is that the problem statement will lead to research that solves the marketing problem.

Research Hypotheses

Our problem definition process ends with research hypotheses. **Research hypotheses** tentatively state the marketing topic in a form for empirical testing. Some examples of hypotheses are:

- Competitors' reimbursements for cooperative advertising averaged less than $1000 per retailer.
- A reduction in the compensation limit on cooperative advertising from 3 percent to 2 percent of billed sales would not upset retailers.
- Bigger retailers took advantage of cooperative advertising allowances less frequently than smaller retailers.

Each of these statements can be supported or not supported by marketing research results, using tests of varying rigor and sophistication.

---

[8]Adapted from Ralph H. Kilmann and Ian I. Mitroff, "Problem Defining and the Consulting/Intervention Process," *California Management Review* 21 (Spring 1979): 26–33.

Research hypotheses follow research objectives. For example, all the preceding hypotheses came from a single research objective: "Describe marketing actions that reduce cooperative advertising costs without affecting sales." As should be obvious, a single marketing research study contains numerous hypotheses. In fact, it should contain at least one hypothesis for each separate variable present in the study. If it does not, then very likely those variables lacking hypotheses should not be a part of the study.

Chapter Summary

Problem definition activities distinguish the more important from the less important performance discrepancies, what probably influenced them, and what may be done about them. Like many of the later steps in the marketing research process, problem definition always compromises. It never completely, precisely, and with certainty states the true marketing problem. However, the information in this chapter should help us define marketing problems systematically and reasonably.

Problem definition activities are less structured and more intuitive than the steps in the subsequent implementation of market research. They are also more frustrating. That is, time spent defining the problem seems less productive than later steps in the marketing research process, probably because it is least near research "task completion." Because of this, some researchers and decision makers tend to speed through problem definition to execute the research design as quickly as possible. They should not.

No other more important step in the marketing research process exists than defining the problem. A problem definition influences every following step in the marketing research process: identifying data sources and data collection methods, designing data collection forms, designing the sample, collecting the data, analyzing and interpreting the data, and reporting and following up the research. Making perfect decisions in each of these steps cannot help a decision maker if the steps pertain to the wrong problem. Moreover, an adequate problem definition narrows the scope of a research design and allows it to be executed more efficiently. An adequate problem definition prevents research "dead ends," and it ensures that marketing research will be relevant.

Problem definition activities depend on the complexity, importance, and singularity of the problem. If the problem is complex, important, and unique, activities to define the problem constitute formal exploratory marketing research. In this situation, the entire marketing research process produces descriptions that allow a better understanding of the problem and research hypotheses. If the problem is less complex, less important, and less unique, activities lead to either descriptive or causal marketing research studies; such problem definition activities are more informal and could be called preliminary research to determine research design.

Chapter Review

Performance parameter	Controllable fixed costs	**KEY TERMS**
Performance discrepancy	External environment	
Problem awareness	Problem statement	
Controllable variable costs	Research hypotheses	

1. Describe any differences you perceive in defining the marketing problem for exploratory, descriptive, and causal research designs.   **DISCUSSION QUESTIONS**

2. The client firm would be able to observe the performance consequences of some potential solutions to the problem more quickly than the consequences of others. What implications does this have in designing marketing research?

3. What personal characteristics should the researcher exhibit in problem definition activities?

4. Illustrate how an adequate problem definition "narrows the scope of a research design."

5. Could a researcher ever base a problem definition on a favorable performance variance?

6. Why doesn't the region's fair share of corporate research and development costs appear in Table 3.2?

7. Which is better—assessing the adequacy of problem definition before conducting marketing research, or after? Why?

8. Consider a hearing aid manufacturer selling its products through independent specialty stores and a national chain. The firm incurs standard manufacturing costs of $75 per unit and pays a 10 percent sales commission on all sales made to specialty stores. Other data for last year follow:

	Through specialty stores	*Through national chain stores*
Co-op Advertising Costs	$158,000	$232,000
Total Revenue	$484,000	$532,000
Unit Sales	4,002	4,840

a) Perform a segment contribution analysis. With which distribution channel does the problem lie? On what assumptions do you base your answer?

b) Supposed planned performance is as shown on page 68:

	Through specialty stores	Through national chain stores
Revenues		
Unit Sales	4,200	4,500
Unit Price	$120	$115
Revenues	$504,000	$517,500
Market		
Total Market Unit Sales	420,000	1,100,000
Share of Market	10.0%	0.4%
Cost per Unit		
Standard Manufacturing Cost	_____	_____
Sales Commissions	_____	_____
Unit Contribution	_____	_____
Advertising Costs	$168,000	$202,500

Fill in the blanks. With knowledge that actual market size was 400,000 units for specialty stores and 1,000,000 units for national chains, complete a performance variance analysis for both channels. Which channel now appears responsible for the problem? What research questions might you investigate?

Additional Readings

Abell, Derek F., and Hammond, John S. *Strategic Market Planning: Problems and Analytical Approaches*. Englewood Cliffs, N.J.: Prentice-Hall, 1979.

See Chapter 2 for an excellent discussion of five ingredients needed to define marketing problems: consumers, competitors, market characteristics, environmental trends, and company capabilities. This discussion extends our knowledge of both the organization's internal and external environments.

Leavitt, Harold J. "Beyond the Analytic Manager." *California Management Review* 17 (Part I, Spring 1975): 5–12, (Part II, Summer 1975): 11–21.

Here are alternatives to "rational" styles of thought in problem finding, problem solving, and solution implementing; they show there are more ways than one to get things done.

Locander, William B., and Cocanougher, A. Benton, eds. *Problem Definition in Marketing*. Chicago: American Marketing Association, 1975.

This short monograph somewhat parallels our discussion on the problem definition process. It clarifies the obligations of both researcher and decision maker in performing problem definition activities.

Pounds, William F. "The Process of Problem Finding." *Industrial Management Review* 11 (Fall 1969), 1–19.

This article extends our treatment of performance models that identify marketing problems.

4

Secondary Data: Sources and Collection

After defining the marketing problem, the marketing research process continues with the researcher selecting data sources. A **data source** is simply something or someone that provides information useful in solving the problem. We begin by examining secondary data sources and collection in Chapter 4. We take up the collection of primary data in Chapters 5 through 11.

Secondary data sources are those repositories of literature or statistics originally collected for some other purpose than to solve the marketing problem at hand. Secondary data contribute so much to the effectiveness of marketing research that most projects should, and indeed do, begin with their thorough review. Secondary data perform these functions:

1. provide some or all information needed to meet marketing research objectives;

2. help to define and refine the problem;

3. illustrate proper research designs; and

4. serve as a basis of comparison for interpreting and evaluating primary data.[1]

---

[1]Points 3 and 4 come from Jerry E. Drake and Frank J. Millar, *Marketing Research: Intelligence and Management* (Scranton, Pa: International Textbook Co., 1969), p. 227.

Secondary data do all these things while taking less time, money, and people to collect than primary data. In addition, some secondary data may be more accurate and more complete than corresponding primary data. For example, a consumer may answer a sensitive question one way on a Census Bureau data collection form and another way or not at all on a commercially used form.[2]

However, these strengths of secondary data are undermined to some extent by three inherent weaknesses.

First, secondary data often apply to times long past.

This does not mean older secondary data are irrelevant. Indeed, all data in marketing research, whether secondary or primary, suffer from this weakness to some degree. Most secondary data suffer to a greater degree than most primary data and some secondary data suffer more than others. Regardless of data type, we should evaluate this "dated data" problem by identifying factors influencing the data since their collection. Moreover, we should make estimates of more current data values whenever factors seem sizeable.

Second, secondary data often only partly satisfy research objectives because of differences between them and the current research project in definitions, categories, and geographic areas.

Differences in definitions occur at both conceptual and operational levels. **Conceptual-level definitions** describe research variables in theoretical terms. See, for example, the first section of Chapter 8 where we conceptually define consumer beliefs and attitudes. **Operational-level definitions** describe research variables in measurement terms. One such definition may state, for example, that a consumer's attitude toward a new product in a particular study is (and only is) the sum of her or his beliefs on eight agree/disagree statements. Problems arise when the conceptual or operational definitions we are currently using do not agree with those in existing secondary data; data simply do not fit as well as we would like.

Differences in categories breaking down variables in our research and those breaking down secondary data lead to more problems. For example, we may desire information on families with incomes between $20,000 and $30,000, but earlier research breaks at $20,001 to $25,000 and $25,001 to $35,000. Sometimes we can adjust for category differences by adding, subtracting, or interpolating; sometimes not.

Differences in geographic areas lead to still more problems. Often it is an **aggregation problem**: we find data for a state but need it for parts of several counties. Again, we may be able to adjust data to generate more appropriate data. Other times it will be a **distance problem:** we find the

---

[2]Harper W. Boyd, Jr., Ralph Westfall, and Stanley F. Stasch, *Marketing Research*, 4th ed. (Homewood, Ill.: Richard D. Irwin, 1977), p. 146.

exact data we need but they apply to a geographic area some distance from the one under study. Distance problems make data either totally irrelevant or somewhat pertinent—it's a matter of judgment.

Third, secondary data may be inaccurate.

This weakness, like the first, applies to primary data too but with one important difference. When we collect primary data, we know a great deal about research design and execution. When we collect secondary data, we know far less. Quite simply, other researchers may lack our knowledge, diligence, and objectivity. If we find quite limited discussion—or none— of research definitions, sampling methods, analytical techniques, and other design aspects accompanying secondary data, it usually indicates sloppy research[3] or ignorance.

Secondary Data: Inside Sources

Secondary data originate either inside or outside the decision maker's organization. Inside sources include marketing plans, company reports, and marketing information systems (MKIS) reports. Outside sources include government units, professional publications, and commercial services, among others. We examine each.

Firms produce, assemble, distribute, and store enormous amounts of internal literature and statistics. (Retrieval may be another matter, however.) Sometimes this secondary data will be conveniently assembled in the form of a marketing management report. Such reports range from a simple one-page warehouse shipment summary, for example, to a 200-page monster describing industries for potential expansion.

More often, internal secondary data will be separately found in its "raw" state, as provided by individuals in departments. Personnel in the accounting and sales departments probably provide the most. To generalize further, all internal secondary data relevant to marketing research relate to the practice of marketing management in the firm: planning, leading, and controlling strategies that deal with product, price, distribution, and promotion.

STRATEGIC MARKETING PLANS

Decision makers in well-managed firms often formulate strategic marketing plans for various organizational levels and units. **Strategic marketing plans** describe the organization's external environment, internal organizational environment, and internal marketing environment concerning the topics identified in Tables 3.7, 3.8, and 3.9 (see pages 58, 60, 61). They also present short-run marketing tactics, time plans for marketing actions,

---

[3]Gilbert A. Churchill, Jr., *Marketing Research*, 2nd ed. (Hinsdale, Ill.: The Dryden Press, 1979), p. 131.

marketing personnel requirements, marketing budgets, and management control procedures.[4] Such plans supply important secondary data in helping to understand circumstances surrounding the marketing problem.

COMPANY REPORTS Annual reports supply similar information although on a more aggregate level. For example, a quick look at the 1978 annual reports for K-Tel International, Inc., and John Deere and Company shows that 27.0¢ and 1.0¢, respectively, of every sales dollar was spent on advertising. Further reading shows slightly over 25 percent of sales for K-Tel, and slightly over 70 percent for Deere, coming from United States operations. Annual reports often provide information on advertising expenditures and on sales by product group and by season; of course, they also present cost of goods sold, accounts receivable, and management strategy decisions. All such information may interest an industrial marketing researcher employed by either the firm in question or one of its competitors.

Another useful internal source of secondary data is old marketing research reports. Someone in the firm usually keeps these on file. Their review adds insight in defining the problem, in making research design decisions, and in interpreting research results.

MKIS SECONDARY DATA All the preceding sources of internal secondary data share a common characteristic: they originate to solve a specific problem that may or may not be marketing in nature. On the other hand, the MKIS secondary data originate to solve no one specific problem, but rather to support many marketing decisions. For example, we would expect to find MKIS data on product, price, distribution, and promotion activities in the firm; more completely, MKIS data would cover the topics in Tables 3.7, 3.8, and 3.9.

The data will consist of both literature and statistics: a great deal of MKIS data appear in newspaper clippings, magazine articles, and research and development division reports. Not all MKIS data have to be stored on a computer. Much data are, of course, but much more can be found in libraries and in collections cared for by technical specialists in the firm. To qualify as part of an MKIS requires only that the literature (and statistics) meet our definition in Chapter 1: data must be structured and flow in an orderly fashion to decision makers in specified areas of marketing management.

MKIS data apply to the past, present, and future; often data for all three periods appear side by side to make comparison easier. Often future or forecasted data appear at three levels: optimistic, realistic, and pessi-

---

[4]Robert J. Williams and Colin F. Neuhaus, "A Model for a Strategic Marketing Plan," in *Contemporary Marketing Thought*, ed. B. A. Greenberg and D. N. Bellenger (Chicago: American Marketing Association, 1977), p. 523.

mistic. A good MKIS allows users to make their own forecasts based on their own assumptions and on a number of forecasting models.

Finally, MKIS data are going to consist of both useful and superfluous information. Which MKIS data fall into which category changes from user to user, decision to decision, and time to time. Systems coping with this problem necessarily "overkill"; that is, they include too much data at too low levels of aggregation. The answer is there but difficult to find.[5] When we are lucky, MKIS data are centrally located and easily modified in a user-oriented system.[6]

Secondary Data: Outside Sources

More general, more diverse, and simply *more* secondary data exist in sources outside the decision maker's firm. Sources include government units, professional publications, commercial services, and others.

Federal and state government units provide much useful literature and statistics—so much, in fact, that they collectively account for more secondary data than any other source we discuss in this chapter.

GOVERNMENT UNITS

The Censuses.   At the federal level, most secondary data relevant to marketing researchers come from censuses conducted by the Bureau of the Census in the Department of Commerce. Most people know about the census of population, taken every ten years since 1790; few know about the census of housing, taken at the same time since 1940. Fewer still know about nine other censuses taken at five-year intervals: agriculture, construction, governments, manufactures, mineral industries, retail trade, service industries, transportation, and wholesale trade. While all of these eleven censuses aid marketing researchers, seven are more useful than the others.

Census of Population	This census enumerates (counts) people. Volumes detail the number of consumers by age, sex, race, marital status, income, and other characteristics for the nation, states, counties, cities, and smaller geographic areas. Volumes also contain cross-classifications by population characteristics for larger areas.

[5]Charles D. Schewe, Roger J. Calantone, and James L. Wiek, "Using Benefit Segmentation to Increase Marketing Information System Usage," in *Marketing: 1776–1976 and Beyond,* ed. K. L. Bernhardt (Chicago: American Marketing Association, 1976), p. 630.

[6]Jack D. Sparks, "Taming the 'Paper Elephant' in Marketing Information Systems," *Journal of Marketing* 40 (July 1976): 83–86.

Census of Housing	This census enumerates housing units. Volumes detail the number of rooms, persons per room, rent paid, plumbing characteristics, structural characteristics, fuels, major appliances, and other characteristics for housing units.
Census of Manufactures	This census enumerates firms that mechanically or chemically transform materials or substances into new products. Volumes detail the number, employment, production worker hours, cost of materials, volume of shipments, capital expenditures, and inventories of firms competing in 452 industries.
Census of Retail Trade	This census enumerates firms primarily engaged in selling merchandise to the general public for personal or household consumption. Volumes detail numbers of firms, sales, employment, sales by merchandise line, and other statistics for about 100 retail business classifications.
Census of Service Industries	This census enumerates firms engaged in providing services to consumers, businesses, government units, and other organizations. Volumes detail the number of firms, revenue, expenses, payroll, employment, size of firm, and other statistics for about 200 service classifications.
Census of Transportation	This census largely samples transportation data from private and commercial truck registrations, consumer households, manufacturing establishments, nonregulated motor carriers, and public warehouses. With regard to consumer households, the 1977 volume details number of persons taking trips, number of trips taken, accommodations used, trip duration, means of travel, destination, and other characteristics for 24,000 U.S. households. Data appear by occupation, education, and family income.
Census of Wholesale Trade	This census enumerates firms primarily engaged in selling merchandise to retailers and repair shops; to industrial, commercial,

Census of Wholesale Trade
(*continued*)

professional or agricultural users; to other wholesalers; and to agents and brokers. Volumes pertain to about 125 different wholesaling classifications—detailing number of firms, sales, payroll, employment, operating expenses, inventories, and other statistics. Data appear by type of wholesale operation.

These short descriptions cannot do justice to the breadth and depth of secondary data in these censuses, but a firsthand perusal of each census would make their worth apparent.

Census publications reach the public as quickly as possible in various forms. Preliminary and advance reports for each state appear first, followed by more detailed microfiche final reports, paperback final reports, clothbound final reports, and computer tapes. For example, for the 1977 Census of Retail Trade (taken in 1978), advance and microfiche final reports began to appear in May of 1979. Paperback final reports followed about a month later and preceded clothbound, final reports and computer tapes by some six months.

Apart from this eighteen-month data collection and processing lag, censuses are always out of date because of their periodic nature. To diminish this problem, the bureau of the Census publishes numerous **interim reports** each week, month, quarter, and year. We identify those of interest in Table 4.1. Each report, with the exception of *County Business Patterns*, actually consists of several series of reports on topics reported on in one or more censuses. For example, *Current Business Reports* consists of eleven series including *Monthly Retail Trade, Monthly Depart-*

TABLE 4.1
Census and Interim Report Title

Census	Interim Report Title
Population	Current Population Reports
Housing	Current Housing Reports
Manufactures	Annual Survey of Manufactures
	County Business Patterns
	Current Industrial Reports
Retail Trade	County Business Patterns
	Current Business Reports
Service Industries	County Business Patterns
	Current Business Reports
Transportation	County Business Patterns
Wholesale Trade	County Business Patterns
	Current Business Reports

ment *Store Sales, Monthly Selected Service Receipts,* and *Monthly Wholesale Trade.* All contain more current statistics than corresponding censuses, with each appearing about forty-five days after the end of each reporting period.

Census publications must aggregate at some level to facilitate data reporting and use. (Interim reports contain the most aggregated data.) Consumer-oriented data are most often aggregated to city, county, state, national, SMSA, and SCSA levels. SMSA stands for **Standard Metropolitan Statistical Area,** an area of roughly one or more counties that contains a city with 50,000 or more inhabitants. SCSA stands for **Standard Consolidated Statistical Area,** an area containing one SMSA of at least 1,000,000 inhabitants plus other, adjacent SMSAs. In 1979 there were over 300 SMSAs and 13 SCSAs in the United States.

Business-oriented census data aggregate on similar levels as well as by SIC code. The SIC, which stands for the **Standard Industrial Classification** system,

> divides the nation's economic activities into broad industrial divisions, 2-digit major groups, 3-digit industry subgroups, and 4-digit detailed industries [for example]:

Division	Manufacturing	SIC Code
Major Group	Good and Kindred Products	20
Industry Subgroup	Canned and Preserved Fruits and Vegetables	203
Detailed Industry	Frozen Fruits, Fruit Juices, and Vegetables[7]	2037

Beyond 4-digit detailed industries, we will often find data on 5-digit product classes (for example, 20371 stands for frozen fruits, juices, and ades). We may even find data on 7-digit products (20371 71 stands for frozen orange juice, concentrated). Table 4.2 shows 2-digit SIC ranges that comprise each of the business-oriented censuses described in the list of censuses. Thus, if the only thing we know about a firm is its SIC code, we can tell immediately from the first two digits whether it is a manufacturer, wholesaler, retailer, or something else.

Aggregated data often do not apply exactly to a given marketing problem. Data may appear for counties and we need it for blocks. Or, data may appear for durable goods and we need it for refrigerators. To diminish this problem, the Bureau of the Census makes available more detailed microfiche versions of tables not published in its usual reports. It also provides computer tapes and Bureau consultants who perform special analyses, both on a cost basis.

---

[7]Adapted from U.S. Department of Commerce, Bureau of the Census, *Mini-Guide to the 1977 Economic Censuses* (Washington, D.C.: Government Printing Office, 1978), p. 3.

TABLE 4.2
SIC Codes (2-digit) by Census

Census	SIC Code Range
Manufactures	20 to 39
Retail Trade	52 to 59
Service Industries	70 to 89
Transportation	40 to 49
Wholesale Trade	50 to 51

Source: U.S. Department of Commerce, Bureau of the Census, *Mini-Guide to the 1977 Economic Censuses* (Washington, D.C.: Government Printing Office, 1978), p. 3.

Other Government Publications.   Many other federal government publications complement those we have discussed. Just scratching the surface, we find some of the most relevant periodicals: *Business Conditions Digest, Construction Review, Federal Home Loan Bank Board Journal, Federal Reserve Bulletin, Monthly Labor Review,* and the *Survey of Current Business.* This last periodical provides quarterly GNP statistics and monthly sales, income, inventory, price, advertising, population, employment, and many other useful business-related statistics for the nation. A companion publication, *Weekly Business Statistics,* provides even more current data.

A multitude of sporadically issued federal government special reports also complement census publications. We consider only three, just to get a feeling for the variety. One noteworthy report, the Department of Labor's *Consumer Expenditure Survey* (1977), details how consumers spend their money. Data came from a sample of over 20,000 families that kept purchase diaries for a two-week period sometime between July 1972 and June 1974. Data summaries report how much money families of various income levels spent on, for instance, potato chips, nuts, and other snacks. The Conference Board revised expenditure data and updated demographic characteristics in 1979 to make findings more useful to marketing researchers.[8]

Another report, the *U.S. Industrial Outlook,* annually describes current conditions and forecasts the future for 200 domestic industries.[9] Each section identifies factors that have an impact on the industry—including exports, imports, government regulations, new technology, labor conditions, and the like. Such descriptions quickly provide a researcher with an overview of the decision maker's external environment.

[8]Complete citations are: U.S. Department of Labor, Bureau of Labor Statistics, *Consumer Expenditure Survey: Diary Survey, July, 1972–June 1974* (Washington, D.C.: Government Printing Office, 1977) and Fabian Linden and Helen Axel, eds., *Consumer Expenditure Patterns* (New York: The Conference Board, 1979).

[9]U.S. Department of Commerce, Industry and Trade Administration, *1979 U.S. Industrial Outlook* (Washington, D.C.: Government Printing Office, 1979), p. 220. Many commercial research agencies also provide industry reports of varying detail and cost.

A last noteworthy report consists of individual disclosure reports that publicly held firms file with the Securities and Exchange Commission. The 10K report interests us most because each is filed by an individual firm with the purpose of identifying its principal products, markets, methods of distribution, research and development expenses, advertising expenses, and other data beyond the detail found in annual reports. Such information can be quite useful in following the actions of competitors.

To conclude our consideration of secondary data published by the federal government, we can examine in Box 4.1 a recommended search process.

At the state level, our search for relevant secondary data is simpler because data come from a smaller number of sources. Titles of the sources vary but will be something like state department of planning or of health or of vital statistics. One or another will publish annual population estimates for the state and smaller divisions. Look for departments of planning or revenue or treasury or commerce to publish both annual estimates of income and actual receipts of various state sales taxes. Tax data provide very accurate consumption information—for alcoholic beverages, tobacco products, and hunting and fishing activities. Look also for departments of labor or human resources or employment to publish useful employment statistics. And look, not necessarily last, for bureaus of business and economic research at state universities to publish summaries and forecasts of these data and more.[10]

PROFESSIONAL PUBLICATIONS

Professional publications provide a means to exchange information between people having common, work-related interests. One type of publication cuts across industries and exchanges ideas between marketing people, usually with an intellectual orientation. The other type focuses on a particular industry and exchanges both ideas and statistics between decision makers, usually with a pragmatic orientation. Let us label the first type **academic publications** and the second, **trade publications.**

Academic Publications.   Academic publications take a variety of literary forms. Some, like the *Marketing News,* look like newspapers and report current marketing events and issues. Others, such as the *Journal of Marketing* and *Journal of Marketing Research* contain greater detail and are of greater interest. Descriptions of these last follow:

Journal of Marketing—Articles in the *Journal of Marketing* present new theoretical work, critical reviews and syntheses of past ideas,

---

[10]See U.S. Department of Commerce, Domestic and International Business Administration, *Measuring Markets: A Guide to the Use of Federal and State Statistical Data* (Washington, D.C.: Government Printing Office, 1979) for an extensive treatment on topics in this paragraph.

BOX 4.1

A Search Process for Secondary Data Published by the Federal Government

1. If you have absolutely no idea about where to find data, start with the most recent edition of the *Statistical Abstract of the United States.* This annual publication summarizes social, political, and economic statistics for the nation and states in each of its more than thirty sections. You may find the data you seek in one or more of the nearly 2000 tables contained in these sections. If not, you will find *references at the foot of each table* leading to more complete and less aggregate sources. Pursue them.

2. If you know that data belong to a particular census, by all means start instead with those publications. Look for more current data in appropriate interim report series (listed in Table 4.1).

3. If you have found nothing so far, check appropriate *subject bibliographies* issued by the Superintendent of Documents. Over 270 are currently available, free—individually treating such subjects as marketing research, the *Census of Population,* educational statistics, how to sell to government agencies, patents and trademarks, prices and the cost of living, retirement, statistical publications, and women, for example. All refer to thousands of reports, articles, and statistical sources of potential interest to marketing researchers.

4. If you still have found nothing, begin the somewhat tedious task of searching through cumulative issues of the *Monthly Catalog to U.S. Government Publications.* This monthly publication indexes by author, by title, and by subject, everything the U.S. government disseminates to the public. It functions as the card catalog as well, giving you call numbers to locate the publication in your library.

   Searching a privately published work, the *Index to U.S. Government Periodicals,* completes this step. This monthly publications indexes articles in over 160 federal government periodicals, including those we mentioned earlier. Entries identify subject, author, title, periodical, and *Monthly Catalog* entry number to allow retrieval.

   Step 4 is mandatory to locate government literature as distinct from government statistics.

5. If you meet little success so far, contact the appropriate government unit directly. Most offer help quite willingly; the Bureau of the Census even employs data "ombudsmen" and publishes a list of "Telephone Contacts for Data Users" as services for information seekers.

substantive and generalizable empirical findings, and new marketing operations methods to advance the science and practice of marketing. Each issue also summarizes: marketing articles in other journals, legal developments in marketing, new marketing books, and current marketing issues.[11]

Journal of Marketing Research—The *Journal of Marketing Research* focuses on the methodological, conceptual, and technical areas of marketing research.[12] Articles discuss research methods and research findings. In addition, each issue abstracts or summarizes useful computer programs and reviews new books.

These two journals are published quarterly by the American Marketing Association. They appear in Table 4.3 along with other journals of interest to marketing researchers.

Beyond these journals, many general business journals publish marketing articles often enough to warrant our attention. As examples, see: *Business Horizons, Business Topics, California Management Review, Harvard Business Review, Journal of Business,* and the *Journal of Business Research.*

Another very useful form of academic publications is the **proceedings** of professional meetings, which are collections of the papers presented there. Marketing academicians and practitioners author these papers, whose contents parallel those of journal articles. Professional associations both sponsor the meetings and publish the proceedings. Copies of proceedings go to members and business libraries across the country so it should be possible to find annual proceedings of the American Marketing Association Fall Educators' Conference, the Academy of Marketing Science Annual Conference, and the Association for Consumer Research Annual Conference. In addition, the American Marketing Association also publishes proceedings of narrower, "theme" meetings. Such meetings (and proceedings) focus on a single marketing topic in great detail.

A last very useful form of academic publication we term special publications. These include research reports, monographs, working papers, and the like. For example, the Marketing Science Institute publishes over 300 such publications concerning aspects of marketing management, industrial marketing, consumer services marketing, communications and consumer behavior, marketing and economics, retail and wholesale distribution, marketing models and methods, marketing and the public interest, and marketing education. Many cover the same topics appearing in journals and proceedings but in more detail. Bureaus of business and economic research, as well as marketing departments at major universities, also make available similar special publications. Finally, the Ameri-

---

[11]Yoram Wind, "From the Editor," *Journal of Marketing* 43 (January 1979): 9–12.

[12]"Manuscript Format for AMA Publications," *Journal of Marketing Research* 16 (May 1979).

TABLE 4.3
Academic Journals of Interest to Marketing Researchers

Marketing Journals	Journals in Related Fields
Journal of Advertising	Decision Sciences
Journal of Advertising Research	Journal of the American Statistical Association
Journal of the Academy of Marketing Science	Journal of Applied Psychology
Journal of Consumer Research	Journal of Consumer Analysis
Journal of Marketing	Public Opinion Quarterly
Journal of Marketing Research	
Journal of Retailing	
Industrial Marketing Management	
Marketing Science	

can Marketing Association provides a series of very important special publications in its bibliography series. One series, "Marketing Doctoral Dissertation Abstracts," lists and briefly describes most marketing doctoral candidates' dissertations. Another series consists of bibliographies that summarize hundreds of professional publications dealing with a particular topic. Such bibliographies greatly reduce the time needed to locate relevant information.

To help us find relevant secondary data in academic publications, we can use the recommended search process in Box 4.2. Throughout the search, a good business librarian will prove invaluable. Most know the literature extremely well and delight in helping the beginner.

Trade Publications.   Another type of professional publications we identified was trade publications. Trade publications contain applied literature and statistics for specific industries. Some circulate to manufacturers, others to wholesalers, and still others to retailers. Some circulate nationally while others circulate only regionally, or within states, or even within cities. While diverse, most trade publications contain articles describing trends in their industry, case histories of successful firms, procedures to improve a firm's performance, and industry statistics. Most are listed in *Business Publication Rates and Data,* a publication of Standard Rate & Data Service, Inc.[13] Each of the over 3000 entries in this publication shows a trade publication's address, issuing and closing dates (for accepting advertisements), advertising costs, circulation, and much other useful information.

Further, just about any industry we can think of has at least one trade association. The most complete source of information on trade associations, the *Encyclopedia of Associations,* lists and briefly describes over

---

[13]Standard Rate & Data Service, *Business Publication Rates and Data* 61 (May 24, 1979).

BOX 4.2

A Search Process for Secondary Data in Academic Publications

1. Start your search by examining current marketing texts. Consult both introductory texts and advanced texts, as well as texts on component parts of marketing: consumer behavior; marketing management; marketing research; and product, price, distribution, and promotion strategy. Use tables of contents and indexes in these books to locate the topic. Depending on the level of the text and its scholarship, you will find varying levels of topic treatment. In the more rigorous texts, you will find footnotes and suggested readings that lead to more detailed sources.

2. Pursue these footnoted and other referenced sources. Read them but also use them to search for work published later and earlier. If the source is a journal, check later and earlier annual indexes usually found as part of the last issue of each journal's annual volume. If the source is a proceedings, check later and earlier editions by scanning their tables of contents and indexes. While reading, be alert for other references to other related work.

3. Be especially alert for literature review articles and annotated bibliographies referenced in the preceding sources. Both of these identify and describe (and often evaluate) past research on the topic.

4. Refer to other published guides to academic publications, three of which are described here: One is the "Marketing Abstracts" section found in each issue of the *Journal of Marketing*. This section summarizes marketing literature in over 200 journals, trade magazines, university monographs, government reports, and business persons' speeches. Entries appear in numerous classes under seven main headings; they report details on the articles' original publication, summarize the article, and often comment on its significance.* The second is a separate publication, *The Marketing Information Guide*. This periodical reviews over 100 marketing-related books, journals, pamphlets, and government reports every other month. Entries summarize the articles, appear in numerous classes under three main headings, and show original sources, including addresses and reprint prices. Finally, try the *Business Periodicals Index*. This monthly publication indexes nearly 300 business journals and trade magazines. It does not summarize indexed articles.

5. Obtain and review publications brochures of the American Marketing Association and Marketing Science Institute. Both of these list and describe special publications on many marketing topics.

---

*Walter Gross, "Research and Other Applications of the Marketing Abstracts," *Journal of Marketing,* 42 (April 1978): 32–37.

BOX 4.3

A Search Process for Secondary Data in Trade Publications

1. Start by using *Business Publication Rates and Data* to identify appropriate trade periodicals. Locate issues of relevant periodicals by visiting your library or by contacting publishers.

2. Finish by identifying appropriate trade associations in the *Encyclopedia of Associ-*

   ations. An alternate work, *National Trade and Professional Associations of the United States and Canada,* provides similar information, if the *Encyclopedia* is unavailable. Contact trade associations to determine data accessibility.

3000.[14] Each entry contains the association's name, address, date of founding, and number of members. Each also describes association purpose, membership, and publications. Often a request to a trade association results in the receipt of many of the same newsletters, directories, and special reports as do association members. This is a quick way to obtain a wealth of data about the industry and the aggregate performance of its members. Disclosure of a specific firm's performance in the industry, of course, seldom occurs.

Our recommended search procedure for secondary data in trade publications is much simpler and appears in Box. 4.3.

COMMERCIAL SERVICES

Commercial services outside the decision maker's organization supply vast quantities of secondary data. Such services sell their data basically to any firm willing and able to pay. This practice, and the idea that data exist to solve no one client's particular marketing problem, is what distinguishes the commercial supplier of secondary data.[15] Such suppliers usually release secondary data to their clients on monthly, quarterly, and annual bases. Most data describe details relating to sales of consumer packaged products and to advertising.

Commercial Services for Consumer Packaged Products. Consumer packaged products consist of frequently purchased food and nonfood

---

[14]Mary Wilson Pair, ed., *Encyclopedia of Associations,* 12th ed. (Detroit: Gale Research Co., 1978), pp. 1–235.

[15]See Donald R. Lehmann, *Market Research and Analysis* (Homewood, Ill.: Richard D. Irwin, 1979), Chap. 8 for an introduction to several firms that perform such activities.

items intended for household consumption. Examples include breakfast cereal, deodorant, and furniture polish and exclude such items as fresh meat, water skis, and automobiles. Commercial services supply manufacturers with estimates of unit sales, market shares, and prices for both their own and competing products. Estimates apply to individual market areas, regions, and the nation. Estimates also apply to sales at wholesale, retail, and consumer levels.

At the wholesale level, the largest supplier of consumer packaged product data is Selling Areas—Marketing Incorporated, better known as SAMI® (Sammy).[16] SAMI collects monthly reports of warehouse shipments from major food wholesalers in thirty-nine major markets accounting for 77 percent of U.S. food sales. Within each market, reporting wholesalers average about 75 percent of the all-commodity volume of distributed food products. SAMI's basic report to a manufacturer shows average shelf prices, case and dollar volumes, and market shares (based on dollar volume) for both the preceding 4-week and 52-week periods. Subscribing manufacturers receive this information thirteen times per year. Costs depend both on the scope of information desired (market area, region, or the nation) and depth of information desired (one product, competing products, historical sales trends, and so on). Often a subscriber spends more than $100,000 per year.

At the retail level, the largest supplier is A. C. Nielsen Company. Nielsen collects sales data by auditing inventory at 1300 retail food stores across the country.[17] Every two months, Nielsen auditors record inventory quantities and purchases made by each store since their last visit. By adding last visit's inventory to purchases and subtracting current inventory, Nielsen obtains a sales figure for the period. Their basic report parallels that of SAMI; so do their costs.

At the consumer level, one of the largest suppliers is NPD Research, Inc.[18] Each day NPD's national panel, consumers in over 13,000 U.S. households, record their packaged product purchases in a 17-page diary. We see a typical page in Exhibit 4.1. Each month NPD collects this data and reports the following:

1. brand share (including complete brand and private label detail)—by outlet

2. industry and brand volume (lbs., units, equivalent cases, etc.)—by outlet

3. number of households buying (projected to U.S. total)

---

[16]For more detail, see "The Facts of SAMI and SARDI" (New York: Selling Areas—Marketing Incorporated, 1978).

[17]For more detail, see "Management with the Nielsen Retail Index System" (New York: A. C. Nielsen Co., 1978).

[18]For more detail, see "Sharpening Marketing Decisions with Diary Panels" (New York: NPD Research, Inc., 1978).

4. penetration (percent of area households buying)

5. buying rate (units per buying occasion)

6. purchase frequency (number of purchases within a period)

7. percent of volume on deal

8. type of deal

9. dollars and dollar share, and

10. average price paid (by deal as compared to non-deal sales).

Manufacturers obtain these reports for each of thirty-five separate local markets, various regions, and the entire United States. Typical costs run $35,000 to $50,000 per product category per year.

Such data at the wholesale and retail levels shed light on the overall effectiveness of a firm's marketing strategy. Consumer level data likewise illuminate but they go further by describing household behavior over time. For example, consumer-level data allow a manufacturer to determine if its 8 percent market share over six months came from the same consumers buying repeatedly or from new consumers buying in place of old. Such information aids significantly in estimating the success of new product introductions and old product reformulations.

Because of this advantage, several commercial services have moved rapidly to collecting data at the consumer level. The most exciting methodology uses Universal Product Code scanners at selected retailers to record purchases of a consumer panel. Data take little time to collect, few errors occur, and panel members experience little inconvenience. The only drawback pertains to sampling representativeness in selecting retail and consumer panel members. Nielsen, SAMI, and several others began to collect such data for commercial use late in the 1970s.

Space restrictions prevent a more extensive discussion of commercial services supplying data on consumer packaged product sales. SAMI, Nielsen, and NPD do much more than we describe in these few pages. Moreover, many other companies, including the Marketing Research Corporation of America (MRCA), Audits & Surveys, and National Family Opinion (NFO), also supply similar data.

Commercial Services for Advertising. Commercial services for advertising provide audience data and much other useful advertising information. Nielsen, for example, supplies its subscribers with detailed information about who watches which network and local television programs. Data come from Nielsen's two television panels—one using Audimeters® and the other using a viewing diary.[19] The Audimeter panel consists of

---

[19]For more detail, see "The Nielsen Ratings in Perspective" (New York: A. C. Nielsen Co., 1978).

CODES FOR SPECIAL OFFERS & PRICES

COUPON OFFERS	NON-COUPON OFFERS
CODE	CODE
01 FROM STORE AD-NEWSPAPER/FLYER	11 CENTS OFF – PRINTED ON PACKAGE
02 FROM MANUFACTURERS NEWSPAPER AD	12 STORE SALE
03 FROM PRIOR PURCHASE OF SAME ITEM	13 MORE OF THE SAME FREE/BONUS SIZE
04 FROM PURCHASE OF OTHER PRODUCT	14 GIFT OR PREMIUM ATTACHED TO PACKAGE
05 RECEIVED IN MAIL	15 DAMAGED OR OPEN CONTAINER
06 FROM MAGAZINE	16 OTHER SPECIAL OFFER
07 OTHER COUPON OFFER	

HOT CEREALS

DATE of PURCHASE	BRAND	MANUFACTURER	HOW MANY OF EACH KIND DID YOU BUY?	TOTAL CASH PAID (do not include taxes) $	¢	NO ✓ / here	SPECIAL OFFER/ SPECIAL PRICE? SEE CODES ABOVE ENTER BELOW ALL CODES THAT APPLY THAT	TOTAL CENTS OFF (if any)	NAME of STORE or COMPANY	GROCERY OR FOOD	OTHER Write in

KETCHUP, MUSTARD, STEAK SAUCE, BURGER SAUCE, BARBECUE SAUCE

and Other Condiments used for Hamburgers, Hot Dogs, Steaks, etc.

MAYONNAISE Including **MAYONNAISE STYLE SALAD DRESSING**

MARGARINE, BUTTER

Include: Diet Margarine, Imitation Margarine, and Other Similar Spreads.

STORE TYPE / GROCERY OR FOOD / HOME DELIVERY / OTHER Write in

EXHIBIT 4.1
Sample NPD Purchase Diary Page

Source: NPD Research, Inc. Used by permission.

NOTE: Extra space below Index. Free Gifts and Samples on Back Cover.

HOT CEREALS BREAKFAST TIPS

- Tell us about the special flavors and fruits included in the package, not those added at the table.

- If the purchase was made primarily for individual family members, be sure to write in the ages of family members. If item was purchased for general family use, check (✓) the appropriate box.

- Tell us whether cereal is instant, quick or regular. Read label.

WEIGHT (SIZE) SHOWN ON LABEL / NUMBER OF OUNCES OR POUNDS PER CONTAINER	DOES PACKAGE SAY: Check (✓) One			HOW PREPARED FOR EATING? Check (✓) One					KIND (✓) One				DOES THE CEREAL INCLUDE ANY SPECIAL FRUITS, FLAVORS, OR SPICES ALREADY IN THE CONTAINER?		WHO EATS THIS CEREAL BRAND?								HOW WILL THIS PURCHASE BE USED? Check (✓) One		
	INSTANT	QUICK	REGULAR	PREPARED IN BOWL, ONLY ADD HOT LIQUID	REQUIRES 3 MINUTES OR LESS	REQUIRES 4–5 MINUTES	REQUIRES 8 MINUTES OR MORE		WHEAT	OATS	FARINA	OTHER	IF YES, WRITE IN ALL FRUITS, FLAVORS OR SPICES (Copy from label)	IF NO Check (✓) here	IS THIS CEREAL PURCHASED FOR SPECIFICALLY ONE FAMILY MEMBER? IF YES, write in age and sex	NO (✓)	IF PURCHASED FOR MORE THAN ONE FAMILY MEMBER WRITE IN AGES OF ALL WHO USE FEMALES AGE / AGE / AGE			MALES AGE / AGE / AGE			AS CEREAL	AS BAKING OR COOKING INGREDIENT	BOTH WAYS

WEIGHT SHOWN ON LABEL / NUMBER OF OUNCES PER CONTAINER	TYPE Check (✓) One or Write In						MAIN INGREDIENT (BASE) Check (✓) One or Write In					SPECIAL FLAVOR
	KETCHUP (CATSUP)	MUSTARD	BURGER SAUCE	STEAK SAUCE	BARBECUE SAUCE	CHILI SAUCE	OTHER Write In	TOMATO BASE	MUSTARD BASE	MAYONNAISE BASE	VINEGAR BASE	OTHER Write In
												IF SPECIAL FLAVOR, SUCH AS: HOT, HICKORY, SMOKY, GARLIC, ONION, MUSHROOM, ETC. Write In

WEIGHT SHOWN ON LABEL / NUMBER OF OUNCES PER CONTAINER	KIND Check (✓) One		IS IT LOW CALORIE OR DIETETIC? Check (✓) One		DOES LABEL SAY IMITATION? Check (✓) One		WHERE DID YOU FIND THIS IN THE STORE? Check (✓) One		MANUFACTURER'S CODE WRITE IN ALL NUMBERS OF THIS 6 OR 10 DIGIT CODE IF AVAILABLE
	MAYONNAISE	SALAD DRESSING	YES	NO	YES	NO	IN REFRIGERATED OR DAIRY CASE	ON REGULAR SHELF OR COUNTER NOT REFRIGERATED	Example 54000 85300

WEIGHT / NUMBER OF POUNDS AND OUNCES PER PACKAGE	TYPE Check (✓)			HOW PACKAGED? Check (✓) or Write In						KIND (✓) All That Apply				DOES LABEL SAY SPREAD? Check (✓)		MANUFACTURER'S CODE WRITE IN ALL NUMBERS OF THIS 6 OR 10 DIGIT CODE IF AVAILABLE
	BUTTER	MARGARINE	OTHER SIMILAR SPREADS	SOLID BLOCK	2 STICKS	4 STICKS	6 STICKS	8 STICKS	2 TUBS	1 TUB	OTHER INCLUDING PURCHASE OF LESS THAN FULL PACKAGE Write In	REGULAR	DIET OR LOW CALORIE	WHIPPED	UNSALTED	YES	NO	Example Copy This Number 54000 85300

approximately 1200 households selected nationwide for a five-year period. An Audimeter automatically records channel setting and viewing times for each TV receiver used inside or outside (backyard battery portables) each household during any time of day. The diary panel, however, reports *who* is watching, information that allows Nielsen summaries to describe socioeconomic characteristics of program audiences.

Weekly summaries describe audiences for a two-week period ending two weeks before the summary appears. However, Nielsen also offers its clients "day-after" summaries for Audimeter data and several-days-after service for other data when needed. Networks, advertising agencies, and advertisers all take an intense interest in these results.

Arbitron also collects television audience data but with a more local emphasis.[20] Seven times a year, Arbitron measures television audiences in each of seventy-five major markets across the country. Another 138 lesser market areas are measured once a year. Arbitron randomly selects households from current telephone directories and contacts each via letter. A telephone call follows to obtain cooperation; those agreeing receive a viewing diary for each television set in the household. In it household members record viewing behavior for themselves and visitors for a one-week period. After supplying some socioeconomic information, a household member mails completed diaries back to Arbitron. Arbitron reports estimates of each station's audience by time period and day of week—in terms of age, sex, and market boundaries.

Arbitron similarly collects radio audience data four times a year for major markets and once a year for lesser markets.[21] In cooperating households, each person age 12 and over receives a diary by mail. In it they record station listened to, listening time, and whether listening occurred at home or away. At the end of the one-week diary period, each indicates his or her age, sex, and address and then mails the diary back to Arbitron. Arbitron estimates each station's audience by age, sex, and time period, as illustrated (in part) in Exhibit 4.2.

Starch INRA Hooper (SIH) provides information on magazine advertising readership.[22] For magazines being studied, SIH interviewers locate readers who meet age, sex, and occupation guidelines. Interviewers then page through the magazines with each reader and, for each advertisement in the study, ask "Did you see or read any part of this advertisement?" If "Yes," the interviewer asks more questions to determine the reader's observation and reading of component parts of the ad (illustrations, head-

---

[20]For more detail, see "Inside the Arbitron Television Report" (1977) and "Description of Methodology" (February 1979)—both published by Arbitron.

[21]For more detail, see "Undertaking and Using Radio Audience Estimates" (1976), published by Arbitron.

[22]For more detail, see "Starch Message Report: Scope, Method, and Use," undated, published by Starch INRA Hooper, Inc.

line, signature or brand name, and copy blocks). SIH reports results as reader categories of: "noted," "associated," and "read-most."

"Noted" Reader: A person who remembered having previously seen the advertisement in the issue being studied.

"Associated" Reader: A person who not only "noted" the advertisement but also saw or read some part of it which clearly indicates the brand or advertiser.

"Read-Most" Reader: A person who read half or or more of the written material in the ad.

Advertisers and advertising agencies use these and other SIH data to evaluate ads of different campaigns, sizes, and colors for similar products.

LNA (Leading National Advertisers, Inc.) supplies data on a completely different advertising topic—expenditures.[23] Four times a year LNA summarizes advertising expenditures estimates by industry, product class, company, and brand. LNA reports expenditure estimates by six media: magazines, newspaper supplements, network television, spot television, network radio, and outdoor. An example of an LNA summary for the breakfast cereal industry appears in Exhibit 4.3. Among others, competitors in the industry find such data quite interesting.

Numerous other commercial services supply a variety of advertising data. Not to downplay their importance but just to save space, we can only give them cursory attention:

Simmons Market Research Bureau (SMRB)	SMRB annually publishes data on mass media audiences of surprising richness. Data describe magazine and TV audiences by demographics, usage rate, purchase intentions, and psychographics.
Standard Directory of Advertising Agencies	This annual directory lists over 4000 U.S. and foreign advertising agencies, their billings by media, their officers, and other useful information.
Standard Rate & Data Service (SRDS)	SRDS publishes monthly volumes that summarize advertising rates and much other useful information about almost all newspapers and magazines, television stations, and radio stations in the United States. Volumes also provide useful market statistics for cities, counties, and SMSAs served by publishers and broadcasters.

All find wide acceptance in the industry.

---

[23]For more detail, see *Class/Brand YTD $*, Leading National Advertisers, Inc., Volume 5, Number 3, 1978, or any current edition.

EXHIBIT 4.2

Average Quarter-Hour and

FLINT
APRIL/MAY
1978

STATION CALL LETTERS	ADULTS 18 +						ADULTS 18-34						ADULTS 18-49					
	TOTAL AREA		METRO SURVEY AREA				TOTAL AREA		METRO SURVEY AREA				TOTAL AREA		METRO SURVEY AREA			
	AVG. PERS. (00)	CUME PERS. (00)	AVG. PERS. (00)	CUME PERS. (00)	AVG PERS RTG.	AVG. PERS. SHR.	AVG. PERS. (00)	CUME PERS. (00)	AVG. PERS. (00)	CUME PERS. (00)	AVG PERS RTG.	AVG. PERS. SHR.	AVG. PERS. (00)	CUME PERS. (00)	AVG. PERS. (00)	CUME PERS. (00)	AVG PERS RTG.	AVG. PERS. SHR.
WAMM	36	78	36	78	1.0	4.7	8	33	8	33	.5	2.1	30	56	30	56	1.2	5.7
WFDF	78	235	76	213	2.2	9.9	31	106	30	92	1.9	8.0	39	125	38	111	1.5	7.3
WGMZ	88	186	86	170	2.5	11.2	30	67	30	67	1.9	8.0	46	108	44	92	1.8	8.4
WKMF	90	237	85	220	2.4	11.1	36	88	31	74	2.0	8.3	56	149	51	135	2.1	9.8
WLQB	1	5	1	5		.1												
WOAP	14	44	10	38	.3	1.3												
WOAP FM	1	18	1	18		.1												
WTAC	45	169	21	106	.6	2.7	26	124	18	88	1.1	4.8	34	148	21	106	.9	4.0
WTRX	60	154	54	148	1.5	7.0	31	100	31	100	2.0	8.3	59	148	53	142	2.1	10.2
WWCK	85	223	84	219	2.4	11.0	69	178	68	174	4.3	18.2	81	212	80	208	3.2	15.3
WFMK	71	141	65	119	1.9	8.5	67	115	61	93	3.9	16.4	70	136	64	114	2.6	12.3
WGER	179	343	43	99	1.2	5.6	49	79	14	32	.9	3.8	100	184	26	55	1.1	5.0
WHNN	91	253	14	58	.4	1.8	82	228	14	58	.9	3.8	88	245	14	58	.6	2.7
WJR	98	332	57	217	1.6	7.4	14	45	14	45	.9	3.8	36	123	26	89	1.1	5.0
WKCQ	88	277	14	49	.4	1.8	30	111	8	30	.5	2.1	47	177	8	30	.3	1.5
WRIF	2	10											2	10				
WVIC	9	29	9	25	.3	1.2	6	21	6	17	.4	1.6	9	29	9	25	.4	1.7
WVIC FM TOTAL	9	29	9	25	.3	1.2	6	21	6	17	.4	1.6	9	29	9	25	.4	1.7
WWJ	8	21	8	21	.2	1.0							2	10	2	10	.1	.4
WWWS	29	75	25	56	.7	3.3	25	50	22	35	1.4	5.9	29	75	25	56	1.0	4.8
METRO TOTALS			766	1774	21.9				373	855	23.7				522	1193	21.2	

Footnote Symbols: (*) means audience estimates adjusted for actual broadcast

Note: "Avg. Pers. (00)" estimates the average number of persons who listened at home and away to a station for a minimum of 5 minutes within the identified time period. "Cume pers. (00)" estimates the number of different persons who listened under the same conditions.

Other Outside Sources of Secondary Data. Marketing researchers sometimes use outside sources of secondary data other than government, professional, and commercial service publications. For example, public utilities in a community often supply monthly information on the number of new customer hookups and related data.[24] Banks often report monthly

[24]See George C. Hepburn, Thomas H. Mayor and James E. Stafford, "Estimation of Market Area Population from Residential Electrical Utility Data," *Journal of Marketing Research* 13 (August 1976): 230–36 for an application.

Cume Listening Estimates

SATURDAY
10.00AM-3.00PM

STATION CALL LETTERS	ADULTS 25-49						ADULTS 25-54						ADULTS 35-64					
	TOTAL AREA		METRO SURVEY AREA				TOTAL AREA		METRO SURVEY AREA				TOTAL AREA		METRO SURVEY AREA			
	AVG. PERS. (00)	CUME PERS. (00)	AVG. PERS. (00)	CUME PERS. (00)	AVG. PERS. RTG.	AVG. PERS. SHR.	AVG. PERS. (00)	CUME PERS. (00)	AVG. PERS. (00)	CUME PERS. (00)	AVG. PERS. RTG.	AVG. PERS. SHR.	AVG. PERS. (00)	CUME PERS. (00)	AVG. PERS. (00)	CUME PERS. (00)	AVG. PERS. RTG.	AVG. PERS. SHR.
WAMM	28	45	28	45	1.6	8.4	31	53	31	53	1.5	7.8	28	45	28	45	1.8	8.8
WFDF	21	66	21	66	1.2	6.3	27	93	27	93	1.3	6.8	35	103	34	95	2.2	10.7
WGMZ	21	64	19	48	1.1	5.7	29	81	27	65	1.3	6.8	37	83	35	67	2.3	11.0
WKMF	55	137	50	123	2.8	14.9	65	165	60	151	2.9	15.0	50	140	50	137	3.3	15.8
WLQB							1	5	1	5		.3	1	5	1	5	.1	.3
WOAP													8	18	8	18	.5	2.5
WOAP FM														6		6		
WTAC	18	93	10	63	.6	3.0	21	104	10	63	.5	2.5	19	45	3	18	.2	.9
WTRX	47	115	41	109	2.3	12.2	48	121	42	115	2.1	10.5	29	54	23	48	1.5	7.3
WWCK	13	38	12	34	.7	3.6	16	43	15	39	.7	3.8	16	45	16	45	1.0	5.0
WFMK	41	85	40	81	2.2	11.9	42	90	41	86	2.0	10.3	4	26	4	26	.3	1.3
WGER	96	166	25	45	1.4	7.5	120	220	34	65	1.7	8.5	115	245	29	67	1.9	9.1
WHNN	37	99	5	25	.3	1.5	40	107	5	25	.2	1.3	9	25				
WJR	34	113	24	79	1.3	7.2	49	172	33	110	1.6	8.3	65	215	30	117	2.0	9.5
WKCQ	40	133	6	18	.3	1.8	43	148	6	18	.3	1.5	34	105				
WRIF	2	10					2	10					2	10				
WVIC WVIC FM TOTAL	6	15	6	15	.3	1.8	6	15	6	15	.3	1.5	3	8	3	8	.2	.9
	6	15	6	15	.3	1.8	6	15	6	15	.3	1.5	3	8	3	8	.2	.9
WWJ	2	10	2	10	.1	.6	5	15	5	15	.2	1.3	8	21	8	21	.5	2.5
WWWS	25	60	21	45	1.2	6.3	25	60	21	45	1.0	5.3	4	25	3	21	.2	.9
METRO TOTALS			335	763	18.8				400	925	19.6				317	726	20.6	

schedule (+) means AM-FM Combination was not simulcast for complete time period.

ARBITRON   *Source:* "Audience Estimates in the Arbitron Market of Flint," *Arbitron Radio Report* (April/May 1978) 44. Used with permission.

debits for summary and distribution to interested parties. All make possible very current estimates of population and economic conditions in local market areas.

Secondary Data Collection

We have seen the diversity of secondary data available to the marketing researcher. Further, we know of search processes that speed the collection of secondary data. Here we complete our discussion by considering

91

EXHIBIT 4.3

LNA Advertising Estimates for Seven Competitors in the Breakfast Cereal Industry, 1978 ($000)

Brands by Classification	Class	6-Media Total
General Mills, Inc.		
Bran Plus Cereal	F122	242.2
Buc-Wheats Cereal	F122	1,922.0
Cheerios Cereal	F122	9,810.8
Cocoa Puffs	F122	2,016.7
Count Chocula Cereal	F122	1.3
Crazy Cow Cereal	F122	4,185.0
Crispy Wheats n Raisins Cereal	F122	539.9
Franken Berry Cereal	F122	6.9
General Mills Cereals	F122	178.5
General Mills Monster Cereals	F122	3,242.1
Golden Grahams Cereal	F122	5,990.9
Golden Grahams Cereal & Fisher Nuts	F122	149.6
Golden Grahams Cereal Sweepstakes	F122	127.1
Kix Cereal	F122	280.5
Lucky Charms Cereal	F122	3,751.0
Lucky Charms & Frosty O Cereals	F122	8.3
Nature Valley Granola	F122	6.1
Nature Valley Granola Raisin & Bran Cereal	F122	37.6
Total Cereal	F122	6,263.3
Trix Cereal	F122	4,571.6
Wheat Hearts Cereal	F122	62.0
Wheaties Cereal	F122	5,100.6
International Multifoods Corp		
Kretschmers Wheat Germ	F122	863.6
Kretschmers Wheat Germ & Dannon Yogurt	F122	11.6
Kellogg Co		
Kelloggs All Bran	F122	1,805.1
Kelloggs All Bran & Bran Buds	F122	495.7
Kelloggs Apple Jacks Cereal	F122	2,840.9
Kelloggs Bran Cereals	F122	985.5
Kelloggs Cereals	F122	864.9
Kelloggs Cereals/Amtrak Offer	F122	180.6
Kelloggs Cocoa Krispies	F122	1,543.7
Kelloggs Corn Flakes	F122	4,946.8
Kelloggs Corny-Snaps Cereal	F122	136.2
Kelloggs Cracklin Bran Cereal	F122	3,802.7
Kelloggs Crunchy Loggs Cereal	F122	69.4
Kelloggs 40% Bran Flakes	F122	70.4
Kelloggs Froot Loops	F122	4,401.7
Kelloggs Frosted Mini-Wheats	F122	4,079.0
Kelloggs Frosted Rice	F122	2,812.0
Kelloggs Graham Crackos Cereal	F122	552.1
Kelloggs Most Cereal	F122	1,038.3
Kelloggs Product 19 Cereal	F122	2,430.1
Kelloggs Raisin Bran	F122	3,888.5
Kelloggs Raisin Bran & Sugar Frosted Flakes	F122	1,337.0
Kelloggs Rice Krispies	F122	5,473.0
Kelloggs Snack Pak	F122	3.9
Kelloggs Special K	F122	4,794.6
Kelloggs Sugar Frosted Flakes	F122	6,592.0
Kelloggs Sugar Pops	F122	1,638.2
Kelloggs Sugar Pops & Froot Loops	F122	.2
Kelloggs Sugar Smacks	F122	2,980.2
Kelloggs Toasted Mini-Wheats	F122	428.2

Source: LNA Class/Brand YTD $, Leading National Advertisers, Inc., Volume 5, Number 3, p. 176. Used by permission.

Magazines	Newspaper Supplements	Network Television	Spot Television	Network Radio	Outdoor
86.5	–	–	155.7	–	–
539.3	–	966.0	416.7	–	–
710.3	–	4,289.4	4,811.1	–	–
–	–	477.6	1,539.1	–	–
–	–	–	1.3	–	–
–	–	1,978.3	2,206.7	–	–
11.8	–	–	528.1	–	–
–	–	–	6.9	–	–
–	–	–	178.5	–	–
–	–	1,118.6	2,123.5	–	–
131.9	–	3,626.2	2,232.8	–	–
149.6	–	–	–	–	–
–	127.1	–	–	–	–
37.8	–	–	242.7	–	–
–	–	1,425.1	2,325.9	–	–
–	–	–	8.3	–	–
–	1.9	–	4.2	–	–
–	1.4	–	36.2	–	–
247.2	–	5,059.2	956.9	–	–
–	–	1,207.4	3,364.2	–	–
62.0	–	–	–	–	–
–	–	4,247.7	852.9	–	–
460.1	34.8	–	368.7	–	–
–	11.6	–	–	–	–
–	–	1,304.1	501.0	–	–
17.7	–	419.0	59.0	–	–
167.4	–	1,313.7	1,359.8	–	–
–	–	939.3	18.8	27.4	–
313.8	–	454.6	58.2	27.0	11.3
–	180.6	–	–	–	–
–	–	1,057.4	486.3	–	–
190.9	–	3,573.4	1,182.5	–	–
–	–	132.3	3.9	–	–
–	–	2,895.4	907.3	–	–
–	–	–	69.4	–	–
69.6	–	–	.8	–	–
143.8	–	2,158.0	2,099.9	–	–
–	–	3,403.2	675.8	–	–
–	–	1,491.5	1,320.5	–	–
–	9.0	–	543.1	–	–
65.8	22.6	–	949.9	–	–
111.6	–	1,655.9	662.6	–	–
–	–	3,440.6	447.9	–	–
–	–	1,309.6	27.4	–	–
291.6	–	3,737.0	1,415.0	29.4	–
–	–	–	3.9	–	–
–	–	3,279.3	1,515.3	–	–
516.8	–	4,281.6	1,793.6	–	–
–	–	927.2	711.0	–	–
–	–	–	.2	–	–
–	–	1,427.7	1,552.5	–	–
–	295.6	132.6	–	–	–

research practices that enhance the quality of data we collect. Eight guidelines appear in Box 4.4, to show us superior secondary data collection techniques.

As a necessary precondition for the application of these guidelines, we must agree to use a form on which to record secondary data. The form need be little more complex than a sheet of ruled paper with preprinted headings to record identification details of the source. Even for less structured exploratory research the form can contain headings and spaces suitable to record the source's title, edition, applicable page numbers, and library location. Such standard information allows the researcher (or someone else) to find the source more quickly in the future. In addition, headings may also indicate spaces for the source's author or editor, publisher, and publication date if there is likely to be a reference to it in the final report. The form should also, of course, provide ample space in which to record data clearly and completely. Given this form, then, we turn to our guidelines in Box 4.4.

BOX 4.4

Research Practices That Enhance the Quality of Secondary Data Collected

1. Consult the **original source** whenever practical. For example, *Current Population Reports* (Series P-25) is an original source of secondary data because it presents data (estimates of U.S. population) for the first time. Another secondary data source, the *Statistical Abstract,* is an **acquired source** because it reprints, abridges, aggregates, or otherwise modifies this data some time later. Consulting the original source reduces the chance that your data will contain typographical and copying errors that occur as editors transfer data from an original to an acquired secondary data source. Moreover, consulting an original source will give you increased understanding about how that research originally produced the data. Such methodological detail seldom appears sufficiently in an acquired source to allow more than a cursory evaluation.

2. Consult the most current original source whenever practical. Often when you search for secondary data you find original sources that have appeared over time. All other things being equal, you prefer the most current. However, all other things may not be equal because of your evaluation of the source; in that case, you may prefer to use or extend data from an older source. In such instances, you may quite properly record data from both sources, noting constancies and differences as part of your evaluation.

3. Understand the data. Before you record secondary data, read it and comprehend it. For tabular secondary data, you would

usually read the table's title first. Reread the title until you know basically what the entries in the table will represent. Next, read table headings to learn specifically what entries in the table will represent. Finally, be sure you understand what any abbreviations and symbols appearing in the table mean by reading identifications and definitions at the foot of the table. For textual secondary data, again take the effort to understand what the author intends. This means you may wish to take separate notes on scratch paper until the author's logic (or lack of it) surfaces and you feel capable of summarizing the research method, findings, and interpretations.

4. Understand the data's context. That is, know who collected the data, where, when, how, and why. You need such an understanding to evaluate the credibility, indeed, the usefulness, of any secondary data. To illustrate, consider a researcher employed by a manufacturer of hair spray who conducted some research as a defense against a potential charge of deceptive advertising. Consider also another researcher employed by the Federal Trade Commission who conducted similar research for purposes of potential prosecution. Comparing the two research reports, we would not be too surprised to learn that even though they studied the same product, the same advertisements, the same consumer segments, and at nearly the same time and in nearly the same market areas, their findings and interpretations differ—perhaps extensively.

Now consider the more common case—in which different researchers have conducted less similar research on less related topics, yet have produced research reports that yield bits and pieces of data relevant to your own topic. Because the researchers used different research designs but, more importantly, because they possessed different frames of references, you must record their findings in a persistently skeptical manner.† That is, you must carefully scrutinize their conceptual and operational definitions of research variables, primary data sources, sampling methods, data collection methods, and data analysis methods—along with their research objectives and affiliations—to learn why results appear as they do. You then must decide which reports summarize research projects that meet your own particular research standards, accept them, and discard the rest as interesting but untrustworthy.

5. Stay alert for trends and supporting and contradicting secondary data.‡ After rigorously examining each separate research report's context, you should look for relationships between secondary data in those you judge acceptable. Often you will want to identify and extend these trends to more current times and to more immediate geographic areas. You also will want to note supporting and contradicting secondary data to provide more perspective.

6. Stay alert to changes to research designs that have produced secondary data over time. Such changes, if you fail to notice them, may cause you to be puzzled by the data or even embarrassed by the findings you base on them. An illustration will make the point: because of minor definitional changes in 1974 to the assigning of SIC codes to wholesalers of electrical apparatus and equipment (SIC 5063), you cannot compare any pre-1974 Bureau of Census statistics for this industry with statistics for

---

†Boyd, Westfall, and Stasch, *Marketing Research,* p. 150.

‡Nathalie D. Frank, *Data Sources for Business and Market Analysis,* 2nd ed. (Metuchen, N.J.: The Scarecrow Press, Inc., 1969), p. 19.

1974 and later.§ Yet you can cautiously compare values of the Consumer Price Index for periods before 1978 (at least back to 1964) with values for 1978 and later, despite major changes in research design.‖ Careful researchers document changes in their research designs and expect colleagues to do likewise.

7. Make careful manipulations of secondary data and recognize assumptions underlying them. Often secondary data appear in a form not exactly suited to your needs. For example, suppose you found the following Pittsburgh data in the 1977 *Census of Retail Trade.*

	All Establishments		Establishments with Payroll	
	Number	Sales ($000)	Number	Sales ($000)
Retail Bakeries	80	13,354	66	12,707
Baking and Selling	* *	* *	42	8,152
Selling Only	* *	* *	24	4,555

The symbols * * indicate data are not available; you are disappointed because you had hoped to find the total number of Pittsburgh retail bakers that both bake and sell. However, if you assume the proportion of bakeries that both bake and sell is the same for all baking establishments as it is for only those with payroll, you could estimate this number by taking (42/66) times 80 and rounding the result to 51. Further, you might also assume that because the 66 baking establishments with payroll account for $12,707/$13,354 (which is over 95 percent of sales for all baking establishments), the 14 without payroll are much smaller and, hence, less likely to both bake and sell. Consequently, you might estimate the total number of retail bakeries that both bake and sell as some number between 42 and 48. You might use both figures—as lower and upper bounds in your research.

8. Weigh each item of secondary data against the needs and goals of your research.# We saved the best guideline for last: that is, you should make an exhaustive search for secondary data but record only data that in the end advance the research design. To record interesting but irrelevant secondary data wastes resources, confuses the analysis, and reflects poorly on you as a researcher.

§U.S. Department of Commerce, Bureau of the Census, *County Business Patterns 1977 Minnesota* (May 1979), p. VIII.

‖U.S. Department of Labor, Bureau of Labor Statistics, *The Consumer Price Index, Concepts and Content Over the Years,* Report 517 (May 1978).

#Frank, *Data Sources,* p. 19.

Chapter Summary

We begin the summary with this generalization: no matter what the marketing problem, someone, somewhere has faced a similar problem and has some useful secondary data. The trick lies in tracking this source down.

To limit the scope of our search, we identified over eighty unique sources of internal and external secondary data. Most are classified as external; these further divide into government, professional, commercial service, and other publications. Which source we will use more frequently than others is impossible to state. Many we will never use, some we will use once or twice, and a select few we will use until they are dog-eared.

The recommended search process varies by secondary data class. Always we should seek out people who are familiar with the class—MKIS managers, librarians, commercial service representatives, and others. But we should do this after trying extensively to find the data on our own. Such practice increases our skills as researchers, allows us eventually to ask more directed questions of these experts, and otherwise gives us a sense of independence and achievement. Throughout our searching, we must analyze each source's currency, relevancy to research objectives, and accuracy. Accept nothing on faith.

Some bibliographies and guides to published secondary data appear as Additional Readings at the end of this chapter. As with all the sources we discussed earlier, to appreciate these bibliographies and guides, one must see them firsthand.

Chapter Review

KEY TERMS

Secondary data source	**Professional publications**
Operational-level definition	**Commercial service**
Conceptual-level definition	**SMSA**
Strategic marketing plan	**SIC code**
Interim report	

DISCUSSION QUESTIONS

1. Why is the appropriate starting point in a data collection plan the review of secondary data?

2. Why types of data might an MKIS regularly report?

3. Library search questions:

   a) List the most current populations for all of the SMSAs in Texas.

   b) List the most current populations for all the SCSAs in the United States.

   c) How much have consumer prices risen in the United States since 1970?

   d) How many three-bottom plows did how many U.S. manufacturers produce in 1977?

   e) What percent of households in the United States contain at least one sewing machine?

   f) Estimate the 1985 population of Knoxville, Tennessee.

   g) Describe the major subject headings of the "Marketing Abstracts" section of the *Journal of Marketing*.

4. Describe a search process to locate current literature on the influence of consumer attitudes on product purchase.

5. Why do independent commercial services for consumer packaged products and advertising exist; that is, why don't large advertisers and advertising agencies simply collect their own data?

6. Discuss Arbitron's television and radio data collection methodology. What limitations or cautions would you give users of these data?

7. "You don't need to know the answer; all you need to know is who already knows it." Why is this a shortsighted way to go through life in general and secondary data collection in particular?

8. We said that each step in the marketing research process interrelates with the others. Illustrate this for the collection of secondary data.

9. Use the commercial services for advertisers to complete these tasks:

   a) Looking at Exhibit 4.2, what radio station would you recommend to an advertiser who is trying to reach young adults, age 18–25? On what assumptions do you base your answer?

   b) In Exhibit 4.3, compare advertising expenditures for each medium as a percentage of the six-media total for Kelloggs All Bran, Kelloggs Apple Jacks, and Kelloggs Toasted Mini-Wheats. Why are percentages so different for these products?

10. Support, then criticize, this statement: Data collection operations for collecting secondary data really reduce to knowing what is in the library.

Additional Readings

Each of the more than eighty sources of secondary data identified in this chapter makes interesting reading. Here we look at some bibliographies and guides to those and other sources.

Business Periodicals Index. New York: H. W. Wilson Company.
   This monthly publication indexes nearly 300 business periodicals, including many that publish marketing-related articles. Listings appear by subject.

Predicasts Funk and Scott Index of Corporations and Industries. Cleveland: Predicasts, Inc.
   This weekly index includes most of the publications indexed in the Business Periodicals Index along with selected government documents, trade journals, and pamphlets. Part One indexes by SIC code, Part Two by company name.

Goeldner, C. R., and Dirks, Laura M. "Business Facts: Where to Find Them." *MSU Business Topics,* Summer 1976, pp. 23–36.
   This article annotates well over 100 secondary data sources and guides to them. Many of the sources and guides apply to marketing topics. Especially noteworthy is the article's discussion of the statistical issues of trade publications.

"Marketing Abstracts." *Journal of Marketing.* Chicago: American Marketing Association.

Each quarterly issue of the JM contains a "Marketing Abstracts" section. Abstracts identify, summarize, and often comment on the significance of marketing articles originally appearing in a variety of publications.

The Marketing Information Guide. Garden City, N.Y.: Trade Marketing Information Guide, Inc.

Issues of this publication identify and summarize marketing-related articles, books, and government publications. Issues classify these materials into three groups: marketing function, policy, methodology, operations; areas and markets; and industries and commodities. Issues also report addresses and prices to obtain these materials.

U.S. Department of Commerce, Bureau of the Census. *Statistical Abstract of the United States.* Washington, D.C.: Government Printing Office, published annually.

Over 2000 tables and charts summarize social, political, and economic statistics for the nation and states. Over 200 government, private, and international organizations provide the data. References at the foot of each table or the Abstract's "Guide to Sources" lead to more detail. No serious marketing researcher should be without a copy.

U.S. Department of Commerce, Bureau of the Census. *Business Statistics Data Finder.* Washington, D.C.: Government Printing Office, undated.

This short pamphlet describes: the various economic censuses; the Current Business Reports series for retail and wholesale trade and selected service industries; and other Bureau of the Census products to aid researchers. It even identifies "subject matter specialists" and their telephone numbers in case the reader wants more personal advice.

For more detail without the personal touch you may want to read these:

U.S. Department of Commerce, Bureau of the Census, Mini-Guide to the 1977 Economic Censuses, *undated.*
U.S. Department of Commerce, Domestic and International Business Administration, Measuring Markets: A Guide to the Use of Federal and State Statistical Data, *August 1979.*
U.S. Department of Commerce, Domestic and International Business Administration, Retail Data Sources for Market Analysis, *undated.*

5

Primary Data Collection: Surveys

Primary data collection activities gather original information for the specific purpose of solving the marketing problem at hand. Activities are almost always in the form of one of four basic methodologies: survey, experiment, observation study, or simulation. Original information usually comes from people, as consumers and as organization members; it less frequently comes from objects, such as products, advertisements, and stores. We discuss surveys in this chapter; experiments, observation studies, and simulations are the subject of Chapter 6.

Surveys collect primary data by mail, telephone, and personal interview. Distinctions between these pure types of surveys are sufficiently obvious that we need no definitions. However, in actual practice, distinctions between types can become blurred when a study uses more than one, or none. For example, a researcher may "intercept" a woman at a shopping mall, ask three questions, and hand her a questionnaire to return by mail. Or, an interviewer may ring the respondent's doorbell, obtain permission to leave a questionnaire, and return to pick it up four days later. We consider both examples to approximate a mail survey because the respondent completes the form without assistance. In telephone and personal interview surveys, an interviewer completes the form.

Our next section discusses the collection of survey data through mail, telephone, and personal interviews. We follow with an examination of some criteria useful in evaluating how well respondents and interviewers complete the survey forms. We then look at factors affecting these criteria and conclude with a comparison of mail, telephone, and personal interviews as survey alternatives.

Collecting Survey Data

MAIL SURVEYS Of the three survey methods—mail, telephone, and personal interviews—mail requires the least discussion of data collection operations. This is true largely because relatively few others assist the researcher in the process. Depending on the size of the mailing, it usually takes only two or three assistants to:

1. assemble the questionnaires,

2. address and sign cover letters,

3. address envelopes,

4. stuff each envelope with the cover letter, questionnaire, incentive, and return envelope,

5. stamp and seal the envelopes, and

6. mail them.

Assistants may be employed by either the researcher's organization or a separate firm that specializes in such activities. As assistants perform these rather routine activities, the researcher supervises.

One aspect of the researcher's supervision concerns timing. All questionnaires usually should be mailed at one time, allowing three to six weeks for sample members (the respondents) to complete and return them. Mailing all at one time makes possible the calculation of response trends (discussed later with Figure 5.2) and simplifies the recordkeeping process which begins with delivery of the questionnaires to the post office.

At the post office, the researcher should request a dated receipt showing the number of pieces mailed as evidence of the original sample size. Recordkeeping continues with the return of undeliverable mailings. Some undeliverable mailings are the result of errors in typing from the mailing list; speed in checking against the list, readdressing, and remailing will increase actual sample size. Other undeliverable mailings result from errors in the list itself; these questionnaires usually cannot be salvaged. Still, the researcher needs a record of their number to calculate the true response rate and to evaluate the list. Moreover, if the researcher purchased the mailing list from a commercial supplier, he or she can use such validated undeliverable mailings to obtain credit.[1] A form such as the one shown in Figure 5.1 facilitates the recordkeeping process. Finally, the researcher often also keeps records of the strengths and weaknesses of each member of the research team. Such information often proves helpful in future projects.

---

[1] The most complete source describing such suppliers is *Direct Mail List Rates and Data* (Skokie, Ill.: Standard Rate & Data Service, Inc.) which is published biannually.

Daily Returns Record

Client _____   Job Name _____

Project Director _____   Assistant
                                     Project Director _____

Mailing Data

Initial Mailing Date _____   Quantity _____

1st Follow-up Mailing Date _____ Quantity _____

2nd Follow-up Mailing Date _____ Quantity _____

Returns Data

Date	Quantity	Cumulative Returns	Date	Quantity	Cumulative Returns

Cumulative Undeliverables

FIGURE 5.1
Example of mail survey returns record
Source: Adapted from Paul L. Erdos, *Professional Mail Surveys* (New York: McGraw-Hill, 1970), p. 154.

Another aspect of the researcher's supervision concerns protecting the anonymity of sample members. Only assistants who need to know the identity of sample members in order to perform data collection activities (or, for that matter, all other research activities), should know. This constraint requires the researcher to explain the confidential nature of the research to members of the research team and to maintain the integrity of returned questionnaires. Policies with respect to the disposition of returned questionnaires vary from firm to firm and from project to project. However, it is always true that returned questionnaires should be kept in one place, apart from questionnaires used in other projects, and under control of the researcher. Upon completion of data analysis the questionnaires may safely be destroyed. Sometimes their destruction will be quite important, especially "if the information is such that someone might want to subpoena it later."[2]

The researcher pays close attention to detail during mail survey data collection operations. Each envelope must contain the proper number of items. If addresses are organized into subsamples, each envelope must receive its appropriate special treatment—be it a different cover letter, different questionnaire, or different incentive. If a personalized cover letter is used, each envelope must correspond with the address and salutation appearing on its cover letter. If follow-up requests to respond are used, they should be sent only to nonrespondents.

TELEPHONE AND PERSONAL INTERVIEW SURVEYS   Telephone and personal interview surveys find the researcher assisted by many others, employed by either the researcher's organization or one or more outside suppliers. While all help, such additional members of the research team also complicate data collection operations because the researcher has to show evidence of polished supervisory skills. Such skills center on topics of hiring, training, motivating, and controlling.

Telephone Surveys.   For hiring telephone interviewers, we note four useful criteria; the applicant must be able to read questions fluently, accurately, and without regional accent; must possess an understandable and pleasant voice on the telephone; must possess a quiet speaking voice (to avoid disturbing other telephone interviewers who work nearby); and must be able to answer respondent questions "in a manner consistent in quality and tone with the remainder of the interview."[3] In sum, in addition to being a good reader and a good speaker, a telephone interviewer should be poised and quick thinking. Researchers often judge these qualities by having applicants conduct practice telephone interviews with some expert playing the role of the respondent.

Once hired, telephone interviewers must be trained. If the interviewer has conducted telephone interviews before, training is often little more than an item-by-item explanation of the data collection form, as well as the execution of one or two practice interviews with feedback, along with an explanation of company policies and work rules. Trainers usually stress that each question must be asked as written and in the order shown on the data collection form. If the interviewer has never conducted telephone interviews before, training has to be more extensive. For instance, training must cover these items: how to operate timing, recording, and other equipment; how to clarify responses; how to probe for better responses; and how to counter refusals. To acquire these skills requires texts, lectures, discussions, exercises, still more practice interviews, and

---

[2]John B. Lansing and James N. Morgan, *Economic Survey Methods* (Ann Arbor, Mich.: Institute for Social Research, University of Michigan, 1971), p. 108.

[3]Donald A. Dillman, *Mail and Telephone Surveys: The Total Design Method* (New York: John Wiley & Sons, 1978), p. 257.

time—a minimum of six hours training, followed by close, on-the-job supervision, is often necessary. Such supervision also benefits experienced telephone interviewers who regularly need someone to answer both their own questions and those of skeptical respondents. Further, as a check on training effectiveness, supervisors often listen and **dual-record** responses in as many as 15 percent of each interviewer's calls.

Telephone interviewing is difficult because it often involves sporadic employment, odd hours, psychologically taxing efforts, and low wages. Consequently, the researcher's most difficult supervisory skill is that of motivating interviewers. Partly, interviewers' motivations depend on adequate hiring and training practices—higher quality interviewers make motivation that much easier. But beyond hiring and training, the supervisor often takes other actions to increase motivation. One is to establish completed interview quotas for each interviewer per hour or per shift. For this quota system to work, the supervisor must tell interviewers the level of their quotas and their performance relative to them. Often the supervisor will post each interviewer's performance on a bulletin board in the telephone center. Thus, high performance is rewarded through peer recognition, or even prizes, bonuses, and higher compensation. At the same time, the supervisor watches that interview quality is maintained at an acceptable level and that quotas do not affect interviews adversely. Finally, a last motivating action consists of the supervisor's exhibiting good work habits and attitudes.

The last supervisory skill area necessary in telephone surveys is control. With so many interviewers working as members of the research team, the supervisor must watch carefully that interviewers' actual behaviors closely parallel those planned. He or she can check that they do by use of several of the supervisory actions noted earlier in the paragraphs on training and motivating interviewers. That is, the researcher achieves control by:

1. establishing quotas and deadlines,

2. tying compensation to performance,

3. dual-recording some of the interviews,

4. **validating** or verifying a sample of responses by a later telephone call (usually to 10 or 15 percent of the sample), and

5. daily editing (examining completed questionnaires for errors).

Quite clearly, interviewers' knowledge that all of these actions will be taken by a capable supervisor further achieves control.

Personal Interview Surveys. For hiring personal interviewers, somewhat more extensive criteria apply because of the more complex and face-to-face nature of these interviews. Thus, in addition to possessing above average reading skills, a pleasant voice, and an ability to answer respondent questions, the successful candidate must be able to read a map quickly and accurately, have regular access to a car, and be willing to work in most neighborhoods in all types of weather. The good candidate is a self-motivated, self-starting individual who likes meeting strangers in unfamiliar surroundings without benefit of an introduction. Finally, she or he must exhibit a pleasant yet ordinary appearance, acceptable to a wide range of respondents.

Much of the training for telephone interviewers applies to personal interviewers as well: they, too, need to know the content of the data collection form, company policies, quantity and quality quotas, that questions must be asked as written, and that their work will be monitored. They, too, must possess skills necessary to record and clarify responses, to probe, and to counter refusals. However, there may be a need for additional training to instruct personal interviewers on the use of product samples and other visual aids for use with the interview. Still more training may show interviewers how to observe and record respondents' nonverbal communications and details of respondents' neighborhoods, residences, and personal appearances.

Personal interviewing is at least as difficult as telephone interviewing. But because personal interviewers work far removed from any central office, control and motivation are the two most important supervisory areas. However, adequate control and motivation are achieved by the same actions in personal interviewing as in telephone interviewing. Even dual-recording occurs in personal interviewing, although in a manner slightly different from that of telephone interviewing: that is, a research firm may actually employ several respondents as **plants** in the population, to evaluate interviewer performance. Ethical considerations require the researcher to inform interviewers before they collect data that they might interview plants.

SUMMARY OF DATA COLLECTION METHODS Data collection operations for mail surveys largely call for the researcher to supervise something other than people. Such supervision usually concerns deadlines, recordkeeping, protection of respondent information, and attention to numerous other details. In contrast, data collection operations for telephone and personal interview surveys demand that the researcher supervise people. Such supervision usually centers on hiring, training, motivating, and controlling these additional members of the research team. Beyond these basic survey activities, we shall learn of more researcher responsibilities in our next two major sections.

Survey Evaluation Criteria

How can one tell a good survey from a bad survey? Basically, it depends on what good and bad mean and how well the survey measures up to these criteria. For our use, survey evaluation criteria are the quantity of the survey data, the quality of the survey data, and survey performance on special criteria.

Consider a research study that attempted to survey 400 Detroit purchasing agents on the telephone. Of the 400, only 360 could be reached after three callbacks; of the 360, only 300 consented to be interviewed; and of the 300, only 240 answered every question. These departures from a 100 percent response rate compromise the survey's data quantity criterion.

SURVEY DATA QUANTITY

Nonresponse Errors. The three departures noted in the preceding paragraph reflect survey nonresponse errors of two types: not-at-homes and refusals; refusals break further into complete refusals and item refusals (the latter are a topic for Chapter 7). Not-at-home errors much more frequently plague telephone and personal interviews than mail surveys. Refusal errors plague all three survey methods—mail surveys the most.

In general, survey respondents compared to nonrespondents tend to be better educated and possess higher socioeconomic status.[4] Respondents tend to be more interested in the research topic than nonrespondents. They tend also to be more outgoing, tolerant, and intellectual.[5] On balance, however, well designed and well executed surveys should minimize the size of these respondent factor differences and their effect on research results. Methods of estimating their effect follow.

Estimating Nonresponse Errors. The differences between an obtained data value and the value found if all designated sample members had responded are **nonresponse errors.** The simplest method of estimating nonresponse errors involves the researcher's and others' subjective estimates. Either separately or jointly these experts compare responses from sample segments and raise or lower values to estimate results for the entire sample.

A second, more complex, method of estimating nonresponse errors uses intensive effort to obtain responses from a random sample of nonrespondents. If the researcher can secure a high response rate from this sample, he or she then generalizes results to all nonrespondents. Then the researcher combines these results with initial results to arrive at an estimate for the entire sample. Usually this method requires personal or telephone interviews, with **callbacks** or repeated attempts to interview and strong pleas for participation. Beyond cost and time considerations, the method often suffers from an inability to secure a high response rate from the sample of nonrespondents, many of whom refused in the first place.

---

[4]Leslie Kanuk and Conrad Berenson, "Mail Surveys and Response Rates: A Literature Review," *Journal of Marketing Research* 12 (November 1975): 448–49. F. L. Filion, "Estimating Bias Due to Nonresponse in Mail Surveys," *Public Opinion Quarterly* 39 (Winter 1975–76: 483. Michael J. O'Neil, "Estimating the Nonresponse Bias Due to Refusals in Telephone Surveys," *Public Opinion Quarterly* 43 (Summer 1979): 218–32.

[5]Kanuk and Berenson, "Mail Surveys," p. 449.

A third method of estimating nonresponse errors works only with mail surveys employing follow-up appeals to nonrespondents. Such **follow-ups** take the form of letters, postcards, or telephone calls to respondents stressing the importance of everyone's cooperation. Usually follow-ups go out in two or three waves, with the first wave sent two to three weeks after mailing the survey. The second wave follows two to three weeks later and then the third wave, if used, two to three weeks after that.

Researchers plot response trends generated by the initial survey and by each follow-up wave to extrapolate or estimate responses for nonrespondents. A regression analysis (see Chapter 17) may express the trend in terms of its intercept and slope; or the researcher can use one of these three simpler methods:[6]

1. The "last-wave" method assumes nonrespondents are like the average respondent generated by the last follow-up wave.

2. The "last-respondent" method assumes nonrespondents are like the projected last respondent generated by the last follow-up wave.

3. The "projected-respondent" method assumes nonrespondents are like the projected respondent at the midpoint of the nonresponse group.

Figure 5.2 illustrates differences between these three methods for a mail survey that used two follow-ups at four and eight weeks. Researchers comparing these three methods favor the last-respondent method because it uses only data already received; that is, it uses no projections.[7]

Like subjective estimates, both callback generalizations and trend extrapolations assume that nonrespondents would respond much as certain respondents have done. This assumption may be untrue, especially for certain survey items; that is, some items might yield responses sharply different from those of callback or follow-up respondents if only the nonrespondent would make his or her response known. To summarize, then, we borrow a conclusion from the Bureau of the Census:

> We consider the efforts taken to achieve small nonresponse rates are of much greater importance than the particular procedure used to make the adjustments for the nonresponse that does occur.[8]

---

[6]Filion, "Estimating Bias," pp. 482–92. The simpler methods come from J. Scott Armstrong and Terry S. Overton, "Estimating Nonresponse Bias in Mail Surveys," *Journal of Marketing Research* 14 (August 1977): 399.

[7]Armstrong and Overton, "Estimating Nonresponse," p. 400.

[8]U.S. Bureau of the Census, *The Current Population Survey—A Report on Methodology: Technical Paper Number 7 (1963)* (Washington, D.C.: Government Printing Office, 1967), p. 53.

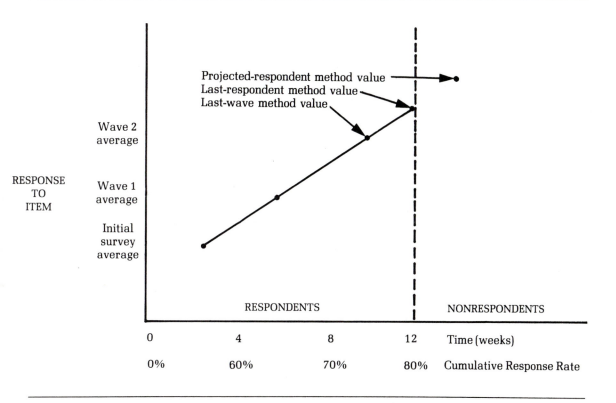

FIGURE 5.2
Response trend projection methods
Source: J. Scott Armstrong and Terry S. Overton, "Estimating Nonresponse Bias in Mail Surveys," *Journal of Marketing Research* 14 (August 1977): 399.

We agree, and we shall spend considerable time in consideration of the factors reducing nonresponse errors later in the chapter.

In contrast to survey data quantity (which "appears" in the findings as nonresponse data), survey data quality appears in the collected data. The extent to which survey data contain response errors compromises the survey's data quality criterion. **SURVEY DATA QUALITY**

Response errors are the differences between actual variable values and true, unknown variable values for survey respondents. Response errors attend every measurement process. To cite an extreme example— a mail survey of 450 consumers once found an average of 48 percent reporting a brand of margarine as their "most often bought brand." Yet their purchase diaries for the previous six months indicated the brand had never been bought![9] Probably the survey, the diary, or both contained response errors.

Response errors come from only three sources: respondents, the research task expected of respondents, and the researcher. Of these, the researcher controls only the last two. That is, the researcher may design, administer, and interpret a survey consistent with proper research practice. Yet because of respondents' boredom, faulty memories, or desires to appear socially acceptable, for example, data can contain uncontrollable response errors.

Researchers regularly attempt to reduce response errors. Some of the rest of this chapter and much of Chapters 7 through 11 discuss research practice on the topic. One point we make now is that some survey practices that attempt to decrease nonresponse error may actually increase response error. For example, a highly personalized mail survey cover letter can lead to respondents reporting distorted incomes and occupational statuses.[10] However, other mail survey variables, apart from assurances of anonymity, seem to have little effect.[11]

Rarely do researchers attempt to estimate the size of response errors. One estimating method compares actual response information to perfect information as available in aggregate form from censuses and the like. An alternate method uses the reliability coefficient (discussed in Chapter 11) to calculate "confidence zones" about obtained variable values.[12] This process is somewhat comparable to estimating sampling errors by calculating confidence intervals about sample means; however, such confidence zones consider only random response error.

SPECIAL CRITERIA   A last basis for evaluating surveys consists of several special criteria. For some studies, these criteria may be more important than data quantity and quality. We discuss two here and others later in the chapter.

One is speed of response.[13] Usually researchers and decision makers need data in a hurry. Huge quantities of high-quality data are worse than worthless if data arrive too late. Moreover, external events occurring part way through data collection may affect the replies of later respondents, making later responses more difficult to interpret.

Another criterion is respondent cooperation, willingness to perform

---

[9]Yoram Wind and David Lerner, "On the Measurement of Purchase Data: Surveys versus Purchase Diaries," *Journal of Marketing Research* 16 (February 1979): 43.

[10]Roger Kerin and Robert Peterson, "Personalization, Respondent Anonymity, and Response Distortion in Mail Surveys," *Journal of Applied Psychology* 62 (February 1977): 86–89.

[11]Michael J. Houston and Neil M. Ford, "Broadening the Scope of Methodological Research on Mail Surveys," *Journal of Marketing Research* 13 (November 1976): 401.

[12]Jum C. Nunnally, *Psychometric Theory*, 2nd ed. (New York: McGraw-Hill, 1978), pp. 239–41.

[13]Houston and Ford, "Broadening the Scope," p. 397.

special activities relating to the survey.[14] One such activity might be to participate in future research studies, that is, a primary objective of an interview may be to secure respondents' participation in a future survey. Another activity may require respondents to search records or cupboard shelves or otherwise expend special effort to make a response. Yet another consists of respondents' volunteering information beyond that asked by a survey question. And, still other special criteria may apply to a particular research study.[15]

Researchers will never know completely why some consumers fail to respond, why some responses contain unacceptable response errors, and why some surveys fail to rate well on special evaluation criteria. Of the three shortcomings, researchers have intensively studied the first two. We discuss their findings in our next section.

SUMMARY OF EVALUATION CRITERIA

Tactics Increasing Survey Data Quantity and Quality

Many research tactics increase survey data quantity and quality. Some apply equally well to mail, telephone, and personal interview surveys, while others work best—or only—with a particular method. Further, as we see at the end of this section, some cost more than others. Always the researcher should consider the tradeoff between the costs of improving data quantity and quality and the benefits such improvements bring to decision making. A researcher need not strive to collect data completely free of nonresponse and response errors. However, there is no excuse for failing to attempt to secure the best data possible, given resource constraints.

Conducting interviews at different times during each day of the week reduces not-at-home errors, yet certain times and certain days will find more consumers home than others. Data provided by the Bureau of the Census support these statements.

REDUCING NOT-AT-HOME ERRORS

Table 5.1 indicates that the chance of finding a male consumer at home at 9:10 A.M. on a Monday morning is slightly less than 1 in 4. Before 4:00 P.M., the chance of finding a female consumer at home is roughly twice that for finding a male. However, as females continue to enter and stay in the work force, this difference will continue to diminish. Indeed,

---

[14]Stephen P. De Vere, Alvin C. Burns, and Ronald F. Bush, "Broadening the Scope of Methodological Research on Telephone Surveys," in *1979 Educator's Conference Proceedings*, ed. Neil Beckwith et al. (Chicago: American Marketing Association, 1979), p. 16

[15]Theresa F. Rogers, "Interviews by Telephone and in Person: Quality of Responses and Field Performance," *Public Opinion Quarterly* 40 (Spring 1976): 51–65.

TABLE 5.1
Proportion of Persons at Home During Interviewer's First Weekday Visit, by Sex

Time of Day	Male (%)	Female (%)
8:00– 8:59 A.M.	.12	.50
9:00– 9:59 A.M.	.22	.47
10:00–10:59 A.M.	.23	.47
11:00–11:59 A.M.	.24	.48
12:00–12:59 P.M.	.24	.48
1:00– 1:59 P.M.	.23	.46
2:00– 2:59 P.M.	.24	.46
3:00– 3:59 P.M.	.30	.57
4:00– 4:59 P.M.	.36	.59
5:00– 5:59 P.M.	.45	.67
6:00– 6:59 P.M.	.62	.72
7:00– 7:59 P.M.	.62	.59
8:00– 8:59 P.M.	.57	.70

Source: U.S. Bureau of the Census, *Who's Home When,* Dean Weber and Richard C. Burt, Working Paper No. 37 (Washington, D.C.: 1972), p. 5.

the overall chance of finding anyone at home during working hours dropped about 10 percentage points between 1960 and 1970.[16] A larger drop probably occurred between 1970 and 1980.[17]

With respect to day of week, more consumers tend to be not-at-home during the business week. But both employed consumers and unemployed consumers, as well as interviewers, dislike weekend interviews. Consequently, many marketing research interviews are conducted in the evening.

Callbacks reduce not-at-home errors, as Table 5.2 shows. We can see that making no callbacks would bias the sample in favor of older, lesser educated, widowed, and poorer consumers. However, making three callbacks (the fourth-call column) results in much the same distribution of family characteristics as making seven or more calls. Usually researchers require interviewers to make two or three callbacks. Callbacks consume resources at a high rate, particularly if personal interviewers perform the survey. Like first calls, the callbacks should be scheduled at varying times for maximum effectiveness.

Scheduling interviews in advance also reduces not-at-home errors. Such practice is especially appropriate in industrial marketing research

---

[16]U.S. Bureau of the Census, *Who's Home When,* Dean Weber and Richard C. Burt, Working Paper Number 37 (Washington, D.C.: Government Printing Office, 1972), p. 2.

[17]M. F. Weeks et al. "Optimal Times to Contact Sample Households," *Public Opinion Quarterly* 44 (Spring 1980): 101–14.

TABLE 5.2
Cumulative Distributions of Family Characteristics after the First, Fourth, and Seventh or Later Call (%)

	First Call	Fourth Call	Seventh or Later Call
Age of Family Head			
Under 25	5.1	6.1	6.5
25–34	13.5	17.2	17.7
35–44	14.4	18.9	19.2
45–54	17.7	19.8	19.6
55–64	15.9	15.4	15.8
65 and over	33.4	22.6	21.2
Education of Family Head			
0–5 grades	12.2	7.8	7.6
6–8 grades	27.3	22.3	21.8
9–11 grades	16.7	17.9	18.3
High school	12.8	16.1	17.0
High school and noncollege	9.5	11.1	10.8
Some college	10.0	11.8	11.9
College, B.A. degree	8.2	9.0	8.6
Advanced degree	3.3	4.0	4.0
Marital Status			
Single	6.2	6.9	7.6
Married	68.6	72.1	71.9
Widowed	18.4	14.1	13.5
Divorced	4.2	4.2	4.1
Separated	2.6	2.7	2.9
Family Income ($)			
0 to 2,000	20.4	12.6	11.8
2,000 to 4,000	20.8	15.9	15.4
4,000 to 6,000	16.2	14.9	14.9
6,000 to 7,500	9.7	12.5	12.9
7,500 to 9,000	13.2	17.1	17.6
10,000 to 15,000	12.9	18.5	18.7
15,000 and over	6.8	8.5	8.7

Source: Adapted from William C. Dunkelberg and George S. Day, "Nonresponse Bias and Callbacks in Sample Surveys," *Journal of Marketing Research* 10 (May 1973): 160–68.

because respondents are persons who constantly schedule their time. It is also more appropriate in small sample projects, for which the resulting interview schedules stay manageable. Like callbacks, conducting personal interviews according to a schedule convenient to respondents consumes resources. It may be faster and cheaper to make the first, second, and third calls without appointments and to use schedules only for those remaining incomplete.

What about another research tactic to reduce not-at-home errors—substitution? If no one answers the telephone on the second callback, for example, why not just substitute another number? In answer to that question consider that such a practice assumes that substituted at-homes differ in no significant way from original not-at-homes with respect to their responses to research questions. Yet we have already seen from Tables 5.1 and 5.2 that the two groups do differ with respect to many socioeconomic characteristics. Thus, substitution usually is a less desirable tactic than varying interview times and using callbacks and appointments.

A procedure that addresses the factor of the not-at-home is the Politz-Simmons approach; each completed interview is weighted by the inverse of the probability of finding that respondent at home. This probability is typically estimated by asking how many of the previous five nights the respondent was at home.[18] Thus, if a respondent says she was at home on none of the preceding five nights, her responses would be weighted by a factor of 6. (During the current 6-day period, she was at home on only the night of the interview.) To be most effective, the method requires a large sample of consumers with superior memories.

Finally, researchers have used one other tactic with some success to reduce not-at-home errors: for a certain few studies, a personal interviewer may leave the questionnaire at not-at-home residences with a stamped return envelope and a request for cooperation. The practice requires identification numbers on questionnaires to avoid callbacks at households that complete and return the questionnaire. More importantly, the practice requires a questionnaire simple enough that the proper consumer in the residence can accurately complete it. This last condition is seldom met in most personal interview studies.

REDUCING REFUSAL ERRORS

Reducing refusal errors has been much studied in mail surveys. Survey design factors and research premises that researchers have employed appear in Exhibit 5.1. As we might suspect, some research premises found more support in the research than others. Two outstanding reviews of this research largely agree with premises on advance notification, follow-ups, premiums, postage type, and sponsor identity.[19] Application of these factors to a mail survey project should find fewer than 30 percent of potential respondents refusing.

That other design factors, particularly questionnaire length, do not appear to affect refusal rates may seem surprising. Common sense seems to dictate that the longer the questionnaire, the more refusals. Yet most research has simply not supported this speculation. However, before we start designing 26-page mail questionnaires, consider the following. Longer questionnaires may result in more response errors and in more don't-know responses; they may be returned more slowly; they may cost

---

[18]Tyzoon T. Tyebjee, "Telephone Survey Methods: The State of the Art," *Journal of Marketing* 43 (Summer 1979): 72.

[19]Kanuk and Berenson, "Mail Surveys," p. 450; and Arnold S. Linsky, "Stimulating Responses to Mailed Questionnaires: A Review," *Public Opinion Quarterly* 39 (Spring 1975): 99–100.

EXHIBIT 5.1
Mail Survey Design Factors and Response Rate Research Premises

Mail Survey Design Factor	Research Premise
Advance Notification	Alerting consumers before they receive the survey decreases refusals.
Anonymity Promise	Promising consumers that their responses cannot be connected with them personally decreases refusals.
Cover Letter Appeals	Stressing the need for each consumer's help and the importance of his or her participation decreases refusals.
Cover Letter Personalization	Dated, individually typed, and personally signed cover letters with the respondent's name in the salutation decrease refusals.
Deadlines	A time limit to return the survey decreases refusals.
Follow-ups	Reminders in the form of postcards, telephone calls, or a letter that includes another copy of the questionnaire decrease refusals.
Premiums	Incentives accompanying the questionnaire decrease refusals.
Questionnaire Appearance	Page color, printing method, and question precoding affect refusal rates.
Questionnaire Length	Shorter questionnaires decrease refusals.
Postage Type	More expensive mailing methods and the use of stamps instead of postage meters for outgoing and return envelopes decrease refusal rates.
Sponsor Identity	Positive consumer attitude toward the organization sponsoring the survey decreases refusals.

more to print, mail, and analyze; and their additional data may confuse more than help solve the research problem. Thus, a good rule still is to keep questionnaires short.[20]

Far less research has studied the refusal errors that occur in telephone surveys. Here refusals occur as **break offs,** typically after the interviewer introduces the study but before the first question. Break offs seldom occur after the first question, even though respondents are certainly able to "hang up at the slightest whim, a far easier act than ordering an interviewer away from one's home."[21]

---

[20]Keep them also uncluttered. It is better to use normal margins, normal-sized paper, and eye-pleasing white space than to cram everything onto one oversized page.

[21]Don A. Dillman, Jean Gorton Gallegos, and James H. Frey, "Reducing Refusal Rates for Telephone Interviews," *Public Opinion Quarterly* 40 (Spring 1976): 68.

Looking back at Exhibit 5.1, we see seven mail survey design factors that might apply as well to reducing break offs. Researchers could notify consumers in advance, promise them anonymity, appeal for their help and stress the importance of their participation, make interviews very personal, offer a premium, use short questionnaires, and identify the study sponsor. As with mail survey research, telephone survey research could be expected to show that only the factors of advance notification, premiums, and sponsor identity affect the break off rate. Unfortunately, research to support or not support this expectation has yet to be conducted. Only one study has investigated the effects of personalization, appeals stressing the importance of participation, premiums, and advance notification;[22] only the last factor had a significant effect, cutting refusals from nearly 14 percent to nearly 8 percent.

We must note a most important design factor present in telephone surveys but absent in mail surveys—the interviewer. Some interviewers undoubtedly manage to have fewer break offs than others; evidence supporting this probability comes from a study of a related primary data collection method, personal interviews.

The Bureau of the Census conducted the research on 802 interviewers to determine if interviewer characteristics affected response rates.[23] Findings showed that response rates generally increased as interviewer income decreased. Response rates also increased as interviewer experience decreased and if the interviewer believed the asking of the question to be "appropriate."

Returning to other personal interview design factors and again to Exhibit 5.1, we note that the seven survey research design factors that may apply to telephone surveys may also apply to personal interviews. Unfortunately, none have been critically tested and reported in the literature. Voluminous research on personal interviews has focused instead on response errors.

REDUCING RESPONSE ERRORS

Reducing response errors proves a more difficult task than reducing not-at-home and refusal errors. For one thing, researchers often cannot tell if their actions result in responses closer to or further from the truth. For another, response errors consist of both stable and random discrepancies. Last of all, response errors consist of both unmotivated and motivated discrepancies; sometimes response errors occur because of memory lapses, for example, and sometimes because of respondents' lying.

Little mail survey research has studied the reduction of response errors. Exhibit 5.2 shows survey design factors and research premises

---

[22]Ibid., 66–78.

[23]Barbara Bailar, Leroy Bailey, and Joyce Stevens, "Measures of Interviewer Bias and Variance," *Journal of Marketing Research* 14 (August 1977): 342.

EXHIBIT 5.2
Mail Survey Design Factors and Response Error Research Premises

Mail Survey Design Factor	Research Premise
Advance Notification	Allowing respondents time to organize and prepare for the questionnaire reduces response errors.
Anonymity	An anonymous respondent makes fewer response errors.
Cover Letter Appeals	Stressing the need for honest answers reduces response errors.
Cover Letter Personalization	A personalized cover letter increases response errors for sensitive or threatening items.
Premiums	Incentives accompanying the questionnaire have no effect on response errors.
Length	Shorter questionnaires reduce response error.
Sponsor Identity	The organization sponsoring the survey and consumers' knowledge of it affect response errors.

regarding error reduction; of these, research done so far supports the premises for anonymity, cover letter personalization, and premiums.[24] Other premises await future research.

Even less telephone survey research has studied the reduction of response errors. Studies have focused on question form and topic rather than on the relevant survey design factors (Exhibit 5.2). Because question form and topic so markedly influence response error in all types of surveys, we reserve further comments on them for Chapters 7, 8, and 9. No telephone survey research has examined the effect of advance notification, introductory appeals, personalization, premiums, length, and sponsor identity on response error.

In contrast, much personal interview research has studied response errors.[25] But, again, rather than focusing on the relevant survey design factors (such as those in Exhibit 5.2), research has instead investigated the

---

[24]Carol Fuller, "Effect of Anonymity on Return Rate and Response Bias in a Mail Survey," *Journal of Applied Psychology* 59 (June 1974): 292–96. Kerin and Peterson, "Personalization, Respondent Anonymity, and Response Distortion." Michael S. Goodstadt et al., "Mail Survey Response Rates: Their Manipulation and Impact," *Journal of Marketing Research* 14 (August 1977): 391–95. William J. Whitmore, "Mail Survey Premiums and Response Bias," *Journal of Marketing Research* 13 (February 1976): 46–50. Stephen W. Brown and Kenneth A. Coney, "Comments on Mail Survey Premiums and Response Bias," *Journal of Marketing Research* 14 (August 1977) pp. 385–87. William J. Whitmore, "A Reply on Mail Survey Premiums and Response Bias," *Journal of Marketing Research* 14 (August 1977): 388–90.

[25]See Harper W. Boyd, Jr., and Ralph Westfall, "Interviewer Bias Once More Revisited," *Journal of Marketing Research* 7 (May 1970): 249–53 and their earlier reviews for a summary of this research.

influence of the interviewer on responses. The influence is described as **interviewer effects** or **interviewer bias.** It results from

> [the] ability of the interviewer to alter the questions, his appearance, his manner of speaking, the intentional and unintentional cues he gives, and the way he probes. . . . It means, in effect, each respondent may receive a slightly different interview.[26]

Moreover, different respondents react differently to a change in the interviewer's behavior during an interview.

All this leads to response error. To reduce it requires careful selection, training, and controlling of interviewers, as we discussed earlier in this chapter. Further, researchers should assign interviewers to interviews randomly[27] and then control their performance quickly and regularly. Field editors should validate and check daily the accuracy of a sample of each interviewer's work to correct flaws and reward good performance. Later, central office editing should also validate a sample (usually 10 to 15 percent) of each interviewer's completed work. Sometimes interviewers use tape recorders to record responses as both a way to decrease response errors and as a control procedure. Sometimes two interviewers conduct each interview as a team for the same purposes. Occasionally researchers also use "plants" to reduce response errors caused by interviewers who cheat.

DATA QUANTITY, QUALITY, AND COSTS

Apart from question form and topic, we have seen that the researcher makes many survey design decisions that affect data quantity and quality. Our point in summary is that some design decisions also greatly influence survey costs.

To illustrate, suppose a researcher is responsible for a survey research project where approximately $5,000 is budgeted for data collection. He could use a "bare-bones" mail survey consisting of only a questionnaire and a good cover letter. Or he could use a more expensive design consisting of an advance notification postcard, a 50-cent piece accompanying the questionnaire as a premium, and two waves of postcards as follow-ups. From past research he estimates the questionnaire with a good cover letter will yield a 50 percent response rate. Without follow-ups, the expensive design would produce about a 65 percent response rate. About 40 percent of the original sample would receive the first follow-up and raise the response rate to 75 percent. About 30 percent

---

[26]Donald S. Tull and Del I. Hawkins, *Marketing Research: Meaning, Measurement, and Method* (New York: Macmillan, 1976), p. 382.

[27]John Freeman and Edgar W. Butler, "Some Sources of Interviewer Variance in Surveys," *Public Opinion Quarterly* 40 (Spring 1976): 91.

TABLE 5.3
Estimated Results of Two Mail Survey Designs

Factor	Bare-Bones Design	Expensive Design
Attempted Sample Size	2,000	1,060
Response Rate	50%	80%
Realized Sample Size	1,000	850
Costs		
Advance Postcard	0	$1,590
Questionnaire	$5,000	2,650
Premium	0	530
First Follow-up	0	127
Second Follow-up	0	95
Total Cost	$5,000	$4,992

of the original sample would also receive the second follow-up and raise the response rate to 80 percent. He estimates the per unit costs to produce and mail the advance postcard, questionnaire, and follow-up postcard at $1.50, $2.50, and $0.30, respectively.

Very easily the researcher determines that the bare-bones design provides for an original sample of 2,000. He determines that the expensive design allows only a sample of 1,060. However, with different response rates, the two designs yield more similar numbers of estimated returns— 1,000 and 850. Table 5.3 summarizes the two designs under consideration.

The issue now, of course, is whether the additional quality present in the expensive design is worth the reduction in quantity. The answer depends on differences between respondents and nonrespondents. If they are small, he would prefer the bare-bones design; if large, he would prefer the expensive design. To make a decision, he needs an intensive research effort on a sample of nonrespondents. Lacking this, he notes that the expensive design allows an estimate of nonresponse error by extending the trends. He also thinks that past research on similar marketing problems may provide further help.

Comparing Mail, Telephone, and Personal Interview Surveys

In this final section we compare mail, telephone, and personal interview surveys. What we have discussed about data quantity, data quality, and special criteria form the bases for comparison. To begin, we assume that a researcher needs data to solve a defined marketing problem, and we know the researcher can collect data by mail, telephone, or personal interviews. We shall see that each survey method has somewhat unique strengths and weaknesses.

Mail surveys generally produce lower response rates than telephone surveys, which generally produce lower response rates than personal interview surveys. Table 5.4 gives response rates achieved by researchers using two or all three survey methods to collect the same data. In addition to comparing response rates, we should consider also the composition of nonrespondents. In mail surveys, nonrespondents consist almost entirely

TABLE 5.4
Survey Methods and Response Rates (%)

Study	Mail	Telephone	Personal Interview
Columbotos[a]	—	64*	68*
Groves[b]	—	70*	74
Hochstim[c]	81	72	90
	75	79	89
Jordan, Marcus, and Reeder[d]	—	49	64
Klecka and Tuchfarber[e]	—	92	96
Locander, Sudman, and Bradburn[f]	—	90	76
Shosteck and Fairweather[g]	70	—	74
Siemiatycki[h]	70	74	84
Wiseman[i]	49	64	60
Average	69	73	78

*Estimated

[a]J. Colombotos, "Personal Versus Telephone Interviews: Effect on Responses," *Public Health Reports* 84 (1969): 773–82.

[b]Robert M. Groves, "Actors and Questions in Telephone and Personal Interview Surveys," *Public Opinion Quarterly* (Summer 1979), pp. 190–205.

[c]Joseph R. Hochstim, "A Critical Comparison of Three Strategies of Collecting Data from Households," *Journal of the American Statistical Association* (September 1967), pp. 976–89.

[d]Lawrence A. Jordan, Alfred C. Marcus, and Leo G. Reeder, "Response Styles in Telephone and Household Interviewing: A Field Experiment," *Public Opinion Quarterly* (Summer 1980), pp. 210–22.

[e]William R. Klecka and Alfred J. Tuchfarber, "Random Digit Dialing: A Comparison to Personal Surveys," *Public Opinion Quarterly* (Spring 1978), pp. 105–14.

[f]William Locander, Seymour Sudman, and Norman Bradburn, "An Investigation of Interview Method, Threat and Response Distortion," *Journal of the American Statistical Association* (June 1976), pp. 269–75.

[g]Herschel Shosteck and William R. Fairweather, "Physician Response Rates to Mail and Personal Interview Surveys," *Public Opinion Quarterly* (Summer 1979), p. 214.

[h]Jack Siemiatycki, "A Comparison of Mail, Telephone, and Home Interview Strategies for Household Health Surveys," *American Journal of Public Health* (March 1979), pp. 238–45.

[i]Frederick Wiseman, "Methodological Bias in Public Opinion Surveys," *Public Opinion Quarterly* (Spring 1972), pp. 105–08.

of refusals. In telephone and personal interview surveys, nonrespondents consist of both not-at-homes and refusals. Between telephone and personal interview surveys there seems to be little difference in refusal rates.[28]

In summary of the table, we can arrive at a response rate guideline: well designed and well executed mail, telephone, and personal interview surveys should produce minimum response rates of 70, 75, and 80 percent, respectively. When considering costs, a researcher may accept lower response rates, especially when differences between respondents and nonrespondents are slight.

All survey methods contain response errors of largely unknown frequency, direction, and level. Rogers, for example, reports no difference between responses from two samples of consumers—one interviewed by telephone and the other in person—to complex knowledge and attitudinal items and to selected behavioral and socioeconomic items, including income.[29] Other researchers report similar socioeconomic results.[30] However, Locander, Sudman, and Bradburn report research suggesting that the personal type of survey methods, like personal and telephone interviewing, may induce more overreporting of socially desirable acts than the less personal ones. Less personal methods may induce underreporting of socially undesirable acts.[31] Also, Jordan, Marcus, and Reeder report differences between telephone and personal interview samples in response style to attitudinal items.[32] We conclude that no survey method always produces better quality data.

Apart from using other data collection methods than surveys, researchers can do little to reduce response error caused solely by respondents. However, they can do much to reduce response errors caused instead by researchers and research tasks, as we shall consider in Chapters 7 through 11.

DATA QUALITY AND SURVEY METHODS

---

[28]Rogers, "Interviews by Telephone and In Person," pp. 59–60. William R. Klecka and Alfred J. Tuchfarber, "Random Digit Dialing: A Comparison to Personal Surveys," *Public Opinion Quarterly* 42 (Spring 1978): 108. Conflicting results are reported by Lawrence A. Jordan, Alfred C. Marcus, and Leo G. Reeder. "Response Styles in Telephone and Household Interviewing: A Field Experiment," *Public Opinion Quarterly* 44 (Summer 1980): 210–22.

[29]Rogers, "Interviews by Telephone and In Person," pp. 59–60.

[30]Robert M. Groves, "Actors and Questions in Telephone and Personal Interview Surveys," *Public Opinion Quarterly* 43 (Summer 1979): 190–205. Klecka and Tuchfarber, "Random Digit Dialing." Jordan, Marcus, and Reeder, "Response Styles."

[31]William Locander, Seymour Sudman, and Norman Bradburn, "An Investigation of Interview Method, Threat, and Response Distortion," *Journal of the American Statistical Association* 71 (June 1976): 269–75.

[32]Jordan, Marcus, and Reeder, "Response Styles."

SPECIAL CRITERIA AND SURVEY METHODS   Earlier we identified speed of response as one special criterion in evaluating surveys. Here we use it and four others—cost, data collection control, sampling control, and versatility—as special criteria to compare mail, telephone, and personal interview surveys.

Speed of Response.   Speed of response, as we have seen, refers to the time between selection of a survey method and completion of data collection operations. Holding budget and other survey design aspects constant, mail and telephone surveys increase the speed of response compared to personal interviews. Telephone surveys usually outperform mail surveys for short questionnaires and small samples. Mail surveys usually outperform telephone surveys under opposite conditions.

Cost.   In this context, cost refers only to expenses connected with survey data collection. Such expenses are usually totaled and expressed as an amount per usable questionnaire collected in the survey. For most surveys, variable expenses include paper, printing, and collating costs. Mail surveys introduce additional costs of envelopes, clerical activities (folding, stuffing, sealing, stamping), and postage. Telephone surveys substitute for these costs interviewers' wages and benefits, supervisors' wages and benefits, and telephone expenses. Personal interview surveys require similar wage and benefit costs but substitute travel for telephone expenses.

Other aspects of the survey design being equal, mail surveys cost less than telephone and personal interview surveys. Actual costs depend on survey design details, but estimated costs per usable questionnaire would be $3 to $10 for mail, $3 to $12 for telephone, and $5 to $25 for personal interviews.[33]

Data Collection Control.   Data collection control refers to a survey method's potential for gathering information according to procedures established by the researcher. For example, the researcher may want personal interviews conducted in low-income areas during evening hours. And he or she certainly will want the questions asked as written and in the order they appear on the data collection form. Yet the researcher may realize neither desire to the extent specified by the research design because of a lack of control over data collection.

Mail and telephone surveys offer somewhat more data collection control, even though neither can claim it as a particular strength. With mail surveys the only factors frustrating data collection control are the respondent and the research task. Telephone and personal interview surveys add the interviewer, who also must be controlled. Of the two, telephone surveys allow more control: telephone interviewers generally work in a

---

[33]Thomas C. Kinnear and James R. Taylor, *Marketing Research An Applied Approach* (New York: McGraw-Hill, 1979), p. 436.

central location and are easily monitored; personal interviewers remove themselves to scattered job sites.

Sampling Control.   Sampling control describes the ability of the survey to collect data from and only from members of the target population. Adequate sampling control depends on the questionnaire reaching the right person and obtaining her or his complete responses.

This occurs most easily with a telephone survey. Researchers usually find it simple to select a telephone number, dial it, and conduct the interview. Over 95 percent of all U.S. households have one or more telephones.[34] While not all list their numbers, all can be reached by randomly dialing sample telephone numbers (a topic we introduce in Chapter 13). Sampling control suffers somewhat in telephone surveys (compared to mail surveys) because of not-at-homes. However, reaching not-at-homes through telephone callbacks uses far fewer resources than personal interview callbacks.

Adequate sampling control occurs less easily with personal interviews than with telephone interviews, even though most consumers live in households potentially reachable by interviewers.[35] While not all households appear on a list, most can be selected by cluster sampling of units of area (also a topic for Chapter 13). However, we have seen that personal interviewers tend to be difficult to control. They may mistakenly or intentionally interview the wrong person in the right household or interview some other improper person and household combination. They may avoid interviews in certain neighborhoods, at certain times of the day, and on certain days of the week. However, with conscientious interviewers, rigorous control and validation procedures, and a higher budget, sampling control in personal interviews can approach that for telephone surveys.

Such is not the case for mail surveys. Apart from the generally lower response rate, sampling control suffers in mail surveys for two reasons. First is the lack of an adequate list of mailing addresses for members of the target population. Even the best available list fails to include current addresses of all members once and only once. Second is the inability to control the identity of the actual respondent. A teenage son can complete a mail questionnaire as a favor for mom and the researcher will be none the wiser.

Versatility.   Versatility describes a survey method's potential to apply to a variety of marketing problems. It is a method's ability to meet all sorts

---

[34]U.S. Bureau of the Census, *Statistical Abstract of the United States: 1978*, 99th ed. (Washington, D.C.: Government Printing Office, 1978), p. 590.

[35]Many "transients and social isolates" (admittedly a rare population in a marketing research study) have no household, and any survey method to collect data from such a population lacks sampling control. See Klecka and Tuchfarber, "Random Digit Dialing," p. 106.

TABLE 5.5
Relative Strengths and Weaknesses of Mail, Telephone, and Personal Interview Surveys

Evaluation Criteria	Mail	Telephone	Personal Interview
Data Quantity	W	N	S
Data Quality	N	N	N
Special			
Speed of Response	N	N	W
Cost	S	S	W
Data Collection Control	N	N	W
Sampling Control	W	S	N
Versatility	W	N	S

Key: S = relative strength, W = relative weaknesses,
    N = neither a relative strength or weakness.

of research objectives, to measure many types of concepts in valid and reliable manners, to measure much information per respondent, and to work well in different cultures.

The most versatile survey uses personal interviews. Personal interviews can collect data on just about any research topic from just about any population. Interviewers can ask probing questions to get beneath vague and superficial responses. They can follow complex instructions to conduct the interview. They can present research materials that appeal to senses of sight, sound, taste, smell, and touch. They can simultaneously confirm responses to some purchase behavior and socioeconomic questions by careful observation during the interview. Personal interviews can last for perhaps as long as ninety minutes.

Less versatile surveys use telephone interviews. Telephone interviews measure most variables, even knowledge and attitudes, from most populations that personal interviews can reach.[36] Telephone interviewers can also probe and follow complex instructions. However, for the most part they can present only auditory research materials. And, they cannot confirm responses simultaneously during the interview. Telephone interviews can last for as long as fifty minutes, but usually take less than twenty.

Still less versatile surveys use mail questionnaires. While mail surveys can measure most variables from most populations, they largely cannot ask probing questions, use complex instructions, or present other than printed research materials. They cannot confirm responses. Nor can they

---

[36]Rogers, "Interviews by Telephone and In Person." See also Eugene Telser, "Data Exorcises Bias in Phone Versus Personal Interview Debate," *Marketing News* (September 10, 1976), pp. 6–7.

BOX 5.1

How the Minicomputer Works for Telephone Surveys

Many marketing research firms have begun to change their survey methods because of the minicomputer. Several now conduct "on-line interviewing" where interviewers sit at video display terminals and conduct telephone interviews. The terminal displays each telephone number, times to call by time zone, and keeps track of when to try again. It also displays each question and its allowable responses, often in a rotating order to lower sequence and timing problems.

As the respondent answers, the interviewer enters her response directly into the computer, using either the terminal keyboard or a "light pen" that enters any response it touches on the terminal display. This reduces errors normally produced by coding and keypunching. It also results in some other advantages according to Clare Brown, president of Clare Brown Associates, Inc., a marketing research firm.

For one, the interviewer doesn't have to be concerned with skip instructions that direct the interviewer past irrelevant questions. Computer programs simply identify which question to ask for even the most complicated skip patterns. For another, once interviews end, results can be quickly analyzed with important tables appearing on the client's desk the next morning. Perhaps the most interesting advantage is that a minicomputer can easily personalize a question based on a respondent's earlier answer. For example, a respondent might report driving a 1981 Ford. Sixteen questions later the terminal might display this question: "What kind of mileage does your 1981 Ford get?"

Clare Brown concludes "This is the way interviewing is going. On-line offers many advantages and interviewers love the terminals because they can concentrate better on the interviewing job."

Source: Adapted from Henry T. Teller, "Lower Prices, Improved Hardware/Software Will Marry Minicomputer to Marketing Research," *Marketing News* (November 16, 1979), p. 3.

---

go much beyond eight pages in length for studies of the general population.[37]

SUMMARY OF SURVEY METHODS

No survey method emerges as superior to the others on all survey evaluation criteria. Table 5.5 illustrates the point and summarizes the information in the last few pages. Because no clear-cut winner emerges, researchers regularly use different methods in numerous research designs. Moreover, they often use more than one in a single design.

THE FUTURE OF TELEPHONE INTERVIEWS

To end our treatment of survey techniques, we look to what the future holds for telephone survey methods with the coming of the minicomputer. Box 5.1 is a description of how the computer can be used to assist the interview process.

---

[37]Paul L. Erdos, *Professional Mail Surveys* (New York: McGraw-Hill, 1970), p. 12.

Chapter Summary

Researchers collect primary data using mail, telephone, and personal interview survey methods. Each survey method requires detailed and careful planning. When planned against a particular marketing problem and research budget, each may be evaluated in terms of the quantity and quality of data it will produce. Each may further be evaluated in terms of the expected performance on special criteria. No survey method consistently betters the other two.

Because surveys have been the foundation of marketing research does not mean they have ceased to develop. Supplanting the traditional mail, telephone, and personal interview surveys are newer practices such as **mall intercepts** and **on-line interviewing.** We started the chapter with a mall intercept example; we ended it with an on-line telephone survey example. (Even beyond these developments, some firms now conduct on-line mall intercepts; a few even conduct on-line mall intercepts using a prominently displayed computer terminal without an interviewer! Consumers approach, press a key to initiate the interview, and enter their responses as directed. This practice clearly is experimental, and sampling control problems have not been resolved.[38])

Chapter Review

KEY TERMS

Nonresponse error

Response error

Survey follow-up wave

Survey quality indicators

Callbacks

Break offs

Speed of response

Data collection control

Sampling control

Survey versatility

On-line interview

DISCUSSION QUESTIONS

1. Consider the following survey data:

Age Group	Daily Coffee Consumption (oz.)	Sample Size (n)	Response Rate (%)	Population Size (N, 000)
18–24	3	40	50	500
25–29	5	60	60	400
30–34	6	60	80	400
35–39	7	80	80	400
40–49	8	70	70	600
50 and over	4	50	70	200

[38]For simple research questions, sampling control may not be a problem. See Ernest R. Cadotte, "TELLUS Computer Lets Retailers Conduct In-store Market Research," *Marketing News* (December 12, 1980), p. 17.

Estimate the average ounces of coffee consumed per person in the total population. What assumptions underlie your estimate?

2. Why is it usually easier to estimate nonresponse error than it is to estimate response error?

3. Why do you suppose research on mail surveys has focused on response rates and research on personal interviews has focused on response errors?

4. What is right and what is wrong about a researcher trying to match interviewer characteristics with interviewee characteristics before assigning interviews?

5. Consider the following survey designs: Design A uses an advance notification telephone call, a one-dollar incentive accompanying a mail questionnaire, and two follow-up telephone calls to 35 percent and 25 percent of the original sample to achieve an overall response rate of 85 percent. Design B uses only a good cover letter for a response rate of 50 percent. If the research budget is $20,000 and costs of each telephone call $4, and each letter $3, which design do you prefer? Why?

6. With the cost of first class postage less than $0.50 per ounce, how can a mail survey possibly cost $10 per usable return?

7. What survey data collection method would you use to collect:
   a) a lot of simple information about Tucson consumers, quickly, at low cost?
   b) exploratory research data on Yamaha's brand image?
   c) a wide variety of data from 250 San Francisco purchasing agents?
   d) data showing the influence of flavor intensity on consumer reaction to a new soft drink?

8. Which survey method is best? Discuss.

Additional Readings

Ferber, Robert, ed. *Readings in Survey Research*. Chicago: American Marketing Association, 1978.

> *Forty-three serious articles and one farcical article detail what is known about survey research. Articles discuss everything from nonresponse error to drop-off questionnaire delivery.*
>
> *For a less empirical, less current, but quicker summary see these treatments in the Handbook of Marketing Research, Ferber, Robert, ed. (New York: McGraw-Hill, 1974).*
> *Paul L. Erdos, "Data Collection Methods: Mail Surveys," Section 2: 90–104.*
> *Stanley L. Payne, "Data Collection Methods: Telephone Surveys," Section 2: 105–23.*
> *Charles S. Mayer, "Data Collection Methods: Personal Interviews," Section 2: 82–90.*

Tyebjee, Tyzoon T. "Telephone Survey Methods: The State of the Art." *Journal of Marketing* 43 (Summer 1979): 68–78.

> *This article brings us up to date on telephone surveys. It does not appear in Readings in Survey Research but probably would have had it been written early enough.*

Primary Data Collection: Experiments, Observation Studies, and Simulations

Experiments, observation studies, and simulations represent newer, less traditional ways to produce primary data than the survey method. Used seldom before 1960, these three new methods seem destined to become more popular. Especially for larger firms, experiments and simulations will increasingly take the place of surveys in marketing research designs. Yet, for now, the majority of designs continue to collect primary data through surveys. We learn why at the end of the chapter.

Collecting Experimental Data

An **experiment** investigates the extent to which a change in one variable (called the independent variable) leads to a change in another (the dependent variable) for an identified population under controlled conditions. Key works in the definition are "controlled conditions"; that is, researchers attempt to regulate or control the situation surrounding an experiment in such a way that most variables that have the potential to influence the dependent variable actually do not. All such attempts contrast sharply with surveys, in which researchers allow most influencing variables to operate without restraint. Experiments take place in somewhat synthetic but highly controlled research rooms or in more realistic but accordingly less regulated real world surroundings. The former we call laboratory experiments and the latter, field experiments. Let us look more closely.

129

LABORATORY EXPERIMENTS   Suppose we want to determine the effects of a 25 and a 50 cents off coupon, good for a consumer's next purchase of Flavor Fiesta coffee, before distributing one of the two nationally. We might design an experiment as follows:

1. Using random digit dialing, invite 200 Philadelphia coffee drinkers to a central laboratory, without telling them the specific purpose of the experiment. (This means the screening process would include other questions of product consumption in addition to one for coffee.)

2. Randomly assign 100 subjects to a Treatment A room and 100 to a Treatment B room in the laboratory as they arrive.

3. In the Treatment A room show ten slides of coupons for various products, including the 25 cents off coupon. In the Treatment B room, show the same slides, except substitute the 50 cents off coupon for the 25 cents off coupon.

4. In both rooms, measure each subject's intention to buy each couponed product after each slide appears.

5. Measure socioeconomic and buyer behavior characteristics of each subject.

6. Debrief subjects and compensate them.

Of course, other experimental designs are possible, too. Instead of massing 100 subjects in each room at the same time, we might conduct the experiment with individuals, using closed circuit television screens that randomly display only seven coupons. Or we might present individual subjects with a sealed envelope containing twelve coupons and ask each to open his or her envelope and select the ones they would be likely to use. Our point is this: no matter the experimental design, data collection operations for experimental data proceed in an orderly way—sequentially and without improvisation.

Such data collection operations carefully control the experimental instructions, treatments, experimenters, and facilities.

Instructions to Subjects. Instructions to subjects must describe the nature of the experiment so that they know generally what to expect, when, where, and from whom; yet instructions must not disclose the specific purpose of the experiment if this knowledge might influence subjects' reactions. For example, the purpose of our coffee coupon experiment might be described in the instructions as a study of consumer reactions to various marketing promotions (not as a study of consumer reactions to a Flavor Fiesta cents off coupon). Instructions should further tell of the need for subjects to respond independently and to view the coupons naturally, as if the subjects were alone in their own homes.

Instructions should clearly explain the mechanics of filling out data collection forms; and they should appear in clear, complete, and standardized language. Unless they do, resulting data may reflect the effect of different instructions rather than the effect of different experimental treatments. Some researchers even recommend the use of only written, audiotaped, videotaped, or filmed instructions—to minimize instructional effects.[1]

Experimental Treatments. Experimental treatments are the specific forms or levels of intensity of the independent variable or variables whose effects are under investigation. In our coffee coupon experiment, we have two treatments: the 25 cent coupon and the 50 cent coupon. Treatments are assigned to subjects either on a random or a deterministic basis. That is, either chance alone or chance plus subjects' possession of certain characteristics determine to which treatment they will be exposed.

Treatments further must seem sufficiently real to subjects that it is justifiable for the researcher to generalize results to the real world.[2] Unless the design requires otherwise, multiple treatments applied to one group of subjects should be assigned in random order for each subject.

Experimenters. Research has shown that apart from their already mentioned influence in giving instructions, experimenters affect research results in other intentional and unintentional ways.[3] An intentional influence is blatantly unethical conduct and deserves no further consideration here. But unintentional influence should be discussed. One unintentional way in which experimenters affect some research results is through their own socioeconomic characteristics: their sex, age, race, religion, and social status. Another is through their sociopsychological characteristics: their anxiety, need for approval, hostility, and warmth. Another is through situational experimenter factors: their prior familiarity with subjects, their own experience as an experimenter, and the way in which they are directed by the researcher. And yet another is the expectancy each experimenter has of how subjects will respond to treatments; such expectations may color each experimenter's behavior and observation during the experiment and even distort the researcher's data interpretations upon completion. See Box 6.1 for an illustration of this effect.

To minimize the effect experimenters have on research results, a researcher might, whenever possible, employ a large number of experienced experimenters, preferably hiring those of different sexes, ages, races, religions, and social classes. The researcher should train them well

---

[1]Robert Rosenthal, *Experimenter Effects in Behavioral Research* (New York: Appleton-Century-Crofts, 1966), pp. 374–76.

[2]E. Aronson and J. M. Carlsmith, "Experimentation in Social Psychology," in *Handbook of Social Psychology,* vol. 2, ed. G. Lindzey and E. Aronson (Reading, Mass.: Addison-Wesley, ley, 1968), pp. 22–28.

[3]This discussion draws from Rosenthal, *Experimenter Effects,* pp. 3–140.

BOX 6.1

Illustration of Experimenter Expectancy Effect

Robert Rosenthal documented existence of the experimenter expectancy effect by the following experiment. He instructed ten students in an undergraduate experimental psychology course to serve as experimenters. Each was told exactly how to present to approximately twenty different subjects the same series of ten photographs of people. Each subject rated the person in each photograph on a 20-point scale, anchored at −10 with "extreme failure" and at +10 with "extreme success." Rosenthal's only departure from equal treatment was to tell five of the ten experimenters that their photographs would average about a −5 rating and to tell the other five experimenters that their photographs would average about a +5 rating.

Average ratings obtained from the subjects appear opposite for the two groups of experimenters. The difference between overall averages for the two groups of experimenters is statistically significant. Such a result is surprising because experimenters were carefully instructed to read written instructions to subjects and to say nothing else than hello and goodbye. Yet other experiments have generally supported Rosenthal's findings. [*]

	Expected Ratings	
	−5.0	+5.0
Average ratings recorded	.18	.66
	.17	.45
	.04	.35
	−.37	.31
	−.42	.25
Overall average	−.08	+.40

[*] For a critical evaluation of this support, see Kenneth R. Graham, *Psychological Research: Controlled Interpersonal Interaction* (Monterey, Calif.: Brooks/Cole, 1977), pp. 168–72.

Source: Robert Rosenthal, *Experimenter Effects in Behavioral Research* (New York: Appleton-Century-Crofts, 1966), pp. 143–46.

but avoid disclosing the specific purpose of the experiment. The researcher should control their behaviors through well-written, complete instructions, and through monitoring systems such as one-way mirrors, closed circuit television, and the like. The researcher should design the experiment to minimize contact and interaction between experimenter and subject. And, finally, the researcher should watch for trends in research results that seem to occur as experimenters become more experienced.

Facilities.   Facilities for the experiment also concern the researcher during data collection operations. The researcher wants facilities, like treatments, to appear sufficiently real that subjects behave as if in a normal setting.[4] For some experiments, this may require only a room, extensive instructions, and a paper and pencil measurement of the dependent variable. For other experiments, this may require a 10,000-square-foot mockup of a supermarket, few instructions, and several Universal Product Code scanners to record product selections.

Whatever the experiment, a researcher will usually assess the extent to which experimental facilities influence responses; she or he makes this assessment by raising questions during both the pretest and the experiment itself. The researcher will want to know the experimenters' impressions of how the subjects experienced the realism of the setting; the researcher will discard data from those subjects who found the facilities extremely artificial. A researcher may also ask subjects, during debriefing, to learn firsthand their impressions of experimental realism; the researcher uses this information to both edit and interpret data and to improve future experiments.

Beyond these points, the researcher should recognize the need for unchanging facilities for similar experiments over time. As long as facilities for such experiments remain static, their effect on research results should not operate differentially from one experiment to the next. Consequently, the researcher can compare results over time with more confidence.

FIELD EXPERIMENTS

Data collection operations for field experiments—as much as in laboratory experiments—cause researchers to be concerned about control in the areas of instructions, treatments, experimenters, and facilities. But in the field, distance greatly complicates communications and control in each area. Other differences also appear, as we shall see.

Instructions to Experimenters.   Instructions for field experiments apply not usually to subjects but to field experimenters, who work either for the researcher's firm or for some other. For example, suppose we also want to test the effect of three different point-of-purchase displays on sales of Flavor Fiesta coffee over a three-month period before we specify one display for national distribution. Suppose we select nine supermarkets in Chicago, match or block them into similar groups of three (based on their size), and, within each group, randomly assign the three displays. Now, if we live in

---

[4]Beyond our discussion of realism here, other laboratory characteristics may directly influence subject responses. See Rosenthal, *Experimenter Effects*, pp. 98–101 for details.

Chicago, such efforts would complicate our lives little more than those associated with our earlier laboratory experiment. However, if we live in Atlanta or Boston, we begin to see the sorts of communication and control problems our instructions must solve. That is, someone probably outside our firm must select representative stores, secure their cooperation, set up displays, stock them with coffee, monitor their performance, and remove displays upon study completion. Throughout these activities, this someone will need instructions on how to deal with store managers, shelf stockers, union regulations, and even actions of competitors (who may try to sabotage the test either by cutting prices or by buying so much Flavor Fiesta coffee from one display that they distort the test).

Experimental Treatments.   Treatments again must be available, as with laboratory experiments, in sufficient quantity, quality, and realism. Only the first two criteria much concern researchers in field experiments; that is, realism occurs nearly as a matter of course. The challenge is to get enough satisfactory treatments, an objective that often requires huge investment and expense. In particular, a field experiment for a new product (a **test market**) may demand expenditures for package design, advertising support, and distribution services beyond what may already be massive investments for new production equipment and high variable costs for pilot production. Such expenditures may well exceed a million dollars. Finally, treatments must appear untainted by competitive action. This may require secrecy, fast execution, and perhaps tacit understandings not to disrupt a competitor's field experiment.

Experimenters.   Experimenters in the field, like laboratory experimenters, may influence experimental results, but not so much through their characteristics as through their situational behaviors not covered by instructions. For example, experimenters for our point-of-purchase displays, if not instructed otherwise, might do any of the following:

1. select only stores that have cooperated enthusiastically in the past and are located near a major freeway;

2. place displays in a different area in each store; or

3. arrange stock differently from one display to another.

All operate to confound results of the experiment. That is, all of these uncontrolled behaviors may influence coffee sales far more than experimental treatments could do. Thus, the need to give field experimenters complete instructions, training, frequent communication opportunities, and close control becomes apparent. In this sense, field experimenters are much like personal interviewers in a survey design.

Facilities.   Facilities for a field experiment naturally appear real and subjects usually respond in a normal manner. As an aside, such natural circumstances and responses, while they lead to more generalizable results, usually consume more research resources than would a laboratory experiment with a similar purpose. That is, information that takes months to collect in a field experiment may take only days in the laboratory. In any event, a researcher selecting facilities for a field experiment chooses both geographic areas and specific entities or firms. In choosing geographic areas, the researcher considers two criteria: the area's representativeness and its potential for control. An area's representativeness depends on its consumers, distribution channels, advertising media, and competition. Consumers should reflect national markets in terms of selected socioeconomic and buyer behavior characteristics. Wholesalers and retailers in the area should exist in typical numbers and operate like their counterparts across the country. Advertising media available should also reflect the national market. So should the number, identity, marketing practices, and market shares of competitors.

The geographic area should be controllable with respect to measurement of dependent variables used to estimate the effect of experimental treatments. Beyond sales, the researcher will also measure retailer and consumer acceptance data. Further, the researcher must be able to control advertising exposure, keeping unwanted messages sponsored by his or her firm in other markets out and test messages in. The researcher must also be able to control distributors, keeping the product in only the test market area so that sales can be accurately measured. The researcher achieves this control in smaller, more isolated markets that yet possess a wealth of historical sales data. Box 6.2 identifies some popular test market areas, of two different types.

In choosing specific entities for field experiments, again the researcher considers each firm's representativeness and its potential for control. That is, selected wholesalers or retailers should represent the area, should freely cooperate, and have historical data available to help interpret results. Often the researcher will look for firms that promise both especially high cooperation and secrecy from competitors.

BOX 6.2

Popular Test Markets

Marketers frequently test new products or elements of their marketing plans in the following areas. *Standard markets* are those in which the company sells the product through its regular distribution channels and monitors the results, usually by hiring an auditing service. *Controlled markets* (also referred to as "mini markets" or "forced-distribution test markets") are those in which the entire test program is handled by an outside service. The service pays retailers for shelf space and therefore can guarantee distribution to stores representing a predetermined percentage of the market's all-commodity volume.

Standard Markets

Albany-Schenectady-Troy
Amarillo
Atlanta
Birmingham, Ala.
Boston
Buffalo
Charlotte
Chattanooga
Cincinnati
Cleveland
Columbus, Ohio
Dallas-Fort Worth
Denver
Des Moines
Fort Wayne
Green Bay, Wis.
Hartford
Houston
Indianapolis
Jacksonville
Kansas City
Lubbock, Texas
Memphis
Miami
Milwaukee
Minneapolis-St. Paul
Nashville
New Orleans
Oklahoma City
Omaha
Orlando-Daytona Beach
Peoria, Ill.
Phoenix
Pittsburgh
Portland, Ore.
Providence
Quad Cities: Rock Island &
    Moline,Ill.; Davenport &
    Bettendorf, Iowa (Davenport-
    Rock Island-Moline SMSA)
Rochester, N.Y.
Rockford, Ill.
Sacramento-Stockton

St. Louis
San Antonio
San Diego
Savannah
Seattle-Tacoma
South Bend
Spokane
Syracuse
Tampa-St. Petersburg
Tucson
Tulsa
Wichita

Controlled Markets
Burgoyne, Inc.

Albuquerque
Binghamton, N.Y.
Dayton
Fort Wayne
Fresno
Grand Rapids-Kalamazoo
Green Bay, Wis.
Lansing, Mich.
Lexington, Ky.
Lima, Ohio
Madison, Wis.
Modesto, Cal.
Omaha
Peoria, Ill.
Portland, Me.
Quad Cities: Rock Island & Moline,
    Ill; Davenport & Bettendorf,
    Iowa
Rockford, Ill.
South Bend
Spokane
Tucson

Marketest, division of Market
    Facts
*Binghamton, N.Y.
*Erie, Pa.
*Fort Wayne

*Fresno
*Little Rock
*Spokane
*Syracuse
*Wichita

Nielsen Data Markets
*Bangor, Me.
*Boise
*Charleston, S.C.
*Green Bay, Wis.
*Peoria, Ill.
*Portland, Me.
*Savannah, Ga.
*Tucson

Telesis Group
*Albany, Ga.
*Austin
*Boise, Idaho
*Burlington, Vt.
*Eugene, Ore.
*Santa Barbara, Cal.
*Sioux Falls, S.D.

ParaTest Marketing
Austin
Binghamton, N.Y.
Charlotte
Chattanooga
Erie, Pa.
Evansville, Ind.
Fresno
Lexington, Ky.
Lubbock, Texas
Madison, Wis.
Omaha
Peoria, Ill.
Spokane
Wilkes-Barre

*Indicates cities in which the company maintains per-
manent distribution, merchandising, and auditing
services.

Source: Sales and Marketing Management (New York:
Bill Publications) (March 17, 1980), p. 63. Used by
permission.

Compared to observation studies, simulations, and surveys, laboratory and field experiments proceed with more structure and control. Structure and control apply to experimental instructions, treatments, experimenters, and facilities. Greater structure and control allow researchers greater assurance when making causal inferences from experimental data. This is an experiment's primary advantage.

SUMMARY OF EXPERIMENTS AND CAUSAL INFERENCES

Such causal inferences deduce the likelihood of cause-and-effect relationships between experimental treatments and the dependent variable. For example, one causal inference might state that increasing the value of a cents off coupon for Flavor Fiesta coffee from 25 to 50 cents leads to a 30-percentage point increase in intention to buy. If this inference came from an observation study, simulation, or survey, we would feel less sure of its truth than we do when it comes from an experiment.

The primary disadvantage of experiments is their limitation to well-defined, narrow, and immediate marketing problems. Problems must reduce to a few underlying factors that can be controlled or manipulated as experimental treatments. Problems must extend over a relatively short time period to allow measurement of the dependent variable in an economical fashion.

We shall say more about the relative merits of different experimental designs, types of experimental errors, and experimental data analyses in Chapter 19.

Collecting Observation Data

Observation studies differ from surveys in that researcher and sample members share no spoken or written communication during data collection. The researcher collects data not by questions but by perceptions. For example, a researcher might measure the effectiveness of two point-of-purchase displays by observing the proportion of passing shoppers who buy the displayed product. Another might determine a radio station's audience share by observing radio dials in cars parked at a local shopping center. These examples complement one other type of observation study about which we already know a great deal—secondary data research: the researcher collects secondary data too, only through observation.

Observation studies, including secondary data research, can be classified along six basic dimensions that describe what is observed, how, when, and where. Figure 6.1 shows these basic dimensions.

What is observed ranges from physical to physiological behavior. Physiological behavior consists of involuntary processes internal to sample members. For example, a marketing researcher might observe a consumer's galvanic skin response (resistance to a small electrical current passing between electrodes along the skin). Marked lowerings of resistance imply arousal or alertness to stimuli; for example, responses to ver-

PHYSICAL AND PHYSIOLOGICAL BEHAVIORS

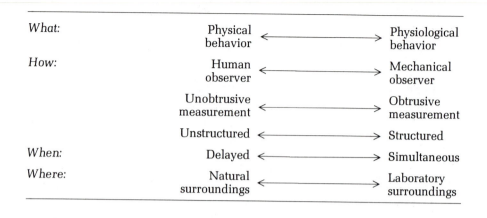

What:	Physical behavior	⟷	Physiological behavior
How:	Human observer	⟷	Mechanical observer
	Unobtrusive measurement	⟷	Obtrusive measurement
	Unstructured	⟷	Structured
When:	Delayed	⟷	Simultaneous
Where:	Natural surroundings	⟷	Laboratory surroundings

FIGURE 6.1
Six dimensions of observation studies

sions of an advertisement. Some physical behavior or voluntary aspect of external behavior may also be observed to corroborate findings—such as eye fixation frequency or eye fixation duration on parts of advertisements.[5]

Researchers usually observe larger physical behaviors than eye movements. That is, they usually observe consumer behavior acts connected with product search, purchase, use, and disposal. In industrial marketing research, they may observe employee behavior acts like the ones Box 6.3 describes for a study of several financial institutions. Beyond illustrating the less extensive structure and control inherent with observation studies, Box 6.3 also shows the compatibility of observation with the survey method.

Such larger units of physical behavior lie closer to the marketing problem than do those observed as physiological behavior: decision makers regard them as more actionable and researchers can observe them more easily. Observations of physical behavior normally require little costly, complicated equipment. Moreover, until equipment improves, observations of physiological behavior must be made with the subject's cooperation. Some subjects do not cooperate, of course, creating nonresponse problems that observations of physical behavior may not possess.

However, observed physical behavior may represent less valid behavior than physiological because acts are large, voluntary, and subject to outside influences. An observation study of consumers passing, and buying from, a point-of-purchase display illustrates this problem: the display may influence certain consumers very little yet they purchase

[5]Werner Kroeber-Riel, "Activation Research: Psychobiological Approaches in Consumer Research," *Journal of Consumer Research* 5 (March 1979): 240–50.

BOX 6.3

Financial Institution Study

Interviewer Role: You are acting the part of the wife of an automobile mechanic, recently moved into an apartment near the freeway. You need information on:

1. checking account costs and minimum balance levels,

2. conventional passbook savings rates,

3. CD rates and sizes (you have about $3,500 to invest),

4. a safety deposit box,

5. a loan for a used car "if you can find a job."

Check your watch as you enter the bank
_____ :_____ A.M.   Date ____/____/____
                  P.M.

1. About how many minutes did it take for you to find out who you should speak to? _____ minutes

2. What was this person's name?
   Mr./Ms. _____
   (circle)

3. How long did you have to wait to see this person? _____ minutes

4. Write the names of each other person to whom you were referred during your visit and how long you had to wait to see each one.

                              Waiting
                              Time (mins.)

   Mr./Ms. _____ _____

   Mr./Ms. _____ _____

   Mr./Ms. _____ _____

   Mr./Ms. _____ _____

5. For the person with whom you spent the *most time,* make the following evaluations:

	Very Poor		Average			Good	
Warm, friendly greeting	1	2	3	4	5	6	7
Businesslike	1	2	3	4	5	6	7
Personal appearance	1	2	3	4	5	6	7
Technical competence	1	2	3	4	5	6	7
Showed interest in you	1	2	3	4	5	6	7
Courteous	1	2	3	4	5	6	7

6. How many times did this person attempt to sell you on this bank? _____

7. Overall, describe in a few sentences how you were treated in this bank.

Time as you leave the bank _____ :_____ A.M.
                                              P.M.

because of habit, price, or even error. It may influence other consumers immensely yet they do not purchase because of limited budgets, sufficient inventory already owned, or insufficient space in the shopping cart. Thus, the physiological measure of consumer response would seem to be a truer or more valid measurement than the physical measurement.

HUMAN AND MECHANICAL OBSERVATION

How the study collects observations forms the second dimension classifying observation studies. Observations may be made unaided or with the help of some device. For example, either a researcher or a mechanical counter could record street traffic patterns at potential store locations. Either consumers at home with a purchase diary or personnel at a supermarket with an automated checkout scanner could record purchases.[6]

Beyond these examples, the number of mechanical and electrical devices aiding marketing research observation is quite large. We mention stopwatches, digital scales, Audimeters®, psychogalvanometers, eye movement monitors, and pupilometers; we will take up the last three briefly. A psychogalvanometer records skin resistance to the small electrical current mentioned earlier. An eye movement monitor tracks consumer eye fixations necessary to receive visual stimuli. Both produce measures indicating consumer interest and information processing relative to the stimulus. A pupilometer records the dilation or size of a consumer's pupils, which shows attention, mental effort, information-processing load, and anxiety.[7] All three devices find frequent use in advertising research.

Mechanical observers produce fewer random and systematic observation errors than do human observers. They require no training, work odd hours at low cost, and seldom quit. Moreover, they measure things humans physically or socially cannot: without the aid of a mechanical device, human observers find great difficulty measuring time, galvanic skin resistance, and channel selection of a consumer's bedroom television set. On the other hand, human observers add a richness to observation data that escapes machines. Human observers can subjectively interpret and react variably to subtleties in observed behavior. Such ability prescribes their use in unstructured observation studies, which will be discussed later.

OBTRUSIVE AND UNOBTRUSIVE MEASUREMENTS

How the study collects data can be described also in terms of obtrusive and unobtrusive measurement. **Obtrusive measurements** are those made of sample members who are told of the study's existence before being observed. **Unobtrusive measurements** come from sample members unaware of their participation. Sometimes they are told after being observed (for purposes of follow-up research) and sometimes they are never told.

---

[6]For a practitioner's view of which is better see "New 'BehaviorScan' System ties Grocery Sales to TV Ads," *Marketing News* (September 21, 1979), p. 7.

[7]Kroeber-Riel, "Activation Research," p. 243.

The major strength of unobtrusive measurement is that it produces no guinea pig effect on the part of sample members—they react naturally. Sample members also tend to better represent the population under study because none refuse to participate. However, sample members tend to be less like others observed at different study times and locations because similar people tend to cluster together. Therefore, unobtrusive measurement studies should be conducted at several locations and times to secure a representative sample.

Unobtrusive measurements may take longer to collect data. With regard to the point-of-purchase display discussed earlier, suppose further that we desire sample members of only certain ages, incomes, and occupations. Thus, perhaps only 1 person in 20 who pass the display may actually qualify as a sample member. Moreover, consider that not all shoppers are going to pass the display—perhaps only 1 in 3 will actually go down our aisle.

Finally, how the study collects data can be described according to measurement structure. Structured observation studies are those that measure very specific behaviors with a well-defined procedure. Observers know exactly what to look for, perhaps even that they are to look in a prescribed sequence. Baseball umpires, real estate appraisers, and tax assessors make fairly structured observations, as does the interviewer in Box 6.3.

STRUCTURED AND UNSTRUCTURED MEASUREMENTS

Unstructured observation studies are those that measure behaviors specified in a loosely defined manner. Observers have an idea about what they should record, a blank sheet as a data collection form, and little else. An engaged couple searching for their first apartment makes fairly unstructured observations.

Like extremes in other dimensions, both sorts of measurement structure have their place in marketing research. Unstructured studies work best in exploratory marketing research, where the researcher is trying to define the problem. Structured studies work best in descriptive and causal research, where the researcher seeks answers to specific questions.

Another dimension classifying observation studies consists of the time interval between behavior and observation. Observation can occur simultaneously (as in the use of a pupilometer) or years later (as in secondary data research). Between the two extremes lie delayed observations not of behavior but of **behavioral artifacts** or objects that imply the behavior took place. For examples, finding an empty liquor bottle implies its consumption in the household whose trash container holds it. Noting that one retail store when compared to a competitor rents 1.7 times more space and averages 2.1 times as many cars parked in its lot allows an estimate of relative sales. Tallying addresses on checks received in payment for merchandise provides a retail manager with a measure of the store's trade area.

DELAYED AND SIMULTANEOUS OBSERVATION

In general, simultaneous observation yields richer data. Subtleties that disappear over time have a chance of survival if researchers observe them as they happen. Simultaneous observation also leads to more confidence in the data: what was true five years ago may not be so today.

However, simultaneous observation will interfere with sensitive behavior if sample members know they are being observed (and, ethically, sample members must know). Delayed observation cancels this weakness of sensitive behavior being distorted; one observes instead only the aftermath. Delayed observation also collects more data faster: a month's worth of simultaneous observation can be accomplished in less than a day by reading an existing research report.

NATURAL AND LABORATORY SURROUNDINGS

Where observation occurs is the last dimension classifying observation studies. Just as with experiments, observation studies may occur in artificial, secluded research rooms or in real world, natural surroundings. Thus, exactly the same comments made about laboratory and field experiments apply to observation studies conducted in laboratory and natural surroundings. To summarize, natural compared to laboratory surroundings permit less structure and control but produce data more generalizable to the real world.

SUMMARY OF OBSERVATION STUDIES

With knowledge of the different types of observation studies, we now summarize the technique's strengths and weaknesses. Observation studies work well in defining the problem because experiments, simulations, and surveys require far more knowledge and structure. Observation studies produce data free from question wording and consumer memory deficiencies. In addition, if studies use unobtrusive measurement in natural surroundings, they produce data free from consumer cooperation and guinea pig problems.

Sometimes observation studies are the only primary data collection method possible for certain populations:

> Most small children cannot be questioned very successfully. Even among studies of human group processes [interactions between people and the results of such interactions], it is extremely difficult to gather useful information by questioning respondents. Their involvement in a group process is usually such that they are unable to report accurately what happened.[8]

To populations of most small children and human group processes, we add competitors.

---

[8]C. William Emory, *Business Research Methods* (Homewood, Ill.: Richard D. Irwin, 1976), p. 288.

Observation's primary weakness is its inability to uncover *why* the observed behavior took place. The observer knows only what happened under observed conditions and must use questions to discover what lies behind the behavior. More specifically, observation studies cannot measure psychological characteristics—such as consumer knowledge, beliefs, attitudes, and satisfaction. Observation studies apply only to behaviors that have occurred in the past or at the time of observation. Observation studies cannot measure intentions of future behavior. Nor can they economically measure sporadic, diverse, and lengthy behaviors: using observation studies to find out how often middle-class families in Florida charter fishing boats makes poor use of the technique.

These strengths and weaknesses imply that observation is best used with, rather than instead of, other primary data collection techniques. Indeed, because its strengths and weaknesses complement those possessed by the other methods, observation usually precedes the design and execution of experiments, simulations, and surveys. For any primary data study to rely only on observation would be rare.

Collecting Simulation Data

As an infrequent alternative to experiments and observation studies, simulations can be used to produce primary data. A **simulation,** in a simplified, organized, and meaningful fashion, represents a marketing problem.[9] It represents the problem by isolating and interrelating a few concepts to aid the decision maker in understanding the process and the consequences. Some concepts are designated as inputs to the simulation and some as outputs. When researchers supply a range of values for input concepts, the simulation produces a range of output values. These become primary data for analysis of the problem.

As a simple example, consider that a formula for price elasticity of demand simulates a marketing problem. It uses only one input concept, price changes, to forecast one other, unit sales changes, for a specified price elasticity coefficient. Different price changes and different price elasticities lead to different estimates of unit sales. For a more complex example, let us look at a new product simulation (NEWPROD); the simulation predicts first year market shares for recently purchased consumer goods.[10] It provides weekly share estimates based on input values for company advertising, sampling, and couponing expenditures, as well as for consumer advertising awareness, trial purchase, and repeat purchase

---

[9]Gerald Zaltman, "The Structure and Purpose of Marketing Models," in *Behavioral Models for Market Analysis: Foundations for Marketing Action,* ed. Francesco M. Nicosia and Yoram Wind (Hinsdale, Ill.: The Dryden Press, 1977), pp. 29–31.

[10]Gert Assmus, "NEWPROD: The Design and Implementation of a New Product Model," *Journal of Marketing* 39 (January 1975): 16–23.

rates. The simulation applies to hypothetical values of these variables as supplied by researchers and managers before test marketing. It applies also to actual values obtained from either test markets or national market results.

Simulations represent all sorts of marketing problems. They help determine prices, allocate advertising budgets, determine salesforce size, set inventory levels, and explain buyer behavior. They range from simple, judgmental, qualitative statements to complex, data-based, computer programs. All propose to aid decision makers, not to replace them.[11]

THREE TYPES OF SIMULATIONS   Despite this diversity, all marketing simulations reduce to three types: descriptive, predictive, and prescriptive. **Descriptive simulations** require the researcher to identify relevant concepts and, thus, clarify marketing problems. Descriptive simulations help decision makers make better decisions because they:

1. transform data into more meaningful forms;

2. indicate areas for search and experimentation;

3. generate hypotheses for testing;

4. provide a framework for measurement;

5. aid in systematic thinking about the problem; and

6. provide bases of discussion that will lead to common understanding of the problem.[12]

Predictive simulations like NEWPROD go beyond descriptive simulations by forecasting the future. They require researchers not only to identify relevant concepts but to specify concept relationships—with each other and with predicted concepts. In addition to forecasting, predictive simulations also validate or verify the choice of concepts in descriptive simulations. Predictive simulations also allow the researchers to determine which concepts affect predicted concepts more than others.[13] This last function is often termed a sensitivity analysis.

Prescriptive simulations are more specific about the future; they tell decision makers what action to take. Of course decision makers may not follow this advice but a prescriptive simulation still provides an exact, often optimized value for decision action. Other prescribed actions often

---

[11]David B. Montgomery and Charles B. Weinberg, "Modeling Marketing Phenomena: A Managerial Perspective," *Journal of Contemporary Business* (Autumn 1973), p. 21.

[12]Zaltman, "Structure and Purpose," p. 30.

[13]Ibid.

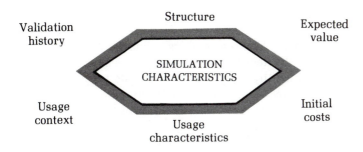

FIGURE 6.2
Six types of simulation characteristics, which can be the basis for evaluation

follow from other levels of input concepts (or from other simulations) to provide the decision maker with perspective. Prescriptive simulations may or may not embody aspects of descriptive and predictive simulations. For example, a prescriptive simulation may tell decision makers exactly what to do but only after considering one concept out of the seven available. Such a simulation may be valid but often lacks credibility with decision makers, who may not use it.[14] Our next section discusses criteria that decision makers use to evaluate these three types of simulations.

Larréché and Montgomery provide a most complete evaluation framework for simulations.[15] They see six types of simulation characteristics, as shown in Figure 6.2, which they use as evaluation criteria.

**EVALUATING
A SIMULATION**

On Structure.   Decision makers may judge a simulation's structure in five areas: adaptability, completeness, ease of testing, ease of understanding, and robustness. Adaptability describes the ease of changing the simulation to adapt to new conditions. Completeness refers to the simulation's descriptive scope, its inclusion of all important and relevant concepts underlying the problem. Ease of testing refers to the facility with which decision makers can assess the simulation's applicability to the problem. Ease of understanding needs no explanation. Robustness is the simula-

---

[14]A. S. C. Ehrenberg and G. J. Goodhardt, "Decision Models and Descriptive Models in Marketing," Working Paper, Marketing Science Institute, 1976, p. 2.

[15]Jean-Claude Larréché and David B. Montgomery, "A Framework for the Comparison of Marketing Models: A Delphi Study," *Journal of Marketing Research* 14 (November 1977): 489–91.

tion's ability to produce plausible results from input data values that lie beyond a certain range.

On Expected Value.   Decision makers primarily judge the simulation's expected value by the decision-making resources it saves and the benefits it produces. Additionally, they may estimate its value for training new decision makers—mistakes made while training on a simulation are certainly preferable to those made while on the job.

On Initial Costs.   Decision makers evaluate initial or startup costs incurred in several areas. If the simulation originates outside the organization, purchase or lease costs form a large portion of initial costs. If the simulation originates inside the organization, development costs form a similar or even larger portion. For sophisticated, computer-based simulations, purchase or development costs can easily exceed several hundred thousand dollars. Regardless of origin of the simulation, initial costs also are generated by the costs of adaptation, including those to train the decision maker and others to use the simulation. Finally, costs to gather and input initial data also contribute to initial costs, often substantially.

On Usage Characteristics.   Decision makers evaluate the simulation's usage characteristics in these areas: running costs, ease of communication, ease of control, input volume, and response time. Running costs are the simulation's operating costs for one complete use. Very expensive simulations may cost more than $1000 per use. Ease of communication refers to the facility with which decision makers can input data and interpret output. Ease of control refers to the facility with which decision makers can identify changes in particular input data that produce desired changes in output. Input volume describes the quantity of data the simulation requires to complete one use. Response time describes how long the decision maker must wait for output after supplying input data.

On Usage Context.   Decision makers also evaluate the simulation's usage context—the problem environment to which the simulation applies. Areas of usage context include: problem area, importance of the problem, and frequency of use. Problem area includes the type of decision the simulation aids in making and the problem's boundaries. To be evaluated favorably, the simulation's problem boundaries should coincide with those that limit the decision maker, as assigned by the organization. Decision makers also evaluate usage context according to the significance of the problem and its frequency of occurrence.

On Validation History.   Finally, decision makers evaluate a simulation's validation history according to its concepts, structure, and record of successful use. Other decision makers should have evaluated the simulation positively and benefited from it.

Simulations possess several advantages over other primary data collection methods: (1) Simulations answer a large number of "what if" questions sooner. That is, they provide expected results of potential marketing actions more quickly and cheaply than experiments, observation studies, and surveys. (2) Simulations operate in the relatively secure environments of the firm.[16] No consumer, retailer, wholesaler, or competitor need be aware of pending, simulated marketing actions. (3) Simulations encourage creative decisions by allowing "the emergence of politically unmentionable solutions."[17] Blaming the simulation for such "mistakes" is usually easier than identifying them as your own.

SIMULATION SUMMARY

All this occurs along with a few disadvantages. Prime among them is initial cost. Simulations usually cost much more to construct and adapt than do other primary data collection methods. Thus, unless the need for a simulation is continuing, experiments, observation studies, and surveys will require fewer resources. Further, researchers need more detailed, structured knowledge of the marketing problem before constructing a simulation. Finally, decision makers may avoid using a simulation because they do not understand it or because they feel threatened by it.

A Comparison of Primary Data Collection Methods

In the past two chapters, we have learned about and evaluated four primary data collection methods separately. Illustrative as this has been, it is not the way a researcher views surveys, experiments, observation studies, and simulations. Rather, a researcher views them simultaneously—as alternative ways to solve a defined marketing problem using data sources that have already been specified. He or she sees them in the context of anticipated research decisions in sampling, data collection operations, and data analysis. In other words, a researcher views primary data collection methods as competing decision choices in the third step of an integrated marketing research process.

We will match the researcher's vision in this section by comparing the four methods relative to marketing problems, data sources, and anticipated research decisions. Let us recognize at the outset that different marketing problems, different data sources, and different anticipated research

---

[16]Thomas C. Kinnear and James R. Taylor, *Marketing Research: An Applied Approach* (New York: McGraw-Hill, 1979), p. 126.

[17]Montgomery and Weinberg, "Modeling Marketing Phenomena," p. 21.

decisions usually favor different methods. Let us recognize further that a single problem, single data source, and single anticipated research decision usually allow more than one method.

MARKETING PROBLEMS

Assume a researcher faces an important problem requiring marketing research. The problem compares to similar problems that occur at an estimated frequency. It compares to similar problems in its complexity and in how well it is understood. These three problem considerations—similar problem frequency, problem complexity, and degree of understanding—help the researcher to select a primary data collection method.

If any similar problems occurred in the past, the researcher often will select the same data collection method used then. Such practice makes it easier to interpret results and provides more confidence in recommendations. If many similar problems occurred in the past or likely will occur in the future, the researcher will favor simulation. Time and expense involved to construct a simulation will be offset by the simulation's frequent use. If no similar problems ever occurred, the researcher will favor experiments, observation studies, and surveys.

For complex problems, the researcher usually decides on a survey. We define a complex problem as one having a large number of potential causes, solutions, environmental limitations, and environmental implications. Less complex problems allow simulations. Simple problems allow observation studies and experiments. These last two primary data collection methods simply cannot tolerate large numbers of causes, solutions, limitations, and implications as well as surveys can.

Simulations require well-understood problems. Experiments and surveys require less understanding, and observation studies require the least. We should see why: To construct a simulation, the researcher must specify both key variables in the problem and their relationships. To construct either an experiment or a survey requires only the specification of the variables. To construct an observation study requires neither.

We can see a summary of problem considerations in the selection of primary data collection methods in Table 6.1.

TABLE 6.1
Problem Considerations and Primary Data Collection Methods

	Similar Problem Frequency	Problem Complexity	Problem Understanding
Use experiments	low	low	moderate, high
Use observation studies	low	low	low
Use simulations	high	low, moderate	high
Use surveys	low, moderate	low, moderate, high	moderate, high

TABLE 6.2
Data Source Considerations and Primary Data Collection Methods

	Expected Diversity	*Expected Cooperation*
Use experiments	low	high
Use observation studies	low, moderate	low, moderate
Use simulations	low, moderate	low
Use surveys	low, moderate, high	high

Two data source considerations influence the selection of primary data collection methods: expected diversity and expected cooperation. Expected diversity describes the heterogeneity between data sources on factors affecting their reaction to research variables. The researcher may estimate that data sources are very alike or very diverse or anything in between. Expected cooperation describes the willingness of data sources to comply with research instructions. Some data sources cooperate more completely than others, depending on the instructions.   **DATA SOURCES**

Experiments work best when data source diversity is low. Only when this is the case can the researcher feel confident that the experiment's typically small sample is representative. Observation studies and simulations generally work well with data sources of low to moderate diversity. Surveys apply to any degree of data source diversity.

Both experiments and surveys work best when data sources are expected to exhibit high cooperation. Observation studies do not require as much cooperation, especially unobtrusive observation studies, which do not require any. Simulations, after their construction, also require no cooperation.

We summarize data source considerations and the selection of primary data collection methods in Table 6.2.

Research decisions yet to be made also influence the selection of primary data collection methods. Such anticipated research decision considerations include sampling, data collection operations, and data analysis.   **ANTICIPATED RESEARCH DECISIONS**

Sampling Considerations.   Two sampling considerations influence the choice of primary data collection methods: availability of a sampling frame and expected sample size. A sampling frame lists elements of the population under study. Researchers use a sampling frame as the source from which they select population elements for measurement. The number of elements that likely will supply measurements is the expected sample size.

Experiments and surveys generally require a sampling frame, observation studies sometimes do, and simulations seldom do. To understand

TABLE 6.3
Sampling Considerations and Primary Data Collection Methods

	Sampling Frame	Sample Size
Use experiments	available	small
Use observation studies	not available	small
Use simulations	not available	small
Use surveys	available	small to large

why, consider that experiments and surveys require the researcher to identify individual data sources before the act of measurement. Once identified, the researcher seeks each individual's consent before proceeding. Such practice occurs much less often in observation studies—as unobtrusive observation and observation of behavioral artifacts exemplify. It never occurs in simulations, except in their construction.

Experiments, observation studies, and simulations generally use small samples. Experiments and simulations do so because they emphasize intensive learning about variables under investigation, while observation studies do so because they usually cost much per measurement. Surveys use samples of any size.

We summarize sampling considerations on the selection of primary data collection methods in Table 6.3.

Data Collection Operations Consideration. Only one consideration about data collection operations influences selection of primary data collection methods: data collection control. The term, we said, refers to a research method's potential for gathering information according to procedures established by the researcher. Some primary data collection methods offer more data collection control than others.

Simulations offer the highest degree. Aside from time, budget, and technology influences, the researcher has complete control. Experiments offer the next most control; however, the researcher must now control instructions, treatments, experimenters, and facilities. Observation studies offer less, especially unobtrusive observation; and surveys offer the least.

Table 6.4 summarizes data collection control and the selection of primary data collection methods.

Data Analysis Considerations. Two data analysis considerations influence selection of primary data collection methods: analysis objectives and analysis structure. Analysis objectives parallel the research design's focus. We said in Chapter 2 that a design could have an exploratory, descriptive, or causal focus—such terms also describe the three kinds of analysis

TABLE 6.4
Desired Data Collection Control and Primary Data Collection Methods

	Desired Data Collection Control
Use experiments	moderate
Use observation studies	low, moderate
Use simulations	high
Use surveys	low

objectives. That is, some analyses intend to explore data, others to describe data sources, and still others to infer causation.

Analysis structure describes the rigidity of analytical procedures. Some primary data collection methods use rather rigid analytical procedures. Analysis of experimental data, for example, proceeds in almost a lockstep fashion. Other methods use more flexible procedures; analysis of observation data, for example, often proceeds somewhat creatively.

We summarize data analysis considerations in selecting primary data collection methods in Table 6.5.

At the start of this comparison, there was a statement that experiments, observation studies, simulations, and surveys compete as primary data collection methods. At the finish, we concur but add that the four methods also complement each other. Each has its own strengths and weaknesses depending on the problem, data sources, and anticipated research decisions. Each finds its own best application.

On the subject of applications, Table 6.6 summarizes some research on the usage of primary data collection methods. Although observation studies to collect primary data were not researched, observation studies to collect secondary data were reported as used by nearly 90 percent of the firms. The table supports our own conclusions, stated here as promised at the chapter opening: the most versatile and widely used primary data collection method is surveys.

SUMMARY OF PRIMARY DATA COLLECTION METHODS

TABLE 6.5
Data Analysis Considerations and Primary Data Collection Methods

	Analysis Objectives	*Analysis Structure*
Use experiments	infer causality	high
Use observation studies	explore and describe	low, moderate, high
Use simulations	explore and describe	high
Use surveys	explore and describe	moderate, high

TABLE 6.6
Use of Primary Data Collection Methods in 269 U.S. Firms

Method	Firms Using (%)
Personal Interviews	76
Telephone Surveys	74
Mail Surveys	70
Focus Group Interviews	47
Informal Experimental Designs	35
Test Markets	35
Consumer Panels	31
Store Audits	28
Simulations	21
Formal Experimental Designs	16

Source: Barnett A. Greenberg, Jac L. Goldstucker, and Danny N. Bellenger, "What Techniques Are Used by Marketing Researchers in Business?" *Journal of Marketing* 41 (April 1977): 64–65.

Chapter Summary

Each major section in this chapter contains a summary. We should reread them. Beyond their discussion, there is only one more point: many concepts discussed separately with a primary data collection method apply quite well to one or several other methods. For example, survey nonresponse errors in the form of refusals affect both experiments and observation studies; response errors of all forms affect experiments. Observation concepts of structure, time interval between behavior and measurement, and measurement setting all equally apply to surveys. And, like marketing simulations, all experiments are by nature descriptive, predictive, or prescriptive. We should look for these broadened applications as we review both Chapter 6 and Chapter 5.

Chapter Review

KEY TERMS

Experiment

Experimental treatment

Observation study

Unobtrusive measurement

Physiological behavior

Unstructured measurement

Marketing simulation

DISCUSSION QUESTIONS

1. How do a researcher's concerns vary depending on whether he executes a laboratory or a field experiment?

2. In selecting cities for a test market, what should a researcher look for?

3. A veteran of numerous test markets remarks that "you always should use at least two cities per experimental treatment." Why?

4. What ethical issues accompany unobtrusive measurement by a researcher in each situation:

   a) counting traffic passing by a billboard?

   b) counting empty soft drink bottles in trash collected from a neighborhood?

   c) counting empty gin bottles in trash collected from a neighborhood?

   d) checking a retail competitor's operation by posing as a customer?

5. Why can't observation measure "psychological characteristics like consumer knowledge, beliefs, attitudes, and satisfaction?"

6. Compare and contrast data collection operations using humans as observers with those that use machines.

7. "Observation studies generally use small samples because they usually cost much per measurement." On what assumption is this statement based?

8. Is Larréché and Montgomery's framework in Figure 6.2 a descriptive, predictive, or prescriptive simulation or model? Explain your answer.

9. The concerns of a researcher in collecting simulation data are much like those in collecting secondary data. Discuss.

10. Which primary data collection method is best? Discuss.

11. What research decisions usually made after deciding on a primary data collection method partly influence this decision? Discuss the nature of their influence.

12. Which primary data collection methods require high cooperation from potential respondents? What can researchers do to increase cooperation?

Additional Readings

Kotler, Phillip. *Marketing Decision Making: A Model Building Approach.* New York: Holt, Rinehart and Winston, 1971.

> *This book is the standard treatment on prescriptive marketing simulations—applied, mathematical, and readable.*

Neter, John, and Wasserman, William. *Applied Linear Statistical Models.* Homewood, Ill.: Richard D. Irwin, 1974.

> *Chapters 13 through 24 discuss details of experimental design and analysis. The book lucidly presents almost everything you need to know about these topics.*

Webb, Eugene J., Campbell, Donald T.; Schwartz, Richard D.; and Sechrest, Lee. *Unobtrusive Measures: Nonreactive Research in the Social Sciences.* Chicago: Rand McNally, 1966.

> *While containing few marketing examples, this classic book quite completely describes unobtrusive observation. The book merits—at the least—a scanning before you either dismiss the technique or use it.*

Cases for Part II

1. Daisy Chain Discount Stores*

"Let's see what Jerry has come up with," thought Virginia Atkins. She looked at two tables packed with numbers. "What I need are the top four or so cities in terms of their discount store potential." Eventually, of course, she would have to reduce this list to two cities in which to locate two new Daisy Chain discount stores. Each would begin operation about 18 months from now, in the summer of 1982. Each would contain about 50,000 square feet of selling space, for products ranging from automotive accessories to women's wear.

For now, Virginia noted that Jerry Osmond in Marketing Research had done a thorough job in collecting data on the ten cities of interest. Table C1.1 presented trends in population and in effective buying income—based on Census and *Sales and Marketing Management* data. Effective buying income represented disposable personal income and appeared as median values per household. Table C1.2 contained total retail and general merchandise sales trends from the same two sources.

A quick telephone call to Jerry confirmed Virginia's suspicion that general merchandise stores included, in addition to discount stores,

TABLE C1.1
Population and Median Effective Buying Income (EBI) per Household

	POPULATION (000)				EBI/HOUSEHOLD ($000)		
SMSA	1972	1977	1977*	1979*	1974*	1977*	1979*
Austin, TX	349	474	484	506	11.0	14.6	18.2
Baton Rouge, LA	386	435	437	457	12.0	16.1	19.7
Corpus Christi, TX	298	303	305	304	10.5	13.7	17.1
El Paso, TX	374	435	442	453	10.4	13.9	16.5
Killeen-Temple, TX	NA	209	221	210	9.1	11.9	14.3
Little Rock-North Little Rock, AR	336	369	380	388	11.1	15.2	17.9
Lubbock, TX	NA	200	209	205	10.7	14.4	18.5
Oklahoma City, OK	736	769	777	809	11.4	14.5	17.9
Shreveport, LA	340	357	359	364	10.0	13.2	16.1
Tulsa, OK	560	610	607	642	11.3	14.1	17.2

Sources: Data in columns headed with an * come from *Sales and Marketing Management,* Survey of Buying Power issues: July 21, 1975; July 24, 1978; and July 28, 1980; reprinted by permission. Other data come from the *Statistical Abstract of the United States,* 1974 and 1979 editions.

*Tyler Artz and Linda Novotny, graduate research assistants at the University of Minnesota, helped write this case.

TABLE C1.2
Retail Sales and Sales of General Merchandise

SMSA	RETAIL SALES $(000,000)				SALES OF GENERAL MERCHANDISE ($000,000)		
	1972	1977	1977*	1979*	1974*	1977*	1979*
Austin, TX	840	1703	1734	2299	112	160	300
Baton Rouge, LA	874	1595	1357	1987	190	232	402
Corpus Christi, TX	602	1044	1188	1385	97	131	181
El Paso, TX	785	1350	1496	1744	217	277	281
Killeen-Temple, TX	NA	502	595	665	56	76	75
Little Rock-North Little Rock, AR	863	1412	1513	1722	197	235	290
Lubbock, TX	474	873	810	1134	107	132	137
Oklahoma City, OK	1806	3030	3139	3674	336	413	474
Shreveport, LA	730	1227	1203	1469	147	186	231
Tulsa, OK	1283	2288	2316	2802	183	229	368

Sources: Data in columns headed with an * come from *Sales and Marketing Management,* Survey of Buying Power issues: July 21, 1975; July 24, 1978; and July 28, 1980; reprinted by permission. Other data come from the *Census of Retail Trade,* volumes for 1972 and 1977.

department and other stores. Jerry said he knew of no source that published sales data for only discount stores. Jerry also gave her his rough estimate of the 1972 population for the Killeen-Temple and the Lubbock, Texas, markets as 175,000 and 180,000, respectively. His best estimate for Killeen-Temple's 1972 retail sales was "in the neighborhood of $325 million."

Armed with the data, Virginia knew her decision would look convincing to her boss. However, it also looked to be more complex than she had first thought. "Let's see, I need at least $6 million in sales to break even, and I want to locate in fast growing markets. . . . What else?" She took out her calculator.

2. Polk County Daycare Centers*

Late one January afternoon, Chris Watkins sat in his office in downtown Des Moines. Slowly he turned over in his mind the forces that affected demand for child daycare centers in Polk County, Iowa. On the one hand, there are more young mothers working than ever. At least 40 percent of all young mothers in Des Moines and the surrounding Polk

*Tyler Artz and Linda Novotny, graduate research assistants at the University of Minnesota, helped write this case.

County area work at either part-time or full-time jobs. Chris thought too, about the increases in the divorce rate and in inflationary pressures. The percentage of working mothers could easily rise to 50 percent. On the other hand, there is a growing population of singles, and trends toward higher ages at first marriage and reduced fertility rates. Perhaps the two hands balanced; Chris did not know.

Such reflection on the changing nature of the market was no idle exercise. As Executive Director of the Polk County Daycare Center Directors Association, Chris was charged with forecasting demand from now (1980) through the end of the century. He decided that he would state demand as the number of preschoolers in Polk County, ages 2 to 5. However, several of Chris's members were interested in expanding their market to include toddlers, ages 1½ to 2. In fact, one was even considering providing infant daycare for children age 6 months to 1½. Chris decided that all members might be interested in the numbers of these age groups too. As long as he was at it, he might as well forecast everything.

3. Ghost Manor*

As he set his morning coffee down, Phil Herschel noticed something new on his desk. It was a memo from Duke Willard, his boss, evidently placed there after Phil had gone home yesterday. Phil read with some concern that Mr. Willard had selected KDWB-AM as cosponsor of this year's Ghost Manor. KDWB-AM's selection meant that Ghost Manor radio advertising would continue to focus on twelve- to seventeen-year-olds rather than on Phil's choice, eighteen- to twenty-four-year-olds. Mr. Willard's memo concluded:

> Without any numbers to the contrary, it's probably best to stay with what we've used in the past. Don't you agree?

At least, Phil thought, I can agree with half of his conclusion: we don't have *any* numbers to base *any* promotion decision on. Perhaps if I think about it, we might be able to do something about this for next year.

BACKGROUND   Phil had received a BS in business administration in June of 1980. After graduation, he had accepted a position with the Minneapolis Northstar Chapter of the Multiple Sclerosis Society as special projects coordinator. Since starting three months ago, Phil had worked on planning, organizing, and coordinating several local fundraising projects. Proceeds from

*Bruce Pastorius, undergraduate student at the University of Minnesota, helped write this case.

all projects went toward supporting the care of multiple sclerosis (MS) victims and toward finding the cause and cure of MS.

The Minneapolis Northstar Chapter of the Multiple Sclerosis Society was founded in 1953 and currently supports the care of over 2,000 patients. Duke Willard is its executive director and Phil's immediate supervisor.

GHOST MANOR

Ghost Manor is a "haunted house," an annual fundraising project operated by the Northstar Chapter in October. While it initially had been an outstanding success, the past two years found revenues declining nearly forty percent and attendance falling by about thirty-five percent.

Ghost Manor can best be described as a specialized thematic theatrical production. Like any theatrical production, its success depended on a few key factors: location, stage and sets, actors and direction, and promotion. However, there is a major difference—the audience actually moves about on the Ghost Manor stage and becomes part of the act. That is, while the audience moves from stage to stage, set to set, volunteer Ghost Manor "employees" startle them, causing much fear and screaming. Consequently, audience control becomes important to keep people moving and to protect the actors and sets.

For his first year of heading up the Ghost Manor project, Phil decided that the haunted house should continue to operate in its present location, an old Victorian house located at the intersection of a major artery leading downtown and a well-traveled crosstown parkway. Ample parking was nearby and a large public park sat across the street. Phil thought the location to be at least equal to most competing haunted houses and quite superior to one eight blocks away.

To build the stage and sets, local businesses and theater groups had donated materials, labor, and expertise. Volunteers had cleaned and gutted the house and then installed partitions and stairways to form a "free-flow" pattern that allowed large numbers of customers to walk through continuously. Phil felt the stage and sets bettered those found in competing haunted houses.

Phil's primary responsibility during the four-week operation of Ghost Manor would be to coordinate and control volunteer help. About thirty teenagers would be available to staff about fifteen jobs required each night.

Despite the importance of location, stage and sets, and actors and direction, Phil felt the key to the project's success was promotion. People simply will not attend an event if they do not know about it. Moreover, any promotional message must be both informative and motivational—make the target segment aware and interested in attending. Timing of the promotion would be important, too, he felt. Messages should "heavy up" during the opening week of Ghost Manor and again near Halloween to stimulate attendance. Phil also felt it important to use a variety of media, including radio, TV, newspapers, posters, and direct mail to get broad market coverage and repetition. Thus, promotion plans had occupied a lot of Phil's time over the past two weeks.

PROMOTION PLANS Some of Phil's time had been spent in considering which radio station should be cosponsor of the project. This station would supply up to two 30-second spots per hour at the height of the promotion in free public service announcements (PSAs). This station would also supply facilities, materials, and expertise in making sound tapes for use in Ghost Manor. In return, the station's call letters, logo, and cosponsor relationship would appear in almost all promotions.

In the past several years, KDWB-AM had cosponsored Ghost Manor. KDWB-AM's programming was essentially a top-40 format aimed at twelve- to seventeen-year-olds in the Minneapolis–St. Paul market. Until now, Phil had only talked briefly to KDWB-AM's personnel and had learned of their continued interest and support. However, over the summer, he had worked closely with KQRS-AM & FM personnel on other Northstar Chapter PSAs and, in the process, had discussed their potential cosponsorship. Programming for KQRS-AM & FM was aimed at eighteen- to twenty-four-year-olds in the Minneapolis–St. Paul market. Many twelve- to seventeen-year-olds listened also and Phil wondered if KQRS-AM & FM might not be a better choice. Some Arbitron listenership data from last summer gave him further food for thought (see Table C3.1).

Beyond the cosponsor PSAs, Phil planned to run a lesser number of a slightly different PSAs at other radio stations whose programming was different from that of the cosponsor's, and thus, essentially, noncompeting. Three of the five local television stations also would run a commer-

TABLE C3.1
Average Quarter-Hour and Cume Listening Estimates-ADI*

Station	AVERAGE PERSONS (00)		CUME PERSONS (00)	
	12–17	18–24	12–17	18–24
KDWB-AM	92	40	1,631	1,274
KQRS-AM	8	20	233	477
KQRS-FM	45	100	777	1,268

*ADI stands for Area of Dominant Influence, a geographic area within which Minneapolis–St. Paul television stations receive a majority of viewing.

Average persons refers to the estimated number of persons who listened to a station at least 5 minutes during the quarter hour.

Cume persons refers to the estimated number of *different persons* who listened at least 5 minutes during the quarter hour.

Source: Adapted from "Audience Estimates in the Arbitron Market of Minneapolis–St. Paul," *Arbitron Radio,* April/May 1979, p. 121. Used by permission.

cial supplied by the National MS Society. In addition, Phil planned to
send weekly press releases to community, junior high school, senior high
school, college, and religious publications before and during the event.
He also planned to coupon in several local "entertainment guide" type
newspapers and in most of the market area's 7-11 stores and
McDonald's restaurants, and in the other haunted house operations.

The same 25 cents off coupon (from the normal admission price of
$1.75) would also be distributed by his volunteer work force to friends
and relatives. Volunteers would also place posters describing Ghost
Manor in schools, playgrounds, laundromats, supermarkets, and meeting
places. Further, Phil planned to advertise by direct mail to numerous
church, school, Cub Scout, Boy Scout, Girl Scout, Camp Fire Girl, and
YMCA groups in the market area. The mailer would include a different
coupon, offering 50 cents off to each customer arriving in a group of 15
or more. Such groups in the past had accounted for about twenty-five
percent of total attendance.

All in all, the planned promotion had been warmly received by
everyone responsible. Phil felt that it was much more extensive and
aggressive than that used in the past—this year's revenues and attendance would not decline.

CONSUMERS

Mr. Willard knew little about consumers and Phil knew even less. Two
weeks ago as Phil began work on Ghost Manor, Mr. Willard had
summed up his impressions in a conversation:

> I've been involved in this event for three years now and it seems to
> me that most of our customers are twelve- to seventeen-year-olds.
> These kids come, get scared half out of their wits, tell their friends,
> and that's where all our business comes from.

> But, I guess at the same time, a lot of them come for the social end
> of it. They like to meet old friends and make new friends standing
> in the line, going through the house, hanging around afterwards, . . .
> if you know what I mean.

Phil had thought he knew and agreed; but he reminded Mr. Willard that
population trends seemed to show that the size of this segment was getting smaller. Moreover, an older audience might be easier to control, he
had mentioned, and would allow later hours of operation, perhaps closing at 12:30 A.M. instead of 11:00 P.M.

MARKETING RESEARCH

Finishing his coffee, Phil thought he saw the solution: marketing
research. That is, there was not much he could do now about cosponsor
choice other than go along with Mr. Willard. However, next year, with
the proper data, he might be in a better position. Consequently, he spent
the rest of the morning designing a personal interview questionnaire to

Ghost Manor Survey

Weekday: M T W TH F   Weekend: SAT. SUN.   Weather: GOOD BAD

1. Sex: Male / Female

2. Age: 7–11 / 12–14 / 15–18 / 19–24 / 25–35 / 36 and up

3. Occupation: Student: Grades 1–6 / Grades 7–9 / Grades 10–12 / College Student
   Professional / Clerical / Technical / Trade / Unemployed

4. Marital Status: Single / Married

5. White / non-White

6. Is this your first time going through the Ghost Manor? yes / no

7. If no, how many times previously? 1 2 3 4 5 6

8. Have you ever attended a haunted house sponsored by another organization? yes / no

9. Do you think that the admission is fair? yes / no too high / too low

10. How did you hear about the Ghost Manor?

    a) Radio
       Which station? _____

    b) TV
       Which station? _____

    c) Newspaper
       Which one? _____

    d) Poster? _____

    e) Friend? _____

    f) Other? _____
       What? _____

11. What is your favorite radio station? _____

12. Did you come in a group? yes / no

13. How many in your group? 2–5 / 6–10 / 11+

14. Did you use public transportation or your own? public / own

15. How many miles did you travel: (approx.) <1 1–5 6–10 11–15 16+

collect data on haunted house customers (see above).

Phil figured that one volunteer, specially selected and trained, could survey approximately fifty customers every other night as they stood in line waiting for Ghost Manor to open. (Mr. Willard had said that such lines were common, even during the week.) Phil planned to have data collected for each night of the week to eliminate biases. As an incentive to complete the questionnaire, the interviewer would give each respondent a coupon good for a free soft drink at the refreshment stand on the grounds of Ghost Manor. This ought to work, Phil thought, although I might check my marketing research text tonight when I get home.

4. Lehand Distributing*

Jim Lehand had just finished locking up for the evening and was about to turn off the lights. His mind went back to last week's sales figures lying on his desk. It was now clear that despite projections of an 18 percent minimum market share (which seemed conservative a couple of years ago), Lehand's was barely going to claim a meager 14 percent— and this with a line of beers that only three years previous had acquired almost one-fourth of the market.

BACKGROUND

Lehand had purchased the distributorship two years ago for $1,400,000 and had since put another $200,000 into it. His territory (six counties in southeastern Missouri) contained approximately 300,000 consumers of legal drinking age, consuming on the average about twenty-five gallons of beer each per year. The territory contained about 950 retail outlets. Each sold at least two brands of beer either "on" or "off premises." Grocery and liquor stores typically carried at least twenty brands each, and bars and taverns often carried about half that number.

Lehand sat down at his desk and shook off the sinking feeling that comes with the realization that something is definitely wrong. "After all," he thought, "I've been in other businesses for a long time and faced other hard times; but why is my market share so low? Maybe it's advertising—but I know that the brewery spends as much on advertising as anyone else in the industry. And I think I spend almost as much on promotion support as John's and Riley's. It must be my routemen; they just aren't pushing hard enough. No, darn it, the retailers buy what sells and if our beer was selling they'd buy. Maybe I need more specials—weekend pushers—but it seems like that's all I'm doing and the cost is staggering." Last month, for example, his use of specials had reduced Lehand's gross revenue per gallon of beer to about $3.05. The net was perhaps $0.10 per gallon.

THE MARKET

"Maybe I need some more information about the beer business locally. I really should have a better feel for the market." As Lehand's thoughts continued to mull over possibilities, he absently turned to his files to see what data were available to help him with the dilemma. All beer, wine, and liquor wholesalers filed monthly sales figures by product with the State Revenue people and this is public information. Lehand found the information contained in Table C4.1.

He knew other data were probably available, but what data should he be looking for? "That's it! I'll run a survey! But what to ask? 'Why

*Ronald W. Lundquist, Associate Professor of Management at Montana State University, wrote this case.

TABLE C4.1
Wholesalers' Market Shares

	Percent of Market						
Distributor	1975	1976	1977	1978	1979	1980	1981 (thru Oct)
John's	36.3	36.1	33.0	37.1	43.1	48.6	50.3
Riley's	34.5	35.1	39.9	37.4	36.1	35.0	34.9
Highland	10.1	7.8	5.5	3.1	0.3*	—	—
Lehand	19.1	21.0	21.6	22.4	20.5	16.4	14.8
	100.0	100.0	100.0	100.0	100.0	100.0	100.0

*Went out of business in January

don't you buy my beer?' No, I've got to get more organized than that. And what type of survey should I run? Telephone? Mail? Interview?"

THE PHONE CALL   As Lehand stared at the file cabinets, the phone rang. "Jim, what's the problem? I thought we had an appointment to talk with some of my marketing students about the beer business." Lehand's heart jumped. "Sorry Frank—got tied up at the office, but I'll be there in ten minutes. By the way, in return for my free lecture, perhaps your students could do me a favor!"

5. Southwestern Montana Coors, Inc.

Larry Brownlow was just beginning to realize the problem was more complex than he thought. The problem, of course, was giving direction to Manson and Associates regarding which research should be completed by February 20, 1976, to determine market potential of a Coors beer distributorship for southwestern Montana. With data from this research, Larry would be able to estimate the feasibility of such an operation before the March 5 application deadline. Larry knew his decision on whether or not to apply for the distributorship was the most important career choice he had ever faced.

LARRY BROWNLOW   At 29, Larry was just completing his M.B.A. and, from his standpoint, the Coors announcement of expansion into Montana could hardly have been better timed. He had long ago decided the best opportunities and rewards were in small, self-owned businesses and not in the jungles of corporate giants.

Larry knew he was lucky to be in a position to consider small business opportunities such as the Coors distributorship. An inheritance of approximately $200,000 was held in trust for Larry, to be dispersed when he reached age 30. Until then, Larry and his family lived on an annual trust income of about $8,000. It was on this income that Larry decided to leave his sales engineering job and return to graduate school for his M.B.A.

The decision to complete a graduate program and operate his own business had been easy to make. While he could have retired and lived off investment income, Larry knew such a life would not be to his liking. Working with people and the challenge of making it on his own, Larry thought, were certainly preferable to an early retirement.

Larry would be 30 in July, about the time money would actually be needed to start the business. In the meantime, he had access to about $2,500 for feasibility research. While there certainly were other places to spend the money, Larry and his wife agreed the opportunity to acquire the distributorship could not be overlooked.

COORS, INC.

Coors history dated back to 1873 when Adolph Coors built a small brewery in Golden, Colorado. Since then, the brewery had prospered and become the fifth largest seller of beer in the country. All facilities are still located in Golden, which is centrally located for the eleven western states in which Coors is marketed. Coors is still family operated and controlled. The company recently expanded into the Texas market and issued its first public stock, $127 million worth of nonvoting shares. The issue was enthusiastically received by the financial community despite its being offered at the bottom of the 1975 recession.

Coors unwillingness to compromise on the high quality of its product is well known both to its suppliers and to its consuming public. Coors beer requires constant refrigeration to maintain this quality, and wholesalers' facilities are closely controlled to ensure proper temperatures are maintained. Wholesalers are also required to install and use aluminum can recycling equipment. Coors was one of the first breweries in the industry to recycle its cans.

Larry was aware of Coors' popularity with consumers. Coors consumers were characterized as almost fanatically brand loyal despite the beer's premium price. As an example, ticket counter employees at the Denver airport regularly report seeing out-of-state passengers carrying one or more cases of Coors on board for home consumption in non-Coors states. Local acceptance, Larry thought, would be no less enthusiastic.

Because of this high consumer acceptance, the Coors company spent less on advertising than competitors. Consumer demand seemed to pull the product through the distribution channel.

MANSON RESEARCH PROPOSAL

Because of the press of studies, Larry had contacted Manson and Associates in January for their assistance. The firm was a Spokane-based general research supplier which had conducted other feasibility studies in the Pacific Northwest.

Larry had met John Rome, Senior Research Analyst for Manson, and discussed the Coors opportunity and appropriate research extensively in the January meeting. Rome promised the formal research proposal for the project, which Larry now held in his hand (see Exhibit C5.1 and Tables C5.1 to C5.9). It certainly was extensive, Larry thought, and it reflected the professionalism he expected. Now came the hard part,

EXHIBIT C5.1
Manson and Associates Research Proposal

January 16, 1976

Mr. Larry Brownlow
1198 West Lamar
Pullman, WA 99163

Dear Larry:

It was a pleasure meeting you last week and discussing your business and research interests in Coors wholesaling. From further thought and discussion with my colleagues, the Coors opportunity appears even more attractive than when we met.

Appearances can be deceiving, as you know, and I fully agree some formal research is needed before you make application. Research that we recommend would proceed in two distinct stages and is described below:

Stage One Research Based on Secondary Data:

Study A: National and Montana Per Capita Beer Consumption for 1973, 1974, and 1975
Description: Per capita annual consumption of beer for the total population age 21 and over in gallons is provided.
Source: Various Publications
Cost: $100

Study B: Population Estimates for 1975–1980 for Five Montana Counties in the Market Area
Description: Annual estimates of total population and population age 21 and over is provided for the period 1975–1980.
Source: U.S. Bureau of Census and Sales Management Annual Survey of Buying Power
Cost: $150

Study C: Coors Market Share Estimates for 1977–1980
Description: Coors market share based on total gallons consumed in the five county market area is estimated for each year in the period 1977–1980. This data will be projected from Coors' experience in Idaho, Colorado, California, Oklahoma, and Texas.
Source: Various Publications
Cost: $200

Study D: Estimated Liquor and Beer Licenses for the Market Area 1976–1980
Description: Projections of the number of on-premise sale operations and off-premise sale operations is provided.
Source: Montana Department of Revenue, Liquor Division
Cost: $100

Study E: Beer Taxes Paid by Montana Wholesalers for 1974 and 1975 in the Market Area
Description: Beer taxes paid by each of the five presently operating competing beer wholesalers is provided. This can be converted to gallons sold by applying the state gallonage tax rate (10.5¢ per gallon).

Source: Montana Department of Revenue, Liquor Division
Cost: $400

Study F: Financial Statement Summary of Wine, Liquor, and Beer Wholesalers for 1975
Description: Composite balance sheets, income statements, and relevant measures of performance provided for 152 similar wholesaling operations is provided.
Source: Robert Morris Associates Annual Statement Studies 1976 ed.
Cost: $13.50

Stage Two Research Based on Primary Data

Study G: Consumer Study
Description: Study G involves focus group interviews and a mail questionnaire to determine consumer past experience, acceptance, and intention to buy Coors beer. Three interviews would be conducted in three counties in the market area. From this data, a mail questionnaire would be developed and sent to 1,000 adult residents in the market area utilizing direct questions and a semantic differential scale to measure attitudes towards Coors beer, competing beers, and an ideal beer.
Source: Manson and Associates
Cost: $1,100

Study H: Retailer Study
Description: Focus group interviews would be conducted with six potential retailers of Coors beer in one county in the market area to determine their past beer sales and experience and their intention to stock and sell Coors. From this data, a mail questionnaire would be developed and sent to all appropriate retailers in the market area to determine similar data.
Source: Manson and Associates
Cost: $600

Study I: Survey of Retail and Wholesale Beer Prices
Description: Study I involves in-store interviews with a sample of 15 retailers in the market area to determine retail and wholesale prices for Budweiser, Hamms, Michelob, Olympia, and a low-price beer.
Source: Manson and Associates
Cost: $500

Examples of the form of final report tables are attached [Tables C5.1 to C5.9]. This should give you a better idea of the data you will receive.

As you can see, the research is extensive and, I might add, not cheap. However, the research as outlined will supply you with sufficient information to make an estimate of the feasibility of a Coors distributorship, the investment for which is substantial.

I have scheduled 9:00 next Friday as a time to meet with you to discuss the proposal in more detail. Time is short, but we firmly feel the study can be completed by February 20, 1976. If you need more information in the meantime, please feel free to call.

Sincerely,

John Rome
Senior Research Analyst

TABLE C5.1
Study A Results: National and Montana Resident Annual Beer Consumption, 1973–1975 (Gallons per capita)

	U.S. CONSUMPTION		MONTANA CONSUMPTION	
Year	Based on Entire Population	Based on Population Over Age 21	Based on Entire Population	Based on Population Over Age 21
1973				
1974				
1975				

Source: Study A

choosing the more relevant research from the proposal because he certainly couldn't afford to pay for it all. Rome had suggested a meeting for Friday which gave Larry only three more days to decide.

Larry was at first overwhelmed. All the research would certainly be useful. He was sure he needed estimates of sales and costs in a form allowing managerial analysis, but what data in what form? Knowledge

TABLE C5.2
Study B Results: Population Estimates for 1975–1980 for Five Montana Counties in Market Area

County	PROJECTED ENTIRE POPULATION					
	1975	1976	1977	1978	1979	1980
A						
B						
C						
D						
E						

County	PROJECTED POPULATION AGE 21 AND OVER					
	1975	1976	1977	1978	1979	1980
A						
B						
C						
D						
E						

Source: Study B

TABLE C5.3
Study C Results: Coors Market Share Estimates for 1977–1980[a]

Year	Market Share (%)
1977	
1978	
1979	
1980	

[a]Coors 1975 market shares for Idaho, Colorado, California, Oklahoma, and Texas are   %,   %,   %,   %, and   %, respectively.
Source: Study C

TABLE C5.4
Study D Results: Liquor and Beer License Estimates for Market Area for 1976–1980

Type of License	1976	1977	1978	1979	1980
All Beverages					
Retail Beer and Wine					
Off-Premise Beer Only					
Veterans Beer and Liquor					
Fraternal					
Resort Beer and Liquor					

Source: Study D

TABLE C5.5
Study E Results: Beer Taxes Paid by Beer Wholesalers in the Market Area, 1974 and 1975[a]

Wholesaler	1974 Tax Paid ($)	1975 Tax Paid ($)
A		
B		
C		
D		
E		

[a]Montana Beer Tax is 10.5¢ per gallon.
Source: Study E

of competing operations' experience, retailer support, and consumer acceptance also seemed crucial for feasibility analysis. For example, what if consumers were excited about Coors and retailers indifferent or the other way around? Finally, several of the studies would provide information also useful in later months of operation in the areas of promotion and pricing, for example. The problem now appeared more difficult than before!

TABLE C5.6
Study F Results: Financial Statement Summary fo 152 Wholesalers of Wine, Liquor, and Beer in 1975

Assets	%	Ratios
Cash		
Marketable Securities		
Receivables Net		
Inventory Net		
All Other Current		
Total Current		
Fixed Assets Net		
All Other Noncurrent	_____	Ratios
Total	100.0	Quick
		Current
Liabilities		Debts/Worth
Due to Banks—Short Term		Sales/Receivables
Due to Trade		Cost Sales/Inventory
Income Taxes		% Profit Before Taxes
Current Maturities LT Debt		Based on Total Assets
All Other Current		
Total Current Debt		
Noncurrent Debt. Unsub.		
Total Unsubordinated Debt		
Subordinated Debt		
Tangible Net Worth	_____	
Total	100.0	
Income Data		
Net Sales		
Cost of Sales		
Gross Profit		
All Other Expenses Net	_____	
Profit Before Taxes		

Note: Robert Morris Associates cannot emphasize too strongly that its figures *may not* be representative of the entire industry for the following reasons:
1. The only companies with a chance of being included in this table are those for whom their submitting banks have recent figures.
2. Even from this restricted group of potentially includable companies, those which are chosen, and the total number chosen, are not determined in any random or otherwise statistically reliable manner.
3. Many companies in this table have *varied* product lines. Bankers have categorized them by their *primary* product line and some "impurity" in the data will be introduced.

Thus, the figures should not automatically be considered as representative norms.

Source: Study F (Robert Morris Associates © 1976)

TABLE C5.7
Study G Results: Consumer Questionnaire Results

	Yes %	No %
Consumed Coors in the Past:		

	%
Attitudes Toward Coors:	
Strongly Like	
Like	
Indifferent/No Opinion	
Dislike	
Strongly Dislike	_____
Total	100.0

	%
Weekly Beer Consumption:	
Less than 1 can	
1–2 cans	
3–4 cans	
5–6 cans	
7–8 cans	
9 cans and over	_____
Total	100.0

	%
Intention to Buy Coors:	
Certainly Will	
Maybe Will	
Not Sure	
Maybe Will Not	
Certainly Will Not	_____
Total	100.0

	%
Usually Buy Beer at:	
Liquor Stores	
Taverns and Bars	
Supermarkets	
Corner Grocery	_____
Total	100.0

	%
Features Considered Important When Buying Beer:	
Taste	
Brand Name	
Price	
Store Location	
Advertising	
Carbonation	
Other	_____
Total	100.0

Semantic Differential Scale[a]

	Extremely	Very	Somewhat	Somewhat	Very	Extremely	
Masculine	_____	_____	_____	_____	_____	_____	Feminine
Healthful	_____	_____	_____	_____	_____	_____	Unhealthful
Cheap	_____	_____	_____	_____	_____	_____	Expensive
Strong	_____	_____	_____	_____	_____	_____	Weak
Old Fashioned	_____	_____	_____	_____	_____	_____	New
Upper Class	_____	_____	_____	_____	_____	_____	Lower Class
Good Taste	_____	_____	_____	_____	_____	_____	Bad Taste

[a]Profiles would be provided for Coors, three competing beers, and an ideal beer.

Source: Study G

It would have been nice, Larry thought, if he only had some time to perform part of the suggested research himself. There just was too much in the way of class assignments and other matters to allow him that luxury. Besides, using Manson and Associates would give him research

TABLE C5.8
Study H Results: Retailer Questionnaire Results

Brands of Beer Carried:	%	1975 Beer Sales	%
Olympia		Olympia	
Budweiser		Budweiser	
Rainier		Rainier	
Hamms		Hamms	
Brand E		Brand E	
Brand F		Brand F	
Brand G		Brand G	
		Others	
		Total	100.0

Semantic Differential Scale[a]

	Extremely	Very	Somewhat	Somewhat	Very	Extremely	
Masculine	___	___	___	___	___	___	Feminine
Healthful	___	___	___	___	___	___	Unhealthful
Cheap	___	___	___	___	___	___	Expensive
Strong	___	___	___	___	___	___	Weak
Old Fashioned	___	___	___	___	___	___	New
Upper Class	___	___	___	___	___	___	Lower Class
Good Taste	___	___	___	___	___	___	Bad Taste

Intention to Sell Coors: Certainly Will   %
                           Maybe Will
                           Not Sure
                           Maybe Will Not
                           Certainly Will Not   ___
                                               100.0

[a]Profiles would be provided for Coors, three competing beers, and an ideal beer.

Source: Study H

results from an unbiased source. There would be plenty for him to do once he received the results.

INVESTMENT AND OPERATING DATA

Larry was not completely in the dark regarding investment and operating data for the distributorship. In the past two weeks he had visited two beer wholesalers in his hometown of Pullman, Washington who handled Olympia and Hamms beer; he wanted to get a feel for their operation and marketing experience. It would have been nice to interview a Coors wholesaler, but Coors management had strictly informed all their distributors to provide no information to prospective applicants.

TABLE C5.9
Study I Results: Retail and Wholesale Prices for Selected Beers in the Market Area

Beer	Wholesale Six Pack Price ($)	Retail Six Pack Price ($)
Budweiser		
Hamms		
Michelob		
Olympia		
Low-Price Special		

Source: Study I

While no specific financial data was discussed, general information had been provided in a near-cordial fashion because of the noncompetitive nature of Larry's plans. Based on his conversations, Larry made the estimates shown in Table C5.10 (see page 172).

A local banker had reviewed Larry's financial capabilities and saw no problem in extending a line of credit on the order of $200,000. Other family sources also might lend as much as $200,000 to the business.

As a rough estimate of fixed expenses, Larry planned on having four route salesmen, a secretary, and a general warehouse man. Salaries for these people and himself would run about $75,000 annually plus some form of incentive compensation he had yet to determine. Other fixed or semifixed expenses were estimated at:

Equipment Depreciation	$20,000
Warehouse Depreciation	8,000
Utilities and Telephone	8,000
Insurance	6,000
Personal Property Taxes	5,000
Maintenance and Janitorial	2,800
Miscellaneous	1,200
	$51,000

According to the two wholesalers, beer in bottles and cans outsold keg beer by a three to one margin. Keg beer prices at the wholesale level were about 45 percent of prices for beer in bottles and cans.

MEETING

The entire matter deserved much thought. Maybe it was a golden opportunity, maybe not. The only thing certain was that research was needed, Manson and Associates was ready, and Larry needed time to think.

Today is Tuesday, Larry thought, only three more days until he and John Rome get together for direction.

TABLE C5.10
Estimates of Investments

Inventory		$120,000
Equipment		
Delivery Trucks	$76,000	
Fork Lift	10,000	
Recycling & Misc. Equip.	10,000	
Office Equipment	4,000	
Total Equipment		100,000
Warehouse		160,000
Land		20,000
Total Investment		$400,000

PART

Asking and Evaluating Research Questions

CHAPTER 7

Questions of Fact: Behavior and Socioeconomic Characteristics

Do you own a car? Where did you buy your bicycle? Who went with you when you last ate out? How old are you? What is your zip code? We could continue for a long time, asking questions of behavior and socioeconomic characteristics, but these few are enough to reveal the nature of our topic for this chapter.

Questions of Fact

Questions of behavior and socioeconomic characteristics can also be called questions of fact. Our primary interest is in questions of fact that apply to people. Usually our interest will be in people as consumers, but occasionally it will be in people as salespersons, wholesalers, retailers, and others in various organizations. A secondary interest is in questions of fact that apply to organizations. For example, we may want to determine an organization's 1981 gross sales, the size of its salesforce, and how much it spent on radio advertising. When we understand what there is to know about questions of fact asked of people, we will find it easy to extend this knowledge to questions of fact asked of organizations. The same problems and solutions are present because people in organizations still provide the answers.

The major types of marketing research questions concerning behavior and socioeconomic characteristics appear in Exhibit 7.1.

EXHIBIT 7.1
Marketing Research Questions of Behavior and Socioeconomic Characteristics

Behavior Questions	Socioeconomic Characteristic Questions
Purchase/Ownership	Age
Usage rate	Sex
Decision maker identity	Income
Payment method	Occupation
Information sources	Education
Shopping patterns	Family size
Media exposure patterns	Stage in family life cycle
Advertising exposure	Marital status
Specific behavior patterns	Race
	Geographic location

BEHAVIOR QUESTIONS

At the outset it is important to realize that **behavior questions** ask for reports of past and current behavior and not for intentions of future behavior. The first are questions of fact while the second are questions of psychological characteristics, a topic for our next chapter.

Purchase/Ownership Questions. Perhaps the most important behavior question in marketing research is that of purchase or ownership of a product or service. For services and nondurable goods the question of purchase is more relevant; questions of ownership usually apply to durables. Question form is quite simple:

- Do you own your home?
- Have you bought an unsweetened breakfast cereal in the past two weeks?
- What typewriter makes and models have you purchased for your firm in the past six months?

As we see, basic purchase/ownership questions are often embellished by references to time periods, product models, brand names, stores, and other frames of reference.

In fact, most other types of behavior questions in Exhibit 7.1 are really only refinements of the basic question about purchase or ownership. Most frequently asked of these are usage rate questions.

Usage Rate Questions. Here the marketing researcher often tries to identify the heavy user of a product or service. Heavy users are important to marketing decision makers because they consume product amounts greatly disproportionate to their number. For example, less than 40 percent of all consumers account for 80 percent of all cake mix purchases. Less than 20 percent of all consumers account for over 90 percent of all beer purchases.[1] Clearly marketing decision making can be more effective if marketing research can identify such consumers.

Again, question form is straightforward. Questions simply ask consumers to report the number of times a particular usage behavior occurred during a specified time period:

- How many times did you serve a hot breakfast cereal in the past week?
- On the average weekday, how many miles do you drive your car?
- How many different times each day do you chew gum?

Little more need be said.

Decision Maker Identity Questions.   In Exhibit 7.1, decision maker identity refers to questions that determine who in the purchasing unit specifies what will be purchased, where, when, and how. Often this person is different from the actual user, and even from the buyer, of the product. A typical question asks the consumer to rate degree of involvement for family members across stages in the decision process. Here is an example:

> Thinking back to the last time you ate out as a family, indicate how involved your *children* were in deciding to eat out in the first place.

Other questions might measure children's involvement in providing information on various restaurants, in deciding how much would be spent, and in making a final decision. Similar questions would apply to the involvement of mothers and fathers.

Payment Method Questions.   Payment method questions in Exhibit 7.1 refer to whether payment is made by cash, check, or credit. Also measured may be type of credit card used and identity of its issuer.

Information Source Questions.   Information source questions in Exhibit 7.1 determine the importance of general and marketer dominated information sources.[2] General information sources consist of other people or the mass media. Marketer dominated sources consist of the various promotion forms—advertising, personal selling, and sales promotion activi-

---

[1]Dik W. Twedt, "How Important to Marketing Strategy is the Heavy User?" *Journal of Marketing* 28 (January 1964): 71–72.

[2]This framework and following discussion is essentially that of James F. Engel, Roger D. Blackwell, and David T. Kollat, *Consumer Behavior*, 3rd ed. (Hinsdale, Ill.: The Dryden Press, 1978), pp. 245–56.

ties. Consumers frequently use both kinds of sources in a given purchase decision; usually the research issue is to assess their relative importance.

Care should be taken that questions measure both exposure to the information source and its effectiveness in providing information. These sorts of questions are typically asked:

- Do you recall seeing this ad in yesterday's newspaper?
- How did you find out about our grand opening?
- Suppose your neighbor told you that _____ was the best place to eat in Portland. How believable is her opinion?

Notice that the third question really asks not about consumer facts but about consumer opinions of information source credibility or effectiveness. We shall have much more to say in the next chapter on questions that deal with opinion.

Shopping Pattern Questions.   Shopping pattern questions of fact measure both in-store and out-of-store consumer behavior. In-store behavior questions measure such variables as amount purchased, usage of unit pricing information, time spent in the store, and coupon redemption. Out-of-store behavior questions measure such variables as number of stores shopped, distances traveled, transportation mode, and the extent of mail order, telephone, and door-to-door buying. Short questions usually ask for simple reports of these behaviors.

Media Exposure Pattern Questions.   Questions about patterns of media exposure refer to contact with the various mass advertising communication channels: television, radio, magazine, newspaper, outdoor, transit, yellow pages, and direct mail. Questions measure consumers' exposure to a particular communication channel, relative channel usage, channel exposure by time of day, exposure to a particular channel element (a specific radio station, for example), and channel effectiveness.

Question form varies, depending on which communication channels are part of the research. For example, broadcast media questions measure either simultaneous or historical audiences—are respondents listening to the radio right now, or, did they watch the evening news last night? Print media questions may deal with whether or not respondents subscribe to a particular magazine, if they read the latest issue, and whether or not they subscribe to the Sunday paper. A second question often *qualifies* respondents by asking for a specific detail to make sure the respondent is telling the truth. For example, a radio listener might be asked to describe what is now playing on the station she says she is listening to; a magazine reader might be asked to describe an article appearing in last week's issue.

Advertising Exposure Questions.   This item in Exhibit 7.1 measures contact with a particular advertisement. Here a researcher might be interested in the number of people who read a particular page of a magazine or newspaper on which an advertisement appears. Or, the researcher might want to know who stayed in the room when a television commercial was on or who looked out the car window at a passing billboard. Usually these questions are **aided-recall** questions. That is, usually respondents are asked an advertising exposure question and then given some help before answering; the help is designed to stimulate their long-term memory of advertisements. Help may be limited, such as identifying only the product category of interest and asking if respondents can recall advertising for any products in the category. Or, help may be extensive, such as presenting the advertisement itself and asking if respondents recall it. In both instances, additional detail may also be asked—to qualify responses.

Specific Behavior Pattern Questions.   The final type of behavior question indicated in Exhibit 7.1 is used when researchers try to determine the existence of other specific behavior patterns. These sorts of questions look like purchase or usage rate questions, but they deal with larger aspects of behavior somewhat removed from purchase or usage of a specific product. For examples:

- In an average month, how many times do you bake bread?
- Do you golf?
- Have you tried lowering your thermostat at night to save heating costs?

As we can see, the number of possible behavior questions of interest to marketers is large.

Although we recognize the importance of behavior questions, it is socioeconomic characteristic questions that provide perspective and meaning. For example, it is easy to see that a marketing decision maker finds little value in the knowledge that heavy users consume four times as much of the company's product as light users. The real issue is who these heavy users are. Similarly, it is of little value for a marketing decision maker to know that women buy more men's shirts than men do. The real issue is which women and which men, because the market may be segmentable on certain socioeconomic characteristics.

SOCIOECONOMIC CHARACTERISTIC QUESTIONS

As Exhibit 7.1 indicates, marketing researchers frequently ask one or more of ten socioeconomic characteristic questions: age, sex, income, occupation, education, family size, stage in the family life cycle, marital status, race, and geographic location. Answers allow the researcher to comment on sample representativeness, to explain consumer behavior, and to segment the market. Determining sample representativeness is perhaps the lowest level of use for socioeconomic information. Still, the researcher will almost always want to compare sample member characteristics with known population characteristics and make statements about significant differences.

At a higher level, marketing researchers will try to explain consumer behavior from selected socioeconomic characteristics. Age, for example, explains most of the purchases of baby food, acne medications, and hearing aids. Sex determines consumption of certain health and beauty aids, cigarette brands, and magazines—even though both sexes could find many of the different products quite usable.

At the highest level, socioeconomic questions help segment a market into homogeneous subgroups, each having largely unique responses to marketing strategies and each having largely similar socioeconomic characteristics.[3] For example, marketing managers commonly speak of a youth market, a black consumer market, an economy car market, a pre-sweetened breakfast cereal market, and so on. To be most useful, segment definition should include socioeconomic characteristics; without them, product, pricing, promotion, and distribution decisions would be difficult.

Most socioeconomic questions are quite simple:

- What is your age (as of your last birthday)?
- Are you male or female?
- What was your 1981 gross income?
- What is the age of your youngest child currently living at home?
- What is your zip code?
- How many salespeople does your firm currently employ?

As we'll see in the next section, the complexity of the researchers' concerns in writing these questions contrasts greatly with the apparent simplicity of the questions.

Only the occupation, stage in the family life cycle, and geographic location questions in Exhibit 7.1 require further explanation. Occupation questions generally require the respondent to write a specific, complete, but short description of what he or she does for a living. The researcher then classifies or converts this information to a number representing occupational status. Basis for the conversion would be one of several currently available "master lists" of occupational status.[4]

A family's position in the family life cycle depends on the spouses' ages and the presence and age of the youngest child now living at home. Starting with young singles living alone, a family life cycle proceeds to young marrieds without children, young marrieds with youngest child under age 6, young marrieds with youngest child over age 6, older marrieds with older children, older marrieds without children, and solitary

---

[3]The literature on marketing segmentation is voluminous. For a state-of-the-art review see the August, 1978 issue of the *Journal of Marketing Research*.

[4]See Engel, Blackwell, and Kollat, *Consumer Behavior*, pp. 116–22 for an identification of frequently used lists of occupational status.

survivors.[5] Numbers 1 through 7 are usually assigned as labels to families classified in each of the respective family life cycle stages.

Geographic location questions contain terms of spatial identification. The questions are often asked in terms of political boundary units—such as states, counties, cities, suburbs, and the like. Alternatively, these questions sometimes use units of distance or units of travel time from some well-known location. Increasingly popular with marketing researchers is the measuring of location by zip codes: zip code responses produce geographic location units of meaningful sizes, easily identifiable boundaries, high respondent familiarity, and high computer compatibility.

Marketing researchers often ask both behavior and socioeconomic questions in a single marketing research study. By asking both types of questions, researchers learn, for example, which communication channels urban heavy users use in gathering information on a product—or which payment methods young, limited-income marrieds use that their more wealthy counterparts do not. Such combinations of the two types of questions yield the most information to marketing decision makers.

Developing Questions of Fact

Although questions of fact are simple in form and content, their development is not. What complicates the process are concerns about the two concepts we introduce here but discuss more completely in Chapter 11: measurement validity and measurement reliability.

Measurement validity refers to the ability of any question (of fact or psychological characteristic) to measure the concept it is meant to measure. For example, everyone agrees that a speedometer measures velocity, but what do we measure when asking a wholesaler for an estimate of 1981 selling costs? In part, responses measure 1981 selling costs. But, responses also measure the respondent's understanding of the term "estimate," the concept of "1981," and what constitutes "selling costs." Responses further measure the respondent's memory, motivation to respond, and intelligence, among several other concepts (all apart from the one intended).

Measurement reliability refers to the absence of random errors in responding to any question. A reliable question produces repeatable, stable, and consistent responses for each respondent. To illustrate, consider that even responses to such a straightforward question as "How old are you?" lack complete reliability because some respondents lie about their age, the question itself may be interpreted to mean age as of either a last

VALIDITY AND
RELIABILITY

---

[5] For an extensive discussion of family life cycle and its influence on consumer behavior, see Fred D. Reynolds and William D. Wells, *Consumer Behavior* (New York: McGraw-Hill, 1977), Chaps. 3–7. See also Patrick E. Murphy and William A. Staples, "A Modernized Family Life Cycle," *Journal of Consumer Research* 6 (June 1979): 12–22 for a proposed revision to the seven stages.

or a nearest birthday, and researchers sometimes misrecord responses. Responses to more complex questions show even greater potential for unreliability.

Thus, responses to any question always depend on the respondent, the research task expected of respondents (here, the question itself), and the researcher. Four examples from the literature illustrate:

- Consumer recall of the number of television news stories watched less than three hours prior to questioning was more than three times higher when aided-recall instead of unaided-recall questions were asked.[6]

- When words referring to a hairpiece were added, a wig ownership question found reported ownership to drop by almost 90 percent for two samples of German women.[7]

- Two only slightly different religious affiliation questions found 5 percent of a single sample reporting different affiliations on two different occasions.[8]

- An identical age question when repeated after an 8- to 10-day interval produced an age difference of one or more years for 10 percent of a single consumer sample.[9]

More examples could be cited.

The rest of this chapter covers some factors that influence validity and reliability and some research tactics that minimize their effect on questions of fact.

SOCIAL DESIRABILITY AND ITEM NONRESPONSE   Two such influential factors are social desirability and item nonresponse. **Social desirability** describes a tendency for respondents to answer questions in a manner consistent with core-cultural values. That is, people often lie or otherwise "fake good" to varying degrees when responding to sensitive questions (either fact or psychological questions). A similar occurrence is when respondents determine the identity of the research project's sponsor and alter their responses because of this knowledge.

Researchers employ several tactics for minimizing the effect of social desirability. Most common is the pretesting of questions in order to determine which questions people feel are too sensitive and personal for them

---

[6]W. Russell Neuman, "Patterns of Recall Among Television News Viewers," *Public Opinion Quarterly* 40 (Spring 1976): 115–23.

[7]Elisabeth Noelle-Neumann, "Wanted: Rules for Structured Questionnaires," *Public Opinion Quarterly* 34 (Summer 1970): 197–98.

[8]Kathleen McCourt and D. Garth Taylor, "Determining Religious Affiliation Through Survey Research: A Methodological Note," *Public Opinion Quarterly* 40 (Spring 1976): 124–27.

[9]Gladys Palmer, "Factors in the Variability of Response in Enumerative Studies," *Journal of the American Statistical Association* 38: 143–52.

TABLE 7.1
Item Nonresponse to Questions of Fact

Question Type	Nonresponse Mean Percentage
Age	1.5
Education	1.7
Occupation	1.8
Marital Status	1.9
Income	6.0
Sex	8.4

Source: C. Samuel Craig and John M. McCann, "Item Nonresponse in Mail Surveys: Extent and Correlates," *Journal of Marketing Research* 15 (May 1978):285–89.

to answer without bias. It may be possible to reword these questions or to change response categories to minimize their threatening nature (as we discuss later in this chapter). Another common tactic is to avoid disclosing both sponsor and precise research purpose. General terms often describe research purpose and questions unrelated to research objectives often intermingle with pertinent questions to disguise the study. We should not deliberately mislead respondents in this process, however. A third tactic is to employ an attitude scale in the data collection form to identify people who respond in a socially desirable manner.[10] Once identified, data from these individuals may be completely removed from the study or analyzed apart from that of other respondents.

Beyond these tactics, researchers may need to change from surveys to a completely different data collection method. Observation, simulation, and qualitative data collection methods all show lower potentials for social desirability errors.

Nonresponse in this chapter concerns item nonresponse as distinct from complete nonresponse, a topic we discussed in Chapter 5. In particular, here we want to examine consumer nonresponse to questions of fact. Craig and McCann show that item nonresponse in marketing surveys is the rule rather than the exception.[11] Reviewing seven mail surveys of over 17,000 respondents, they found only one respondent in four returned a completely filled out questionnaire. About 2 to 8 percent of all fact questions were left blank. Table 7.1 shows the distribution of item nonresponse to six types of fact questions in their research. As we might expect, it shows respondents more likely to refuse to answer sex and income questions than other fact questions.

---

[10]See the Social Desirability Scales by Crowne and Marlowe, and those by Edwards, both in *Measures of Social Psychological Attitudes* John P. Robinson and Phillip R. Shaver eds., (Ann Arbor, Mich.: Institute for Survey Research, 1969), pp. 640–47.

[11]C. Samuel Craig and John M. McCann, "Item Nonresponse in Mail Surveys: Extent and Correlates," *Journal of Marketing Research* 15 (May 1978): 285–89.

Surprisingly, Craig and McCann found item nonresponse unrelated to questionnaire length, which ranged from 71 to 166 items in the seven surveys. However, nonresponse did appear to be affected by age and educational background of the respondents: nonresponse rates for older and less educated respondents were significantly higher. Craig and McCann conclude that:

> [I]t is important to test questionnaire design and response enhancing techniques that increase the likelihood that older individuals and those with less education will complete more items. Such devices might include question simplification, larger type, repetition of important questions with slight variation in format, increased specification in the instructions, threat of checking all returned questionnaires for completeness, and providing incentives for completeness rather than for return of the questionnaire (or in addition to the initial incentive). Also, during questionnaire pretesting stages particular attention should be paid to older individuals and those with less education to identify questions that pose potential item nonresponse problems.[12]

FACT QUESTION CONSTRUCTION GUIDELINES[13]   Three aspects of fact questions require construction guidelines: question topic, question wording, and response format. **Question topic** refers to the basic behavior or socioeconomic variable measured by the question. **Question wording** refers to the choice of terms or language. **Response format** refers to the method by which respondents indicate answers. We examine each in turn.

Question Topic Issues.   Our first issue concerns topic selection. How do we know which variables to include as questions of fact? Obviously, there are many such variables we could consider for inclusion—as Exhibit 7.1 shows. Recognition of the need to choose among them leads to our first guideline:

> *Include only variables that relate to research objectives.*

Consideration of the research objectives may show the variable under consideration to be completely unrelated. It sometimes happens that the

---

[12]Ibid., p. 289.

[13]There are several sources offering similar advice when writing questions. A good one is by Arthur Kornhauser and Paul B. Sheatsley, "Questionnaire Construction and Interview Procedure," in Claire Selltiz et al., *Research Methods in Social Relations*, rev. ed. (New York: Holt, Rinehart, and Winston, 1966), pp. 552-74.

researcher is intrigued by a very interesting research variable, sufficiently tempting that it finds its way onto the data collection form. Often the researcher reasons that "as long as we're conducting the study, it won't hurt to add one or a few more questions."

Avoid this practice. Extra questions increase the length of the data collection form and the cost of the project, especially for data collected with personal or telephone interviews. Extra questions may influence responses to pertinent questions, or confuse the analysis. Extra questions are shotgun research, a practice unworthy of someone who has read this book.

Reference to research objectives may show the variable to be related but of little practical use. For example, suppose the research objective is to determine which radio stations to use for advertising a new hair spray in forty cities. We collect data for a sample of three cities and find product usage concentrated among higher income females who live in households of five or more persons. When it comes time to use these results, however, we find that no radio station in any of the cities collects data on audience income by household size. Thus, only the sex data really relate to research objectives.

Sometimes a fact question is irrelevant with respect to the research objectives because it is redundant. Researchers usually notice identical questions and remove duplicates; they occasionally miss more subtle redundancies. Consider these two questions:

- What are the ages of all dogs living at this address?
- How many dogs live at this address?

A little thought reveals that the second question is unneeded—its answer is supplied by the first.

Our first guideline has only one exception. That is, marketing researchers frequently use one or a few unrelated but interesting questions to disguise the study or to gain a respondent's interest and cooperation. Often this is the nature of the first question in a study because of its importance in creating respondent interest. Mostly, however, they discard irrelevant or redundant questions.

Recognize that we have considered only relevancy errors of commission. Even more serious are relevancy errors of omission—asking too few questions usually means bigger problems in meeting research objectives than asking too many. To minimize errors of omission requires the researcher to have intimate knowledge of past research, consumer behavior literature, the decision maker, the organizational environment, and the marketing problem. Even then, experienced researchers sometimes inadvertently omit an important question. Take care that this happens infrequently.

Our second guideline for selecting topics in questions of fact concerns the respondents:

> *Include only variables that are meaningful to respondents.*

Respondents see a question as meaningless if it is unrelated to their personal experience. If we ask teenagers to identify their favorite denture adhesive or childless couples to recall what brand of baby food they last purchased, we deserve the sorts of answers we will get. More important, one or two such meaningless questions will cause many people to lose interest in our research and stop participating.

To avoid meaningless questions researchers often use filtering questions, along with skip instructions, to screen respondents for subsequent questions.

Some typical examples are:

4. Are there children living at this address under 10 years of age?

Yes   No ⟶ TERMINATE INTERVIEW,
                       ERASE AND REUSE FORM

5. Do you ever serve them instant pudding for dessert or a snack?

Yes   No ⟶ GO TO QUESTION 12

6. What brands of instant pudding would we find on your cupboard shelf right now?

Only if the consumer answers yes to the filtering questions (4 and 5) does he or she answer following questions that would otherwise be meaningless.

Questions that require unrealistic effort and extreme memory in responding also seem meaningless to respondents. Asking where respondents have vacationed in the past 5 years or what they ate for dinner the last 7 evenings will likely get a researcher blank stares, inaccurate answers, or worse. If it is necessary to ask these sorts of questions, we should instruct respondents to refer to easily available records. Alternatively, we might use a different research design with diaries to collect data.

Respondents also consider a question to be meaningless if it contains too many variables. Consider this question:

Do you or your spouse use newspaper advertisements, coupons, shopping lists, and unit price information to buy food?

Apart from the question's length, many respondents will find the question confusing because they could answer "yes" to one part of it and "no" to another. Moreover, their answers are simply uninterpretable. A "yes" response could indicate the respondent, spouse, or both use advertisements, coupons, lists, and unit prices. A "no" response could indicate that neither uses one, two, three, or four of the four shopping aids. Because the question contains two subjects and four verb objects, it lacks meaning. Keep questions simple!

Question Wording Issues.   After determining question topics we must choose the words. Two guidelines help; the first is:

> *Choose words that respondents understand.*

Several factors can prevent a respondent from understanding a question. One is the use of ambiguous terms. Words that lack precision and clarity confuse respondents and result in no answer or misinformation. Suppose we ask:

<u>Where</u> do you <u>usually shop</u> for <u>clothes</u>?

All four underlined words create confusion. Does "where" refer to a department within a store, a particular store, store type, shopping mall, city, or state? All are acceptable answers. Does "usually" refer to the last purchase, two out of the three last purchases, a favorite store, or what? Does "shop" include window shopping, impulse buying, and gift buying, or does it mean buying only after carefully comparing prices and quality? Does "clothes" mean work clothes, casual clothes, dress clothes, underwear, accessories, or something else? Are there other interpretations to this simple seven-word question?

Notice also that the question assumes that the respondent "usually" performs the behavior in question—yet some consumers don't "usually" do anything. That is, some consumers form loyalties to several stores and shop an equal amount at all of them. Some shoppers seek even more variety by being loyal to none. Questions containing "usually" or similar words are often defective on this basis.

The net effect of four ambiguous words is to make the question too general. We should avoid this by striving for specificity in our questions. Make them concrete. Thus, the question could be better written as:

In the past five days, how much have you spent for casual clothes at the following stores? Be sure to include casual clothes purchased for yourself, other family members, and as gifts.

While we recognize this question is not perfect, it is an improvement over the first. Writing such questions takes several drafts and comes more quickly with practice. We'll see in Chapter 11 that a pretest helps, too.

Another factor that prevents respondents from understanding the question is the use of jargon. Jargon is a technical term that the researcher understands but most people do not. Consider these examples: distribution channel, specialty store, marketing mix, case goods, point-of-purchase display, premiums, syncratic decision making, decision criteria, and brand loyalty. Such terms find little use among consumers; they do not belong on a data collection form without clear explanation.

A closely related problem is the use of involute, polysyllabic, and obfuscating words. People have a difficult time understanding words like these. Remember that most consumers do not have the same facility with the language as recent college graduates. A picture or other graphic presentation may make the question more understandable, especially for young consumers.

A last factor that clouds the meaning of a question is failure to specify the frame of reference appropriate for the answer. These two questions illustrate:

- How many television sets are owned by members of this family?
- Which shopping center, Rosewood or Ferndale, is closer to you?

The first question fails to provide a spatial frame of reference. Respondents could report either the number of television sets at that address or the number owned by all family members, including those owned by sons and daughters living away from home. The second question fails to provide either a spatial or temporal frame of reference. Respondents could report being closer in space to one shopping center while being closer in time to the other. Both questions, then, would benefit by the addition of a short phrase that provides a clear frame of reference.

As much as possible, questions should be worded so that consumers do not distort their responses. This forms the basis for our next guideline:

Write questions with neutral words.

We want to avoid leading questions, emotion-laden words, and stereotypes. Consider these questions:

- Are you, like most consumers, having occasional quality-related problems with newly purchased small electrical appliances?
- Have you personally been exposed to the recent nationwide trend of retailers using deceptive advertising?

Clearly, answers to such leading questions represent biased reporting (that the writer likely intended in the first place). Such practice gives decision makers bad information and marketing research a bad name.

The use of impartial words in questions is equally at issue. Each of these descriptions of a product—as cheap, less expensive, or more economical—will lead to a different consumer reaction. Using "rich" to describe a new food product is different from calling it "fattening." Asking consumers if they have been exasperated, or upset, or inconvenienced by telephone salespeople will yield different responses. Words have precise meanings. A good thesaurus and dictionary helps the researcher prevent unintentional bias.

Finally, writing questions with neutral words means avoiding stereotypes. Living in a socially conscious society, we should not have to be reminded of consumers' religious, race, sex, age, and national origin sensitivities. Questions that reflect prejudices in these areas have no place in marketing research.

Response Format Issues.   Responses to questions of fact may be made in two fashions, unstructured and structured. **Unstructured responses** are made to free-answer (open-ended) questions. Here are some examples:

- At what store have you purchased sporting goods in the past week?
- What magazines are delivered to this household each month?
- Describe how you reached your decision to vacation in Aspen.

With most questions of fact, answers are short phrases; but some require long, detailed essays. We quickly recognize the third question above as one of this last sort.

Structured responses are made to dichotomous and multiple choice questions. The respondent or interviewer need only make a check mark or other small effort in indicating an answer. Some examples are:

- Circle the following SEX identification that applies to you:
  Male   Female

- Circle one of the following MARITAL STATUS descriptions that applies to you:
  Single   Married   Widowed   Divorced   Separated
  (Never
  Married)

- Estimate the TOTAL FAMILY INCOME BEFORE TAXES for 1981 by making an X in the appropriate circle to the right. Include income from all sources such as full- and part-time employment, savings and investments, pensions, social security, alimony, unemployment compensation, welfare and other sources. You may want to refer to tax or other records, if easily available.

  ○ $10,000 or less
  ○ $10,001 to $15,000
  ○ $15,001 to $17,500
  ○ $17,501 to $20,000
  ○ $20,001 to $22,500
  ○ $22,501 to $25,000
  ○ $25,001 to $30,000
  ○ $30,001 to $40,000
  ○ $40,000 and over

Both types of response formats have advantages and disadvantages. Because open-ended questions allow consumers to answer in their own words, data contain more variety. Things that pass unsaid in a structured format come to the surface when responses are free form. Open-ended questions do not force responses into categories, and, therefore, more reflect consumers' true answers. Open-ended questions require less effort and information to write; that is, sometimes we have to use open-ended questions simply because we know too little about the question topic to allow construction of structured responses. All these advantages favor the use of open-ended questions in either basic or applied exploratory research.

A disadvantage of open-ended questions is that often a forgetful respondent could provide a more complete answer if the question provided key words in a structured format. If the question requires a long essay answer, it will take much time to analyze and interpret responses. Respondents also consider such questions to take more effort to answer than structured response questions. These last two points usually limit the use of very broad free-answer questions to small samples, again consistent with exploratory research.

Structured response formats, in contrast, are generally fast and easy both for respondents to use and for researchers to analyze. Most important, structured response formats reduce memory and motivation problems in responding.

Some researchers hold that structured response formats make it psychologically less threatening for people to answer sensitive questions. That is, having respondents check an income category instead of writing an income amount should result in higher response rates and more accurate answers. Blair and his associates make a convincing case that this is only partly correct. They found that structured responses, compared to free-answer responses, are associated with slightly higher response rates but with more socially desirable answers. Specifically, reported amounts of wine, beer, and hard liquor consumed by consumers increased as much as 70 percent when open-ended questions were substituted for multiple choice questions—while response rates dropped less than 10 percent.[14]

Other disadvantages of structured response formats include more opportunity for respondent and researcher clerical error (such as when a college student circles the wrong answer to a multiple choice exam question by mistake). Because more words appear (in the form of response categories), responses potentially contain more errors caused by ambiguity, semantics, jargon, and inadequate frames of reference. Consumers also find it easier to guess when they don't know an answer.

Structured response formats may also lead to a **response sequence,** or **position bias, problem.** Obviously, we must array response categories

---

[14]Ed Blair et al. "How to Ask Questions About Drinking and Sex: Response Effects in Measuring Consumer Behavior," *Journal of Marketing Research* 14 (August 1977): 316–21.

in a logical, defensible order instead of jumbling them together. But this decision to array response categories in either ascending or descending order can create position bias; that is, this decision can have a significant impact on responses.

Locander and Burton describe research on separate telephone samples of approximately 250 consumers, each of whom was asked to indicate her or his 1974 income.[15] One group was given six income categories in ascending order, starting with "more than $5,000" and ending with "more than $25,000." Another group was given the same six response categories, but in descending order. And what was the effect? Much more than we might think—the first group reported an income of $12,711 while the second reported $17,184! The Census estimate for both groups was $15,235. Such results are unusual. Analyzing results from 1332 personal interviews, Powers and his associates report insignificant income, age, education, and marital status differences between two (reversed) response-option forms.[16] Carp reports similar results for personal interviews with 899 consumers age 65 and over.[17]

On balance, we realize we must be alert for potential response sequencing problems when we pretest the data collection form. If the problems are significant, we can control for them by varying response order in the questions on different versions of the final data collection form. Separate subsamples, then, would each receive a different form, allowing us to measure and adjust for response position bias in the final data analysis.

A more clear-cut disadvantage of structured response formats is the additional effort they take to construct. Not only do we need detailed knowledge to write the question, we need detailed knowledge to specify the responses. Usage rate questions, for example, require that we know maximum, minimum, and normal amounts of usage to select both the size and the number of response categories. Also, we should recognize that some fact questions could have unmanageably numerous response categories: consider identifying all possible magazines as potential responses to a magazine readership question, or listing all Chicago drug stores for a shopping pattern question.

It is no wonder, then, that many structured response formats contain an "other" category to simplify preparation. Usually this category asks respondents who check it to describe the nature of their response with a short phrase. This aids considerably in data collection form design, data analysis, and interpretation.

---

[15]William B. Locander and John P. Burton, "The Effect of Question Form on Gathering Income Data by Telephone," *Journal of Marketing Research* 13 (May 1976): 189–92.

[16]Edward A. Powers et al. "Serial Order Preference in Survey Research," *Public Opinion Quarterly* 41 (Spring 1977): 80–85.

[17]Frances M. Carp, "Position Effects on Interview Responses," *Journal of Gerontology* 29:581–87.

All of this discussion leads us to our fifth question construction guideline:

> *Prefer structured response formats to unstructured; use either with caution.*

Advantages of structured response formats usually outweigh those of unstructured if the sample is large and response alternatives are known, few in number, nonthreatening, and largely immune to response sequencing problems. Fortunately, these conditions exist for most marketing research fact questions.

Because structured response formats predominate, we should look at their construction in more detail. This discussion really started two paragraphs ago; to finish requires our last guideline:

> *Response categories should be meaningful to both respondent and researcher.*

There are several considerations. Each respondent must be able to indicate a response in one and only one category. Income response categories of $5,000 to $10,000 and $10,000 to $15,000, for example, fall short on this point. (In which category does an individual earning $10,000 place a mark?) If the question topic allows, response categories should be constructed so that responses will distribute across several categories and not cluster in just one or two: our income question some pages ago illustrates both of these ideas by using different-sized, nonoverlapping income categories across the entire income range.

Certain fact questions may be made more meaningful with the use of a "Don't Know" category. Dichotomous response categories are best used only for questions of fact that have easily recalled, concrete, and truly dichotomous answers. In other situations, response categories should include a "Don't Know" alternative.

Only in rare instances should a question of fact have more than six to eight response categories. More than this gives the data collection form a cluttered look, wastes space, and confuses some respondents. We should ask ourselves if we really need the detail provided by ten response categories—just how much more useful is it than six? More often than not our answer will favor a smaller number of response categories.

Our earlier comments on making questions meaningful are every bit as relevant here in making response categories meaningful. Response categories should relate to the respondent's experience and be free of ambiguous, jargonistic, and obscure words. Categories should not be biased to favor a desirable result. A last and very important concern is that response categories reflect research objectives. If we plan to make final report statements on families earning between $30,000 and $40,000, for example, we should use response categories that allow it.

Survey Communication Method Influences Question Form

So far we have treated questions of fact largely without regard to survey communications method. If it seemed that we were discussing only mail questionnaires, change this assumption for the second reading. We'll see from the rest of this chapter that some questions of fact take slightly different forms between mail, telephone, and personal interview methods.

MAIL SURVEY QUESTIONS OF FACT

Using a mail survey means having no interviewer, which requires having simpler questions. We must use fewer filtering questions and fewer skip instructions, shorter words, and shorter questions. Even with this advice, we should expect more consumer response error in returned questionnaires. Instead of having 100 trained interviewers each completing 50 interviews, for example, we have 5000 unskilled respondents each completing 1. An absorbing concern is for simplicity.

Having no interviewer also means a greater need for interesting initial questions to gain cooperation. The entire data collection form must look shorter, more pleasant, professional, and cohesive.[18]

Mail questionnaires use proportionately more structured response questions than personal interviews. To do otherwise requires large amounts of blank space next to each question. This white space discourages potential respondents who think, quite correctly, that much effort is needed to respond. The use of structured responses reduces this (often wasted) space and, consequently, reduces postage.

TELEPHONE SURVEY QUESTIONS OF FACT

Compared to mail surveys and personal interviews, telephone surveys are a much more abstract situation. The interviewer communicates only by voice for only a short time period. And he or she communicates without the benefit of pictures or other aids to make questions concrete. Because of this, telephone surveys tend to have fewer structured response questions and fewer response alternatives. One authority recommends limiting the number of response alternatives to not more than four or five.[19]

---

[18]A more complete discussion of mail survey questionnaires can be found in Paul L. Erdos, "Data Collection Methods: Mail Surveys," in *Handbook of Marketing Research*, ed. Robert Ferber (New York: McGraw-Hill 1974), Section 2:90–104.

[19]Stanley L. Payne, "Data Collection Methods: Telephone Surveys," in Ferber, ed., *Handbook of Marketing Research*, Section 2:105–123.

Exceeding this number confuses certain respondents and wastes precious time while interviewers read both questions and potential responses.

Open-ended questions in telephone surveys should elicit short answers. Respondents get anxious, bored, and uncooperative if the interviewer has to write more than fifteen or twenty words after each question. (This problem disappears with ethical use of a tape recorder.)

Because the interviewer is trained, telephone surveys make extensive use of filtering questions and skip instructions. Indeed, it is imperative they do so to conserve time.

PERSONAL INTERVIEW QUESTIONS OF FACT

The distinguishing feature of a personal interview survey method is the physical presence of another human being. Impact of this social situation is primarily on socially desirable responses to sensitive or threatening fact questions. Two specific questioning techniques counter this problem.

The first asks long, open-ended, and familiarly worded questions. Long questions contain more than 30 words, at least 15 of which are prefatory and counter biasing. For example, instead of asking "What was your 1981 family income?" a researcher might state:

> Some families that I interview earn lots of money each year from salaries, interest, and other sources. Other families earn very little. What is your best estimate of your family's 1981 income before taxes?

Doing so should provide less biased answers.

Familiarly worded questions use words supplied by the respondent for the sensitive topic. Thus the question is stated partly in the respondent's own words to make him or her more comfortable and to improve reporting. A first question obtains the respondent's own words:

> Different words can be used to describe the total amount of money a family earns each year from jobs and all other sources. So that you will know what I mean and feel more comfortable when I ask you, what word or words would you use?

The interviewer then substitutes the respondent's wording for income words in the income question.

Blair and his associates used this technique in their study of beer, wine, and liquor consumption cited earlier. They found the consumption almost doubled when compared to that reported with short, structured response questions that were standardly worded.[20] Even so, their reported amounts were far less than those derived from liquor tax reports.

Another way to ask sensitive fact questions in personal interviews is

---

[20]Blair et al., "Questions about Drinking and Sex."

by a **randomized response technique.** The technique presents both a sensitive and an innocuous question to respondents, who randomly respond to one question without telling the interviewer which. Suppose the two questions are:

- On the average, how many cans of beer do you drink in a 24-hour period?
- How many times have you moved from one address to another in the past ten years?

The interviewer instructs consumers to flip a coin in secret and answer the first question if it is heads, the second if it is tails. An answer is given and the interview proceeds. At no time does the interviewer know either the result of the coin flip or which question was answered.

Suppose survey results show an overall average response to both questions of 4.4. If we know from other research that the average number of address changes (the answer to the second question) is, say, 4.8, then the average number of beers consumed must be 4: All we did was reason that the sum of 4.8 plus the number of beers consumed when divided by 2 must equal 4.4; then we solved this equation. In symbols, the overall average is given by the formula:

$$\overline{X}_{overall} = (P)\overline{X}_{sensitive} + (1 - P)\,\overline{X}_{innocuous}$$

Solving, we get:

$$\overline{X}_{sensitive} = \frac{\overline{X}_{overall} - (1 - P)\,\overline{X}_{innocuous}}{P}$$

It is easy to substitute known values in the second equation for the overall average ($\overline{X}_{overall}$), and for the innocuous question average ($\overline{X}_{innocuous}$), and for P (the probability that a consumer is expected to answer the sensitive question), and confirm our answer.

Researchers can use the randomized response technique even if they do not know the average for the innocuous question—but in this case, the technique requires that they use two samples instead of one and slightly different formulas. Another variation of the randomized response technique estimates sensitive proportions instead of averages; and a third version estimates averages for only those consumers who actually engage in the sensitive behavior.[21]

Researchers should exercise a great deal of care in using the randomized response technique because results depend heavily on the method. For example, researchers have found that higher respondent cooperation

---

[21]These variations are detailed by James E. Reinmuth and Michael D. Geurts, "The Collection of Sensitive Information Using a Two-Stage, Randomized Response Model," *Journal of Marketing Research* 12 (November 1975):402–07.

TABLE 7.2
Fact Questions and Survey Communication Methods

	Question Complexity	Response Format	Response Emphasis	Techniques for Sensitive or Threatening Questions
Mail Surveys	Simple	Structured	Short answers	Long questions, open-ended responses
Telephone Surveys	Simple	Structured with few categories, or unstructured	Short, moderate answers	Long questions, familiarly worded questions, open-ended responses
Personal Interview Surveys	Simple to complex	Structured to unstructured	Short to long answers	Long questions, familiarly worded questions, open-ended responses, randomized response technique

occurs when the innocuous question deals with a socially responsible behavior, also when the respondent fully understands the randomizing device (the flip of a coin or other random process). Extensive pretesting of respondent instructions is needed for the researcher to be sure the technique will work.[22]

Validated applications of the technique—that is, usage where researchers compare randomized response results with known, true data—have been limited. Lamb and Stem report good results when estimating the number of failed courses by college students.[23] Locander, Sudman, and Bradburn report mixed results for estimating voter registration, library card ownership, bankruptcy involvement, and drunken driving violations. Their conclusion can perhaps serve as a workable generalization: the randomized response technique appears to be best used to reduce "under-reporting of socially undesirable acts" rather than to reduce "over-reporting of socially desirable acts."[24]

Until more research is completed, we cannot decide that either the randomized response technique or the long, open-ended, familiarly worded question technique is superior. Both appear to be definite improvements over the usual questioning methods—when sensitive or threatening questions must be asked.

To sum, fact questions differ from mail to telephone to personal interview surveys. We emphasize our points of comparison in Table 7.2.

---

[22]S. M. Zdep and Isabelle N. Rhodes, "Making the Randomized Response Technique Work," *Public Opinion Quarterly* 40 (Winter 1976–77):531–37.

[23]Charles W. Lamb, Jr., and Donald E. Stem, Jr., "An Empirical Validation of the Randomized Response Technique," *Journal of Marketing Research* 15 (November 1978):616–21. See also Zdep et al., "The Validity of the Randomized Response Technique," *Public Opinion Quarterly* 43 (Winter 1979): 544–49.

[24]William Locander, Seymour Sudman, and Norman Bradburn, "An Investigation of Interview Method, Threat, and Response Distortion," *Journal of the American Statistical Association* 71 (June 1976): 269–75.

Chapter Summary

Marketing researchers constantly measure both respondent behavior and socioeconomic characteristics. The former term identifies what the respondents do; the latter, who they are. Many types of questions exist within each of these two categories—for short, we call all of them questions of fact.

Concerns in developing questions of fact center on validity and reliability. In addition to social desirability and item nonresponse, such things as question topic, wording, and response format also influence validity and reliability. This influence can be minimized by proper research practice, that is, by employing certain research tactics and adhering to our six guidelines for fact question construction. We'll see in the next two chapters that the same six guidelines aid in writing questions of psychological characteristics.

How questions of fact are asked partly depends on how they are communicated. Mail surveys, telephone interviews, and personal interviews all require subtle differences in questions of fact. Personal interviews, in particular, may seek answers to sensitive fact questions by using either long, open-ended, familiarly worded construction or the randomized response technique.

Chapter Review

KEY TERMS

Questions of fact

Validity

Reliability

Filtering question

Skip instruction

Free-answer question

Aided-recall question

Social desirability

Item nonresponse

Multiple choice question

Response position bias

Familiarly worded question

Randomized response technique

DISCUSSION QUESTIONS

1. What distinguishes a question of fact from a question of psychological characteristics?

2. Why should a marketing segment almost always be described partly in socioeconomic terms?

3. Why does observation as a data collection method show a lower potential for social desirability problems?

4. Of the three aspects of fact questions that require guidelines—question topic, wording, and response format—which is the most crucial in obtaining accurate data from consumers?

5. How do research objectives influence questions of fact?

6. How do data collection methods influence questions of fact?

7. Why does the randomized response technique work better when the innocuous question concerns a socially responsible behavior rather than a neutral or sensitive behavior? What should be true about frequency distributions of responses to the innocuous question and the sensitive question?

8

Questions of Psychological Characteristics: Qualitative Data

What do you think about Ford automobiles? In the next seven days, do you intend to go to a movie? Overall, how satisfied are you with your new Gillette hair drier? How long does the warranty last for your new Sansui receiver?

These four questions illustrate our topic for Chapters 8 and 9—the measurement of consumer attitudes, purchase intentions, satisfaction, and knowledge. All are psychological characteristics. All are central variables in models that explain consumer behavior.[1] To guide our discussion, a shortened model of consumer behavior appears in Figure 8.1.

Psychological Characteristics That Influence Buying Behavior

In the model, **knowledge** is the consumer's awareness and understanding of past consumption experiences. It is acquired information about products, stores, advertisements, prices, and other marketing activities. Consumers' knowledge of these things greatly influences marketing decision makers as they design products and packages, measure advertising effectiveness, and set prices.

---

[1]Standards on the topic are James F. Engel, Roger D. Blackwell, and David T. Kollat, *Consumer Behavior*, 3rd ed. (Hinsdale, Ill.: The Dryden Press, 1978) and John D. Howard, *Consumer Behavior: Application of Theory* (New York: McGraw-Hill, 1977).

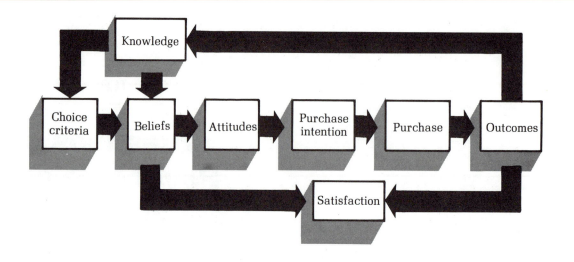

FIGURE 8.1
A shortened model of consumer behavior

Choice criteria are attributes of consumption alternatives that consumers use to make comparisons. For example, choice criteria in selecting a department store (one such consumption alternative) may include such attributes as distance, prices, merchandise carried, service, store layout, and parking. Choice criteria in choosing a bottle of salad dressing are obviously much different.

Beliefs are consumer views of a consumption alternative's performance on various choice criteria. They are views, or convictions, that join a consumption alternative (for example, one of several accessible department stores) to each choice criterion. In our department store example, a consumer may have several beliefs about the consumption alternative (often called a belief object); he or she may believe that store A is the closest, that store A's prices are higher than competitors', that it carries a wider assortment of merchandise, and so on.

The model shows that knowledge influences both the choice criteria and the beliefs of a consumer. Certainly. Suppose someone has extensive knowledge and experience relating to car stereos. In fact, suppose he even worked part-time selling them and can cite performance specifications for every major brand and model. It's easy to see that his car stereo choice criteria and beliefs would differ greatly from those of a first-time purchaser. Similarly, knowledge influences all choice criteria and beliefs that consumers use to purchase any product.

Choice criteria and beliefs combine to form attitudes. We define an

attitude as simply a consumer's overall like or dislike of an alternative. More precisely, an attitude is a "learned predisposition to respond consistently in a favorable [or unfavorable] manner with respect to a given alternative."[2] "Alternative" in the definition continues to mean products, stores, advertisements, salespersons, price, and other aspects of marketing. "Learned" means that an attitude is a result of both general and specific experience with the alternative. "Predisposition to respond" means the behavioral likelihood of response, where the response may be anything from a consumer's verbal statement to actual purchase and use. "Consistently" means the response is stable over time and consonant with other psychological characteristics. Finally, "favorable" (or unfavorable) means that responses reflect elements of like (or dislike) with respect to the alternative.

It is important for us to distinguish between an attitude toward an alternative and an attitude toward some behavior connected with the alternative. The first is truly an attitude while the second is more correctly an intention. While the distinction may seem small, it is significant—it is the difference between liking something and intending to do something about it. A person may like an advertisement very much but not intend to buy the advertised product. Or, she may dislike the advertisement very much but intend to buy the product anyway.

Managers consider consumer choice criteria, beliefs, and attitudes extremely important in making marketing decisions. The attributes that consumers include in their choice criteria, how the consumers rate each attribute's importance, and how beliefs differ by consumer segment are all common and important marketing research topics. In particular, consumer beliefs about a product and competing products have significant implications for product design, advertising, and pricing decisions. Marketing decision makers may attempt to change the choice criteria, the beliefs, and consequently, the attitudes of consumers toward both their own and other firms' products. Or, decision makers may attempt to change their products to conform to these psychological characteristics.

An attitude leads to or influences purchase intention. By **purchase intention** we mean the consumer's subjective probability of product purchase during some specified time period. As seen by the consumer, a purchase intention is how likely it is that she or he will buy. Decision makers find such information useful again in evaluating the effect of marketing strategies, either before or after putting them into operation. Purchase intentions also help forecast future demand.[3]

Purchase in the model consists of the behavioral act of buying. It is

[2]Engel, Blackwell, and Kollat, *Consumer Behavior*, p. 388.

[3]Donald G. Morrison, "Purchase Intentions and Purchase Behavior," *Journal of Marketing* 43 (Spring 1979): 65–74.

the only part of the model that can be directly seen by a researcher; all other parts are mental. Obviously, marketing decision makers consider purchase a behavior of great importance.

Outcomes we limit to mean mental results of buying. Two outcomes interest us: knowledge (previously discussed) and satisfaction. **Satisfaction** results from the consumer's comparison of prepurchase beliefs with postpurchase performance. If differences are noted, the consumer is either pleased or displeased. Because marketers have only recently become explicitly interested in satisfaction, its measurement is less well formalized than other psychological characteristics in the model. Despite this, satisfaction is an important concept in evaluating a marketing strategy. Low satisfaction usually means a low level of repeat purchases.

We can readily see that all these consumer psychological characteristics apply further to explaining *industrial* buyer behavior. For example, we could be interested in measuring attitudes, purchase intentions, and satisfaction from samples of retail buyers, industrial engineers, or purchasing agents. These people also possess knowledge, choice criteria, and beliefs relevant to purchases and satisfaction.

Thus, like behavior and socioeconomic characteristics in Chapter 7, psychological characteristics show widespread application. However, psychological characteristics do differ from behavior and socioeconomic characteristics. For one thing, psychological characteristics are more abstract: they may not be seen, touched, or otherwise directly sensed. For another, their measurement almost always requires tailor-made instead of standard questions. This happens because psychological characteristics exist only with respect to some object or class of objects that changes from one research project to the next. One time we might be interested in peanut butter and consumer behavior, the next time it may be banks. Clearly, we require different questions.

What we'll soon see is that despite project differences in measurement content, there are constancies in measurement process. In fact, we measure all these psychological characteristics for either consumers or industrial buyers using only two basic methods: qualitative or quantitative measurements. Let us proceed with a discussion of these two methods without further introduction—nothing can be more interesting than learning how to find out about people.

Qualitative Psychological Research

Qualitative psychological research measures psychological characteristics not by numbers but by words. Such research is often described as subjective, unstructured, and intensive when compared to quantitative psychological research. Differences are more in degree than in kind, however.

Qualitative research has three basic purposes:

1. To generate or select hypotheses about consumer behavior for later investigation by quantitative psychological research.

2. To investigate aspects of consumer behavior when quantitative psychological research is inappropriate.

3. To understand consumers from the standpoint of consumers.[4]

Projects having purposes other than these ought not to use qualitative psychological research methods.

The first qualitative method we discuss is a depth interview. Suppose that a consumer is meeting privately with an interviewer in a comfortable marketing research setting. After becoming acquainted and discussing writing instruments in general, the interviewer determines that she uses Bic pens, then asks her to tell him about them. She might respond that they are pretty good writing instruments, and always work, but that she really hasn't thought that much about them. The interviewer says that that's not unusual and that she seems to feel they are reliable. She agrees, explaining that they never clog up or run out of ink without warning. The interviewer asks what she means by warning. She explains that the clear barrel of the pen is nice because she can judge fairly well when she needs a new one.

DEPTH INTERVIEWS

A short pause follows. After a while, the interviewer asks if there's anything more she could say about Bic pens. They're really cheap, she offers. Is this important? She answers, and the interviewer asks if cheap is more important than reliable. She responds at length while the interviewer listens. Finally the interviewer asks if there are other things she considers important when she buys a pen. She answers. When satisfied that the consumer can go no further on this line of questioning, the interviewer asks about competing pens and what she thinks of them. The two of them proceed in this relatively unstructured manner until the interviewer calls a halt after over an hour together. A summary of the interviewer's behavior appears in Exhibit 8.1.

The interview is tape recorded (with the respondent's prior permission, of course) and perhaps even video taped. The entire process is fairly interesting, flexible, and personal. Later someone transcribes all respondents' responses for reading by trained consumer psychologists. They subjectively interpret what was said (and not said) in the interviews, based on their understanding of consumer behavior theory. They may identify and count key words and thoughts from the transcripts as part of a more quantitative, content analysis.

[4]Bobby J. Calder, "Focus Groups and the Nature of Qualitative Marketing Research," *Journal of Marketing Research* 14 (August 1977): 353–64.

EXHIBIT 8.1
Interviewer Behavior in a Depth Interview

Provides a comfortable environment.

Allows the interview to proceed along respondent's train of thought in respondent's own words.

Reflects respondent's feelings as summary statements.

Occasionally asks probing questions to investigate new topics or clarify meaning.

May use a topic outline but only to make sure certain topics are covered sometime during the interview.

Avoids evaluative comments or other inhibiting behaviors.

Waits out pauses to allow respondent time to think.

Lets respondent do the talking.

FOCUS GROUP INTERVIEWS

We can conclude from our depth interview example that the interviewer functions mostly to listen. We might further conclude that the interviewer could just as easily listen to a group of consumers as to only one—to save time and money. Such a group situation is called a focus group interview and is used in marketing research more commonly than depth interviews.

A typical **focus group interview** consists of an interviewer or moderator questioning and listening to a group of eight to twelve consumers, again in a comfortable setting. With participants' prior approval, a hidden observer or mechanical device might be used to record behaviors that the moderator could miss because of the number of participants.

Before the interview, group members are screened to make sure all have had experience with the focus group topic. All group members ought to have not participated in other focus group interviews for at least six months before the session—unless the research design requires it.[5] All group members ought to be strangers. If the basic purpose of the focus group interview is to understand the consumer from his or her standpoint, all group members should have similar socioeconomic characteristics (social class, stage in the family life cycle, sex, and age). To obtain a representative sample of the general population, then, requires several different groups. Our other qualitative research purposes noted in the list at the beginning of this section tolerate more diverse people in a group.[6]

---

[5]Reasons cited by a practitioner for a focus group's meeting more than once include the need to let ideas form over time, the assignment of take-home tasks that require home activity, and insufficient trust and rapport developing during the first session; see Robert J. Kaden, "Incomplete Use Keeps Focus Group from Producing Optimum Results," *Marketing News* (September 9, 1977), p. 4. Advocating new members for each focus group session is Myril D. Axelrod, "10 Essentials for Good Qualitative Research," *Marketing News* (March 14, 1975), pp. 10–11.

[6]Calder, "Focus Groups," p. 362.

Thousands of focus group interviews are conducted each year. Some specific applications include:

- Identifying products that a major gasoline producer might sell in its service stations to increase sales.
- Identifying consumer reactions to a bank's planned introduction of a new, fully automated bank teller machine.
- Determining key phrases consumers use to describe needs satisfied by soft drinks.
- Determining why test market results for a new carbonated fruit juice found low levels of repeat purchase.
- Identifying tire retailers' reactions to a new fiber glass radial tire in order to design sales and merchandising aids.
- Identifying bases for consumer resistance to a utility company's planned price increase.
- Identifying potential reasons for a sales decline of a firm's luncheon meats and wieners.
- Determining sexual connotations of cigar smoking that could be used for advertising cigars.[7]

Note that two of the applications show focus group interviews being conducted after management action and not before. This highlights a growing application of focus group interviews—that of interpreting previously collected quantitative data. Notice also that focus group members can be people other than consumers. Middlemen, decision makers, and others in an organization make excellent focus group members when a researcher faces our first qualitative research purpose, generating or selecting hypotheses.

Even though focus group members do most of the talking, group moderators decidedly influence the interview's success. The moderator should be able to establish a feeling of trust and confidence in the group. She or he must be flexible and well prepared, having studied a topic outline that shows an understanding of both the consumer and the marketing problem. She should be an excellent listener and able to elicit comments from shy members. Moderators attain such skills only after training and practice.

Success depends in particular on the moderator and qualitative

---

[7]The first five applications come from Danny N. Bellenger, Kenneth L. Bernhardt, and Jac L. Goldstucker, *Qualitative Research in Marketing*, (Chicago: American Marketing Association, 1976), pp. 20–23. Applications 6 and 7 come from Keith K. Cox, James B. Higginbotham, and John Burton, "Applications of Focus Group Interviews in Marketing," *Journal of Marketing* 40 (January 1976): 77–80. Application 8 comes from Eleanor Holtzman, "Use Groups for Parity Products, Those Meeting Psychological Needs," *Marketing News* (August 12, 1977), p. 6.

research purpose. If the purpose is to understand the consumer from his or her standpoint (the third purpose listed), the moderator must be able to place herself in the consumer's shoes. She must "become the consumer" and experience consumer feelings, interpretations, and decisions. In contrast, if research purpose is to generate hypotheses (the first purpose on the list) or to investigate consumer behavior when quantitative research is inappropriate (the second purpose), the moderator must stay removed from the consumer. She must be aloof, objective, and "possess a high degree of sophistication with scientific theory."[8] Such theory would include consumer behavior, psychology, sociology, social psychology, and even managerial economics. The interviewer needs much training and practice for these research purposes.

The moderator's interviewing technique is very important in meeting our second research purpose, when research is being conducted because quantitative research cannot be. This often happens when consumers' real feelings and motivations are at least partly subconscious and they provide superficial responses to direct questions. It also occurs when consumers provide socially desirable responses. In both cases, the focus group moderator conducts the interview much as a highly skilled clinical psychologist would, with the result that group members "reveal their inner experience in a way that is susceptible to clinical judgment and therefore clinical scientific interpretation."[9] This result is the usual outcome of most depth interviews as well.

PROJECTIVE METHODS

The third and last qualitative research method we discuss consists of a group of related procedures called projective methods. They, like depth and focus group interviews, were borrowed from clinical psychology and adapted for marketing research. Projective methods measure psychological characteristics when disclosure is unlikely with the other qualitative (and quantitative) psychological research methods. For example, no matter how capable the interviewer, a consumer might resist divulging choice criteria, beliefs, and intentions when asked about a highly personal product. Because of the extremely sensitive and subconscious nature of these psychological characteristics, the consumer may find it psychologically impossible to provide information. Such research topics occur frequently enough in marketing research to warrant our discussion.

Three commonly used projective methods are word association, sentence completion, and construction. All apply one or more special procedures in the attempt to measure true psychological characteristics. One such procedure is to note the speed of the response: if the respondent takes too much time, responses likely contain rationalizations instead of truth. A second is disguised content: if neutral research topics are mixed

---

[8]Calder, "Focus Groups," p. 362.
[9]Ibid. pp. 357–58.

with sensitive topics, consumers are less likely to feel threatened by the sensitive topics. A third is asking consumers to respond from the viewpoint of some generalized other person: instructions may ask consumers to answer "the way most women on your block would answer instead of how you would personally." A fourth is using ambiguous research materials that allow consumers to make a subjective and also less threatening interpretation.

Word Association.   The word association method asks individual consumers to respond to a stimulus word or phrase with the first word or phrase that comes to mind. After the response, a second stimulus word follows and the process repeats. Suppose a researcher is interested in people's beliefs about hair pieces. Stimulus words might be:

- Coffee . . .
- Ford automobiles . . .
- Tea . . .
- Hair pieces . . .
- Volkswagens . . .

A representative sample of consumers individually listens to each word and makes a response. An interviewer records each response before reading the next word. If a response follows the stimulus word by more than two or three seconds, it is disregarded: the consumer is probably not giving his true reaction.

Information from a word association test is rather limited. The researcher would usually supplement word association results with later depth or focus group interviews. Of the two, depth interviews are probably better, allowing each consumer to explain responses to perhaps one neutral word and the research topic word privately.

Sentence Completion.   A sentence completion method simply extends the word association technique to sentence stems. Consumers, either individually or in a group, listen to or read sentence stems and then complete them. In a group, consumers usually write their responses on separate data collection forms. Continuing our hair piece example, sentence stems might be:

- A good cup of coffee . . .
- Most Ford automobiles . . .
- Iced tea at our house . . .
- People who buy a hair piece . . .
- Volkswagens last . . .

Time limits may or may not be imposed for responses to each stem.

Notice that sentence completion uses a more directed set of stimuli than word association. Thus, researchers can find out what consumers think about people who buy hair pieces or what consumers think about hair piece quality or about any pertinent hair piece attribute.

Construction.   The construction method simply extends sentence completion by asking consumers to make a longer response to a more ambiguous stimulus. Instead of completing just a sentence, a sample member might respond at length orally or write a paragraph or two about the stimulus. For example, a bald man might be shown a cartoon, drawing, or photograph of someone putting on a hair piece and asked to summarize what that person is thinking. Or, he might be presented with the hair piece itself, told to examine it, and then asked to write a description of its owner. Underlying the method is the assumption that

> the respondent's story about the stimulus is based on personal experiences and observations from conscious and unconscious images, even though he is relating a story about the people in the picture. Thus, the pictures serve to encourage projection and delve into important attitudes and motivations.[10]

Even though each consumer's interpretation of the stimulus is different, certain thoughts and words from a sample of consumers will recur. These become the basis for interpretation when trained consumer psychologists make an analysis.

PERSPECTIVE ON QUALITATIVE METHODS   Depth interviews, focus group interviews, and projective methods have some common features. All attempt to learn about a few consumers in great detail. All result in rich and varied data expressed in consumers' own words. Most require one or more trained consumer psychologists who subjectively analyze and interpret results.[11]

All qualitative methods share three common purposes, which limit their application. Currently, by far the dominant method is focus group interviews, used to understand the consumer from her or his viewpoint. Properly conducted, focus group interviews offer several advantages over depth interviews and projective techniques. Several come from the group interaction process itself:

- Synergism—the group's ability to produce results in greater quantity and diversity than the sum of separate individual efforts.

---

[10]Bellenger, Bernhardt, and Goldstucker, *Qualitative Research in Marketing*, p. 35.

[11]On the other hand, focus group interviews frequently use paper and pencil quantitative measures as part of their data collection. Two researchers report the use of only quantitative measures in their projective research: Dan H. Robertson and Robert W. Joselyn, "Projective Techniques in Research," *Journal of Advertising Research* 14 (October 1974): 27–31.

- Snowballing—the group's ability to take a small point made by one member, add to it, and reveal significant insights.
- Stimulation—the elements of general excitement, enthusiasm, and even competition created by a group of similar consumers or other members.
- Security—the feeling of safety in numbers that allows a member to discuss sensitive topics with group support.
- Spontaneity—the idea that after the moderator asks a question, only interested members respond, making answers more meaningful, less forced, and less conventional.[12]

Additionally, we noted earlier that focus groups allow researchers to collect data from several consumers at once, saving time and money.

Improperly conducted, focus groups can be worse than no research at all. Focus groups contain shy group members reluctant to participate, small sample sizes, nonrandomly selected members, and only participants able to spend at least 1½ hours at a central research facility. The moderator affects what group members say by the questions he asks, his facial expressions, and his background and training. Results often depend on who interprets the data and on what the interpreter considers important enough to report.

Despite these shortcomings, focus group interviews are extremely popular—so popular, in fact, that they may be "smothering" other more appropriate techniques.[13] This inappropriate application happens, for example, when the results of focus group interviews lead to management decisions that should have used quantitative research results. This happens more than it should: decision makers, it seems, are often prone to take focus group results and run with them. This is a misuse of qualitative research if the marketing problem can be better solved with quantitative research.

Collecting Qualitative Data

Beyond producing data in a common form, data collection operations for qualitative psychological research methods share several other features: All try to avoid anything that would inhibit consumer responses. All lack the structure that is so prominent in collecting experimental and survey data. All take much time to collect detailed information from rather small samples. All require special facilities and need highly trained interviewers. Let us look more closely at these last two similarities.

---

[12]John M. Hess, "Group Interviewing," in *New Science of Planning*, R. L. King ed. (Chicago: American Marketing Association, 1968), p. 194.

[13]Sid Levy, "Focus Group Magic may be Smothering Other Research Tools," *Marketing News* (October 24, 1975), p. 1 ff.

FACILITIES FOR COLLECTING QUALITATIVE DATA

One characteristic of facilities for collecting qualitative data is privacy. Because qualitative data always describe personal beliefs, feelings, and reactions and because qualitative data occasionally describe sensitive topics, facilities must show consideration for participants' privacy. This means that rooms should be separate, relatively soundproof, and secure from interruptions.

A second characteristic is that facilities be comfortable. Comfortable facilities help break down barriers to communication between interviewer and consumers. Moreover, because qualitative data collection generally takes much time, comfortable facilities delay the point at which consumers become restless, tired, and prone to error. Thus, many depth interview and projective technique facilities will look more like a lounge than a laboratory. Many focus group interview facilities will look like tidy living rooms in a middle-class home. Such facilities usually contain upholstered furniture, coffee tables, pictures, plants, and other furnishings. Some even have an adjoining kitchen to prepare refreshments for the group or to test new food products.

A third characteristic is that facilities allow unobtrusive monitoring of data collection operations. Rooms will usually be fully wired for audio and video recording and also contain a one-way mirror for unobtrusive observation (known to consumers before participating). Wiring and mirrors also allow other researchers and even the decision maker to draft pertinent comments and questions for transmittal to the moderator at a suitable time during the session.

INTERVIEWERS FOR COLLECTING QUALITATIVE DATA

A researcher must hire, train, motivate, and control interviewers in collecting qualitative data. For projective techniques, the hiring criteria are similar to those discussed with other primary data collection operations (experiments, telephone interviews, and personal interviews), and apply almost completely. And even for depth and focus group interviews, we see some commonality in hiring criteria. That is, good depth and focus group interviewers should have pleasant appearances and voices, like to meet people, take direction well, and possess a genuine interest in the project. Here, we noted that they should be able to reflect and summarize a respondent's feelings, wait out pauses, avoid evaluative comments, and establish a feeling of trust and confidence. They also should be quick thinkers and good listeners. Finally, in addition (and depending on research purpose), focus group moderators must be able either to take the role of the consumer or to remain aloof and objective. Socioeconomic characteristics seem much less important than possession of these abilities, almost all of which require training.

The training of depth and focus group interviewers consists partly of exposure to both general and specific topic matter. At the minimum, general topic matter would include undergraduate courses in psychology, sociology, social psychology, buyer behavior, and marketing research.

Specific topic matter would include decision maker operations, responsibilities, and expectations of the research. Training should also discuss objectives for the qualitative research and the outline sheet that guides the interviews. The latter item should show a schedule of interview processes, including blocks of time for warmup, actual discussion, and summary, besides listing specific topics to be covered in the interview. Training should also teach certain skills. In addition to possessing those skills noted as hiring criteria, interviewers must also be able to probe for true responses, to stimulate creative thinking and responding, and to summarize and report results. Acquiring these skills will require several weeks for instruction, practice, and on the job training. Finally, training should consist partly of forming professional attitudes. Well-trained interviewers should see themselves as professionals who conduct the interview in an ethical manner and provide the decision maker with an unbiased service.

Motivating and controlling depth and focus group interviewers occurs in much the same manner as with telephone and personal interviewers. That is, the researcher should hire and train competent interviewers, set deadlines, and insist on the freedom to observe sessions along with the decision maker. However, professional interviewers may sometimes insist that such observers attend either all sessions "including the briefing and debriefing sessions or stay away completely" to prevent their making quick decisions based on only partial results.[14] Of course, the use of audio or video tape that is largely unique to depth and focus group interviews also functions as a control mechanism. And, because of these techniques' much smaller sample sizes, it is quite important that the researcher use some sampling procedure that controls participant characteristics.

Chapter Summary

A model of consumer behavior should include such variables as consumer attitudes, knowledge, purchase intentions, purchase, and satisfaction. Of these, only the behavioral act of purchase is not a psychological characteristic. Marketing researchers commonly measure psychological characteristics either qualitatively or quantitatively.

Qualitative measurement methods produce data largely expressed in words. Such results fulfill one of three qualitative research purposes:

1. To generate or select hypotheses about consumer behavior for later investigation by quantitative psychological research.

2. To investigate aspects of consumer behavior when quantitative psychological research is inappropriate.

3. To understand consumers from the standpoint of consumers.

---

[14]The quotation is attributed to Richard A. Drossler, Drossler Research Corporation, in "Moderators Focus on Groups," *Marketing News* (September 10, 1976), p. 14.

To satisfy these purposes, marketing researchers use depth interviews, focus group interviews, and projective methods. Most used are focus group interviews to understand the consumer from her or his viewpoint. Beyond method details, the three methods require researcher attention to facilities and interviewers. Good facilities should be private, comfortable, and allow unobtrusive monitoring of activities. Capable interviewers should be well trained, motivated, and controlled.

In contrast, quantitative measurement methods produce data largely expressed in numbers. Our next chapter discusses several such methods, as rating scales for psychological characteristics.

Chapter Review

KEY TERMS

Knowledge	Qualitative psychological research
Choice criteria	Satisfaction
Beliefs	Depth interview
Attitude	Focus group interview
Purchase intention	Projective methods

DISCUSSION QUESTIONS

1. In our shortened model of consumer behavior, which variable is most important to marketing decision makers? On what does your answer depend?

2. What advantages does a focus group interview have over a depth interview?

3. A good focus group interviewer should possess much the same characteristics as members in the group. Discuss.

4. A depth interview following a word association test might discuss a consumer's responses to one neutral word and to the research topic word. Why discuss responses to the neutral word?

5. A Philadelphia-based researcher finds it necessary to conduct some focus group interviews with housewives in New Holland, Pennsylvania. What is wrong with holding interviews in a motel room?

6. Interviewers for qualitative research are born, not made. Discuss.

7. Qualitative measurement of psychological characteristics largely lacks scientific methodology. Discuss.

Additional Readings

Bellenger, Danny N.; Bernhardt, Kenneth L.; and Goldstucker, Jac L. *Qualitative Research in Marketing*. Chicago: American Marketing Association, 1976.
   This short book covers all types of qualitative research in marketing from both a descriptive and an applied point of view. Included is an edited tran-

script of an actual focus group interview followed by hypotheses derived from the interview for purposes of later quantitative research.

Engel, James F.; Blackwell, Roger D.; and Kollat, David T. *Consumer Behavior,* 3rd ed. Hinsdale, Ill.: The Dryden Press, 1978.

As the standard work in consumer behavior, this book discusses elements of our shortened model of consumer behavior much more completely. It also provides similar discussion for a host of other psychological and sociological characteristics.

Questions of Psychological Characteristics: Quantitative Data

Beliefs, attitudes, purchase intentions, satisfaction, and knowledge are usually measured in marketing research by quantitative psychological research. The conventional method uses some type of paper and pencil rating scale presented to a large sample of people. Each person privately checks or makes a similar response to items on the scale. The interpreter of the test gives each response a numerical score which becomes part of a mathematical analysis. Compared to qualitative methods, rating scales show more objectivity, structure, and detail. They yield numeric, narrow, and piecemeal descriptions of psychological characteristics rather than the nonnumeric, broad, and holistic descriptions produced by qualitative methods.

We proceed by examining decisions that attend the construction of all rating scales. We then focus on specific rating scale applications—that is, on the use of rating scales to measure beliefs, attitudes, purchase intentions, satisfaction, and knowledge. We conclude the chapter with sections discussing the quantitative measurement of consumer life styles and some guidelines in psychological characteristic measurement.

Rating Scale Construction

A **rating scale** contains a set of items having response categories that indicate relative intensity of a psychological characteristic. To illustrate, suppose we want to learn consumers' beliefs about Duncans, a large   215

EXHIBIT 9.1

Semantic Differential Scale to Measure Consumers Beliefs About Duncans Department Store

	Extremely	Quite	Some-what	Some-what	Quite	Extremely	
Fair prices	☐	☐	☐	☐	☐	☐	Unfair prices
Messy	☐	☐	☐	☐	☐	☐	Neat
Friendly personnel	☐	☐	☐	☐	☐	☐	Unfriendly personnel
Inconvenient location	☐	☐	☐	☐	☐	☐	Convenient location

department store. After we determine relevant attributes on which consumers compare stores, we might construct a semantic differential rating scale like the one in Exhibit 9.1.

A **semantic differential scale** consists of a set of opposite terms or phrases separated by a stepped set of response categories. Each pair of opposites (that is, each rating item) describes an attribute of the object to be rated (in this case, the object is Duncans). Consumers would be instructed to place an X in the box that most closely represents their feelings for each pair of opposites. For example, a respondent believing that Duncans had "somewhat fair" prices would mark the third box; another believing that Duncans had "somewhat unfair" prices would mark the fourth. Our scale is "forced choice" in that it has no middle position to allow a neutral response.

Another example of a rating scale appears in Exhibit 9.2. Suppose here we want to determine the relative importance of the various store choice attributes in Exhibit 9.1. Consumers would be instructed to circle the designation that most closely represents the importance each attribute has in deciding at which store they shop.

In contrast with the simplicity of the instructions to consumers

EXHIBIT 9.2

A Rating Scale to Measure Relative Importance of Choice Attributes

	Not Important	Slightly Important	Important	Very Important	Extremely Important
Fair prices	NI	SI	I	VI	EI
Neat	NI	SI	I	VI	EI
Friendly personnel	NI	SI	I	VI	EI
Convenient location	NI	SI	I	VI	EI

responding to the scale, the construction of the scale is complicated and exacting work. Our two examples result from three major scale construction decisions: response anchor selection, number of response categories, and rating item selection.

The choice of **response anchors** (the words used to describe the response categories) depends on what the scale measures and how consumers interpret the anchors themselves. We see from our two examples that what the scale measures changes from intensities of feelings about the four choice criteria (as applied to Duncans Department Store) to intensities of importance of these choice criteria (in deciding at which store consumers shop). We'll see from the rest of this chapter that several other types of anchors are possible, depending on what the scale measures.

RESPONSE ANCHOR SELECTION

Equally important, response anchors depend on consumer interpretations. All other things being equal, we would like consumers to interpret anchors as nearly equal-sized measurement steps or gradations. As an aid in anchor selection, Table 9.1 presents mean scale values and standard

TABLE 9.1
Scale Value Means and Standard Deviations of Selected Adjectives

Adjective	Mean (s.d)	Adjective	Mean (s.d.)
Terrible	1.28 (0.53)	O. K.	10.94 (2.12)
Horrible	1.37 (0.83)	Slightly good	11.67 (2.44)
Awful	1.39 (0.74)	All right	11.76 (1.94)
Exceptionally poor	1.81 (0.93)	Nice	12.76 (1.86)
Extremely poor	2.02 (0.96)	Reasonably good	13.48 (2.42)
Very bad	2.06 (1.00)	Pleasant	13.80 (2.04)
Very poor	2.06 (0.98)	Fairly good	13.82 (2.29)
Unacceptable	2.80 (2.52)	Moderately good	14.26 (1.93)
Unusually poor	2.82 (1.51)	Good	14.96 (1.81)
Remarkably poor	2.91 (1.46)	Fine	15.35 (2.78)
Quite poor	3.13 (1.56)	Delightful	15.65 (3.13)
Bad	3.72 (1.57)	Quite good	15.78 (1.80)
Unpleasant	4.15 (2.08)	Very good	17.32 (1.77)
Poor	4.39 (1.77)	Unusually good	17.76 (2.15)
Reasonably poor	5.00 (1.52)	Wonderful	17.83 (2.39)
Moderately poor	5.41 (1.90)	Terrific	18.00 (2.77)
Not very good	5.43 (2.36)	Remarkably good	18.19 (1.76)
Fairly poor	5.57 (1.94)	Exceptionally good	18.50 (2.04)
Slightly poor	6.46 (2.34)	Extremely good	18.57 (1.86)
Mediocre	8.82 (2.22)	Tremendous	18.78 (2.37)
So-so	9.44 (1.76)	Outstanding	18.85 (2.11)
Neutral	10.28 (1.42)	Excellent	19.26 (1.89)
Average	10.33 (1.83)	Fantastic	19.26 (2.07)
Acceptable	10.59 (2.12)	Superb	19.35 (1.74)
Fair	10.71 (2.25)	Superior	19.80 (1.52)

Source: Albert R. Wildt and Michael B. Mazis, "Determinants of Scale Response: Label Versus Position," *Journal of Marketing Research* 15 (May 1978): 262.

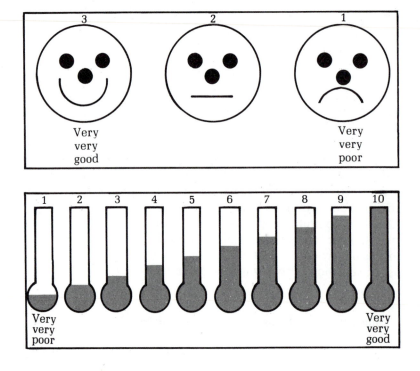

FIGURE 9.1
Face and thermometer anchors

deviations for fifty adjectives. These values were supplied by a group of undergraduate college students who rated each adjective on a 21-point scale labeled "the best (worst) thing I can say about a product" at the endpoints.[1] Similar research with other groups of subjects should produce similar results.[2]

If we intended the scale for young children, we would need different anchors. "Faces" and "thermometer" anchors are usually more appropriate than the more symbolic word anchors; see Figure 9.1 for examples. Even then, the scale will need careful explanation, especially for children under age 8.[3]

[1] Albert R. Wildt and Michael B. Mazis, "Determinants of Scale Response: Label Versus Position," *Journal of Marketing Research* 15 (May 1978): 261–67.

[2] See James H. Myers and W. Gregory Warner, "Semantic Properties of Selected Evaluation Adjectives," *Journal of Marketing Research* 5 (November 1968): 409–12; and Robert A. Mittelstaedt, "Semantic Properties of Selected Evaluative Adjectives: Other Evidence," *Journal of Marketing Research* 8 (May 1971): 236–37.

[3] Fred Cutler, "To Meet Criticism of TV Ads. Researchers Find New Ways to Measure Children's Attitudes," *Marketing News* (January 27, 1978), p. 16.

A second major decision in rating scale construction concerns how many response steps or categories will yield the best, and most manageable, portrait of consumer response. More categories provide finer measurement; a simple analogy illustrates the point: suppose we have rules marked in inches, with no smaller gradations. Measuring the length of anyone's foot with such an instrument yields coarse results, except for the few who happen to be lucky. The same is true when rating scales use just a few categories. The small number of categories forces respondents to "round" their responses to the next higher or lower category and thereby introduces random, rounding error.[4] In addition, some respondents so dislike being forced into coarse categories that they make their response between two categories, producing a coding dilemma.

Another disadvantage of using only a few categories is that it artificially restricts the range of correlation coefficients calculated from the data. Because we have not yet discussed correlation as a data analysis method, we limit our discussion here (see Chapter 16 for more detail). Consider this as an introduction: a correlation coefficient could be calculated between heights and weights as measured from a group of consumers. Or, in our first rating scale example, a correlation coefficient could be calculated between consumer's price beliefs and their location beliefs. The resulting correlation coefficient is a number between -1.0 and $+1.0$ that expresses the amount of agreement. A correlation coefficient of 0.9 indicates high agreement, one of 0.1 indicates almost none, and one of -0.9 indicates high disagreement.

Martin has shown that correlation coefficients between two 6-category rating scale items actually has an upper limit of 0.828 when the true correlation is 0.900.[5] With the same true correlation, an actual maximum correlation for two 2-category items is only 0.711. The danger, then, in using scales with only a few categories is that a researcher may interpret a correlation coefficient as indicating only a modest relationship when it is actually much stronger.

Now, before constructing a rating scale with 26 response categories, we should be alerted to some other considerations. Scales having a large number of response categories obviously take up more room on the data collection form. They increase the time it takes for consumers to make a response, they tire consumers, and they increase item nonresponse. Consequently, a good guideline is to construct rating scales having 5 to 9 response categories.[6] Most applied marketing research projects use rating scales having 4, 5, 6, or 7.

---

[4]Donald R. Lehmann and James Hulbert, "Are Three-Point Scales Always Good Enough?" *Journal of Marketing Research* 9 (November 1972): 444–46.

[5]Warren S. Martin, "Effects of Scaling on the Correlation Coefficient: Additional Considerations," *Journal of Marketing Research* 15 (May 1978): 304–08.

[6]Eli P. Cox, III, "The Optimal Number of Response Alternatives for a Scale: A Review," *Journal of Marketing Research* 17 (November 1980): 420.

A related but less important issue is whether the number of response categories should be odd or even. An odd number allows consumers to indicate a neutral, or neither, response; an even number forces them one way or the other. If the population under study could reasonably be expected to have a neutral reaction, odd is better. Such would be the case when many consumers lack the knowledge on which to base their responses. With an odd number of response categories, however, some consumers use the neutral category as an easy way to avoid making decisions. On balance, an even number of categories is generally better, especially if there are 6 or 8 categories. But, for the sake of perspective, if the only error in a marketing research project is the use of 5 categories instead of 6, results should not be dramatically affected.[7]

RATING ITEM SELECTION

The third major decision in rating scale construction concerns the choice of rating items. How do we know which topics to include? There are numerous topics possible and some selection is always needed.[8] Our answer comes directly from the research problem statement, which was discussed in Chapter 3; that is, the problem statement should identify most relevant topics.

Often relevant topics consist of consumers' choice criteria (the attributes of consumption alternatives consumers use to make consumption decisions). Indeed, most of our rating scale examples in this chapter support this statement. Determining relevant topics usually begins, in the absence of any past research, with consumer interviews. Either depth or focus group interviews with a number of representative consumers will produce common ideas and terms. Researchers continue to conduct these interviews until few new topics surface.

Researchers interview the decision maker and others in the organization as well. These "experts" also have ideas about rating scale topics; to neglect their potential contributions can, from their point of view, easily result in completely irrelevant rating scales. For example, if a store manager is concerned about clerks' personal appearances, an item in a rating scale should contain this topic.

A related and equally important issue concerns the actual choice of words used in the rating items. Look at the Likert rating scale in Exhibit 9.3. As we can see, a **Likert rating scale** consists of a set of belief statements, each to be rated in one of a number of agree/disagree response categories. Instructions to consumers would be to circle the response that most closely represents their feelings about each statement.

---

[7]Stanley Presser and Howard Schuman, "The Measurement of a Middle Position in Attitude Surveys," *Public Opinion Quarterly* 44 (Spring 1980): 70–85.

[8]John Dickson and Gerald Albaum, "A Method for Developing Tailormade Semantic Differentials for Specific Marketing Content Areas," *Journal of Marketing Research* 14 (February 1977): 87–91.

EXHIBIT 9.3
A Likert Scale to Measure Consumer Beliefs About Duncans Department Store

Item	Strongly Agree	Agree	Agree a Little	Disagree a Little	Disagree	Strongly Disagree
Duncans Department Store has lower prices than competitors'.	SA	A	AL	DL	D	SD
Merchandise displays at Duncans Department Store are messy.	SA	A	AL	DL	D	SD
Clerks at Duncans Department Store are not very friendly.	SA	A	AL	DL	D	SD
The downtown Duncans Department Store is a convenient location.	SA	A	AL	DL	D	SD

Notice that two of the belief statements in Exhibit 9.3 appear in a favorable form while the other two appear in an unfavorable form. This is called balancing the loading of the statements and is done to give consumers the feeling of impartiality. It also leads them to read statements more carefully before responding.

Balancing must be done carefully. Research has indicated that balancing with the use of the word "not" as in the third statement, seems particulary troublesome.[9] Two studies report significant response differences to positive and negative versions of an identical belief statement when presented to two similar consumer samples. If a pretest indicates a balancing problem, the researcher can counter by using two different final data collection forms: one would contain a positive version of the statement and the other a negative version. Versions of each statement would be randomly assigned to each form. An alternative solution, of course, is to use a semantic differential scale, in which avoiding the use of not is not difficult. One should still balance loadings by randomly placing favorable and unfavorable terms on the same side of the scale.

Another alternative solution would be to use a **Stapel scale.** The format of a Stapel scale appears in Exhibit 9.4. Instructions to consumers would ask them to circle one number either above or below each term that most accurately describes their feelings about the store.

Stapel scales look quite similar to semantic differential scales but use as rating items only one word or phrase instead of two. This is an advantage of Stapel scales because we do not have to worry about phrase bipo-

[9]John R. Nevin, "Statement Polarity in Attitude Studies: Additional Evidence," in *Contemporary Marketing Thought*, ed. B. A. Greenberg and D. N. Bellenger (Chicago: American Marketing Association, 1977), pp. 337–40. Alfred M. Falthzik and Marvin A. Jolson, "Statement Polarity in Attitude Studies," *Journal of Marketing Research* 11 (February 1974): 102–05.

EXHIBIT 9.4
A Stapel Scale to Measure Consumer Beliefs About Duncans Department Store

Duncans Department Store			
+3	+3	+3	+3
+2	+2	+2	+2
+1	+1	+1	+1
Fair prices	Messy	Friendly personnel	Inconvenient location
−1	−1	−1	−1
−2	−2	−2	−2
−3	−3	−3	−3

larity—a +3 is truly opposite to a −3 and so on. Moreover, using numbers instead of words as response categories at least suggests that consumers will interpret category divisions as equal. Another advantage is that Stapel scales show strong promise for measuring beliefs over the telephone, a communication model less workable with Likert and semantic differential scales.[10]

Actual appearance of any rating scale—whether it is arranged vertically or horizontally on the page, whether it uses boxes or blanks to check, and so on—is largely unimportant from a measurement standpoint.[11] We do want the scale to be understandable, professional, and brief in appearance. Beyond this, scale appearance is a matter of personal preference.

Rating Scale Applications

Now that we appreciate construction details of several kinds of rating scales, we discuss applications. Likert, semantic differential, and Stapel scales find wide use in measuring consumer beliefs and attitudes. More specialized scales measure purchase intentions, satisfaction, and knowledge. Finally, a last application of Likert scales occurs as the measurement of consumer life styles.

BELIEFS AND ATTITUDES Likert scales, semantic differential scales, and Stapel scales measure beliefs that can be combined into a quantitative measurement of attitude. We start by scoring the belief items. We simply assign numbers 1 through 6 to each response category according to the degree of favorability in the response. Let us arbitrarily agree that favorable beliefs should get high

[10]Del I. Hawkins, Gerald Albaum, and Roger Best, "Stapel Scale or Semantic Differential in Marketing Research?" *Journal of Marketing Research* 11 (August 1974): 318–22.

[11]Jum C. Nunnally, *Psychometric Theory*, 2nd ed. (New York: McGraw-Hill, 1978), p. 598.

TABLE 9.2
Belief and Attitude Scores

	BELIEF SCORES:				ATTITUDE SCORES
Individual	*Fair Prices*	*Neat*	*Friendly Personnel*	*Convenient Location*	
A	4	5	6	6	21
B	6	6	5	5	22
C	1	1	2	5	9
D	3	3	3	3	12
E	1	2	1	2	6
F	4	3	4	4	15
G	6	4	6	1	17
H	1	1	1	2	5
I	5	5	5	6	21
J	3	4	5	4	16
Averages	3.4	3.4	3.8	3.8	14.4

scores and unfavorable low. This means we score a "strongly agree" response to our earlier Likert scale as 6 if the statement itself is favorable and as 1 if the statement is unfavorable. We score a "somewhat" response to our semantic differential scale either as 4 or 3 depending on its distance from the favorable anchor. For our Stapel scale, we score a "+2" response to "Friendly personnel" as 5. Scoring item responses in this fashion simplifies keypunching operations and prevents negative averages for the items, which in turn simplifies data interpretation. However, our primary concern in this process is that scoring should consistently reflect the intensity of favorableness of each belief as indicated by each item's response.

We finish by totaling belief scores for each consumer involved in the research and call each consumer's total an attitude score. Consumers with high attitude scores, then, have more favorable attitudes than those with low scores. Table 9.2 shows some scores for a small group of consumers (assume they responded to the semantic differential scale).

A researcher might focus on either attitude or belief scores in Table 9.2. An attitude score forcus would identify behavioral and socioeconomic characteristics of consumer groups having favorable, neutral, and unfavorable attitudes. This analysis would be helpful in understanding the store's clientele.

Alternatively, a researcher might focus on belief scores and attempt to understand attitude structure. Average belief scores at the bottom of Table 9.2 indicate that consumers consider the store's personnel and location more favorably than its prices and neatness. Just as with attitudes, it would be worthwhile to examine behavioral and socioeconomic characteristics associated with consumer groups having favorable and unfavorable beliefs on each choice criterion.

More meaning can be obtained if the research uses more choice criteria. Instead of only four, studies commonly use upwards of ten or twenty choice criteria. And, instead of measuring beliefs about only one store, studies commonly include competing stores as well. The usual analysis presents "profiles" of average belief scores for each store in the study. Figure 9.2 shows an example of profiles for three stores. It's easy to see on which choice criteria Duncans outperforms its competition and on which it needs improvement. Having attitude scales on competitors also produces a worthwhile side benefit: it makes it more difficult for consumers to determine who is sponsoring the research. More accurate data should result.

More meaning can be obtained if the research also examines choice criteria structure. Some choice criteria in Figure 9.2 are probably more

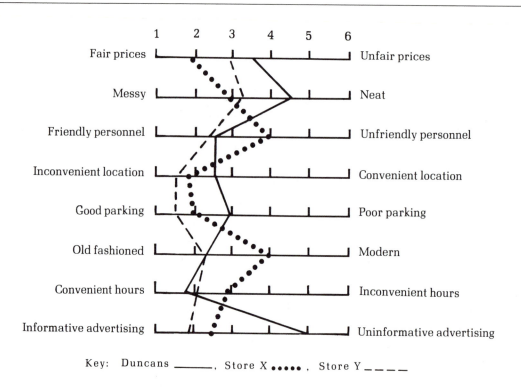

Key: Duncans _____, Store X •••••, Store Y _ _ _ _

FIGURE 9.2
Belief profiles for three department stores

important than others; it would be unfortunate if a decision maker took action on unimportant criteria and neglected the important. Consequently, marketing research studies often attempt to measure choice criteria importance with a rating scale similar to the rating scale example we saw in Exhibit 9.2. Studies may then examine choice criteria structure for different socioeconomically or behaviorally defined groups. Studies may also combine an item's choice criterion importance score with a corresponding belief item score as a more sophisticated, two-component measurement of each consumer's attitudes.[12]

Likert or Stapel scale items can easily be used to construct profiles similar to those in Figure 9.2. And, instead of presenting belief score profiles for different stores, another form of analysis presents profiles for a single store as derived from different groups. Such groups might be light, moderate, and heavy users, or males and females, or any other groups as designated by managerially useful behavior or socioeconomic characteristics.

Attitude rating scales are extremely versatile. While our example was always Duncans Department Store, it could just as easily have been a product, package, warranty, advertisement, salesperson, point-of-purchase display, price, or other marketing decision. All that would have changed are the topics used as rating items. And, while our respondents were always consumers, they could just as easily have been retail buyers, sales engineers, or corporate vice presidents.

Marketing researchers use a number of purchase intention scales, the simplest being a single-item scale:

PURCHASE INTENTIONS

How likely is it that you will buy _____ on your next shopping trip?	Definitely buy it	Probably buy it	Might or might not buy it	Probably not buy it	Definitely not buy it

Instructions would ask consumers to circle the response that most closely represents their intentions. If the scale is used in new product development, the favorable responses are of special interest:

Certain rough rules of thumb have evolved for the two most favorable answers, "definitely buy it" and "probably buy it." For instance, a concept statement should receive 80% to 90% favorable answers to encourage subsequent developmental work. A prototype product that the respondents can actually use should receive 70% to 80% favorable answers for development to continue. And a finished

---

[12]James F. Engel, Roger D. Blackwell, and David T. Kollat, *Consumer Behavior*, 3rd ed. (Hinsdale, Ill.: The Dryden Press, 1978), pp. 389–409.

product in a finished package will rarely be successful in actual test marketing if it does not receive at least 60% to 70% favorable answers. (These norms are based on experience with over 100 brands in many product categories.)[13]

Of course, the scale could also obtain consumer reaction to the modification of a current product or to other marketing decisions (an advertisement, for example).

For existing products, a more complicated but more accurate scale measures purchase intention relative to competing brands.[14] A typical scale asks each consumer to allocate 100 points among five competing brands, according to the estimated likelihood of a given brand being the next purchase. Each brand's average number of points when divided by 100, then, represents future purchase probability. This method counters a common consumer response bias that inflates or overestimates purchase intention when consumers rate each brand separately.

When using these or other purchase intention scales, a strong concern is for consumer understanding. Consumers find it difficult to respond to purchase intention scales more sophisticated than the two discussed here. In particular, consumers find it difficult to make direct, subjective probability estimates of purchase. When the scale uses, say, eleven equally spaced numerical response categories ranging from 0.0 to 1.0 to indicate purchase likelihood, the consumers may well be uncertain of how to respond. Many consumers are simply "too ignorant of even the simplest probability concepts, or may lack any explicit probabilistic framework in their lives which can be characterized in terms of subjective probability estimates."[15]

Purchase intention scales usually contain a time frame of reference. Time frames for consumer goods scales are usually short and stated in terms of a consumer's "next purchase" or her "next shopping trip." Alternatively, they may be stated in temporal terms—for example, "within the next 7 days" or "within the next 14 days." Purchase intention scales for consumer durable goods or in industrial marketing research may use a time frame as distant as one year.

CONSUMER SATISFACTION   Interest in consumer satisfaction only recently resulted in its formal measurement. For years, decision makers took informal measures of satisfaction in the form of letters of praise or complaint from outspoken consumers. It was not until the mid-1970s, however, that marketing

---

[13]James W. Taylor, John J. Houlahan, and Alan C. Gabriel, "The Purchase Intention Question in New Product Development: A Field Test," *Journal of Marketing* 39 (January 1975): 90.

[14]John Pavasars and William D. Wells, "Measures of Brand Attitudes Can Be Used to Predict Buying Behavior," *Marketing News* (April 11, 1975), p. 6.

[15]Boris W. Becker and Marshall G. Greenberg, "Probablity Estimates by Respondents: Does Weighting Improve Accuracy?" *Journal of Marketing Research* 15 (August 1978): 485.

EXHIBIT 9.5
A Typical Satisfaction Rating Scale

Item	Much More Than I Expected	Somewhat More Than I Expected	About What I Expected	Somewhat Less Than I Expected	Much Less Than I Expected
Price	____	____	____	____	____
Chocolate flavor	____	____	____	____	____
Sweetness	____	____	____	____	____
Moistness	____	____	____	____	____

researchers began to develop satisfaction rating scales to apply to all consumers.

Today, satisfaction rating scales abound,[16] largely because researchers use a variety of conceptualizations in describing satisfaction as a psychological characteristic. To illustrate, Hunt summarizes eight conceptualizations of consumer satisfaction, only one of which is our "comparison of prepurchase beliefs with postpurchase performance evaluations."[17] Our definition is a micro conceptualization, more useful in measuring consumer satisfaction with a firm's products and communications than their satisfaction with an industry or economic system. For example, a typical satisfaction rating scale for a cake mix might look like Exhibit 9.5. Instructions would ask consumers to place an X in the blank beneath the statement that best describes their feelings about the characteristic in question.

Several comments parallel our earlier discussion on rating scales in general. Satisfaction scales may use different anchors, more or fewer response categories, but always employ integer scoring. Selection of choice criteria used as scale items again depends on consumers and decision makers, with depth or focus group interviews helping to limit the numerous criteria. Choice criteria structure should again be examined to determine relative importance—otherwise, satisfaction on certain criteria may be misleading.

Rather than measure satisfaction on several separate choice criteria, it may be more appropriate to measure satisfaction in a less detailed fashion. For instance, suppose we want to measure product engineers' satisfaction with twenty products made by a large industrial goods manufacturer. After determining that each engineer had recently been responsible for the purchase of at least one of each product, we might measure satis-

---

[16]See H. Keith Hunt, ed., *Conceptualization and Measurement of Consumer Satisfaction and Dissatisfaction* (Cambridge, Mass.: Marketing Science Institute, 1977).

[17]H. Keith Hunt, "Consumer Satisfaction and Dissatisfaction and the Public Interest: Conceptualization, Measurement Problems, and Applications," in *Marketing and the Public Interest*, ed. John F. Cady (Cambridge, Mass.: Marketing Scence Institute, 1977), pp. 251–66.

faction by using response categories phrased as "Performed much better than I expected, Performed somewhat better than I expected," and so on. The four choice criteria items of Exhibit 9.5 would be replaced in this case with the twenty products. Later research might well examine satisfaction details for selected products on separate choice criteria. To have instead measured satisfaction on separate choice criteria for all twenty products would have resulted in an excessively long data collection form.

KNOWLEDGE   Knowledge is a consumer's awareness and understanding of past consumption experiences—where experiences can mean anything from advertisement exposure to repeated product purchase. At its most basic level, knowledge is awareness. As an example, a researcher might ask a consumer to name as many brands of men's shirts as he could. At its most complex level, knowledge is understanding. As an example, a researcher might ask what a product is, how it operates, and what benefits it produces. Beyond examining knowledge alone, often marketing researchers try to explain knowledge by simultaneously examining consumer behavior and socioeconomic variables. For example, they may test whether brand awareness of a product is higher among consumers who have seen one advertisement than among consumers who have seen another.

Actually, you as college students should be intimately familiar with the concept of knowledge and its measurement because of your student background. Similar procedures to those you have experienced measure consumer knowledge: open-ended, fill-in blanks, true-false, and multiple choice questions. Scoring generally proceeds on a 0-or-1 basis for each question. Each question's score is then totalled to indicate knowledge scale scores for each individual.

As in your student experience, a good knowledge scale to measure consumer understanding requires careful construction. It must include questions that measure all relevant topics of interest. It should not be so easy that most consumers score perfectly: if it does, all a researcher can conclude in this situation is that these consumers possess identical knowledge. This is unlikely. Nor should it be so difficult that most score poorly because, again, the scale fails to distinguish between consumers with varying amounts of knowledge. A good knowledge scale invariably needs a pretest using a representative sample of consumers. Here the researcher would present questions of different difficulties for each knowledge topic of interest.

Most consumer knowledge scales in marketing research measure awareness. Some examples:

- Name as many brands of cat food as you can.
- Which brands of cat food come in a can?
- What brand of cat food advertises with cats in a chorus line?

Such questions primarily measure long-term memory aspects of knowledge.

Our chapter on consumer psychological characteristics would not be complete without a discussion of consumer life style measurement. Earlier, we approached the topic of consumer life styles when we discussed certain behavioral characteristics and when we discussed attitudes. Without further introduction, let us define **life style** measurement as statements that measure consumer activities, interests, opinions, needs, and values.[18] Thus, when we discussed shopping, media exposure, and specific behavior patterns in Chapter 7, we were really discussing aspects of life style. The same is true when we discussed belief measurement in this chapter, because beliefs can be considered synonymous with opinions.

CONSUMER LIFE STYLES

    Marketing researchers usually measure life style using a large number of consumers who respond to a large number of Likert statements about their activities, interests, opinions, needs, and values. Here is an example of each.

Activities: Our family eats out frequently.

Interests: I like to read cookbooks.

Opinions: Most fast-food restaurants are equally clean.

Needs: When I cook a meal at home, I feel important.

Values: A family that eats together is basic to our society.

Consumers record their responses to each item using a set of agree/disagree categories. The typical life style data collection form contains some 200 to 300 similar statements on a variety of topics—such as money, jobs, hobbies, family, products, social issues, and the like.[19] Sample sizes in the thousands are common. Responses generate rich descriptions of consumer segments that are then analyzed in terms of selected behavior and socioeconomic characteristics.

    One analysis simply cross-classifies life style data with purchase. Life style statements that distinguish between heavy users and other consumers, for example, can subsequently help construct more complex descriptions for users in general or for users of a particular brand. Another analysis segments the market by combining life style data with socioeconomic characteristics to produce some very actionable descriptions. In Exhibit 9.6 Wells describes four stomach remedy user segments,

---

[18]Fred D. Reynolds and William D. Wells, *Consumer Behavior* (New York: McGraw-Hill, 1977), p. 34.

[19]Joseph T. Plummer, "The Concept and Application of Life Style Segmentation," *Journal of Marketing* 38 (January 1974): 34.

EXHIBIT 9.6
Segmentation of Stomach Remedy Users

The Severe Sufferers

The Severe Sufferers are the extreme group in the potency side of the market. They tend to be young, have children, and be well educated. They are irritable and anxious people, and believe that they suffer more severely than others. They take the ailment seriously, fuss about it, pamper themselves, and keep trying new and different products in search of greater potency. A most advanced product with new ingredients best satisfies their need for potency and fast relief, and ties in with their psychosomatic beliefs.

The Active Medicators

The Active Medicators are on the same side of the motivational spectrum. They are typically modern suburbanites with average income and education. They are emotionally well adjusted to the demands of their active lives. They have learned to cope by adopting the contemporary beliefs [sic] of seeking help for every ill, and use remedies to relieve even minor signs of ailments and every ache and pain. In a modern product, they seek restoration of their condition and energy, mental recovery, and a lift for their active lives. They are influenced by a brand's reputation and by how well it is advertised. They tend to develop strong brand loyalties.

The Hypochondriacs

The Hypochondriacs are on the opposite side of the motivational spectrum. They tend to be older, not as well educated, and women. They have conservative attitudes toward medication and a deep concern over health. They see possible dangers in frequent use of remedies, are concerned over side effects, and afraid of remedies with new ingredients and extra potency. To cope with their concerns, they are strongly oriented toward medical authority, seeking guidance in treatment, and what products they should use. They hold rigid beliefs about the ailment and are disciplined in the products they use, and how frequently. They want a simple, single-purpose remedy, which is safe and free from side effects, and backed by doctors or a reputable company.

The Practicalists

The Practicalists are in the same extreme positions on this side of the motivational spectrum. They tend to be older, well educated, emotionally the most stable, and least concerned over their ailment discomforts as a part of life, without fuss and pampering. They use a remedy as a last resort, and just to relieve the particular symptom. They seek simple products whose efficacy is well proven, and are skeptical of complicated modern remedies with new ingredients and multiple functions.

Source: William D. Wells, "Psychographics: A Critical Review," Journal of Marketing Research 12 (May 1975): 203.

TABLE 9.3
Stomach Remedy Brand Use

	PERCENT WHO USE BRAND MOST OFTEN			
BRAND	Severe Sufferers	Active Medicators	Hypochondriacs	Practicalists
A	6	3	1	1
B	32	23	10	8
C	16	17	12	5
D	16	19	24	8
E	5	29	37	51

Source: William D. Wells, "Psychographics: A Critical Review," *Journal of Marketing Research* 12 (May 1975): 203.

taken from some research by Pernica.[20] These segments have strikingly different brand usages, as Table 9.3 shows.

Beyond helping us to understand consumer segments, life style data directly contribute to many marketing decisions. Applications include selecting advertising appeals and media, product features, and package design—all of which might otherwise result from other data collection methods.[21] In other words, as Exhibit 9.6 and Table 9.3 show, life style data yield a qualitative understanding of the consumer based on large samples and quantitative analyses instead of small samples and qualitative analyses.

Guidelines in Psychological Characteristic Measurement

Guidelines that we discussed in Chapter 7 on writing questions of fact apply to writing questions of psychological characteristics. We should reread the last half of Chapter 7 with this in mind. To save space, our discussion here is limited largely to summary statements consistent with this material.

Fact question guidelines are concerned with question topics, wording, and response formats. Topics, we learned, should be relevant with respect to respondents and to research objectives. Similarly, psychological scale items must both contain relevant topics and result in managerially actionable responses. Scale items must use simple construction so that consumers can understand them and so that researchers can interpret responses. For example, the Likert statement that "Product X contains too

[20]William D. Wells, "Psychographics: A Critical Review," *Journal of Marketing Research* 12 (May 1975): 202–03. Wells also cites other interesting case histories of life style research applied to marketing decisions and details five different types of life style data analysis.

[21]Ibid., p. 208.

much sugar and artificial preservatives" may be understandable but, for all responses indicating disagreement, uninterpretable.

Again words should be precise, clear, and commonly used. If appropriate, the question should contain a frame of reference; the difficulty arises most often from comparative sorts of questions:

- Do you think Brand X is too sweet?
- Is the price too high?

For both, a proper reaction on the part of respondents is "compared to what?" Bases for answering these questions (bases that the researcher had in mind when writing them) should be provided to minimize confusion. Usually the researcher would use such short phrases as "compared to most products on the market" or "compared to the brand you last bought" or similar words to begin the question. Finally, it should go without saying that items must use neutral words that do not lead consumers to a "right" response.

Words used for response anchors and the relative position of each anchor to its endpoint make a difference in scale response frequency. For example, the anchor "average" has one meaning when it is positioned this way:

| Extremely good | Average | Moderately poor | Quite poor | Extremely poor |

and another when positioned here:

| Extremely good | Very good | Good | Average | Extremely poor |

Even the decision to order Likert anchors from "agree" to "disagree" instead of from "disagree" to "agree" affects response frequencies.[22] Both position and order effects can largely be ignored, however, if we consistently use one response format and make relative comparisons between consumers' reactions to different scale items. To compare responses from different response formats invites error.

The choice between unstructured and structured response formats in psychological characteristic measurement largely reduces to the choice between qualitative and quantitative methods. Table 9.4 summarizes major differences between the two. As the table indicates, both qualitative

---

[22]David Sheluga, Jacob Jacoby, and Brenda Major, "Whether to Agree–Disagree or Disagree–Agree: The Effects of Anchor Order on Item Response," *Advances in Consumer Research* vol. 5, ed. H. Keith Hunt (Ann Arbor, Mich.: Association for Consumer Research, 1978), pp. 109–13.

TABLE 9.4
Qualitative and Quantitative Psychological Characteristic Measurement

QUALITATIVE MEASUREMENT	QUANTITATIVE MEASUREMENT
Questions are fast to assemble	Questions are slow to assemble

Responses
  are slowly made
  are made in respondents' own words
  contain much variety
  require more effort to make
  contain less social desirability
  have more memory problems
	Responses
	  are quickly made
	  force respondents to categorize
	  contain less variety
	  require less effort to make
	  contain more social desirability
	  have fewer memory problems

Analysis is
  slow
  capable of subjective interpretation
  largely incapable of statistical analysis
	Analysis is
	  fast
	  capable of objective interpretation
	  quite capable of statistical analysis

Application is characterized by
  flexible procedure
  small samples
  usually preceding any quantitative techniques
  exploratory research focus
	Application is characterized by
	  rigid procedure
	  large samples
	  usually following qualitative techniques
	  descriptive, causal research focus

and quantitative psychological characteristic measurement occupy unique places in marketing research.

Finally, we mention again a common basis for all fact and psychological characteristic measurement guidelines—the desire for valid and reliable procedures. Such is the topic matter for an extensive discussion in Chapter 11 after we discuss data collection form design.

Chapter Summary

Quantitative measurement of psychological characteristics largely results in data expressed in numbers—numbers that represent consumer responses to some type of rating scale. A rating scale consists of a set of rating items having response categories that indicate the relative intensity of the psychological characteristic. Some particular types of rating scales are the Likert, semantic differential, and Stapel scales. These rather universal scale types can be applied to measure consumer beliefs, attitudes, and life styles. More specialized rating scales measure the importance of choice criteria, knowledge, purchase intentions, and satisfaction. All require careful construction; the guidelines we discussed in Chapter 7 also apply here.

Chapter Review

KEY TERMS	Rating scale	Belief item score
	Response anchor	Attitude score
	Semantic differential scale	Consumer life style
	Likert scale	Belief profile scores
	Stapel scale	

DISCUSSION QUESTIONS

1. Distinguish between qualitative and quantitative research on psychological characteristics.

2. How do data sources influence rating scale construction?

3. What is wrong with using "excellent, terrific, good, average, and poor" as response categories to measure consumer reaction to a new soft drink?

4. Outline major differences between Likert, semantic differential, and Stapel scales.

5. Interpret Figure 9.2.

6. Explain why a "finished product in a finished package will rarely be successful in actual test marketing if it does not receive at least 60% to 70% favorable" responses to a purchase intention scale administered to consumers during a product screening test.

7. Of what use is life style data in making advertising decisions?

Additional Readings

Hughes, G. David. *Attitude Measurement for Marketing Strategies.* Glenview, Ill.: Scott, Foresman, 1971.

Although short, this book provides an extensive discussion on attitudes as psychological characteristics and their numerous measurement techniques.

Hunt, H. Keith, ed. *Conceptualization and Measurement of Consumer Satisfaction and Dissatisfaction.* Cambridge, Mass.: Marketing Science Institute, 1977.

This book summarizes theory and research on consumer satisfaction. Contents are of interest to consumer behavior theorists, marketing mangers, and public policy makers.

Morrison, Donald G. "Purchase Intentions and Purchase Behavior" *Journal of Marketing* 43 (Spring 1979): 65–74.

This article provides a framework for collecting, analyzing, and interpreting purchase intentions data.

Wells, William D. "Psychographics: A Critical Review," *Journal of Marketing Research* 12 (May 1975): 196–213.

In this article are case histories of five somewhat different uses of psychographics or life style research. It critically reviews the status of research in the field, basing the review on a bibliography of 148 entries.

10

Research: Questions, Data, and Collection Forms

Research Questions and Data

Obviously, research questions are intimately linked with research data. Questions of fact produce fact data; questions of psychological characteristics produce psychological characteristic data. But beyond these simple linkages based on question topic lie more complex linkages based on variable conceptualization and question form. These more complex linkages are our topic matter for the first half of this chapter.

Marketing research **data** are facts and figures about people, things, events, concepts, or organizations. Our first reaction, of course, is that data consist of numbers or quantities. This idea is incomplete. Remember that in Chapter 8 we discussed the collection of qualitative data or data that are expressed in words. Thus, our definition of data includes both facts and figures with facts often expressed in words or other symbols.

MARKETING RESEARCH DATA

Data depend on variable conceptualization and on question form. More precisely, data depend on variable conceptualization and variable measurement.[1] Table 10.1 identifies the various ways in which researchers conceptualize and measure variables. As we can see, a variable can be

---

[1]G. C. Helmstadter, *Research Concepts in Human Behavior* (New York: Appleton-Century-Crofts, Educational Div., Meredith Corp. 1970), pp. 177–80.

TABLE 10.1
Variable Conceptualization and Measurement Method

Variable Conceptualization	Variable Measurement Method
Nonordered	Nominal
Ordered	
Discrete	Ordinal, Interval, Ratio
Continuous	Ordinal, Interval, Ratio

conceptualized as nonordered or ordered. Ordered variables can be further conceptualized as either discrete or continuous. Four methods of measurement can be identified: nominal, ordinal, interval, and ratio. The paragraphs that follow will explain what these terms mean and how they are related.

How a variable is conceptualized means how the researcher theoretically views or pictures a concept involved in the research. For example, suppose we do research on comparison shopping among breakfast cereal consumers. We could conceptualize such behavior as an either/or phenomenon. That is, either consumers comparison-shop or they don't. On the other hand, we could conceptualize all consumers as falling into one of five categories of comparison shoppers—never, seldom, sometimes, often, and always. Still different, we might think of consumers as existing at any point on an unbroken line ranging from no comparison shopping to always comparison shopping. Any of these or other conceptualizations of comparison shopping could form the object of a research study.

Measurement of this concept involves a different, more operational problem. Here we ask how shall we word questions to collect information on the variable under study—shall we use this measurement procedure or some other? Measurement always assumes that some element of respondent behavior (the real world) demonstrates the theoretical concept. In other words, measurement deals with reality, conceptualization with theory.

Nonordered Variables and Nominal Measurement.   Researchers conceptualize **nonordered variables** as those that do not allow expression of ordered relationship to be made between variable values. Consider the variable of marital status. Suppose a researcher allows it to take on values of 1 for never married consumers, 2 for married, and 3 for all others (widowed, divorced, or separated). Such variable values do not permit expressions of ordered relationships between variable categories. We cannot, for example, consider a widowed consumer to possess more marital status than a married consumer because the assigned value 3 is greater than 2. In fact, the assignment could be made in an opposite fashion (or by assigning the values 1, A, and * to the three categories of marital status) and data would be just as meaningful. In short, allowed values are nothing more than *names* indicating presence or absence of a characteristic—hence, the description of nominal measurement.

Many variables in marketing research are conceptualized as nonordered, and all of these use questions that measure in a nominal fashion. Examples include questions of buyer status (buyers, nonbuyers), home ownership, sex, race, religion, employment status, zip code, personality types, and subcultural membership. Some of these variables have only two permissible values while others take on many more.

Ordered Variables and Ordinal, Interval, and Ratio Measurement. Researchers conceptualize **ordered variables** differently. Here variables take on values that meaningfully reflect possession of the variable in "more than or less than" amounts. Thus, researchers can express an ordered relationship between variable values. Consider the variable of age. Allowed variable values range from, say, 1 to 100 and a meaningful ordered relationship between values can be stated. A 22-year-old consumer possesses more age than a 19-year-old; a 14-year-old more than a 12-year-old; and so on. An ordered variable always has this property of direction or order.

Ordered variables break into two classes: discrete and continuous. **Discrete ordered variables** are conceptualized as having only a limited number of distinct values and no others. For example, the variable "cars owned" can take on only the values 1, 2, 3, 4, 5 and so on up to the maximum value in the population under study. Another example is the variable "number of stores shopped" where possible values range from 0 to some maximum value. In both examples, it is impossible to assign the values 1.17, 2.8, 3.639, or any value other than integers or whole numbers.

On the other hand, **continuous ordered variables** are conceptualized as having an infinite number of values limited only by the precision of measurement. All values of the variable between population extreme values are meaningful. For example, two consumers' ages could be measured at 21.78 and 22.09 years or two attitude scale scores could be measured at 26 and 28 and represent meaningful continuous ordered data.

The last example, attitude scale scores of 26 and 28, looks suspiciously like discrete data with its whole number values. Remember, we are discussing how the variable is conceptualized and not how it is measured. Attitudes are usually conceptualized as an unbroken line or continuum from strongly favorable to strongly unfavorable. It is just an artifact of the measuring process that whole number scores result. Looking at it another way, it would be meaningful to speak of attitude scores of 26.48 and 28.10, because these values exist on the attitude continuum if only questions could measure in such precision.

Much marketing research uses questions that produce either continuous or discrete ordered variable values. Examples of continuous variable values are responses to questions measuring age, store and brand attitudes, purchase intentions, social class, dwelling size, amount of product consumed, time spent watching television, and stage in the product life cycle. Examples of discrete variable values are responses to questions measuring family size, number of stores shopped, brands purchased, cars owned, and income. Marketing researchers often treat income as a continuous ordered variable even though it is, strictly speaking, discrete.[2] Usually little problem results in this instance.

Both continuous and discrete ordered variables may be measured by questions based on either ordinal, interval, or ratio methods. Each method uses special procedures and results in data with special properties.[3]

Ordinal Measurement. Ordinal measurement measures or assigns values only on the basis of "more than or less than" possession of the variable. This process is often called *ranking* or *rank ordering*. For example, suppose we ask a sales manager to rank the dollar sales of five similar products for last year. Product A is ranked first, followed in order by products C, D, E and B. All we know when examining this data is that property of order. We don't know, for example, that product A sold twice as well as product B (or ten times as much, for that matter). Nor do we know if sales of product A less sales of product C is the same as the difference between any other two adjacently ranked products. We know only that the sales manager reported product A selling more than C, C more than D, and so on.

Interval Measurement. Interval measurement assigns values also on the basis of "more than or less than." However, the assignment is made now on the basis of equal units between measurement reference points. Again, suppose we have five products and wish to determine relative performance for last year. The sales manager might take each product's sales and subtract from it the company's average product sales. These differences are reported to us as +$48,220, −$10,110, +$37,123, +$12,020, and +$527 for products A, B, C, D, and E, respectively.

Clearly we can determine that product A sold best, that product C sold second best, and so on, as we could with ranking. But now, however, we can subtract one product's sales from another's to determine the amount of relative difference. For example, product A and C differ by $11,097, an amount that is less than the difference between the second and third place products. We can also make other comparisons between any

---

[2]Income varies in one-cent increments. In reality, marketing researchers seldom strive to collect income information more accurate than the nearest hundred dollars and consider the variable to be continuous.

[3]There are numerous sources discussing measurement procedures and properties. An excellent introduction can be found in C. William Emory, *Business Research Methods* (Homewood, Ill.: Richard D. Irwin, 1976), pp. 112–17. A more sophisticated treatment can be found in Jum C. Nunnally, *Psychometric Theory*, 2nd ed. (New York: McGraw-Hill, 1978), Chap. 1.

two or more products. About the only thing we can't determine is the ratio of one product's sales to another's. We can't state, for example, that product A sold 110 percent more than product C.

Ratio Measurement.   To do this, we need an absolute zero point in addition to equal units between measurement points. In the last example we had an arbitrary zero point, average company sales per product, that helped measure individual performance. Suppose this average was $824,000—how would we evaluate the lowest performing product? Or, suppose the average was $82,400—now how would we evaluate the lowest performing product? It's clear that using an arbitrary zero point can lead to erroneous conclusions about the relations between observation values if we're not careful.

We solve the problem with an absolute zero point. Suppose the five product's actual sales for last year are known to be $248,220, $189,890, $237,123, $212,020, and $200,527 for A, B, C, D, and E, respectively. The absolute zero point is $0 of sales, and now we can perform a complete analysis of relative performance. For example, not only do we know that the first place product outsold the second place product by $11,097 (as before) but we now can determine that the second place product sold $237,123/$248,220 or 95.5 percent of the first place product's sales. Now we can compute any ratio of one product's sales to another.

As is probably clear, this last measurement is called ratio measurement. Ratio measurement is clearly superior to all others in terms of information that can be extracted from the data.

Consider nominal data again—what information can we glean from it? About the only thing we can determine from nominal data is equality. If two measurement objects have the same variable value, they are equal in the eyes of the researcher on that variable. Different values, obviously, imply inequality.

MEASUREMENT METHOD AND INFORMATION

Ordinal data allow the determination of order—"more than or less than"—to be made in addition to the determination of equality. A measurement value of 12, for example, indicates more possession of the variable than the value 9.

Interval data provide still more information. Here we can determine equality, relative possession of the variable, and distances between measurement objects. That is, we know that a value of 12 is as far from a value of 9 as 9 is from 6—or that the distance from 12 to 6 is twice as much as the distance from 12 to 9 or from 9 to 6.

Finally, with ratio data we can determine equality, order, distance, and the ratio of one value to another. We can state, for example, that one individual has twice as much income as another or that it took three times longer to find a clerk at one store as it did at another.

Certainly marketing researchers should attempt to use the measurement method that yields the most information, all other things being equal. But writing questions that produce interval or ratio level data is not always possible. For example, the variable itself may have no meaningful absolute zero point. Consider such variables as consumer reactions to a new product taste test, or their price–quality perceptions, or their social class. A complete absence of these variables is impossible as long as the consumer is alive!

Or, consider a six-step Likert scale for measuring consumer attitudes toward a store. Here we could argue that an absolute zero point exists (completely neutral attitudes, say) but in truth there are not equal units between the measurement reference points. Examine the six steps—strongly agree, agree, agree a little, disagree a little, disagree, strongly disagree—by asking how a consumer might see the difference between two adjacent steps. We simply aren't sure that a consumer perceives the same distance between strongly agree and agree, for example, as between disagree a little and disagree. Moreover, for any single pair of adjacent steps, different consumers may perceive different distances between them.

Thus, how an ordered variable is measured depends really on two things: the basic nature of the variable itself and the sophistication of the measurement procedure, that is, the question and its response format. In general, it is possible to achieve interval or ratio measurement in marketing research only when measuring a few socioeconomic and buyer behavior variables. For most psychological variables in marketing research, we usually end up with ordinal data.

MEASUREMENT METHOD AND DATA ANALYSIS DEPENDENCY

We should not view the preceding discussion on measurement as abstract or sterile. Rather, recognize that how we measure a variable greatly influences how we analyze it. Stated simply, most of the commonly used statistical operations and analyses we have studied require interval or ratio data. Yet we've just said that often marketing research questions produce only nominal or ordinal data. What can be done?

The answer is not simple. As part of the answer, we will examine in Chapters 15 through 19 some lesser known analytical tools that may be easily applied to nominal or ordinal data. Beyond them, there will be many instances when it will be convenient to apply to ordinal data an analysis procedure that requires interval or ratio data. This does not mean that the data analysis procedure will not work. Rather, it means that analysis procedures by themselves are oblivious to measurement procedures and to what the numbers they manipulate actually represent. We, of course, should not be oblivious.

Our concern rests on interpretability of results. Numerous scientists have also concerned themselves with this point and have largely divided themselves into two camps: mathematical purists and analytical pragmatists. Purists hold that data requirements of analysis procedures cannot be violated without loss of interpretability:

... statistical tests, which use means and standard deviations (i.e., which require the operations of arithmetic on the original scores), ought not to be used with data in an ordinal scale.... When only the rank order of scores is known, means and standard deviations found on the scores themselves are *in error* to the extent that the successive intervals (distance between classes) on the scale are not equal. When [these] parametric techniques of statistical inference are used with such data, any decisions about hypotheses are doubtful.[4]

Marketing researchers holding this position see the use of "interval scale statistics for ordinal scale data" as a subtle sin in much marketing research.[5]

Pragmatists hold a more liberal view from two bases:

1. "that most psychological and educational scales approximate interval equality fairly well"[6] and

2. that "it is unlikely that the decision to assume interval measurement when it does not exist will lead to the spurious overestimation of results."[7]

In fact, pragmatists hold that using analysis procedures designed for interval or ratio data on interval data *usually* has "very little" effect at all.[8]

The position taken in this book is that of analytical pragmatists. However, there is more to it than this. We should be aware, as previously noted, of the many simple analysis procedures for nominal and ordinal data that we discuss later. We should also take care to measure ordered variables in an interval or ratio fashion whenever it is possible. That is, we should write questions that attempt to measure at the interval rather than at the ordinal level of measurement sophistication. For example, suppose we are measuring consumer reaction to a new soft drink. We test three different versions. We ought to avoid questions that have consumers rank which version they like best, second best, and least as ordinal measurements. Instead, we should favor questions that have consumers rate each version on a Likert-type like/dislike stepped scale or other similar measure that approximates interval measurement. Often we will face this

---

[4]Sidney Siegel *Nonparametric Statistics for the Behavioral Sciences* (New York: McGraw-Hill, 1956), p. 26.

[5]John A. Martilla and Davis W. Carvey, "Four Subtle Sins in Marketing Research," *Journal of Marketing* 39 (January 1975): 8.

[6]Fred N. Kerlinger, *Foundations of Behavioral Research*, 2nd ed. (New York: Holt, Rinehart and Winston, 1973), p. 440.

[7]George W. Bohrnstedt, "Reliability and Validity Assessment in Attitude Measurement," in *Attitude Measurement*, ed. Gene F. Summers (Chicago: Rand McNally, 1970), p. 82.

[8]Nunnally, *Psychometric Theory*, p. 28.

choice between ordinal or interval measurement in constructing many measurement scales. Finally, we should also stay alert for serious departures from interval scale assumptions and should exercise caution in interpreting such data.

Assembling the Data Collection Form

When done writing questions, the researcher begins assembling them into a data collection form. As much care as was exercised in their writing should accompany their assembly. Care rests on the issues of question sequence, question timing, data collection form instructions, and data collection form layout.

QUESTION SEQUENCE AND TIMING

The issue of **question sequence** considers the extent to which a question's response is influenced by preceding items; the issue of **question timing** considers an item's response as influenced by respondent boredom and fatigue. To show the measurement problems that question sequence and timing can cause, these examples serve well:

- The percentage of college students identifying themselves as political independents after first being asked their parent's political preferences was one-third higher than when question order was reversed.[9]
- Responses to 46 belief statements in a 168-item questionnaire had significantly more blanks, smaller standard deviations, more modal responses, and fewer extreme responses when items were located among the last half of all items than when they were among the first half.[10]

Both sequence and timing issues attend the location of unitary portions within the data collection form and the location of questions inside a unitary portion. A **unitary portion** is a set of questions measuring either a single respondent characteristic or several very closely related characteristics.

Question Sequence.   Question sequence causes problems because people sometimes respond using an inappropriate frame of reference. This

---

[9]D. H. Willick and R. K. Ashley, "Survey Question Order and the Political Party Preferences of College Students and Their Parents," *Public Opinion Quarterly* 35 (Summer 1971): 189–99.

[10]Allen I. Kraut, Alan D. Wolfson, and Alan Rothenberg, "Some Effects of Position on Opinion Survey Items," *Journal of Applied Psychology* 60 (December 1975): 774–76. These results conflict with the findings of Craig and McCann, cited in Chapter 7.

easily occurs when they misinterpret, overlook, or ignore data collection form instructions. It happens again when they discover the research purpose or the sponsor's identity from earlier questions and make responses partly based on this knowledge. In short, people respond with an inappropriate frame of reference whenever any earlier instruction or question in the data collection form distorts responses to any later question. For example, consider first using twenty Likert statements to measure consumer beliefs on twenty different choice criteria and then asking an open-ended brand satisfaction question. Such a sequence will result in far more detail and variety in participants' responses to the satisfaction question than if we reverse question order.

Another situation in which people respond with an inappropriate frame of reference occurs as the **halo effect:** when a data collection form measures beliefs about more than one attribute of some object, people may allow their responses to be influenced by a general feeling toward the object rather than by a specific reaction to each question. If a man likes Campbell's soup, for example, he may generally rate all its attributes more favorably than if he stopped to think critically about each attribute being rated. Of course, if he dislikes Campbell's soup, his responses may instead reflect a negative halo effect.

Question sequence contributes to the halo effect if the data collection form gathers in one place all belief items dealing with one object, and then presents all items dealing with the next object, and so on.[11] If, instead, the form presents all items dealing with one attribute for all objects in the study and then presents all items dealing with the next attribute for all objects (until the form presents all attributes for all objects), question sequence minimizes the halo effect.

Question Timing.   We have much less to say about the question timing issue: people simply get bored and tired during the data collection process. This means they give later questions in the data collection form less consideration than earlier questions.

Controlling Sequence and Timing Effects.   To control sequence and timing effects we can apply a general principle: as viewed by the respondent, organization of the data collection form should show a logical, professional, and short sequence of measurements. In theory, a logical and professional sequence means beginning the data collection form with the more general questions and proceeding to the more specific. It also means proceeding from the simple to more complex questions, from the innocuous to more sensitive, from the interesting to more boring, and from the

---

[11]William L. Wilkie, John M. McCann, and David J. Reibstein, "Halo Effects in Brand Belief Measurement: Implications for Attitude Model Development," in *Advances in Consumer Research*, ed. S. Ward and P. Wright (Urbana, Ill,: Associaton for Consumer Research, 1974), p. 280–83.

more important to less important. However, contrasting with this theoretical simplicity is the difficulty of putting such guidelines into operation. For example, more important questions tend to be more sensitive. More boring questions tend to be more simple. To resolve the difficulty, the researcher usually ends up trading one guideline off against another.

In practice, a logical and professional sequence also means organization consistent with suggestions in the rest of this section. Considerations include items and their response behaviors, respondents, past research, research objectives, fellow researchers, pretests, and data analysis.

Items that measure psychological characteristics and that use identical response behaviors should usually be randomly combined as a unitary portion. This means we usually would randomly assemble all agree/disagree statements together, all important/unimportant statements together, and so on.

Different unitary portions should be positioned with an understanding of the effect of previous unitary portions on respondents. For example, measuring consumers' beliefs before their purchase behaviors often leads to their knowledge of research purpose. Such knowledge may then influence responses to the purchase questions. A much smaller influence may occur by reversing the order of unitary portions.

Past research may already have established an accepted measurement sequence. For example, data collection forms measuring consumer attitudes toward a specific behavior typically include measures of values, beliefs, attitude, and behavioral intention in that order.[12] If we intend to compare our measurement results to past research, a logical and professional sequence should employ past measurement order. Along with this advice, we should note that most data collection forms start with one or two interesting questions to generate respondent enthusiasm and most end with socioeconomic questions because of their boring yet sensitive nature. Income questions are often asked last.

Research objectives may require one or two initial qualifying questions to screen inappropriate from appropriate respondents. An interview that intends to measure beliefs of heavy users is wasted if the last question shows the consumer never has used the product.

While assembling a draft of the form, the researcher can ask fellow researchers for their impressions. When the form is complete, sequencing and timing problems become one concern for a pretest. That is, a pretest may use several different versions of the data collection form to check for sequence influence on responses. Each pretest form could repeat at one-page intervals the same open-ended question asking respondents how they feel about the measurement process, to find out if and when they

---

[12]Paul W. Miniard and Peter R. Dickson, "Item Order Effects in Expectancy-Value Attitude Instruments" (Working Paper #16, Center for Consumer Research, College of Business Administration, University of Florida, February 1979).

become bored. Such a topic can also be a part of a focus group debriefing session for pretest respondents. At the end of the pretest form and during the focus group interview, respondents should be asked who they think is sponsoring the study. Other frequently asked questions include what respondents think is the study's intended purpose and what in the form led them to this conclusion. We take up some other concerns of pretests in the next chapter.

Pretest results influence design of the final data collection form. If the final form is short, contains interesting topics that are measured by some variety in response behaviors, and otherwise represents a logical and professional product, the impact of question sequence and timing ought to be slight. Beyond these points, the final form may rotate both unitary portions and items within a unitary portion to average out some sequence and timing influence during data collection. This requires either printing different forms or instructing interviewers to start at different locations on each form. Both are common practices.

Finally, some researchers note that belief score averages and attitude score totals are less sensitive to sequence and timing effects than are frequency distributions of item responses.[13] Thus, we can partly mitigate the effects of sequence and timing by using averages or total scores in our data analysis.

Our next design issue addresses data collection form instructions. We organize our discussion about instructions found on interviewer- and on self-administered forms. Interviewer-administered forms often contain fairly detailed instructions describing sampling, form administration, and validation procedures. Such instructions sometimes exceed forty pages of single-spaced, technical prose. Self-administered forms, as used in a mail survey, for example, contain only simple form administration instructions.

DATA COLLECTION FORM INSTRUCTIONS

Interviewer-Administered Forms: Sampling Instructions. Personal interview forms regularly include **sampling instructions** telling the interviewer how to select both a household and a respondent. To select a household, the interviewer needs a list of starting points or a route map to keep her within an assigned area. She also must have a definition of what constitutes a household and a set of selection procedures that apply equally well to a neighborhood of single-family dwellings and a complex of 500 apartments. She needs clearly detailed procedures to handle not-at-homes, refusals, and callbacks along with instructions telling the proper days and hours to canvass.

To select a respondent within a household, instructions must discuss screening criteria, which usually consist of standards based on selected behavior and socioeconomic characteristics. Sometimes any consenting

---

[13]Kraut, Wolfson, and Rothenberg, "Effects of Position," p. 776.

BOX 10.1

Screener Instructions

(IF CONSUMER AGREES TO PARTICIPATE, ASK:)

Does anyone living at this address work for:

    an advertising agency?

    a marketing research agency?

    a manufacturer of frozen foods?   (IF YES TO ANY, TERMINATE, AND REUSE FORM)

Has the child/children eaten any of these <u>frozen foods</u> at home during the past <u>5 days</u>?

pot pies	1
tv dinners	2
pizza	3
Mexican dinners	4

(IF NEITHER, TERMINATE, ERASE, CIRCLE LOWEST UNCIRCLED NUMBER BELOW, AND REUSE FORM)

How many children between the ages of 6 and 12 live at this address?

0 ————————→ (TERMINATE AND REUSE FORM)

1

2

3

4

5 or more

01 02 03 04 05 06 07 08 09 10 11 12 13
14 15 16 17 18 19 20 21 22 23 24 25 26
27 28 29 30 31 32 33 34 35 36 37 38 39
40 41 42 43 44 45 46 47 48 49 50 51 52
53 54 55 56 57 58 59 60 61 62 63 64 65
66 67 68 69 70 71 72 73 74 75 76 77 78
79 80 81 82 83 84 85 86 87 88 89 90 91
92 93 94 95 96 97 98 99 100 (USE NEW FORM)

---

respondent satisfies screening criteria; more often than not only certain ones will do. See Box 10.1 for an example.

    Why, when the last question in Box 10.1 has no positive response, does the interviewer circle the lowest uncircled number at the bottom of the instruction? Consider, for example, a completed form having the number 24 circled. What this means is that, before talking with this family, the interviewer screened out 24 others with children (whose parents did not work at the three sorts of firms) who did not eat either frozen pizza or Mexican dinners. Some simple arithmetic (with the total of these numbers and the number of completed forms) provides us with an estimate of the two products' consumption frequency in the population. The same procedure also tallies the number of refusals and not-at-homes in many marketing research studies.

Of course, personal interview sampling instructions may leave little decision freedom to the interviewer. Respondent identity, interview times, and other sampling details can be fully specified but only at great cost. Such specification is much more economically used with telephone interviews, but even here research practice often allows some interviewer decision on respondent selection.

Summary sampling instructions to personal and telephone interviewers often state that great effort went into sample design and that instructions must be followed exactly. If the interviewer does not understand a sampling detail, a summary instruction should reference a field supervisor or other authority. An instruction should also tell the interviewer to note on the data collection form any unusual field circumstances that made a selection decision difficult.

Interviewer-Administered Forms: Form Administration Instructions.
Form administration instructions tell the interviewer how to use the questionnaire once a qualified person consents to be interviewed. Some general form administration instructions outline the importance of the study and describe its purpose in broad terms. To avoid biasing interviewer behavior, instructions disclose neither the exact research objectives nor the specific marketing problem.

General administration instructions also stress the importance of understanding form administration procedures and of following them to the letter. Question sequence departures, wording changes, casual remarks, and other variations serve only to distort results. At the same time, instructions usually tell the interviewer of the need to put the respondent at ease early in the interview. General administration instructions also should identify a member of the research team who can answer questions about administering the form. The approximate time an interview takes should be told and to whom completed forms should be returned. Interview quotas and completion dates should be detailed. An instruction to protect disclosure of consumer identity can also be stressed if anonymity is part of the study.

Following general administration instructions, specific instructions cover each unitary portion of the form. Instructions usually discuss specific questions and present examples of properly recorded responses. Instructions always explain probing and open-ended questions where responses are more difficult to record. Specific instructions also explain stimulus materials such as cards, pictures, or product samples that accompany certain questions. They also tell interviewers of the need to conduct the interview at a table, if one is needed to present stimulus materials

---

BOX 10.2

Validation Instructions

(START)
Could I please have your name so that I feel more comfortable when we talk? Also, someone may call you later in the week to confirm 1 or 2 questions and she will need your name too.

Respondent's Name (PRINT)

_____

Address (CONFIRM DIRECTORY ADDRESS) _____

_____

Telephone Number (AREA CODE AND NUMBER)
(   ) _____

Interview Date ____/____/____ (MONTH/DATE/YEAR)

Interview Starting
Time _____ A.M. P.M. (CIRCLE)

Interview Ending Time ____ A.M. P.M. (CIRCLE)

Interviewer Signature _____

_____

(OFFICE USE)
Validated by _____ Date _____
Time _____ A.M. P.M. (CIRCLE)

---

while recording responses. They should also tell interviewers how to complete time sheets and other record keeping forms for accounting purposes.

Interviewer-Administered Forms: Validation Instructions. Validation instructions describe procedures necessary to collect information confirming interview results. Researchers usually confirm 10 to 15 percent of each interviewer's work—to check on her or his performance. Most of this information and its accompanying instructions are straightforward; see Box 10.2 for an example from a telephone survey. Similar validation instructions usually appear at the end of a personal interview form. Interviewers should know that their work will be validated. Spaces on the form provide for the interviewer's and validator's signatures as proof of an acceptable interview.

Validation instructions may ask the interviewer to draw a map of the route she took to obtain her interviews. Key instructions should tell how to indicate households that she skipped, contacted, and called back and how to show ones that participated and ones that refused. If the interviewer is to use a tape recorder for validation, its operations must be explained here along with language to introduce the device to the consumers.

Summary of Interviewer-Administered Forms. Like fact questions, sampling, form administration, and validation instructions for interviewer-administered forms are certain to improve if fellow researchers review them. However, with experience each researcher will develop good instructions and find that they become fairly standard across numerous projects.

Interviewers who regularly are inactive between studies or who participate in many studies may not find them so standard. Consequently, many projects require training or briefing sessions to clarify instructions and answer questions about the form. Some role-playing interviews also allow interviewers to practice and become familiar with procedures.

Self-Administered Forms.   Instructions for self-administered forms parallel those for interviewer-administered forms but are much simpler. Some general instructions, often on the cover letter or cover page of the form, describe an overview of the research and the importance of each person's participation, how long it takes to complete the form, who should fill it out, when to fill it out, and what to do with the completed form. General instructions also state the need for careful, honest answers and the researcher's intent not to disclose any respondent's identity. Instructions often ask the respondent to complete the form at one sitting, during a time likely to be free of interruptions. Always a last "instruction" on the form thanks the respondent for completing the form.

Specific instructions accompany each unitary portion of the form. See Box 10.3 for some examples.

Our last issue in the design of the data collection form addresses the form's **layout** or physical appearance. Most our interest lies with self-administered and not interviewer-administered forms. Erdos outlines some rules: **DATA COLLECTION FORM LAYOUT**

1. The layout should give the impression of a neatly printed page that is both easy to read and simple to fill out. Do not crowd questions or responses.

2. Simplify the form by consistently placing questions on one side of the page and response categories on the other. For each unitary portion in the form, align response categories vertically or horizontally on the page.

3. Provide lines instead of blank space for responses to open-ended questions.

4. Number questions within unitary portions of the questionnaire, returning to 1 for the first question of each unitary portion. This avoids using high numbers for later questions in a long questionnaire.

BOX 10.3

Examples of Instructions on Self-Administered Forms

Now we would like your impressions of the bank where you keep your <u>largest savings account</u>.

Write the name of that bank here: _____

Place an X between each of the 12 pairs of phrases below in the space that most closely represents your feelings about this bank. For example, if you feel this bank has extremely friendly tellers and quite crowded parking, your responses to the first two pairs of phrases would look like this:

Now we would like to know what you think about Harrisons Bicycle Shop. For each of the 16 statements below, circle a response to the right of each statement that most clearly represents your feelings.

Now we would like some background information about you and your family. These questions are for statistical purposes only. Do not put your name anywhere on this or any other page.

	Extremely	Quite	Somewhat	Somewhat	Quite	Extremely	
1. Friendly tellers	___	___	___	___	___	___	Unfriendly tellers
2. Crowded parking	___	___	___	___	___	___	Uncrowded parking

Read each pair of phrases carefully and remember to place an X between each pair.

5. Print mail survey forms that are longer than one page on both sides of the paper to save postage.

6. Use illustrations in mail survey forms only as absolutely necessary to clarify or shorten questions. Consumers may confuse illustrated questionnaires with direct mail advertisements.[14]

Overall, the final form should look "professional but not slick."

Typographic and spelling errors, poorly worded questions, and poorly worded instructions cannot be tolerated. As a matter of policy, someone

---

[14]Paul L. Erdos, "Data Collection Methods: Mail Surveys," in *Handbook of Marketing Research*, ed. Robert Ferber, (New York: McGraw-Hill, 1974), Section 2: 95.

other than the person drafting the form should proofread every final draft before printing. Normally, the form need only be professionally typed and not typeset. Key words on the form should be emphasized by using different typefaces, capital letters, underlines, or other methods, much as our examples on preceding pages.

Beyond writing questions, we see there is much a researcher must do in assembling the data collection form before finally using it. Assembling involves locating questions in unitary portions and locating the unitary portions in a data collection form. It also involves writing instructions to aid interviewers or respondents in recording answers, as well as physically designing the form to help achieve that purpose.

SUMMARY OF DATA COLLECTION FORM ASSEMBLY

One last activity a researcher performs in assembling the data collection form is to pretest it. Because pretests apply not just to assembly but to the entire measurement development process, we wait until the next chapter for a more complete discussion.

Chapter Summary

This chapter makes two major points:

1. Research data depend on research questions.

2. Assembling research questions into a data collection form is as important as the nature of the questions.

Let us summarize our discussion on each point in the next two paragraphs.

Research data come from research questions. Research questions reflect both the researcher's conceptualization of the variables being measured and his or her selection of measurements method. A researcher conceptualizes a variable as either ordered or nonordered, depending on whether or not measurement objects can be considered to possess greater or lesser quantities of the variable (ordered) or can be considered merely to possess or lack the variable (nonordered). Ordered variables break further into continuous and discrete variables, depending on whether the measurement objects can possess any quantity of them or only integer quantities. A researcher measures variables using nominal, ordinal, interval, and ratio methods. Each uses different rules to assign numbers as measurements; each produces data possessing different properties. Such properties become especially important in selecting a data analysis technique. All other things being equal, a researcher prefers questions that produce interval or ratio data.

In assembling questions into a data collection form, a researcher must consider the potential for response errors caused by question sequence and timing. Controlling for these errors is a matter of organizing the data collection form in a logical and professional manner. Considerations include item content, item response behaviors, respondents, past research, and pretest results. Response errors also result when faulty instructions accompany the data collection form and when the layout is confusing. All contribute to invalid and unreliable measurement, a topic we shall examine in Chapter 11.

Chapter Review

KEY TERMS

Data	Question sequence
Nonordered variable	Question timing
Ordered variable	Halo effect
Nominal measurement	Unitary portion
Ordinal measurement	Sampling instructions
Interval measurement	Form administration instructions
Ratio measurement	Screening criteria
Ordered relationship	Validation instructions
Continuous variables	Self-administered form
Discrete variables	Data collection form layout

DISCUSSION QUESTIONS

1. Think of twelve variables you would like to measure in a marketing research study. Which if these did you conceptualize as nonordered? Which are discrete? Which are continuous? Try to list four variables in each category.

2. Identify the following measurements as either nominal, ordinal, interval, or ratio data:
   - temperature measured by a centigrade thermometer
   - numbers on the backs of football players
   - an intention-to-buy scale using integers from 0 to 10 as responses
   - a semantic differential scale measuring brand image
   - cubic volume of a new package design

3. Could an ordered variable ever be measured in a nominal fashion?

4. What happens when you collapse relatively continuous measurements into crude, discrete categories—for instance, suppose you convert consumers' actual incomes into one of four categories. What are the consequences?

5. On what bases could someone criticize the organization of a data collection form?

6. Of what use to the researcher is a sampling instruction, "If consumer refuses to participate, circle lowest uncircled number below and reuse the form."

7. Illustrate how construction of a data collection form is based on decisions reached at earlier stages in a marketing research design.

Additional Readings

Emory, C. William. *Business Research Methods.* Homewood, Ill,: Richard D. Irwin, 1976.
   Chapters 5 and 9 provide an excellent introduction to research questions and the data such questions produce.

Nunnally, Jum C. *Psychometric Theory.* 2nd ed. New York: McGraw-Hill, 1978.
   This is the standard work on the measurement of psychological characteristics. See Chapters 1, 2, 15, and 16 for more detailed discussions than ours in this chapter.

11

Measurement Process Evaluation

The time comes to focus a critical eye on the entire measurement process. We want to consider fact questions, psychological characteristic questions, and data collection form assembly as sources of truth and sources of error. In this discussion we employ two measurement concepts: validity and reliability. After discussing them, we conclude with a section presenting a recommended procedure for measurement development.

Measurement Validity

In Chapter 7 we defined **validity** as the measurement process's ability to measure the concept or the concepts it is meant to measure. Three examples of marketing research questions illustrate validity:

- How likely are you to purchase a can of tuna fish the next time you buy groceries?
- Starting tomorrow when you get up, use this diary each day to record the number of times you use baking soda to brush your teeth, bathe, and bake.
- What things were important to you when you selected your obstetrician?

257

Ask yourself what answers to these questions will represent—will they represent data about the intended variables of interest? Or will they represent something else?

TYPES OF VALIDITY   The first question is meant to measure consumers' future purchase behaviors. The extent to which consumers show future purchase behaviors different from the intentions they expressed by their responses represents the extent of invalid measurement. (The influence of just asking the question itself causes some degree of future purchase behavior; this also represents invalid measurement.) Only to the extent that responses actually represent estimates of undistorted future behavior do we have valid measurement. Such a situation is described by one type of validity called **predictive validity**, applicable when researchers intend to foretell some future event.

The second question is meant to measure consumers' usage of an item. However, a moment's thought reveals that consumers use baking soda for many purposes other than those few noted in the question. Consequently, their responses only partly indicate usage of baking soda and the question is only partly valid. This situation is described by a second type of validity called **content validity**, applicable when researchers intend that a measurement's content represent the universe of all possible measurement content.

The third question is meant to identify consumer choice criteria. Because of a host of factors (see our next paragraph, for example), some responses will identify choice criteria while others will not. And because choice criteria exist as abstract, unobservable psychological characteristics, the researcher will meet difficulty in distinguishing valid responses from the invalid. This situation is described by a third type of validity, called **construct validity**, applicable when researchers intend to measure psychological characteristics or constructs that have no direct, concrete manifestation.

The "something else" that our research questions may measure actually consists of a variety of things. For one, the questions partly measure consumers' relative understanding of the English language: people who understand a question better than others may respond differently. For another, the questions partly measure consumers' motivations or reasons for responding: some responses will come not from a desire to provide the truth but from a desire to protect the self or to please the researcher or to conclude the interview as quickly as possible. For other examples of the "something else," consider that the questions partly measure consumers' short- and long-term memories and their abilities to articulate past experiences. These marketing research questions may measure even more things; these extras will become apparent when we discuss measurement reliability.

That the questions measure things other than what the measurement process was meant to measure is not unusual; marketing research measurement is always partly valid and partly invalid. Whether predictive, content, or construct in nature, validity is always a "matter of degree rather than an all-or-none property."[1] What we attempt as marketing researchers is to design measurements having maximum validity for the use to which results will be put, given resource constraints.

Establishing predictive and construct validity involves examining response frequencies and relationships. To illustrate the process for predictive validity, let us return to our question of tuna fish purchase intentions. A researcher would begin by combining the question with other questions (including some for purposes of disguise) and pretest the resulting data collection form on a representative sample of consumers. Suppose that eighty housewives in Cleveland compose the sample. The researcher instructs each housewife to respond to the form and to record her grocery purchases for the following four weeks in a purchase diary. Results appear in Table 11.1. Examining intention categories and the percentages purchasing tuna fish, we see support for the question's predictive validity—the higher the intention, the greater the percentage purchasing.

ESTABLISHING VALIDITY

Instead of response frequencies, an alternative procedure examines the relationship between purchase intentions and purchase behavior. Because the researcher conceptualized and measured purchase intentions as a continuous, ordinal variable and purchase behavior as a discrete, ratio variable, the relationship may be expressed by Goodman and Kruskal's gamma. For data in Table 11.1, we have gamma = 0.65, which indicates moderate scale validity. (We can easily confirm this answer after reading a section describing gamma in Chapter 16.)

Establishing construct validity is more difficult because of the nature

TABLE 11.1
Tuna Fish Purchase Intentions and Purchase Behavior

Purchase Intentions	Number of Housewives	Housewives Actually Purchasing	Percent Actually Purchasing
Definitely buy	10	9	90
Probably buy	20	12	60
Might or might not buy	20	8	40
Probably not buy	20	5	25
Definitely not buy	10	1	10

[1]Jum C. Nunnally, *Psychometric Theory*, 2nd ed. (New York: McGraw-Hill, 1978), p. 87.

of a psychological characteristic or construct. We said that a researcher cannot see or otherwise directly sense the construct because a psychological characteristic has no direct, concrete manifestation. Rather, a psychological characteristic exists only as an organization of mental activities. To say, then, that a question or set of questions actually measures a psychological characteristic requires two things: measurements of behaviors that can be seen and an assumption that such behaviors reflect the construct.

A researcher usually can choose from a wide variety of behaviors assumed to manifest the construct. Consider our choice criterion question that was meant to measure things important to women when selecting an obstetrician. Potential behaviors include conversations, gestures, galvanic skin responses, pencil marks on a data collection form, and real world choice behavior, among others. Consider just paper and pencil measurement. Potential behaviors include circling a response category, filling in a blank, completing sentences, and writing short paragraphs. Even within one of these activities we could identify different potential behaviors based on the sorts of instructions given and the sorts of questions asked. How do we establish construct validity for such a wide range of behaviors?

The answer, of course, is that we don't. Rather, what we do is establish construct validity for one or a few behaviors that eventually will become part of the final data collection form. This establishment process proceeds in three ways.

The first looks for positive relationships between two different behaviors that are both meant to measure the same construct. For example, we might conduct depth interviews with fifteen women on the obstetrician selection topic and list in descending order the number of times different choice criteria appear. We then might ask another group of women to rank-order a scrambled version of the list according to how they think most women would feel. An expression of the relationship between the two sets of ranks would estimate construct validity.

A second way to establish construct validity looks for predicted measurement differences between two different consumer groups. For example, we might identify an obstetrician charging high prices and one charging low prices. Rank orderings of choice criteria by the two obstetricians' patients should show that the relative importance of price is different for the two groups—and in the predicted direction. Results to the contrary would indicate an invalid measure.

A third way of establishing construct validity applies if the measuring method contains several items that are meant to measure the same construct. Taken together, these items should show high internal consistency reliability for a representative consumer sample. We discuss internal consistency reliability in the next section, but the idea behind it is appropriate now: if the construct is meaningful for the group under study, items that measure the same construct should show at least moderate relationships with each other. Alternatively, if many of the relationships between items are quite small, items probably do not measure the same construct. Or, at best, they measure little of it and more of something else. Evidence of high internal consistency reliability indicates only that the items measure something but not necessarily what we intend. In other words, high internal consistency reliability is a necessary but not a sufficient condition that supports construct validity.[2]

In establishing predictive and construct validity, the researcher is not limited to evidence obtained by just two behavior measurements from just two groups. Obviously, the more measurements and groups used, the more evidence is accumulated. Also accumulated is more cost. At some point the researcher determines that a measurement method has sufficient validity to warrant its use as a research tool and she or he proceeds to use it. At that time the validity of the method cannot be described as "proven" but rather as "established and adequate" for the use to which the method will be put.

Establishing content validity is easier. It is established judgmentally from reference both to the domain or universe of all possible item content and to the measurement items. The researcher's concern is simply one of adequacy in selecting a sufficient and representative number of items. For example, to establish the content validity of our baking soda question, a researcher might begin by conducting several focus group interviews with consumers to determine how they use baking soda. Suppose consumers report fourteen different uses. From this universe of all possible item content, the researcher might select the three uses most frequently mentioned to serve as measurement items. Such a procedure leads to a valid measurement, in the researcher's judgment.

For perspective on this subject of validity, consider that marketing researchers most often concern themselves with predictive validity, and the form of behavior most often used to establish validity is sales. Is the reaction of a laboratory group of consumers the same as that of consumers in a supermarket? Does a test market really forecast eventual sales of a new product? Can vocational interest tests predict success as a salesperson? All of these reflect predictive validity issues and need to be addressed in any assessment of research relevancy.

Measurement Reliability

Apart from the concept of validity stands the concept of reliability—the absence of random error in measurement. **Reliability** means that measurement results are repeatable at different times (assuming that what we measure does not change), that they are repeatable by different researchers, and that they are repeatable by different measurement items that we intend to measure the same concept.

---

[2]Ibid., p. 103.

CAUSES OF RANDOM ERROR IN MEASUREMENT

Random error in measurement comes from three general sources: respondents, the research task, and researchers. Examples of specific causes appear in Table 11.2.

Respondents themselves are perhaps the largest source of random error. Often they become anxious during the measurement process and respond differently from the way they otherwise would. Some have an articulation problem—that is, they know what they want to say but cannot say it. Others answer questions haphazardly because of boredom. Respondents sometimes make a clerical mistake and indicate an unintentional answer; they occasionally guess and make a response for which they truly have no basis. Some indicate a wrong answer because of memory lapses or because of a headache developed halfway through the measurement process. Actually, these respondent causes of random error should be well known to anyone beyond his or her first college midterm.

The research task as embodied in the data collection form also causes random errors in measurement. The form's layout may influence answers by confusing people. Response categories might be so few in number that they cannot measure accurately what the research means to measure, or response categories might not be mutually exclusive and exhaustive. A question's position with respect to other questions might influence responses to it or to other questions. Item wording may be vague, subject to semantic confusion, have an unspecified frame of reference, or tip people off as to the sponsor of the research and its purpose. Another aspect of the research task, the research environment, also causes random error. Poorly written instructions, too little time, and, for example, faulty air conditioning can all lead to unreliable responses. So can casual and formal remarks made by peers and interviewers.

TABLE 11.2
Some Causes of Random Error in Measurement

Respondents as Source	Research Task as Source	Researchers as Source
Anxiety	Data collection form	Clerical
Articulation	Layout	Data processing
Boredom	Response categories	Interpretation
Clerical	Question sequence	
Guessing	Question wording	
Memory	Research environment	
Physiology	Instructions	
	Time pressure	
	Physical environment	
	Social environment	

Even researchers cause random error. They may make clerical errors in data coding, analysis, and reporting. They may make more significant mistakes in data interpretation: different researchers may provide different interpretations, just as a single researcher might for the same data on different occasions. Errors by machines (particularly computer hardware) should also be noted as a source of random error, although machines are usually quite reliable. And, as if our discussion so far were not enough, we should recognize that interactions between respondents, research tasks, and researchers provide a last source of random error. Imagine a poorly designed questionnaire being completed by an anxious consumer for analysis by an absent-minded researcher!

The concept of reliability considers causes in Table 11.2 as sources of random or unrepeatable measurement error. Yet some, if not most, look disturbingly like potential sources of stable or repeatable measurement error, which is partly the topic of validity. For example, a consumer's memory abilities represent both a "temporary and specific characteristic" (reliability issue) and a "lasting and general characteristic" (validity issue).[3] Thus, what reliability really considers is general error causes as they specifically lead to unpredictable inaccuracies. These inaccuracies are incapable of being reproduced by a second, third, or later measurement.

ESTIMATING RELIABILITY

Estimating reliability for a particular measurement is, like establishing validity, a process of examining response frequencies and relationships. And, like validity, reliability should describe only unitary portions of the data collection form rather than the form as a whole. Thus, we should speak of the reliability of an income question or the reliability of a store image semantic differential scale rather than the reliability of an entire questionnaire.

To estimate reliability for a unitary portion of a data collection form, we discuss two commonly used procedures: **alternate form reliability** and **internal consistency reliability**. The first applies to most measurement processes in marketing research and requires two different versions of the items whose reliability we wish to assess. Usually a sample of people responds to one version and two weeks later responds to an alternate version. Reliability is then estimated by the agreement between the two sets of response scores.

Internal consistency reliability is more specialized and can be used only to estimate the reliability of a multiple-item scale that measures a single characteristic. Most often the scale measures a psychological characteristic but nothing prevents the procedure from being applied to any multiple-item measuring device, as long as each item attempts to measure

[3]Julian C. Stanley, "Reliability," in *Educational Measurement*, 2nd ed., ed. R. L. Thorndike (Washington, D.C.: American Council on Education, 1971), p. 363–69.

the same aspect of the same thing. This procedure requires only one sample of people who respond only once to the items. Reliability is estimated by the agreement between item response scores.

Let us use two examples to illustrate the two procedures.

Example of Alternate Form Reliability. Suppose we want to estimate the reliability of a single consumer behavior question, "What brand of toothpaste did you last purchase?" Because our question is a single-item measurement, alternate form reliability is the proper procedure. We embed the question in a data collection form, assemble a representative sample of 140 consumers, measure their responses, and tabulate results. Two weeks later we repeat the process with the same sample but use another questionnaire with an alternative item: "Circle the brand of toothpaste below that you bought most recently." Suppose purchase frequencies for the 106 consumers who did not buy toothpaste during this two-week period look as in Table 11.3.

Table 11.3 shows, for example, that of the 24 consumers who answered brand A to the original question, 18 gave the same response to the alternate question. Adding all main diagonal frequencies (18 + 18 + 23 + 9 + 14) we find 82 of 106 consumers (77.4 percent) answered the two questions identically. As an aside, notice that the alternate question finds reported purchases decreasing for leading brands (A, B, and C) and increasing for less popular brands (D and all others). This is typical for responses to an aided-recall question when compared to those for an unaided-recall question.

Instead of examining purchase frequencies, alternate form reliability could be estimated by examining the relationship between responses to the two questions. Because we conceptualize brands purchased as a non-ordered variable, the two questions produce nominal data. A proper expression for the relationship is Goodman and Kruskal's lambda. (Just as

TABLE 11.3
Toothpaste Brand Purchase Frequencies

		Brand Purchased by Alternate Question					
		A	B	C	D	All Others	Totals
Brand	A	18	0	1	1	4	24
Purchased	B	0	18	0	0	0	18
by Original	C	1	0	23	2	8	34
Question	D	0	0	0	9	1	10
	All Others	1	0	4	1	14	20
Totals		20	18	28	13	27	106

with our gamma expression of relationship earlier in this chapter, we must accept this on faith or jump ahead to read parts of Chapter 16.) For our data, we have lambda equal to 0.68. Because lambda has a minimum of 0 and a maximum of 1.0, we consider our question to show moderate reliability.

Now consider internal consistency reliability with our second example.

Example of Internal Consistency Reliability. Suppose a record manufacturer wishes to measure consumer satisfaction with the quality of its records using a six-item Likert scale. Items are randomly combined with thirty-four other statements about records, given to a representative sample of 100 consumers; responses are indicated by scores of 1 to 6. Now, if we have a reliable satisfaction scale, what should be true about each consumer's response to each satisfaction item? The answer is that responses should be related or internally consistent, because each item attempts to measure a part of some unknown record quality attitude possessed by sample members.

To estimate internal consistency reliability for our satisfaction scale requires correlation coefficients calculated between all item pairs. Because we consider responses to be interval data, an ordinary correlation coefficient is appropriate. (We may want to refer to Chapter 16 for justification and a computing formula.) Suppose the matrix of correlation coefficients looks like the presentation in Table 11.4 (i rows, j columns).

A formula for calculating the internal consistency reliability coefficient (r_{tt}) is:[4]

$$r_{tt} = \frac{k\bar{r}_{ij}}{1 + (k-1)\bar{r}_{ij}}$$

TABLE 11.4
Matrix of Correlation Coefficients

		Item					
		1	2	3	4	5	6
Item	1						
	2	0.22					
	3	0.30	0.20				
	4	0.41	0.21	0.48			
	5	0.17	0.31	0.21	0.15		
	6	0.27	0.26	0.40	0.26	0.35	

[4]Nunnally, *Psychometric Theory*, p. 211.

where $\bar{r}_{ij}$ is the average correlation between the k items in the scale. For our data we have:

$$\bar{r}_{ij} = (0.22 + 0.30 + 0.20 + \cdots + 0.35)/15$$

$$= 0.28 \text{ and}$$

$$k = 6$$

Thus,

$$r_{tt} = \frac{6(0.28)}{1 + (6 - 1)(0.28)} = 0.70$$

This indicates moderate internal consistency reliability, perhaps barely adequate for most applied marketing research studies. More desirable would be an internal consistency reliability coefficient of 0.80 or greater.[5]

To achieve this level of reliability we can use two approaches: increasing the number of items in the scale or increasing their average correlation. Using both, a little arithmetic shows that eight scale items having an average correlation between them of 0.40 results in a reliability coefficient of 0.84. This increased reliability should make sense. A scale whose items show higher correlations between them means that it measures more of the same thing (and is subject to less random error). Also, more such items means that the scale has more measurement repeatability. The scale measures more of the intended concept more times.

For perspective, we should realize that internal consistency reliability is easier to estimate than alternate form reliability: only one data collection form is needed at only one point in time. Moreover, truly equivalent alternate data collection forms are difficult to construct and difficult to apply. That is, when responding to the alternate form, some people remember some of their responses made to similar items on the original form. This artificially inflates the reliability estimate.

Alternate form and internal consistency reliability each have a less rigorous counterpart. Instead of correlating response scores from alternate data collection forms, **test/retest reliability** correlates scores from the same form. Unless the number of items is large, respondent memory artificially increases the correlation. Instead of examining a scale's individual item score correlations, **split-half reliability** examines the correlation between total scores from one half of the items with total scores from the other half. How the scale is halved (randomly, first half items versus second half, odd-numbered versus even-numbered, etc.) influences total scores and, hence, the reliability estimate. Test/retest and split-half reliability estimation procedures should generally be avoided.

---

[5]J. Paul Peter, "Reliability: a Review of Psychometric Basics and Recent Marketing Practices," *Journal of Marketing Research* 16 (February 1979): 15.

A Model for Measurement Development

Our last section models the process of developing valid and reliable measurements in marketing research. We discuss a measurement development model that coordinates previously discussed material and treats one new topic: item to total score correlations.

The model applies primarily to new data collection forms—that is, to research situations that demand measurement novel to the researcher. Such situations can consist of new questions, new populations, or both. The model appears in Figure 11.1.

DISCUSSION OF THE MODEL

Review Characteristics to be Measured. The model's first step asks us to review the behavior, socioeconomic, and psychological characteristics potentially a part of the data collection form. From this large number and variety, we want to select only those characteristics that help solve the marketing problem, keeping in mind already specified data sources and collection methods. In other words, review of the characteristics to be measured is made partly in light of decisions reached earlier in the marketing research design.

Review of these characteristics is also made partly in light of how selected characteristics can be measured. Regularly we will face some general measurement alternatives: Will open-ended or structured response questions be better? Is a Likert scale or another measurement method more appropriate? Does a published scale used by other researchers meet our needs? Decision bases again include earlier steps in the research process and add a later one, data analysis methods. That is, we must collect data in a form that allows the use of intended analytical techniques—the time to find that an intended analysis is impossible is not when we begin to interpret results of the first computer run.

Construct First Draft. After that extensive review process comes the second step—writing a first draft of the data collection form. The draft should show an understanding of the mechanics of measurement as discussed in this and the previous four chapters. The draft should include only relevant characteristics; to include others only creates confusion.

Actually, we may write several versions of the first draft, each having alternate instructions, questions, and response behaviors. At this stage of measurement development we may not know which measurement method is best, so we must compare different versions of the form. We should write each version separately at a single sitting, allowing a large block of uninterrupted time. We should write complete unitary portions at one time instead of first writing a usage rate question, then a belief statement, then a purchase intentions question and so on.

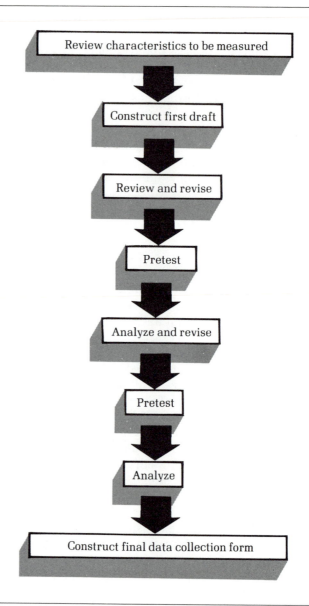

FIGURE 11.1
A measurement development model

Write two or three different versions of each item to be used in a psychological characteristic scale. For example, consider the development of our record quality satisfaction scale. Suppose several focus group interviews, conducted as part of our first model step, identified four relevant quality choice criteria as factory scratches, improper mixing, warped records, and unsatisfactory return policies. For the first choice criterion, we might write such statements as:

- Most new records have too many scratches.
- Consumer complaints about factory scratches on new records are greatly exaggerated.
- Most record companies could easily make new records with fewer scratches.

These statements would be randomly combined with other satisfaction and belief statements (including some pertinent to research purpose and some for disguise purposes) as part of one data collection form rough draft.

When this step is complete, put all first drafts aside for a few days and work on something else. We should use this time to let associates review our efforts while we regain some perspective.

Review and Revise.   The third step reviews and revises the rough draft. If we considered several measurement methods, now is the time to settle on one better way. This should be possible in most applied marketing research studies. Our own fresh outlook, other researchers, and the decision maker should help our decision. After agreement, the draft should look like the final form, for most behavior and socioeconomic characteristic questions. Psychological characteristic scales, however, contain a large number of quite similar items.

Pretest.   In the fourth step the data collection form draft is pretested by a small sample of representative respondents. Our primary interest is in their response problems. Do they understand data collection form instructions? Are any items hard to understand? Equivocal? Sensitive? When did they begin to guess the identity of the research sponsor? Are all response categories meaningful? Answers to these and other questions can be obtained by having respondents make notes in the form's margin as they respond. Focus group interviews conducted after the participants have responded also prove worthwhile in determining where and how to improve the form.

Analyze and Revise.   When we analyze pretest results, the fifth step in our measurement development process, these response problems in the pretest affect the data's validity and reliability. For now, the concern is validity: we must first determine that the questions mostly measure the concepts we mean to measure before we consider how accurately the questions measure them.[6] Consequently, we examine pretest fact question results to see if they correspond with actual, validated behavior for the

---

[6]Stanley, "Reliability," p. 357.

pretest group whenever possible. We examine different pretest groups, defined in terms of behavior or socioeconomic characteristics, to see if they respond differently to psychological characteristic items, as we had predicted they would. We also examine different measures of the same and of different psychological characteristics as taken from one pretest group, to confirm other predictions.[7]

Estimating reliability during this step can only be begun. Sources of random error should clearly be removed as discovered, but to go beyond and calculate internal consistency or alternate form reliability is usually improper. This is so because members of the first pretest group were asked both to respond to the form and to note what they found "wrong" with it. This dual purpose instruction artificially increases random error because it makes their research task more complex. These respondents have more on their minds than those who participate in the next pretest.

Pretest.   In our sixth step, the revised data collection form is subjected to a second pretest. Here our concern is almost entirely with measurement reliability. A larger sample of representative persons responds , following instructions that will appear the same way on the final form. We require one sample, one form, and one set of responses if we intend to investigate internal consistency reliability. We require one sample, two alternate forms, and two sets of responses taken two weeks apart if we intend to investigate alternate form reliability. In either case, the form should be quite similar to the final data collection form except that it still has two or three times more psychological characteristic items than we expect to use in the final form.

Analyze.   Our seventh step discards the less reliable psychological characteristic scale items and then estimates reliability for each scale and other unitary portions of the data collection form. To illustrate, let us return to our record quality satisfaction scale as one such portion. Suppose that fifteen items (including the three on factory scratches) were written in step two and randomly combined with twenty-five others as part of the pretest data collection form. Response categories are scored one to six, with higher scores again indicating more satisfaction with record quality, for the second pretest sample (consisting of 120 consumers). As with the first pretest, scoring is reversed for negatively loaded scale items. Table 11.5 shows part of the raw data matrix obtained from this pretest.

A **raw data matrix** simply shows each consumer's response score for each data collection form item. We have edited this matrix to show in Table 11.5 only response scores for three of the consumers on the fifteen satisfaction scale items. Also shown for convenience are total satisfaction

---

[7]Discussion in the paragraph is basically that of Nunnally, *Psychometric Theory*, Chap. 3.

TABLE 11.5
Record Quality Satisfaction Scale Item Scores and Total Scores

Consumer	Item Response Score for Item Number:															Total Satisfaction Score
	1	4	5	8	11	15	17	22	24	25	26	30	33	36	40	
A	6	4	1	3	2	4	5	5	3	4	2	6	1	1	2	49
B	5	3	2	4	4	6	5	4	2	5	1	6	2	2	3	54
C	6	4	3	3	3	5	5	5	3	5	2	5	2	2	5	58
.																.
.																.
.																.
$n = 120$																

scale scores for these consumers. Total scores show consumer C to be the most satisfied, consumer A the least, and consumer B in between.

We proceed by calculating each item's **item to total score correlation coefficient**. Recall that we intend each scale item to measure a part of this psychological characteristic called satisfaction. If one does, for example, it should agree or correlate with the total satisfaction scale score which we accept as a summary or more complete measure. Thus, we should obtain high correlation coefficients between each column of item response scores and the last column of total scale scores. If a correlation coefficient is low or even slightly negative, that item probably does not measure satisfaction very well. By correlating each column of item response scores with the total score column we obtain fifteen item to total score correlations in all.

Suppose we rank-order these correlations and they look like the listing in Table 11.6 (using r_{iT} to stand for the correlation between item i and total scores). Now, if we wanted to choose only six items to measure con-

TABLE 11.6
Rank Orderings of Item to Total Score Correlation Coefficients

Rank	Item	r_{iT}	Rank	Item	r_{iT}
1	24	0.81	8	17	0.64
2	4	0.75	9	8	0.62
3	33	0.72	10	11	0.61
4	36	0.69	11	5	0.57
5	15	0.67	12	30	0.53
6	25	0.65	13	26	0.48
7	40	0.65	14	22	0.43
			15	1	0.37

sumer satisfaction, which ones would they be? Quite right, we would pick the top six items in terms of their item to total score correlations.

How reliable a scale do we have? The question can be answered most easily by calculating an internal consistency reliability coefficient. All we need is a matrix of correlation coefficients for all item pairs involving these six items and the use of our formula for r_{tt}. If the resulting internal consistency reliability coefficient is below our standard of 0.8, we add more items. (Which item would we add first?) Only if we performed earlier measurement development steps ineptly should we be unable to achieve satisfactory reliability.

Alternate form reliability could also be estimated during this step for unitary portions of the form requiring its use. As noted earlier, reliability of single-item measures can be investigated only with this procedure. All we do is compute frequencies and correlation coefficients for responses to the different alternate form items. We should achieve correlations 0.8 or higher.

Construct Final Data Collection Form. Our last step in measurement development is to construct the final data collection form. This should proceed rather mechanically, owing to our measurement development efforts. Our only new consideration is the idea of adjusting scale content to reflect particular research interests. That is, basing item selection solely on item to total score correlations and achieving acceptable internal consistency reliability might result in a scale containing some near duplicate items. At the same time, it might omit others of more interest. For example, a six-item scale would contain items 24, 4, 33, 36, 15, and 25 according to our procedure. However, suppose items 4, 33, and 25 deal with record scratches and no items concern warpage. Thus, we may justifiably drop item 25 from the scale and replace it with the warpage item having the highest item to total score correlation of all remaining items. Usually this adjustment will have little effect on scale reliability. This statement does not excuse us from calculating a revised coefficient, however.

SUMMARY OF THE MODEL FOR MEASUREMENT DEVELOPMENT

Our model implies expending much effort and resources in developing new measurements. While it is tempting to offer the opinion that certain steps in the model be bypassed for the sake of expediency, it is difficult to describe when this can be done. Speaking of a similar model, Churchill states that applied researchers "perhaps cannot afford the execution of each and every stage, although many of their conclusions are likely to be nonsense, one-time relationships."[8] The same is true with our model; it is hard to see how we can afford not to use it.

Perhaps only if a measurement has an empirical history of being very "right" could we consider not investigating its validity and reliability as

---

[8]Gilbert A. Churchill, Jr., "A Paradigm for Developing Better Measures of Marketing Constructs," *Journal of Marketing Research* 16 (February 1979): 73.

above. Even here we must be careful because we may not understand why and how the measurement works, only that it does. Additionally, if we intend to use this measurement for other than its present use, we do so at a considerable risk. No measurement is valid and reliable for universal application.

Consider our model to be moderately sophisticated. To simplify, the first thing we would remove would be item to total correlations in our seventh step; we would select final items based only on item correlations and content. To make it more complex, we would add a factor analysis of responses in our fifth and seventh steps (just before computing item to total score correlations). This would allow us to be more sure that all items in a scale measure the same thing, and not something else—which could occur despite their having high correlations.

Chapter Summary

A valid measurement measures what we mean to measure: predictions of future behavior, some specified domain of content, or some abstract psychological characteristic. These three types of validity are called, in order: predictive, content, and construct validity. Establishing predictive and construct validity focuses on pretest responses—in contrast to establishing content validity, which focuses on item content. A reliable measurement consistently yields similar results. Internal consistency and alternate form reliability procedures provide estimates of reliability by examining response frequencies and relationships.

Our model for measurement development encompasses all material in Chapters 7 through 11. It is complex, resource consuming, and largely uncompromising. It stresses the worth of measurement pretesting, a recurring topic in this and preceding chapters. In evaluating the model, we note again its purpose, to assist researchers in developing valid and reliable measurements. Most marketing researchers would agree that most marketing measurements would benefit from a more thorough investigation of what and how well they measure.

On this last point, we note that marketing researchers can calculate r_{tt} both during measurement development and after *actual use* of a multiple-item scale. This last calculation is quite important. It allows researchers to estimate reliability of each such scale used in their data collection, from the actual sample of respondents in the study.

Chapter Review

Validity	**Reliability**	**KEY TERMS**
Predictive validity	**Alternate form reliability**	
Content validity	**Internal consistency reliability**	
Construct validity	**Raw data matrix**	

DISCUSSION QUESTIONS

1. The validity of a measurement depends on the use to which its results will be put. Discuss.

2. Apply the concepts of content, predictive, and construct validity to a college midterm examination that is given in an introductory marketing course.

3. Which of the causes in Table 11.2 could cause stable measurement error? Illustrate each with an example.

4. Why are two pretests needed in our model for measurement development?

5. Instead of using internal consistency reliability and item to total score correlations to discard less reliable items, show how you would proceed using alternate form reliability.

6. An instructor would like you to develop a set of questions to measure students' likes and dislikes of her teaching methods. How would you proceed?

7. What "things" might a purchase diary actually be measuring beyond purchases?

8. A researcher in a large bank compares 318 consumers who have defaulted on their new car loans with a random sample of 300 promptly paying consumers. Results show marked differences on three socioeconomic variables: debt outstanding, income per family member, and length of employment. Why would screening all new applicants for all loans on these variables produce largely invalid measurements?

9. Estimate the internal consistency reliability for a five-item knowledge scale whose item correlations appear below:
How would you improve the scale's reliability?

	1	2	3	4	5
1					
2	.48				
3	.37	.26			
4	.29	.19	.61		
5	.43	.48	.50	.35	

10. Validity depends on the use to which measurement results will be put, but reliability is absolute and constant as long as the measurement process itself does not change. Discuss.

Additional Readings

Journal of Marketing Research (February, 1979).
   Most of the articles in this issue discuss research applications of validity and reliability.

Nunnally, Jum C. *Psychometric Theory* 2nd ed. New York: McGraw-Hill, 1978.
   This is the standard work in psychometric methods. Chapters 3, 6, and 7 provide extensive treatments on measurement validity and reliability.

Sudman, Seymour, and Bradburn, Norman M. *Response Effects in Surveys.* Chicago: Aldine Publishing, 1974.

This is a comprehensive and pragmatic discussion of stable and random response effects in surveys. The authors estimate both the direction and magnitude of these effects on survey measures of behavior and attitude.

Cases for Part III

6. Seville Community College*

"I see a great potential here at Seville for new continuing education programs. The problem is how to get started."

The speaker was Dr. Eleanor Digrazia, President of Seville Community College, a two-year public institution which offered a number of courses in the liberal arts and various vocational fields leading to an associate's degree. Founded in 1961, the college was located in Magraw, a growing city with a population of about 250,000 in a southwestern state. In 1972, the college had completed the final phase of a planned expansion program and boasted modern, air-conditioned buildings on a small, attractive campus, easily accessible from most parts of the city. The college had good parking facilities and was served by two bus lines which operated on thirty-minute headways until 11:30 P.M., Monday through Saturday.

Concerned about rising costs and an apparent reluctance on the part of elected state and county officials to increase community college budgets, Dr. Digrazia was evaluating other ways of increasing revenues. A study of existing course schedules and extracurricular activities showed that college facilities were underutilized in the evenings and on Saturdays. The campus was normally closed from 5:00 P.M. Saturday until 7:00 A.M. Monday unless a special event (such as a concert or community meeting) was scheduled.

On the basis of some preliminary enquiries, Dr. Digrazia believed that professional programs in fields such as law and real estate offered good potential for Seville. Real estate activity had always been significant in the region and was beginning to move into high gear again as the economy recovered from the recession. She knew that many practicing and would-be realtors traveled over thirty miles to Fairfax State University. The law school there offered a number of evening and weekend courses in special topics for lawyers and paralegal assistants. Continuing education programs in law and real estate were also sponsored by professional associations in both Fairfax (a city of 400,000 people) and Dos Rios, forty five miles in the opposite direction, which had a metropolitan population of over a million. President Digrazia had met several local lawyers and realtors who had expressed a desire to see such courses offered closer to home.

Getting part-time faculty would not be a problem, the President believed, since she knew a number of well-regarded professionals who had expressed an interest in teaching.

"I believe that there's a good market out there," said Dr. Digrazia. "We've got a nice facility here and a good location. Perhaps our main drawback is that many people see community colleges as just an extention of high school—13th or 14th grade if you know what I mean."

7. Powder Ridge Ski Area

"Another questionnaire to design," thought David Hamel, "but this one should be more interesting than most—and more difficult." Hamel picked up his pen. His mind went back to yesterday's meeting with Ted Friendly at Powder Ridge. Friendly had spent some time describing what he knew or thought he knew about the Powder Ridge skier. As Friendly saw it, "Our problem is that we only know who our customers are and not *why* they are." Further conversation had disclosed that Friendly knew who his customers were only in terms of where they came from, and little else for sure.

POWDER RIDGE

Powder Ridge was located in the heart of the Colorado Rockies, about four hours' driving time from Denver. It was a large destination ski area with many chair lifts and numerous advanced, intermediate, and beginner runs. It contained over 4,000 beds in several lodges and condominiums, with another 3,000 available at nearby motels and condominiums outside its control.

Powder Ridge was also a "mature" ski area. Some changes were always under way, of course; but primarily operations went smoothly, according to plan, and almost repetitively from year to year. In fact, Friendly had wondered if operations weren't too repetitive, especially when it came to his area of responsibility, marketing.

Friendly's concern centered on advertising. Each year Powder Ridge spent a sizeable amount of money on advertising aimed at two consumer segments, local and out-of-state skiers. About 30 percent was spent in Denver and other Colorado cities to attract the local skier to the slopes. Advertisements appeared in newspapers and on television, radio, and billboards. About 50 percent was spent in two ski magazines to reach out-of-state skiers. For the current ski season (which started in about a month), Friendly had budgeted over $100,000 to produce and place these ads. Another 15 percent was spent to reach both local and out-of-state skiers as they attended public ski shows during October and November each year in Denver, Minneapolis, Chicago, Kansas City, Houston, and other cities. Powder Ridge usually exhibited at these shows, passing out literature and advice to interested skiers.

Powder Ridge also spent a sizeable amount of money on trade promotion aimed at travel agents in many western and midwestern cities. Each year the firm sent packets of literature explaining Powder Ridge as a vacation experience to over 6,000 travel agents. The materials described Powder Ridge skiing, lodging, and entertainment in various packaged combinations at several price levels. Such materials were necessary to educate travel agents who, in turn, would "sell" the area to consumers. Even further, Friendly often invited travel agents to spend two days at Powder Ridge, courtesy of the area. Usually only one agent would be invited from an agency, to arrive at an off-peak time. Cooperating airlines would "comp" the air fare and Powder Ridge would do the same for lodging and lift tickets. During their stay, agents would attend several hours of meetings and tours of the operation. Powder Ridge's out-of-pocket costs for such promotion was almost equal to that for its advertising aimed at consumers.

CONSUMER SEGMENTS   Powder Ridge skiers divided neatly into local and out-of-state segments. According to Friendly, locals skied much more frequently on the weekend, usually arriving early Saturday and leaving late Sunday. However, some came only for one day. Locals were usually better skiers and took fewer ski school lessons. Those spending the night often stayed in private condominiums or in nearby motels. Of course, some spent a week at Powder Ridge as a regular winter vacation but most, he felt, came for a day or two on a sporadic basis. Few used travel or rental car agencies.

In contrast, out-of-state skiers usually arrived late Saturday, skied for six days, and left the following Saturday. They often came as families on vacation, stayed at Powder Ridge, and spent large sums of money on rooms, meals, ski lessons, lift tickets, and souvenirs. Total expenses for a family of four on these items could easily exceed $2,000. Air fares would add another $1,500 or more, depending on where the family came from. Here Friendly had some fairly reliable data based on a sample of last year's lodging receipts. He had made the following estimates on the origin of Powder Ridge lodgers:

Texas	26%	Missouri	9%
California	16%	Illinois	9%
Oklahoma	13%	New York	8%
Kansas	10%	Other States	9%

Apart from these data, Friendly had realized that much of his consumer analysis was based on casual observation and common sense. What he lacked was some formal marketing research.

THE MEETING   This realization had led to yesterday's meeting between Friendly and Hamel. To begin, Hamel had pressed for the real reason Friendly had contracted for the study. Friendly had responded, "I guess why you're here is that we just don't know that much about our consumers. Who they are, how much they spend, why they come here, whether they'll come back, and so on, are all questions we'd like an answer to."

"Who's 'we'?" Hamel had asked.

"Well, there's me, of course; I'm interested in answers primarily from the advertising end of it. But Ken Olson, you know Ken, don't you? You don't? Ken's our lodging manager, responsible for everything indoors except food and beverages. He's after some feedback on how satisfied his guests are with their lodging experience. I guess I'd like that too."

"What for?"

"Well, I want to advertise the things that are important to our consumers and stress those that we're doing a good job on. And, I want to know the things that we aren't doing so well on—because then I can go to Ken or Sarah or George or whoever is responsible." Friendly had then described Sarah Jackson's responsibilities, the food and beverage service in the several eating and drinking areas. George Raymond's responsibilities included everything outdoors—from the ski runs themselves to the parking lots. Friendly had concluded, "At Powder Ridge, I represent consumers more than anyone else. I want to know what makes them tick, what they like, and what they don't like."

A long discussion had followed. Hamel had finally convinced Friendly that an encompassing data collection form—that is, one that would address both advertising issues and the details of lodging, food and beverage service, ski terrain and conditions, lifts, and parking lots—would be just too long. The best they could do, Hamel had said, was to design a form to make next year's advertising decisions easier and to measure overall satisfaction in the other areas. That seemed to placate Friendly, who had urged that he be able to compare consumer satisfaction across all areas on an "apples and apples" basis.

Near the end of the meeting, Friendly had listed what he thought brought local and out-of-state skiers to Powder Ridge. "Our ski conditions, first of all. We have the best snow-making and grooming equipment anywhere in the state. Second, our people, from lift operators to ski school instructors to cocktail waitresses, are well trained, friendly, and courteous. Third, we have attractions to suit just about everyone—like fine dining, live music, and even the Teen Connection room. And, last and probably most important, we are Powder Ridge. I think a lot of out-of-state skiers, especially, come here just because they want to be able to tell their friends that they skied Powder Ridge."

On the other hand, Friendly had thought that prices and lift lines were two reasons not to come to Powder Ridge. Powder Ridge prices were at or near the top of the list of competing ski areas (and there were many in Colorado, Utah, New Mexico, and even Montana) for lift tickets, lodging, and probably food and beverages. Waits in the lift lines, especially during Christmas and the month of February, probably averaged forty-five to sixty minutes, maybe more on the weekends. Rather than expand the area, Powder Ridge had raised prices in an attempt to control lift lines. Friendly had wondered about how this tactic sat with consumers.

THE DATA COLLECTION METHOD

The meeting had concluded with a brief discussion of tentative data collection procedures. Hamel thought that at random times throughout the ski season two interviewers on skis would approach the pair of skiers last in a lift line. Interviewers would ask if the skiers would mind participating in a short interview on skiing. The incentive to participate would be an immediate "cut" to the front of the lift line, through the ski school lane as if the four were members of a class. One interviewer and one skier would pair up for the first chair and the other two would follow in the next. Interviewers would ask questions and record responses on a clipboard, in full view of respondents, during the approximately 12-minute ride to the top of the lift. If necessary, the interview could be continued for a brief period off the lift.

Interviewers would identify themselves as employees of Rocky Mountain Research, Hamel's firm. They would be trained and able to probe for details, but they could record only short answers.

THE DATA COLLECTION FORM

The meeting had left the next step up to Hamel. He had promised a draft of the data collection form on Friendly's desk within a week. The form probably could not exceed two pages in length because of the proposed data collection procedures. It would have to reflect his expertise in marketing research as well as his understanding of Friendly's request for research. "You know, it might be a good idea for me to pretest this one myself," thought Hamel. "After each interview, I'd get a free run down the mountain!"

8. Alabama CPAs

"Actually, now it's just a matter of reading the articles," thought Beverly Harris as she scanned a list in front of her. That and, of course, being sure that the data collection form reflected her conversation last week with Clinton Frazee. Frazee was Executive Director of the Alabama Society of CPAs.

THE SOCIETY

Members of the Alabama Society of CPAs were current state residents who had passed the CPA exam and paid nominal annual dues. They numbered about 4,000 out of an estimated potential membership of near 7,000. All were separately listed on a membership roster that was fairly accurate and current.

Apart from these similarities, members exhibited some striking differences. Many worked for public accounting firms, but a large number were employed by government agencies and private businesses. Those working for public accounting firms separated into employees of local CPA firms and employees of large, national accounting firms that operated Alabama offices (primarily in Birmingham). All performed a variety of duties: auditing the activities of organizations, preparing tax-related documents for organizations and individuals, and consulting with management at all organizational levels. Their clients consisted of large and small: manufacturers, wholesalers and retailers, services, financial institutions, transportation firms, and firms in most other Alabama industries, including agriculture and construction.

Most employees of public accounting firms practiced their profession. However, for a few, the work was mainly managing other accountants; an even smaller number mostly directed the business, usually as a senior partner or corporate officer. Their ages, experiences, and salaries differed greatly.

Last Thursday, Harris had met with Frazee to discuss a contract for some research on Alabama CPAs' attitudes toward advertising. It was only since March 31, 1978 that the American Institute of CPAs had relaxed rule 502 of its code of professional ethics to permit advertising by public accounting firms. Frazee had said that CPAs' reaction to the new rule seemed to range from indifference to enthusiasm, with most seeming to move very cautiously to favor advertising.

THE CONVERSATION

Frazee was quite concerned about the role of advertising with respect to it replacing "practice development" activities—do CPAs feel that advertising will largely replace such activities as distributing brochures that describe the firm's services and personnel, sending newsletters to clients, or even performing public and community service? Further, he had wondered about their thoughts on advertising and the profession's image—do CPAs feel advertising will hurt or help the profession's image? Of equal concern was their general belief about advertising and its effectiveness—will advertising lead to new business or will it merely increase each firm's operating expenses? He also had wondered what CPAs thought about the proper advertising message—should it inform or persuade its audience? Finally, he had wondered about potential differences in beliefs among different CPA groups. It was possible to group CPAs in various ways—by age, job title, experience, or by the firm's line of business, size, competitive environment, and level of current advertising expenditures. How did these groups feel about advertising?

Harris had promised a research proposal before the end of next week, followed by a meeting to discuss a draft of the data collection form. She planned to use a telephone survey, with each call lasting upwards of ten minutes and preceded by an advance notification letter.

The letter would identify the survey's research topic and its data collection period. Scanning her notes, she realized that Frazee's concerns could easily be measured using a relatively simple data collection form. Perhaps as few as six belief questions followed by a like number of fact questions should do the job.

However, Harris decided to review what other researchers had already done. Other researchers, she felt, had probably faced a similar problem in other market areas, had written some good belief questions, and then reported their findings; her knowledge of their work would allow her to incorporate some of their research variables in her data collection form. Frazee could then add to, subtract from, or otherwise alter this more complete data collection form during their meeting.

Results of the research were intended to interest most Alabama CPAs as well as to aid those who currently make advertising decisions. It was this latter group, Frazee felt, who should benefit most from the results. These CPAs regularly make decisions on advertising objectives, budgets, copy, media, and the like. Frazee planned to make copies of the final report available at distribution cost to all members. He further planned to summarize portions in the Society's newsletter. He wanted to be sure the Society got its money's worth on the project.

THE LIST   Harris had spent the better part of the morning searching business publications for relevant articles. She had developed a surprisingly long list—given that accounting firms had been free to advertise for less than three years now. Undoubtedly, some articles would be more useful than others, she thought.

Articles in the *Journal of Accountancy:*

> John R. Darling, "Attitudes Toward Advertising by Accountants" (February 1977), pp. 48–53.
>
> Gerald A. Hanggi, Jr., "Media Advertising as a Practice Development Tool" (January 1980), pp. 54–58.
>
> John G. Keane, "The Marketing Perspective: The CPA's New Image" (January 1980), pp. 60–66.
>
> Wallace Olson, "Is Professionalism Dead?" (July 1978), p. 78.
>
> Bradford E. Smith, "Reaching the Public: The CPA's New Image" (January 1980), pp. 47–52.
>
> Thomas D. Wood and Donald A. Ball, "New Rule 502 and Effective Advertising by CPAs" (June 1978), pp. 65–70.

Articles in the *CPA Journal:*

> Max Block, "Any Limits to 'Marketing' CPA Services?" (August 1980), pp. 35–40.

James R. Hickman, "A Marketing Plan for CPA Firms" (July 1978), pp. 35–37.

Jack Schwersenz, "Marketing Your Services" (October 1979), pp. 11–15.

W. Douglas Sprague, "The Advertising Dilemma" (January 1977), pp. 27–30.

Donald M. Zuckert, "Think About Your Advertising Program" (October 1977), pp. 11–13.

Articles in other publications:

Paul N. Bloom and Stephen E. Loeb, "If Public Accountants are Allowed to Advertise," *Business Topics* (Summer 1977) pp. 57–64.

M. Robert Carver, Jr., Thomas E. King, and Wayne A. Label, "Attitudes Toward Advertising by Accountants," *Management Accounting* 47 (October 1979), 10 ff.

John R. Darling and Donald W. Hackett, "The Advertising of Fees and Services: A Study of Contrasts Between, and Similarities Among, Professional Groups," *Journal of Advertising* (Spring 1978), pp. 23–24.

J. B. Wilkinson, "Advertising Passes 'Go': Do CPAs Collect a 'Marketing Opportunity'?" *Akron Business and Economic Review* 9 (Winter 1978), 26–32.

9. KPAD Radio*

Cal Jensen looked carefully again at the three research proposals lying on his desk. The only thing clear was that KPAD badly needed data in order to assess its marketing strategy. Assessment was needed because KPAD's local competitor, KLJN, seemed to have developed a substantial audience in the two years it had been operating—and it was soon going to triple its broadcasting power. Getting data now would provide a useful base against which to measure the effects of this power boost as well as any action KPAD might take in response. Data would also help salesmen convince prospective advertisers of the benefits to be gained from advertising on KPAD. The big question now, Jensen thought, is: Which data? Each of the three proposals seemed to have some strengths and some weaknesses with respect to the data they would produce.

BACKGROUND

KPAD was a typical small-town AM radio station with a daytime broadcasting power of 5,000 watts at radio frequency. At night it reduced its power to 1,000 watts. The station had remained with the owner (and

*This case was written by Professor James L. Brock, Montana State University.

founder) from 1948 until six months ago, when Jensen and two silent partners had purchased it for a sizeable sum. The new owners had continued the station's format as adult country and popular music, with a heavy emphasis on local news and events. For example, they daily offered 12 minutes of air time free to consumers who would call in live to describe articles for sale, rent, or giveaway. They had broadcast all high school football games live and would soon do the same for basketball.

When KLJN had started some twenty months ago, it had caused KPAD some problems. To begin with, the KPAD station manager and its top disc jockeys had jumped ship and gone to work for the new station, taking many faithful listeners with them. This naturally had led many advertisers to move their advertising, partially or completely, to KLJN. It also had meant a heart attack for KPAD's owner, who sold the station and took an early retirement.

KLJN was an FM station and played mostly soft or mellow rock, targeted at 25- to 34-year-olds, with few commerical interruptions and fairly little news. What news there was seemed about evenly divided among national, state, and local stories.

Both KPAD and KLJN served a small agricultural and light industrial community of about 20,000 people in northeast Iowa. Waterloo was about sixty miles away and contained some 150,000 people. Jensen suspected that many of KPAD's and KLJN's listeners shopped for major durables in Waterloo but lacked data to back this up. If his suspicion could be proved true, perhaps Jensen could convince some Waterloo advertisers to buy space on KPAD. Local advertisers were mainly small retailers and services, most of which were independently owned and operated. There were a few national chains, which seemed better managed than the independent counterparts, most of which operated without advertising objectives and budgets. The chain stores, in particular, wanted hard data on radio audiences; until they had it, they would devote the bulk of their advertising to the local newspaper, a weekly with a circulation of about 6,000.

ASSIGNMENT FOR THE RESEARCH AGENCY Jensen and his partners had been wrestling for some time with the problem of generating cost-effective audience data. They had quickly dismissed Arbitron and other listenership services as providing data insufficiently detailed and too expensive for KPAD. Such data generally would describe only who listened when, in demographic terms, and would cost at least $5,000. The station had always been run on a shoestring and the new owners simply could not afford much more than half this amount.

Jensen had located a small market research agency in Waterloo which seemed eager for the business. During a luncheon meeting with the owner some two weeks ago, he had outlined the kind of data KPAD needed:

1. Listenership data—including market shares for KPAD and KLJN, listener demographics, most and least liked programs, and an overall idea of KPAD's image.

2. Other data that KPAD's salesforce could use to persuade clients to buy more time, including listener shopping habits in the local community and in Waterloo.

The agency owner had promised a proposal in two weeks.

THE PROPOSALS

Jensen actually received more than he wanted—three proposals! The cover letter explained that he could contract for any one or all three of the described projects and that only the station owners could best decide on which was best. The cover letter continued:

> Each project will yield different kinds of data at different costs and in different time frames. Finally, it may be argued from a cost-effectiveness perspective that each is best, depending on your budget and the required precision of your information needs.

The letter concluded with a hope that KPAD and the research agency would agree on one or more of the three proposals, modified if necessary.

As Jensen looked over the three proposals (Exhibits C9.1, C9.2, and C9.3), several questions came to mind:

1. Which of the three is likely to yield the "best" data?

2. Which will yield the best data per dollar of cost?

3. What should he recommend to his partners? Should he contract for the third proposal alone, the second alone, or perhaps the second and first together? Should he look for another research agency?

Jensen's decision was awaited by his business partners.

EXHIBIT C9.1
The Vehicle Radio Survey

Objective: To determine the proportion of vehicle radio dials set at KPAD and KLJN frequencies.

Method and Data Generated:
Four interviewers will record radio dial settings for 300 cars and light trucks at separate locations in the community. They will ask the driver one question, "What

station is your radio tuned to?" They will record the response and also the driver's sex, apparent age, and vehicle make and model. Where possible, interviewers will note the proportion of vehicles equipped with FM radios. Interviewers will be instructed as to procedures and purposes of the study. They will carry clipboards and standardized forms for data recording.

Half of the sample will be generated on a weekday between 10:00 A.M. and 3:00 P.M. The other half will be generated on a Saturday, during the same hours. Approximately 60 percent of the sample will be drawn from the community's business district. The remainder will be drawn from residential areas in the community. Although the sample will not be drawn in a statistically random fashion, every effort will be made to select a sample representing all areas of the community.

Tabulations will present listenership data by sex, age, and vehicle value.

Costs will be $320. Research will be completed two weeks after approval.

EXHIBIT C9.2
The Telephone Survey

Objective: The overall objective of this research proposal is to complete a survey of area listenership to determine market characteristics. Specific objectives are:

- to determine the market shares of KPAD and KLJN;
- to determine peak listening times;
- to determine where local residents shop for hard goods, soft goods, groceries, and entertainment; and
- to determine demographic characteristics of the audience.

Method and Data Generated:
The sample will consist of 300 households (with telephones) in the local market area. A list of numbers will be selected at random from the local telephone directory. To allow unlisted numbers an equal chance of being dialed, the last digit in the phone number selected will be increased by one. This will result in researchers reaching a greater number of commercial numbers or numbers not in service, but the effort will be continued until 300 "eligible" households have been contacted.

Telephone calls will be placed between 5 P.M. and 9 P.M. on a weekday evening and between 1 P.M. and 4 P.M. on a Saturday afternoon. Each call will last about ten minutes. The subject will be whoever answers the phone, excluding children under the age of 13. The respondent will remain anonymous and the identity of the client will not be disclosed. A sample questionnaire is included with this proposal.

Collected data will be processed by computer, appropriate cross-tabulations will be compiled, and results will be reported in a final written document.

Cost will be $3,600. Research will be completed two weeks after approval.

Sample Telephone Questionnaire

1. What is your favorite type of radio programming?

    (a) News   (b) Sports   (c) Call-in   (d) Top rock   (e) Progressive rock

    (f) Country   (g) Classical   (h) Religious   (i) Jazz   (j) Easy listening   (k) Other

2. When you are in your car, what radio station do you listen to most often?

3. My car radio is equipped with:
   (a) AM only   (b) AM/FM   (c) No radio

4. What radio station do you listen to most often at home? _____

5. What station do you tune into for news and weather information? _____

6. During what time period do you most often listen to the radio?
   (a) 6–9 A.M.   (b) 9 A.M.–noon   (c) noon–4 P.M.   (d) 4–7 P.M.   (e) 7–10 P.M.
   (f) 10 P.M.–6 A.M.

7. On the average, about how many hours a day do you spend listening to the radio?
   (a) less than 1   (b) 1–3   (c) 3–5   (d) 5–7   (e) 7–9   (f) Over 9

8. Do you read a newspaper regularly?
   (a) Yes   (b) No

9. What newspapers do you most often read? _____

   _____

10. Do you subscribe to cable television?
    (a) Yes   (b) No   (c) Not available

11. Which TV station do you watch for news? _____

12. At what times of the day do you most often watch TV? (a) Morning
    (b) Daytime   (c) Evening   (d) Late night

13. In the past two weeks, where have you shopped for groceries? (Names of
    stores/towns) _____

14. Where did you shop the last time you bought clothing? (town)_____

15. Where did you shop the last time you bought a car or major appliance?
    (washer, dryer, TV, etc.) (town) _____

16. The last time you went out for entertainment (say, a movie, or dinner and
    dancing), where did you go? (town) _____

17. Age: (a) Under 25   (b) 25–34   (c) 35–44   (d) 45–54   (e) 55 or older

18. Sex: (a) Male   (b) Female

19. Occupation: _____

20. Last year's gross family income: (a) Under $10,000
                                      (b) $10,001–$15,000
                                      (c) $15,001–$20,000
                                      (d) $20,001–$25,000
                                      (e) over $25,000

21. Marital status: (a) S   (b) M   (c) S/D   (d) W

22. Number of people in your household? _____

EXHIBIT C9.3
The Radio Diary Study

Objectives:
- To determine listenership of area radio stations by program, time of day, and day of week.
- To determine respondent shopping habits and demographic characteristics.
- To determine any relationships between listenership, shopping habits, and demographic characteristics.

Method and Data Generated:

An area sample of 200 households will be drawn from the listening area. Researchers will personally place diary booklets in selected homes, explaining how they are to be maintained. Diary booklets will consist of a cover sheet with instructions and separate pages for each day of the week, with columns for time, station, and place of listening (at home, away from home). One person in each household will complete a questionnaire that elicits data similar to that for the telephone survey proposal.

As an incentive to participation, subjects will be promised, upon completion of the diary, a gift certificate for $5.00 worth of merchandise from a KPAD advertising client. (Note: these will be purchased at cost from a cooperating client. Approximate cost will be $2.50 each.)

Stamped return envelopes will be provided to participants. Completed diaries will be mailed to our offices. Respondents whose diaries have not been received one week after the diary completion date will receive follow-up phone call reminders.

Tabulations will present listenership data by time of day and day of week, and by shopping and demographic characteristics of respondents.

Costs, including the incentive gift (at $2.50 each) will be $4,450. Research will be completed within five weeks after approval.

Sampling

CHAPTER 12

Introduction to Sampling

Let us set the stage for our three-chapter discussion on sampling by re-stating a definition from Chapter 2: **Sampling** is simply the process of selecting some secondary or primary data sources in the population of interest for measurement. Sampling contrasts with a **census,** the latter a process taking measurements from all secondary or primary data sources in the population of interest. Sampling occurs more frequently than a census in marketing research because it requires less time, money, and fewer people. To illustrate these differences and to show the diversity and complexity of sampling in practice, Box 12.1 presents three examples of sampling scope and purpose.

Although not obvious now, the examples contain applications of four sampling concepts: population of interest, sampling frame, sampling procedures, and sample size. After we take up these concepts in the next section we may want to return to Box 12.1 and identify applications of each.

The Sampling Planning Process

Taken together, the four concepts describe a sampling planning process.[1] Such a process specifies decision activities a researcher completes in designing data source selection procedures. Figure 12.1 illustrates the process and maps our discussion.

---

[1]Similar sampling planning processes appear in Thomas C. Kinnear and James R. Taylor, *Marketing Research: An Applied Approach* (New York: McGraw-Hill, 1979), pp. 181–85, and in Donald S. Tull and Del I. Hawkins, *Marketing Research: Meaning, Measurement, and Method* (New York: Macmillan, 1976), pp. 153–69.

BOX 12.1

Three Sampling Examples

Example 1. The Bureau of Census 1976 Survey of Institutionalized Persons (SIP)[*]

The SIP sample consisted of administrators, staff, and residents in six types of long-term residential care institutions: psychiatric, physically handicapped, mentally handicapped, children, nursing homes, and others. Also included in the sample were residents' next of kin.

Because no list of potential sample members existed, researchers started by obtaining a list of institutions. Their list identified 26,003 nonhospital residential care facilities in the United States as of 1973, the most current year then available. They classified each institution into one of six classes on the basis of the type of care it provided, and into one of three classes on the basis of its size (the number of beds). If an institution provided more than one type of care, researchers identified each part of the facility as a separate sampling unit. Within each of the eighteen resulting care/size classes, researchers systematically sampled institutions by selecting every jth one after a random start somewhere within the first j institutions. An institution's chance of being selected was proportionate to its size.

Interviewers in the field continued the sampling process by selecting residents, next of kin, administrators, and staff. They obtained a list of current residents at each selected institution. After assigning each resident on the list a number, they systematically selected every kth one, beginning with a random start within the first k

entries. If the institution's identification number on the list of 26,003 institutions was even, next of kin of all even numbered sample residents were selected for the next of kin sample. If the institution's identification number was odd, opposite selection procedures were used. Administrators and staff at sampled institutions were selected not randomly but purposively based on their job responsibilities. The final sample included 855 institutions, 9,046 residents, 3,327 next of kin, and an unspecified number of administrators and staff.

Example 2. The Nielsen Retail Index Sample[†]

Sample members consist of 1,300 retailers of food products, home care products, proprietary drug products, health and beauty aids, and alcoholic beverages. Nielsen selects sample members from its list of over 240,000 such stores. The list stays current through Nielsen's own efforts and data found in the *Census of Retailing* and *Current Business Reports*.

Like the SIP, Nielsen stratifies or groups data sources into classes before taking a probability sample. Nielsen stratifies according to geographic area of the country, county population, store size, and store type. Also like the SIP, Nielsen systematically selects data sources with probabilities proportionate to their size (measured in terms of their annual sales). See the following data:

[*]U.S., Department of Commerce, Bureau of the Census, *1976 Survey of Institutionalized Persons: Methods and Procedures,* Technical Paper 42 (Washington, D.C.: Government Printing Office, June 1978), pp. 6–14.

[†]*Management with the Nielsen Retail Index System* (Northbrook, Ill.: A.C. Nielsen Company, 1978), pp. 8–11.

Store Type	Percent of Stores (%)		Average Store Annual Sales ($000)	Take Ratio
	In Population	In Nielsen Sample		
Chain	21.6	46.7	3,700	1 out of every 40
Large Independent	10.5	21.9	1,600	1 out of every 67
Medium Independent	29.8	19.0	222	1 out of every 220
Small Independent	38.1	12.4	45	1 out of every 400

Unlike the SIP, Nielsen uses sampling proportionate to size not only for reasons of sample representativeness but also for cost. To take 1 out of every 100 stores, for example, would lead to an excessively large and costly sample. Also unlike the SIP, Nielsen sample members provide data regularly rather than only once.

Example 3. Durable Goods Buyers‡

Sample members consisted of 236 buyers of major household appliances (refrigerators, freezers, washing machines, clothes dryers, ranges/ovens, and dishwashers) in metropolitan

‡Robert A. Westbrook and Claes Fornell, "Patterns of Information Source Usage Among Durable Goods Buyers," *Journal of Marketing Research* 16 (August 1979): 303–12.

Detroit. To have been considered an eligible data source, a consumer must have purchased a major appliance within the two months preceding the study. Because no list of data sources existed, researchers used three selection methods:

1. Intercepts of purchasers on the floor of four leading retail outlets;

2. Lists of recent purchasers supplied by the outlets; and

3. A random survey of telephone subscribers with listed numbers.

The three methods each produced sample members having similar socioeconomic characteristics.

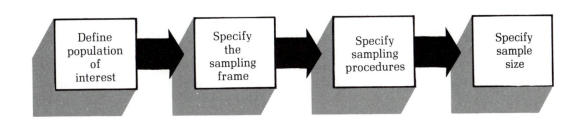

FIGURE 12.1
The sampling planning process

DEFINE THE POPULATION OF INTEREST A **definition of the population of interest** theoretically describes data sources (people, objects, or organizations) that the researcher expects to provide measurements. Descriptions generally contain a specification of population elements, extent, and time. To illustrate, we describe the SIP population(s) of interest as:

> Elements: Administrators, staff, and residents of long-term residential care units, plus residents' next of kin.
>
> Extent: In the United States.
>
> Time: In 1976.

Thus, the term **population elements** describes single, identifiable data sources. **Extent** describes the population elements' geographic limits; **time** describes their temporal limits.

Researchers must exercise great care in defining a population of interest. For example, the casual "people owning stereos in Los Angeles" leaves much to be desired. Most obvious is a temporal limit, but the definition lacks also a specific geographic limit. Does "Los Angeles" encompass only areas inside its legal limits or areas inside its Standard Metropolitan Statistical Area or inside its Area of Dominant Influence[2] or inside some other boundary? Does "owning" mean only stereos owned outright and exclude stereos being purchased on time? Does "people" mean only people as private citizens and exclude people (and organizations) owning stereos as business assets? And, what does "stereo" mean? Different answers and, hence, different definitions of the population of interest would dramatically influence sampling frame specification, our next step.

SPECIFY THE SAMPLING FRAME A **sampling frame** operationally describes data sources. Descriptions contain a specification of sampling units and, again, extent and time. We return to the SIP:

> Primary Sampling Unit: A facility or part of a larger facility that offers one of the six distinct types of long-term residential care at one or more locations. "Long-term" means length of stay per patient must average thirty days or more.
>
> Secondary Sampling Unit: Administrators, staff, and residents of the primary sampling unit, including residents' next of kin.

---

[2]An Area of Dominant Influence defines a market as the collection of counties in which local television stations receive a majority of viewers. See *Description of Methodology,* Arbitron Television Market Reports, February 1979, published by the Arbitron Company for more detail.

Extent: In the United States.

Time: In 1973.

Thus, a **sampling unit** consists either of one population element or a group of population elements available for sample selection. If a sampling unit contains a group of population elements, like the SIP's primary sampling units, actual selection proceeds by stages. At each stage before the final one, a sampling frame *lists* all sampling units available for selection within the frame's extent and time boundaries. At the final stage, a sampling frame lists all population elements available for selection, again within the frame's extent and time boundaries.

A strong correspondence should exist between a sampling frame (or frames) and the study's population of interest. Each frame's sampling units should either represent or contain in an unbiased fashion all population elements; extents and times should match. Yet sampling practice may find these ideals frequently violated because of resource constraints. For example, SIP researchers found their list of 26,003 institutions failed to include about two-thirds of the residential care psychiatric wards in hospitals. They found their list also contained:

1. an unknown number of duplicate entries;

2. an unknown number of separate population elements represented by only a single entry; and

3. several entries representing institutions not a part of the population of interest.

And, we have already shown clearly the disparity between their sampling frame and their population with respect to time. Often such sampling frame problems have no economical solution.

Researchers strive to use sampling frames that adequately represent populations of interest, given resource constraints. Beyond this, they sometimes adjust or weight data to partly overcome sampling frame problems (much as they adjust for nonresponse). Ethical considerations require them to report frame problems, data adjustment procedures, and the estimated impact of these deficiencies on research results. Such discussions usually appear as parts of either the methodology or appendix sections in the final report.

After defining the population of interest and specifying a sampling frame, the sampling planning process continues by specifying sampling procedures. **Sampling procedures** describe how sampling units will be selected from the sampling frame. The researcher chooses between two basic procedures: probability and nonprobability methods.

Probability methods use sampling procedures in which each sam-

SPECIFY SAMPLING PROCEDURES

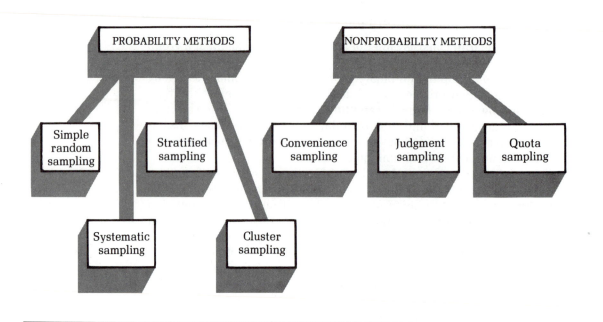

FIGURE 12.2
Probability and nonprobability sampling methods

pling unit has a known chance of being selected. Procedures select sampling units solely by chance according to rigid rules. **Nonprobability methods** use sampling procedures in which each sampling unit has an unknown chance of being selected. Such procedures select sampling units largely by the researcher's judgment. We identify the major probability and the nonprobability methods in Figure 12.2.

After our discussion of the sampling planning process and a review of sampling statistics, we will examine these eight sampling methods in detail. For now, we note that the choice between probability and nonprobability sampling methods results in sample data being either theoretically or judgmentally projectable to the entire population of interest. Probability samples use statistical theory as a projection basis; nonprobability samples use judgment. The two projection procedures may lead to quite different estimates.

SPECIFY SAMPLE SIZE The last step in the sampling planning process specifies **sample size,** that is, the number of population elements expected to provide measurements. There are numerous considerations, fitting under headings of classical, study-specific, and Bayesian.

Classical considerations include three major factors associated with key variables of interest in the research: desired precision, population variability, and desired confidence coefficient. Usually a researcher selects a few variables on which the management decision hinges; for each, he states desired precision limits, he estimates population variability, and he selects a confidence coefficient. Placing values for each factor in a formula, the researcher quickly arrives at a sample size estimate for each key variable. A fourth factor, population size, usually affects sample size only when the research deals with small populations.

Study-specific considerations include the research design classification, resources available, response rates expected, and data analysis methods planned. For example, a study proposing to explore a marketing problem almost always uses a smaller sample than a study proposing to solve it. So do studies facing smaller rather than larger budgets and studies expecting larger rather than smaller response rates. Planned data analysis methods influence sample size estimates in a less generalizable manner. Some methods work well with small samples, some require a sample of at least size 30, and some need a sample in the thousands.

Bayesian considerations include expected monetary values associated with research findings and estimated sampling costs. By subtracting the latter from the former, a researcher arrives at an expected net gain of sampling. All other considerations equal, a researcher prefers the sample size that achieves the highest expected net gain.

SAMPLING PLANS OR CENSUS PLANS

The sampling planning process—define the population of interest, specify the sampling frame, specify sampling procedures, specify sample size—accompanies all marketing research projects that use sampling. However, some projects may instead use a census. That is, some projects select, instead of some, all data sources for measurement. This might happen if the population of interest were small, research budgets high, or time constraints distant. Under such conditions, a **census planning process** substitutes for our sampling planning process. This planning process entails only two decision activities: define the population of interest and specify a census frame. Considerations in these activities are largely as discussed for sampling, however.

Researchers summarize sampling or census decision activities as sampling or census plans. Such plans apply to a specific research project and usually occupy one or two pages. Sections use headings corresponding to major decision activities in the sampling or census planning processes.

Our discussions in Chapters 12 and 13 focus on the last two parts of a sampling plan: specifying sampling procedures and specifying sample size. Such lack of balance does not imply that defining the population of interest and specifying the sampling frame are unimportant. Indeed, these two decision activities may influence research results to a greater degree than those for procedures and size. Such lack of balance does imply that procedures and size decision activities enjoy greater theoretical and practical understanding. It also implies the infrequent use of a census in marketing research. Our remaining discussion in this chapter summarizes statistical theory necessary to understand the rather technical presentations in Chapters 12 and 13. Much, if not all, of this summary should be in the nature of a review.

Sampling and Statistical Theory

Let us begin by identifying terms, meanings, symbols, and formulas that apply to populations and samples; see Exhibit 12.1. Calculated terms in Exhibit 12.1 applying to population concepts are called **population parameters.** Calculated terms applying to sample concepts are called **sample statistics.** Good sample statistics represent population parameters in unbiased and efficient fashions.[3]

EXHIBIT 12.1
Population and Sample Concepts

Term	Meaning	Symbol	Formula
Population size	Total number of population elements	N	
Sample size	Number of population elements in the sample	n	
Population mean	Arithmetic average derived from all population element values	μ	$\mu = \dfrac{\sum\limits_{i=1}^{N} X_i}{N}$
Sample mean	Arithmetic average derived from population element values in the sample	$\overline{X}$	$\overline{X} = \dfrac{\sum\limits_{i=1}^{n} X_i}{n}$
Population variance	Dispersion of population element values about the population mean	σ^2	$\sigma^2 = \dfrac{\sum\limits_{i=1}^{N} (X_i - \mu)^2}{N}$
Sample variance	Dispersion of population element values in the sample about the sample mean	s^2	$s^2 = \dfrac{\sum\limits_{i=1}^{n} (X_i - \overline{X})^2}{n-1}$
Population standard deviation	Positive square root of population variance	σ	$\sigma = +\sqrt{\sigma^2}$
Sample standard deviation	Positive square root of sample variance	s	$s = +\sqrt{\sigma^2}$

[3]Two other terms that also apply to good sample statistics are "consistent" and "sufficient." See John Neter, William Wasserman, and G. A. Whitmore, *Applied Statistics* (Boston: Allyn and Bacon, 1978), pp. 229–32.

Let us illustrate the application of these concepts with an example. Con- **AN EXAMPLE**
sider an industrial marketing researcher employed by an automobile tire
manufacturer who wishes to analyze 1981 sales to wholesalers in Pennsylvania. Table 12.1 summarizes the data as a census.

Rather easily the researcher calculates μ as

$$\mu = (29 + 116 + 14 + 51 + 84 + 79 + 150 + 98 + 45)/9$$

$$= \$74,000$$

Almost as easily she calculates σ^2 as

$$\sigma^2 = [(29 - 74)^2 + (116 - 74)^2 + (14 - 74)^2 + \ldots + (45 - 74)^2]/9$$

$$= 1,700$$

Taking the square root, she finds σ as

$$\sigma = \sqrt{1,700} = \$41,000$$

But suppose it takes time and other resources to total up sales to each
wholesaler and arrive at the figures shown in Table 12.1. Instead of a census, then, let us have the researcher take a sample of three wholesalers
(suppose A, E, and H) to save resources and calculate sample statistics to
estimate population parameters. Cutting data collection costs by about
two-thirds, she calculates:

$$\overline{X} = (29 + 84 + 98)/3$$

$$= \$70,000$$

$$s^2 = [(29 - 70)^2 + (84 - 70)^2 + (98 - 70)^2]/2$$

$$= 1,300$$

$$s = \sqrt{1,300} = \$36,000$$

TABLE 12.1
Census of 1981 Sales to Pennsylvania Wholesalers ($N = 9$)

Wholesaler [i]	1980 Sales ($000) [$X_i$]
A	29
B	116
C	14
D	51
E	84
F	79
G	150
H	98
I	45

Notice what happens. The sample mean, variance, and standard deviation values fall below their population parameter values. However, if the researcher were to choose another sample (say D, G, and I) the opposite might well occur (it will). Thus, how well sample statistics represent population parameters partly depends on which population elements find their way into the sample. The other things that sample representativeness depends on will appear in Chapter 13.

SAMPLING DISTRIBUTIONS OF $\overline{X}$

Continuing our train of thought, we recognize that our researcher could take a large number of samples of size 3 in a population of size 9. To be exact, she could take 84.[4] To prove a point, let us do just that and calculate the sample mean for each one. Table 12.2 summarizes.

Data in Table 12.2 show the exact sampling distribution of $\overline{X}$ for our population of nine wholesalers. As we see, the **exact sampling distribution of $\overline{X}$** is nothing more than a census of means taken from all possible samples of a specified size from a specified population. We more clearly describe the exact sampling distribution as in Table 12.3.

To describe the exact sampling distribution of $\overline{X}$ further, we can treat it as a population and calculate its parameters from data in either Table 12.2 or 12.3. Let us use Table 12.2. We calculate the population mean of the exact sampling distribution of $\overline{X}$ as

$$(53 + 65 + 76 + \ldots + 98)/84 = \$74,000$$

This is the identical value to that obtained for the mean of the original population of wholesalers. Such is no accident: $\overline{X}$ is an unbiased estimator of μ. That is, the mean of the sampling distribution of $\overline{X}$ always equals the mean of the population from which samples were drawn if all possible sample combinations of size n have an equal chance of being selected. Our exact sampling distribution of $\overline{X}$ clearly meets this criterion; each sample combination of three wholesalers had one chance in eighty-four of being selected.

We calculate the variance of our population of sample means in Table 12.2 as

$$[(53 - 74)^2 + (65 - 74)^2 + \ldots + (98 - 74)^2]/84 = 420$$

The standard deviation is $\$21,000$. In comparing these two numbers to those calculated earlier for the population of nine wholesalers, we see no other apparent correspondence than that sample values appear lower. However, statistical theory provides exact expressions of correspondence, more easily calculated than the preceding.

We show them below, letting $\sigma_{\overline{X}}^2$ symbolize the variance of the exact

---

[4]The number of combinations of N objects taken n at a time equals $\dfrac{N!}{n!\,(N-n)!}$.

TABLE 12.2
Means of All Possible Samples of Size 3 in a Population of 9 Wholesalers (A–I)

Sample	Wholesalers in Sample	Sample Mean ($000)	Sample	Wholesalers in Sample	Sample Mean ($000)
1	ABC	53	43	BEI	82
2	ABD	65	44	BFG	115
3	ABE	76	45	BFH	98
4	ABF	75	46	BFI	80
5	ABG	98	47	BGH	121
6	ABH	81	48	BGI	104
7	ABI	63	49	BHI	86
8	ACD	31	50	CDE	71
9	ACE	42	51	CDF	48
10	ACF	41	52	CDG	72
11	ACG	64	53	CDH	54
12	ACH	47	54	CDI	37
13	ACI	29	55	CEF	59
14	ADE	55	56	CEG	83
15	ADF	53	57	CEH	65
16	ADG	77	58	CEI	48
17	ADH	59	59	CFG	81
18	ADI	42	60	CFH	64
19	AEF	54	61	CFI	46
20	AEG	88	62	CGH	87
21	AEH	70	63	CGI	70
22	AEI	53	64	CHI	52
23	AFG	86	65	DEF	71
24	AFH	69	66	DEG	95
25	AFI	51	67	DEH	78
26	AGH	92	68	DEI	60
27	AGI	75	69	DFG	93
28	AHI	57	70	DFH	76
29	BCD	60	71	DFI	58
30	BCE	71	72	DGH	100
31	BCF	70	73	DGI	82
32	BCG	93	74	DHI	65
33	BCH	76	75	EFG	104
34	BCI	58	76	EFH	87
35	BDE	84	77	EFI	69
36	BDF	82	78	EGH	111
37	BDG	106	79	EGI	93
38	BDH	88	80	EHI	76
39	BDI	71	81	FGH	109
40	BEF	93	82	FGI	91
41	BEG	117	83	FHI	74
42	BEH	99	84	GHI	98

TABLE 12.3
Frequency Distribution of Sample Means

Sample Means ($)	Frequency	Relative Frequency (%)
20 to 30	1	1
30 to 40	2	2
40 to 50	7	8
50 to 60	13	15
60 to 70	10	12
70 to 80	17	20
80 to 90	14	17
90 to 100	11	13
100 to 110	5	6
110 to 120	3	4
120 to 130	1	1
Total	84	99*

*Does not equal 100 because of rounding.

sampling distribution of the mean and $\sigma_{\overline{X}}$ symbolize the standard deviation:

$$\sigma_{\overline{X}}^2 = \frac{\sigma^2}{n}\left(\frac{N-n}{N-1}\right) \quad \text{and} \quad \sigma_{\overline{X}} = \frac{\sigma}{\sqrt{n}}\left(\frac{N-n}{N-1}\right)^{1/2}$$

Researchers usually call $\sigma_{\overline{X}}$ the **standard error.** Substituting population values directly derived from Table 12.1 into each formula we get

$$\sigma_{\overline{X}}^2 = \frac{1,700}{3}\left(\frac{9-3}{9-1}\right) = 420$$

and

$$\sigma_{\overline{X}} = \frac{41}{\sqrt{3}}\left(\frac{9-3}{9-1}\right)^{1/2} = \$21,000$$

This is exactly equivalent to our results above.

Careful readers will have noted that our discussion so far treats only the exact sampling distribution of $\overline{X}$. An exact sampling distribution of $\overline{X}$ obtains in theory only for finite populations and in practice only for small, finite populations. For the large finite and infinite populations usually encountered in marketing research, we can only estimate the sampling distribution of $\overline{X}$. To do so we would take a large number of samples of size n (several hundred, say) rather than all possible samples.

Apart from this and one other difference, our summary of the estimated sampling distribution of $\overline{X}$ would proceed as before. We would still calculate a mean for each sample and describe all means in a frequency distribution. The mean of this frequency distribution would come very close to the usually unknown population mean if all possible combinations of population elements of size n had an equal chance of being selected. We would also calculate a variance and standard deviation from the frequency distribution or use the more easily calculated expressions of correspondence if population parameters were known. However, because sample size is now so small compared to population size, we modify the expressions to

$$\sigma_{\overline{X}}^2 = \frac{\sigma^2}{n} \quad \text{and} \quad \sigma_{\overline{X}} = \frac{\sigma}{\sqrt{n}}$$

That is, we remove the $(N - n)/(N - 1)$ term, called a **finite population correction factor.** We can easily see why. If N is large relative to n, $(N - n)/(N - 1)$ approximates 1. In practice, researchers ignore $(N - n)/(N - 1)$ and use the shortened formulas above unless sample size exceeds 5 percent of the population.

Let us summarize our discussion in four statements.

1. The mean of the sampling distribution of $\overline{X}$ equals the usually unknown population mean, μ.

2. The variance of the sampling distribution of $\overline{X}$ either equals σ^2/n times $[(N - n)/(N - 1)]$ or σ^2/n depending on sample size relative to population size.

3. The standard deviation of the sampling distribution of the mean either equals $\sigma/\sqrt{n}$ times $[(N - n)/(N - 1)]$ or $\sigma/\sqrt{n}$ depending on sample size relative to population size.

4. The above statements hold true only if the sampling distribution of $\overline{X}$ is derived from a sampling process that allows all possible sample combinations of size n an equal chance of being selected.

Given the fourth statement, note the powerful implications of the first three. Statement (1) implies that if we know the mean of the sampling distribution of $\overline{X}$, we know the mean of the population. Statement (2) implies that if we know the variance of the sampling distribution of $\overline{X}$, we know the variance of the population. Statement (3) implies that if we know the standard deviation of the sampling distribution of $\overline{X}$, we know the standard deviation of the population. Thus, if we take all possible samples or a large number of samples, we learn some important characteristics about the population providing the samples.

Such a conclusion still satisfies us only somewhat. We simply do not get very excited about the idea of taking all possible samples or even a large number of samples. Samples consume resources and taking even a small number of them may require too much time, money, and help.

Moreover, we know or strongly suspect that a researcher usually takes only one sample per research study. How does this practice square with our discussion? We find the answer in our next two sections.

PROBABILITY DISTRIBUTIONS AND THE CENTRAL LIMIT THEOREM

Let us look at one other way of describing the sampling distribution of $\overline{X}$ —its probability distribution. See Figure 12.3. As we can see, a probability distribution pictures a sampling distribution of $\overline{X}$. To construct one, we merely draw rectangles in each class interval for the variable under study along the horizontal axis with heights equal to the percentage or relative frequency of population elements in each class. We interpret each height or percentage as the probability associated with its respective class interval.

For example, Figure 12.3 shows a probability of 0.08 that a sample of three wholesalers will have placed orders averaging between $40,000 and $50,000 in 1981. It shows a probability of 0.08 + 0.02 + 0.01 or 0.11 that a sample of three wholesalers will have placed orders averaging less than

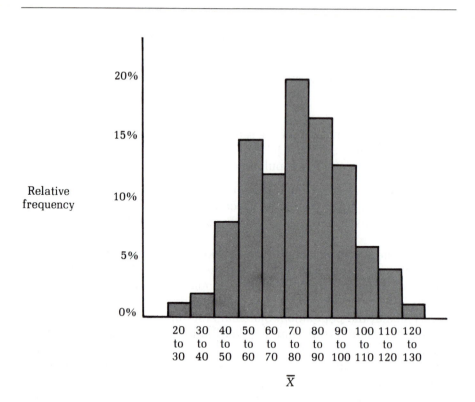

FIGURE 12.3
Probability distribution of sample means

$50,000. It shows a probability of 0.24 that a sample of three wholesalers will have placed orders averaging more than $90,000. And so on.

The probability distribution in Figure 12.3 looks like a normal probability distribution. We should remember studying normal probability distributions as smooth, bell-shaped curves. An example appears in Figure 12.4, superimposed over our probability distribution of the sampling distribution of $\overline{X}$. As we can see, our probability distribution approximates the normal probability curve fairly well.[5]

This fit of specific case and abstraction is not unusual. The probability distribution of many variables in marketing research approximates a normal probability distribution. Even more important, the probability distribution of the sampling distribution of $\overline{X}$ derived from samples of almost any population approximates a normal probability distribution if all pos-

---

[5]Statistical procedures to test whether or not a probability distribution approximates a normal distribution appear in most introductory statistics texts. See Neter, Wasserman, and Whitmore, *Applied Statistics*, Chap. 16.

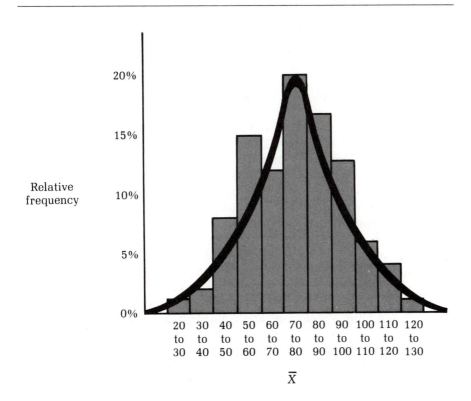

FIGURE 12.4
The normal curve and a probability distribution of sample means

sible sample combinations have an equal chance of being selected and sample size is sufficiently large. Such states the **Central Limit Theorem,** a proposition we accept without proof.

In support of the Central Limit Theorem, Figure 12.5 shows four population distributions of various shapes and, for each, sampling distributions of $\overline{X}$ as derived from samples of size 2, 5, and 30. Note that for the first three populations the sampling distribution of $\overline{X}$ approximates a normal probability distribution more closely as n increases. Note also that a sample taken from a normal population produces a normal sampling distribution of $\overline{X}$ regardless of sample size. Both statements hold true for many populations other than those in Figure 12.5.

The fact that the probability distribution of the sampling distribution of $\overline{X}$ approximates a normal distribution provides us with a great deal of knowledge. We know that areas under a normal probability distribution curve represent probabilities. We know also that exactly half the area under a normal probability distribution curve lies to the left of its mean and half lies to the right. Thus, we would expect to find about 50 percent of all sample means lying below and about 50 percent lying above the population mean. (Remember that the mean of the sampling distribution of $\overline{X}$ equals the usually unknown population mean.) Further, we recall that a normal probability distribution curve has about 68.3 percent of its area beneath it and within one standard deviation on either side of its mean. Thus, we would expect to find about 68.3 percent of all sample means to lie less than ± 1 standard error ($\sigma_{\overline{X}}$) from the population mean.

Reference to a table of Z (the **standard normal variable**) values such as the one abridged in Table 12.4 allows us to form other expectations. Using Table 12.4, we would expect about 34.1 percent of all sample means to be contained in the interval between the population mean and one standard error above it. Because Z is distributed symmetrically, we make the same statement for the interval between the population mean and one standard error below it. As a last example, we would expect slightly less than one percent of all sample means to exceed 2.33 standard errors.

All such statements about sample means imply their close correspondence with Z and μ. We illustrate the correspondence in Figure 12.6 by showing a line representing the range of $\overline{X}$ values taken from its sampling distribution directly below a similar line of Z values taken from its standard normal distribution. As we can see, Z has a mean of 0 and a standard deviation of 1. Sample means have a mean of μ and a standard deviation of $\sigma_{\overline{X}}$. To lend more precision, Z is a linear transformation of $\overline{X}$, of this form:

$$Z = \frac{\overline{X} - \mu}{\sigma_{\overline{X}}}$$

This relationship between Z and $\overline{X}$ allows us to make probability statements and to write confidence intervals about $\overline{X}$ and μ. Our next section shows how.

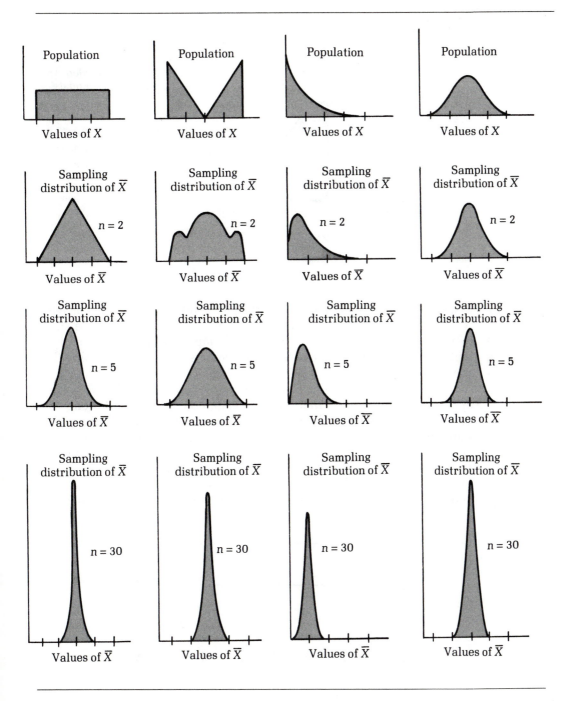

FIGURE 12.5
Sampling distribution of $\overline{X}$ for four populations and three sample sizes

Source: Ernest Kurnow, Gerald J. Glasser, and Frederick R. Ottman, *Statistics for Business Decisions* (Homewood, Ill.: Richard D. Irwin, © 1959), pp. 182–183. Used by permission

TABLE 12.4
Abridged Table of Normal Curve Areas

	When Z Equals:	Shaded Area Equals:
	0.00	0.0000
	1.00	0.3413
	1.65	0.4505
	1.96	0.4750
	2.00	0.4772
	2.33	0.4901
	2.58	0.4951
	3.00	0.4987

-3   -2   -1   0   +1   +2   +3

Z

Note: A more complete table of Z values appears in Table 2 in the Appendix.

PROBABILITY STATEMENTS AND CONFIDENCE INTERVALS

Instead of making statements about the percentage of sample means lying within specified distances of the population mean, we may make statements about the probability that a single sample mean will be contained within a range of values. Such statements are called **probability statements.**

To illustrate, let us now consider a larger population of 2,000 owners of large dogs, who report their pets' consumption of dog food for one day. The population average daily consumption, μ, equals 25.4 ounces with a standard deviation, σ, equal to 12.2 ounces. Suppose we take a large number of samples of size 49 from this population, making $\sigma_{\bar{X}}$ equal to $12.2/\sqrt{49}$ or 1.7 ounces. Given our discussion in the last two sections, we can state that the probability that a single sample mean $\bar{X}$ will be contained in the range between $25.4 - 2(1.7)$ and $25.4 + 2(1.7)$ ounces—which

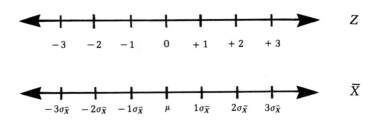

FIGURE 12.6
Correspondence between Z and $\bar{X}$

is 22.0 to 28.8 ounces—is 2(0.4772), which is a probability of 0.9544. (This is the same as stating that the probability that Z is contained in the range −2.00 to +2.00 is 0.9544; right?)

We can replace this somewhat cumbersome prose with a more convenient shorthand:

$$P[22.0 \leq \overline{X} \leq 28.8] = P[-2.00 \leq Z \leq +2.00] = 0.9544$$

The P in our notation stands for "probability of". Expressions in brackets specify ranges either for $\overline{X}$ or Z. Both P[ ] expressions hold true 95.44 percent of the time, or with a 0.9544 probability.

By definition and by Table 12.4 we know that $P[-2.00 \leq Z \leq +2.00]$ equals 0.9544. However, we may not see so clearly where the range for $\overline{X}$ comes from. Recall that Z equals $(\overline{X} - \mu)/\sigma_{\overline{X}}$. This allows us to rewrite the range for Z as

$$-2.00 \leq \frac{\overline{X} - \mu}{\sigma_{\overline{X}}} \leq +2.00$$

Substituting dog food population values for μ and $\sigma_{\overline{X}}$, we get

$$-2.00 \leq \frac{\overline{X} - 25.4}{1.7} \leq +2.00$$

which rearranges to

$$22.0 \leq \overline{X} \leq 28.8$$

To derive the general form of all probability statements for $\overline{X}$, we start with this symbolic expression which is directly equivalent to that empirically discussed above:

$$P\left[-Z \leq \frac{\overline{X} - \mu}{\sigma_{\overline{X}}} \leq +Z\right] = 1 - \alpha$$

where $1 - \alpha$ denotes the probability of obtaining a correct confidence interval of the range specified within the brackets. $1 - \alpha$ is commonly called the **confidence coefficient.** Rearranging terms in the inequalities, we get

$$P\left[\mu - Z\sigma_{\overline{X}} \leq \overline{X} \leq \mu + Z\sigma_{\overline{X}}\right] = 1 - \alpha$$

Inequalities inside the brackets in this probability statement form a **confidence interval** for $\overline{X}$. Such a confidence interval will contain $(1 - \alpha)100$ percent of all $\overline{X}$s in the sampling distribution. Or, such a confidence interval has a $1 - \alpha$ probability of containing any one $\overline{X}$.

While interesting and perhaps intellectually satisfying, the expression seems to hold little practical significance. Usually in marketing research μ and $\sigma_{\overline{X}}$ are unknown. Indeed, usually in marketing research our purpose is to estimate or infer from known sample statistics the values of these unknown population parameters. Thus, we would rather have probability statements and confidence intervals not about $\overline{X}$ but about μ.

Nothing could be easier. With some simple algebra we rearrange bracketed symbols in our inequalities:

$$P[\overline{X} - Z\,\sigma_{\overline{X}} \leq \mu \leq \overline{X} + Z\,\sigma_{\overline{X}}] = 1 - \alpha$$

Now the bracketed expression constitutes a confidence interval about the unknown population mean. It requires just one sample to derive $\overline{X}$, a specified Z value, and a given $\sigma_{\overline{X}}$. Together they specify a range of values within which μ will lie with a $1 - \alpha$ probability.

Such confidence intervals still satisfy us only somewhat because it appears we have gained only a little. To calculate $\sigma_{\overline{X}}$ requires σ, and to calculate σ requires μ. Our solution to this hidden circularity involves replacing $\sigma_{\overline{X}}$ with its estimate, $s_{\overline{X}}$. This estimate of the standard deviation of the sampling distribution of $\overline{X}$ or the estimated standard error of $\overline{X}$ is given by

$$s_{\overline{X}} = \frac{s}{\sqrt{n}}\left(1 - \frac{n}{N}\right)^{1/2}$$

Like our expression for $\sigma_{\overline{X}}$, the $(1 - n/N)$ term is a correction factor for use with finite populations. In practice, researchers ignore it whenever sample size totals less than 5 percent of the population.

Using $s_{\overline{X}}$, our probability statement becomes

$$P[\overline{X} - Z\,s_{\overline{X}} \leq \mu \leq \overline{X} + Z\,s_{\overline{X}}] = 1 - \alpha$$

The bracketed expression forms a confidence interval about the unknown population mean, μ, using a specified Z value and calculated values from one sample for $\overline{X}$ and $s_{\overline{X}}$. We cannot overstate the importance of this probability statement; researchers use it or one quite similar in nearly every research study in which they participate.

SMALL SAMPLES   A research study having a small sample ($n \leq 30$) uses one quite similar probability statement. With such small samples, the sampling distribution of $\overline{X}$ no longer approximates the standard normal distribution. Instead, it approximates a t distribution.

We recall that similarity of a t to the Z distribution depends on the former's degrees of freedom. As degrees of freedom become larger, t becomes closer to Z. With infinitely large degrees of freedom, t equals Z. In Figure 12.7, we can see one t distribution having 5 degrees of freedom with the Z distribution. It is apparent that t distributes quite similarly to Z, but more flatly.

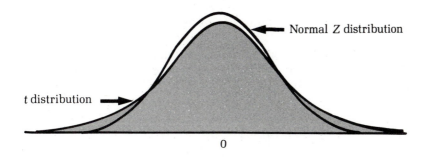

FIGURE 12.7
The Z and a t distribution with 5 degrees of freedom
Source: William Mendenhall and James E. Reinmuth, *Statistics for Management and Economics*, 3rd ed. (North Scituate, Mass.: Duxbury Press, 1978), p. 281.

All t distributions possess properties quite like the Z distribution. All t distributions are symmetrical. Areas under all of them represent percentages, which we might state as probabilities. The means of all t distributions equal 0. However, their variances depend on their **degrees of freedom,** ν. We define ν as $n - 1$ and the variance of a t distribution as $\nu/(\nu - 2)$ for all $\nu > 2$ (a t distribution's variance is undefined for $\nu \leq 2$).

For example, a sample of size 8 has 7 degrees of freedom. Variance of a t distribution with 7 degrees of freedom is $7/(7 - 2)$ or 1.4. Variance of a t distribution for a sample size of 20 is 19/17 or 1.1 and for size 30 is 29/27 or 1.07. Thus, as sample size increases, we can see how properties of t approach those of Z. (Recall that Z has a mean of 0 and a variance of 1.)

We may also want to compare entries in Table 3 in the Appendix showing values for t with those derived from Table 2 for Z. We make a

TABLE 12.5
Correspondence of t and Z by Sample Size and $1 - \alpha$

Sample Size	$t_{(1-\alpha)}$			
	$t_{(0.950)}$	$t_{(0.975)}$	$t_{(0.990)}$	$t_{(0.995)}$
10	1.81	2.23	2.76	3.17
30	1.70	2.04	2.46	2.75
60	1.67	2.00	2.39	2.66
120	1.66	1.98	2.36	2.62
Z	1.65	1.96	2.33	2.58

brief comparison in Table 12.5 on page 311. Again the similarity of t to Z is apparent. In practice, researchers use t values from Table 3 in their confidence intervals until sample size exceeds 30 and then Z values from Table 2 thereafter.

To formalize our discussion, we say that $(\overline{X} - \mu)/s_{\overline{X}}$ distributes approximately as t with $n - 1$ degrees of freedom. This allows us to write a probability statement of the form

$$P\left[-t \leq \frac{\overline{X} - \mu}{s_{\overline{X}}} \leq +t \right] = 1 - \alpha$$

Solving it for μ we get

$$P\left[\overline{X} - ts_{\overline{X}} \leq \mu \leq \overline{X} + ts_{\overline{X}} \right] = 1 - \alpha$$

The bracketed expression forms a confidence interval about the unknown population mean μ, using a specified t value and calculated values for $\overline{X}$ and $s_{\overline{X}}$ from a sample. The interval contains μ with a probability of $1 - \alpha$. The probability statement holds true only if the sampling procedure used to derive $\overline{X}$ and $s_{\overline{X}}$ allows all possible sample combinations of size n population elements an equal chance of being selected. Equally important, it holds true only if the population itself is normal.

We did not meet this restriction in discussing Z. Fortunately it is, "of little consequence as it can be shown that the distribution of ... [$(\overline{X} - \mu)/s_{\overline{X}}$] possesses nearly the same shape as the theoretical t distribution for populations that are nonnormal but possess a mound-shaped probability distribution."[6] To be safe, researchers examine the distribution of the variable about which probability statements will be made in the population to see that it is not skewed. They also avoid exceedingly small samples.

DICHOTOMOUS VARIABLES   A research study employing dichotomous variables also uses a quite similar probability statement. Dichotomous variables are conceptualized as those discrete nonordered and ordered variables that take on only two values. Examples include buyer status (buyers or nonbuyers), home ownership, and sex. Measurement of dichotomous variables assigns either a 1 or a 0 according to presence or absence of one of the two variable values. Population elements cannot possess other quantities of the dichotomous variable.

Statistical terms, meanings, symbols, and formulas for dichotomous populations appear in Exhibit 12.2. We see that dichotomous variables have a population mean, variance, and standard deviation defined similarly to those of continuous variables. Usually these population parame-

---

[6]William Mendenhall and James E. Reinmuth, *Statistics for Management and Economics*, 3rd ed. (North Scituate, Mass.: Duxsbury Press, 1978), p. 283.

ters are unknown and a researcher estimates π, σ^2, and σ from a sample. Like our earlier discussion, a researcher could take a large number of different samples. For each, the researcher could calculate $\bar{p}$, s^2, and s as estimates. Usually in calculating σ^2 and s^2, the researcher uses two shortcut formulas:

$$\sigma^2 = \pi (1 - \pi) \quad \text{and} \quad s^2 = \frac{\bar{p} (1 - \bar{p}) n}{n - 1}$$

EXHIBIT 12.2
Population and Sample Concepts that Apply to Dichotomous Variables

Term	Meaning	Symbol	Formula
Population proportion	Arithmetic average derived from all population element values	π	$\pi = \dfrac{\sum\limits_{i=1}^{N} X_i}{N}$
Sample proportion	Arithmetic average derived from population element values in the sample	$\bar{p}$	$\bar{p} = \dfrac{\sum\limits_{i=1}^{n} X_i}{n}$
Population variance	Dispersion of population element values about population proportion	σ^2	$\sigma^2 = \dfrac{\sum\limits_{i=1}^{N} (X_i - \pi)^2}{N}$
Sample variance	Dispersion of population element values in the sample about sample proportion	s^2	$s^2 = \dfrac{\sum\limits_{i=1}^{n} (X_i - \bar{p})^2}{n - 1}$
Population standard deviation	Positive square root of population variance	σ	$\sigma = +\sqrt{\sigma^2}$
Sample standard deviation	Positive square root of sample variance	s	$s = +\sqrt{s^2}$

As with $\bar{X}$, a sampling distribution of $\bar{p}$ exists. It also approximates a normal distribution if all possible combinations of population elements have an equal chance of being selected for the sample and the sample size is sufficiently large (another statement of the Central Limit Theorem).[7] The mean of the sampling distribution of $\bar{p}$ equals π. The variance of the sampling distribution of $\bar{p}$ is symbolized by $\sigma_{\bar{p}}^2$. Like $\bar{X}$, the variance of the

---

[7]Sample size must be sufficiently large that $n(\pi)$ and $n(1 - \pi)$ exceeds 5.

sampling distribution of $\bar{p}$ is derived by dividing the population variance by n. Thus, we have

$$\sigma_{\bar{p}}^2 = \frac{\sigma^2}{n}\left(\frac{N-n}{N-1}\right)$$

Usually a researcher estimates $\sigma_{\bar{p}}^2$ by $s_{\bar{p}}^2$, which is given by

$$s_{\bar{p}}^2 = \frac{s^2}{n} = \frac{\bar{p}(1-\bar{p})}{n-1}\left(1-\frac{n}{N}\right)$$

Again, the last terms are finite population correction factors that researchers ignore whenever n/N is less than 5 percent. The estimated standard deviation of the sampling distribution of $\bar{p}$ or the estimated standard error of $\bar{p}$ equals the positive square root of the sample variance divided by n. That is,

$$s_{\bar{p}} = +\left[\frac{\bar{p}(1-\bar{p})}{n-1}\right]^{1/2}\left[1-\frac{n}{N}\right]^{1/2}$$

With this knowledge, we state a probability statement for π of the form

$$P\left[\bar{p} - Zs_{\bar{p}} \leq \pi \leq \bar{p} + Zs_{\bar{p}}\right] = 1 - \alpha$$

Such a probability statement holds true with a $1 - \alpha$ probability.

SUMMARY ON STATISTICS REVIEW We have quickly reviewed much of a one-term course in statistics. As a last step, we can look at Exhibit 12.3 which shows statistical concepts that apply to sampling distributions. Anyone who lacks understanding of anything in our statistics review should study a basic statistics text before she or he continues through the rest of this book.[8]

One final point. It may appear that our review treats topics somewhat removed from sampling. Not so. Underlying the entire review are probability sampling procedures that allow each combination of population elements of size n an equal chance of being selected. The term given such procedures is simple random sampling, our first topic for Chapter 13.

Chapter Summary

Sampling in marketing research is the process of selecting some secondary or primary data sources for measurement. The sampling planning process consists of four steps: define the population of interest, specify the sam-

---

[8]See Chapters 8, 9, 10, and 11 of Neter, Wasserman, and Whitmore, *Applied Statistics* or Chapters 7, 8, and 9 of Mendenhall and Reinmuth, *Statistics for Management and Economics.*

EXHIBIT 12.3
Statistical Concepts that Apply to Sampling Distributions

Term	Meaning	Symbol	Formulas for Finite Populations	Formulas for Infinite Populations
Standard error of $\overline{X}$	Standard deviation of the sampling distribution of $\overline{X}$	$\sigma_{\overline{X}}$	$\sigma_{\overline{X}} = \dfrac{\sigma}{\sqrt{n}}\left(\dfrac{N-n}{N-1}\right)^{1/2}$	$\sigma_{\overline{X}} = \dfrac{\sigma}{\sqrt{n}}$
Estimated standard error of $\overline{X}$	Estimated standard deviation of the sampling distribution of $\overline{X}$	$s_{\overline{X}}$	$s_{\overline{X}} = \dfrac{s}{\sqrt{n}}\left(1 - \dfrac{n}{N}\right)^{1/2}$	$s_{\overline{X}} = \dfrac{s}{\sqrt{n}}$
Standard error of $\overline{p}$	Standard deviation of the sampling distribution of $\overline{p}$	$\sigma_{\overline{p}}$	$\sigma_{\overline{p}} = \dfrac{\sigma}{\sqrt{n}}\left(\dfrac{N-n}{N-1}\right)^{1/2}$	$\sigma_{\overline{p}} = \dfrac{\sigma}{\sqrt{n}}$
Estimated standard error of $\overline{p}$	Estimated standard deviation of the sampling distribution of $\overline{p}$	$s_{\overline{p}}$	$s_{\overline{p}} = \dfrac{s}{\sqrt{n}}\left(1 - \dfrac{n}{N}\right)^{1/2}$	$s_{\overline{p}} = \dfrac{s}{\sqrt{n}}$
Large sample confidence interval for $\overline{X}$ ($n > 30$)	Limits within which μ is contained with a $1 - \alpha$ probability	$\overline{X} - Z\sigma_{\overline{X}} \leq \mu \leq \overline{X} + Z\sigma_{\overline{X}}$ $\overline{X} - Zs_{\overline{X}} \leq \mu \leq \overline{X} + Zs_{\overline{X}}$		
Small sample confidence interval for $\overline{X}$ ($n \leq 30$)	Limits within which μ is contained with a $1 - \alpha$ probability	$\overline{X} - t\sigma_{\overline{X}} \leq \mu \leq \overline{X} + t\sigma_{\overline{X}}$ $\overline{X} - ts_{\overline{X}} \leq \mu \leq \overline{X} + ts_{\overline{X}}$		
Large sample confidence interval for $\overline{p}$ [$n\pi$ and $n(1 - \pi)$ greater than 5]	Limits within which π is contained with a $1 - \alpha$ probability	$\overline{p} - Z\sigma_{\overline{p}} \leq \pi \leq \overline{p} + Z\sigma_{\overline{p}}$ $\overline{p} - Zs_{\overline{p}} \leq \pi \leq \overline{p} + Zs_{\overline{p}}$		

pling frame, specify sampling procedures, and specify sample size. Decisions in the first step produce somewhat abstract descriptions of whoever or whatever is expected to supply measurements on variables of interest. Decisions in the second step make those in the first operational.

Decisions in the third step reduce to a choice between nonprobability and probability sampling methods. Nonprobability sampling methods consist of convenience, judgment (or purposive), and quota sampling. All are widely used in marketing research, especially to explore the problem and to develop data collection forms. All result in data that can be only judgmentally generalized to the population of interest.

Probability methods consist of simple random, stratified, systematic, and cluster sampling. All these methods of sampling are widely used in marketing research, especially in descriptive and causal research. All use statistical theory, particularly the normal distribution and probability statements, to generalize sample results to the population.

Chapter Review

KEY TERMS

Sampling planning process	Population mean
Population of interest	Population variance
Population element	Population standard deviation
Sampling frame	Sample mean
Sampling unit	Sample variance
Probability sample	Sample standard deviation
Nonprobability sample	Sampling distribution of $\overline{X}$
Census	Standard error
Central Limit Theorem	Confidence coefficient
Probability statement	Sample proportion
Confidence interval	

DISCUSSION QUESTIONS

1. What's wrong with this statement: Sampling consists of a set of decisions taken to randomly select consumers for purposes of marketing research.

2. What are characteristics of a good sampling frame?

3. Identify three marketing research populations of interest, for which obtaining a good sampling frame would be easy, somewhat difficult, and next to impossible.

4. What advantages are there to sampling versus taking a census of population elements? What disadvantages? (Hint: Part of your answer may reflect material discussed in Chapter 7.)

5. What sampling method does a researcher use when:

   a) selecting adjective pairs for a semantic differential scale?

   b) choosing time periods to make telephone calls in marketing survey?

6. A nonprobability sample of 1,000 may be just as good as a probability sample of 500. Discuss.

7. For a sample of size 30 and confidence coefficient of 0.95, would t or Z provide a smaller confidence interval? Why?

8. Suppose you found yourself in a large auditorium classroom facing 250 classmates. Why would closing your eyes, swinging your arm around, stopping to point out an individual, and repeating the process 20 times not produce a probability sample of students?

9. Sampling theory may be confirmed in statistics laboratories using samples of numbered marbles drawn from a known population that have been thoroughly mixed in a container. What problems are absent in such conditions but present when you sample people in the real world?

10. "Perfect" sampling procedure and sample size decisions may compensate for incomplete definitions of the population of interest and inadequate sampling frames. Discuss.

PROBLEMS

1. Fill in the blanks in the probability statements below.

$P[-3.00 \leq Z \leq 2.00] =$ _____

$P[-1.00 \leq Z \leq$ _____$] = .0833$

$P[Z \leq 1.72] =$ _____

$P[-1.725 \leq t \leq +1.725] =$ _____ for 20 d.f.

$P[t \leq$ _____$] = .0500$ for 15 d.f.

2. What are Z values such that:

a) 80 percent of all sample means lie above Z?

b) 20 percent of all sample means lie between Z and the population mean?

c) 99.44 percent of all sample means lie below Z?

3. For the population of six students below, compute the sampling distribution of average summer income for samples of size 2.

Student	Summer Income ($000)
Betty	6
Charles	8
David	2
Eunice	4
Frank	4
Gloria	6

a) Show that the mean of the sampling distribution equals μ.

b) Show that the standard deviation of the distribution equals

$$\frac{\sigma}{\sqrt{n}} \left[\frac{N-n}{N-1} \right]^{1/2}$$

c) What is the probability that a sample of size 2 will produce a mean summer income of $4,000 or less?

4. For our population of dog food owners ($\mu = 25.4$ ozs., $\sigma = 12.2$ ozs.), what is the probability that a sample of size 49 will produce an average consumption figure in the range of 26 to 28 ozs.? Show your work.

5. Take simple random samples of sizes 2, 3, 4, and 5 from the population of nine tire wholesalers in Table 12.1. Calculate 95 percent confidence intervals for each sample. What seems to be happening?

6. Consider a marketing researcher interested in estimating the population proportion of consumers who have tried a new brand of breakfast sausage substitute. He takes a telephone sample of 100 consumers and calculates the proportion of triers as 0.08. State a 95 percent confidence interval for π.

Additional Readings

Kish, Leslie. *Survey Sampling*. New York: John Wiley and Sons, 1965.

Just about anything anyone would want to know about sampling is in this book. You'll find everything from simple random sampling to sampling rare populations, from unequal cluster sampling to sampling costs, from incomplete sampling frames to field sampling instructions. Topics receive an elementary to sophisticated treatment in both theoretical and practical terms.

Neter, John; Wasserman, William; and Whitmore, G. A. *Applied Statistics*. Boston: Allyn and Bacon, 1978.

The book presents an introductory discussion on applied statistics but with more theory, rigor, and clarity than usually found in such texts. It contains almost everything we discuss in Chapters 12 through 19 but in more detail. This book makes an excellent reference.

Sudman, Seymour. *Applied Sampling*. New York: Academic Press, 1976.

Here is a shorter, simpler, and more pragmatic book than Kish's. Yet it contains some Bayesian sampling discussions not treated in that work. It makes an excellent introduction to sampling.

13

Probability Sampling Methods

Probability sampling methods select sampling units on the basis of chance. We discuss simple random, stratified, systematic, and cluster sampling as four such methods in this chapter. Throughout the discussion we should be sensitive to the rigidity of rules detailing chance selection decisions. Chance selection means not haphazard choice but probabilistic determination. Only with chance selection can the researcher employ well-founded theory to generalize sample results to the population of interest.

Simple Random Sampling

Actually we have seen **simple random sampling** (SRS) defined several times already in Chapter 12: SRS selects population elements such that each combination of population elements of sample size n has an equal chance of being selected. In marketing research, SRS almost always occurs without replacement; that is, once the sampling procedure selects a population element it cannot do so again. In this and in all following sampling discussions we assume sampling proceeds without replacement.

To apply SRS to a population involves four steps: **SRS PROCEDURE**

1. Identify each population element.

2. With equal probability, randomly select one population element for the sample.

3. With equal probability, randomly select one remaining population element for the sample.

4. Repeat step (3) until the desired sample size is reached.

Taken repeatedly, such steps would produce a large number of different combinations of population elements of size n as samples within any large population. All would appear with equal probability.

To comment on step (1)—identifying population elements usually means giving them serial identification numbers. Each population element receives a different number beginning with 1 and proceeding in order until reaching the population size N. However, sometimes population elements already have unique identification numbers. For example, consider a population of purchase orders issued during a particular month by a large wholesaler. Each purchase order form comes with its own pre-printed number. To sample from such a population, a researcher need not assign identification numbers but may instead base selection on existing numbers. To do so, the researcher need know only the maximum and minimum existing numbers present in the population. The range between the two need not be serial, that is, it may contain gaps.

Order of population elements as they receive identification numbers makes no difference in SRS. That is, sampling frames may be in alphabetical, geographic, random, or any other order without the order influencing sample representativeness. Other probability methods do not share this characteristic.

To comment on steps (2) and (3)—the term **random selection** is used for the first time. Random selection means chance or probabilistic selection, selection without apparent pattern. Each random selection should occur independently of any and all others. Each simple random selection should occur with the same probability. To achieve these properties requires well-specified procedures that researchers follow without exception. Thus, the simple random selection process and not the researcher actually selects population elements. To illustrate, Box 13.1 shows the use of a table of random digits in SRS.

A wide variety of other procedures may be used for the random selection process. For example, numbering slips of paper, placing them in a goldfish bowl, mixing them thoroughly, drawing one out, remixing, redrawing, and so on constitutes a random selection process. So does shaking dice or cutting cards, as long as we get a fair shake or a fair shuffle. Computers also make fine random number generators; some researchers even own pocket calculators with the same capability.

Whatever random selection procedure we use should follow along the lines of the description in Box 13.1. That is, we make a random start, generate random numbers corresponding to population identification numbers, and then select those population elements for the sample until reaching n. Our choice of a random selection procedure does not influ-

BOX 13.1

Simple Random Selection With a Table of Random Digits

Suppose a firm needs a simple random sample of twenty-five salespeople (from a salesforce of 632) to participate in a training exercise reducing sexual stereotyping among employees. Following step (1), we assign each salesperson a unique identification number from 001 through 632.

We proceed with the help of Table 1 in the Appendix. Table 1 contains 2,500 random one-digit numbers, that is, each digit appears without pattern with equal probability. No trends, cycles, regular and frequent changes in direction, or changes in variability accompany the digits. *

Suppose our seed led us to the circled group of random numbers that follows (we reproduce only part of Table 1 to save space). As we see, random numbers appear in blocks of five digits. Yet we need random numbers of only three digits, to correspond to our three-digit identification numbers. Our solution is simply to reblock random numbers into groups of three, using light pencil marks or lines.

Proceeding down the first column of 3 numbers including the circled group, we select salespersons 146, 105, 196, and 570 (we disregard 881 because it exceeds N). Proceeding

(14648)	77210	12923	53712	87771
10597	17234	39355	74816	03363
19660	03500	68412	57812	57929
88102	30176	84750	10115	69220
57022	52161	82976	47981	46588

We enter the table in a random fashion. For example, we might note the last two digits on the license plate of a car in the company parking lot. Or, we might close our eyes and stab Table 1 with a pencil to produce the two digits. In any event, we use these two digits as a "seed" to locate a row and a column in the table as a starting point. For instance, if our two digits were 5 and 2, we would start in row 5, column 2.

down the next column of 3 (directly to the right of the first), we select salespersons 487, 600, 023, and 225 (disregarding 971.) We continue in this fashion until all 25 sample members are selected. If any random number appears twice, we disregard the second selection and replace it with a new number. If any random number lacks a corresponding salesperson, that is, if the list of population elements contains gaps, we disregard that number and proceed to the next.

As an alternative, we could work our way across the page until achieving an n of 25. We would select a different sample but this does not matter. The only important thing is that we specify a procedure and then follow it rigidly.

* John Neter, William Wasserman, G. A. Whitmore, *Applied Statistics* (Boston: Allyn and Bacon, 1978), p. 383.

ence sample representativeness as long as the procedure itself is truly random. However, different selection procedures will consume different quantities of research resources. Large sophisticated samples usually favor the computer.

SRS EVALUATION   SRS requires just three things: a list of population elements, knowledge of their number, and some random selection procedure. Yet despite this simplicity, researchers use SRS less than other probability sampling methods. Our three sampling examples starting Chapter 12 support this statement; none used SRS.

A reason for this lack of popularity is that typically researchers lack either a list of population elements or knowledge of their number. For example, they may know from Census Bureau data the number of population elements but not their identities. Or, they may simply find population elements too numerous (and too costly) to count. To illustrate, consider a researcher who desires a sample of 150 San Diego teenagers: only a special census could provide the sampling frame. Thus, one reason for this lack of popularity is the want of an adequate, economical sampling frame.

Another reason stems from researchers' desires of producing a **representative sample.** A representative sample depends on decisions reached in the last three steps of the sampling planning process. That is, a sample can represent a defined population of interest only if it meets these requirements:

1. The sampling frame should correspond to the defined population in terms of its sampling units, extent, and time.

2. The sampling procedure should produce small sampling errors.

3. The sample size should also produce small sampling errors.

We define a **sampling error** in requirements (2) and (3) as the difference between a sample and a census result (researchers estimate sampling error for the mean by $Zs_{\bar{x}}$ or $ts_{\bar{x}}$ with a $1 - \alpha$ confidence coefficient). Stated simply, for a given sampling frame, sample size, and confidence coefficient, other probability sampling procedures than SRS may produce smaller sampling errors.

Yet another reason comes from researchers' desires that particular classes or groups of population elements provide sample members. Often these classes may be small in number yet have a disproportionate influence on research results. For example, a researcher for a manufacturer of track shoes may want to be sure that a sample of fifty high schools contains at least five of the twenty-five large schools out of a state's total of 970. But an SRS of the schools may include none of the large ones.

SRS is part of a family of probability sampling methods that selects sample members with known probabilities. SRS selects population elements as sample members—randomly with equal probability. Our next several sections discuss other probability methods that possess other characteristics.

    SRS underlies much of our course work in statistics. Like this work, *our statistics and formulas in Chapter 12 assumed that all data came from SRS.* We'll see that most of these other probability sampling methods derive their statistics from different formulas.

Stratified Sampling

Stratified sampling first divides all population elements into separate strata or classes. Each stratum or class is composed of population elements that possess like quantities of some **stratification variable** identified by the researcher. Within each stratum, the researcher then takes a probability sample of population elements. For example, a researcher employed by an importer of food processors might classify a population of sixty retail accounts into small, medium, and large strata, using past sales as the stratification variable. Within each of the three strata, the researcher might then take a simple random sample of five stores for measurement on the variable of interest.

    The application of stratified sampling to a population proceeds in general in five steps:

1. Identify each population element and estimate its relative possession of the stratification variable.

2. Divide all population elements into mutually exclusive and exhaustive strata or classes based on each population element's possession of the stratification variable.

3. Within each stratum or class, randomly and with equal probability select one population element for the sample.

4. Within each stratum or class, randomly and with equal probability select one remaining population element for the sample.

5. Repeat step (4) until the sample reaches desired sizes for each stratum or class.

Except for steps (1) and (2), stratified sampling uses identical activities to those for SRS.

Beyond steps (1) and (2), the major difference between SRS and stratified sampling lies with procedures to derive sample statistics. Exhibit 13.1 provides the necessary statistical concepts; the last two combine to form confidence intervals about the usually unknown population mean, μ. The

EXHIBIT 13.1
Statistical Concepts for Stratified Sampling

Term	Meaning	Symbol	Formula
Stratum size	Number of population elements in stratum i	N_i	
Population size	Total number of population elements in L strata	N	$N = \sum_{i=1}^{L} N_i$
Stratum sample size	Number of population elements selected in the sample in stratum i	n_i	
Total sample size	Total number of population elements selected in the sample	n	$n = \sum_{i=1}^{L} n_i$
Stratum sample mean	Arithmetic average derived from population element values in the sample in stratum i	$\overline{X}_i$	$\overline{X}_i = \dfrac{\sum_{j=1}^{n_i} X_{ij}}{n_i}$
Stratum sample variance	Dispersion of population element values in the sample in stratum i about the stratum sample mean	s_i^2	$s_i^2 = \dfrac{\sum_{j=1}^{n_i} (X_{ij} - \overline{X}_i)^2}{n_i - 1}$
Estimated population mean	Average population element value derived from stratum size/population size weights	$\overline{X}_{st}$	$\overline{X}_{st} = \sum_{i=1}^{L} \dfrac{N_i}{N} \cdot \overline{X}_i$
Estimated standard error	Standard deviation of the sampling distribution of $\overline{X}_{st}$	$s_{\overline{X}_{st}}$	$s_{\overline{X}_{st}} = \left[\sum_{i=1}^{L} \dfrac{N_i^2}{N^2} \cdot \dfrac{s_i^2}{n_i} \cdot \dfrac{(N_i - n_i)}{N_i} \right]^{1/2}$

interval is of a familiar form:

$$\overline{X}_{st} - Z s_{\overline{X}_{st}} \leq \mu \leq \overline{X}_{st} + Z s_{\overline{X}_{st}}$$

The interval holds true with a $1 - \alpha$ probability for any stratified sample. All n_i must exceed 1, and n must exceed 30 for the confidence interval to apply.

An Example.   We need an example to illustrate use of these concepts: let us return to our importer of food processors. He sells to sixty retailers in California, Oregon, and Washington. Suppose a researcher wishes to estimate the average dollar amount of co-op advertising allowances paid by the importer to these retailers in 1981. On the basis of 1980 sales, the researcher places ten, twenty, and thirty retailers respectively into large, medium, and small classes. Within each of these strata, he takes a simple random sample of a size proportionate to the stratum's size in the population. We can see this in Table 13.1 with selected retailers circled. For illustrative purposes, we use a sample of only size 12.

TABLE 13.1
Co-op Advertising Allowances Claimed in 1981 by Retailer Size

	LARGE		MEDIUM		SMALL
Retailer	Co-op Advertising ($000)	Retailer	Co-op Advertising ($000)	Retailer	Co-op Advertising ($000)
1	38	⑪	27	㉛	13
2	36	12	26	32	13
③	33	13	25	33	13
4	27	14	20	34	12
⑤	29	15	21	35	11
6	26	16	21	36	13
7	24	⑰	23	37	14
8	31	18	24	38	11
9	29	19	20	㊴	11
10	28	20	17	40	10
		21	18	41	10
		㉒	20	42	10
		23	18	㊸	9
		24	18	44	10
		25	15	㊺	8
		26	14	46	10
		㉗	17	㊼	8
		28	14	48	7
		29	15	49	6
		30	13	50	6
				51	8
				52	6
				53	5
				�554	5
				55	4
				56	4
				57	4
				58	3
				59	1
				60	1

Using a formula from Exhibit 13.1, our researcher calculates the mean co-op advertising allowance paid in the large retailer stratum as

$$\overline{X}_1 = \frac{\sum_{j=1}^{n_1} X_{1j}}{n_1} = \frac{33}{2} + \frac{29}{2} = \$31,000$$

He similarly calculates the variance in this stratum as

$$s_1^2 = \frac{\sum_{j=1}^{n_1} (X_{1j} - \overline{X}_1)^2}{n_1 - 1} = \frac{(33 - 31)^2 + (29 - 31)^2}{2 - 1} = 8.0$$

TABLE 13.2
Co-op Advertising Statistics

	Symbol	Large Retailers	Medium Retailers	Small Retailers
Stratum	i	1	2	3
Stratum size	N_i	10	20	30
Stratum sample size	n_i	2	4	6
Stratum sample mean ($000)	$\overline{X}_i$	31.0	21.8	9.0
Stratum sample variance ($000)^2	s_i^2	8.0	18.2	7.6

We summarize results for all strata in Table 13.2. Again using a formula from Exhibit 13.1, our researcher estimates the population mean as

$$\overline{X}_{st} = \sum_{i=1}^{L} \frac{N_i \overline{X}_i}{N} = \frac{10}{60}(31.0) + \frac{20}{60}(21.8) + \frac{30}{60}(9.0)$$

$$= \$17,000$$

The standard error of this estimate is

$$s_{\overline{X}_{st}} = \left[\sum_{i=1}^{L} \frac{N_i^2}{N^2} \cdot \frac{s_i^2}{n_i} \cdot \frac{(N_i - n_i)}{N_i} \right]^{1/2}$$

$$= \left[\left(\frac{10}{60}\right)^2 \left(\frac{8.0}{2}\right)(0.8) + \left(\frac{20}{60}\right)^2 \left(\frac{18.2}{4}\right)(0.8) \right.$$

$$\left. + \left(\frac{30}{60}\right)^2 \left(\frac{7.6}{6}\right)(0.8) \right]^{1/2}$$

$$= \$860$$

Thus, a 95 percent confidence interval for the unknown mean value of co-op advertising allowances claimed by the population of sixty retailers is

$$17,000 - 1.96(860) \leq \mu \leq 17,000 + 1.96(860)$$

or

$$\$15,000 \text{ to } 19,000$$

Comparison to Statistics in Simple Random Sampling. It is most illuminating to compare these results to those obtained from simple random sampling in the same population. Let us suppose the researcher instead had taken a simple random sample without stratification. To compare results on an equivalent basis, let us have the simple random sample select the exact same twelve population elements. The mean of this sample is exactly the same as before:

$$\bar{X} = \frac{\sum_{i=1}^{n} X_i}{n} = (33 + 29 + 27 + \ldots + 5)/12$$

$$= \$17,000$$

However, the standard error becomes

$$s_{\bar{X}} = \left[\frac{\sum_{i=1}^{n} (X_i - \bar{X})^2/(n-1)}{n} \right]^{1/2} \left[1 - \frac{n}{N} \right]^{1/2}$$

$$= \left[\frac{87.9}{12} \right]^{1/2} [0.8]^{1/2} = \$2,400$$

And, a corresponding 95 percent confidence interval is $12,000 to $22,000. What happened?

The obvious answer is that our standard error grew nearly three times larger. We explain this result by examining the two procedures for computing standard error. In simple random sampling, we take each sampled population element value, subtract from it the sample mean, and square the result. We note that some sampled values lie some distance from the sample mean and lead to large $(X_i - \bar{X})^2$ values. In stratified sampling, we take each sampled population element value, subtract from it its respective stratum mean, and square the result. However, sampled values lying some distance from the total sample mean will almost always lie much closer to their respective stratum mean. Thus, a stratified sample will produce sampling error that is equal to or less than that of a simple random sample of the same size.

Another way of explaining the result involves the idea of combinations of population elements as sample members. In stratified sampling, only certain sample combinations are allowed. The researcher in our example could select no more and no less than two large retailers, four medium retailers, and six small retailers. Values for $\bar{X}_{st}$ resulting from all samples using this procedure (that is, the sampling distribution of $\bar{X}_{st}$) would necessarily group closely together. However, in simple random sampling, the researcher could conceivably select the twelve largest or the twelve smallest retailers as his sample. Thus, for samples of the same size, the sampling distribution of $\bar{X}$ would contain more extreme sample means lying further from the population mean than would the sampling distribution of $\bar{X}_{st}$. This results in more sampling error.

Dichotomous Variables. For the sake of completeness and with the comment that our discussion to this point also applies, we present in Exhibit

EXHIBIT 13.2
Statistical Concepts for Stratified Sampling With Dichotomous Variables

Term	Meaning	Symbol	Formula
Stratum sample proportion	Arithmetic average derived from population element values in the ith stratum	$\bar{p}_i$	$\bar{p}_i = \dfrac{\sum\limits_{j=1}^{n_i} X_{ij}}{n_i}$
Stratum sample variance	Dispersion of population element values in the ith stratum about the stratum sample proportion	s_i^2	$s_i^2 = \dfrac{(\bar{p}_i)(1 - \bar{p}_i)n_i}{n_i - 1}$
Estimated population proportion	Average of all L stratum sample proportions weighted by stratum size/population size	$\bar{p}_{st}$	$\bar{p}_{st} = \sum\limits_{i=1}^{L} \dfrac{N_i}{N} \bar{p}_i$
Estimated standard error	Standard deviation of sampling distribution of $\bar{p}_{st}$	$s_{\bar{p}_{st}}$	$s_{\bar{p}_{st}} = \left[\sum\limits_{i=1}^{L} \dfrac{N_i^2}{N^2} \cdot \dfrac{(\bar{p}_i)(1 - \bar{p}_i)}{n_i - 1} \cdot \dfrac{(N_i - n_i)}{N_i} \right]^{1/2}$

13.2 statistical concepts for the stratified sampling of dichotomous variables. Such concepts would apply if our researcher were interested in the proportion of retailers using television advertising, for example.

STRATIFIED SAMPLING IN PRACTICE It seems we get something for nothing with stratified sampling. Actually, we do not: costs of stratification may outweigh benefits derived from decreased sampling error. For example, it takes research resources to choose both a stratification variable and the number of strata in a reasonable manner. Kish provides some guidelines.[1]

1. For any variable used in stratification, measurement information must be available on all population elements. However, if a few lack measurement on the stratification variable, a researcher might place these elements in a "miscellaneous" stratum. A researcher might also stratify part of the population using one stratification variable and stratify another part using another.

2. Stratification produces greater gains if it uses coarse divisions of several stratification variables rather than fine divisions of one. We would expect smaller sampling errors when we stratify using one

[1] Leslie Kish, *Survey Sampling* (New York: John Wiley & Sons, 1965), pp. 88–106.

variable as 1980 sales (having three categories) jointly with another variable as advertising aggressiveness (having two categories) than when we stratify using six categories of 1980 sales.

3. Stratification produces greater gains if it uses several stratification variables related to research variables of interest but unrelated to each other.

4. Using a single stratification variable, sampling errors for most research variables show marked reduction as the number of strata increases to three or four. Sampling errors show little reduction beyond ten strata.

5. Stratification produces little gain unless separate strata variances on the variable of interest are greatly below the variance in the unstratified population.

Beyond choosing stratification variables and the number of strata, it takes more research resources to classify all population elements into the various strata before sampling. It takes more research resources to draw the simple random sample L times in the population instead of only once. It takes more research resources to calculate estimates of population parameters. And because stratified sampling requires more researcher decisions, the possibility of nonsampling errors also increases.

Occasionally researchers stratify population elements *after* their selection by a simple random sample. The practice is called **poststratification.** Poststratification avoids the tedious classification process associated with stratifying large populations because classification applies only to population elements in the much smaller sample. It also allows stratification if knowledge of individual population elements' possession of the stratification variable is unknown before sampling. Researchers still need information on the relative sizes of resulting strata in the original population (N_i values), however. Little else from our stratified sampling discussion changes except for a slight modification to the standard error formula. Researchers usually ignore this modification for moderately large n_i values.[2]

Occasionally researchers stratify population elements and then, in contrast to our example, take a **disproportionate simple random sample** within each stratum. That is, instead of using $n_i = nN_i/N$, which we rewrite as $n_i/n = N_i/N$, a disproportionate sample uses $n_i/n = W_i$. W_i may be any number between 0.0 and 1.0, subject to

$$\sum_{i=1}^{L} W_i = 1$$

---

[2]Kish, *Survey Sampling*, pp. 90–92.

Nothing else changes from our stratified sampling discussion. Why would a researcher want to do this? Basically, for one or more of four reasons:

1. Variances of a key research variable across the L strata differ by sizeable amounts.

2. Desired standard errors within the L strata on a key research variable differ by sizeable amounts.

3. Costs of sampling across the L strata differ by sizeable amounts.

4. Numbers of population elements in the L strata differ by sizeable amounts.

To explain the first, consider a population divided into two strata. In one stratum, suppose population elements show no variation with respect to measurement values on a key research variable. In the other, suppose population elements show much variation. A sample of size 2 provides all the information potentially available from the first stratum. (We need a sample of at least size 2 to estimate variance.) Taking a small sample here allows us to take a large sample in the second stratum and still satisfy a given sampling budget.

To explain the second, suppose a researcher is also interested in estimating a mean value in one of the two strata. Taking a large sample in one stratum and a small sample in the other will produce a smaller confidence interval for the first stratum's mean. The researcher obtains greater precision within a stratum of interest for a given sampling budget.

To explain the third and fourth, suppose one stratum has quite high sampling costs per population element and the other has quite low. For a given sampling budget, then, we might prefer to sample more elements in the cheap stratum than in the expensive stratum. Likewise, if one stratum contains many population elements, we might prefer to take a larger sample in it than in one containing only a few.

Notice that we need more prior information about the population before proceeding with a disproportionate sample.[3] Not only do we need all information required for proportionate stratified sampling, we also need estimates of strata variances and sampling costs. Moreover, note that most research studies involve several key research variables of interest. It is entirely possible that one may show a decreasing pattern of variances and costs across the L strata, another show a stable pattern, and yet another show an increasing pattern. Under such conditions, selecting optimum stratum sample sizes will be impossible.

---

[3]"Prior information" hints at a Bayesian approach to disproportionate stratified sampling. See Seymour Sudman, *Applied Sampling* (New York: Academic Press, 1976), pp. 121–30. for an introduction to the topic.

Occasionally researchers use stratified sampling solely to ensure that samples contain population elements from certain groups. Quite often this occurs in populations "naturally" stratified in a recordkeeping process. For example, suppose co-op advertising allowance claims are filed by state by retailer and that our researcher desires a sample of seven California, three Washington, and two Oregon retailers. Suppose further that retailer location is unrelated to co-op advertising usage. Stratified sampling compared to SRS in such instances will neither decrease nor increase sampling error. It will only make certain the composition of the sample.

Stratified sampling proportionate to stratum size requires the same information as simple random sampling—plus knowledge of each population element's possession of the stratification variable and knowledge of strata sizes in the population. If stratification occurs after sampling, we alter these requirements to knowledge of each sampled population element's possession of the stratification variable and knowledge of strata sizes. In either case, obtaining this information consumes more resources than is usually expended in simple random sampling. Yet researchers may benefit because both types of stratified sampling usually reduce sampling errors. And both provide research results not just for the population of interest as a whole but for specific strata in the population.

STRATIFIED SAMPLING SUMMARY

Similar statements apply to stratified sampling disproportionate to stratum size. Disproportionate stratified sampling often produces even smaller sampling errors but almost always at considerably greater cost. Conditions favoring its use (unequal variances, unequal desired standard errors in strata, unequal costs, unequal stratum sizes) occur most often not with consumers as population elements but with organizations. Organizations more often show great variance differences on variables of interest across strata based on size. Some class or classes of organizations often interest the decision maker more than others. Organizations more often show great cost differences for sampled population elements, based on geography. However, we make no general statement about their stratum sizes. As a rule, researchers should avoid disproportionate stratified sampling unless variances and costs differ roughly by a factor greater than two across several strata.[4]

Somewhat as an aside, our discussion in this section hints at a basic trade-off between sampling errors and sampling costs. The two concepts share an inverse relationship: one generally decreases while the other generally increases. In Chapter 14 we discuss this trade-off as a major consideration in estimating sample size.

---

[4]Kish, *Survey Sampling*, p. 94.

All types of stratified sampling are quite compatible with probability sampling methods other than simple random sampling. We examine one of them, systematic sampling, in our next section.

Systematic Sampling

Systematic sampling proceeds differently and more simply. A researcher merely:

1. Lists population elements; and

2. Selects every kth element after a random start within the first k elements.

To illustrate, consider again our importer of food processors. Suppose a researcher were interested in estimating the average shop time taken to repair a unit returned under warranty in 1981. Suppose 2,815 units were returned and completely repaired that year. Each had received a shop ticket, which was later collected and stored in a file drawer. Each ticket showed the amount of time required to repair the processor in the shop. The researcher wishes to draw a sample of fifty tickets.

Rather easily she calculates $N/n = 56.3$ as the desired **sampling interval** k. To simplify, she rounds k to 56. Using Table 1 in the Appendix, she determines her random start as 12 and, thus, selects shop tickets starting with number 12, then 68, then 124, and so on through 2,812. Those readers who are quite empirically oriented might determine that our researcher ends up with a sample of fifty-one tickets. Had the random start been any number from 16 through 56 she would have achieved an n of fifty. Usually a sample size of either n or $n + 1$ presents no problem in marketing research.[5]

SYSTEMATIC SAMPLING AND STATISTICAL THEORY Despite this simplicity, systematic samples are quite complex statistically, with procedures to calculate unbiased estimates of their standard errors that are beyond our scope.[6] However, using the following discussion, we may apply to systematic samples the same statistical concepts and formulas from Chapter 12 that we applied to simple random samples.[7] The discussion concerns the distribution of the variable of interest among units as they appear in the sampling frame.

---

[5]See Kish, *Survey Sampling*, pp. 115–6 for procedures when $n + 1$ is irksome.

[6]For formulas and their development see Kish, *Survey Sampling*, pp. 118–20.

[7]The discussion follows the one in Richard L. Scheaffer, William Mendenhall, and Lyman Ott, *Elementary Survey Sampling*, 2nd ed. (North Scituate, Mass.: Duxbury Press, 1979), pp. 177–84.

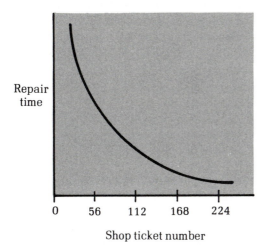

FIGURE 13.1
Shop tickets ordered by a decreasing exponential trend

If this distribution is random or near random, concepts and formulas apply without reservation. That is, systematic sampling from a random or near random distribution of variable values essentially produces a simple random sample.

If this distribution is ordered, as either an increasing or decreasing trend line, concepts and formulas apply as follows. First, the researcher instead of randomly starting between 0 and k should purposely start near or at $k/2$. To illustrate, suppose the researcher in our repair shop ticket example faced the sampling frame in Figure 13.1. (Such a frame would be typical if 1981 were the shop's first year of operation—repair personnel would have become more efficient at some constant rate.) If the researcher were to start at random, a number close either to 0 or to 56 might result and the ensuing sample would either overestimate or underestimate the unknown population mean. However, if the researcher were to start with ticket number 26, 27, 28, 29, or 30, the sample would quite accurately estimate the population mean. Second, the researcher should recognize that use of the simple random sample formula to estimate the standard error always overstates the value for a systematic sample drawn from an ordered sampling frame.[8] Resulting confidence intervals will be too wide or confidence coefficients too low.

If the distribution of variable values fluctuates in a periodic manner,

---

[8]Scheaffer, Mendenhall, and Ott, *Elementary Survey Sampling*, p. 178.

concepts and formulas apply as follows. First, as long as the fluctuation's period does not equal k, or some integral multiplier of k (such as $2k$, $3k$, etc.), or some integral fraction of k (such as $k/2$, $k/3$, etc.), the researcher should use earlier concepts and formulas without reservation. Second, under those rare and opposite conditions, the researcher should change the random start frequently during the course of the systematic sample. See Figure 13.2 showing another sampling frame for our example; in this one, the variable values are ordered in a fluctuation whose period equals 28. This could happen if the shop manager, when opening each crate of 28 returned units, assigned repair tickets first to those more easily fixed. Failure to change the random start (frequently) in this sampling frame would lead either to overestimates or underestimates of the population mean and to underestimates of sampling error.

SYSTEMATIC SAMPLING AND RESEARCH PRACTICE

Systematic sampling produces samples much faster and much cheaper than does simple random sampling or stratified sampling. Researchers need only a list of population elements and only one number as a start.

Sometimes they need only the start, as when sampling from infinite populations or continual processes. For example, a researcher may select every kth candy bar beginning with the 814th as they slide down a production line as a systematic sample. The following day he may select every kth bar again (or every jth bar, for that matter) after a different random start.

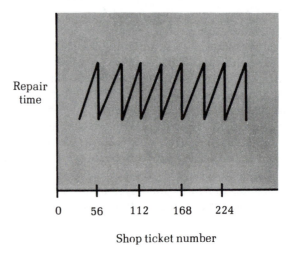

FIGURE 13.2
Shop tickets ordered by a fluctuation with period equal to 28

Systematic sampling occasionally meets a problem when sampling from an uncounted, finite population. If the application of k produces too big a sample, a researcher will need a second probability sample of these elements to achieve n. If k produces too small a sample, the researcher will need to start over again, using a new sampling interval $k' < k$. Sometimes starting over will be impossible as, for example, when the researcher desires a sample of shoppers at a supermarket on a particular date.

Systematic sampling allows easier validation of sampling activities. All a researcher needs to confirm that someone has drawn a proper systematic sample is knowledge of k, the start number, and the identification numbers of selected population elements. This contrasts with simple random and stratified sampling where checking is often quite tedious and occasionally impossible.

Finally, systematic sampling works well as a substitute for simple random sampling in stratified sampling. (See again the SIP example in Box 12.1.) Systematic sampling also works well with cluster sampling, our last probability sampling method. (See also the Random Digit Dialing discussion in Box 13.2 later.)

Cluster Sampling

Cluster sampling differs from simple random, stratified, and systematic sampling because cluster sampling selects not individual population elements but clusters or groups of population elements. Why would a researcher want to do this? One reason is cost. A researcher usually finds it more economical to select groups than to select individuals. The other reason is frequently the lack of an adequate sampling frame. That is, often a researcher cannot find a current list of individual population elements containing no duplicates, omissions, and outsiders. However, often the researcher can find an adequate list of groups of population elements in the form of a list of organization names or units of area.

Consequently, researchers use cluster sampling, of either single or multiple stages. A **single-stage cluster sample** randomly selects groups of population elements and then collects measurements from every population element in each group. A **multi-stage cluster sample** similarly selects groups of population elements but then collects measurements from a probability sample of population elements in each group. Either a simple random, stratified, or systematic sample may be used as the probability sample.

Consider as an example a researcher interested in consumer reaction in Miami to a new dishwashing liquid. From a sampling frame listing residential blocks, the researcher randomly selects six and places the product in all 115 households as a single-stage cluster sample. Alternatively, the researcher might have randomly selected twenty-four residential blocks and then randomly selected five households in each block as a two-stage cluster sample. In either case, to apply cluster sampling to a population, the researcher:

1. Lists clusters or groups, and

2. Randomly selects clusters in sufficient quantity to produce n measurements.

However, the price of this simplicity comes in the form of increased sampling error as we discuss below.

CLUSTER SAMPLING AND SAMPLING ERROR Cluster samples almost always produce larger sampling errors than other probability samples of the same size. They do so primarily because cluster samples make comparatively fewer independent sampling selections.

If the researcher in our test of the new dishwashing liquid randomly selects six residential blocks and places the product in all 115 households, she really makes only 6 independent selections. If she randomly selects twenty-four blocks and then randomly selects 5 households on each, she makes not 120 but only 24 independent selections.[9] In either case, the selection of households on any block depend on that block being selected.

To see how a reduction in number of independent selections increases sampling error, we need some symbols as follows:

Symbol	Meaning
a	Number of primary or first level clusters selected in the sample
A	Total number of primary or first level clusters in the population
b	Number of population elements selected in each primary or first level cluster
B	Total number of population elements in each primary or first level cluster

Note that symbols require equal sized primary clusters. With these and other, more familiar symbols we can present relevant statistical concepts, including sampling error for cluster sampling, as in Exhibit 13.3.

Look carefully at the formula to calculate the variance of a cluster sample. We can see that it looks much like its counterpart for a simple random sample. We show both below to highlight the similarity.

$$s^2 = \frac{\sum_{i=1}^{n} (X_i - \overline{X})^2}{n - 1} \quad \text{and} \quad s_{Cl}^2 = \frac{\sum_{j=1}^{a} (\overline{X}_j - \overline{X}_{Cl})^2}{a - 1}$$

[9]Kish, *Survey Sampling*, p. 161.

EXHIBIT 13.3
Statistical Concepts for Cluster Sampling

Term	Meaning	Symbol	Formula
Cluster mean	Arithmetic average derived from population element values selected in the jth primary cluster	$\overline{X}_j$	$\overline{X}_j = \dfrac{\sum\limits_{i=1}^{b} X_i}{b}$
Sample mean	Arithmetic average of primary cluster means	$\overline{X}_{Cl}$	$\overline{X}_{Cl} = \dfrac{\sum\limits_{i=1}^{a} \overline{X}_j}{a}$
Sample variance	Dispersion of primary cluster means about the sample mean	s_{Cl}^2	$s_{Cl}^2 = \dfrac{\sum\limits_{i=1}^{a} (\overline{X}_j - \overline{X}_{Cl})^2}{a-1}$
Estimated standard error	Standard deviation of the sampling distribution of $\overline{X}_{Cl}$	$s_{\overline{X}_{Cl}}$	$s_{\overline{X}_{Cl}} = \left[\dfrac{s_{Cl}^2}{a} \left(1 - \dfrac{a}{A} \right) \right]^{1/2}$

Such correspondence implies that we can think of a cluster sample as a simple random sample whose sample members consist of means calculated from the a clusters.

An Example.   As an example to illustrate and extend our discussion, consider a large population of consumers in which we select two primary clusters of eight population elements each. Let their measurements and their means on a variable of interest be as shown below:

									$\overline{X}_j$
Cluster 1	5	6	5	8	9	2	6	7	6
Cluster 2	12	14	13	11	17	12	15	18	14

We have

$$\overline{X}_{Cl} = \sum_{j=1}^{a} \frac{\overline{X}_j}{a} = \frac{6 + 14}{2} = 10$$

$$s_{Cl}^2 = \sum_{j=1}^{a} \frac{(\overline{X}_j - \overline{X}_{Cl})^2}{a - 1} = \frac{(6 - 10)^2}{1} + \frac{(14 - 10)^2}{1} = 32$$

and the estimated standard error, $s_{\overline{X}_{Cl}}$ is

$$s_{\overline{X}_{Cl}} = \left[\frac{s_{Cl}^2}{a} \right]^{1/2} = \left[\frac{32}{2} \right]^{1/2} = 4$$

Now, let us keep the same sample members but double the number of independent selections by doubling the number of primary clusters. Let the clusters, their measurements, and their means now be

					$\overline{X}_j$
Cluster 1	5	6	5	8	6.0
Cluster 2	9	2	6	7	6.0
Cluster 3	12	14	13	11	12.5
Cluster 4	17	12	15	18	15.5

We have the same value as before for $\overline{X}_{Cl}$:

$$\overline{X}_{Cl} = (6.0 + 6.0 + 12.5 + 15.5)/4 = 10.0$$

but now

$$s^2_{Cl} = \frac{(6 - 10)^2}{3} + \frac{(6 - 10)^2}{3} + \frac{(12.5 - 10)^2}{3} + \frac{(15.5 - 10)^2}{3}$$

$$= 22.8$$

Consequently

$$s_{\overline{X}_{Cl}} = \left[\frac{22.8}{4} \right]^{1/2} = 2.4$$

a quantity much smaller than our original estimated standard error. Thus, we see how sampling error in cluster sampling depends on a; the more primary clusters that are sampled, the smaller the error.

Note the relative lack of variability of measurements within these four clusters. Each measurement seems fairly close to others in its cluster—a characteristic common to many samples using natural clusters of people. That is, people of similar ages, incomes, occupations, interests, and so on tend to group together—as residents in the same neighborhood, as shoppers in the same retail store, as attendants of the same social event, as human beings. Often such inherent similarity leads to a decrease in variability between measurements made on research variables of interest in each cluster. For example, a consumer group whose members have somewhat similar incomes will show somewhat similar reactions to a price increase. Thus, cluster samples will naturally show somewhat similar measurements within each cluster.

This lack of variability in natural clusters is a secondary reason why cluster samples compared to simple random samples show larger sampling errors. To see this, let us increase the variability inside our clusters (but not inside our sample) by transposing measurements in the fourth cluster with those in the fourth column. Our transposed clusters and their means now look like this:

					$\overline{X}_j$
Cluster 1	5	6	5	17	8.25
Cluster 2	9	2	6	12	7.25
Cluster 3	12	14	13	15	13.50
Cluster 4	8	7	11	18	11.00

We find $\overline{X}_{Cl}$ still equals 10. We expect a smaller estimated standard error, and are not disappointed:

$$s^2_{Cl} = \frac{(8.25 - 10.0)^2}{3} + \frac{(7.25 - 10.0)^2}{3} + \frac{(13.5 - 10.0)^2}{3} + \frac{(11.0 - 10.0)^2}{3}$$

$$= 7.96$$

$$s_{\overline{X}_{Cl}} = \left[\frac{7.96}{4} \right]^{1/2} = 1.4$$

Thus, we see how sampling error in cluster sampling also depends on variability within the clusters;[10] the more variability, the smaller the error.

Comparison to Statistics in Simple Random Sampling. Suppose we had instead taken a simple random sample of the same size. To compare sampling errors on an equivalent basis, let us have the simple random sample select the same sixteen population elements. We calculate $\overline{X}$ again as 10, and s^2 as

$$s^2 = \frac{\displaystyle\sum_{i=1}^{n} (X_i - \overline{X})^2}{n - 1} = \frac{(5 - 10)^2}{15} + \frac{(6 - 10)^2}{15} + \dots + \frac{(18 - 10)^2}{15}$$

$$= 22.1$$

and $s_{\overline{X}}$ as

$$s_{\overline{X}} = \left[\frac{s^2}{n} \right]^{1/2} = \left[\frac{22.1}{16} \right]^{1/2} = 1.2$$

Such results showing the relative efficiency of simple random sampling over cluster sampling are typical. A stratified sampling procedure would produce even smaller sampling errors.[11]

---

[10]For a more formal treatment on cluster sample variability see Kish, *Survey Sampling*, pp. 161–78 or Sudman, *Applied Sampling*, pp. 73–78.

[11]Cluster sampling from a stratified sampling frame is also possible. The relative reduction in sampling error here with cluster sampling is greater than with ordinary stratified sampling. See Kish, *Survey Sampling*, pp. 164–66.

Cluster samples produce confidence intervals of an expected form:

$$\overline{X}_{Cl} - Zs_{\overline{X}_{Cl}} \leq \mu \leq \overline{X}_{Cl} + Zs_{\overline{X}_{Cl}}$$

Such intervals hold true for any cluster sample with a $1 - \alpha$ probability. Such intervals generally require $a \geq 30$.

Dichotomous Variables. We complete our discussion by presenting in Exhibit 13.4 statistical concepts for cluster sampling with dichotomous variables. Our comments to here apply equally well to such variables.

CLUSTER SAMPLING IN PRACTICE A researcher using cluster sampling desires the largest number of primary clusters of the greatest variability for a given sampling budget. Of the two desires, a researcher can usually control only the number of primary clusters. But, by specifying their large number, a researcher significantly increases sampling costs if personal interviewers collect the data. Increases come mostly from higher travel costs claimed by interviewers—it costs more to find 100 households scattered over 400 blocks than to find the 100 concentrated in only 10. Lesser increases also occur if the researcher employs more interviewers and spends more on their training and supervision in order to complete the research in a given time. Thus, in personal interviewing, cluster sampling is used either to reduce data collection costs or when the researcher cannot economically obtain a list of population elements as the sampling frame.

EXHIBIT 13.4
Statistical Concepts for Cluster Sampling With Dichotomous Variables

Term	Meaning	Symbol	Formula
Cluster proportion	Arithmetic average derived from population element values selected in the jth cluster	$\overline{p}_j$	$\overline{p}_j = \sum_{i=1}^{b} \dfrac{X_i}{b}$
Sample proportion	Arithmetic average of cluster proportions	$\overline{p}_{Cl}$	$\overline{p}_{Cl} = \sum_{j=1}^{a} \dfrac{\overline{p}_j}{a}$
Sample variance	Dispersion of cluster proportions about the sample proportion	s_{Cl}^2	$s_{Cl}^2 = \dfrac{\sum_{j=1}^{a} (\overline{p}_j - \overline{p}_{Cl})^2}{a-1}$
Estimated standard error	Standard deviation of the sampling distribution of $\overline{p}_{Cl}$	$s_{\overline{p}_{Cl}}$	$s_{\overline{p}_{Cl}} = \left[\dfrac{s_{Cl}^2}{a} \left(1 - \dfrac{a}{A} \right) \right]^{1/2}$

Specifying either a large or a small number of primary clusters usually affects sampling costs little in mail and telephone surveys. In such research, cluster sampling is used primarily for want of an economical sampling frame.

Cluster Definitions and Other Decisions. To apply cluster sampling to a population requires, in addition to a definition of the population of interest, a definition of the clusters. Earlier we said that cluster definitions may be conceptualized in either organization or area terms. For example, we could think of young children in a city either as students at its fifty-one elementary schools or as inhabitants of its 12,430 residential blocks. In any such cluster sampling, cluster definitions must meet two criteria: (1) every population element must belong in one and only one cluster; and (2) the number, or a good estimate of the number, of sampling units available for selection in each cluster must be known. Definitions failing on either criterion will lead cluster samples to under- or overrepresent certain population elements.

A cluster sample also requires decisions on the number of stages and on sample size and sampling method in each stage. Most natural clusters consisting of organizations or units of area usually contain population elements in excess of the desired sample size and, thus, require two-stage or multi-stage cluster sampling. In each but the final stage, clusters are selected with a predetermined probability or sampling fraction. In the final stage, it is the population elements that are so selected.

Sometimes sampling fractions at each stage are equal for all sampling units. To illustrate:

Sampling Stage	Sampling Unit	Sampling Fraction
Primary	Elementary School	1/20
Second	Teacher	1/4
Final	Student	1/6

Such a sampling procedure would select 1/20 of the elementary schools, 1/4 of the teachers in these schools, and 1/6 of the students in their classrooms. The overall probability of a student being selected is given by

$$\frac{1}{20} \cdot \frac{1}{4} \cdot \frac{1}{6} = \frac{1}{480} = 0.0021$$

An identical probability results from sampling fractions of 1/2, 1/8, and 1/30 or from many other suitable combinations. Using a frame consisting of elementary schools, we could also achieve the same probability in a two-stage cluster sample by selecting 1 school in 20 and then selecting 1 student in 24. Stating cluster sampling procedures in sampling fractions emphasizes the method's compatibility with systematic sampling.

However, the procedure just described has two drawbacks: First, primary clusters contain an unequal number of population elements, in violation of our formulas in Exhibit 13.3;[12] second, the total sample size depends on which primary and later stage clusters find their way into the sample. For example, if the sampling fraction of 1/20 selects two schools in the population and they happen to be somewhat larger than average, then the following sampling fractions lead to a larger than expected sample. As Kish discusses, this not only makes budgeting, cost control, and field work difficult, it also leads to increased sampling error. Therefore, researchers try to avoid this "uncontrolled random sampling of clusters with large size variations; e.g., cities, blocks in big cities, and establishments."[13] For such populations they use cluster sampling with **probabilities proportional to size (PPS)**.

PPS Sampling.   PPS sampling selects clusters at any stage not with equal sampling fractions but with fractions based on each cluster's size. For example, consider an automobile dealer serving a small city that is surrounded by seven suburbs. Suppose a researcher wishes to interview a sample of 150 residents age 18 and over, in their homes, to determine the dealer's image compared to images of competitors. Suppose population projections from the most recent census indicate that 28,000 people over age 18 live in the city and 24,800 live in the suburbs.

The researcher decides to interview eighty city residents, that is, she selects this cluster with certainty. Cluster sample size for a cluster selected with certainty is given by n/N times the cluster size. She further decides to select two suburbs with PPS in which to interview the other seventy.

Suppose population projections for the seven suburbs appear as follows:

Suburb	Projected Population Age 18 & over	Cumulative Projected Population Age 18 & over
A	4,100	4,100
B	1,000	5,100
C	800	5,900
D	3,800	9,700
E	5,600	15,300
F	1,500	16,800
G	8,000	24,800

To proceed, the researcher would draw two random numbers between 1 and 24,800 and select those two suburbs having the lowest cumulative populations that exceed the random numbers. For example, if the random numbers are 4,832 and 8,314, she would select suburbs B and D.

---

[12]See Kish, *Survey Sampling*, Chap. 6 for a discussion on sampling with unequal clusters.
[13]Kish, *Survey Sampling*, pp. 217–18.

In each suburb she would randomly select 35 residents over age 18 for interview. The probability associated with these final selections in each suburb is the probability of selecting the suburb times the probability of selecting a resident within the suburb (that is, the sampling fraction for the suburb). For suburb B, we calculate that probability as

$$\frac{(2)(1,000)}{24,800} \cdot \frac{35}{1,000} = 0.0028$$

For suburb D, we have

$$\frac{(2)(3,800)}{24,800} \cdot \frac{35}{3,800} = 0.0028$$

For all suburbs, the probability of resident selection is given by n/N or 70/24,800 which, not surprisingly, equals 0.0028. Thus, PPS samples produce equal selection probabilities despite their selecting samples of equal sizes in clusters of unequal sizes. However, PPS samples still use primary clusters of unequal sizes and, thus, require special formulas for purposes of estimating population parameters.

As a last comment on cluster sampling in practice, we should realize that it is important that data collection forms and computer cards carry a number designating cluster origin. This obviously facilitates calculations of desired cluster statistics. It also allows us to weight data in the various clusters because of both differing accuracies in estimating cluster sizes before sampling and differing response rates after. Minor differences, on the order of 10 percent or so, between clusters would usually not require weighting.

CLUSTER SAMPLING SUMMARY

Cluster sampling differs from other probability sampling methods because it selects groups of population elements. It uses a sampling frame composed of either organizations or units of area. This creates time and cost economies and, at the same time, greater sampling errors. Time and cost economies are usually far greater for personal interview than for mail and telephone surveys.

Cluster sampling is quite compatible with simple random, stratified, systematic, and PPS sampling. For example, a researcher may stratify primary clusters before taking a systematic sample of them. He may continue by stratifying second-stage clusters with a different stratification variable before taking a PPS sample of them. Benefits of stratification will appear in reduced final estimates of sampling error as long as stratification variables correlate with the research variable of interest.[14] He may then select population elements in the final stage with a simple random sample. Box 13.2 further illustrates this compatibility.

---

[14]With PPS sampling, the stratification variable should not be cluster size. PPS sampling automatically produces a sample stratified by cluster size.

BOX 13.2

Random Digit Dialing

A procedure that employs aspects of stratified, systematic, and cluster sampling designs is **random digit dialing (RDD)**. The basic idea behind RDD is simple random sampling: a researcher randomly generates 7- or 10-digit telephone numbers (depending on whether the sample is local or national in scope), then makes the calls. Interviews may take place during these calls or their occasion used as a "foot in the door" to gain cooperation in a later mail or personal interview survey.

However, the basic practice of RDD often relies on stratified, systematic, and cluster sampling because of an inherent condition: simply generating 7- or 10-digit random numbers leads to a high percentage of nonworking and nonresidential numbers, often as high as 60 percent. Employing these more complex sampling methods often reduces the percentage of unsuitable numbers to approximately 30 percent. For example, a researcher may systematically select every nth household listing in a telephone directory and add 1 to the last digit—to allow unlisted numbers a chance to be selected (much as in the study by E. Laird Landon and Sharon K. Banks, "Relative Efficiency and Bias of Plus-

One Telephone Sampling." *Journal of Marketing Research,* 14 (August, 1977): 294–99).

In a national sample, a researcher might stratify by area code, 3-digit prefix, and exchange size and take a cluster sample of adjacent numbers whenever a working number is produced (Robert M. Groves, "An Empirical Comparison of Two Telephone Sample Designs," *Journal of Marketing Research,* 15 (November 1978): 633–31). Such practice may cut the cost per interview as much as one-half with little decrease in statistical efficiency (K. Michael Cummings, "Random Digit Dialing: A Sampling Technique for Telephone Surveys," *Public Opinion Quarterly,* 43 (Summer 1979): 233–44).

Like other telephone surveys, RDD selects no households without telephones, currently about 5 percent of all U.S. households. Unlike other telephone surveys, RDD selects households with unlisted numbers, currently about 30 percent of all U.S. households. RDD also proportionately selects households having more than one working number, currently about 2 percent of all U.S. households.

Chapter Summary

We have continued our three-chapter discussion of sampling in marketing research with an investigation into four probability sampling methods. The first, simple random sampling, selects population elements such that each combination of populaton elements of size n has an equal chance of being selected. It requires a list of population elements, knowledge of their number, and some random selection process. Because of cost difficulties connected with the first two requirements, it is less widely used in marketing research than other probability methods.

The other three probability sampling methods contrast with simple random sampling by organizing their sampling frames into groups of population elements, either explicitly as in the case of stratified and cluster sampling or implicitly as in the case of systematic sampling, before the researcher draws the sample. In stratified sampling, the researcher selects individual population elements randomly from separate strata or classes of population elements. In cluster sampling, the researcher selects groups of population elements randomly from a frame composed of groups. In systematic sampling, the researcher selects every kth individual population element (thus, only k unique samples can possibly be drawn and the population implicitly consists of k groups). Thus, all three methods further contrast with simple random sampling by allowing only certain combinations of population elements as sample members.

All four probability methods enjoy the support of extensive statistical theory. Such theory allows statistical generalization of their sample results to the population of interest using confidence intervals of similar form. No such ability attends nonprobability sampling methods, a topic for Chapter 14. There we will also discuss decisions in the fourth step of the sampling planning process, those specifying sample size.

Chapter Review

		KEY TERMS
Simple random sampling	**Systematic sampling**	
Random digits	**Sampling interval**	
Sampling error	**Cluster sampling**	
Sample representativeness	**Multi-stage cluster sampling**	
Stratified sampling	**PPS sampling**	

DISCUSSION QUESTIONS

1. Under what conditions will a stratified sample produce a smaller sampling error than a simple random sample of the same size?

2. Suppose that, instead of drawing 1 slip of paper from 1,000 in a goldfish bowl 20 times, you draw 2 slips of paper 10 times. Is this a simple random sample?

3. Why might a researcher take samples of sizes 20, 40, and 140, respectively, in three strata of size 1,000 each?

4. There might be a problem in systematic sampling of a population of home mortgages whose elements appear in a sampling frame ordered by time. How so?

5. Stratified samples produce lower sampling errors as stratum sample members become more alike on the variable of interest. Cluster samples produce lower sampling errors as cluster sample members become more different on the variable of interest. Why?

PROBLEMS

1. Use the random numbers that follow to take both a simple random sample and a stratified sample from the population of sixty retailers in Table 13.1. What confidence intervals for estimating the average co-op advertising allowance result from the two samples (use $\alpha = 0.05$)?

   01 08 15 23 24 30 37 42 43 44 51 58

2. Compute a 95 percent confidence interval for the mean, using the following sample measurements taken from a very large population.

   Measurements

Cluster 1	8	2	7	12	15	10
Cluster 2	15	19	18	26	24	22

   a) How does the interval compare to that which would be produced by four clusters consisting of the first and last three measurements in each of the original two clusters?

   b) Consider the twelve measurements to have come instead from a simple random sample. Now what confidence interval results?

3. Suppose you need a simple random sample of 18 students out of a class of 126. Enter Table 1 in the Appendix in a random fashion and:

   a) identify your starting point;

   b) describe your selection procedure; and

   c) identify those students you select.

4. Take a systematic sample of every fourth retailer in Table 13.1, beginning with retailer number 1. Calculate a 95 percent confidence interval for the mean cooperative advertising allowance.

5. A researcher divides a population of 3,000 savings accounts into sixty groups of size 50. He randomly selects eight groups, within which he takes a systematic sample of every twentieth account, using a different random starting point between 1 and 20. Results appear below.

Group:	1	2	3	4	5	6	7	8
Balance ($):	10	800	13	1,100	50	1,843	6	2,002
	48	232	39	408	817	155	178	178
			485	307				756

   a) Identify values for a, A, b, and B for cluster sampling.

   b) Calculate a 95 percent confidence interval for the unknown population mean balance.

Additional Readings

In addition to the sampling texts by Kish and by Sudman (noted at the end of Chapter 12), see:

Scheaffer, Richard L.; Mendenhall, William; and Ott, Lyman. *Elementary Survey Sampling*, 2nd ed. North Scituate, Mass.: Duxbury Press, 1979.

  This text contains an excellent treatment of both simple random and the more complex survey sampling methods—yet the level of instruction remains basic, the discussion pragmatic, and the presentation lucid.

Sudman, Seymour. "Improving the Quality of Shopping Center Sampling." *Journal of Marketing Research* 17 (November 1980): 423–31.

> This article describes rigorous procedures with which researchers may take a probability sample of people at shopping centers within a market area. Apart from its advice to researchers, the piece is worth reading because it helps us appreciate the logic and completeness of rules leading to chance selection.

14

Nonprobability Sampling Methods and Sample Size Estimation

In contrast to our lengthy involvement in Chapter 13 with probability sampling methods, we spend little time here with nonprobability methods. Nonprobability sampling methods are less complex, lacking the theoretical underpinnings that attend probability methods. They produce samples whose results generalize to populations of interest only through the researcher's judgment. After we have seen this, we spend more time with the last step in the sampling planning process—sample size estimation. We take up numerous considerations grouped under three headings: classical, study-specific, and Bayesian. The first and third apply only to estimates of sample size for probability methods; parts of the second may apply to estimates for nonprobability methods.

Nonprobability Sampling Methods

Three nonprobability sampling methods find wide use in marketing research: convenience, judgment or purposive, and quota samples. All use selection procedures based not on chance but on ease for the researcher, on judgment, or on sampling unit characteristics. Because chance is not involved, they are classified as nonprobability sampling methods.

CONVENIENCE SAMPLING

In **convenience sampling,** a researcher selects sampling units on the basis of ease. For example, researchers at Pillsbury regularly test new food products on fellow employees who volunteer for the experience. Telephone calls and more formal requests regularly produce the necessary samples: consent is the only selection criterion. As another example, consider a marketing researcher studying attitudes of Procter and Gamble sales representatives. To help define the problem, the researcher decides to interview five sales representatives and two unit managers. Presence in the district office when the researcher arrives may be the only selection criterion.

The problem with such convenience samples lies with the possibility that they do not represent their populations of interest. Fellow employees possess socioeconomic, behavioral, and psychological characteristics different from those of all consumers. Whoever consents depends on whoever is asked, whoever has the time, and so on. Thus, convenience samples almost always fail in some fashion, to some degree, to represent their populations of interest.

But, in the researcher's judgment, such unrepresentativeness is more than compensated for by time and cost considerations. A convenience sample needs no definition of its population of interest, uses no sampling frame, requires few procedural decisions, and often involves only cursory sample size estimates. Consequently, a convenience sample represents a fast and cheap sampling method, useful for certain research objectives.

Usually these objectives relate to defining the marketing problem, developing hypotheses for later research using probability samples, pretesting data collection forms, and the like. Even in such situations, researchers use them cautiously; they avoid them when attempting to represent the population of interest in descriptive and causal research.

JUDGMENT OR PURPOSIVE SAMPLING

In **judgment** or **purposive sampling,** a researcher selects sampling units on the basis of some expert's judgment that selected units satisfy a stated purpose. Often the expert is the researcher and often the purpose is to represent the population of interest. For example, researchers assembling the durable goods buyers sample in Box 12.1 might judge it representative of people living in Detroit. They might judge it so because no socioeconomic differences appeared between buyers selected by the researchers' three methods, one of which was a random sample of telephone subscribers. As another example, consider that any researcher's selection of any secondary data in marketing research constitutes a judgment sample. Researchers judge that selected secondary data adequately represent the population.

Occasionally the purpose may be completely different. For example, the SIP sample in Box 12.1 selected administrators and staff based on their job responsibilities, not on representativeness considerations. Selected sampling units had to have firsthand knowledge of the randomly selected resident.

Compared to convenience samples, judgment samples tend to take more time and money to assemble. Such increased demands on research resources tend to be offset by judgment sampling's better representing their populations of interest. Yet judges may err; thus their samples would misrepresent populations of interest. Like convenience samples, then, judgment samples often accompany exploratory research and the pretesting of questionnaires. They occasionally accompany descriptive and causal research.[1]

In **quota sampling,** a researcher selects sampling units on the basis of their possessing certain characteristics such that the sample will exactly represent the population of interest on these characteristics. For example, suppose we need a sample of one hundred Kansas teenagers to measure their reaction to a new gardening magazine (appealing to youthful gardeners with larger yards, perhaps). Referencing the *1970 Census of Population,* we determine the facts assembled in Table 14.1. To proceed, we need quotas or totals of the number of teenagers in each age category by sex and population density.

QUOTA SAMPLING

We begin by determining the probability that a teenager is age 15 and under, male, and a rural resident. We then determine the probability that a teenager is age 16 and over, male, and a rural resident. And so on, until we determine probabilities for all eight age, sex, and population density categories. Results appear as percentages in Table 14.2.

We now take each entry times our sample size of 100 and derive our quotas. Results appear in Table 14.3 (rounded to the nearest integer). Instructions to interviewers would be to collect data from individuals possessing the required age, sex, and population density characteristics until

TABLE 14.1
Number of Teenagers by Age, Sex, and Population Density

Age	Total	SEX		POPULATION DENSITY	
		Male	Female	Rural	Urban
15 and under	135,462	69,562	65,900	49,535	85,927
16 and over	171,906	86,454	85,452	55,739	116,167
	307,368				

Source: Adapted from U.S. Department of Commerce, Bureau of the Census, *1970 Census of Population,* Vol. 1, *Characteristics of the Population,* Number 18, Kansas, pp. 60–61.

[1]A good example of judgment sampling accompanying causal research is a test market or field experiment. Here the researcher judgmentally selects a small number of cities, typically two to four, to test combinations of marketing strategies.

TABLE 14.2
Percentages of Teenagers by Age, Sex, and Population Density

Age	MALES		FEMALES	
	Rural	Urban	Rural	Urban
15 and under	7.66	14.71	7.43	14.27
16 and over	9.72	18.67	9.43	18.11

TABLE 14.3
Sample Sizes of Teenagers by Age, Sex, and Population Density

Age	MALES		FEMALES	
	Rural	Urban	Rural	Urban
15 and under	8	15	7	14
16 and over	10	19	9	18

they reach these quotas. Thus, quota sampling shows potential for more representative samples than convenience or judgment sampling.

However, the sample may still not represent the population of interest because we have not controlled for household income (or geographic location or gardening interest or some other characteristic). To remedy the situation, suppose we control first for household income by breaking each quota into categories—above the median and below the median. This sample should better represent the population of interest; controlling for still other characteristics should improve the sample even more.

It will, but it will also create two new problems. First, we encounter a rounding problem that either compromises our quotas or increases our sample size (or forces us to interview only part of a sampling unit!) The problem increases as the number of quota characteristics and their number of categories increases. Second, and more important, interviewers find it difficult to locate sampling units that meet such detailed quotas. This problem leads some interviewers to cheat and record responses of someone in one category as if the person were in another.

Notice further that nothing in either of our quota sampling procedures prevents interviewers from approaching and interviewing only sampling units that exhibit, for example, smiling faces and neat appearances. Thus, failure of this sort of quota sampling to control for interviewers interviewing only sampling units they like or only those they think will cooperate creates an additional problem. Still, such quota samples show higher potential compared to the other nonprobability methods in representing the population of interest on selected, objective characteristics. Furthermore, quota samples that are more sophisticated, setting specified travel patterns for interviewers within randomly selected geographic areas, produce data that behave much like those from a full probability sample.[2]

Three nonprobability sampling methods—convenience, judgment or purposive, and quota—select sampling units on bases other than chance. Convenience samples use ease. Judgment or purposive samples use an expert's opinion that units satisfy some stated purpose. Quota samples use selected sampling unit characteristics.

NON-PROBABILITY SAMPLING METHODS SUMMARY

Often the dividing line between the three nonprobability methods is thin. Most convenience samples involve some sort of judgment; most judgment samples involve some implicit quotas. Thus, research practice frequently employs hybrids using elements of all three. For example, while at a shopping mall (a convenient location) a teenager may be approached by an interviewer (whose decision to approach was based on her judgment); the interviewer's first questions could measure age or zip code or number of siblings (to fill a quota).

Nonprobability methods find wide use in marketing research. However, because of their potential for inadequately representing the population of interest, we should use them cautiously. They are best used in exploratory research. If we use them in descriptive and causal research, we must critically evaluate the degree and direction of sampling differences from population values or be prepared to pay the consequences. We should take care that our evaluation concerns key and not peripheral research variables. We care less if the sample misrepresents the population on variables of lesser importance, but we care a great deal if our sample misrepresents on variables central to meeting research objectives.

Sample Size Estimation

We conclude our discussion of the sampling planning process by examining the estimation of sample size. Like defining the population of interest, determining the sampling frame, and specifying sampling procedures, the estimation of sample size requires the researcher's learned, analytical judgment. A researcher makes such judgments using three decision approaches: classical, study-specific, and Bayesian. We discuss the first

[2]C. Bruce Stephenson, "Probability Sampling With Quotas: An Experiment," *Public Opinion Quarterly* 43 (Winter 1979):477–96. See also Seymour Sudman, "Probability Sampling with Quotas," *Journal of the American Statistical Association* 61 (September 1966):749–71 and Seymour Sudman, *Applied Sampling* (New York: Academic Press, 1976), pp. 191–200.

two approaches in the following sections, but the complexity and infrequent use[3] of Bayesian estimation make it more suitable for separate treatment in a chapter appendix.

CLASSICAL ESTIMATION OF SAMPLE SIZE

Consider the end result of a research study to be an average value for some key research variable. Examples might be the average number of brands consumers can recall, or their average score on a measure of purchase intention, or their average ounces of mustard consumed, or whatever. For any study, the classical approach to estimating sample size starts with this basic question:

> How large a confidence interval about the unknown population average value for this variable do I want?

We call the answer, when divided by two, **desired precision.** Desired precision for the average value of a key research variable depends on two things—expected variability associated with the variable and expected confidence associated with the confidence interval. Let us examine desired precision, expected variability, and expected confidence in detail to see how they combine to determine sample size.

Precision, Variability, and Confidence.   We begin with a statement of a confidence interval for the mean of a variable whose measurements derive from a large simple random sample:

$$\overline{X} - Zs_{\overline{X}} \leq \mu \leq \overline{X} + Zs_{\overline{X}}$$

Alternatively, we might state that μ is contained in the confidence interval:

$$\overline{X} \pm Zs_{\overline{X}}$$

Both forms of confidence interval statements hold true for $(1 - \alpha)100$ percent of all simple random samples and with a $1 - \alpha$ probability for any one. Both forms also apply the concepts of precision, variability, and confidence.

Precision is half of the confidence interval's range or, in symbols, $Zs_{\overline{X}}$. Smaller values of $Zs_{\overline{X}}$ make the estimate of the unknown population mean, μ, more precise; larger values make the estimate less. A researcher design-

---

[3]Probably fewer than 10 percent of all firms conducting marketing research use Bayesian analysis to estimate sample size. See Gerald Albaum, Donald S. Tull, and James W. Hanson, "The Expected Value of Information: How Widely Is It Used in Marketing Research" in *1979 Educators' Conference Proceedings,* ed. Neil Beckwith et al. (Chicago: American Marketing Association, 1979), pp. 32–34. See also Barnett A. Greenberg, Jac L. Goldstucker, and Danny N. Bellenger, "What Techniques are Used by Marketing Researchers in Business" *Journal of Marketing* 41 (April 1977):62–68.

ing a sample finds desired precision reflected by such decision maker statements as:

> I would like to estimate the average number of brands that consumers recall, within one brand.
> I would like to estimate the average purchase intention score, within one half of a scale point.
> I would like to estimate average ounces of mustard consumed, within 0.03 ounces.

With some little thought, we should posit that the greater the desired precision, the larger the estimated sample. We shall confirm this shortly.

Variability in a confidence interval is reflected by the value of the estimated standard error, $s_{\bar{X}}$. Recall that $s_{\bar{X}}$ equals $s/\sqrt{n}$ which, when squared, estimates the variance or variability associated with the sampling distribution of $\bar{X}$. Smaller values of s or larger values of n (when combined with Z or t) produce less sampling error and, hence, greater precision. Larger variability and smaller samples do the opposite.

Confidence in a confidence interval is the $1 - \alpha$ probability associated with the confidence interval containing μ. It is the area beneath the standard normal curve bounded by the $\pm Z$ values. (It is twice the shaded area shown in Table 2 in the Appendix.) Smaller values of Z correspond to lesser confidence and greater precision; larger values correspond to greater confidence and lesser precision. Such should agree with our intuition. We ought to have less confidence that a narrow confidence interval contains the unknown population mean and more that a wide one does.

To formalize our discussion, we express precision as

$$\text{precision} = Zs_{\bar{X}} = \frac{Zs}{\sqrt{n}}$$

Using the last expression to solve for n, we get

$$n = \frac{Z^2 s^2}{\text{precision}^2}$$

This is the basic formula for estimating the size of a simple random sample.

To illustrate its use, consider a researcher who wishes to estimate average ounces of mustard consumed by a population of families during January. Suppose he desires the sample to show a precision of 0.03 ounces; he estimates s at 0.2 ounces and specifies a confidence coefficient of 0.95, making Z equal to 1.96. He quickly estimates n by

$$n = \frac{(1.96)^2 (0.2)^2}{(0.03)^2} = 170.7$$

Thus, a sample of 171 families will produce a precision of ± 0.03 ounces, if s equals 0.2 ounces. If s turns out to be less than 0.2 ounces, the resulting confidence interval will have greater precision, a higher confidence coefficient, or both. If s turns out to be greater than 0.2 ounces, the opposite occurs.

Now suppose he decides to double the desired precision to see what effect this has on estimated sample size. He desires that variability and confidence stay as before and estimates n by

$$n = \frac{(1.96)^2(0.2)^2}{(0.015)^2} = 682.95$$

Thus, he needs a sample of 683 families or an n four times greater than before. We generalize from this experience that relative changes in precision influence sample size by their square. To be twice as precise, we need a sample four times as large and so on.

Now suppose further that he keeps both desired precision at 0.03 ounces and s at 0.2 ounces but specifies a confidence coefficient of 0.99, making Z equal to 2.58. Because of the increased confidence, we expect n to grow from our original estimate, and it does:

$$n = \frac{(2.58)^2(0.2)^2}{(0.03)^2} = 295.8$$

This larger n and Z value will produce the same precision as originally if s continues to equal 0.2 ounces. We might do well to confirm this as a check on our understanding.

Finally, let us suppose the researcher estimates that the population will show more variability than reflected by an s of 0.2 ounces. Suppose he estimates s at 0.3 ounces but keeps desired precision at 0.03 ounces and Z at 1.96. We expect n to grow, this time by the square of the relative change in s, and again find our expectation confirmed:

$$n = \frac{(1.96)^2(0.3)^2}{(0.03)^2} = 384.2$$

A similar formula and identical discussion apply to estimating sample size when the key research variable is dichotomous. For the sake of completeness, we show the formula below:

$$n = \frac{Z^2 \bar{p} (1 - \bar{p})}{\text{precision}^2}$$

Here $\bar{p}$ estimates the proportion of the sample that possesses one of the dichotomous variable's two characteristics. Precision is stated as some small decimal, as the allowable distance from $\bar{p}$.

Population Size Considerations. We might feel uneasy because our discussion seems to have overlooked population size as an influence on sample size. Precision, variability, and confidence bear no relationship to population size, and we feel intuitively that something is missing. Both the intuition and the "oversight" are justified: population size influences sample size, but only when populations are small and samples large.

In such situations, our formulas overestimate sample size because they neglect the finite population correction factor. To adjust for this, a researcher will compare the estimate of n with population size N. If n/N exceeds 0.05, the researcher will revise n to n' where

$$n' = n/(1 + n/N)$$

Thus, a sample originally estimated at 40 in a population of 400 is reduced by a factor of $1 + 40/400$ or 1.1 to 36.4. We round upward to 37 to make sure the actual confidence interval is equal to or smaller than that originally desired. Apart from this slight influence, population size has no effect on sample size.

Estimates of $\overline{X}$ and s^2.   We could also feel uneasy because our discussion on estimating sample size, like our discussion on disproportionate stratified sampling, implies that a researcher possesses some prior information about $\overline{X}$ and s^2. Clearly, a researcher cannot know $\overline{X}$ and s^2 exactly before sampling or there would be no need to sample. But, just as clearly, a researcher must know $\overline{X}$ and s^2 approximately or estimates of sample size become impossible. As support for knowledge of $\overline{X}$, consider that statements of desired precision implicitly require some value of $\overline{X}$ for perspective—a desired precision of 0.03 ounces means one thing when we expect $\overline{X}$ to be 40 ounces and quite another when we expect $\overline{X}$ to be 0.04 ounces. And, as support for knowledge of s^2, we have only to look at the formulas to estimate sample size. Estimates explicitly depend on estimates of s^2.

To obtain estimates of $\overline{X}$ and s^2, researchers can rely solely on their own experience and subjective judgment. Researchers often have measured the same or a similar variable of interest in the same or a similar population; they can equally often expect like values for $\overline{X}$ and s^2. More objectively, researchers can instead use values obtained from final pretests of their data collection forms. As long as they execute pretests under representative conditions, such values estimate $\overline{X}$ and s^2 fairly accurately. Researchers can also use values from reports of studies completed by other researchers using similar variables and populations.

If all these efforts meet failure, often researchers can still estimate $\overline{X}$ and s^2 by taking advantage of the concepts' statistical properties. The value of $\overline{X}$ equals the midpoint of a variable's range of values if its distribution of values is symmetrical. The approximate value of s^2 for a continuous variable equals 1/16 of its range squared.[4] The value of s^2 for a dichotomous variable stays fairly constant as long as the estimated value

---

[4]William Mendenhall and James E. Reinmuth, *Statistics for Management and Economics*, 3rd ed. (North Scituate, Mass.: Duxbury Press, 1978), p. 613.

of $\bar{p}$ lies between 0.3 and 0.7. Further, the value of s^2 for a dichotomous variable reaches an absolute maximum (hence, so does the estimate of n) whenever the estimated value of $\bar{p}$ equals 0.5. However, such "armchair" estimates of $\bar{X}$ and s^2 will usually contain more error than those derived from pretests and other studies. Consequently, a prudent researcher relying on only them will make conservative adjustments to estimates of sample size.

Complex Sampling Methods and Cost Considerations.[5]   Sample size estimates for systematic, stratified, and cluster samples present little additional complication. In fact, systematic samples from frames as discussed in Chapter 13 present none; our preceding simple random sampling formulas and discussion apply here as well. And, with some slight modification, we can extend formulas to stratified and cluster samples.

Our basis for the modification consists of a comparison between the square of the standard error expected from the more complex sample to the square of the standard error expected from a simple random sample of the same number of population elements. Researchers call the ratio of these two squared standard errors the **design effect.** We denote it by de

$$de = \frac{(se')^2}{(s_{\bar{X}})^2}$$

which may be rewritten as

$$de = \frac{(se')^2}{\left(1 - \dfrac{n}{N}\right)\dfrac{(s^2)}{n}}$$

where se' represents the expected standard error of the complex sample and $s_{\bar{X}}$ the expected standard error of the simple random sample. For our second formula, we recall that s^2 is the sample variance for a simple random sample of size n taken in a population of size N.

As examples, recall our stratified sample of sixty retailers of food processors discussed with Table 13.1. There we calculated

$$s_{\bar{X}_{st}} = \$860$$

and

$$s_{\bar{X}} = \$2,400$$

The design effect, then, is

$$\frac{(\$860)^2}{(\$2,400)^2} = 0.13$$

---

[5]This section draws from Leslie Kish, *Survey Sampling* (New York: John Wiley & Sons, 1965), pp. 254–68.

Recall also our cluster sample of consumers in Chapter 13 where we compared standard errors for one design having 2 clusters of size 8 and two designs having 4 clusters of size 4 with one design consisting of a simple random sample of size 16. Our values for standard errors appear below along with design effects, neglecting the $1 - n/N$ terms because of the large population.

Sample	Standard error	Design effect
2 clusters of size 8	4.0	11.1
4 clusters of size 4	2.4	4.0
4 clusters of size 4	1.4	1.4
simple random sample of size 16	1.2	

Such results are typical. For most stratified samples, the design effect will lie between 0 and 1.0; for most cluster samples, the design effect will exceed 1.0.

Like estimates of $\overline{X}$ and s^2, researchers estimate design effects from their experience, pretests, and reports of other research. For example, after pretesting a cluster sample design, a researcher can easily calculate se'. Just as easily, the researcher could consider the same pretest sample values to have come instead from a simple random sample and calculate $s_{\overline{x}}$. It is now a simple matter to estimate the design effect.

With such an estimate, our researcher can estimate the number of independent selections needed for a complex sample to produce a desired precision. The estimation formula looks like this:

$$n_{\text{Ind}} = \left[\frac{Z^2 s^2}{\text{precision}^2} \right] [de]$$

To illustrate its use, let us extend our food processor example from Chapter 13. Suppose the importer in that example shared co-op advertising expenditures with a total of 612 retailers in its fifteen-state market area. A researcher wishes to estimate the average advertising allowance the importer paid using a stratified sample drawn from large, medium, and small accounts (classified by sales over the past twelve months). The estimate should not differ from the unknown population mean value by more than \$1500 with a 95 percent confidence coefficient. The researcher begins by taking a pretest sample of twelve retailers with results in Table 14.4.

We have (neglecting the finite population correction factor because $n/N < 0.05$):

$$s^2_{\overline{X}_{st}} = \sum_{i=1}^{L} \frac{N_i^2}{N^2} \cdot \frac{s_i^2}{n_i}$$

$$= \left(\frac{94}{612} \right)^2 \left(\frac{8.0}{2} \right) + \left(\frac{237}{612} \right)^2 \left(\frac{18.2}{4} \right) + \left(\frac{281}{612} \right)^2 \left(\frac{7.6}{6} \right)$$

$$= \$1.0(1{,}000)^2$$

TABLE 14.4
Co-op Advertising Statistics from Pretest

	Symbol	Large Retailers	Medium Retailers	Small Retailers
Stratum	i	1	2	3
Stratum Size	N_i	94	237	281
Stratum Sample Size	n_i	2	4	6
Stratum Sample Mean ($000)	$\overline{X}_i$	31.0	21.8	9.0
Stratum Sample Variance ($000)²	s_i^2	8.0	18.2	7.6

Suppose the researcher now treats the 12 sampling unit values as if they came from a simple random sample and calculates:

$$s_{\overline{X}}^2 = \frac{s^2}{n} = \frac{87.9}{12} = \$7.3(1,000)^2$$

We have for the design effect:

$$de = \frac{\$1.0(1,000)^2}{\$7.3(1,000)^2} = 0.14$$

Because of the small pretest sample, the researcher somewhat conservatively (and arbitrarily) decides to round this value upward to 0.2. Thus, to estimate the number of independent selections needed by the stratified sample, we have

$$n_{\text{Ind}} = \left[\frac{(1.96)^2(87.9)}{(1.5)^2}\right](0.2)$$

$$= 30$$

The researcher would now allocate this sample proportionately over the three strata and draw the stratified sample.

As another, shorter illustration, suppose we want a cluster sample, whose design effect we estimate at 1.4, to equal the precision of a simple random sample of sixteen consumers. We estimate the variance of the simple random sample at 22.1. Using a Z value of 2.58, we have for the precision of the simple random sample:

$$\text{precision} = \frac{Zs}{\sqrt{n}} = \frac{2.58(22.1)^{1/2}}{\sqrt{16}} = 3.0$$

To achieve this same precision with the same confidence in our cluster sample, we estimate n_{Ind} at

$$n_{\text{Ind}} = \left[\frac{(2.58)^2(22.1)}{(3.0)^2}\right](1.4) = 22.9 \text{ or } 23.$$

However, in cluster sampling n_{Ind} stands for the number of primary or first level clusters selected and not for the number of population elements, because only primary clusters are selected independently. Thus, we estimate that we need 23 primary clusters that produce a design effect of 1.4—not 23 population elements. Such results reflect the lesser statistical efficiency of cluster sampling.

Because of greater economic efficiency (lower sampling costs per sample member) we may prefer a statistically inefficient sample to a statistically efficient one. That is, a cluster sample may achieve greater overall efficiency compared to a stratified sample because of the former's lower sampling costs. For comparison, we can look at one design's per-member sampling costs times its design effect divided by that of another design. If the ratio exceeds 1.0, we prefer the design corresponding to the denominator. If the ratio is less than 1.0, we prefer the design corresponding to the numerator. For example, suppose a cluster sample of 23(4) or 92 population elements costs $240 and produces a design effect of 1.4. Suppose a stratified sample of the 23 population elements in the same population costs $500 and produces a design effect of 0.2. For the ratio between the two designs we have:

$$\frac{\left(\dfrac{240}{92}\right) 1.4}{\left(\dfrac{500}{23}\right) 0.2} = 0.84$$

Thus, we prefer the design reflected in the numerator—the cluster sample.

Number of Key Research Variables Considered. To this point, we have simplified the estimation of sample size by limiting the process to only one key research variable. For this one variable, a researcher specifies desired precision, estimates s^2, chooses Z, and estimates the design effect if planning a complex sample; n then appears with little further judgment. Yet because a planned study might contain 5, 8, or 15 key research variables, a researcher usually exercises considerable judgment. That is, because of both different estimated variances and different desired precisions for each key research variable, any number of them more than one means an equivalent number of estimated sample sizes.

In this more common situation, the researcher chooses from one of three basic options after estimating sample sizes.

1. Use the largest sample resulting from the estimation process. This means that actual precision, confidence, or both will exceed that desired for all key research variables but one. This may be satisfactory if sampling costs are mostly fixed.

2. Compromise by choosing some sample size between the largest and smallest resulting from the estimation process. This means actual precision and confidence will sometimes exceed and sometimes fall short of that desired, depending on key research variable. This option may be favored when sampling costs are mostly variable.

3. Use the exact sample size resulting from the estimation process for each key research variable. This means that some sample members will be asked more research questions than other sample members. Analyses using more than one key research variable at one time will be limited to the smallest subsample of respondents answering research questions in common.

Summary on the Classical Estimation of Sample Size. Statements of desired precision, estimates of s^2, and specifications of Z combine in classical statistics to estimate n. A researcher usually makes several estimates of n for a single key research variable, holding Z constant, and varying both desired precision and estimates of s^2. A researcher then usually makes several additional estimates of n based on the same concepts as applied to other key research variables. A final estimate of n often appears at three levels—low, medium, and high—based on the researcher's assumptions in the process: optimistic, realistic, and pessimistic.

Notice that the classical estimation of sample size merely substitutes for the question of "how large a sample" that of "how big a confidence interval."[6] Such emphasis on expected research results makes classical estimation relevant to researchers and decision makers. However, its failure to give similar emphasis to sampling costs often leads to less than economically optimum results. That is, maybe a smaller sample will lead the researcher and decision maker to the same conclusion at less cost. More on the topic of costs in our next section and in our chapter appendix.

STUDY-SPECIFIC INFLUENCES ON SAMPLE SIZE

Peculiar to any research study are other considerations that exert as much influence on sample size as those already discussed. We call them **study-specific considerations.** Unlike the classical estimation of sample size, study-specific considerations enjoy no detailed theory to prescribe specific research action. Instead, they influence sample size in a general way—usually on an ad hoc basis—affecting n only a little in some studies and much more in others. Moreover, which of four types of study-specific considerations influence sample size more than others also varies from one study to another.

One such type of study-specific consideration is the study's research

---

[6]Sudman, *Applied Sampling*, p. 89.

design classification. In Chapter 2 we said that all research designs fall into one of six classes:

Such classifications, based on the design's primary objective and research focus, influence sample size in a broad, pervasive manner. Generally, basic research in marketing uses smaller samples than applied research. Exploratory and causal research use smaller samples than descriptive research.

Another type of study-specific consideration consists of resources available. Obviously, small budgets, limited numbers of research personnel, and immediate deadlines call for a small sample. Only somewhat less obvious, opposite quantities of research resources may still call for the same sample. That is, larger quantities of research resources do not require larger samples; they only allow them. We have seen from classical estimation that increases in sample size beyond some value for n affect precision and confidence very little. Yet they may add much to sampling costs.

On sampling costs, we note that such expenses are either fixed or variable. **Fixed costs** consist of those out-of-pocket expenses whose total stays constant while sample size changes. Examples of fixed costs include those associated with constructing the questionnaire, choosing a sampling method, and managing such activities. **Variable costs** consist of those out-of-pocket expenses whose total varies directly with sample size. Usually such costs are stated in terms of dollars per sampling unit. Examples include costs associated with interviewer compensation and travel, questionnaire reproduction, and the coding of responses.

For some researchers, costs influence sample size estimation in the extreme, as Lehmann describes:

> When all the scientific talk subsides, someone always asks how much money is available for the study. If this is known, the easiest way to calculate the sample size is to take the budget (SP), subtract the fixed costs of the study (EN) plus any dinners, trips, or expenses we can charge to it (D) and then divide by the variable cost of a sample point or interview (IT). This leads to the very scientific formula:
>
> $$n = \frac{SP - EN - D}{IT}$$

This formula is in reality every bit as important in determining sample size as those relating to the statistical precision of the results.[7]

Another quite obvious type of study-specific consideration in estimating sample size is the expected response rate. That is, after estimating sample size using classical procedures a researcher will almost always want to adjust n to reflect an estimate of the percentage of questionnaires returned. The adjustment is quite simple. The researcher merely divides the original estimate of n by the expected response rate and uses this higher value in the study. For example, if the researcher originally estimates the optimal sample size at 832 and the expected response rate at 75 percent, the revised estimate of n becomes 832/0.75 or 1,110. The same simple procedure applies to planning subsample sizes for strata or for quota categories based on different response rates per subsample.

A last type of study-specific consideration in estimating sample size consists of planned data analysis methods. Actually, planned data analysis methods already have influenced our estimation of sample size—we used it when we discussed desired precision of means for key research variables. That is, our planned data analysis method was always the one-by-one examination of these means. If, instead, our planned data analysis method were the simultaneous comparison of two or more of these means, slightly different estimation procedures would apply.[8]

Also influencing estimates of sample size are theoretical requirements of the planned test statistics. As examples, a test of differences between sample means using Z usually requires samples greater than size 30 so that the distribution of differences approximates a normal distribution. For a similar reason, a test between sample proportions requires an n such that both $n\pi$ and $n(1 - \pi)$ equal or exceed 5. A test using chi-square requires all expected category cell sizes to be greater than 2 and most greater than 5, although some statisticians relax this to allow up to 5 percent of the expected cell sizes to only exceed 1. These and other influences of planned data analysis methods on sample size will be discussed in later chapters. Here they illustrate again the interdependency between decisions made in different stages of the marketing research process.

A last comment on estimates of sample size concerns planned data analysis methods for subsamples. If the analysis plans to examine separate groups of sampling units within the entire sample, these subsamples also must contain a sufficient number of population elements with respect

---

[7]Donald R. Lehmann, *Market Research and Analysis* (Homewood, Ill.: Richard D. Irwin, 1979), p. 259.

[8]See, for example, John Neter, William Wasserman, and G. A. Whitmore, *Applied Statistics* (Boston: Allyn and Bacon, 1978), pp. 272–87 for details. See also John Neter and William Wasserman, *Applied Linear Statistical Models* (Homewood, Ill.: Richard D. Irwin, 1974), pp. 492–501, 601–02, and 734–35.

to desired precision, sampling costs, research purpose, resources available, expected response rates, and planned data analysis methods. In other words, all our discussion up to this point on estimating sample size applies to subsamples as well.

Chapter Summary

Three nonprobability sampling methods select data sources with less than complete reliance on chance: convenience, judgment or purposive, and quota sampling. These methods generally provide quicker and cheaper data than probability methods can provide. Data so generated may be extended to a population of interest only through the researcher's judgment; consequently, these methods find their greatest use in exploratory research, in pretesting data collection forms, and in research of similar purpose.

Most of our discussion on estimating sample size applies to probability sampling methods, where data extend to a population of interest through confidence intervals. Influencing the size or precision of any confidence interval are sample size, variability in the population, and confidence associated with the interval. In the classical estimation of sample size, a researcher will state desired confidence with some desired precision in the interval and then estimate population variability. Other considerations influencing the estimation of sample size change from study to study: the basic research design classification, resources available, expected response rates, and planned data analysis methods. Further, as our chapter appendix discusses for the Bayesian estimation of sample size, a researcher can estimate both an expected monetary value of marketing research and the cost of sampling at various sample sizes in order to maximize an expected net gain of sampling. Thus, estimated sample size can depend on a number of factors.

As the researcher selects sampling methods and makes estimates of sample sizes, errors naturally occur. Usually the researcher considers the level of sampling error or precision to reflect these errors and neglects any judgmental mistakes. Moreover, usually the researcher neglects judgmental mistakes in defining the population of interest and in specifying sampling frames, the first two steps in the sampling process.[9] Such practice is unfortunate because errors in these early stages of sample design can easily overshadow those inherent in sampling. Thus, our concern throughout the sampling planning process, like that in the entire research design, should be one of minimizing total error at an acceptable cost.

---

[9]Charles S. Mayer, "Assessing the Accuracy of Marketing Research," *Journal of Marketing Research* 7 (August 1970):285.

Chapter Review

KEY TERMS   Nonprobability sample   Precision
               Convenience sample   Design effect
               Judgment sample   Fixed costs of sampling
               Quota sample   Study-specific considerations

DISCUSSION   1. Estimating sample size is as much an art as it is a science. Discuss.
QUESTIONS
             2. What are similarities and differences between probability and nonprobability samples?

             3. A quota sample is much the same as a stratified sample. Discuss.

             4. Why do study-specific considerations influence the estimation of sample size as much as or more than classical considerations?

PROBLEMS   1. A researcher wishes to estimate the average age, within one year, of U.S. consumers classified into a particular segment. She estimates s at three years and desires a 95 percent confidence coefficient.

             a) How large a sample do you estimate she needs?

             b) Suppose the actual sample produces an s of only two years. How does this affect the actual confidence interval?

             c) How large a sample do you estimate she needs if she wishes to estimate average age in the segment within two years?

             2. Calculate the design effect for the two- and four-cluster sample appearing in Problem 2 in Chapter 13.

             3. A researcher is considering the following sample designs in a population of Indiana teenagers.

             Design A: A simple random sample of names drawn from a purchased mailing list, at a cost of $8.50 per sample member.

             Design B: A systematic sample of names drawn from a purchased mailing list, at a cost of $6.25 per sample member.

             Design C: A cluster sample of high schools drawn from a list compiled by the researcher. Cost per sample member is $2.50 and the estimated design effect is 2.2.

             If all samples are the same size, which do you recommend and why?

             4. A researcher wishes to estimate the proportion of single-family dwellings located in zip code 55456 that change ownership during a one-year period.

             a) Assuming a 70 percent response rate, how many telephone numbers must be selected for the survey to produce a precision of 0.01?

             b) What other assumptions must the researcher make to answer question part (a)?

Appendix: Bayesian Analysis

Bayesian analysis is a decision-making approach useful for solving a variety of problems. Here we apply it first to estimate expected values associated with the execution of proposed research designs. We then compare expected values with sampling costs associated with each design and choose the design that maximizes the net gain or difference. Thus, Bayesian analysis as used here is actually a fourth procedure to examine the costs and benefits of proposed marketing research designs, a topic begun in Chapter 2.

Problem Requirements

Bayesian analysis requires a marketing problem to be stated in terms of decision alternatives that are related to states of nature or events beyond the decision maker's control. Consider a new product introduction where a decision maker must decide which of three new products—identified as A, B, and C—will be introduced. Obviously, the products are decision alternatives because the decision maker has complete control over their selection. Suppose product A is a cheap, low-margin, and highly advertisable product that should find wide consumer acceptance. Let C be an expensive, high-margin product that has to be aggressively sold by dealers. Let B be described as a product fitting somewhere in between A and C.

Let the states of nature be identified as three levels of dealer acceptance. Dealers could be enthusiastic, so-so, or negative toward the new product, depending on their evaluation of its features. Dealer acceptance may be partly influenced by the decision maker but ultimately it is beyond the decision maker's control.

States of nature and decision alternatives can be combined using estimated payoffs or benefits. These payoffs or benefits can be described as the present value of a stream of profits associated with each decision alternative and state of nature. All this information is usually presented in tabular form along with the subjective probabilities of each state of nature's likely occurrence. Table 14A.1 is a payoff table for our example; it shows that if product A is introduced and dealer reaction is enthusiastic, the decision maker realizes a discounted profit of $250,000. If product C were introduced instead and dealer reaction similar, a discounted profit of $300,000 is estimated.

Probabilities associated with the negative, so-so, and enthusiastic states of nature are 0.2, 0.5, and 0.3, respectively. We can interpret these numbers as the estimated likelihood, as seen by the decision maker, of each state of nature's occurrence. Most likely is a so-so reaction, followed by an enthusiastic acceptance, with a negative reaction being the least likely.

TABLE 14A.1
Payoff Table for New Product Introduction (in thousands of dollars)

DECISION ALTERNATIVES	STATES OF NATURE		
	Dealer Reaction		
	Negative $(P = 0.2)$	So-So $(P = 0.5)$	Enthusiastic $(P = 0.3)$
Product A	100	220	250
Product B	150	150	150
Product C	50	80	300

Some comments of clarification are in order: The word *estimate* has been much used already in our Bayesian discussion and it is important that we understand its meaning. An estimate is a subjective judgment based on the best current information available to the decision maker without conducting any formal marketing research. For example, subjective probabilities for each state of nature may be derived from past experience, from the advice of peers and experts, and from structured observation. Benefits or payoffs may come from similar sources or from detailed cost, volume, and profit estimates based on market share assumptions. The point is that these are not weak, arbitrary, and "out of the blue" opinions but rather calculated and analytical judgments open to question and discussion.

It is important that we recognize that more states of nature could be identified, as could more decision alternatives. Three of each are used here to keep calculations manageable. Also, it is important to recognize that payoffs in Bayesian analysis are absolute and not differential (as in the present-value method discussed in Chapter 2). Here the payoff figures are just estimated profits associated with decision alternatives. They are not estimated differential profits (which are returns of decision alternatives with research minus returns of alternatives without research). Thus, decision makers might find it easier to make profit estimates in Bayesian analysis than in the present-value method.

Finally, we do not want to lose sight of our first objective in Bayesian analysis, which is to estimate the expected value or benefit associated with the execution of a proposed marketing research design. We should be asking now: what would be the objective of this research? To tell the decision maker which product to introduce is perhaps our first response. Notice from Table 14A.1 that product selection is a difficult decision. Introducing the wrong product implies a loss (called an *opportunity loss* or *regret*) when its payoff is compared to that for the right product. For example, if the decision maker were to introduce product A and dealer reaction were enthusiastic, a $50,000 loss would occur compared to what she or he would have realized from product C. Clearly, the decision maker would appreciate some research estimating dealer reaction, because with this information the decision about which product to introduce becomes easy. It is to this topic of information that we now turn.

Decisions Without Research Information

A first step is to calculate each decision's expected monetary value without conducting research. Expected monetary value for a decision is, as its name implies, profit a decision maker would expect to make given that decision choice. For example, if the decision maker chose product A, he or she would make $100,000 an estimated 20 percent of the time, $220,000 an estimated 50 percent of the time, and $250,000 the rest of the time. In other words, expected monetary value for each decision is the sum of the products of a decision's payoffs times each payoff's respective probability of occurrence. In our example, the following *expected monetary values* (*EMVs*) result (we drop the dollar sign and thousands digits for the sake of convenience in our calculations):

- $EMV_A = 100(0.2) + 220(0.5) + 250(0.3) = 205$
- $EMV_B = 150(0.2) + 150(0.5) + 150(0.3) = 150$
- $EMV_C = 50(0.2) + 80(0.5) + 300(0.3) = 140$

Expected monetary values for products A, B, and C are 205, 150, and 140 respectively. In the absence of any marketing research, the decision maker would do well to introduce product A because of its highest expected monetary value. However, consider that there is a 50 percent chance of states of nature occurring that imply either product B or C should have been introduced.

Suppose a marketing researcher interrupts at this point and announces, "I propose a research design that is 90 percent accurate on forecasting dealer reaction. And it will cost you only $13,500." Should the decision maker proceed with the research? The answer to that question involves our next few steps.

Decisions With Perfect Information

The second step is to calculate the expected monetary value of a decision made under conditions of perfect information or certainty. Here the decision maker is absolutely sure of which state of nature will occur and it is just a matter of selecting the best decision alternative. Suppose in our example we know for sure that dealer reaction will be negative; what product should we introduce? Obviously, product B. Now suppose we know for sure that dealer reaction will be so-so; our decision is clearly product A. If we know for sure dealer reaction will be enthusiastic, we would choose product C. These three statements describe decision making under certainty and the choices lead to payoffs of 150, 220, and 300 respectively. However, we must consider that we make 150 only 20 percent of the time, 220 only 50 percent of the time, and 300 only 30 percent of the time when we make decisions under conditions of certainty. Thus we must weight payoffs expected under conditions of certainty by the probabilities associated with each respective state of nature. We have, then,

$$EMV_{Certainty} = 150(0.2) + 220(0.5) + 300(0.3) = 230$$

This can be interpreted as the discounted profit a decision maker can expect if states of nature could be predicted with certainty.

How much is this "perfect information" worth? *The answer is called the expected monetary value of perfect information and its derivation is our third step.* The expected monetary value of perfect information is simply defined as the expected monetary value of certainty minus the expected monetary value of the best decision alternative without conducting research. In our example:

$$EMV_{Perfect\ information} = EMV_{Certainty} - EMV_{Best\ alternative}$$
$$= 230 - 205 = 25$$

The expected monetary value of perfect information is, in a sense, a *general* upper limit to pay for marketing research. A decision maker would never pay more than $25,000 for *any* marketing research study because it simply is not worth it. With no marketing research at all the decision maker realizes a payoff of $205,000; with certainty, profits rise only to $230,000. Clearly it is bad business in this example to pay $50,000, say, for marketing research that is always imperfect to some degree.

Decisions With Research Information

We continue to our fourth step which is to determine the expected value of a specific marketing research design "that is 90 percent accurate." We should recognize that statements of estimated accuracy are subjective estimates too and are made with the same qualifications, bases, and other comments noted earlier.

Eventually, what we want to end up with is an equation for the EMV of research information. Such an equation should be quite similar to that for perfect information; it looks like this:

$$EMV_{Research\ information} = EMV_{Research\ "certainty"} - EMV_{Best\ alternative}$$

The EMV for research information represents the maximum amount to pay for a specific marketing research study. Because we already know the EMV for the best alternative ($205,000), we need only calculate the EMV for research "certainty." This EMV is quite similar to the EMV we previously calculated for certainty. However, now it represents discounted profits realized from decisions made with research results of limited accuracy instead of with certainty as before. We should ask ourselves: What should be the relationship between the EMV for certainty and the EMV for research "certainty"? The EMV for research "certainty" must be smaller, we conclude, because it is based on partly inaccurate results.

To proceed, we need conditional, joint, and revised probabilities. Conditional probabilities could be called error and accuracy probabilities. They are the probabilities of a marketing research finding or conclusion given actual states of nature. For example, a conditional probability answers this question: "What is the chance that marketing research will conclude that dealer reaction will be negative when it will, in fact, actually be negative? Or when it will, in fact, be so-so? Or, enthusiastic?" With the first state of nature or dealer reaction, a conditional probability represents an accuracy probability (0.90 in our example). However, a research conclusion of negative dealer reaction when reaction actually will be so-so or enthusiastic represents error probability. We shall estimate these probabilities at 0.05 each. We should readily see that the sum of these conditional probabilities is 1.0. This says that the likelihood of research being either accurate or in error is unity.

CONDITIONAL PROBABILITIES

Instead of research concluding that dealer reaction will be negative, we could have research concluding that reaction will be so-so. Again, actual reaction could be either negative, so-so, or enthusiastic. Conditional probabilities associated with this research conclusion and these states of nature are 0.05, 0.90, and 0.05, respectively. We easily see why. Clearly the so-so research conclusion coupled with a so-so actual dealer reaction represents research accuracy which we said was 0.90. Just as clearly, when research concludes a so-so reaction, a negative or an enthusiastic reaction represents error. Error probabilities, we recall, were set at 0.05 and 0.05 for each mistake.

The third possible research result is a conclusion of an enthusiastic dealer reaction. Actual reaction could again be negative, so-so, or enthusiastic. If the last reaction is true, research is accurate, and there is a 0.90 probability of this happening. Errors occur when actual dealer reaction will be negative or so-so. Conditional or error probabilities associated with this are still 0.05 and 0.05.

For summary purposes, the three marketing research conclusions, actual dealer reactions, original probabilities, and conditional probabili-

TABLE 14A.2
Marketing Research Conclusions and Conditional Probabilities

Marketing Research Conclusion	Actual Dealer Reaction	Original Probability	Conditional Probability
Negative dealer reaction	Negative	0.2	0.90
	So-so	0.5	0.05
	Enthusiastic	0.3	0.05
So-so dealer reaction	Negative	0.2	0.05
	So-so	0.5	0.90
	Enthusiastic	0.3	0.05
Enthusiastic dealer reaction	Negative	0.2	0.05
	So-so	0.5	0.05
	Enthusiastic	0.3	0.90

ties are shown in Table 14A.2. From this table we shall easily be able to calculate joint and revised probabilities for each marketing research conclusion.

JOINT PROBABILITIES Joint probabilities for each marketing research conclusion must be calculated next in our determination of maximum research costs. We can remember from our statistics background that a joint probability is the chance that two or more events will all occur. In Bayesian analysis, a joint probability continues to mean this: It is the chance of a given research conclusion and a given state of nature both happening at once. For each research result, joint probabilities are obtained by multiplying each original probability in Table 14A.2 (column 3) by each conditional probability (column 4). Results appear in Table 14A.3 along with revised probabilities.

Notice that the joint probabilities for each research conclusion have been summed in Table 14A.3. Each of these sums represents the likelihood of occurrence of their respective marketing research conclusions. For example, 0.220 is the overall chance of this research concluding that dealer reaction will be negative. Similarly, 0.475 and 0.305 represent chances of this research concluding a so-so and an enthusiastic reaction, respectively. Notice also that the sum of all the joint probability sums equals 1.0. Not only is this a good check on our arithmetic, it shows that the probability is certain that one of three research conclusions must occur.

REVISED PROBABILITIES Revised probabilities for each marketing research conclusion in Table 14A.3 look somewhat mysterious. They do not end neatly in a 5 or a 0 like all other probabilities we have used. Each set of three revised probabili-

TABLE 14A.3
Joint and Revised Probabilities

Marketing Research Conclusion	Actual Dealer Reaction	Joint Probabilities	Revised Probabilities
Negative dealer reaction	Negative	0.180	0.818
	So-so	0.025	0.114
	Enthusiastic	0.015	0.068
		0.220	
So-so dealer reaction	Negative	0.010	0.021
	So-so	0.450	0.947
	Enthusiastic	0.015	0.032
		0.475	
Enthusiastic dealer reaction	Negative	0.010	0.033
	So-so	0.025	0.082
	Enthusiastic	0.270	0.885
		0.305	

ties seems to total 1.0. And they all are placed at the far right of the table which probably indicates that their derivation is based on joint probabilities. Sound reasoning indeed. Revised probabilities are obtained for each research conclusion by dividing each joint probability by its appropriate sum. The 0.818 figure, for example, results when we divide 0.180 by 0.220; 0.114 when we divide 0.025 by 0.220; and so on.

However, knowing how to calculate revised probabilities is not the same as knowing what they are. They are called revised probabilities because they represent revisions to our original probabilities based on the anticipated research conclusions. Originally, our estimates of probabilities for negative, so-so, and enthusiastic dealer reactions were 0.2, 0.5, and 0.3. But, if research is 90 percent accurate and if this research concludes dealer reaction will be negative, wasn't our original estimate of 0.2 for this state of nature too low? Certainly. Likewise, if this research conclusion occurs, our original probability estimates for both a so-so and an enthusiastic reaction were too high. Consequently, we should use these revised probabilities to calculate new EMVs, given our anticipated research conclusions, for each product for each of the three anticipated research conclusions. These calculations appear as in Table 14A.4.

We come now to the calculation of the EMV for research "certainty." The process is similar to our earlier one for certainty only it is based on revised EMVs. To begin, we identify the payoff expected for each marketing research conclusion. For example, if the marketing research conclusion is

A DECISION TO CONDUCT RESEARCH

TABLE 14A.4
EMVs Calculated for Each Research Conclusion

Marketing Research Conclusion	Revised Expected Monetary Value Calculations
Negative dealer reaction	$EMV_A = 100(0.818) + 220(0.114) + 250(0.068) = 123.88$
	$EMV_B = 150(0.818) + 150(0.114) + 150(0.068) = 150.00$
	$EMV_C = 50(0.818) + 80(0.114) + 300(0.068) = 70.42$
So-so dealer reaction	$EMV_A = 100(0.021) + 220(0.947) + 250(0.032) = 218.44$
	$EMV_B = 150(0.021) + 150(0.947) + 150(0.032) = 150.00$
	$EMV_C = 50(0.021) + 80(0.947) + 300(0.032) = 86.41$
Enthusiastic dealer reaction	$EMV_A = 100(0.033) + 220(0.082) + 250(0.885) = 242.59$
	$EMV_B = 150(0.033) + 150(0.082) + 150(0.885) = 150.00$
	$EMV_C = 50(0.033) + 80(0.082) + 300(0.885) = 273.71$

that dealer reaction will be negative, which product should we introduce? Clearly product B, because it has the highest revised EMV, given that research conclusion. Similarly, we would choose product A if research concluded dealer reaction will be so-so, and product C if research concluded reaction will be enthusiastic. Payoffs associated with these three decisions are $150,000, $218,440, and $273,710 respectively.

However, we make $150,000 only when research concludes that dealer reaction will be negative which, according to Table 14A.3, only happens with a 0.220 probability. Thus, we must weight this payoff by its probability just as we must also weight each of the other two payoffs by their probabilities to arrive at total EMV for research "certainty." The calculations appear below:

$$EMV_{\text{Research "certainty"}} = 150.00(0.220) + 218.44(0.475) + 273.71(0.305)$$

$$= 220.24$$

It is now a simple matter to return to our formula for the EMV of research information and determine its value as below:

$$EMV_{\text{Research information}} = EMV_{\text{Research "certainty"}} - EMV_{\text{Best alternative}}$$

$$= 220.24 - 205.00 = 15.24$$

Thus, $15,240 is the most a decision maker should pay for marketing research that is 90 percent accurate. Because the original research cost was quoted as $13,500, the decision maker should feel reasonably comfortable in going ahead with the project. However, suppose at this point a second researcher interrupts and announces, "I propose a more accurate research design using a larger sample. My design is 98 percent accurate and costs $15,500."

The decision maker's first reaction might be to dismiss the second design because its cost exceeds $15,240. After some quick reflection, the decision maker should realize that a more accurate design would produce a higher EMV for research certainty and might, therefore, be a better decision. This decision proceeds as the Bayesian estimation of sample size, our second objective in Bayesian analysis.

Bayesian Estimation of Sample Size

In the Bayesian estimation of sample size, we explicitly recognize the importance of sampling costs and research benefits. The basic calculation looks like this:

$$\text{ENGS} = \text{EMV}_{\text{Research information}} - \text{CS}$$

We define ENGS as the expected net gain of sampling and CS the cost of sampling.

Behind the apparent simplicity of the formula lies complex theory, the explanation of which we leave to other sources.[1] As a summary of this theory and to introduce its application, let us start with Figure 14A.1. To save some space there and in further discussion, we shorten $\text{EMV}_{\text{Research information}}$ to EMV_{Ri}.

Figure 14A.1 shows that EMV_{Ri} increases at a varying rate with sample size. With a constant increase in n, it rises quite rapidly for small samples but quite slowly for large. Our intuition should support this: adding 15 members to a sample size of 5 should more dramatically affect the value of research information than adding 15 members to a sample of size 500. Notice also that EMV_{Ri} approaches EMV_{Pi}, the expected monetary value of perfect information, for very large values of n. As n nears N, we expect almost perfect information.

Sampling costs show a positive, linear relationship with sample size; as n grows, so does CS. The line for CS also indicates that some C amount of fixed costs is associated with sampling. That is, we incur C costs regardless of n.

ENGS initially is negative because the small EMV_{Ri} cannot compensate for C.[2] It rises to 0 when EMV_{Ri} equals CS and continues to grow as the vertical distance between EMV_{Ri} and CS grows. ENGS falls when increases in sample size produce greater additional CS than greater additional EMV_{Ri}. It becomes negative again when CS exceeds EMV_{Ri}.

Let us expand our discussion of CS and EMV_{Ri} to see why changes in sample size affect them as above.

---

[1]See, for example, Robert L. Winkler, *An Introduction to Bayesian Inference and Decision* (New York: Holt, Rinehart and Winston, 1972), Chap. 6; or Robert Schlaifer, *Introduction to Statistics for Business Decisions* (New York: McGraw-Hill, 1961), Chaps. 20, 21.

[2]There are other reasons why ENGS might initially be negative. See Schlaifer, *Statistics for Business Decisions*, pp. 329–41.

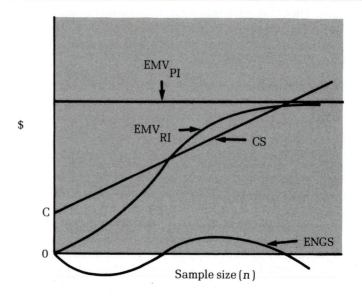

FIGURE 14A.1
Concepts for Bayesian estimation of sample size*

SAMPLING COSTS Suppose fixed and variable sampling costs for proposed research designs in our new product introduction example follow the schedule below:

Fixed Costs (C)		Variable Costs Per Interview (c)	
$1,500	questionnaire design (includes pretest)	$50	interviewer travel
		30	interviewer wages
250	sample design	10	coding, analysis
250	interviewer training	5	survey premium
1,500	overhead	5	other
C = $3,500		c = $100 per interview	

Suppose each interview would be conducted with a retailer who might sell product A, B, or C.

Total sample costs, CS, may be computed as:

$$CS = C + nc$$

Values for CS appear below, for five different research designs using five different sample sizes.

Sample Size (n)	CS ($)
50	8,500
80	11,500
100	13,500
120	15,500
150	18,500

To this point, our Bayesian discussion has recognized no explicit relationship between EMV_{Ri} and sample size. Instead, we have seen that EMV_{Ri} depends on payoffs associated with each decision alternative and on accuracy associated with each research result. Indicators or measures of accuracy were conditional probabilities associated with each anticipated marketing research result, given each state of nature. While payoffs remain constant, conditional probabilities change with sample size, thus changing EMV_{Ri}. That is, the larger the sample size, the more likely it is that research will predict states of nature accurately, and vice versa.

EXPECTED MONETARY VALUE OF RESEARCH INFORMATION

Suppose the researcher estimates the following conditional probabilities and sample sizes for our new product example:

Sample Size	Conditional Probabilities		
50	0.70	0.15	0.15
80	0.80	0.10	0.10
100	0.90	0.05	0.05
120	0.98	0.01	0.01
150	0.99	0.005	0.005

It is now a simple but tedious matter to calculate values for EMV_{Ri} and CS for each sample size and determine a like number of ENGS values. Because of our earlier calculations, we illustrate the procedure for an n of 100 and note that research practice here relies heavily on the computer.[3]

For research "that is 90 percent accurate," we found a value for EMV_{Ri} of $15,240. Given that the 0.90 conditional probability corresponds with an n of 100, we have for ENGS:

ENGS

$$ENGS = EMV_{Ri} - CS$$

$$= \$15,240 - [\$3,500 + 100(\$100)]$$

$$= \$1,740$$

---

[3]Robert Schlaifer, *Computer Programs for Elementary Decision Analysis* (Cambridge: Division of Research, Graduate School of Business Administration, Harvard University, 1971).

TABLE 14A.5
Sample Size and ENGS

Sample Size (n)	Conditional Probabilities			*EMV_{Ri}($)	CS ($)	ENGS ($)
50	.70	.15	.15	−4,250	8,500	−12,750
80	.80	.10	.10	5,500	11,500	−6,000
100	.90	.05	.05	15,240	13,500	1,740
120	.98	.01	.01	23,090	15,500	7,590
150	.99	.005	.005	23,940	18,500	5,440

*EMV_{PI} equals $25,000.

However, some larger or smaller *n* might produce a higher ENGS. To investigate this, we merely replace conditional probabilities of 0.90, 0.05, and 0.05 with those associated with sample sizes of 50, 80, 120, and 150 and undertake four parallel sets of calculations. Results for all five sample sizes appear in Table 14A.5. As we see, ENGS appears to reach a maximum for a sample size between 100 and 150. To determine an optimum sample size would require still further calculations.

Bayesian Summary

With estimates of decision payoffs, probabilities of states of nature, research accuracy, and research costs, a researcher and decision maker may determine an optimum sample size and hence, select a research design. However, it may seem that both parties get an extremely precise answer based on what are, after all, only estimates. This is true and few would fault researchers and decision makers for decisions that differ modestly from Bayesian results.[4] We conclude further that the primary issue in Bayesian analysis is the ability of decision makers to supply these estimates. A current opinion is that this ability is "limited" but that no other method has demonstrated "an equally strong potential for analyzing the returns from marketing research."[5]

[4]Two additional factors that may bear on this decision are the decision maker's utility function and tolerance of risk. A good introduction is in Donald S. Tull and Del I. Hawkins, *Marketing Research: Meaning, Measurement, and Method* (New York: Macmillan, 1976), pp. 42–50.

[5]Gert Assmus, "Bayesian Analysis for the Evaluation of Marketing Research Expenditures: A Reassessment," *Journal of Marketing Research* 14 (November 1977):567.

1. Confirm that the ENGS value of $5,440 is correct in Table 14A.5.

2. Suppose a sample of size 25 is proposed for our new product introduction, having conditional probabilities of 0.60, 0.20, and 0.20. Calculate values for EMV_{Ri}, CS, and ENGS.

Appendix Additional Readings

Enis, Ben M. and Broome, Charles L. *Marketing Decisions: A Bayesian Approach.* Scranton, PA: International Textbook, 1971.

> *This short book provides a complete and very understandable exposition of Bayesian analysis in marketing decision-making.*

Winkler, Robert L. *An Introduction to Bayesian Inference and Decision.* New York: Holt, Rinehart and Winston, 1972.

> *This book provides a basic, somewhat theoretical introduction to Bayesian statistics, including the estimation of sample size. At the end of each chapter you will find an excellent set of references to other discussions on the same and related topics.*

Cases for Part IV

10. Rosco Shoes*

Dallas Holmes sat alone in his office, trying to reach some conclusions about the women's court shoe market. Three things now seemed clear:

- The market for men's court shoes was stagnant.
- The market for women's court shoes was growing rapidly.
- No one at Rosco knew much about women's footwear preferences.

THE MARKET Women's court shoes include shoes for basketball, tennis, racquetball, volleyball, and all other lateral movement sports played on hard surfaces. The shoes differ considerably from women's running shoes, which tend to fall apart quickly under court conditions. Court shoes are purchased by women largely between the ages of 14 and 25.

Purchasers often participate as members of athletic teams in schools and colleges. Including individual participants, as well, Holmes forecast 1980 market size at about 2 million women athletes. Some purchasers undoubtedly would be owners of more than one pair of court shoes; most probably buy about one pair per season. Given the increased public emphasis on physical fitness and the sizeable government concern with women's athletics, Holmes thought the market would grow at about 6 percent per year, maybe even faster.

Four competitors (one much larger than Rosco and two much smaller) currently were marketing women's court shoes using construction methods inferior to the Rosco standards for men's shoes. If Rosco entered the women's market, they would do as they did for men: aim at the top 20 percent of the market in terms of price and quality. This would mean selling shoes only through reputable specialty and department stores. Competitors often sold through discount stores.

THE PROPOSED MARKET ENTRY Certainly the opportunity is there, Holmes thought, or at least the appearance of an opportunity. The problem seemed to lie with Rosco's lack of understanding of the market.

And the problem was significant. At least $400,000 and as much as $1,000,000 might have to be invested in capital equipment and design activities. The amount depended on how aggressively Rosco entered the

*Lori Calahan, graduate student at Montana State University, helped write this case.

market and on how different from the existing line of men's court shoes the new line was designed to be. Moreover, if the new line sold poorly, Rosco would experience a loss from unsold inventory, wasted advertising, and soured dealer relations of an amount at least equal to that invested in capital equipment and design.

Apart from production technology, Rosco's lack of understanding concerned basically everything. Style and price were strong concerns— what should the line look like and could it retail at $39.95? In addition, Holmes wondered about his purchase and ownership assumptions, whether he would need new retail outlets, and what to call the new line. Clearly, before he stuck his neck out further, he would need some basic user data.

Probably the best way to proceed, Holmes thought, was to see the results of some focus group interviews. To this end, he had contacted Warner Research about their conducting no more than ten group interviews with no more than ninety women athletes across the country. Everything seemed to be going smoothly in their research design except securing a representative, random sample.

THE FOCUS GROUPS

11. Montana Automobile Licensing

Tom Alexander thought he finally had all the information necessary to construct a sampling plan. Basically the plan would describe sample procedures and sample sizes for populations of automobile registrations in Montana counties. His goal as a marketing researcher was to be able to estimate the average tax paid per automobile within five dollars for each of twelve counties. Such estimates would be useful to his client, a committee of state legislators, in designing a new statewide uniform license fee system to replace the current license tax system.

About 700,000 motor vehicles (automobiles, trucks, and motorcycles) in the fifty-six Montana counties received licenses in 1981. Fees charged depended on the value of the vehicle and where its owner lived. Actually, "fees" poorly describes their payments. More correctly, motor vehicle owners paid personal property taxes on their vehicles to receive licenses—taxes whose rates differed greatly among the nearly 1,000 tax districts comprising the counties.

As illustrative, Alexander calculated that an owner of a $7,000 value car might pay as much as $370 for an annual license. Another owner of the identical car living several blocks away might pay only $280. Still another owner living several counties away might pay as little as $120. Not only did owners resent the inequity, it led many to report their resi-

BACKGROUND

dence to county license clerks as an address different from their actual address.

The proposed remedy was a statewide uniform fee system based on vehicle value. However, any such system should generate at least equal revenues to those produced by the current system. To this end, Alexander had been approached by representatives of the state legislature to study taxes paid on automobiles registered in twelve of the counties. From a sample of registrations in each county, Alexander could estimate both the average tax paid and the distribution of automobile values. This distribution of values would allow estimates of fees generated by various proposed schedules. Representatives had specified the number of counties based on political considerations; they left the actual selection to Alexander.

THE SAMPLE   Copies of all automobile registrations were kept at the Registry of Motor Vehicles, filed by county in numerical sequence. After a visit to the office, Alexander estimated that it took a clerk about one minute to find a registration and to record both the vehicle's value and its 1980 tax on a FORTRAN coding form.

Right now it seemed the biggest issue was determining which counties belonged in the sample. Because sampling costs were largely independent of the counties selected, Alexander's major concern was representativeness: counties selected should reflect the variety in mill rates currently charged. To aid him in making selections, he had estimated the average mill rates levied in 1980 (see Table C11.1).

Application of these mill rates to an automobile would proceed in general as follows:

1. Determine the automobile's current market value based on a listing of automobile makes and models.

2. Determine 13 percent of the current market value as the automobile's taxable value.

3. Multiply the taxable value times the mill rate to determine the tax (the mill rate is expressed in dollars of tax per thousand dollars of taxable value).

For example, an automobile purchased new in 1979 for $8,000 might show a current market value of $6,000. Its taxable value would be $780. Using the mill rate in Table C11.1, for tax districts in, say, Beaverhead county, the tax would average

$$(\$780)\frac{(\$216)}{(\$1,000)} = \$168$$

TABLE C11.1
1980 Average Mill Rates and Automobile Registrations Per County

County	Average Mill Rates	Automobile Registrations
Beaverhead	216	4,049
Big Horn	101	4,970
Blaine	158	3,087
Broadwater	218	1,817
Carbon	193	4,781
Carter	201	805
Cascade	300	42,892
Choteau	189	3,591
Custer	326	6,734
Daniels	235	1,478
Dawson	282	5,661
Deer Lodge	335	5,941
Fallon	120	1,943
Fergus	247	6,882
Flathead	274	27,827
Gallatin	296	21,663
Garfield	197	741
Glacier	165	4,825
Golden Valley	185	492
Granite	225	1,527
Hill	237	9,031
Jefferson	262	3,581
Judith Basin	209	1,633
Lake	267	9,548
Lewis & Clark	353	22,966
Liberty	175	1,331
Lincoln	233	8,214
Madison	205	3,292
McCone	202	1,336
Meagher	228	1,057
Mineral	337	1,578
Missoula	318	39,108
Musselshell	162	2,344
Park	260	7,765
Petroleum	141	314
Phillips	177	2,465
Pondera	213	3,491

County	Average Mill Rates	Autombile Registrations
Powder River	106	1,401
Powell	228	3,396
Prairie	280	915
Ravalli	221	11,503
Richland	154	6,708
Roosevelt	221	4,491
Rosebud	108	4,803
Sanders	233	4,199
Sheridan	131	3,410
Silver Bow	324	19,651
Stillwater	213	3,212
Sweet Grass	201	1,758
Teton	267	3,655
Toole	159	3,167
Treasure	193	515
Valley	246	4,977
Wheatland	232	1,161
Wibaux	146	851
Yellowstone	294	59,540

In Yellowstone county, the tax would average $229. Alexander estimated that market values ranged from a set minimum of $150 to $10,000 in each county.

THE SAMPLE
DESIGN

Alexander promised the representatives a sampling plan by the end of the week. Apart from selecting the twelve counties, he faced two other issues in developing the plan as: how to estimate sample sizes and how to estimate sampling costs. He would not need identical sample sizes in each county because of expected different variances and population sizes. But he *would* need some assistants—to systematically select registrations in each county; he planned to pay them $6.00 per hour.

12. Fernwood Shopping Center

This year we'll have a better sample, thought Henry Wilson as he left work late one Tuesday afternoon in January. And, really, the sample was the only thing that he needed to change from last year's survey. The rest of the research would stay pretty much the same.

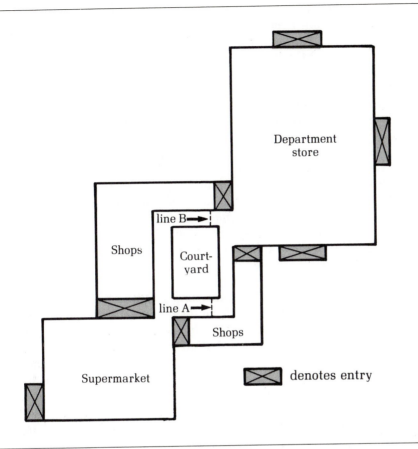

EXHIBIT C12.1
Fernwood Shopping Center

That study had been somewhat of a disaster, he recalled with discomfort. One Sunday, per his instructions, four reasonably well trained interviewers with good intentions had stopped every twentieth shopper passing by the court area in the shopping center (line A on Exhibit C12.1) to request the shopper's participation in the survey. By noon on Wednesday they had filled their quotas for female shoppers; they stopped Saturday evening with quotas for males less than half full. His mistake, Wilson recalled, was designing quotas that matched population characteristics in the market area exactly.

BACKGROUND

Wilson was operating manager for the Fernwood Shopping Center, a small shopping mall in St. Petersburg, Florida. The Center currently held about forty small shops, and was anchored at one end by a large department store and at the other by a national food chain. On the average weekday, about 1,500 shoppers visited the Center. The number grew to about 2,500 on Saturday and fell to about 2,000 on Sunday.

Each year in March since its opening in July 1978, the operating manager had been responsible for a survey of shoppers. The survey determined where shoppers lived, their media preferences and habits, their images of Fernwood shops, their expenditures, and much other useful information. Data were summarized and given to each Fernwood shop, including the two anchors. Wilson had replaced the original operating manager in July 1980. Each year it seemed the survey became more and more refined (and the users of the data more and more demanding). The first year, Wilson understood, had been more or less a fiasco on all counts. The next year found major problems with the questions. These were resolved only to reveal the sampling deficiencies of last year. This year the bugs should be out of everything, and next year it should run itself, Wilson hoped.

DATA COLLECTION PROCEDURES

Data collection should proceed quite simply. Wilson planned again to hire four part-time interviewers from his brother-in-law's marketing research agency. All would report to the Center for a one-week period in March, for which Wilson expected no unusual sales or weather patterns. Interviewers would work in pairs, one at each of two assigned locations (lines A and B on Exhibit C12.1) during their 5½-hour shifts. Each would approach a shopper and attempt to secure the shopper's cooperation for an interview lasting about 15 minutes. Respondents were to receive as compensation one $5.00 coupon for merchandise at any one of six participating shops.

Apart from the attempt to interview too many males, data collection went quite smoothly last year. From the 740 attempts and the 500 actual interviews, Wilson had heard from only 3 upset shoppers. He usually got ten times this number of complaints during the high school art show in April.

THE SAMPLE

This year Wilson again wanted a sample of 500 shoppers. However, rather than a sample that represented the surrounding population, this one should represent just Fernwood shoppers. Ideally, he knew he should sample throughout the year to ensure representativeness. But this was impractical and not needed, according to most shop owners and managers; most agreed that the second week in March would be satisfactory. Most further agreed that sampling procedures must select from all days of the week and from all hours of the operating day.

This confused sampling procedures, Wilson thought, because the Center was much busier at certain hours on certain days than at others. To give him a better understanding of this concentration, an assistant

TABLE C12.1
Estimated Number of Shoppers Crossing Lines A and B by Day and Hour of Operation

Time	Sunday A	Sunday B	Monday A	Monday B	Tuesday A	Tuesday B	Wednesday A	Wednesday B	Thursday A	Thursday B	Friday A	Friday B	Saturday A	Saturday B
10:00–11:00	Closed		40	50	40	50	40	50	50	60	50	60	80	100
11:00–12:00	Closed		50	60	50	60	50	60	50	70	60	80	120	160
12:00– 1:00	150	200	130	150	140	170	120	140	130	140	160	180	170	210
1:00– 2:00	220	270	100	120	110	130	90	110	110	120	140	150	170	230
2:00– 3:00	200	230	60	70	50	70	50	60	60	70	110	130	180	250
3:00– 4:00	280	220	60	70	50	60	50	60	60	70	90	100	210	260
4:00– 5:00	160	200	70	80	60	70	60	70	70	80	90	110	200	250
5:00– 6:00	130	190	80	90	90	110	80	90	90	110	110	140	140	180
6:00– 7:00	Closed		120	140	140	180	110	130	120	150	160	200	110	140
7:00– 8:00	Closed		120	150	130	160	100	110	100	140	150	210	100	110
8:00– 9:00	Closed		80	100	90	100	80	90	90	110	130	170	70	80
Totals	1,140	1,310	910	1,080	950	1,160	830	970	930	1,120	1,250	1,530	1,550	1,970

had estimated the number of shoppers passing the assigned locations in either direction (Table C12.1). Shoppers during the one-week period in March would be counted to form the sampling frame as they crossed one or the other location.

THE ARTICLE

Opening his car door, Wilson recalled a telephone call earlier in the day. It was his brother-in-law, reporting some good news. He had just finished reading an article in the November 1980 issue of the *Journal of Marketing Research*. "It looks like I found the answer for you, Henry," he had said. "Sudman's article discusses the very situation you're up against in that sample of yours." Wilson had thanked him and asked for a copy in today's mail. With it and some careful planning, the bugs should be out of everything.

13. National Research on Consumer Satisfaction*

Throughout the summer of 1978, Dr. Neil Cameron, a member of the business faculty at a leading business school in Canada, became increasingly interested in an idea for a government-financed research project to investigate consumer satisfaction and dissatisfaction (CS/D) with products and services available in Canada. After several informal discussions with academic colleagues and government officials, Cameron felt that this type of project could be instrumental in helping policy makers increase their understanding of consumer problems in Canada.

He was enthusiastic about seeing the idea materialize. In mid-October 1978, with only a week to go before meeting again with government officials, Cameron began to develop a research design which would be the basis of a detailed research proposal to be submitted to the federal government.

BACKGROUND   The late 1960s and 1970s were characterized by a significant increase in government sensitivity to consumer issues and in the level of consumer protection programming. In 1967, the federal government responded to what it perceived as a need for a ministry to promote and protect the interests of the Canadian consumer by forming a new department, Consumer and Corporate Affairs Canada (CCAC). Part of CCAC's function was to design and implement consumer protection programs and to set policies that encouraged business practice and conduct leading to better protection of the consumer. The Consumer Research and Evaluation Branch (CREB) of CCAC was created to provide key information on problems facing consumers and on levels of consumer satisfaction with products and services. This type of information could then be used by CCAC as a basis for designing specific programs and policies.

CCAC was aware of the apparent rise in overall consumer dissatisfaction that was being expressed by complaints covering a broad range of products and services. However, no satisfactory explanation had been offered for this increase. While some studies had been done in the area, CCAC recognized that existing information and research results were incomplete, outdated, and often conflicting. Accordingly, CCAC began to express a need for improved information based on comprehensive research projects. Such information would help CCAC to increase its understanding of the products and services of concern to Canadian consumers as well as to identify characteristics of individuals who seemed to be experiencing relatively higher levels of dissatisfaction. Better understanding of the types of problems confronting Canadian consumers would provide the basis for designing consumer protection programs and setting priorities for corrective actions. Such actions might involve prosecuting violators of consumer protection laws, revising current legislation, or allocating infield government effort in inspection of products and services.

Dr. Cameron was quite familiar with the area of consumer satisfaction and complaining behavior. In addition to his doctoral thesis on the topic, he had published numerous articles on consumer satisfaction and participated in several conference seminars on CS/D. In fact, he was in Chicago in early October 1978 presenting a paper to the Second Annual Symposium on Consumer Satisfaction/Dissatisfaction and Complaining Behavior when he first learned of the Canadian government's active interest in the area. At the conference he met Peter McCall, who was attending on behalf of the Consumer Research and Evaluation Branch of CCAC (he was Chief of the CREB Behavioral Analysis Unit). Cameron and McCall informally discussed existing efforts to measure consumer satisfaction/dissatisfaction and the apparent need for further research. During the conversation, Cameron asked McCall about the possibility of obtaining financial support from CCAC for a research project focusing on CS/D in Canada. In addition, he requested a set of guidelines which could be utilized in the preparation of a detailed research proposal which would then be submitted to CCAC. A few days later, Cameron received a written response from McCall in the form of an outline which summarized the department's procedure for submitting research proposals to the branch (Exhibit C13.1).

After some contemplation, Cameron decided to submit a proposal to CCAC and sat down to develop a research design. At the outset, he believed that the project would probably be of sufficient magnitude to necessitate engaging an outside marketing research firm to collect and process data. Also, he realized that in addition to formulating his research design and proposal, he would have to collaborate with CCAC in developing a request for proposal to invite outside firms to bid for the data gathering contract. To develop such a request, typically, the researcher would outline the information needs and design specification, whereas the government would be responsible for the budget and time-table components.

Dr. Cameron had decided that the research should focus primarily on the postpurchase evaluation of consumer products and services. The ultimate goal of the proposed project would be to gather, analyze, and report the kinds of information that could be used as a basis for diagnosing consumer satisfaction/dissatisfaction and complaining behavior and for improving consumer protection programming. Cameron considered the initial broad objectives of the research to be twofold:

RESEARCH PROBLEM

1. Increasing the understanding of the types of problems confronting consumers (and the kinds of people experiencing them).

2. Providing policy makers in Canada with an expanded information base for products and services of concern.

Cameron developed a detailed list of specific objectives which he believed to be consistent with CCAC's desire to understand the reasons

EXHIBIT C13.1
Outline for Research Proposals

Academics and other researchers from outside government should provide the following information when submitting a proposal for research and seeking financial support from this Branch for its conduct.

1. Project Title;
2. Outline of nature and extent of the problem to be investigated;
3. Statement of research objectives (or hypotheses);
4. Definition of proposed scope (i.e., products, years covered, etc.);
5. A preliminary review of the relevant literature on the topic and its implications for the proposed study;
6. A definition of the methodology to be used in the analysis;
7. An outline of the expected results and/or policy implications for the Department;
8. Proposed timetable for the main tasks to be accomplished (or main phases of the study);
9. Researcher identification:
   a) principal researcher ▪ name
                          ▪ academic qualification
                          ▪ present occupation
                          ▪ faculty, university (or organization)
   b) Same as in a) for associate researcher(s);
10. Budget ▪ Honoraria or Professional fees (and rate)
           ▪ research assistance (and rate)
           ▪ expected travel costs
           ▪ supplies and services (with details if total is significant)
           ▪ University (or organization) overhead
           ▪ Total Cost;
11. Special Requirements for conduct of study (if appropriate)
           ▪ CREB manpower resources required
           ▪ data needs
           ▪ survey or investigation work to be performed
           ▪ computer assistance requirements;
12. Other background information: e.g.
           ▪ other sponsors
           ▪ related activities, other studies
           ▪ publications expected
           ▪ special constraints (material, location, time).

behind the apparent increase in consumer dissatisfaction in Canada. These objectives were as follows:

▪ To identify products and services which are highly important to consumers and to examine the relationship between perceived product/service importance and various levels of satisfaction/dissatisfaction.

- To report levels of satisfaction and dissatisfaction with products and services which have been purchased or used during the recall periods.
- To compare levels of consumer satisfaction and dissatisfaction over various classes of durables, nondurables, and services or intangible products.
- To determine which items appear to have caused the greatest amounts of dissatisfaction among users within the recall periods.
- To identify recurring reasons for dissatisfaction with durables, non-durables, and services or intangible items.
- To compare and contrast consumers who voice complaints with those who are dissatisfied but do not report dissatisfaction.
- To describe how consumers who report dissatisfaction with products and services attempt to resolve their dissatisfaction through alternative courses of private and public action.
- To compare complaining behavior patterns over various classes of durables, nondurables, and services or intangible products.

Cameron considered these objectives to be tentative. He recognized that they were subject to modification depending on their implications for the research design. However, he felt that they provided a solid foundation for planning the project.

Given his assessment of the problem and his stated objectives for the proposed research, Cameron began to think about the actual design of the project. Initially, he wanted to avoid jumping to the conclusion that a marketing research study inevitably meant a questionnaire study. Even though he believed intuitively that a survey would provide the type of information he wanted, Cameron forced himself to review the alternatives. In their simplest form, he recalled, research designs can be separated into two broad categories: exploratory and conclusive studies.

RESEARCH DESIGN

Exploratory research is usually most appropriate when the management problem in question is a relatively new one. Rather than testing hypotheses, exploratory research projects try to generate them. Examples of this type of research are surveys of the literature, secondary data studies, expert opinions, and individual or group depth interviews. Any of these categories seemed a feasible way to study CS/D. Though the area was still new, the literature in Canada and the United States was developing rapidly, as Cameron well knew from his recent DBA studies. Also, there was some potentially useful secondary data available to CCAC through local consumer protection agencies and Better Business Bureaus. Another possibility, focus group interviews (in which a skilled moderator unobtrusively leads a group of eight to twelve people through a discussion of an issue—such as consumer warranties or product quality), was currently achieving considerable acceptance among market researchers and decision makers.

Conclusive research, as the name implies, has the objective of reaching a decision about a hypothesis. Though surveys are the most common kind of conclusive research that is undertaken, they are not the only type. Cameron knew that observational studies (for example, observing consumer shopping behavior) can be conclusive in nature, although they are more frequently used in exploratory projects. Experimental research is another form of conclusive research; it is designed to reach a conclusion about a cause-and-effect relationship. Cameron knew that, so far, observational and experimental research had been used only infrequently by CS/D investigators. For example, very few experiments involving consumer satisfaction had been reported in the literature to date; a typical example involved inducing expectations in subjects about performance of a product, then subsequently confirming or disconfirming these expectations, and measuring subsequent reactions.

Cameron further recognized that the choice was not as simple as merely between exploratory and conclusive research. Not only were there subcategories within each area, but there was also the realistic possibility of using both approaches in a single project—an exploratory phase to formulate the research questions, and a conclusive phase to test them.

Inevitably, Cameron's decision about the broad form of the research design would have ramifications for more specific choices downstream. For instance, he was aware that before writing a research proposal, he would also have to decide on some (or all) of the following: the scope of the project; the precise data collection method; the sampling strategy (i.e., regional allocations); and the sample size.

Scope.   With regard to the scope of the proposed research, there appeared to be two issues at hand. First, should the research be carried out on a regional or a national scale? Second, should the research deal with a small, selective range of products and services or a multitude of products and services available to consumers? Clearly, these decisions involved focusing on the objectives and information needs of study. Just as clearly, these decisions would have a considerable effect on subsequent design decisions and on the eventual timing requirements of the research.

Data Collection Method.   Regardless of whether the research would cover a wide spectrum of product and service categories or just a few, Cameron anticipated a fairly lengthy survey. However, the individual items were not likely to be very complex, consisting mainly of multiple choice and dichotomous questions with very few open-ended queries. He saw three possibilities for gathering the information: personal interview, telephone interview, or self-administration (mail survey or "drop-off/pick-up"). Whichever method he proposed, the design and the preparation of the questionnaire would be largely based on a revision of a similar instrument Cameron had obtained from a pilot study which had been run recently in the United States. A portion of this instrument covering food products is presented in Exhibit C13.2 to show the type of questions he had in mind.

Obtaining a high response rate had always been very important to Cameron when conducting research, and this study would be no exception. Accuracy of information and representativeness, Cameron felt, were largely dependent on the response rate in a project. And despite a potentially lengthy survey, Cameron set the high response rate as a primary criterion for selecting the data collection method.

Sampling Strategy.   Arriving at a sampling strategy that would ensure maximum representativeness on a national or regional basis was clearly

EXHIBIT C13.2
Examples of Survey Questions

SECTION 1. FOOD PRODUCTS

1. This section covers foods and food products of all kinds.

   Read each of the numbered categories in this section, one at a time, and think about your experiences with each of the products listed in that category *in the past year*. If you *never* use *any* item in the category, or if you have *not* bought *at least one* of them *in the past year*, circle the number to the left of the category under "HAVE NOT BOUGHT IT DURING PAST YEAR" and go on to the next category. If you *have* bought one or more products listed in the category in *the past year*, please circle one of the two numbers directly to the right of the category to indicate whether you usually buy the items in the category "SOMETIMES" or "OFTEN", and then circle *one* number from 1 to 4 to indicate how satisfied you have been with that product or group of products *during the past year*. If you have bought one or more items covered by a single category, then think about your experiences with them as a group. Remember, you circle a number to the right of the category *only* if you have bought at least one product from the category in the past year. If in doubt, check the example page (PAGE 1).

Have Not Bought It During Past Year	Categories	I Buy It:		How Satisfied I Am:			
		Sometimes	Often	Almost Always Satisfied	Usually Satisfied	Often Dissatisfied	Almost Always Dissatisfied
-1-	1. Fresh bread, rolls, cakes, cookies or other baked goods	-2-	-3-	1	2	3	4

Have Not Bought It During Past Year	Categories	I Buy It:		How Satisfied I Am:			
		Sometimes	Often	Almost Always Satisfied	Usually Satisfied	Often Dissatisfied	Almost Always Dissatisfied
-1-	2. Frozen bread dough, pizza, cakes, pie crusts	-2-	-3-	1	2	3	4
-1-	3. Flour, cornmeal, rice	-2-	-3-	1	2	3	4
-1-	4. Macaroni and noodle products (raw and prepared)	-2-	-3-	1	2	3	4
-1-	5. Ready-to-eat or cooked breakfast cereals	-2-	-3-	1	2	3	4
-1-	6. Molasses, corn syrup, maple syrup, other syrups, honey	-2-	-3-	1	2	3	4
-1-	7. Sugar, salt, spices, seasonings, flavourings, sweeteners, whiteners	-2-	-3-	1	2	3	4
-1-	8. Cake or cookie mixes, puddings, gelatin desserts, snack or party food of all types	-2-	-3-	1	2	3	4
-1-	9. Margarine, cooking oils, shortening	-2-	-3-	1	2	3	4
-1-	10. Peanut butter, jams and jellies, spreads	-2-	-3-	1	2	3	4
-1-	11. Milk, cream, cheese, yogurt, butter, ice cream and other dairy products	-2-	-3-	1	2	3	4
-1-	12. Eggs and egg products	-2-	-3-	1	2	3	4
-1-	13. Soft drinks, canned or frozen fruit juices, beverage mixes, coffee, tea, cocoa and other non-alcoholic beverages	-2-	-3-	1	2	3	4

the goal. Undoubtedly the particular strategy selected would also have cost and other design implications. Cameron knew further that the selection of sampling points or geographic locations can have a substantial impact on the quality of the information. Depending upon the data collection method he chose, Cameron knew that between 1 percent and 7 percent of the population would not be included in the sampling frame due to inaccessability of their sampling points—that is, the sample would miss persons residing in the far north, on Indian reservations, in mental and penal institutions, etc.

The two basic choices for allocating the sample clearly had different costs because they would employ different numbers of sampling points. The first option was a national probability sample to select respondents across five geographical regions of Canada in proportion to the population of each region. Since British Columbia, for example, contains 11 percent of the nation's population, then 11 percent of the sample would be taken from B.C. Table C13.1 illustrates the population breakdown by regions and the corresponding sample composition for each plan. The first plan results in a majority of respondents being selected from heavily concentrated population areas (Ontario and Quebec). Such concentration requires fewer sampling points than if the respondents were more scattered, and, therefore, results in significantly lower costs. It does not, however, guarantee that representative results would be obtained from the smaller regions.

The second option was a disproportionate probability sample. The sample consists of an equal number of respondents taken from each geographical region of the country. In effect, the sample is drawn in such a way as to overrepresent the less populated regions and produce equivalent sampling error in the results of each. This heavier representation of less densely populated areas would necessitate more sampling points and increase costs by about 15 percent.

Finally, Cameron knew that the procedure he chose for handling callbacks could significantly affect research costs, particularly if personal interviews were used. If he permitted substitution of another similar household in the neighborhood for not-at-homes, he estimated that his costs could be materially reduced. The other option, requiring up to three callback attempts for not-at-homes, could cost twenty to thirty percent extra.

TABLE C13.1
Different Sample Plans: Allocation of Interviews

	British Columbia	Prairie Provinces	Ontario	Quebec	Atlantic Provinces
1. National Probability Sample* (Modified)	11%	17%	36%	27%	9%
2. Disproportionate Probability Sample (Stratified)	20%	20%	20%	20%	20%

*Percentages correspond to the population breakdown by region.

Sample Size.   Before setting out to design the actual data gathering instrument, it was of fundamental importance to make a specific decision about sample size. The research would require surveying consumers who consumed the chosen categories of products and services; but in addition, Cameron wanted adequate representation of different age, sex, income, and occupation groups. Small samples would likely result in insufficient cell-sizes when analyzing specific subgroups of the population (for instance, young, low-income women). Cameron hoped to be able to estimate average satisfaction for most groups within a tenth of a scale point.

CCAC felt that, in order to have a well-balanced representation of different demographic groups, at least 2,000 respondents would be needed. Clearly, the larger the sample size, the more representative the sample and the higher the cost. From past experience with research firms and his knowledge of fixed and variable costs for research projects, Cameron knew that an increase of each 1,000 respondents would not necessarily mean a proportional increase in cost. He estimated that the relationship between sample size and cost would be approximately as below:

Number of respondents	Relative cost
1,000	0.60
2,000	1.00
3,000	1.25
4,000	1.45

Cameron was unsure of what the total costs of the research would be but realized they would be largely determined by what prospective research firms would charge for their role in collecting and processing the data. The request that would be sent to the research firms would essentially be a reproduction of Cameron's research proposal with budget and timetable specifications created by CCAC.

NEXT WEEK'S MEETING   It was clear to Cameron that he should be well prepared for the discussions he would have with the CCAC officials next week. He wanted to be able to demonstrate a good understanding of their research needs, and to present a convincing argument that the design he developed would meet these needs.

V

Analyzing Data

15

Introduction to Data Analysis

In a sense, data analysis is the most interesting stage of the marketing research process, for it is here we finally begin to discover truth. After hours of planning and executing the research design we finally start finding something out. One thing we find out early is that it usually is not very difficult nor very time consuming to perform a properly planned data analysis. The key, of course, is having a detailed plan of what will be done with the data; we return to this topic shortly. Our point here is that we can usually analyze data quite rapidly with a computer.

In fact, because computers are so productive, some marketing researchers tend to "go overboard" in their data analysis and waste resources. As an example, consider a researcher who avoids planning and instead asks the computer to perform all possible cross-tabulations in her data. The researcher might think she saves time by doing this because surely the answer to the marketing problem will surface in the computer output. Probably it will, but hidden among much misleading information as well: that is, if she examines only 15 variables and only 2 of them at a time, the computer will produce exactly 105 cross-tabulation tables, very rapidly. But now she must examine each table, separately and in relation to each other table, for theoretically and managerially meaningful results. This will take huge amounts of time.

A better approach is to plan the data analysis based on existing theory and past research, to hypothesize what variables might be related to each other, and to ask the computer for only these cross-tabulations. Moreover,

399

the researcher should specify the nature of all hypothesized relationships as a further check on results. That is, good theory and results of earlier research often allow the researcher to detail which relationships will probably be positive, which will probably be negative, and which will probably be near zero. Computer and interpretation time will both be reduced.

In this chapter we'll take care of some preliminary matters in data analysis and we'll look at an overview of seven data analysis purposes; then we'll examine in detail the first three, which are: characterizing what is typical in the data, showing data variability, and presenting the distribution of data. These three purposes are almost always present in any data analysis.

Preliminary Matters in Data Analysis

Before beginning data analysis, the researcher should have planned a sequence of analytical techniques, edited the data, and coded them. Of these preliminary matters, the first overshadows the second and third in terms of its importance and its difficulty in execution. That is, the data analysis plan functions as an indispensable roadmap that anticipates and guides the entire analysis process. Its preparation requires knowledge of analytical methods, foresight, and clarity of thought. In contrast, editing and coding the data usually require less of these characteristics.

DATA ANALYSIS PLAN
A **data analysis plan** describes, for each major research variable of interest, analysis procedures the researcher considers appropriate. An example appears in Box 15.1. Notice that in addition to analysis procedures a data analysis plan also identifies major research variables of interest and their measurement methods. Such identification helps make the plan complete and the analysis procedures appropriate for the level of measurement.

Looking at specific measurement methods in Box 15.1, we see that Likert-type scales measure the degree of involvement of family members in the decision to eat out. Evidently some stepped scale of "involvement" serves as response categories. Similarly, a stepped scale of "importance" must measure what features family members consider important in the decision. Also a semantic differential scale using these features as rating items must measure the image of two pizza restaurants. (If these measurement methods and terms appear somewhat alien, a quick review of Chapter 9 is in order.)

Looking at analysis procedures in Box 15.1, we see that several *t*-tests of mean differences are planned on means derived from the Likert-type and semantic differential scales. Yet from our discussion in Chapter 10, we remember that these measurement devices yield ordinal data. Evi-

---

BOX 15.1

Data Analysis Plan for a Study of Pizza Consumers

Variables and Measurement

Variables Measured	Measurement Methods
Decision maker identity	Family member degree of "involvement in the decision" by a Likert-type scale
Features considered important in selecting a pizza restaurant	Feature "importance" measured by a Likert-type scale
Pizza restaurant image	Semantic differential with features used as rating items
Restaurant usage rate	"Number of times" purchased
Socioeconomic characteristics	Open-ended questions

Analysis Procedures

1. Using *t*-tests, examine mean differences for parental and child involvement in the decision to eat out—between heavy users of restaurant A and heavy users of restaurant B.

2. Identify the five most important features in selecting a pizza restaurant.

3. Using *t*-tests, examine mean differences of semantic differential scores on the five most important features for restaurants A and B.

4. Compute sample average ages, incomes, and family sizes; compare to census data for representativeness.

---

dently the researcher has decided that *t*-tests, which require interval data, can be applied here. In general, *t*-tests are quite "robust" and insensitive to measurement differences between ordinal and interval data.

A final comment on any data analysis plan: it is reasonable to feel that such a thing is desirable but difficult to prepare. Absolutely right. In fact, we'll never be fully able to detail all data analysis procedures, but this should not stop us from investigating and describing the major ones. That is, we must investigate and plan various methods of analysis before collecting data to be sure that some procedure is appropriate for each unitary portion of the data collection form. Unless we do this, we will likely end up with too little of the right data, too much of the wrong, and no good way of distilling truth.

DATA EDITING

Before analysis starts, the researcher usually edits raw data as they appear on returned data collection forms. To **edit** raw data means to examine data as originally corrected for errors and then take appropriate action. Errors exist as either the presence of incorrect data or the absence of correct data. But how do we know a particular piece of data, or lack of one, means there is an error?

The answer to this question is not exact and relies on experience, intuition, and motivation. We should recognize that it is easier to find gross or large data errors and that some error will still remain in even the best edited data. Beyond these points, we can identify six guidelines to help to locate errors.

1. Examine the data for extreme values. Look for values (including 0) that lie more than two standard deviations from the average value. A critical pair of eyes and the help of a computer are invaluable here. Further investigation will show some of the extremes to be in error and to require remedial action.

2. Look for inconsistencies in the data. Data that conflict with other data or our own understanding of the research should be investigated as potential errors. For example, we might find one mail questionnaire returned from a total sample of 1,000 Chicago housewives with the respondent's age indicated as 13 years. Or, we might find another questionnaire with the respondent's zip code shown as one appropriate for Madison, Wisconsin. In both instances, further action is warranted to confirm the existence of error.

3. Confirm or validate selected aspects of data collection. As we saw in Chapter 5, researchers regularly check a sample of questions from a sample of respondents for accuracy.

4. Hand-calculate and confirm computer data manipulations. Obviously, we do not want to do the computer's work for it but we can often make some calculations on a subset of data quite easily. At the very least, this activity will confirm that the computer has read the proper data columns on the computer card and that the program works.

5. Every time the data are transferred—from data collection forms to coding forms to computer cards to computer generated transformations—check for accuracy.

6. Finally, try to uncover errors in the data when the analysis is complete by looking for the existence of unusual results. We should investigate results that differ from past research or our understanding of the theory underlying the research problem.

Our goal in editing is to minimize the occurrence of errors—subject to cost and other constraints.

When and Where Editing Occurs.   Editing occurs both during data collection and upon completion of data collection operations. *Field editing* is the term given to the first activity and *central editing* to the second. Of course, field editing is possible only when the research design uses telephone and personal interviews to collect data. Here editing not only uncovers collection errors but helps to reduce their further occurrence before data collection ends. Incomplete answers, illegible answers, fake interviews, and other errors can be discovered and traced to interviewers for remedial action. This activity should be done daily, even hourly, if possible.

Central editing is usually more thorough than field editing because of the availability of time and other resources. The process is tedious, requires attention to detail, and demands that the editor understand research design, project execution, and the data analysis plan. Emory outlines some useful rules for editors:[1]

1. Each editor should be familiar with instructions given to interviewers and coders as well as his own editing instructions.

2. He should not destroy, erase, or make illegible the original entry by the interviewer. Original entries should be crossed out with a single line so as to remain legible.

3. He should make all entries on a data collection form in some distinctive color and in a standardized manner.

4. He should initial all answers he has changed or supplied.

5. He should add his initials and the date of editing on each data collection form completed.

Editor Actions. As Emory indicates, after identifying a particular bit of data as an error, the editor usually takes some action. If the true value can be easily determined, the editor will use it to correct the error. For example, interviewers may incorrectly record interview dates or some other similar bit of information about which the editor has perfect knowledge. Or, the editor may find in a validation interview that the respondent's family has four members and not five as indicated. In both instances the editor simply and immediately corrects the error.

If the true value cannot be easily determined, the editor takes other actions. The most extreme is to discard the respondent's entire data set and exclude it from data analysis. Grounds for such action include the data collection form's containing frivolous or insincere responses, numerous blanks, and quantities of illegible and inconsistent responses.[2] In

[1]C. William Emory, *Business Research Methods* (Homewood, Ill.: Richard D. Irwin, 1976), pp. 338–39.

[2]G. W. Roughton, "Coding, Editing, and Processing of Market Research Data," in *Consumer Market Research Handbook*, ed. Robert M. Worcester (Maidenhead, Berkshire, England: McGraw-Hill (UK) Ltd., 1972), p. 243.

addition, the editor also discards entire data sets produced by sampling units outside the population of interest or by fake interviews.

A less extreme editorial response is to adjust the error to a more accurate, estimated value. For example, zero, when it indicates the presence of nonresponse error for a particular item, may be replaced by an estimate derived from other data that appear on the respondent's or on another respondent's data form. Estimates can be simple—such as finding a complete data set for a respondent of similar socioeconomic characteristics and using those values as appropriate. Or complex—such as constructing a multiple regression model from complete data sets to estimate missing values. A slightly different procedure is to adjust missing data to the mean or average value for a particular group, as defined by the researcher.[3] As with small quantities of nonresponse errors, small quantities of modest-sized response errors can be similarly corrected. However, because of their modest size, these response errors often slip past the editor undetected and, thus, editors tend to focus their efforts on nonresponse errors.

Finally, the least extreme action, frequently undertaken for item nonresponse, is simply to exclude erroneous data from the main body of data analysis and to report all such instances. Reporting usually involves establishing a category of "No Response" in frequency distributions of the data and reporting the actual number of respondents used in various calculations.

All such editorial efforts pose some difficulty. Problems lie in adjusting data to estimate an unknown true value and in excluding item nonresponse. If we adjust by replacing an error with a response from one similar complete data set, we assume the edited response is now more correct than the original. This may not be true. Further, this action almost always increases the variance or amount of variation of that item in our analysis. If our research objective centers on the variability of the population of interest, we damage our ability to meet the objective.

If we adjust by replacing with either a regression derived value or a group mean, the amount of variation decreases. However, regression techniques often consume much time, require that data meet certain assumptions, and call for researcher judgment in selecting respondents and variables having largely complete data sets to use in predicting. If we use a group mean instead as a replacement value, we assume an individual is more similar to the average value for the group than to one single respondent in the group. This may not be true either.

If we exclude nonresponses and perform certain statistical tests and analyses, we must also exercise care. For example, suppose we are investigating the relationship between two variables using correlation analysis. The usual situation is to exclude a respondent from the calculation of a

---

[3]John B. Lansing and James N. Morgan, *Economic Survey Methods* (Ann Arbor: Institute for Social Research, University of Michigan, 1971), pp. 169–70, 233–36.

correlation coefficient if the respondent is missing either value for the two variables. All other respondents having complete data on both variables are used in the calculation. But suppose we now calculate three correlations coefficients from our data and then compare them. Almost certainly the coefficients are based on three slightly different samples because of different patterns of item nonresponse. One respondent, for example, may report his product consumption, age, but not his weight. Another may report her product consumption, weight, but not her age. Thus, a correlation between age and product consumption would include the first individual but not the second in the calculation. Only if item nonresponse is low can this concern be ignored.

A final note of caution should be made if our main data analysis will consist of one or more least squares techniques. Examples are all regression methods, analyses of variance and covariance, discriminant function analyses, principal components and factor analyses, and canonical correlation.[4] Such techniques are susceptible to sample-specific covariation; the use of extreme error values, including zero, often dramatically increases this covariation. The result is a lessening of interpretability and instability of results.

In sum—an editor's treatment of erroneous data depends on the quantity of error contained in the raw data, research objectives, and planned data analysis techniques. Occasionally the editor's treatment has a sizeable influence on research results. However, much more pervasive influences derive from earlier decisions in the research process, especially those in the areas of question design, data collection methods, and selection of research personnel. If such decisions have been made properly, the need for massive editorial correction is unlikely.

DATA CODING

After data have been edited and adjusted where needed, data are ready for coding. To **code** data means to assign numbers (or occasionally other symbols) to data to facilitate analysis. For most quantitative research variables, the assigned or coded value is simply the same as the raw data value. That is, if a consumer reports her family size as "four people" the researcher codes the response as a "4". Only rarely might we code quantitative responses as something other than their original values. One instance occurs as the shortening of lengthy raw data values to speed up keypunching and other data-processing activities. Another occurs as the collapsing of quantitative data into a small set of mutually exclusive and exhaustive categories. Shortening and collapsing during coding are seldom good ideas for at least three reasons: we lose information, we make mistakes, and we work slowly. The last two criticisms are easily elimi-

---

[4]We discuss regression in Chapter 17 and analysis of variance in Chapter 18. For an introduction to the other techniques, see David A. Aaker, ed., *Multivariate Analysis in Marketing: Theory and Application*, 2nd ed. (Palo Alto, Ca.: The Scientific Press, 1981).

nated by having a computer perform these activities—however, we still lose information.

Coding becomes more complex when we process raw data that exist in the form of words; the primary method is that of categorization, which proceeds fairly simply for responses to most research questions of fact. Consider such questions as "What brands of razor blades does the store carry?" or "Are you single (never married), married, widowed, divorced, or separated?" In both instances the coder merely assigns unique integers to unique responses. Gillette may always be coded as 1, Schick as 2, single as 1, married as 2, and so on.

Categorization becomes much more complex when coding qualitative responses to most psychological research questions. Suppose we collect thirty hours of taped interviews from focus groups; how do we proceed? Tull and Albaum cite conditions that categories must meet in such instances:[5]

1. Within categories, responses are sufficiently similar that they can be considered the same.

2. Between categories, responses are substantively different.

3. Categories are based upon one, and only one, relevant dimension of the problem.

4. Categories are mutually exclusive and exhaustive.

The first two conditions require that categories be meaningful in terms of raw data values they contain—in other words, that there be a just sufficient number of categories. There should not be so many that each response is the sole member of its category nor should there be so few that different responses are categorized as identical.

The third condition requires that categories derive from one relevant basis or dimension. To see the need for this, consider a variable whose responses we categorize using two or even three dimensions. For example, suppose we say to a consumer: "Tell me about Store X." We are listening simultaneously for the customer's reactions to store clerks, to store merchandise, and to store cleanliness. Suppose we code negative responses as a 1 and positive responses as a 2. Now consider a coded value of 1 and ask what it represents—we know it represents an unfavorable opinion but we do not know if the opinion is about clerks, merchandise, cleanliness or some combination of the three. We have lost information contained in the raw data.[6]

The fourth condition requires that categories be mutually exclusive

---

[5] Donald S. Tull and Gerald S. Albaum, *Survey Research: A Decisional Approach* (New York: Intext Press, 1973), p. 167.

[6] See Lansing and Morgan, *Economic Survey Methods*, pp. 228–29 for an extended discussion of problems in using more than one dimension in coding responses.

and exhaustive. *Mutually exclusive* means that it must not be possible that a given response could belong in more than one category. *Exhaustive* means that all responses must be categorizable. In other words, every response must belong to only one of the identified categories.

Finally, we end our coding discussion by raising three rather mechanical concerns. The first centers on coders themselves. We must select and train coders and provide them with written, understandable instructions. We usually would select and train as few coders as possible. If we need more than one coder (to complete coding more rapidly), we should organize them as specialists by assigning each a unitary portion of the data collection form. Such practice results in higher coding consistency than assigning each a separate stack of forms. We must also be available to answer coders' questions and to monitor their performance. On the latter point, usually a researcher would check each coder's work daily for adherence to coding instructions. Each coder should be following instructions, every day, on all data collection forms.

The second concern is the preparation of the instructions themselves—the codebook, as it is called. A **codebook** describes the location of variables on the data collection form, presents coding or categorization procedures, and indicates computer card columns where coded values will be keypunched. An abbreviated example appears in Table 15.1, for our study of pizza consumers. Table 15.1 shows, for example, that question

TABLE 15.1
Part of a Codebook for a Study of Pizza Consumers

Question Number	Variable Name	Card/ Column	Coding Procedure	
4a	price importance	1/8	Extremely important	= 1
			Quite important	= 2
			Slightly important	= 3
			Unimportant	= 4
			Missing data	= 9
33	marital status	2/16	Single (never married)	= 1
			Married	= 2
			Widowed	= 3
			Divorced	= 4
			Separated	= 5
			Missing data	= 9
38	occupation	2/22	Professional	= 1
			Managerial	= 2
			Other white collar	= 3
			Clerical and related	= 4
			Skilled blue collar	= 5
			Unskilled	= 6
			Unemployed	= 7
			Retired	= 8
			Missing data	= 9

4a produces a variable called price importance and that it takes on values of 1 through 4, and 9. Values appear on each sample member's first computer card, in the eighth column. Question 38 produces a variable called occupation, whose nine permissible values are punched on each sample member's second computer card, in the 22nd column. Codebooks prove a valuable reference to coders, the researcher, and others, especially in complex research designs and for designs long since completed.

The third concern is about limitations of computer programs planned for data analysis. Particular problems arise from a program's treatment of blanks and zeros; they can be treated as identical or different. For example, suppose responses are coded 0 through 9 for ten categories of educational level and a particular respondent checks none of them. If our program treats blanks and zeros identically there is no acceptable coding procedure for this respondent. Before we devise any coding schemes, we must check computer program limitations.

SUMMARY OF PRELIMINARY MATTERS   With our discussion on preliminary matters complete, we turn to the topic of data analysis. Once we are past preliminaries, we can finally begin to seek truth in the data. We should not be dismayed at this side trip into data analysis plans, data editing, and data coding because it is imperative that we have this understanding; without it, we have only the familiar acronym—GIGO—"garbage in, garbage out." Even though computer output tables look impressive, they can contain worthless information because of inherent errors in the data.

Overview of Data Analysis

Earlier we defined **data analysis** as the summary and manipulation of facts and figures to yield information in a form that will solve the marketing problem. Probably we all can recall from earlier statistics courses a multitude of statistical terms, summarization methods, numerical manipulations, and purposes. If not a multitude, perhaps a few anyway. That's usually the problem—we tend to remember things that have a personal relevancy, and the topic of statistics is seldom one of them. Thus, what we are going to try in this book is to increase the relevancy by examining statistical procedures with an eye on data analysis objectives, on what we want to find out.

Basically, researchers have only about seven purposes or things they want to find out when they analyze data:

- what is typical in the data;
- how much the data vary;
- how the data are distributed;

TABLE 15.2
Data Analysis Purposes and Frequently Used Statistics and Techniques

Data Analysis Purposes	Analysis Statistics and Techniques
What is typical	Means, medians, modes
How data vary	Standard deviations, variances, ranges, average deviations
Presenting the distribution	Frequency distributions, histograms, frequency polygons
Describing relationships	Correlations and other measures of association
Making estimates, predictions, and forecasts	Point and interval estimates, regression, time series
Describing group and variable differences	t-tests, Z-tests, analysis of variance
Showing causality	t-tests, Z-tests, analysis of variance

- what relationships exist between variables;
- what estimates, predictions, and forecasts result from the data;
- what differences exist between groups and variables; and
- what variables likely caused changes in other variables.

Often they call the first three purposes "data summarization" or "data reduction" because they reduce masses of data into only one or a few pieces of information. All seven purposes appear in Table 15.2 along with examples of specific statistics and techniques that marketing researchers frequently use. It should come as no surprise that these and other statistics and techniques are subjects for the rest of our five-chapter discussion on data analysis. Regarding the techniques that businesses use, slightly more than half of all firms conducting marketing research regularly use regression, correlation, and interval estimates; slightly less than half use t-tests, Z-tests, and time series analysis; and about one firm in four uses analysis of variance.[7]

Almost always researchers employ these statistics and techniques with the aid of a computer. Unless data sets are extremely small and analysis purposes extremely simple, data analysis will be much easier with a computer. This does not mean that a researcher must be an accomplished Fortran programmer. It does mean that he or she should be familiar with available computer packages or software that accomplish data analyses efficiently and flexibly. Usually these packages use very simple commands

---

[7]Barnett A. Greenberg, Jac L. Goldstucker, and Danny N. Bellenger, "What Techniques are Used by Marketing Researchers in Business" *Journal of Marketing* 41 (April 1977):62–68.

that perform both simple and complex data analyses and manipulations. For example, SPSS (the *Statistical Package for the Social Sciences*) uses only one command, FREQUENCIES GENERAL, to compute frequency distributions, means, medians, modes, minimums, maximums, standard deviations, and five other statistics for up to 500 variables at one time. Cross-tabulations, *t*-tests, correlations, regressions, and other more complex analyses can be completed just as easily.[8] Other packages offer similar features.

Three final comments before we examine specific analysis techniques in detail: First, much of our discussion will be limited. Data analysis is only part of marketing research, and it is a part to which any user of this text has had some previous exposure. Some material, then, will be in the nature of a review, but there will also be emphasis on analysis techniques we may not have studied but frequently apply to marketing research data. Second, in all our discussion we assume that data being analyzed came from a simple random sample drawn from a very large population. Third, in all our discussion we note the close correspondence of measurement method with statistics and techniques.

Characterizing What Is Typical

To characterize what is typical in the data, we must first know the level of measurement used in data collection. Table 15.3 summarizes the possibilities (review Chapter 10 if measurement level terms appear unfamiliar).

To illustrate the logic underlying Table 15.3, consider the raw data matrix in Table 15.4 for a sample of 10 supermarkets from a population of 200. Assume that "Location" identifies stores in one of four Denver metropolitan areas. Let the "Index of Parking Lot Size" be a categorization of estimating parking lot sizes—with 1 being the smallest and 5 the largest. Let "Brand X Shelf Facings" be the number of boxes of brand X facing the shopper as she walks down the supermarket aisle. Let "Brand X Unit Sales" be the number of units sold during the research period.

MEANS, MEDIANS, AND MODES   Now, let us determine the typical store's unit sales. Because unit sales represent ratio measurement data, Table 15.3 says we have a choice of mean, median, or mode measures of typicalness. We defined a **mean** in Chapter 12 as the sum of all variable values divided by the number of values. Mean unit sales, then, are

$$(62 + 72 + 27 + 34 + 35 + 68 + 112 + 72 + 0 + 58)/10, \text{ or } 54$$

Notice that the mean was not written 54.0 or 54.00; in other words, notice that the mean was written with only two significant digits. We do

---

[8]See William Klecka, Norman H. Nie, and C. Hadlai Hull, *SPSS Primer* (New York: McGraw-Hill, 1975) for an overview of SPSS capabilities. A complete description can be found in Nie, et al., *SPSS: Statistical Package for the Social Sciences*, 2nd ed. (New York: McGraw-Hill, 1975). Another widely used data analysis package is SAS; see *SAS User's Guide* (Raleigh, N.C.: SAS Institute, Inc., 1979).

TABLE 15.3
Measurement Level and Measures of Typicalness

Measurement Level	Measures of Typicalness
Nominal	Mode
Ordinal	Mode, median
Interval, Ratio	Mode, median, mean

this because it would be improper to imply that our calculated mean is accurate to more than two digits or to more than the number of significant digits in the least accurate rounded number or in the sample size involved in the calculation, whichever is smaller. Accuracy of rounded numbers is not at issue here because we are dealing with discrete variables and, therefore, unrounded and exact counts. Our sample size, however, contains two significant digits.

We define the **median** as the value of the middle (n/2) observation when all values have been ordered from least to most or from most to least. If we order values for unit sales, the ten values would look like this:

0   27   34   35   58   62   68   72   72   112

However, we can't find the middle value—is it the fifth value from the left or from the right? The problem occurs because we have an even number of values. If we only had one more or one less value, that is, nine or eleven, finding the middle one would be easy. To compute the median when the number of sample values is even, we simply take the middle two values and compute their average. Thus, for our unit sales data we add (58 + 62), divide by 2, and get a median of 60.

We define the **mode** as the most frequently occurring value in the

TABLE 15.4
Raw Data Matrix

Supermarket	Location	Index of Parking Lot Size	Brand X Shelf Facings	Brand X Unit Sales
A	1	3	3	62
B	2	5	3	72
C	3	2	2	27
D	2	1	1	34
E	2	1	1	35
F	1	4	3	68
G	2	5	3	112
H	3	4	2	72
I	4	4	0	0
J	4	3	2	58

data. The value 72 occurs twice and no other value does so. It then is the mode.

We should be able to calculate a mean, median, and mode for Brand X shelf facings too. However, we cannot calculate all these statistics for the other two variables. Actually, we *can* calculate means, medians, and modes for these variables but two of these statistics lack meaning. What does it mean, for example, to state the mean location is 2.0? Or that the median location is 2.0? Absolutely nothing, because the variable, "location," lacks the property of order. In short, because it is a nominal variable, its only appropriate measure of typicalness is the mode. To see this, consider that means and medians imply being "in the middle of something," of being approximately just as far from one end of the something as the other. If the something has no order or distance associated with it, then being in its middle makes no sense at all. However, it does make sense to say the most frequently occurring location value is 2, that this value occurs twice as frequently as the values 1, 3, and 4, and so on.

Now, consider what is typical for the "Index of Parking Lot Size." Its mode or most frequently occurring value is 4 as we can determine. In addition, because this variable has the property of order (a "5" parking lot is bigger than a "4"), we can also determine its median at 3.5. That is, half the sample possesses variable values more than 3.5 and half less. However, it would be inappropriate to state that its mean is

$$(3 + 5 + 2 + 1 + 1 + 4 + 5 + 4 + 4 + 3)/10, \text{ or } 3.2$$

Why?

The answer stems from the variable's ordinal nature. Its values indicate only "more than or less than" amounts and not distances. Means must be calculated on data that indicate distance expressed in *identical units of measure* between variable values; otherwise, they mislead. To illustrate, suppose that a particular "5" parking lot is actually 100 times bigger than a "1" parking lot. Yet when we use these 1s and 5s in calculating a mean parking lot size, we actually weight the large parking lot only five times heavier. Serious distortions can result.

To summarize, if we have nominal data, the only appropriate measure of typicalness to calculate are modes. If we have ordinal data, we may properly calculate both modes and medians. If we have either interval or ratio data, we may properly calculate modes, medians, and means.

WHICH TYPICALNESS MEASURE TO USE   Other considerations than measurement level also determine which measure of typicalness to use. Assuming we have a choice, means are more attractive than medians because of the wealth of statistical techniques that apply. Medians are more attractive than modes for the same reason.

Means are more dramatically influenced by extreme data values—outliers—than are medians or modes. Consider the set of sample values (4,4,4,4,4,4,4,4,64) and calculate what is typical. Obviously 4 is the most typical value, but the mean is 10! Whenever sample values contain a few extreme values, the median or mode will be a better measure of typicalness than the mean. An example of a variable that frequently has a few extreme values is consumer income.

Notice also that calculation of both the median and mode require data to be ordered. A mean does not require this and thus may be simpler to calculate if the researcher has a moderate-sized data set and no computer to help.[9]

We have made earlier reference to the reporting of results in significant digits. Let us have a brief review: suppose we want to total five salespersons' incomes, reported as *roughly* $25,000, $22,000, $18,250, $14,150, and $14,100. **SIGNIFICANT DIGITS**

It appears that the first two incomes were reported already rounded to the nearest thousand dollars. Thus, a total of all five incomes can be no more accurate than this and should be stated as $93,000 to avoid the appearance of unjustified precision. A decision rule for significant digits in addition or subtraction of rounded numbers is:

> Retain in the results only digits in the position and to the left of the position of the least accurate rounded number in the addition or subtraction.

To do otherwise gives a false sense of accuracy.

A similar rule can be stated in the division or multiplication of rounded numbers. Suppose we want to calculate the average salesperson's income. We add $25,000 + $22,000 + $18,250 + $14,150 + $14,100 and divide by 5. The number of significant digits in the least accurate income is two; our average, then, should contain only two significant digits and be reported as $19,000. The decision rule is:

> Retain in the results only the number of significant digits in the least accurate rounded number involved in the division or multiplication.

But why not report the average to only one significant digit—because we divided by 5, which is only one digit. The answer, of course, is that 5 is not a rounded number; it is an exact count of a discrete variable. (It is not an approximate measurement of a continuous variable.)

However, this brings us to a last consideration in reporting numbers. If our calculation uses sample data, we really should not express results to more significant digits than are found in the sample size.

---

[9]For an excellent discussion on other considerations in choosing measures of typicalness, see John H. Mueller, Karl F. Schuessler, and Herbert L. Costner, *Statistical Reasoning in Sociology*, 3rd ed. (Boston: Houghton Mifflin, 1977), pp. 115–21.

To see this, consider expanding our sample to 6 salespersons and let this last individual report an income of $24,000. A new average income will be determined as $20,000. Or, suppose this sixth salesperson has an income of $17,000, the new average will be $18,000. Thus, our average when expressed to *two* significant digits is subject to instability or change when our *single* digit sample size is altered. If our average were originally expressed as $20,000, no such change would occur. Saying the same thing, if we wanted to express average salesperson income to two significant digits, our sample size ought to contain two significant digits.[10]

Showing Variability in the Data

Our treatment of data variability goes much faster. Researchers commonly choose from four measures: the range, average deviation, standard deviation, and percentile. Their choice depends again on level of data measurement and their particular interests in the variability measure. Let us see how.

FOUR MEASURES OF VARIABILITY The **range** is merely the difference between the smallest and largest variable values in a set of data. Consider two sets of sample values (0,8,8,20,4) and (8,8,8,8,8). The range is 20 for the first set and 0 for the second.

The **average deviation** for a set of sample values is the sum of all absolute values of differences between each sample value and the sample mean divided by sample size. In symbols

$$\text{average deviation} = \frac{\sum_{i=1}^{n} \left| X_i - \overline{X} \right|}{n}$$

The average deviation for the first data set above is (8 + 0 + 0 + 12 + 4)/5 = 4.8 and 0 for the second. Average deviations are seldom used in marketing research.

The sample standard deviation is much more frequently used and is given by a formula from Chapter 12:

$$s = + \left[\frac{\sum_{i=1}^{n} (X_i - \overline{X})^2}{n - 1} \right]^{1/2}$$

In words, the **standard deviation** is the positive square root of the sum of all squared differences between each sample value and the sample mean

---

[10]This position is less widely discussed than the earlier material on significant digits. See Chester R. Wasson and Richard R. Schreve, *Interpreting and Using Quantitative Aids to Business Decision* (Austin, Tex.: Austin Press, Lone Star Publishers, 1976), pp. 50–56.

TABLE 15.5
Measurement Level and Measures of Variability

Measurement Level	Measures of Variability
Nominal	Frequency distribution
Ordinal	Frequency distribution, percentile, quartile
Interval, Ratio	Frequency distribution, percentile, quartile, interquartile range, range, average deviation, standard deviation, variance

divided by the number of values minus one. In other words, the standard deviation is the positive square root of the sample variance.

A last measure of variability is the percentile. A **percentile** is a variable value such that a specified proportion of sample values lies below it. For example, the 20th percentile is a variable value such that 20 percent of the sample has values less than it. In a roundabout way, we already have been introduced to one special percentile as the median or 50th percentile. Other percentiles often of special interest are called **quartiles**—the first, second, and third quartiles are the 25th, 50th, and 75th percentiles, respectively. Often the difference between the first and third quartiles is also of interest, called the **interquartile range.**

Choice of a variability measure also depends on the level of measurement involved in our research. The variability of nominal data is usually expressed by a frequency distribution.[11] With ordinal data, we may properly express variability in a frequency distribution or by percentiles and quartiles. With interval and ratio data, we may use any of the measures of variability discussed above. For convenience, we summarize this information in Table 15.5.

WHICH VARIABILITY MEASURE TO USE

Presenting the Distribution

The major form of presenting the distribution of data in tables is a frequency distribution. A **frequency distribution** simply presents a count of the number of instances that data values fall within specified classes. An example appears as Table 15.6. We can see that additional information often appears as class count percents and as cumulative percents of the total sample. The cumulative percent column shows the total percentage of data values that fall in each class plus all earlier classes.

TABULAR PRESENTATION

---

[11]See Mueller, Schuessler, and Costner, *Statistical Reasoning*, pp. 175–81 for a discussion of their Index of Qualitative Variation, which more completely describes the variation of qualitative or nominal variables.

TABLE 15.6
Brand X Unit Sales Per Day

Unit Sales Class	Number of Supermarkets (f)	Percent (%)	Cumulative Percent (%)
0 to under 20	1	10	10
20 to under 40	3	30	40
40 to under 60	1	10	50
60 to under 80	4	40	90
80 to under 100	0	0	90
100 to under 120	1	10	100
Total	10	100	

Frequency distribution tables are generally easy to construct. Some guidelines to help are:

1. Table titles should clearly identify the variables being presented.

2. Tables should stand on their own. Necessary definitions of table terms and other details should appear at the bottom of the table. The table should show the sample size on which data are based.

3. If the table presents secondary data, a note must appear at the bottom of the table, clearly identifying their source.

4. The number of classes and class sizes should be meaningful to the intended audience.

Only the last guideline deserves more comment. As much as possible, classes should have equal intervals or sizes—at least five classes but usually no more than twelve should appear in a typical table. Class intervals should have whole number midpoints. Basic statistics textbooks can provide details. Class intervals should be constructed with the intended audience in mind: if readers are interested in a certain class interval, be sure the frequency distribution reflects this interest. If readers will largely consist of technical experts, we can use more classes than if we intend the table for a more diverse audience.

GRAPHIC PRESENTATION Researchers commonly use four basic graphic or pictorial presentation forms for showing the distribution of data: the frequency polygon, the histogram, the ogive, and the pie chart.[12] Another term for the ogive is a cumulative frequency polygon. All are really nothing more than pictorial versions of the tabular frequency distribution.

A frequency polygon for the frequency distribution in Table 15.6

---

[12]A most complete discussion of these and other forms of graphic presentation is found in Calvin F. Schmid and Stanton E. Schmid, *Handbook of Graphic Presentation*, 2nd ed. (New York: John Wiley & Sons, 1979).

appears in Figure 15.1. We can see that a **frequency polygon** is made by connecting dots that represent class midpoints and counts for each class. The circled dot in Figure 15.1, for example, represents the three supermarkets that have unit sales between 20 and 40 units. A frequency polygon can easily be turned into a **histogram.** All we do is convert the class midpoint dots to horizontal lines and draw vertical lines to each class limit. An example appears as Figure 15.2.

A **pie chart** may be used to present the same data as in a frequency polygon or histogram. An example for our unit sales data appears in Figure 15.3. To construct it, we merely take each class percent in Table 15.6 times 360 degrees and then draw in resulting angles. For example, the smallest unit sales class contains 10 percent of the number of supermarkets. Thus, the angle formed by its two limits in Figure 15.3 is (0.10)(360) or 36 degrees.

Because a histogram, frequency polygon, and pie chart all present the same data we might wonder whether it matters which we use. The answer is that it really makes very little difference, unless we want to compare two or more frequency distributions at the same time. If this is the case, the best form of graphic presentation is the frequency polygon because we can construct several frequency polygons on the same graph for a more vivid comparison. Obviously, we must use different colors of ink or different line forms to tell the distributions apart. Also, unless the distributions are based on exactly the same sample size, this comparison process will mislead. If different-sized samples are involved, we must first convert the number or counts in each class to percents of the total number in each sample.

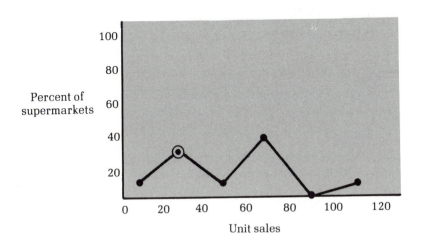

FIGURE 15.1
Brand X unit sales per day (frequency polygon)

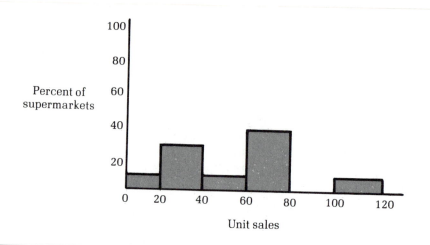

FIGURE 15.2
Brand X unit sales per day (histogram)

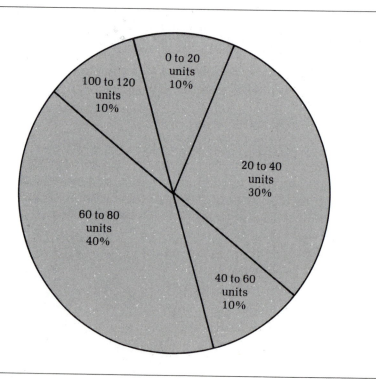

FIGURE 15.3
Brand X unit sales per day (pie chart)

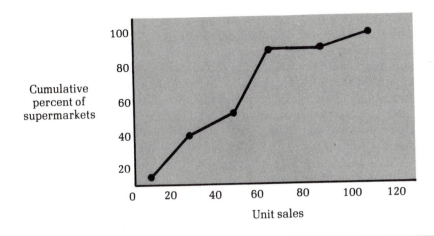

FIGURE 15.4
Brand X unit sales per day (ogive)

The last form of graphic presentation we discuss is called the **ogive** or **cumulative frequency polygon.** Again it illustrates a frequency distribution. However, an ogive is based not on class percents but on cumulative percents. The ogive in Figure 15.4 also presents the distribution of data in Table 15.6. As we can see, several ogives could easily be presented on the same graph for comparison purposes.

How we characterize what is typical in the data and how we show the variance in the data depends primarily on measurement level. Means and standard deviations—respectively the two most popular statistics for these purposes—require interval or ratio measurement. In addition, analytical procedures employed for purposes other than these (but which in some way use the mean or standard deviation) also require interval or ratio data.

    In contrast, the most popular method of presenting the distribution of data—the frequency distribution—requires no special level of measurement. However, the calculation of cumulative percentages does require at least ordinal level measurement of the variable of interest.

    Practically speaking, we should restate that we seldom calculate means and standard deviations or construct frequency distributions by hand. Computers, programmable calculators, or assistants will do the job for us. But we must understand completely what these statistical tools mean and to what uses they may be put. Without this understanding, we would be like mechanics who can identify tools of the trade but do not know when to use which one.

**SUMMARY ON
PRESENTATION
OF DATA**

Chapter Summary

Before beginning data analysis, the researcher completes some preliminary matters, the most central of which is devising a data analysis plan. Such plans describe major research variables of interest, their levels of measurement, and planned procedures for their analysis. Such plans give order and direction to data analysis. Data editing and coding follow, to put data in a form allowing execution of the plan. Apart from correcting non-response and response errors and coding qualitative data, these matters involve somewhat mechanical considerations compared to data analysis planning.

Actual data analysis accomplishes one or more of seven basic purposes, determining: what is typical in the data; how much the data vary; how the data are distributed; what relationships exist between variables; what estimates, predictions, and forecasts result from the data; what differences exist between groups and variables; and what variables are likely causes of changes in other variables. Analytical procedures largely differ for each. Within any one purpose, we often face a decision in selecting from a number of appropriate statistics and techniques. Consequently, we must understand assumptions underlying these statistics and techniques to choose those more appropriate.

Chapter Review

KEY TERMS

Data analysis purposes	Standard deviation
Data analysis plan	Variance
Data editing	Percentile
Data coding	Quartile
Codebook	Interquartile range
Mean	Frequency distribution table
Median	Range
Mode	

DISCUSSION QUESTIONS

1. Why does the mean require interval or ratio data for its calculation?

2. What types of data may use the range as a meaningful measure of variability?

3. Consider the following monthly warranty claim totals for a sample of twenty service centers: $8342, 16167, 4200, 10157, 8154, 9942, 3316, 8690, 2347, 10008, 2460, 7950, 5051, 5000, 4600, 11450, 9278, 1488, 10220, and 6890.

   a) Compute the mean and median amounts.

   b) Compute the range and standard deviation.

4. Describe in words what the interquartile range actually represents.

5. "Much of marketing research is judgmental and not hard and fast." What discussion can you cite from this chapter that would support this statement?

Additional Readings

Perhaps the best additional readings consist of portions of texts used in earlier statistics courses. Review the various statistics and procedures and identify their implicit purpose in data analysis. You should see that all meet one or more of our seven purposes. Beyond these, you may wish to look at:

Nie, Norman H.; Hull, C. Hadlai; Jenkins, Jean G.; Steinbrenner, Karin, and Bent, Dale H. *SPSS: Statistical Package for the Social Sciences.* 2nd ed. New York: McGraw-Hill, 1975.

> This manual contains descriptions of computer programs to perform most analyses described in a basic statistics text. In addition, it also contains discussions that further an understanding of statistics and procedures.

SAS Institute. *SAS User's Guide.* 1979 ed. Raleigh, N.C.: SAS Institute, 1979.

> This manual contains descriptions of computer programs to perform most analyses described in a basic statistics text. It contains less complete descriptions of statistics and procedures than does SPSS.

Schmid, Calvin F. and Schmid, Stanton E. *Handbook of Graphic Presentation.* McGraw-Hill, 1979.

> Here is almost everything you ever would need to know about summarizing data in graphic form—practical, current, readable, and well illustrated.

CHAPTER

16

Relationships Between Variables

Let us begin our discussion of this fourth purpose in analyzing data by reviewing what we mean by a relationship between variables. A **relationship between variables** means that their measurement values, as obtained from a group of sampling units at one point in time, either occur jointly or vary together.[1] Let us explain by considering the two-variable case. If two nominal variables relate, a sampling unit having one measurement value on one variable will tend to have one measurement value on the other. If two ordinal, interval, or ratio variables relate, a sampling unit having a measurement value near the typical value on one variable will tend to have a measurement value near the typical value on the other. Likewise, if two ordinal, interval, or ratio variables relate, a sampling unit having an extreme measurement value on one variable will tend to have an extreme measurement value on the other. A similar discussion holds for the three- and n-variable cases at any measurement level: if any number of variables relate, their measurement values either occur jointly or vary together.

Relationships pervade our everyday experience. For example, a person's sex relates to her or his deodorant brand choice; a day's temperature relates to sales of ice cream at the beach; a study period's length relates to scores on the midterm. Yet we recognize that it would be folly to explain

---

[1] However, we did mention a special case as the relationship between measurement values for a single variable at two points in time as a test/retest reliability coefficient in Chapter 11.

measurement values for each of these second variables solely on the basis of values for each of the first. Our everyday experience tells us that many other variables also relate, some perhaps even more strongly. Moreover, some of these other variables, along with those identified, might actually *cause* joint occurrences or variations in measurement values for each of the second.

So it is with marketing experience, where knowledge of relationships pervades decision making. For example, if a decision maker knows that consumer marital status relates to product usage, then advertising copy decisions become clearer. If a decision maker knows that consumer satisfaction relates to a product's weight but not its color, then product design decisions improve. If a decision maker knows that age, family size, and income relate to product consumption, then territorial sales forecasts become more accurate. Thus, knowledge of relationships leads both to increased understanding of marketing phenomena and to more effective marketing decisions.

Let us make three more formal statements about relationships and marketing experience:

- Marketing researchers express relationships in *numbers* calculated by *explicit rules* that depend on level of variable measurement.
- They state most relationships in terms of their *strength, direction,* and *statistical significance.*
- They recognize that relationships usually mean *association* and *not causation.*

Elaboration of these statements is the substance of this chapter.

Relationships Between Two Nominal Variables

Recall that nominally measured variables show measurement values that indicate only equality or inequality of the sampling units that produced them. In our introductory discussion preceding, we mentioned sex, deodorant brand choice, marital status, and a product's color as examples of

TABLE 16.1
Deodorant Brand Use by Sex

SEX	DEODORANT BRAND USE		
	Brand A	Brand B	Total
Male	782	418	1,200
Female	230	570	800

TABLE 16.2
Deodorant Brand Use by Sex

	DEODORANT BRAND USE		
SEX	Brand A (%)	Brand B (%)	Total (%)
Male	65.2	34.8	100.0
Female	28.8	71.2	100.0

nominal variables. Their measurement values—male, female; Brand A, Brand B, Brand C; single, married, widowed, divorced, separated; blue, red, green, and so on—are really nothing more than labels. Let us see how marketing researchers show relationships using counts of such measurement values as obtained from sampling units.

Consider two nominal variables such as sex and deodorant brand use. More explicitly, suppose a firm currently marketing two brands of deodorant wishes to investigate a relationship between sex and deodorant choice as an aid in making advertising decisions. If a strong relationship exists, the firm might use male models, male-oriented copy, and male-oriented magazines in its print advertisements for one brand and opposite tactics for the other. To investigate the relationship, a researcher collects data on sex and deodorant brand choice from a random sample of 2,000 consumers who use either Brand A or Brand B. Data appear in Table 16.1 as a **cross-tabulation** or **crosstab** table. As we see, a crosstab table shows the joint frequency distribution of two variables as obtained from a single group of sampling units.

NOMINAL RELATIONSHIPS

Examining the table, we see support for a relationship in the form of joint occurrences. Males seem to prefer Brand A while females appear to prefer Brand B. However, because sample sizes for males and females are unequal, we usually will find our examination easier if we convert frequencies in Table 16.1 to percentages, as in Table 16.2.

Notice that entries in Table 16.2 used either the total number of males or the total number of females as denominators to calculate percentages (entries did not use either the total number of Brand A or Brand B users). Such practice implies that our interest lies with males and females as distinct groups (not with Brand A and Brand B users). Moreover, such practice implies that sex partly influences or causes deodorant brand choice (not vice versa). As a general rule, researchers organize crosstab tables with causal variable categories arrayed in a column to the left of data values and caused variable categories arrayed in a row at the top of data values. Researchers then calculate percentages in a fashion to explain behavior of the distinct groups of interest or to understand potential causes of the behavior. Thus, Table 16.2 allows us to state for our sample of deodorant users:

1. If the user is male, the probability that he uses Brand A deodorant is about 0.65.

2. If the user is female, the probability that she uses Brand B deodorant is about 0.71.

However, a critic might contend that some variable other than sex—say, income—more strongly influences deodorant brand use. His contention might be based on both economic theory and empirical observation:

1. consumers exhibit rational, price sensitive behavior;

2. female consumers earn lower incomes than males; and

3. Brand B is cheaper than Brand A.

To answer, we require data on sex and deodorant brand use while controlling for income. That is, to refute the contention, we must see our original relationship hold for consumers in different income categories. Table 16.3 provides the data. As we can see, the relationship between sex and deodorant brand use persists for consumers in both income categories and, thus, we reaffirm our original conclusion. Controlling for still other variables would allow us even more faith in our original conclusion. In fact, if the relationship persisted while all other theoretically meaningful variables were controlled, we would have initial support for establishing causation.

TABLE 16.3
Deodorant Brand Use by Sex, Controlling for Income

| | *INCOME < $20,000* | | | |
| | *DEODORANT BRAND USE* | | | |
SEX	*Brand A (%)*	*Brand B (%)*	*Total (%)*	*n*
Male	65.2	34.8	100.0	400
Female	28.3	71.7	100.0	600
	INCOME > $20,000			
	DEODORANT BRAND USE			
SEX	*Brand A (%)*	*Brand B (%)*	*Total (%)*	*n*
Male	65.1	34.9	100.0	800
Female	28.5	71.5	100.0	200

TABLE 16.4
Deodorant Brand Use by Sex, Controlling for Income

INCOME < $20,000

DEODORANT BRAND USE

SEX	Brand A (%)	Brand B (%)	Total (%)	n
Male	100.0	0.0	100.0	400
Female	20.0	80.0	100.0	600

INCOME > $20,000

DEODORANT BRAND USE

SEX	Brand A (%)	Brand B (%)	Total (%)	n
Male	46.9	53.1	100.0	800
Female	55.0	45.0	100.0	200

We should realize that adding income as a control variable might not have led to such clear-cut support. For example, we might instead have found data such as that in Table 16.4. Examining these data, we see a different relationship obtaining between sex and deodorant brand use within each income category. Lower income males and females exhibit the original relationship more strongly, while their higher income counterparts exhibit an opposite relationship.

Adding income as a control variable might even have led to the original relationship disappearing completely, as Table 16.5 illustrates. Here

TABLE 16.5
Deodorant Brand Use by Sex, Controlling for Income

INCOME < $20,000

DEODORANT BRAND USE

SEX	Brand A (%)	Brand B (%)	Total (%)	n
Male	6.2	93.8	100.0	400
Female	6.7	93.3	100.0	600

INCOME > $20,000

DEODORANT BRAND USE

SEX	Brand A (%)	Brand B (%)	Total (%)	n
Male	93.8	6.2	100.0	800
Female	95.0	5.0	100.0	200

we see almost no relationship at all between sex and deodorant brand use for either income group. Our original relationship appearing in Tables 16.1 and 16.2 apparently came from the influence not of sex but of income. Given data in Table 16.5, a researcher would call our original relationship artificial or spurious. **Spurious relationships** derive not from causal influences but from a common relationship with another, third variable.

Whenever an initial analysis shows a relationship between two variables, researchers usually attempt a more complete understanding. This understanding usually involves adding a third, theoretically meaningful variable as a control. Researchers call the initial relationship a *zero-order relationship*; the relationship when using one control variable, a *first-order relationship*; the relationship when using two control variables, a *second-order relationship*; and so on. For example, we could continue examining the relationship between sex and deodorant brand use while simultaneously controlling for both income and social class. If income contained 2 categories and social class contained 5, this analysis would produce 2 times 5, or 10 second-order crosstab tables. Each would contain 4 cells; each cell would represent 1 combination of the 2 categories of sex and deodorant brand use. In each table, we would look for evidence of the original relationship.

Tables showing first- or higher-order relationships sometimes meet with sample size problems. For example, to examine fourth-order relationships when control variables possess 2, 5, 4, and 4 categories, respectively, and when original variables possess 2 and 3 categories, would produce 160 tables and 960 cells. Even with a sample size of several thousand, we would expect to find many cells empty—owing not to the nonexistence of people exhibiting particular combinations of behaviors but to the "smallness" of the sample. Consequently, researchers seldom look for higher than second-order relationships, nor do they use control variables with numerous categories, unless sound theory makes a compelling case. Moreover, we cannot overstate the worth of sound theory in the initial analysis—to interpret findings and to indicate the identity of control variables.

We must recognize that a somewhat similar discussion also applies to a zero-order table showing no relationship. Here, sound theory may indicate a control variable that, when used, might produce a very strong first-order relationship (just the opposite to a finding of spuriousness). Such a control variable is called a **suppressor variable** because "failure to control for it 'suppresses' the zero-order relationship, making it *appear* weaker than it is."[2]

To return to our ideas at the start of this chapter, we again note that a relationship between two variables in a zero- or higher-order table does

---

[2]Allan G. Johnson, *Social Statistics Without Tears* (New York: McGraw-Hill, 1977), p. 132. His Chapter 7 provides an excellent introduction to relationships, controlling and other types of variables, and causal path analysis.

not show causation. We have only to look at the relationship between sex and deodorant brand use from the standpoint of the latter variable causing the former to see the truth of this statement. Showing a relationship merely sets the stage for establishing causation. Beyond a relationship and before we can make causal statements, we must show that the causal variable preceded the caused variable in time and that some other third variable did not cause *both* variables.

With our discussion on understanding nominal relationships complete, let us now examine in detail how researchers express relationships between two nominal variables. As we said, researchers usually express such relationships in numbers derived from the application of explicit rules and in terms of their strength, direction, and significance. Our next several sections show how.

One way of expressing the relationship between two nominal variables if both contain only two categories is through **phi correlation.** Phi can be calculated very easily by the following formula:

PHI CORRRELATION

$$r_{phi} = \frac{ad - bc}{[(a + b)(c + d)(a + c)(b + d)]^{1/2}}$$

The symbol r indicates correlation and the subscript phi indicates phi correlation, to distinguish it from other forms of correlation which we discuss later. The symbols a, b, c, and d represent cell frequencies in a two-by-two crosstab table. Usually the researcher arranges the table as below, to simplify interpretation.

		variable Y	
		+	−
variable X	+	a	b
	−	c	d

Pluses and minuses signify mere convention, in order to aid the researcher's interpretation. For example, if variable X is advertising exposure and variable Y is product purchase, a would represent the number of consumers in the sample who both saw the ad and purchased the product. That is, the researcher would designate both of these characteristics as positive, or plus, behaviors. For Table 16.1, we have

$a = 782 \qquad b = 418$

$c = 230 \qquad d = 570$

and

$$r_{phi} = \frac{(782)(570) - (418)(230)}{[(1,200)(800)(1,012)(988)]^{1/2}} = 0.357$$

If we had arranged Table 16.1 differently—as in (1), (2), and (3) below—we would have calculated the same absolute value for r_{phi}. However, arrangements (2) and (3) would have led to a negative sign preceding r_{phi}.

570	418
230	782

(1)

230	782
570	418

(2)

418	570
782	230

(3)

Strength of r_{phi}.   Values for r_{phi} range from -1.0 to $+1.0$. Both extremes indicate a perfect relationship between the two variables, while a value of 0 indicates no relationship.

When r_{phi} is squared, the resulting value indicates the proportion of variation in one of the two variables explained by the other. For our data, $(r_{phi})^2 = (0.357)^2$ or 0.127. This indicates that 12.7 percent of the variation in deodorant brand use is explained by the variation in sex.

Not too strong a relationship, we're quite correctly saying to ourselves. To guide interpretations of r_{phi}, we need the following descriptions:

Absolute Value of r_{phi}	Relationship Description
Over 0.80	Very Strong
0.60 to 0.80	Moderate
0.40 to 0.60	Weak
0.20 to 0.40	Very Weak
0.00 to 0.20	Negligible

Thus, we would describe our original value of 0.357 as a very weak relationship.

Further, because $(r_{phi})^2$ represents the proportion of variance explained or shared between the two variables, we may compare two or more values and make meaningful statements about relationship strength. For example, if $(r_{phi})^2$ between sex and deodorant brand use is 0.127 and that between income and deodorant brand use is 0.381, we may state that the second relationship is three times stronger than the first. In other words, $(r_{phi})^2$ produces ratio data.

Direction of r_{phi}.   While we can call phi correlation coefficients with a "$+$" sign positive and those with a "$-$" sign negative, we must realize that such indicators of direction lack the usual meaning of more and less. Nominal variable measurements used by r_{phi} do not become more or less across sampling units; they only become different. Consequently, directionality signs for r_{phi} appear only to aid the researcher's interpretation. For Table 16.1, the positive sign for r_{phi} means that there is a positive relationship between being male and choosing Brand A deodorant. Negative signs associated with r_{phi} for the different table arrangements (2) and (3) still allow this interpretation.

TABLE 16.6
Deodorant Brand Use by Sex

| | DEODORANT BRAND USE | | |
SEX	Brand A	Brand B	Total
Male	782	418	1,200
Female	230	570	800
Total	1,012	988	2,000

Significance of r_{phi}. If we calculate r_{phi} from a census and not from a sample, the significance of r_{phi} is not at issue and the researcher disregards this section. However, the more usual situation finds r_{phi} calculated from a sample and the researcher must determine the probability that sampling error could have produced a phi correlation of the observed strength. The general practice is called a *test of statistical significance*.

A quite simple test of statistical significance for r_{phi} exists, using the χ^2 (read, **chi-square**) test statistic. A formula for the χ^2 test statistic is

$$\chi^2_{test} = \sum_{i=1}^{R} \sum_{j=1}^{C} \frac{(O_{ij} - E_{ij})^2}{E_{ij}}$$

where R = row variable number of categories
C = column variable number of categories
O_{ij} = observed frequency in cell ij
E_{ij} = expected frequency in cell ij

Only the last symbol requires explanation. E_{ij} is the expected cell frequency for the ith row, jth column, assuming independence or no relationship between the row and column variables in a crosstab table. Let us return to Table 16.1 reproduced (with totals now) as Table 16.6, to illustrate the determination of E_{ij}.

Looking at the data, ask how many male Brand A users we can expect if there were no relationship between sex and deodorant brand use. We note that there are 1,012 Brand A users and that males account for 1,200/ 2,000 or 60 percent of the sample. Therefore, we can expect (1,012)(0.60) or 607 male Brand A users in the absence of any relationship. Similarly, we would expect (988)(0.60) or 593 male Brand B users, 405 female Brand A users, and 395 female Brand B users.

Thus, we have

$$\chi^2_{test} = \sum_{i=1}^{R} \sum_{j=1}^{C} \frac{(O_{ij} - E_{ij})^2}{E_{ij}}$$

$$= \frac{(782 - 607)^2}{607} + \frac{(418 - 593)^2}{593} + \frac{(230 - 405)^2}{405} + \frac{(570 - 395)^2}{395}$$

$$= 255$$

Now, what to do with it? Our answer requires a more rigorous discussion of an hypothesis test for the significance of r_{phi}. The test proceeds along four steps:

1. State the null and alternate hypotheses as

    H_0: The population value for $r_{phi} = 0$
    H_1: The population value for $r_{phi} \neq 0$

2. Choose a critical value of χ^2 from Table 4 in the Appendix.

3. Calculate the value for χ^2_{test} as above.

4. Compare the value for χ^2_{test} to the chosen critical value of χ^2 and state conclusions as below:[3]

    If $\chi^2_{test} \leq \chi^2_{critical}$, accept H_0.
    If $\chi^2_{test} > \chi^2_{critical}$, accept H_1.

To illustrate the application of these four steps, let us state hypotheses exactly as above for r_{phi} between sex and deodorant brand use and proceed to step 2. Turning to Table 4 in the Appendix, we find many critical values of χ^2, depending on both degrees of freedom and areas in the right-hand tail. Critical values appear to increase both as degrees of freedom increase and as areas in the right-hand tail decrease.

Degrees of freedom are simply explained as the product of $(R - 1)$ and $(C - 1)$. For Table 16.6, we have

$$(R - 1)(C - 1) = (2 - 1)(2 - 1),$$

or

1 degree of freedom

Equally simple, areas in the right-hand tail denote probabilities of the test rejecting H_0 when it is in fact correct. Such an occurrence, we recall, is called a **Type I error** and is possible only because data derive from a sample. Let us choose this probability as 0.05. Thus, our critical value of χ^2 is 3.841.

It is now a simple matter to take our calculated value for χ^2_{test} at 255 from step 3 and compare it to 3.841 as step 4. Because $\chi^2_{test} > \chi^2_{critical}$, we accept H_1. The population value for r_{phi} is not 0.

We note only one limitation to our test: crosstab table cells should contain expected frequencies of 5 or more. Occasionally this will mean taking larger samples or "collapsing" two or more categories of a variable into one. However, some statisticians relax the limitation to require only

---

[3]Many statistical texts would state the second conclusion as "reject H_0." We prefer to "accept H_1," a more common-sense approach used by John Neter, William Wasserman, and G. A. Whitmore, *Applied Statistics* (Boston: Allyn and Bacon, 1978).

TABLE 16.7
Deodorant Brand Use by Sex

SEX	*DEODORANT BRAND USE*				
	Brand A	*Brand B*	*Brand C*	*Brand D*	*Total*
Male	500	400	280	20	1,200
Female	10	90	200	500	800
Total	510	490	480	520	2,000

that a minimum of 80 percent of all cells contain expected frequencies of 5 or more and that no cell contain an expected frequency of less than 1.[4] To apply this relaxed requirement, tables must contain either more than 2 rows or more than 2 columns. Yet tables that contain more than 2 rows or 2 columns depart from our r_{phi} assumptions. Our next section discusses another measure of relationship between two nominal variables without the 2-by-2 assumption.

Goodman and Kruskal's **lambda**[5] applies to crosstab tables composed of two nominal variables that may have any number of categories. Lambda differs further from r_{phi} in that it is not a correlation method but one of several *proportionate reduction in error* (PRE) methods. PRE methods look at relationships not in terms of explaining variations between the two variables but "in terms of increasing our ability to predict one characteristic from knowledge of another."[6] That is, if a relationship exists, knowledge of one characteristic should help predict the presence or absence of another, for any and all sampling units in the study. If no relationship exists, knowledge of one characteristic should help not at all.

    To illustrate the calculation of lambda, let us broaden our sex and deodorant brand use example to include Brand C and Brand D. Suppose our data now appear as in Table 16.7 and a researcher wishes to examine the relationship between sex and deodorant brand use. Looking at the data, we intuitively feel that it would be easier to predict sex from knowledge of deodorant brand use than to predict deodorant brand use from knowledge of sex. For example, if we know that a consumer uses Brand A or B or D deodorant, we can predict sex with almost perfect accuracy. However, if we know for example that a consumer is male, we can predict brand use far less accurately. Thus, we have a hint of another difference between lambda and r_{phi} (when we apply both to the same table, of

GOODMAN AND KRUSKAL'S LAMBDA

---

[4]W. G. Cochran, "Some Methods for Strengthening the Common Chi-Square Tests," *Biometrics* 10 (1954): 417–51.

[5]Some statistics texts may refer to Guttman's lambda as an identical statistic.

[6]Johnson, *Social Statistics*, p. 94.

course): lambda will usually take on different values, depending on which variable predicts which other variable, while r_{phi} will always take on only one value.

Calculation of Lambda.   One form of lambda (there are two) may be calculated from the formula below

$$\text{lambda}_{asym} = \frac{\sum_{i=1}^{R} f_i - F_j}{n - F_j}$$

The designation lambda_{asym} stands for lambda *asymmetrical* in recognition of lambda's dependency on the choice of predictor and predicted variables. We shall see this explicitly in a bit. For our other symbols,

R = row variable number of categories
f_i = modal row frequency
F_j = modal column total or marginal frequency
n = sample size.

In words, the formula for lambda_{asym} says to sum each row's modal frequency, subtract from this the modal column marginal frequency, and divide the result by the difference between sample size and the modal column marginal frequency.

Let us apply the formula to data in Table 16.7. The modal frequency for the first row is 500, as it is for the second. Thus, we have

$$\sum_{i=1}^{R} f_i = 500 + 500 = 1,000$$

The modal column total or marginal frequency is 520, and n is 2,000. Thus, lambda_{asym} for predicting deodorant brand use from knowledge of sex is

$$\text{lambda}_{asym} = \frac{1,000 - 520}{2,000 - 520} = 0.324$$

To illustrate lambda's dependency on which variable predicts the other, let us rearrange Table 16.7 to predict sex from deodorant brand use. Table 16.7 now looks like this:

		SEX Male	SEX Female
DEODORANT BRAND USE	A	500	10
	B	400	90
	C	280	200
	D	20	500
Total		1,200	800

And we have

$$\sum_{i=1}^{R} f_i = 500 + 400 + 280 + 500 = 1,680$$

$$F_j = 1,200$$

Thus, lambda$_{asym}$ for predicting sex from knowledge of deodorant brand use is

$$\text{lambda}_{asym} = \frac{1,680 - 1,200}{2,000 - 1,200} = 0.600$$

Clearly, we see our earlier intuition of relative predictive power supported by the data.

Now, if we were interested purely in the association between sex and deodorant brand use without regard to which one predicts the other, another form of lambda is appropriate. We identify this form as lambda *symmetrical* and designate it as

$$\text{lambda}_{sym} = \frac{\sum_{i=1}^{R} f_i + \sum_{j=1}^{C} f_j - (F_i + F_j)}{2n - (F_i + F_j)}$$

In the formula,

f_i = modal row frequency
f_j = modal column frequency
F_i = modal row total or marginal frequency
F_j = modal column total or marginal frequency
n = sample size

Applying the formula to data in the original Table 16.7, we get

$$\sum_{i=1}^{R} f_i = 500 + 500 = 1,000$$

$$\sum_{j=1}^{C} f_j = 500 + 400 + 280 + 500 = 1,680$$

$$F_i = 1,200$$

$$F_j = 520$$

Thus, lambda$_{sym}$ becomes

$$\text{lambda}_{sym} = \frac{1,000 + 1,680 - (1,200 + 520)}{4,000 - (1,200 + 520)}$$

$$= 0.421$$

We can consider lambda$_{sym}$ to represent an average or mutual predictability between the two variables. Lambda$_{sym}$ is suitable for situations in which we can make no causal statements about the two variables.

Strength of Lambda.   Values for both forms of lambda range between 0.0 and 1.0. A value of 0.0 indicates no relationship between the two variables, while a value of 1.0 indicates a perfect relationship.

Moreover, because values for lambda indicate the proportionate reduction in prediction errors made, we may compare one value with another and make meaningful statements about relationship strength. For example, suppose we also calculate a lambda$_{sym}$ between marital status and deodorant brand use and that value turns out to be 0.100. We can quite properly divide 0.421 by 0.100 and state that the relationship between sex and deodorant brand use is about 4.2 times stronger than the relationship between marital status and deodorant brand use. Other PRE measures also produce ratio data.

Direction of Lambda.   Because both forms of lambda take on no negative values, they indicate no direction. This should seem reasonable because variables they describe possess no direction.

Significance of Lambda.   Both forms of lambda have a standard error, a sampling distribution, and, thus, a test for statistical significance.[7] However, the procedure goes beyond the scope of this book. Instead let us make a practical compromise and suggest the following approach:[8]

1. Conduct a χ^2 test between the two variables using the following hypotheses:

    H_0: Variable A and variable B are statistically independent

    H_1: Variable A and variable B are not statistically independent

    Apart from these hypotheses, the test proceeds exactly as for testing the significance of r_{phi}.

2. If H_1 is accepted, calculate either form of lambda and interpret it.

If lambda derives from a census instead of a sample, statistical significance of lambda is not at issue.

---

[7]Henry T. Reynolds, *The Analysis of Cross-Classifications* (New York: The Free Press, 1977), pp. 50–52.

[8]Some statisticians provide support. See Johnson, *Social Statistics*, pp. 237–38 and John H. Mueller, Karl F. Schuessler, and Herbert L. Costner, *Statistical Reasoning in Sociology*, 2nd ed. (Boston: Houghton Mifflin, 1970), p. 437.

Numerous other measures of relationship for nominal variables exist. We mention in passing: the contingency coefficient, Yule's Q, Cramér's V, Goodman and Kruskal's tau, Cohen's kappa, Kim's uncertainty coefficient, and Hildebrand's del. The first three generally perform less well than both r_{phi} and lambda and should be used sparingly. The last four generally equal or exceed the statistical performance of both r_{phi} and lambda but require discussion beyond our limited scope. See any of several beginning to advanced statistics texts.[9]

OTHER MEASURES

Relationships Between Two Ordinal Variables

Ordinally measured variables show measurement values that possess properties of equality and order. For example, consider a variable called "performance in a company training program" that describes newly hired sales engineers. That is, suppose all new sales engineers in a firm are ranked on their training program performance—on the basis of a battery of tests and on instructor-supplied comments. For the 20 students completing the program one term, we would expect to find a value from 1 to 20 next to each one's name.

Most of the values would be unique. If one student had a value of 2 and another a value of 4, we would know that the first student's performance was better. Moreover, we would know that the difference between these two students' performances is likely not equal to the difference between that for students who rank 16 and 18. A very few values might be identical, to indicate students whose performances cannot be distinguished from those of others. If this is the case for the two students who performed poorest in the class, each would receive a value of (19 + 20)/2, or 19.5.

Now, consider another ordinally measured variable obtained from a sample of 400 overweight consumers called "intention to buy." Suppose each read a two-paragraph concept statement about a new diet dessert and then responded to a purchase intention scale. Such a scale might have five categories in descending order of buying certainty, with category anchors being such phrases as "definitely buy, probably buy, might buy," and so on. Notice here that a large number of variable values will be identical, to indicate consumers with tied ranks. For example, 200 consumers might indicate they would definitely buy the product, so each would be denoted with a measurement value of 1.

---

[9] See Russell S. Winer and Michael J. Ryan, "Analyzing Cross-Classification Data: An Improved Method for Predicting Events," *Journal of Marketing Research* 16 (November 1979): 539–44 for a comparison of strengths and weaknesses of several PRE measures. See also Johnson's *Social Statistics*, Chaps. 6 and 7 for an excellent introduction. Mueller, Schuessler, and Costner, *Statistical Reasoning*, Chap. 9 as well as Reynolds, *Cross-Classifications*, Chap. 2, provide an indepth discussion.

As we shall see, each type of ordinally measured variable has a different set of rules with which to calculate relationships.

ORDINAL RELATIONSHIPS

Compared to nominal relationships, ordinal relationships are both more complex and more meaningful. This occurs because ordinal variables show measurement values with properties of equality and order instead of only equality. Thus, instead of stating that one category of one variable jointly occurs with one category of another, we can say with ordinal level measures of relationship that the two variables vary together in a particular *direction*. That is, ordinal level measures allow us to say that as one variable increases, the other variable increases—or that as one variable increases, the other decreases. In the first situation, we say the variables vary in a *positive direction*; in the second, we say they vary in a *negative direction*.

To illustrate, let us return to the performance of newly hired sales engineers in a company training program. Suppose the training director would like to examine the relationship between this performance and an evaluation by the sales manager of their job performance at the end of their first year. The training director would hope for a positive relationship to indicate the predictive validity of the program's performance rankings.

Or, let us return to the new diet dessert. Suppose a researcher would like to examine the relationship between consumers' intention to buy and their obesity. The second measurement might possess four response categories, ranging from "grossly overweight" to "slightly overweight." Here the researcher might hope for a negative relationship because more consumers are slightly overweight than grossly overweight.

Apart from the idea of direction, there exist two basic kinds of ordinal relationships. One is the relationship between *two sets of ranks* (as in our sales engineer example); the other is the relationship between *two ordinal variables* (as in our diet dessert example). This latter kind of relationship far more frequently interests marketing researchers than the first. For either, the researcher must organize crosstab tables carefully, arranging categories in consistent order.

We illustrate below the table form for relationships between two sets of ranks. As we can see, basic dimensionality of the table is *n* by *three*

Ranked Object	Method One Rank	Method Two Rank
B	1	2
A	2	3
D	3	1
E	4	5
C	5	4

where n represents the number of ranked objects or rows and *three* the number of columns. Entries in the first column identify objects in perfect rank order according to the first ranking method, as indicated by entries in the second column. Entries in the third column indicate the rank of these objects according to the second ranking method. Ranked objects in marketing research studies may be anything compatible with rank ordering, including people.

The table form for relationships between two ordinal variables appears below. Here dimensionality is *i* by *j* where *i* is the number of row ranks and *j* is the number of column ranks. Entries in each cell *ij* represent counts of sampling units that possess indicated measurement values

	Ordinal Variable B Values				
	1	2	3	4	5
Ordinal Variable *A* Values 1					
2					
3					
4					

on ordinal variables *A* and *B*. Ordinal variables in marketing research studies represent characteristics of either people, objects, or organizations.

Spearman's **rho** measures the relationship between two sets of ranks. Goodman and Kruskal's **gamma** measures the relationship between two ordinal variables. We examine each.

To illustrate the calculation of Spearman's rho, let us use the data in Table 16.8 (we return to our sales engineer example yet again). Inspecting the table, we note support for a positive relationship between the two sets of ranks. In general, those sales engineers who rank high at the end of the training school also rank high at the end of their first year on the job.

SPEARMAN'S RHO

To express this relationship in a single number requires the formula for Spearman's rho, as follows:

$$r_s = 1 - \frac{6 \sum_{i=1}^{n} D_i^2}{n(n^2 - 1)}$$

In the formula

r_s = rho

D_i = the difference between the two ranks assigned to sampling unit *i*

n = sample size

Let us examine the formula's last term more closely. To obtain the numer-

TABLE 16.8
Ranks of 20 Sales Engineers on Training School and Job Performance

Sales Engineer	Training School Rank	Job Performance Rank	Sales Engineer	Training School Rank	Job Performance Rank
Calvin	1	3	Edward	11	9
Susan	2	4	Charles	12	13
Richard	3	1	James	13	8
Kathy	4	7	Henry	14	11
Mary	5	2	David	15	19
Earle	6	12	Ruth	16	17
Jane	7	5	Theodore	17	14
Merick	8	10	Betty	18	20
Wayne	9	6	Alan	19	18
Thomas	10	15	Sheila	20	16

ator, we take each difference between ranks for each sampling unit, square it, sum these values, and multiply the total by 6. For the first six sales engineers in Table 16.8, we have

Sales Engineer (i)	Training School Rank	Job Performance Rank	D_i	D_i^2
Calvin	1	3	2	4
Susan	2	4	2	4
Richard	3	1	2	4
Kathy	4	7	3	9
Mary	5	2	3	9
Earle	6	12	6	36

Proceeding through Sheila and summing D_i^2 values, we find

$$\sum_{i=1}^{20} D_i^2 = 4 + 4 + 4 + \cdots + 16 = 194$$

Using this value, and 20 for n in the formula, we have

$$r_s = 1 - \frac{6(194)}{20(400 - 1)} = 0.85$$

Strength of Rho. Values for r_s range from -1.0 to $+1.0$. A value of -1.0 indicates a perfect negative relationship while a value of $+1.0$ indicates a perfect positive relationship. A value of 0 indicates no relationship. And because r_s is a correlation measure like r_{phi}, we may use the latter's descriptive phrases to describe the strength of r_s.

Moreover, when we square r_s, the resulting value is a PRE measure of relationship like lambda.[10] Thus, we may compare two values of $(r_s)^2$

[10]Mueller, Schuessler, and Costner, *Statistical Reasoning*, pp. 271–73.

and make meaningful statements about their relative strengths, like lambda and like $(r_{phi})^2$.

Direction of Rho.   Rho carries either a positive or negative sign indicating either a positive or negative relationship. A positive sign means that if a sampling unit's rank is high on the first ranking method, it will be high on the second. Also, a positive sign means that if a sampling unit's rank is low on the first ranking method, it will be low on the second. A negative sign means the opposite.

Significance of Rho.   Rho may be easily tested for statistical significance using the following four steps.

1. State the null and alternate hypotheses as

   H_0: The population value for $r_s = 0$

   H_1: The population value for $r_s \neq 0$

2. Choose a critical value of Z from Table 2 in the Appendix.

3. Calculate the value for the test statistic Z as

   $$Z_{test} = \frac{r_s - 0}{1/\sqrt{n - 1}}$$

4. Compare the value for the Z statistic with the chosen critical value of Z and state conclusions as below:

   If $-Z_{critical} \leq Z_{test} \leq +Z_{critical}$, accept H_0.

   Otherwise, accept H_1.

Like earlier tests, these steps apply only when data come from a sample. Let us use the hypotheses as stated, choose a critical value of Z that allows a Type I error probability of 0.01, and test r_s for data in Table 16.8 for significance. We have

$$Z_{test} = \frac{0.85 - 0}{1/\sqrt{20 - 1}} = 3.70$$

and

$$Z_{critical} = 2.58$$

Thus, we accept H_1; the population value for r_s does not equal 0.

We note only two limitations to our test. One, n should equal or exceed 10 ranked objects. And, two, data should contain few ties among ranks. If data contain many ties such as when a large number of sampling units respond to two ordinal variables, Goodman and Kruskal's gamma is more appropriate.

TABLE 16.9
Purchase Intentions by Obesity (n = 400)

		Purchase Intentions				
		1	2	3	4	5
Obesity	1	10	15	20	25	30
	2	15	15	20	25	25
	3	25	20	20	15	10
	4	40	30	25	10	5

GOODMAN AND KRUSKAL'S GAMMA

Goodman and Kruskal's gamma is a PRE measure expressing relationships between two ordinal variables. To illustrate its calculation, let us use Table 16.9 which summarizes responses of 400 overweight consumers to both a purchase intention scale and a self-report index of obesity. Suppose the purchase intention scale used five phrases as response categories in descending order of buying certainty. A scale value of 1 indicates the consumer would definitely buy the product while a value of 5 would indicate almost no chance of purchase. Suppose the obesity scale used four phrases describing degrees of obesity in descending order. From inspection of the data, we would guess that a somewhat negative relationship exists between degree of obesity and purchase intentions.

To express this relationship in a single number requires a formula for Goodman and Kruskal's gamma as below:

$$\text{gamma} = \frac{P - Q}{P + Q}$$

P and Q are simply (if somewhat laboriously) calculated as follows.

To obtain P, we start in the upper left-hand corner and multiply that frequency by the *sum of all frequencies below and to the right of it.* Thus, we have

$$10(15 + 20 + 25 + 25 + 20 + 20 + 15 + 10 + 30 + 25 + 10 + 5)$$
$$= 2,200$$

We then move to the next cell to the right in the first row and repeat the process; that is

$$15(20 + 25 + 25 + 20 + 15 + 10 + 25 + 10 + 5) = 2,325$$

We then move to the next cell to the right

$$20(25 + 25 + 15 + 10 + 10 + 5) = 1,800$$

And to the next

$$25(25 + 10 + 5) = 1,000$$

But we can move no further because the last cell in row 1 has no frequencies below and to its right. However, we can go to the first cell in row 2 and again work our way across. We have

$$15(20 + 20 + 15 + 10 + 30 + 25 + 10 + 5) = 2{,}025$$

then

$$15(20 + 15 + 10 + 25 + 10 + 5) = 1{,}275$$

and so on through the fourth cell in row 3. Summing all of these products, we get 14,725 as the value for P.

To obtain Q, we start in the upper right hand corner and multiply that frequency by the *sum of all frequencies below and to the left of it*. Thus, we have

$$30(25 + 20 + 15 + 15 + 15 + 20 + 20 + 25 + 10 + 25 + 30 + 40)$$
$$= 7{,}800$$

Moving to the next cell to the left and repeating:

$$25(20 + 15 + 15 + 20 + 20 + 25 + 25 + 30 + 40) = 5{,}250$$

We continue in this fashion through the second cell in row 3, sum all products, and call this value Q. Q for Table 16.9 is 30,125. (We may want to confirm these values for P and Q as a check on our understanding of the process.) It is now a simple matter to substitute values in our formula and calculate gamma. We have

$$\text{gamma} = \frac{14{,}725 - 30{,}125}{14{,}725 + 30{,}125} = -0.343$$

Strength of Gamma.   Values for gamma range from -1.0 to $+1.0$. A value of -1.0 indicates a perfect negative relationship while a value of $+1.0$ indicates a perfect positive relationship. A value of 0 indicates no relationship. Moreover, because values indicate the proportionate reduction in prediction errors, we may compare one value of gamma with another and make meaningful statements about their relative strengths.

Direction of Gamma.   Like rho, gamma carries either a positive or a negative sign, with signs having exactly the same meaning.

Significance of Gamma.   Like lambda, gamma has a standard error, a sampling distribution, and, thus, a test for statistical significance appropriate when data come from a sample. Also as with lambda, procedures to derive all of these lie beyond our scope. However, as Reynolds points out, most researchers when analyzing the relationship between two ordinal variables

> should, no doubt, be most concerned with the estimation [strength] and interpretation of the measures. Statistical significance is usually

of secondary interest, especially since many samples are so large that even trivial associations are significant.[11]

OTHER MEASURES   Numerous other measures of relationships between two ordinal variables exist, some with less desirable properties than rho and gamma, some with more.[12] In the former category, we mention Kendall's tau (also called tau_a.) In the latter, we mention Somers' d, Wilson's e, and Kendall's tau_b and tau_c. Space and computational complexity prevent our discussing these measures more than as follows.

We comment only about measures with more desirable properties. All these measures may substitute for either rho or gamma and will generally lead to similar conclusions. All frequently possess maximum and minimum values with a range less than from $+1.0$ to -1.0. Most appear automatically with the use of widely available computer packages. Most exist because of weaknesses in gamma. That is, gamma values tend to overstate the strength of relationships, to increase as the measurement process becomes cruder, and to ignore some relevant information.[13] Consequently, Somers' d substitutes for gamma when researchers consider one variable to have a causal influence on the other. Wilson's e and Kendall's tau_b and tau_c substitute for gamma when researchers make no such consideration.

Relationships Between Two Interval or Ratio Variables

Variables measured in either an interval or ratio manner show measurement values that possess properties of equality, order, and distance.[14] As examples, consider variables that describe ounces of peanut butter consumed per capita, size of a firm's sales force, the population of a county, and dollars a firm spends on advertising. Given measurement values on any one of these variables for any two sampling units, we may state whether the sampling units possess equal values, whether one sampling unit's value exceeds the others, and how far apart the two sampling units lie. Given measurement values on any two of these variables for a number of sampling units, we may state the strength, direction, and significance of the relationship.

---

[11]Reynolds, *Cross-Classifications*, p. 88. See also Robert S. Weiss, *Statistics in Social Research: An Introduction* (New York: John Wiley & Sons, 1968), pp. 269–74 for a lucid discussion on calculating standard errors for gamma and the various forms of tau.

[12]See Reynolds, *Cross-Classifications*, pp. 66–81 for a comparison of these measures to gamma.

[13]Reynolds, *Cross-Classifications*, pp. 74–75.

[14]Variables measured in a ratio manner also show measurement values expressed in equal units of distance from an absolute zero point.

The usual way of examining such relationships is through Pearson **product-moment correlation.** We shall use the symbol, r, to indicate a Pearson product-moment correlation coefficient. Many of us already have calculated values for r in an earlier statistics course; the opportunity presents itself again later in this chapter.

INTERVAL AND RATIO RELATIONSHIPS

Compared to ordinal relationships, interval and ratio relationships provide more information. Not only can we still interpret relationships as either positive or negative, but now we can state that a measured change in one variable relates to a measured change in the other. For example, knowledge of an interval or ratio relationship allows us to state that an increase to a firm's salesforce of two persons relates to an increase in sales revenue of $900,000. Or, that a decrease of 20 percent in the firm's advertising budget for a product relates to a 10 percent drop in consumer brand recall. Note the increased information. Ordinal measures of relationship would allow us to state only that a salesforce increase relates to a sales revenue increase. Or, that an advertising budget decrease relates to a brand recall decrease.

To introduce the measurement of interval and ratio relationships, let us consider a wholesaler of tobacco and candy products which presently serves a 20-county market. Suppose the wholesaler employs 10 salespersons, some of whom live near the center of their sales territory and some of whom live a distance away. Further suppose that a researcher is interested in the relationship between sales revenue per retail account and the account's location (measured in terms of its distance from the salesperson's home). For each salesperson, then, let us have the researcher select a random sample of retail accounts, calculate 1981 sales revenue obtained from each account (in terms of a deviation from an assigned quota), and estimate distance to each account from a map. Thus, the researcher measures sales revenue in an interval manner and distance in a ratio manner. Suppose data for the first salesperson appear as in Table 16.10. From a visual inspection, we would guess that the relationship between the two variables is negative. It appears that the more distant the account, the lower sales revenue is compared to quota. We can see this more clearly with the scatter diagram or scattergram in Figure 16.1.

A **scatter diagram** or **scattergram** provides a pictorial display of the joint distribution of measurement values obtained from sampling units on the two variables. For our data, each dot in Figure 16.1 represents a retail account. Each dot's position in relation to the X-axis and Y-axis indicates its measurement values for distance and sales revenue, respectively. Marketing researchers customarily locate measurement values of the independent or causal variable along the X-axis and measurement values of the dependent or caused variable along the Y-axis.

Dots in Figure 16.1 show the negative relationship more clearly than

TABLE 16.10
1981 Sales Revenue Quota Deviations and Distances to Salesperson's Home by Account

Account Identification Number	Distances (Miles)	1981 Sales Revenue Deviations from Quota ($000)
8	1.0	0.7
19	12.8	1.6
21	9.4	1.9
35	11.2	0.1
48	23.0	−0.8
72	19.4	−0.9
85	18.8	1.6
89	1.5	2.4
98	7.1	−0.2
109	2.5	3.0
130	16.5	0.5
142	24.1	−1.5
148	24.1	0.3
151	4.2	1.9
162	27.2	−1.7
163	6.1	1.5
177	13.1	−0.7
191	13.9	2.0
199	24.9	1.1
204	7.7	0.7

do the numbers in Table 16.10. Their pattern seems to slope downward to the right, indicating that as values for distance increase, those for sales revenue decrease. However, the relationship is far from perfect, as indicated by the dispersion of the dots. Only if all dots fell exactly in a straight line would we have a perfect relationship.

VALUES FOR *r*   Such visual inspection of the data aids our understanding of relationships between two interval or ratio variables. That is, we now know the relationship is negative and that it is not perfect. Further, a visual inspection also allows us to examine the data for some characteristics required as assumptions to calculate r.

Assumptions for r.   Calculations for r assume five basic properties about the data:

1. Data must represent variables the researcher has conceptualized as continuous.

2. Data must represent measurements made in an interval or ratio manner.

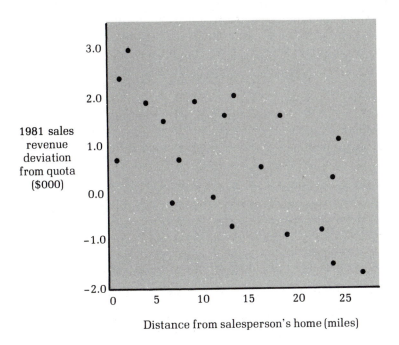

FIGURE 16.1
Scattergram for 1981 sales revenue deviations and distances from salesperson's home

3. The distribution of measurement values for each variable must be normal at all values for the two variables.

4. The joint distribution of measurement values for both variables must show a linear relationship.

5. The joint distribution of measurement values must show equal dispersion at all values for the two variables.

Our data seem to meet these assumptions fairly well. Yet researchers frequently calculate r for variables and measurements that violate these assumptions. With what consequences?

Violating the first assumption—calculating r for one or two discrete variables—artificially restricts the size of the correlation coefficient, as we said in Chapter 9. However, such restrictions average less than 10 percent as long as both variables contain at least six measurement levels.[15] This

[15]Warren S. Martin, "Effects of Scaling on the Correlation Coefficient: Additional Considerations," *Journal of Marketing Research* 15 (May 1978): 304–08.

finding also applies to calculating r for two continuous variables: their measurements should also contain at least six levels.

Violating the second assumption—calculating r for variables measured in an ordinal manner, may artificially inflate or deflate r.[16] However, such departures from the true value of r are usually very small.[17]

Violating the third or fourth or fifth assumptions again usually leads to either slight inflations or slight deflations of r. However, unless such violations are gross, the researcher may compensate for their occurrence by using higher levels of significance in testing hypotheses and more care in data interpretation.[18] We conclude that r is a quite robust statistic.

Calculating r. A formula to calculate r is

$$ r = \frac{n\Sigma XY - \Sigma X \Sigma Y}{\sqrt{n\Sigma X^2 - (\Sigma X)^2} \; \sqrt{n\Sigma Y^2 - (\Sigma Y)^2}} $$

where n = sample size

X = measurement values on one variable for the sampling units

Y = measurement values on the other variable for the sampling units

Let us apply the formula to the data in Table 16.10 to get what is shown in Table 16.11. Taking values from this table and inserting them into our formula, we have

$$ r = \frac{20(45.69) - (268.5)(13.5)}{\sqrt{20(4,969.03) - 72,092.25} \; \sqrt{20(43.01) - 182.25}} = \frac{-2,711}{4,301} $$

$$ = -0.63 $$

Strength of r. Values for r range from -1.0 to $+1.0$. A value of -1.0 indicates a perfect negative relationship while a value of $+1.0$ indicates a perfect positive relationship. A value of 0 indicates no relationship. Because r is a correlation measure, we may use our earlier phrases describing the strength of r_{phi} to describe that of r.

Moreover, the value of r^2 indicates the proportion of variance shared between the two variables. Thus, we may compare two values of r^2 and make meaningful statements about their strengths.

Direction of r. Like most earlier measures of relationship, r carries either a positive or a negative sign. Signs have exactly the same meanings as discussed earlier.

---

[16] George W. Bohrnstedt, "Reliability and Validity Assessment in Attitude Measurement," in *Attitude Measurement*, Gene F. Summers ed. (Chicago: Rand McNally, 1970), p. 82.

[17] Jum C. Nunnally, *Psychometric Theory*, 2nd ed. (New York: McGraw-Hill, 1978), pp. 28–29.

[18] Ibid., pp. 138–39.

TABLE 16.11
Values to Calculate r

Distance X	X^2	Sales Y	Y^2	XY
1.0	1.00	0.7	0.49	0.70
12.8	163.84	1.6	2.56	20.48
9.4	88.36	1.9	3.61	17.86
11.2	125.44	0.1	0.01	1.12
23.0	529.00	−0.8	0.64	−18.40
19.4	376.36	−0.9	0.81	−17.46
18.8	353.44	1.6	2.56	30.08
1.5	2.25	2.4	5.76	3.60
7.1	50.41	−0.2	0.04	−1.42
2.5	6.25	3.0	9.00	7.50
16.5	272.25	0.5	0.25	8.25
24.1	580.81	−1.5	2.25	−36.15
24.1	580.81	0.3	0.09	7.23
4.2	17.64	1.9	3.61	7.98
27.2	739.84	−1.7	2.89	−46.24
6.1	37.21	1.5	2.25	9.15
13.1	171.61	−0.7	0.49	−9.17
13.9	193.21	2.0	4.00	27.80
24.9	620.01	1.1	1.21	27.39
7.7	59.29	0.7	0.49	5.39
$\Sigma X = 268.5$	$\Sigma X^2 = 4{,}969.03$	$\Sigma Y = 13.5$	$\Sigma Y^2 = 43.01$	$\Sigma XY = 45.69$
$(\Sigma X)^2 = 72{,}092.25$		$(\Sigma Y)^2 = 182.25$		

Significance of r.   Values of r may be tested for statistical significance according to the following procedure:[19]

1. State the null and alternate hypotheses as

    H_0: The population value for $r = 0$
    H_1: The population value for $r \neq 0$

2. Choose a critical value of Z from Table 2 in the Appendix.

3. Calculate the value for the test statistic Z as

$$Z_{test} = \frac{1.1513 \log_{10} \frac{1 + r}{1 - r} - 0}{1/\sqrt{n - 3}}$$

[19]This test (and the shortcomings of other tests) is described more completely by J. P. Guilford, *Fundamental Statistics in Psychology and Education*, 4th ed. (New York: McGraw-Hill, 1965), pp. 161–64.

For convenience, values for the expression in the numerator have already been calculated in Table 6 in the Appendix.

4. Compare the value of the test statistic Z with the chosen critical value of Z and state conclusions as below:

If $-Z_{critical} \leq Z_{test} \leq +Z_{critical}$, accept H_0.

Otherwise, accept H_1.

Applying this procedure for the r between distance and sales revenue, we have

$$Z_{test} = \frac{1.1513 \log_{10} \dfrac{0.37}{1.63} - 0}{1/\sqrt{17}} = \frac{-0.741}{0.243}$$

$$= -3.06$$

Assuming we had chosen a critical value of Z at 2.58, we would accept H_1; the population value for r does not equal 0.

This test applies to all values of r calculated for data from all sample sizes. It does not apply to census data.

Additional Comments on Relationships

At this point, we might well feel that we have discussed methods of expressing relationships that apply to every possible research situation. Unfortunately, such is not the case. In this short section, we will identify several situations to which our present methods apply only partly or not at all. To work with many of the methods that do apply here, most of us will need to refer to one or more of the statistics texts listed at the end of this chapter.

OTHER TWO-VARIABLE RELATIONSHIPS Consider a situation in which we measure one variable in a nominal manner and the other in a ratio manner. To be more concrete, suppose the nominal variable is advertising exposure (the respondent has seen ad or not seen ad) and the ratio variable is product consumption rate. How do we express the relationship?

Actually, our last discussed method, Pearson product-moment correlation, works quite well here (as it would if the second variable were instead measured in an interval manner). That is, we would merely score advertising exposure in a 0,1 fashion and use these values plus those for product consumption to compute r. Alternatively, we could calculate another special form of r as the **point-biserial correlation coefficient,** r_{pb}. Both methods lead to measures of relationship having identical strength

TABLE 16.12
Data Arrangement Permitting the Calculation of Lambda

	Income		
Advertising Source Exposure	Low	Medium	High
Radio			
Television			
Newspaper			
Magazine			
Outdoor			

and direction values. However, their tests of statistical significance may differ.[20]

The use of only 0 or 1 to indicate only the presence or absence of a nominally measured characteristic violates none of our assumptions for r. However, if we change the example to use 0, 1, 2, 3, and 4 to now indicate five categories of advertising *source* exposure (radio, television, newspaper, magazine, and outdoor), then we violate our assumptions. That is, calculations for r assume that measurement values for both variables come from a process using measurement scale points showing both direction and equal units of distance. When one or both variables possess measurement values that seriously violate this assumption, r should not be used.[21]

Yet researchers often need to express a relationship between a nominal variable measured in more than two categories and an ordinal, interval, or ratio variable—sufficiently often, in fact, that we state the following as a general procedure:

> Researchers may properly apply a method appropriate in expressing the relationship between two variables measured at any lower level to two variables measured at any higher level, given the proper arrangement of data.

Thus, we may properly calculate lambda for the relationship between advertising source exposure and income, if we arrange data as in Table 16.12. Or, as another example, we could calculate lambda and gamma for the relationship between purchase intention and income if we arrange data as in Table 16.13.

---

[20]See Guilford, *Fundamental Statistics*, p. 322–25 for a discussion of r_{pb}, including its tests of significance.

[21]See Nunnally, *Psychometric Theory*, pp. 28–29 for ideas on what constitutes serious violations.

TABLE 16.13
Data Arrangement Permitting the Calculation of Lambda and Gamma

Purchase Intention	Income		
	Low	Medium	High
Low			
Medium			
High			

Entries in each cell in each table would consist of counts of sampling units that possess the indicated characteristics. Notice that to obtain these entries we merely reduce income measurements from a higher to a lower level. All such reductions lose information. To see this, consider that sampling units located in the same income column now show the income measurement value, even though they originally showed different values.

Notice also that our general procedure allows us to calculate lambda and gamma instead of r to express relationships between two interval or ratio variables. Yet this practice provides less information about the relationship, as explained earlier in the chapter. Consequently, we need a modifier to our general procedure as:

Researchers should always express relationships using the highest level of expression consistent with measurements of both variables.

Now, consider another situation where a scatter diagram shows a curvilinear relationship as in Figure 16.2. Here the use of r will understate the true relationship. However, the understatement will be small if the degree of curvilinearity is slight, as in Figure 16.2A. In contrast, the understatement will be extreme in Figure 16.2B. Thus, whenever the degree of curvilinearity is pronounced, the researcher should express the relationship not by r but by a new measure called **eta, the correlation ratio.**[22]

THREE OR MORE VARIABLE RELATIONSHIPS

As if things were not complicated enough, researchers quite often face a situation for which they wish to express a relationship between three or more variables. Such situations largely reduce to one of two types: examining the relationship between two variables while holding the effect of one or more other variables constant, and examining the simultaneous relationship between three or more variables. Situations of the second type probably occur more frequently in marketing research than do situ-

---

[22]Guilford, *Fundamental Statistics*, pp. 308–17 provides a lucid discussion of eta.

ations of the first. Relationships of both types are commonly called **multivariate relationships** to distinguish them from **bivariate** or two-variable relationships.

Multivariate Partial Relationships.   As we began this chapter we actually discussed multivariate partial relationships for two variables displayed in a crosstab table by the addition of a third or control variable.

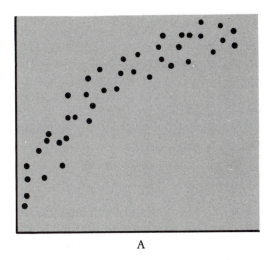

A

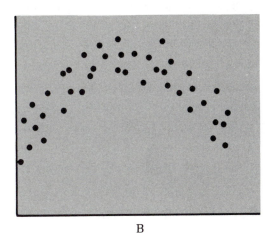

B

FIGURE 16.2
Scattergrams for two curvilinear relationships: A and B

We said that the addition of one or more control variables helps research-ers understand such relationships more completely. We also said that the addition of the first control variable creates a number of new tables equal to its number of measurement levels, identified here by m. The addition of a second control variable with l measurement levels creates m times l new tables. And so on, for as many control variables thought prudent on the basis of sound theory.

One way of expressing the partial relationship between two variables would be to compute the average relationship obtaining in these new tables.[23] For example, suppose we calculate a value for lambda at 0.60 for the zero-order relationship between sex and deodorant brand choice. When we control for the effects of income, measured at six levels, we cal-culate the six values of lambda as 0.40, 0.46, 0.56, 0.54, 0.62, and 0.50. Thus, our estimate of the partial relationship between sex and deodorant brand choice, controlling for income, is the average of these values, or 0.51.

A similar logic extends to interval and ratio measures of relationship, despite what appear to be calculation differences. The measure of partial relationship here is called a **partial correlation coefficient** and we denote and calculate it by:

$$r_{12.3} = \frac{r_{12} - r_{13}r_{23}}{\sqrt{1 - r_{13}^2}\ \sqrt{1 - r_{23}^2}}$$

Subscripts attached to r identify variables in the relationship. The formula applies to calculating a *first-order* partial correlation coefficient, where we control for only one variable, which is identified to the right of the dot. For example, if variable 1 were distance from a salesperson's home to a retail account and variable 2 were 1981 sales revenue for the account, we might have variable 3 as the number of competing brands carried by each account. Suppose zero-order relationships among the three variables look like this:

$$r_{12} = -0.60 \qquad r_{13} = 0.15 \qquad r_{23} = -0.40$$

We have for the first-order partial correlation coefficient:

$$r_{12.3} = \frac{-0.60 - (0.15)(-0.40)}{\sqrt{1 - (0.15)^2}\ \sqrt{1 - (0.4)^2}}$$

$$= -0.73$$

Thus, the relationship between distance and sales revenue increases when we control for the number of competing brands carried by each account. Our original relationship seems not to be spurious.

---

[23]Reynolds, *Cross-Classifications*, p. 102. Reynolds also notes here the calculation of partial lambdas and the possibility of treating ordinal measures of relationship analogously to interval and ratio measures by calculating partial taus and gammas.

Researchers may also calculate second-, third-, and higher-order partial correlation coefficients by holding two, three, and more variables constant. They seldom go beyond second-order partials, however. All partial correlation coefficients range between -1.0 and $+1.0$ with the usual interpretations. All may be tested for statistical significance.[24]

Simultaneous Multivariate Relationships. In contrast to partial relationships, researchers also express relationships between three or more variables with all variables allowed to vary at the same time. Often these situations accompany marketing predicting problems where researchers attempt to predict measurements on one variable from measurements on two or several others.[25] Often predictive power is taken to be the squared value of the coefficient of multiple correlation, R. We defer further comments on R until Chapter 17 where we discuss predictions at length.

Chapter Summary

We have seen that numerous rules exist that allow researchers to express relationships between two or more variables. Which rules researchers apply depends always on how they conceptualized their variables and occasionally on what causal assumptions they were willing to make about them. Once researchers express a relationship, they interpret it, usually in terms of relationship strength, direction, and significance.

We said that researchers study relationships to understand marketing phenomena more completely and to make better decisions. After studying relationships, we find ourselves in a better position to understand this statement. Consider two variables called income and product consumption rate and a researcher interested in how well they "go together." Suppose that if the relationship is strong, positive, and significant, decisions to select retailers become easier. However, to obtain data, the researcher divides a random sample of consumers into two different income groups and computes average consumption rates for each (a procedure not discussed in this chapter).

The researcher then might conduct a test of statistical significance on the difference between the two means. Suppose the test shows that higher

---

[24]Guilford, *Fundamental Statistics*, p. 341 presents formulas for calculating higher-order partials and a test for their statistical significance.

[25]Another instance occurs when researchers attempt to understand variation shared between several independent variables and several dependent variables, all of which are allowed to vary at the same time. Such correlation analysis between sets of variables is called canonical correlation analysis. An introduction and selected references may be found in *Multivariate Analysis in Marketing*, 2nd ed., ed. David A. Aaker (Palo Alto, Calif.: The Scientific Press, 1981), Chap. 24.

income consumers use 8.4 ounces more of the product than lower income consumers. Yet differences of 8.4 ounces or 20 ounces or whatever ounces between 2, 6, or n groups of consumers only partly describe the relationship. What is lacking is a more interpretable measure of relationship strength. Thus, a calculation and interpretation of r would be far more meaningful because it possesses an upper and a lower bound against which its strength may be seen. Moreover, the value of r^2 would describe the proportion of variance shared between the two variables as another measure of relationship strength.

Now, in defense of examining differences between groups, we must recognize this also aids the interpretation of r (and of other measures of relationship). And, we shall see in Chapter 18 that a researcher's interest may focus primarily on groups and their differences with respect to measurement values for a variable. However, our point here is that relationships between variables can best be understood by analysis procedures that possess that primary objective.

In studying the significance of several relationships, we used a test statistic, Z_{test}, to examine whether or not an observed sample relationship equaled 0. We should recognize that often another test procedure may be applied, still using Z_{test} but examining instead whether an observed sample relationship is greater or less than 0. Often researchers state their null and alternate hypotheses in the form of such inequalities and proceed with this more powerful, one-tail test. We discuss such tests in Chapter 17 as they apply to means and medians but the process remains identical for tests of relationships here: compared to a two-tail test, the value of $Z_{critical}$ for a one-tail test moves closer to zero. This allows us to reject H_0 when values of Z_{test} lie closer to zero—hence, the description of a more powerful test.

One final point: researchers almost invariably calculate measures of relationships with the aid of a computer. This does not mean we can dismiss formulas and their discussion in this chapter as outdated. Rather, we must know what the several measures of relationships are, when to use which one, and how to interpret each. Only then can we tell the computer what to do and only then can we attach meaning to what it tells us.

Chapter Review

KEY TERMS		
	Relationship	Relationship strength
	Spurious relationship	Relationship direction
	First-order relationship	Relationship significance
	Suppressor variable	χ^2 statistic
	Phi correlation coefficient	Scattergram
	Goodman and Kruskal's lambda	r

Spearman's rho   **Multivariate relationship**
Goodman and Kruskal's gamma   Partial r

1. Explain the difference between a causal and a noncausal relationship. Give an example of each.

2. What would happen if a researcher arranged a crosstab table as below, instead of in the more conventional manner, and calculated r_{phi}?

	+	−
−	a	b
+	c	d

3. A researcher is interested in the relationship between residence location (measured by five zip codes) and patronage of a shopping center during July (measured 0,1) for 600 Chicago residents.

   a) Lay out the crosstab table, showing title and headings.

   b) What measure(s) of relationship would you use?

   c) Identify a control variable that would be likely to increase the measure of relationship.

4. Instead of calculating r_{phi}, why not just calculate χ^2_{test} as a measure of relationship?

5. A researcher is interested in the relationship between income and consumption rate of milk for consumers between age 18 and 50. Describe how r_{phi} and lambda could be used. Which of the two would likely be a better measure of relationship here?

6. What information does r provide that r_s does not?

7. Two judges evaluating floor exercise routines for twenty gymnasts showed a value for r_s of 0.78. What does this mean?

8. What does a value for gamma of 0.78 mean for the relationship between two ordinal variables?

9. What does a value for r of −0.78 mean for the relationship between two interval variables?

10. Why would it be improper to test the statistical significance of an r obtained from a census of salespeople?

11. What method of expressing relationships would you use to investigate the relationship between the following variables:

    a) family size and savings account balance?

    b) sex and magazine readership for eight different magazines?

    c) tea consumption and national origin?

    d) EPA gas mileage estimates and those obtained by twenty test drivers?

    e) sex and number of impulse purchases per shopping visit to a supermarket?

PROBLEMS   1.   Enter values as indicated below for a χ^2 test of the significance of r_{phi}.

R	C	α	χ^2
3	4	0.05	____
3	4	0.01	____
10	2	0.01	____
2	2	____	3.841
10	3	____	34.805
3	____	0.01	16.812
____	____	____	44.314

2.   A 2-by-3 crosstab table when controlling for two variables having 3 and 4 categories, respectively, produces how many tables? How many cells? How large a sample do you recommend, assuming we expect a weak relationship?

3.   Convert percentages in Table 16.4 to frequencies.

   a) Calculate r_{phi} for both income groups.

   b) Calculate lambda$_{sym}$ for both income groups.

   c) Interpret your results.

4.   Using data in Table 16.5, construct crosstab tables to:

   a) Examine the relationship between income and deodorant brand choice.

   b) Examine the same relationship, this time controlling for sex.

   c) Interpret both tables.

5.   Consider the following sets of ranks for two wine experts tasting six brands of chablis. How well do they agree on their evaluations?

			Brand			
Expert	A	B	C	D	E	F
1	1	2	3	4	5	6
2	2	1	4	5	3	6

6.   **a)** Compute r between variables A and B below.

Individual	Variable A Value	Variable B Value
1	2	1
2	4	5
3	6	8

   b) Add 10 to each of the variable A values and 20 to each of the variable B values and compute r again. What do your results tell you about the sensitivity of r to location of an absolute zero point for measurement values?

7.   A researcher measures stage in the family life cycle on an eight-point scale using anchors as: young singles, young marrieds, young marrieds without children, young marrieds with children, older marrieds with children, older marrieds, retireds, and solitary survivors. She also measures soft drink con-

sumption on a four-point scale using anchors as: nonuser, light user, moderate user, and heavy user. Results appear below for a sample of 12 consumers.

Individual	1	2	3	4	5	6	7	8	9	10	11	12
Stage in Family Life Cycle	1	2	4	3	5	2	3	1	1	4	3	6
Soft Drink Consumption	4	4	2	3	2	3	2	3	3	3	3	1

Describe the relationship between stage in the family life cycle and soft drink consumption.

8. Suppose that r between income and Brand X beer consumption is -0.1, and that r between income and occupational status is 0.6, and r between Brand X beer consumption and occupational status equals -0.7.

   a) What is the relationship between income and Brand X beer consumption—controlling for the effects of occupational status?

   b) Given these data, what term would you apply to the variable "occupational status"?

9. a) Interchange the first two data columns in Table 16.7 and comment on lambda$_{sym}$'s sensitivity to order.

   b) Interchange the first two columns of purchase intentions in Table 16.9 and comment on gamma's sensitivity to order.

   c) Are your findings consistent with your understanding of the two methods? Explain.

Additional Readings

Guilford, J. P. *Fundamental Statistics in Psychology and Education.* 4th ed. New York: McGraw-Hill, 1965.

> *This book provides a complete and readable discussion of all measures of correlation, including r_{phi}, r_s, r_{pb}, r, partial r, and R. See Chapters 6, 14, 15, and 16.*

Mueller, John H.; Schuessler, Karl F.; and Costner, Herbert L. *Statistical Reasoning in Sociology.* 3rd ed. Boston: Houghton Mifflin, 1977.

> *Most social science statistical texts explain relationships better than do most business statistics texts. This one explains them the best. However, it largely avoids tests of statistical significance. See Chapters 8, 9, 10, 14, and 15.*

Reynolds, Henry T. *The Analysis of Cross-Classifications.* New York: The Free Press, 1977.

> *The first four chapters of this book provide an advanced yet readable discussion of most measures of relationship for nominal and ordinal variables. Discussions explain each measure's calculations, statistical tests, and relative strengths and weaknesses.*

Estimates, Predictions, and Forecasts

Our fifth purpose in analyzing data is to make estimates, predictions, and forecasts of typical measurement values for variables. To introduce our topic matter, consider these examples:

1. A researcher would like to estimate the average amount of hair spray used monthly by female consumers between the ages of 13 and 40.

2. A product manager wants to predict the average life of a running shoe in hours, depending on grams of rubber used in a section of the sole.

3. A sales manager for a fertilizer manufacturer would like to forecast sales for each quarter of the next five years.

More explicitly, we shall use **estimates** in this chapter to refer to an expected typical value for a variable based on other values for that variable, as in example 1. **Predictions** will express expected typical values for a variable as derived from values of another or several other variables, as in example 2. **Forecasts** will describe expected typical values for sales data, as in example 3. Knowledge of estimates, predictions, and forecasts—like knowledge of relationships—leads to increased understanding

461

of marketing phenomena and to more effective marketing decisions. Let us see how.

Estimates

Researchers estimate typical measurement values for a variable in two related forms called point estimates and interval estimates. A **point estimate** consists of a single variable value while an **interval estimate** consists of a range of variable values. Five chapters ago, we calculated point and interval estimates for both a population mean and proportion. We shall very briefly review that process here and extend our discussion to medians and modes.

If the variable under analysis has been measured in a nominal or an ordinal fashion, usually researchers calculate only a point estimate.[1] On the other hand, if the variable has been measured in an interval or a ratio fashion, usually researchers calculate both a point and an interval estimate. Variable conceptualization, as either continuous or discrete, technically influences their choice between a point and an interval estimate very little, although researchers calculate interval estimates more often for continuous variables.

Researchers often test point estimates for statistically significant differences from theoretically or historically meaningful values. As with significance tests for measures of relationship, such tests apply only to point estimates calculated from sample data.

NOMINAL AND ORDINAL VARIABLES Quite simply, a point estimate of the typical measurement value for a nominal variable is its modal value. Thus, if we find in a random sample of fifty female consumers of hair spray that twenty-five currently use Brand X, twenty currently use Brand Y, and five currently use Brand Z, our point estimate for the typical value of the variable "hair spray currently used" is Brand X. We would expect more women in the population to use Brand X than any other brand.

Equally simple, a point estimate of the typical measurement value for an ordinal variable may be either its modal or its median value. For an illustration, see Table 17.1, describing data for an ordinal variable, "intention to buy Brand M hair spray," obtained from our sample of 50 women. Our point estimate of the variable's typical value based on the mode is "maybe will buy." However, because we consider measurements to possess ordinal properties, we may assign the numbers 1 through 6 to responses, beginning with the bottom (most negative) response. Now we may take a point estimate based on the median—the number 4.

---

[1] See Wilfred J. Dixon and Frank J. Massey, Jr., *Introduction to Statistical Analysis*, 3rd ed. (New York: McGraw-Hill, 1969), p. 349 for a simple but seldom used procedure to calculate a confidence interval for a population median using sample data.

TABLE 17.1
Intention to Buy Brand M Hair Spray

Response	Frequency	Response Score
Definitely will buy	6	6
Probably will buy	8	5
Maybe will buy	18	4
Maybe will not buy	9	3
Probably will not buy	8	2
Definitely will not buy	1	1

Again equally simple, a point estimate of the typical measurement value for an interval or a ratio variable may be its mode, median, or mean value. As we noted in Chapter 15, means allow the application of more statistical techniques than do medians, which in turn allow the application of more techniques than do modes. Means provide more information but exhibit sensitivity to extreme data values.

INTERVAL AND RATIO VARIABLES

However, usually researchers express the typical measurement value for an interval or ratio variable by an interval estimate. The term, we recall from Chapter 12, is a confidence interval. It takes the form below, assuming that a simple random sample of size greater than 30 is taken in a large population and produces values for $\overline{X}$ and $s_{\overline{x}}$:

$$\overline{X} - Zs_{\overline{x}} \le \mu \le \overline{X} + Zs_{\overline{x}}$$

The value for Z is chosen from Table 2 in the Appendix and corresponds to a value of α such that the inequality holds true $(1-\alpha)100$ percent of the time.

When measurements come from a sample, researchers often test a median or a mean for a statistically significant difference from some specific, meaningful value.[2] We should recall doing so for measures of relationship in the last chapter—the general procedure, again, is called hypothesis testing. When applied to medians and means, hypothesis testing relates closely to calculating confidence intervals but with one important difference. Both confidence intervals and hypothesis tests help to make clear the effects of random selection on values for the sample median or mean. However, confidence intervals estimate the effects of random selection on

HYPOTHESIS TESTS FOR MEDIANS AND MEANS

---

[2]Throughout our discussion here, we save space by continuing to consider proportions as special cases of the mean. Thus, any statements we make about sample and population means apply in general to sample and population proportions. We can find specific details of hypotheses tests for a sample proportion in any introductory statistics text. A particularly good one is John Neter, William Wasserman, and G. A. Whitmore, *Applied Statistics* (Boston: Allyn and Bacon, 1978). See also footnote 5 that follows.

the precision or range of values for the median or mean with a chosen level of confidence. In contrast, hypothesis tests examine the potential falsity of a statement about a specific value for the median or mean, again at a chosen level of confidence. Such statements are called **hypotheses.**

For example, hypotheses for data in Table 17.1 might be (using μ_{md} to denote the median intention-to-buy value in the population)

$H_0: \mu_{md} \geq 3$

$H_1: \mu_{md} < 3$

We call the first hypothesis the null hypothesis and the second the alternate or substantive hypothesis. Instead of as above, we could have stated null and alternate hypotheses as

$H_1: \mu_{md} \leq 5$ or $H_0: \mu_{md} = 2$

$H_2: \mu_{md} > 5$ $H_1: \mu_{md} \neq 2$

or in any meaningful fashion. That is, hypotheses can either use inequalities or use equalities and values of 3, 5, 2, or any other number; the choice depends on their relevancy to the research problem. Thus, form of any hypothesis partly depends on critical values of the problem's performance parameters (as discussed in Chapter 3). Additionally, form of any hypothesis partly depends on the measurement process: an H_0 that $\mu_{md} = 18$ would be meaningless given the measurement process underlying data in Table 17.1. Of slightly more meaning, but with still less than that attending any of our three sets of hypotheses above, would be an H_0 that $\mu = 4$. (An hypothesis involving the mean should be based on interval or ratio data.)

Researchers specifically test the null hypothesis to see if sample data indicate it false. If this occurs, researchers say that sample data "reject" or "do not support" the null hypothesis. Researchers do not say that sample data "prove the alternate hypothesis true" because they did not test H_1. Rather, thay say that data "accept" the alternate hypothesis. If sample data do not indicate the null hypothesis to be false, researchers say that data "accept" the null hypothesis.

To make such statements requires a test of the null hypothesis using sample data. *The test assumes the null hypothesis is true.* That is, the test requires this assumption as it examines the behavior of a sample statistic relative to how the statistic should behave according to statistical theory. If the sample statistic behaves unusually with respect to the theory, researchers reject not the theory but their assumption that the null is true. If the sample statistic behaves as expected, researchers accept the null.

Given this central position of null hypotheses, let us review how they may be stated for medians and means and the nature of their statistical tests. Figure 17.1 summarizes the possibilities. We use the symbol PE to denote either a median or a mean point estimate, c to indicate a meaningful constant value, $(1 - \alpha)$ the confidence coefficient, and Z the value for the standard normal variable from Table 2 in the Appendix.

Hypothesis Form	Type of Test	Critical Region (Shaded)

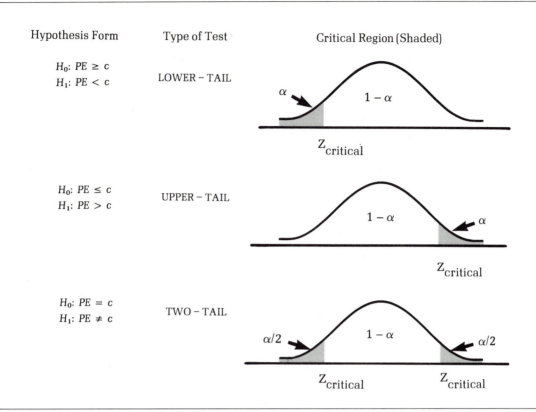

FIGURE 17.1
Hypothesis form, type of test, and critical regions for the mean and median

As we see, null hypotheses may state that a median or mean is more than some constant, less than some constant, or equal to some constant. Corresponding tests are lower-, upper-, and two-tail tests, respectively. If the value of the calculated test statistic, Z_{test}, lies in any shaded area or critical region, we reject H_0. Review an introductory statistics text if these comments seem unclear.[3]

Secure in this knowledge, let us examine statistical tests for specific values of the median and mean.[4] Because these tests apply to data that represent a single variable whose measurement values distribute in one population, they are sometimes called *univariate tests*.

Hypothesis Tests for the Median. Consider a ski manufacturer who places a pair of experimental skis with each of twenty-five testers randomly selected across the country. After two weeks of use, a researcher

---

[3]See Neter, Wasserman, and Whitmore, *Applied Statistics*, Chap. 11 to 13.

[4]There are no common statistical tests for the mode.

collects data via telephone on their experience with the ski, including their overall performance evaluation measured on a scale of 1 to 20. The researcher decides to treat the data as ordinal measurements, skeptical that diverse testers measure overall performance along equal interval scale points. Earlier tests on similar skis had shown that the median overall performance rating should exceed 13 for the public to accept the ski.

To proceed, let us formally describe our test in four steps.

1. State null and alternate hypotheses using one of the three forms in Figure 17.1, consistent with the marketing problem.

2. Choose a critical value of Z from Table 2 in the Appendix.

3. Calculate the value for the test statistic as

$$Z_{test} = \frac{T - n(n+1)/4}{\sqrt{n(n+1)(2n+1)/24}}$$

4. Compare the value of Z_{test} with that for $Z_{critical}$ to see if the former locates in the critical region for the test. State conclusions as

   If Z_{test} lies in the critical region, accept H_1.

   Otherwise, accept H_0.

To apply the test, we need definitions for T and n in the formula, and data. The latter appear in Table 17.2 and definitions follow.

To obtain T begins by our subtracting μ_{md} from each measurement value as in column 3 of Table 17.2. We then rank the absolute value of each nonzero difference in column 4. The number of nonzero differences equals n, a number less than or equal to the sample size. Any tied absolute nonzero differences receive tied ranks—that is the average of ranks they would have received had their differences differed slightly. For example, testers 4, 5, 6, 10, 11, 13, and 21 tied for the lowest seven ranks with absolute differences of 1; they each receive the rank of $(1 + 2 + 3 + 4 + 5 + 6 + 7)/7$, or 4. We then return the sign of the original difference appearing in column 3 to each rank, calling these values signed ranks in column 5. We then sum the positive signed ranks and call this total T.

Proceeding, we state hypotheses as

H_0: $\mu_{md} \leq 13$ (upper-tail test)

H_1: $\mu_{md} > 13$

We select α at 0.05, making $Z_{critical} = 1.65$, and calculate Z_{test}:

$$Z_{test} = \frac{123.5 - (23)(24)/4}{\sqrt{(23)(24)(47)/24}} = -0.44$$

Because the value of Z_{test} did not locate in the critical region, we accept H_0.

TABLE 17.2
Signed Rank Test for Median Performance Ratings by 25 Ski Testers

Tester (i)	Performance Rating (X_i)	$X_i - \mu_{md}$	Rank $\lvert X_i - \mu_{md}\rvert$	Signed Rank −	Signed Rank +
1	19	6	20.5		20.5
2	11	−2	10.0	−10.0	
3	6	−7	22.5	−22.5	
4	14	1	4.0		4.0
5	14	1	4.0		4.0
6	12	−1	4.0	−4.0	
7	15	2	10.0		10.0
8	16	3	14.0		14.0
9	7	−6	20.5	−20.5	
10	14	1	4.0		4.0
11	14	1	4.0		4.0
12	15	2	10.0		10.0
13	12	−1	4.0	−4.0	
14	8	−5	18.5	−18.5	
15	11	−2	10.0	−10.0	
16	13	0	—	—	—
17	20	7	22.5		22.5
18	8	−5	18.5	−18.5	
19	9	−4	16.5	−16.5	
20	11	−2	10.0	−10.0	
21	12	−1	4.0	−4.0	
22	13	0	—	—	—
23	17	4	16.5		16.5
24	16	3	14.0		14.0
25	10	−3	14.0	−14.0	
				T (Total) = 123.5	

Such a test is called a Wilcoxon **signed-rank test.** It assumes that n exceeds 25, although results usually are not seriously distorted as long as n exceeds 10. It also assumes that a continuous variable, X_i, produces differences $X_i - \mu_{md}$, which distribute symmetrically about some typical value.

Hypothesis Tests for the Mean.   Hypothesis tests for the mean proceed similarly to that for the median but use a different test statistic:

1. State null and alternate hypotheses using one of the three forms in Figure 17.1, consistent with the marketing problem.

2. Choose a critical value of Z from Table 2 in the Appendix.

3. Calculate the value for the test statistic as[5]

$$Z_{test} = \frac{\overline{X} - \mu}{s_{\overline{X}}}$$

4. Compare the value of Z_{test} with that for $Z_{critical}$ to see if the former locates in the critical region for the test. State conclusions as:

> If Z_{test} lies in the critical region, accept H_1.

> Otherwise, accept H_0.

Let us apply these steps to overall ski performance data in Table 17.2.

That is, suppose another researcher were willing to accept performance ratings as interval data and wished to test whether the mean performance rating exceeds 13. We state our null and alternate hypotheses as

$$H_0: \mu \leq 13 \quad \text{(upper-tail test)}$$

$$H_1: \mu > 13$$

We choose a critical value of Z as 1.65 as before and calculate

$$\overline{X} = \sum_{i=1}^{n} \frac{X_i}{n} = 12.7$$

$$s = \sum_{i=1}^{n} \frac{(X_i - \overline{X})^2}{n - 1} = 3.56$$

$$s_{\overline{X}} = \frac{s}{\sqrt{n}} = 0.711$$

Thus, we have

$$Z_{test} = \frac{12.7 - 13.0}{0.711} = -0.42$$

and we accept H_0 as before.

SUMMARY OF ESTIMATES   Hypothesis testing permeates data analysis. We applied it earlier to measures of relationship and now to estimates of typical measurement values. We shall soon do it again for predictions, for differences between groups in Chapter 18, and to infer causality in Chapter 19. A most versatile procedure indeed.

---

[5]If hypotheses apply to a population proportion, π, use $Z_{test} = \frac{\overline{p} - \pi}{s_{\overline{p}}}$.

Yet we must recognize that hypothesis testing turns relatively continuous phenomena into strictly dichotomous situations: all potential samples for the test allow Z_{test} to locate any distance from the value of $Z_{critical}$, yet any one sample leads only to acceptance or rejection of the null hypothesis. Thus, we accept H_0 in a lower-tail test when Z_{test} equals -1.62 as surely as when Z_{test} equals 15.7 (assuming $Z_{critical}$ equals -1.65). Researchers recognize this characteristic of hypothesis testing and, consequently, usually report test conclusions along with α values or levels of significance that each test actually achieved. Finally, we note that researchers prefer to state hypotheses with inequalities and use either an upper- or lower-tail test. Such practice makes a more powerful test, reducing levels of significance to half compared to a two-tail test.

Predictions

Predictions express expected typical values for a variable based on values of one or several other variables. Predictions may be made for and from nominal, ordinal, interval, and ratio variables, conceptualized as either continuous or discrete. However, we restrict our discussion here to the prediction of values for one interval or ratio variable conceptualized as continuous (or, if discrete, contains at least six levels) from one or more other variables with similar characteristics.[6] The procedure is called **regression.** Like correlation, regression assumes a straight-line relationship between the dependent and independent variable(s). Somewhat like correlation, regression assumes a normal distribution of dependent variable measurement values for each given value of the independent variable(s). Other assumptions will surface as we examine regression between one dependent and one independent variable, called **simple linear regression.**

SIMPLE LINEAR REGRESSION

Consider an air filter manufacturer about to market a new filter designed to protect the engine of an industrial forklift. As part of product development, an account executive would like to predict filter life until air-borne dirt clogs the paper cartridge. Actual cartridge life depends, of course, on ambient dust conditions and other random phenomena, factors over which the manufacturer has no control. However, actual cartridge life also depends on the amount of filter paper used in the cartridge, a factor over which the manufacturer has complete control. Consequently, the account executive orders a field test of eight different filter models containing different-sized cartridges on eight forklifts in a local warehouse.

---

[6]However, the X variable may be measured by as few as two categories and dummy variable regression used instead. See N. R. Draper and H. Smith, *Applied Regression Analysis* (New York: John Wiley & Sons, 1966), pp. 134–41.

TABLE 17.3
Cartridge Size and Cartridge Life

Cartridge Size (Ft² of Filter Paper)	Cartridge Life (Hours)
5	510
7	440
9	560
11	900
13	880
15	1010
17	1440
19	1350

Test results appear in Table 17.3. In general, we see that the larger the cartridge, the longer the life.

The Scatter Diagram and the Regression Line.   Almost as a matter of habit, we proceed to plot the distribution of cartridge life by cartridge size as the scatter diagram in Figure 17.2. More correctly, we plot the distribution of the two variables to see if data meet two assumptions underlying calculations to derive the regression line which summarizes the pattern of dots in Figure 17.2. The **regression line** is a line of "best fit" between dots in a scatter diagram; it minimizes the sum of the squared vertical deviations between each dot and the line. We shall soon learn of a procedure to calculate an equation describing the regression line.

The first assumption we check in Figure 17.2 is one mentioned earlier—that a straight line accurately depicts the relationship between cartridge life and cartridge size. Cartridge life is designated the *dependent* or *criterion variable* Y and cartridge size the *independent* or *predictor variable* X. Visual inspection of Figure 17.2 shows the linearity assumption well met by our data. The second assumption we check is that dispersion of variable Y values remains equal at all values of variable X. Again visual inspection shows the assumption well met. Beyond these two assumptions, we also assume that both X and Y variables are conceptualized as continuous (or, if discrete, contain at least six levels) and are measured in an interval or ratio fashion. By definition our data support these assumptions. And, again as we said earlier, we further assume that distributions of the variable Y values are normal for all values of variable X[7]. Finally, we must make one further assumption, which it will be best to explain later in our discussion.

[7]See Neter, Wasserman, and Whitmore, *Applied Statistics*, pp. 480–85 for a discussion on the use of inspection and certain statistical tests to investigate assumptions for linearity, equal dispersion, and normality.

Before leaving the scatter diagram, we also make an intuitive interpretation of the regression line. We note that it slopes upward to the right, indicating a positive relationship. It lies close to most of the dots, leading us to expect a strong relationship. And, it summarizes variable X values from 5 to 19, giving us more confidence in predictions for variable Y in this range.

An Equation for the Regression Line. An equation for any straight line may be written as

$Y = a + bX$

where X and Y represent variables and a and b represent constants. The constant b indicates the rate of change in variable Y for a unit change in variable X; the constant a represents the value of variable Y when variable X equals 0.

An equation for any measurement value, Y_i, takes a similar form:

$Y_i = \beta_0 + \beta_1 X_i + \epsilon_i$

In the formula, Y_i and X_i signify measurement values of the dependent and independent variables, respectively, taken from the ith sampling unit. The symbols β_0 and β_1 (read beta zero and beta one) represent the usually

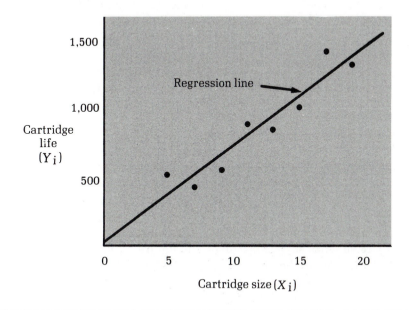

FIGURE 17.2
Cartridge size and cartridge life

unknown regression parameters in the population that describe the regression line. The symbol ϵ_i (read episilon i) denotes random error or scatter, as the vertical distance between Y_i and the value of $\beta_0 + \beta_1 X_i$.

Sample data usually estimate β_0 and β_1 as regression coefficients b_0 and b_1. These point estimates of β_0 and β_1 combine to express *the equation for the regression line as*

$$\hat{Y}_i = b_0 + b_1 X_i$$

Here $\hat{Y}_i$ (read Y hat i) represents the *regression line value* (or the *fitted value* as it is sometimes called) for Y_i based on knowledge of X_i. The difference $Y_i - \hat{Y}_i$ is a point estimate of ϵ_i and is commonly called *prediction error* (or the *residual value*) for the *i*th sampling unit. We denote the difference $Y_i - \hat{Y}_i$ by e_i.

With this notation, we can write formulas to calculate b_1 and b_0:

$$b_1 = \frac{\sum X_i Y_i - \dfrac{\sum X_i \sum Y_i}{n}}{\sum X_i^2 - \dfrac{(\sum X_i)^2}{n}}$$

$$b_0 = \frac{1}{n}(\sum Y_i - b_1 \sum X_i)$$

where Σ denotes the summing process over all sampling units providing values on variables X and Y. Values to calculate b_0 and b_1 for our air filter data appear in Table 17.4.[8] Inserting values into our formulas, we get

$$b_1 = \frac{97,290 - \dfrac{96(7,090)}{8}}{1,320 - \dfrac{9,216}{8}} = 72.68$$

$$b_0 = \frac{1}{8}[7,090 - 72.68(96)] = 14.09$$

Thus, our equation for the regression line in Figure 17.2 is

$$\hat{Y}_i = 14.09 + 72.68 X_i$$

Interpreting the value for b_0, we note that it represents the predicted value for variable Y when X_i equals 0. However, this particular predicted value of 14.09 looks suspicious, given the nature of our problem. That is, if a cartridge contained no filter paper ($X_i = 0$) we would expect it to have 0 hours of life. Consequently, our value for b_0 is more likely an artifact of

---

[8]Notice that we have kept nonsignificant digits throughout to minimize rounding errors in calculating b_0 and b_1 and in calculating values for $\hat{Y}$. Some statisticians recommend keeping at least six digits in all calculations.

TABLE 17.4
Values to Calculate b_0 and b_1

X_i	Y_i	X_iY_i	X_i^2
5	510	2,550	25
7	440	3,080	49
9	560	5,040	81
11	900	9,900	121
13	880	11,440	169
15	1,010	15,150	225
17	1,440	24,480	289
19	1,350	25,650	361
$\Sigma X_i = 96$	$\Sigma Y_i = 7,090$	$\Sigma X_iY_i = 97,290$	$\Sigma X_i^2 = 1,320$
$(\Sigma X_i)^2 = 9,216$			

the calculation process than a statistically and managerially significant value.[9] More often researchers' interests lie with b_1, especially when the value for b_0 is much less than the smallest value of interest for Y_i.

Interpreting b_1, we note that it represents the predicted change in variable Y for a unit change in variable X. Our positive value for b_1 means that we have a positive relationship between variables X and Y; a negative value would have meant the opposite. Beyond these interpretations, researchers regularly test b_1 to see if it represents a β_1 value that is statistically significant from 0. Our next section discusses the procedure.

Statistical Significance of β_1. As preparation for our test, we need a rather lengthy introduction. Consider predicting values for variable Y when we know nothing about values for variable X. Our best prediction under these circumstances would be $\overline{Y}$, the mean value. Predicting $\overline{Y}$ for all sampling units would minimize prediction error, even though errors would be substantial unless all values of variable Y happened to group closely about their mean. Thus, we might take each actual value, Y_i, and subtract $\overline{Y}$ from it, sum the differences, and use this total as a base against which we could compare prediction errors made when we know values of X_i,—that is, the summed differences between Y_i and $\hat{Y}_i$ (the summed values of e_i). Almost.

A problem arises because the sum of $(Y_i - \overline{Y})$, like the sum of $(Y_i - \hat{Y}_i)$, both taken over all sampling units, always equals 0. To resolve it, researchers customarily sum the value of $(Y_i - \overline{Y})^2$ and use it as a base against which they compare the sum of $(Y_i - \hat{Y}_i)^2$. We illustrate graphically

---

[9]A test for the statistical significance of β_0 is described by Draper and Smith, *Applied Regression Analysis*, p. 21. When it is applied to our value of 14.09, we accept the null hypothesis that $\beta_0 = 0$.

the unsquared versions of these two terms in Figure 17.3. We also show a third, $(\hat{Y}_i - \bar{Y})$, as the distance from the regression line to the mean. We can see that, for any value of X_i, we have

$$(Y_i - \bar{Y}) = (Y_i - \hat{Y}_i) + (\hat{Y}_i - \bar{Y})$$

Squaring and summing over all n values, it can be shown that

$$\Sigma(Y_i - \bar{Y})^2 = \Sigma(Y_i - \hat{Y}_i)^2 + \Sigma(\hat{Y}_i - \bar{Y})^2$$

Researchers call the first term the **total sum of squares** *(SSTO)*; the second, the **error sum of squares** *(SSE)*; and the third, the **regression sum of squares** *(SSR)*. Thus, we may rewrite the preceding equation as

$$SSTO = SSE + SSR$$

SSTO needs little further discussion.

Concerning *SSE*, the unsquared values $(Y_i - \hat{Y}_i)$ represent prediction error when we know values for X_i. As we said, these values represent residual values, left over after making our best prediction. The sum of $(Y_i$

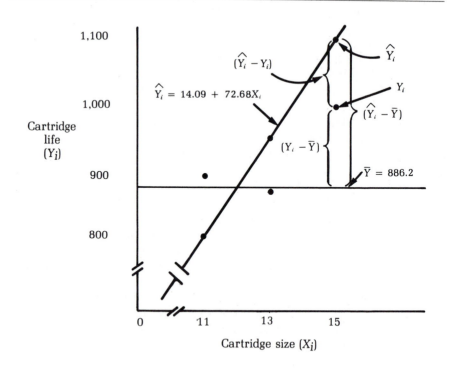

FIGURE 17.3
$\bar{Y}$, **the regression line, and terms** $(Y_i - \bar{Y})$, $(\hat{Y}_i - Y_i)$, **and** $(\hat{Y}_i - \bar{Y})$ **for** X_6

TABLE 17.5
Sums of Squares and Degrees of Freedom for Simple Regression

Sums of Squares	Degrees of Freedom
SSR	1
SSE	$n - 2$
SSTO	$n - 1$

$- \hat{Y}_i)^2$ over all n is a minimum value when our formulas for b_0 and b_1 calculate the equation for the regression line. Hence, our equation for $\hat{Y}_i$ is termed the *least squares expression of relationship* between variables X and Y. Most importantly, when we compute the fraction $(SSTO - SSE)/SSTO$ we find that it equals r_{XY}^2, that is, it equals the square of the correlation coefficient between variables X and Y. For our air filter data, we have

$$r_{XY}^2 = \frac{SSTO - SSE}{SSTO} = \frac{984{,}400 - 97{,}000}{984{,}400}$$

$$= 0.90$$

Concerning SSR, the values $(\hat{Y}_i - \overline{Y})^2$ indicate how much squared variation is explained by the regression line. If the regression line explains or represents the relationship between variables X and Y well, the sum of $(\hat{Y}_i - \overline{Y})^2$ will be quite close to that for $(Y_i - \overline{Y})^2$. In fact, we may take advantage of this logic, and earlier formulas, and write another expression for r_{XY}^2 as

$$r_{XY}^2 = \frac{SSR}{SSTO}$$

which for our air filter data is

$$r_{XY}^2 = \frac{887{,}400}{984{,}400} = 0.90$$

Researchers frequently refer to r_{xy}^2 as the *coefficient of simple determination*.

Each sum of squares has its own degrees of freedom, as shown in Table 17.5. When we divide SSE and SSR by their respective degrees of freedom, we obtain two quantities known as **mean square error** (MSE) and **mean square regression** (MSR). MSE and MSR combine rather simply to test the significance of β_1. We proceed as follows.

1. State the null and alternate hypotheses as

$H_0: \beta_1 = 0$

$H_1: \beta_1 \neq 0$

2. Choose a critical value of F from Table 5 in the Appendix.

3. Calculate the value of the test statistic F_{test} as

$$F_{test} = \frac{MSR}{MSE}$$

4. Compare the value of F_{test} to the chosen critical value of F and state conclusions as below:

   If $F_{test} \leq F_{critical}$, accept H_0.

   If $F_{test} > F_{critical}$, accept H_1.

Only our second step needs explanation. Turning to Table 5 in the Appendix, we see many critical values of F. Values depend on chosen values of α (again representing Type I error), degrees of freedom for the numerator, and degrees of freedom for the denominator. For example, if we wanted to control α at 0.05 and had both numerator and denominator degrees of freedom equal to 5, $F_{critical}$ would equal 5.05. In our test procedure, we choose a value for α but specify numerator and denominator degrees of freedom as those associated with MSR and MSE, respectively.

Continuing our filter example, we choose α at 0.05 for $F_{critical}$ and specify degrees of freedom for its numerator and denominator at 1 and 6. Thus, $F_{critical}$ equals 5.99. We calculate

$$F_{test} = \frac{887,400}{16,170} = 55$$

Because $F_{test} > F_{critical}$, we accept H_1; β_1 is likely not equal to 0.

Researchers customarily summarize their test results in an **analysis of variance (ANOVA)** table. The conventional form appears in Table 17.6. Applying the conventional form to our data, we would report results as Table 17.7. In Table 17.7, the probability value of 0.0000 does not mean there is no chance of making a Type I error when testing $\beta_1 = 0$. Rather, it means that this probability is some positive decimal such as 0.00000146 and that the computer program calculating this probability prints only to four decimal places. Understanding a basic ANOVA table will prove

TABLE 17.6
General Form of the ANOVA Table for Simple Regression

Source of Variation	Sum of Squares	Degrees of Freedom	MS	F_{test}	Probability
Regression	$SSR = \Sigma(\hat{Y}_i - \overline{Y})^2$	1	$MSR = SSR/1$	MSR/MSE	α
Error	$SSE = \Sigma(Y_i - \hat{Y})^2$	$n - 2$	$MSE = \dfrac{SSE}{n-2}$		
Total	$SSTO = \Sigma(Y_i - \overline{Y})^2$	$n - 1$			

TABLE 17.7
ANOVA Table for Air Filter Example

Source of Variation	Sum of Squares	Degrees of Freedom	MS	F_{test}	Probability
Regression	887,400	1	887,400	55	0.0000
Error	97,000	6	16,170		
Total	984,400	7			

quite useful when we discuss multiple regression later in this chapter, mean differences between three or more groups in Chapter 18, and analysis of experimental data in Chapter 19.

Predictions for Y Values.   We can very easily use our knowledge to predict an *average* value for variable Y called $\hat{Y}_h$. That is, $\hat{Y}_h$ denotes this average predicted value when variable X equals X_h.

For example, suppose our account executive promised the forklift manufacturer that, on the average, the new air filter would last for 1,000 hours. We may use this value for Y_h like a regression value for the ith sampling unit $(\hat{Y}_i)$ and write

$$1,000 = 14.09 + 72.68(X_h)$$

Solving, we find $X_h = 13.6$. Cautious because of the small sample size, the account executive prudently rounds X_h upward and specifies a filter whose cartridge contains 14 ft² of filter paper ($X_h = 14$). Such caution increases $\hat{Y}_h$ from 1,000 to 1,030 hours.

However, because variables X and Y relate in a statistical manner, cartridges when $X_h = 14$ will exhibit variability in life. Some will fall short of the 1,030 hour average and some will exceed it. Because we have assumed this variability in variable Y distributes normally, reference to a value for t and the standard deviation for $\hat{Y}_h$ when $X_h = 14$ would allow us to state a confidence interval for our prediction. However, procedures to do so go beyond our scope—as do related procedures to state a confidence interval for a *specific* variable Y value predicted from a variable X value.[10]

Multiple regression parallels simple regression by merely increasing the number of independent or predictor variables. However, in terms of computational complexity, multiple regression requires quite involved mathematics. Few marketing researchers would undertake, say, the prediction of air filter life based on cartridge size, ambient dust conditions, and ware-

MULTIPLE REGRESSION

---

[10]See Neter, Wasserman, and Whitmore, *Applied Statistics*, pp. 465–72 for a discussion of both procedures.

house type without the use of a computer.[11] Yet using a computer makes the complicated mathematics immaterial to the researcher. Accordingly, in this brief section we discuss multiple regression conceptually and present multiple regression results typically produced by a computer.

The Concept of Multiple Regression. Multiple regression predicts values for a single dependent or Y variable from measurement values of two or more independent or predictor X variables. We assume variable Y may be expressed as a straight-line statistical function of each of the predictor variables (plus our earlier assumptions for simple linear regression). The expression takes this form:

$$Y_i = \beta_0 + \beta_1 X_{i1} + \beta_2 X_{i2} + \ldots + \beta_{p-1} X_{ip-1} + \epsilon_1$$

Here we have $p - 1$ predictor variables, each possessing a measurement value for the ith sampling unit. Each predictor variable has an associated β_k coefficient ($k = 1, 2, \ldots, p - 1$) that indicates the mean change in variable Y for an increase by 1 unit in X_k while all other independent variables remain constant. β_0 represents the value of variable Y when all $X_k = 0$ and ϵ_i again represents random error.

Usually population regression coefficients are unknown and the researcher estimates them by b_0 and b_k. These point estimates combine to express the equation for the regression line as

$$\hat{Y}_i = b_0 + b_1 X_{i1} + b_2 X_{i2} + \ldots + b_{p-1} X_{ip-1}$$

Here $\hat{Y}_i$ represents the regression or predicted value for Y_i based on knowledge of measurement values for all $p - 1$ predictor variables. The difference $Y_i - \hat{Y}_i$ again represents a point estimate of ϵ_i and again is called prediction error. As we said, calculations of b_0 and b_k values usually depend on a computer.

Multiple Regression Computer Results. Usually a multiple regression program will produce calculated values for b_0 and each b_k along with an analysis of variance table of the form shown in Table 17.8. As we can see, the only substantive change from Table 17.6 for simple linear regression concerns degrees of freedom. We now have degrees of freedom for regression and error, respectively, as $p - 1$ and $n - p$. All other terms remain as discussed before.

We now test a null hypothesis of this form:

$$H_0: \beta_1 = \beta_2 = \cdots = \beta_{p-1} = 0$$

but use exactly the same F_{test} procedure (except in calculating degrees of

---

[11]Those who read carefully will notice that the variable "warehouse type" is not an interval variable but a nominal variable. Regression analysis accommodates nominal variables by treating them as dummy variables, as we said in footnote 6.

TABLE 17.8
General Form of the ANOVA Table for Multiple Regression

Source of Variation	Sum of Squares	Degrees of Freedom	MS	F_{test}	Probability
Regression	$SSR = \Sigma(\hat{Y}_i - \overline{Y})^2$	$p - 1$	$MSR = \dfrac{SSR}{p-1}$	MSR/MSE	α
Error	$SSE = \Sigma(Y_i - \hat{Y})^2$	$n - p$	$MSE = \dfrac{SSE}{n-p}$		
Total	$SST = \Sigma(Y_i - \overline{Y})^2$	$n - 1$			

freedom) as when testing $\beta_1 = 0$ in simple linear regression. Moreover, the value of R^2 as

$$R^2 = \frac{SSTO - SSE}{SSTO} = \frac{SSR}{SSTO}$$

expresses the proportion of variance of variable Y explained by knowledge of all predictor variables. Researchers refer to R^2 as the *coefficient of multiple determination*; they call its square root, R, the *coefficient of multiple correlation*.

Most multiple regression programs will also provide standard deviation statistics based on t to test the significance of the regression coefficients. Most will provide standard deviation statistics to construct confidence intervals for the average and a specific Y value. Most will print observed, estimated, and residual Y_i values. To explain these rather uncomplicated matters simply exceeds our space available.[12]

SUMMARY OF REGRESSION

Necessarily we have only scratched the surface in discussing regression as a prediction tool. With little effort anyone should be able to find entire volumes that provide more detail. Still, our limited introduction allows us to perform simple linear regression analyses with competence and to understand research reports using either this technique or multiple regression. We should also feel comfortable extending our regression skills through further reading and applications.

One topic we may encounter that we have not covered as yet in this book is sample size. A sample for any regression analysis should contain at least three or four times more sampling units than the number of independent variables present in the regression equation. Such a requirement is necessary because regression, like other least squares techniques, is quite sensitive to outliers or extreme data values, especially when the

---

[12]See Neter, Wasserman, and Whitmore, *Applied Statistics*, pp. 492–505 for a discussion of the tests and confidence intervals. See also Norman H. Nie et al., *Statistical Package for the Social Sciences*, 2nd ed. (New York: McGraw-Hill 1975), Chap. 20 for a discussion of typical computer output.

sample size is small. The consequent use of a large sample relative to the number of independent variables will increase the stability or repeatability of results.

Another topic we may encounter is multicollinearity between predictor variables. **Multicollinearity** exists when two or more predictor variables present in the regression equation correlate highly with each other. Like a small sample size, multicollinearity leads to instability of results for b_k values and their standard deviations. Consequently when the researcher's interests center on determining which b_k predicts more powerfully than others, multicollinearity severely damages the potential for finding that information. However, multicollinearity causes no special problems in forecasting and analyzing $\hat{Y}_h$ values.

Yet another topic we may encounter is the lack of independence of error or residual values. That is, a plot of residual values against $\hat{Y}_i$ values should show the former having a random pattern about 0. A lack of a random pattern about 0 frequently occurs when X_i values come from a sample consisting of time periods. Here we often see the regression line exceeding actual values for several periods in a row only to fall below actual values in several earlier or later periods. Such performance leads to another nonrandom plot of residual values, against time periods, and is called **autocorrelation.** Autocorrelation does not affect values for any b_k but may seriously underestimate its standard deviation. Consequently, a test of the significance of any b_k value may produce an inflated test statistic value leading to an erroneous conclusion. The expectancy of a random pattern of residual values when plotted against $\hat{Y}_i$ values or against time periods is our final assumption underlying simple and multiple regression analysis, alluded to earlier.

Forecasting Sales

Researchers forecast sales for some new territory, product, consumer segment, or time period. Largely we restrict our comments here to forecasts for new time periods but recognize that many methods we discuss apply to these other situations as well. Researchers forecast sales using methods that range in nature from quite subjective to quite objective processes. Subjective processes occur inside the researcher's head and show limited potential for elucidation. In contrast, objective processes occur more in the open and show extensive potential for explanation. Within each of these processes, researchers may make forecasts using only past sales data or using past sales plus additional data. Let us see how.

SUBJECTIVE FORECASTS In one type of subjective forecast, the researcher uses only his own intuition, experience, and judgment in examining data to make the forecast. These naive forecasting procedures or models are informally specified but lead to such expressions as:

On the basis of the last two years of sales data, I predict next month's sales will equal those of the same month last year plus four percent.

Because population in our market area is growing at 6.2 percent per year, our sales for next year will increase 0.5 percent per month.

Often though, the researcher seeks out the opinions or subjective forecasts of others for more expertise, variety, and accuracy.

This other type of subjective forecast, then, comes from surveys of salespersons, executives, or buyers. For example, a researcher employed by a manufacturer of water softeners might forecast next year's sales by polling its twenty-six salespersons and adding up their individual forecasts. Or, the researcher might instead interview the firm's four regional sales managers and add up their forecasts. Yet another approach would be for the researcher to interview a random sample of 150 dealers and measure their intentions to buy. Exhibit 17.1 states some generalities favoring salespersons, executives, or buyers as information sources in subjective forecasting.

No matter what the population of interest is, all subjective forecasts share the element of nonobjectivity—people simply may not respond with honest, dispassionate forecasts. Further, all information sources in all subjective forecasts can explain only approximately how they developed their individual forecasts. Further still, all information sources in all subjective forecasts will have developed their individual forecasts in manners different from those of their peers—using different assumptions, experiences, abilities, and degrees of motivation.

EXHIBIT 17.1
Subjective Forecasting Strengths by Information Source

Salespersons

Salespersons know their customers' needs better than anyone but the customers.

Salespersons' forecasts appear in an unaggregated form, by salesperson.

If salespersons' forecasts lead to sales quotas, salespersons better understand and better accept the quotas.

Executives

Executives know company, industry, and economic trends affecting sales better than anyone else in the firm.

The smaller number of executives means they usually can provide a faster forecast.

Executives' forecasts foster communication and help develop their unified view to the future.

Buyers

Buyers know their own needs (and abilities to pay) better than anyone.

Buyers' forecasts appear in an unaggregated form, by buyer.

Buyers' forecasts allow an understanding of their buying process.

To combat the first and last problems and to reduce the effects of group pressures on subjective forecasts, researchers often resort to a Delphi method. A **Delphi method** asks separated forecasters to each make an initial forecast and to record briefly how they did it. An independent researcher then collects responses in an anonymous fashion, summarizes them, and feeds back results. Usually results will show median, maximum, and minimum forecast values along with a summary of reasoning behind each. A second round of forecasting follows, with summaries of forecasted values and reasoning fed back as before. A third and later rounds follow, until values converge to a managerially useful range. This usually occurs by the end of the third or fourth round. Application of the Delphi method at American Hoist & Derrick reduced their annual sales forecasting error to less than 1 percent.[13] Usually such applications take time and work best with small groups of forecasters.

OBJECTIVE FORECASTS   In contrast, objective forecasts derive from manipulations of data according to quite explicit procedures.

Each set of explicit procedures is called a **forecasting model.** We discuss three very basic types of forecasting models in this section: classic time series models, autoregressive models, and causal models. More exist but an understanding of these will serve us well in many forecasting situations and in preparing us for other, more complex models.[14]

Classic Time Series Model.   The **classic time series model** considers that any observed sales value is the product of four effects or components: long-term trend, cyclical, seasonal, and random. In symbols, letting Y denote observed sales, we have

$$Y = T \cdot C \cdot S \cdot I$$

The symbol T denotes the *long-term trend effect* (either linear or curvilinear) expressed in units of sales. Long-term trend effects result from diverse market phenomena and show steady, continuous growth or steady, continuous decline over time. The symbol C stands for the *cyclical effect*, a pure number oscillating usually between 0.9 and 1.1. Cyclical effects reflect general business and economic conditions that follow a several-year period. The symbol S indicates the *seasonal effect*, again a pure number but ranging usually between 0.5 and 1.5. Seasonal effects complete their cycle within one year and occur because of seasonal influences on buyer demand. The symbol I represents the *random* or *irregular* effect, a pure number very close—we hope—to 1.0.

[13]Shankar Basu and Roger G. Schroeder, "Incorporating Judgments in Sales Forecasts: Application of the Delphi Method at American Hoist & Derrick," *Interfaces* 7 (May 1977): 18–27.

[14]A good introduction is by Steven C. Wheelwright and Spyros Makridakis, *Forecasting Methods for Management,* 2nd ed. (New York: John Wiley & Sons, 1977).

Classic time series forecasting procedures estimate values for T, C, and S. Our limited space allows us to discuss only methods to estimate T and S.[15] However, quite often these two components interest researchers much more than estimates of C. Our forecasting model, then, takes this form:

$$\hat{Y}_t = \hat{T}_t \cdot \hat{S}_t$$

where $\hat{Y}_t$ estimates sales for time period t. (We denote actual unit sales for time period t by Y_t.) $\hat{T}_t$ estimates the trend effect for time period t and $\hat{S}_t$ estimates the seasonal effect for time period t. (We assume C_t equals 1.0.) We will use the sum of the absolute values $|(Y_t - \hat{Y}_t)|$ divided by the sum of Y_t as a summary measure of random or irregular error, I.

An example aids our discussion. Consider an automobile dealer interested in forecasting car sales in units for each quarter of an upcoming year. A researcher collects sales data for each of the preceding twelve quarters as a basis to calculate $\hat{T}_t$ and $\hat{S}_t$ values. We show these data as the *line chart* in Figure 17.4. We can see that sales fluctuate considerably from quarter to quarter but show a slight positive trend over the three years.

Estimating Values for $\hat{S}_t$. The researcher begins by calculating values for $\hat{S}_t$, using a moving average. A **moving average** is simply the sum of sales for m time periods, divided by m, for any m sequential periods. Usually m equals the length of the seasonal cycle; for example, usually m equals 4 if data describe quarterly sales and 12 if data describe monthly sales. Table 17.9 presents unit sales data from Figure 17.4 in tabular form and shows moving averages in columns 5 and 6, based on $m = 4$.

Moving averages in column 5 begin with the value 263.00, calculated as $(155 + 323 + 372 + 202)/4$. The next value of 269.50 results from $(323 + 372 + 202 + 181)/4$, the next from $(372 + 202 + 181 + 364)/4$, and so on—moving one quarter at a time through all 12 sales values. Notice how the 4-Quarter Moving Averages in column 5 remove much of the mystery associated with original sales values. We now see a smooth, almost linear increase in unit sales in the form of the eight moving averages.

Yet, strictly speaking, these eight moving averages represent no identified quarters in our analysis. That is, each 4-quarter moving average in column 5 represents sales for a 3-month period, exactly in the middle of the 12 months involved in its calculation. This 3-month period begins exactly 4½ months into the 12-month period and ends exactly 4½ months before the end of the period; consequently, it represents sales for half of the second quarter plus half of the third quarter of the 12 months involved in the calculation. That is why we show entries in column 5 located vertically in between original unit sales values.

---

[15]See Wheelwright and Makridakis, *Forecasting Methods*, Chap. 6 for a complete discussion.

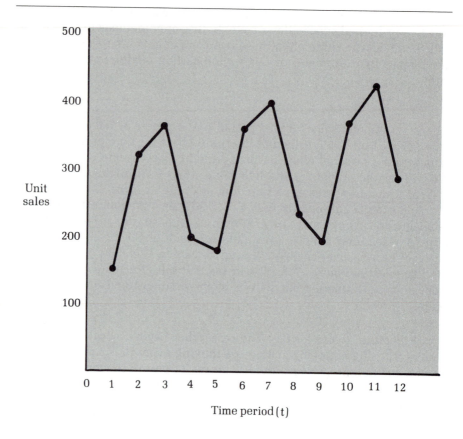

FIGURE 17.4
Quarterly unit sales of automobiles

To obtain a 4-quarter moving average specifically for an identified quarter requires our averaging two adjacent values in column 5. We show these "averages of averages" in column 6 as *Centered* 4-Quarter Moving Averages. The first value of 266.25 results from (263.00 + 269.50)/2, the second from (269.50 + 279.75)/2, and so on. Such centered values are often called **deseasonalized values**, D_t. With these deseasonalized values and our original values, we can calculate values for $\acute{S}_t$.

To proceed, we first calculate values for the actual seasonality effect, S_t, for quarters having a deseasonalized value. S_t is the quotient obtained from dividing an actual sales value for time period t by its deseasonalized value; for example

$$S_3 = \frac{Y_3}{D_3} = \frac{372}{266.25} = 1.40$$

We then define S_Q as the median value of all S_t values associated with

TABLE 17.9
Calculations for $\hat{S}_t$

Year	Quarter	Time Period $(t = X_t)$	Unit Sales (Y_t)	4-Quarter Moving Average	Centered 4-Quarter Moving Average (D_t)	Seasonality Effect (S_t)
1	1	1	155			
	2	2	323			
				263.00		
	3	3	372		266.25	1.40
				269.50		
	4	4	202		274.62	0.74
				279.75		
2	1	5	181		283.62	0.64
				287.50		
	2	6	364		292.00	1.25
				296.50		
	3	7	403		298.38	1.35
				300.25		
	4	8	238		301.12	0.79
				302.00		
3	1	9	196		305.25	0.64
				308.50		
	2	10	371		315.25	1.18
				322.00		
	3	11	429			
	4	12	292			

each unique quarter in the seasonal cycle. Thus, for the first quarter in the cycle, we have

$$S_{first} = (S_5 + S_9)/2$$

$$= (0.64 + 0.64)/2 = 0.64$$

For all quarters, we have

Quarter (Q)	S_Q
First	0.64
Second	1.22
Third	1.38
Fourth	0.76

Values for S_Q estimate the effects of season on unit sales data—that is, values estimate $\hat{S}_t$ in our forecasting model. For example, $\hat{S}_{15}$ denotes the estimated seasonal effect for the third quarter of year 4; we would estimate it by $S_{\text{third}} = 1.38$. Similarly, with the data in Table 17.9, we would estimate $\hat{S}_{19}$, $\hat{S}_{23}$, $\hat{S}_{27}$, and so on by $S_{\text{third}} = 1.38$. However, as actual values S_{19}, S_{23}, and S_{27} become available with the passage of time, the value for S_{third} will probably change.

Estimating Values for $\hat{T}_t$. It remains to estimate the long-term trend effect with $\hat{T}_t$. We do this most easily by assuming the trend effect to be linear and apply the least squares formulas:

$$b_1 = \frac{\Sigma X_t D_t - \dfrac{\Sigma X_t \Sigma D_t}{n}}{\Sigma X_t^2 - \dfrac{(\Sigma X_t)^2}{n}}$$

$$b_0 = \frac{1}{n}(\Sigma D_t - b_1 \Sigma X_t)$$

Such formulas duplicate those for simple linear regression except for notation. That is, we have a simple linear regression situation—the X variable is time periods (X_t) and the Y variable is deseasonalized sales (D_t). The symbols b_0 and b_1 respectively express the intercept and rate of change of the **trend line:**

$$\hat{T}_t = b_0 + b_1 X_t$$

Without showing calculations, we have $b_0 = 249.10$, $b_1 = 6.608$ (as with regression calculations, we carry nonsignificant digits to avoid rounding errors), and

$$\hat{T}_t = 249.10 + 6.608 X_t$$

To predict the trend value for year 4, quarter 1, we have $t = X_{13} = 13$ and

$$\hat{T}_{13} = 249.1 + 6.608(13) = 335.0 \text{ cars}$$

Similarly, for the rest of year 4:

$$\hat{T}_{14} = 249.1 + 6.608(14) = 341.6 \text{ cars}$$

$$\hat{T}_{15} = 249.1 + 6.608(15) = 348.2 \text{ cars}$$

$$\hat{T}_{16} = 249.1 + 6.608(16) = 354.8 \text{ cars}$$

We now may enter these values in our formula for $\hat{Y}_t$ along with values for $\hat{S}_t$ and forecast quarterly sales for year 4:

$$\hat{Y}_{13} = (335.0)(0.64) = 214 \text{ cars}$$

$$\hat{Y}_{14} = (341.6)(1.22) = 417 \text{ cars}$$

$$\hat{Y}_{15} = (348.2)(1.38) = 481 \text{ cars}$$

$$\hat{Y}_{16} = (354.8)(0.76) = 270 \text{ cars}$$

Evaluating the Forecast. How good a forecast do we have? Without data for year 4, we can only guess. However, we can make an educated guess by applying our model to past data and seeing how well these forecasts correspond to our actual unit sales.[16] For example, we have for year 1, quarter 1

$$\hat{T}_1 = 249.1 + 6.608(1) = 255.7 \text{ cars}$$

and

$$\hat{Y}_1 = (255.7)(0.64) = 164 \text{ cars}$$

Proceeding likewise for time periods 2 through 12 we get forecasted $\hat{Y}_t$ values, all of which we show plotted in Figure 17.5. We also show actual unit sales data (Y_t) for comparison. As we can see, forecasted values follow actual values quite closely. If we sum the absolute differences $|(Y_t - \hat{Y}_t)|$ and divide by the sum of Y_t, we get a value for forecast error. As Figure 17.5 shows, this value for our time series model is 3.4 percent, a value quite adequate for most decision-making purposes.

Autoregressive Model. Our discussion of the autoregressive model goes much faster. Like the classic time series model, the autoregressive model predicts future sales from past sales. However, the **autoregressive model** predicts future sales without isolating trend, cyclical, and seasonal effects. The model takes this form:

$$Y_t = \beta_0 + \beta_1 Y_{t-1} + \beta_2 Y_{t-2} + \ldots + \beta_p Y_{t-p} + \epsilon_t$$

It is parallel to the multiple regression model except for assumptions and subscripts that now indicate past time periods. In words, the autoregressive model says that a unit sales figure for any time period, Y_t, equals a constant value, β_0, plus the parameter β_1 times sales for time period $t - 1$, plus the parameter β_2 times sales for time period $t - 2$, and so on. As in multiple regression, values for β_0 and any β_t $(t = 1, 2, 3, \ldots, p)$ may equal 0.

We estimate Y_t by $\hat{Y}_t$ where

$$\hat{Y}_t = b_0 + b_1 Y_{t-1} + b_2 Y_{t-2} + \ldots + b_p Y_{t-p}$$

---

[16]A more severe test would apply the model to past data not used to develop the model.

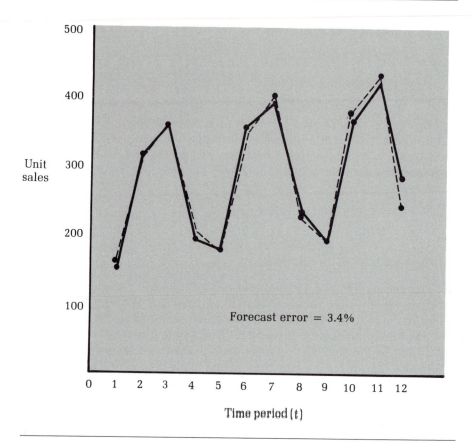

FIGURE 17.5
Actual (————) and forecasted (--------) quarterly unit sales of automobiles using a classic time series model

where b_0 and b_t values derive from least squares estimation procedures. Let us illustrate with an example.

We return to our automobile sales data and again estimate sales for each quarter of year 4. Suppose we use an autoregressive model of this form:[17]

$$\hat{Y}_t = b_0 + b_1 Y_{t-4}$$

That is, we recognize the pronounced seasonality associated with the sales data and decide to use sales from four quarters past as our only predictor.

[17]Numerous autoregressive models are possible. The selection of any one involves considerations beyond the scope of this text. See William Mendenhall and James E. Reinmuth, *Statistics for Management and Economics*, 3rd ed. (North Scituate, Mass.: Duxbury Press, 1978), pp. 546–52 for an introduction.

TABLE 17.10
Autoregressive Forecast Data

Year	Quarter	Time Period (t)	Unit Sales (Y_t)	Lagged Unit Sales (Y_{t-4})	Forecasted Unit Sales $\hat{Y}_t$
1	1	—	155	—	—
	2	—	323	—	—
	3	—	372	—	—
	4	—	202	—	—
2	1	1	181	155	187
	2	2	364	323	352
	3	3	403	372	400
	4	4	238	202	233
3	1	5	196	181	213
	2	6	371	364	392
	3	7	429	403	430
	4	8	292	238	268

Sales from past quarters are often called *lagged sales*. We show our unit sales values and 4-quarter lagged values in Table 17.10. We also show $\hat{Y}_t$ values as calculated from the autoregressive forecasting equation:

$$\hat{Y}_t = 35.24 + 0.9795\,Y_{t-4}$$

Values for b_0 and b_1, 35.24 and 0.9795, derive from the least squares formulas below:

$$b_1 = \frac{\sum Y_{t-4}Y_t - \dfrac{\sum Y_{t-4}\sum Y_t}{n}}{\sum Y^2_{t-4} - \dfrac{(\sum Y_{t-4})^2}{n}}$$

$$b_0 = \frac{1}{n}\left(\sum Y_t - b_1\sum Y_{t-4}\right)$$

In other words, we have a simple linear regression situation in which the X variable is 4-quarter lagged sales and the Y variable is actual sales.

To forecast quarterly sales for year 4, we have:

$$\hat{Y}_9 = 35.24 + 0.9795(196) = 227 \text{ cars}$$

$$\hat{Y}_{10} = 35.24 + 0.9795(371) = 399 \text{ cars}$$

$$\hat{Y}_{11} = 35.24 + 0.9795(429) = 455 \text{ cars}$$

$$\hat{Y}_{12} = 35.24 + 0.9795(292) = 321 \text{ cars}$$

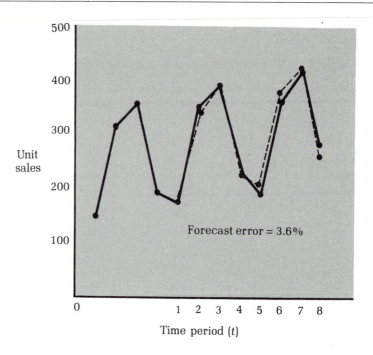

FIGURE 17.6
Actual (——) and forecasted (--------) quarterly unit sales of automobiles using an autoregressive model

Lacking data for year 4, we cannot comment on the accuracy of these forecasts. However, we can comment on the accuracy of forecasts the model produced for periods 1 through 8.[18] A plot of actual and forecasted unit sales appears in Figure 17.6. We can see that our autoregressive model forecasts actual values almost as accurately as our classic time series model does. Again we use the sum of the absolute differences $|(Y_t - \hat{Y}_t)|$ divided by the sum of Y_t as a value for forecast error. Figure 17.6 shows this value to be 3.6 percent.

Causal Models.   Causal models differ fundamentally from classic time series and autoregressive models in that **causal models** forecast sales using variables other than past sales. Such variables are considered influential or causal with respect to sales. For example, we might try to predict quarterly automobile sales based on the market area's bank debits, unemployment rates, and the dealer's quarterly advertising expenses. Or, we

---

[18]A more severe test would apply the model to past data not used to develop the model.

might try to predict sales based only on the number of licensed drivers within a 30-mile radius.

Form of a causal model follows no rigid pattern: some causal models assume only linear causal relationships while others do not. For example, a causal model to predict annual U.S. air travel looks like this:[19]

$$Y_{t+f} = Y_t(1.12)^f \left(\frac{P_{t+f}}{P_t} \right)^{-1.2} \left(\frac{S_{t+f}}{S_t} \right)^{0.2} \left(\frac{I_{t+f}}{I_t} \right)^{0.5} \left(\frac{N_{t+f}}{N_t} \right)^{1.0} \left(\frac{D_{t+f}}{D_t} \right)^{-0.05}$$

where:

- t designates the current year
- f is the number of years in the future
- Y is U.S. domestic revenue passenger miles
- P is price of air travel
- S is average airborne speed
- I is a measure of per capita GNP
- N is U.S. population
- D is the death rate per 100 million passenger miles

A discussion of processes to develop such models goes far beyond the scope of this text. However, we already have discussed processes to develop simpler causal models when we discussed regression analysis earlier in this chapter. As long as we assume straight-line relationships and as long as data meet our other regression assumptions, we may use simple or multiple regression procedures as causal models to forecast sales.[20]

SUMMARY OF FORECASTING[21]

Both subjective and objective forecasting have their place in marketing research. Subjective forecasts involve more people in the firm and, hence, maximize acceptance of forecasting methods and results. Subjective forecasts allow a greater number and variety of variables to be considered in the forecast and a greater variety of relationships to exist between these variables. Subjective forecasting models often take little time to develop.

[19]J. Scott Armstrong and Michael C. Grohman, "A Comparative Study of Methods for Long-Range Market Forecasting," *Management Science* 19 (October 1972): 211–21.

[20]The most frequently occurring violation is autocorrelation of residuals. Frequently researchers may make a simple transformation of their data through the method of first differences and employ regression through the origin to avoid autocorrelation problems. See Neter, Wasserman, and Whitmore, *Applied Statistics*, pp. 648–52 for an introduction.

[21]It might prove helpful to read an alternate summary of sales forecasting by Spyros Makridakis and Steven C. Wheelwright, "Forecasting: Issues and Challenges for Marketing Management," *Journal of Marketing* 41 (October 1977): 24–38. The authors also provide an extensive list of references to published works on forecasting applications.

Subjective forecasts may predict turning points—that is, basic changes in sales patterns—more accurately.

Objective forecasts often take less time to make. Objective forecasts allow more learned criticism and faster teaching of the forecasting procedure. They are often more accurate and more amenable to statistical tests, both of which traits engender more confidence in the procedure. Most important, objective forecasts often allow an understanding of factors influencing the forecast, either as causal variables or as trend, cyclical, and seasonal effects.

Within objective methods, classic time series and autoregressive models when compared to causal models find easier model development, explanation, and use. They require only historical data on one variable—sales—in contrast to causal models, which often require forecasted values for several variables (in addition to historical data on these variables) in order to forecast future sales. More complicated time series and autoregressive models appear to be as accurate as the most complicated causal models;[22] and they seem superior when fundamental changes occur in the market, such that causal relationships no longer hold true.

Chapter Summary

Rather than review this chapter point by point, let us instead consider some summary comments. As we have discussed, making estimates, predictions, and objective forecasts largely reduces to quantitative processes. The researcher assembles a representative sample, collects data, and manipulates numbers to yield an answer. Such manipulations generally proceed according to explicit theory and rules, both of which should have been part of an earlier statistics course (except perhaps as they apply to forecasts).

Our discussion of subjective forecasts differs from this description. Here intuition, judgment, and individual bias combine with personal experience, abilities, and motivation to produce a forecast. Such factors interact to produce subjective estimates and predictions, all the essence of a marketing manager's day. Two points then follow:

1. An equally lengthy discussion exists for qualitative and subjective estimates, predictions, and forecasts but it lacks the theoretical rigor we have seen for the quantitative processes.

2. Processes of both objective and subjective types lend perspective and credence to estimates, predictions, and forecasts. Neither type should be used to the exclusion of the other.

---

[22]Makridakis and Wheelwright, "Forecasting," p. 30. For a conflicting conclusion, however, see Armstrong and Grohman, "Comparative Study," pp. 217–18.

Chapter Review

Estimate	b_0	**KEY TERMS**
Prediction	b_1	
Forecast	*SSTO*	
Point estimate	*MSE*	
Interval estimate	*MSR*	
Regression line	r^2	
Multiple regression	Deseasonalized sales values	
R^2	Classic time series forecasting model	
Multicollinearity	Autoregressive forecasting model	
Autocorrelation	Causal forecasting model	
Simple linear regression		

DISCUSSION QUESTIONS

1. Explain the difference between a confidence interval and a hypothesis test for an unknown population mean, μ.

2. Why do we not discuss procedures to derive an interval estimate for the population modal value?

3. Explain where "specific, meaningful values" come from in hypothesis testing.

4. What information can you glean from a scatter diagram?

5. Suppose an accident damaged a cartridge with 21 ft² of filter paper in our regression example. The filter lasted for 810 hours. What should the researcher do about this when analyzing the data?

6. A marketing manager for a manufacturer of adhesive tape wishes to learn if a promotion aimed at retailers increased sales from their average monthly level of $2,850 per retailer per quarter.

   a) Is this a test of a mode, median, or mean?

   b) State hypotheses that you would test, assuming you collect data from a sample of fifty retailers.

7. Can the Delphi forecasting method work using thirty salespeople as experts, each of whom is responsible for a forecast in his or her territory? Why or why not?

8. What assumptions underlie a multiple regression analysis?

9. What motivations influence individual members of the salesforce as they make annual sales forecasts for their respective territories?

10. What are the relative strengths and weaknesses of the classic time series forecasting model compared to the autoregressive forecasting model?

11. What predictor variables might you include in a causal model to forecast incoming freshmen's first term GPA at your institution?

PROBLEMS **1.** Enter values as indicated below for a test of β_1.

Numerator Degrees of Freedom	Denominator Degrees of Freedom	α	$F_{critical}$
1	10	0.05	____
1	—	0.05	4.17
1	10	0.01	____
1	60	____	7.08

2. Consider the first fifteen ski testers in Table 17.2 to represent a separate sample. Test the following hypotheses for statistical significance, using $\alpha = 0.05$:

$$H_0: \mu_{md} \leq 11$$
$$H_1: \mu_{md} > 11$$

3. Ten sales territories show the following sales revenues and advertising expenditures for Brand L chocolate milk.

Territory	1	2	3	4	5	6	7	8	9	10
Sales Revenues ($000)	46	28	11	17	22	26	32	38	35	27
Advertising Expenditures ($000)	8	6	3	7	7	7	8	5	9	4

a) Identify the independent and dependent variable.

b) Develop a prediction equation or model for sales revenue.

c) How "good" a model is it?

4. Show calculations that determine the values of SSR, SSE, and $SSTO$ for data in Table 17.3.

5. **a)** Complete the ANOVA table below for a multiple regression problem that used 6 predictor variables and 67 sampling units.

Source	SS	df	MS	F_{test}	Probability
Regression	4100	____	____	____	____
Error	900	____	____		
Total	____				

b) Calculate the value for R^2.

6. **a)** Compute values for S_Q from the following data.

Year	1				2			
Quarter	1	2	3	4	1	2	3	4
Unit Sales	100	160	200	80	85	155	185	65

b) Compute values for b_0 and b_1 for the long term trend line.

c) Forecast sales for year 3, quarters 1 and 2 using the classic time series model.

7. With knowledge that quarterly sales for year 0 were 130, 185, 230, and 100 (in sequence), forecast sales for year 3, quarters 1 and 2 in problem 6 above using an autoregressive model of the form:

$$\hat{Y}_t = b_0 + b_1 Y_{t-4}$$

8. Forecast unit sales for each quarter of year 4 for our automobile dealer example, using both the classic time series and autoregressive models developed from unit sales data in Table 17.9. Which forecasting model do you think is better here? Why?

Additional Readings

Mendenhall, William, and Reinmuth, James E. *Statistics for Management and Economics.* 3rd ed. North Scituate, Mass.: Duxbury Press, 1978.

> *As an alternative to Neter, Wasserman, and Whitmore's Applied Statistics, which we suggested for additional reading at the end of Chapter 12, see this book. It provides comparable discussions on making estimates and predictions and a quite superior one on forecasting. Beyond a more complete introduction to autoregressive forecasting models, the book also describes a least squares sinusoidal forecasting model, an exponential smoothing forecasting model, and an exponentially weighted moving-average forecasting model.*

Neter, John, and Wasserman, William. *Applied Linear Statistical Models.* Homewood, Ill.: Richard D. Irwin, 1974.

> *The first twelve chapters discuss regression analyses quite completely and lucidly. Discussions treat the examination of residuals, multiple regression, dummy variable regression, stepwise regression, regression applied to analysis of variance problems, and more.*

Wheelwright, Steven, C., and Makridakis, Spyros. *Forecasting Methods for Management.* 2nd ed. New York: John Wiley & Sons, 1977.

> *This book provides an excellent introduction to sales forecasting. It discusses all major subjective and objective methods, from an applied viewpoint.*

18

Differences Between Groups

We reach in Chapter 18 our sixth purpose in analyzing data: showing differences between groups. As we said at the end of Chapter 16, showing a relationship between two variables borders on showing a difference between groups. For example, if we know that consumers' ages and their coffee consumption rates relate positively, we would expect groups of older consumers to consume more coffee than groups of younger consumers. As another similarity with showing relationships, we also take an interest in the size, direction, and statistical significance of differences between groups.

Yet examining differences between groups exists as a separate purpose in analyzing data. To illustrate, consider a researcher interested in learning per capita consumption of barbecued ribs in eight neighborhoods before locating a take-out rib restaurant in one of them. Here concern lies not with the abstract relationship between neighborhood and consumption rate but with the specific neighborhood showing the highest consumption rate. Or, consider a researcher who finds the near-perfect relationship (between milk consumption and income) shown in Figure 18.1. The coefficient of simple determination, r^2, may be nearly 1.0, yet because the regression line is nearly horizontal, two or more groups of consumers with quite different average incomes will not show very different milk consumption rates. Finally, consider a researcher interested in learning which of two stereo receiver designs show a greater variability in operating life. Both may last equally long on the average, but one may show

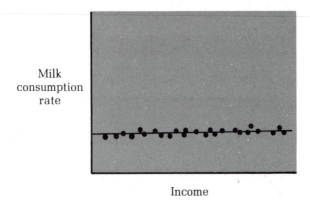

FIGURE 18.1
Income and milk consumption rate

greater variability than the other and, as a result, upset consumers who buy receivers that require early service. Here concern lies with differences in variable variances between groups, a topic quite apart from relationships between variable values.

Consequently, different statistical procedures have been developed specifically for this sixth purpose and we discuss many of them in this chapter. All apply to differences between typical values for variables as measured from one or more groups or samples. The application of any one depends on measurement level associated with each variable. Within measurement level, the application of any one depends on the number of samples and on whether or not samples were drawn independently of each other.

On this last point, measures of typical values can come from either independent or dependent samples. **Independent samples** contain sampling units selected without considering sampling units in any other sample. Two simple random samples illustrate. **Dependent samples** contain sampling units selected so that characteristics of sampling units in one sample match those of sampling units in another sample. Two samples of ten retail stores illustrate, where stores in the second sample are selected to match the sizes of stores in the first. Researchers match sampling units to reduce sampling error in tests for statistical significance of group differences. A special case of dependent samples also occurs when only one group of sampling units provides measurements at two or more points in time. A panel of teenagers whose members provide weekly summaries of record and tape purchases illustrates.

Nominal Measurement Differences Between Groups

We begin by considering a situation in which typical values reflect a nominal measurement process. Such a process, we recall, assigns values to sampling units on the basis of their possession or lack of possession of specified characteristics. Measurement values represent only labels, allowing us to determine only the equality or inequality of sampling units with respect to these characteristics. To express the typical measurement value for a group of sampling units, we count the number of sampling units having each label, find the label with the highest count, and designate that label as the typical value by calling it the mode.

To illustrate, consider a researcher investigating a power tool manufacturer's marketing experience in two sales territories. The researcher randomly selects samples of 100 invoices for 1981 from each of the two territories, with results shown in Table 18.1. The researcher wishes to know if the firm's success with department stores in the first territory holds true in the second. At issue, then, is whether a statistically significant difference between modal values exists for the two territories.

Quite bluntly, the issue cannot be tested. To see this, consider for a moment that data instead represent *censuses* of invoices for the two territories. Clearly we could say that the *population* modal values of "department store" for Territory 1 and "specialty store" for Territory 2 are different. However, when data represent *samples* of invoices, a test for statistical significance would investigate whether one modal value lies sufficiently far from the other that chance, as operating through the sampling process, probably could not have been responsible.

So, how far apart do our two sample modal values lie? Obviously, the question is meaningless because the measurement process producing modal values used neither direction nor distance in assigning measurement values. Consequently, meaningful questions can be raised only with respect to *counts* of modal and other measurement values because counts

TABLE 18.1
Distributions of Invoices by Retailer Type and Sales Territory

| | Sales Territory | | |
Retailer Type	1	2	Total
Department Store	50	40	90
Specialty Store	30	45	75
Discount Store	20	15	35
Total	100	100	200

possess mathematical properties. Thus, when a nominal measurement process describes one or more groups, the researcher can only investigate:

1. Differences between sample proportions possessing a specific modal or other measurement value.

2. Differences between sample distributions of measurement values.

Our next two sections show how.

DIFFERENCES BETWEEN PROPORTIONS Let us begin by discussing differences between proportions in independent populations. Consider again our invoice data in Table 18.1 as taken from two random samples. Suppose the researcher would like to compare unknown population proportions of retailers in the two territories that possess the measurement value "department store." (The procedure we discuss applies to comparisons of any two independent population proportions.) We designate sample proportions possessing the measurement value in the two territories as $\bar{p}_1$ and $\bar{p}_2$ and calculate their values as

$$\bar{p}_1 = 50/100 = 0.5$$
$$\bar{p}_2 = 40/100 = 0.4$$

Two Independent Samples.   The issue, of course, is whether such sample differences likely reflect true differences in the unknown population proportions π_1 and π_2 or likely reflect the sampling process. A simple statistical test resolves the issue.[1]

1. State the null and alternate hypotheses as

$$H_0: \pi_1 - \pi_2 = 0 \quad \text{(two-tail test)}$$
$$H_1: \pi_1 - \pi_2 \neq 0$$

2. Choose a critical value of Z from Table 2 in the Appendix.

3. Calculate the value for the test statistic Z as

$$Z_{test} = \frac{\bar{p}_1 - \bar{p}_2}{(s_{\bar{p}_1 - \bar{p}_2})}$$

4. Compare the value for Z_{test} with that for $Z_{critical}$ and state conclusions as below:

If $-Z_{critical} \leq Z_{test} \leq +Z_{critical}$, accept H_0.
Otherwise, accept H_1.

---

[1] We describe a two-tail test. Alternatively, we could state hypotheses as inequalities and use either a lower- or an upper-tail test parallel to our discussion early in Chapter 17, when we tested an hypothesis about the mean.

Let us apply these steps to our example.

We state hypotheses as above and select a critical value for Z at 1.65, allowing α to equal 0.10. The calculation for Z_{test} proceeds directly, once we know the value of $s_{\bar{p}_1 - \bar{p}_2}$:

$$s_{\bar{p}_1 - \bar{p}_2} = \left[pq \left(\frac{1}{n_1} + \frac{1}{n_2} \right) \right]^{1/2}$$

In the formula, p equals the total number of sampling units in both samples that possess the measurement value of interest, divided by the total number of sampling units in both samples. The measurement value of interest in our data is "department store" and we have

$$p = (50 + 40)/200 = 0.45$$

We define q as $1 - p$ and have

$$q = 1 - 0.45 = 0.55$$

Knowing that n_1 and n_2 indicate sample sizes, we have

$$s_{\bar{p}_1 - \bar{p}_2} = [(0.45)(0.55)(1/100 + 1/100)]^{1/2}$$
$$= 0.070$$

And, because

$$Z_{test} = \frac{0.50 - 0.40}{0.070} = 1.43$$

we accept H_0: the proportion of department store accounts is not significantly different between the two territories.

We make only two assumptions for our test. The first is that n_1 and n_2 each contain sufficient sampling units such that $n\pi$ and $n(1 - \pi)$ exceed 5 for both samples. The second is that samples are taken independently of each other. Our data meet both assumptions.

Three or C Independent Samples.   How do we test for significant differences between three or more sample proportions? Actually, quite easily with a χ^2 test procedure as follows.

To illustrate, suppose we expand our power tool example to sample from five territories and have data as shown in Table 18.2. Now we want to compare proportions of department stores between the five territories. We proceed by *collapsing* retailer types into two categories: department stores and all others, shown in Table 18.3. Proportions for department stores in the five territories may be calculated as:

$$\bar{p}_1 = 50/100 = 0.50$$

$$\bar{p}_2 = 40/100 = 0.40$$

$$\bar{p}_3 = 45/100 = 0.45$$

TABLE 18.2
Distributions of Invoices by Retailer Type and Sales Territory

Retailer Type	Sales Territory					Total
	1	2	3	4	5	
Department Store	50	40	45	60	55	250
Specialty Store	30	45	35	30	35	175
Discount Store	20	15	20	10	10	75
Total	100	100	100	100	100	500

TABLE 18.3
Distributions of Invoices by (Collapsed) Retailer Type and Sales Territory

Retailer Type	Sales Territory					Total
	1	2	3	4	5	
Department Store	50	40	45	60	55	250
All Others	50	60	55	40	45	250
Total	100	100	100	100	100	500

$$\bar{p}_4 = 60/100 = 0.60$$

$$\bar{p}_5 = 55/100 = 0.55$$

The issue is whether such differences likely show true differences in the unknown population proportions π_1, π_2, π_3, π_4, and π_5, or whether the differences likely show results of the sampling process. Our χ^2 test procedure resolves the issue.

1. State the null and alternate hypotheses as

   $H_0: \pi_1 = \pi_2 = \ldots = \pi_C$
   H_1: Not all equalities in H_0 hold

2. Choose a critical value of χ^2 from Table 4 in the Appendix for a desired α and $(R - 1)(C - 1)$ degrees of freedom.

3. Calculate the value for the test statistic χ^2 as

   $$\chi^2_{test} = \sum_{i=1}^{R} \sum_{j=1}^{C} \frac{(O_{ij} - E_{ij})^2}{E_{ij}}$$

4. Compare the value of χ^2_{test} to that of χ^2_{critical} and state conclusions as below:

If $\chi^2_{\text{test}} \le \chi^2_{\text{critical}}$, accept H_0.
If $\chi^2_{\text{test}} > \chi^2_{\text{critical}}$, accept H_1.

Our test (but for statements of hypotheses) is equivalent to one discussed more completely in Chapter 16 to test the significance of r_{phi}.[2] We may wish to review that discussion before proceeding.

Applying the test to data in Table 18.3, we state hypotheses as in step 1 and choose χ^2 for $\alpha = 0.05$ and 4 degrees of freedom at 9.488. We have E_{ij} always equal to 50 and

$$\chi^2_{\text{test}} = \frac{(50 - 50)^2}{50} + \frac{(40 - 50)^2}{50} + \frac{(45 - 50)^2}{50} + \frac{(60 - 50)^2}{50} + \frac{(55 - 50)^2}{50}$$

$$+ \frac{(50 - 50)^2}{50} + \frac{(60 - 50)^2}{50} + \frac{(55 - 50)^2}{50} + \frac{(40 - 50)^2}{50}$$

$$+ \frac{(45 - 50)^2}{50}$$

$$= 10.0.$$

Thus, we accept H_1. Had we instead chosen an α of 0.01, we would have accepted H_0.

With H_1 accepted, our test allows us to say only that one or more proportions do not equal one or more others—we do not know which. To investigate these specific differences between selected proportions requires a contrasting procedure whose explanation goes beyond our scope.[3]

Tests of the proportion of specialty stores or the proportion of discount stores would proceed similarly after appropriate collapsing. Tests need not use equal sample sizes; however, cells should contain minimums noted in Chapter 16. Finally, such tests may also be applied to the case of two independent samples discussed in the last section. They provide identical results to those of the tests using Z.

Two or C Dependent Samples. When data represent dependent samples, everything changes. To explain, let us have a researcher randomly select sixteen power tool retailers in Territory 1 and monitor their activi-

---

[2]Statistics texts refer to the present test as a test of independence. If populations providing samples with which to calculate $\overline{p}_j$s are independent, then all differences between pairs of π_js equal 0. Similarly, if variables whose sample values are used to calculate r_{phi} are independent, then r_{phi} equals 0.

[3]The test is discussed by Leonard A. Marascuilo, *Statistical Methods for Behavioral Science Research* (New York: McGraw-Hill, 1971), pp. 380–82.

ties over three months to see if they display a line of power drills at eye, waist, or knee levels. The researcher would like to compare the proportions of dealers displaying the drills at eye level during each month to learn if a promotion campaign aimed at dealers during the second and third months had any effect. Suppose data appear as in Table 18.4.

The issue is whether proportions (or frequencies) of retailers displaying the tools at eye level differing over the three months is likely because of true differences in the population or likely because of sampling error. Our test to resolve this issue proceeds as follows.

1. State the null and alternate hypotheses as

$$H_0: \pi_1 = \pi_2 = \ldots = \pi_C$$

H_1: Not all equalities in H_0 hold

2. Choose a critical value of χ^2 from Table 4 in the Appendix for a desired α and $C - 1$ degrees of freedom.

TABLE 18.4
Dealers Displaying Drills at Eye Level (1) and Other Levels (0)

Dealer	Month 1	Month 2	Month 3	Total (R_i)
1	0	0	1	1
2	0	1	1	2
3	0	1	1	2
4	1	1	1	3
5	1	1	0	2
6	0	0	1	1
7	0	0	1	1
8	1	0	1	2
9	0	0	0	0
10	0	1	1	2
11	0	1	1	2
12	1	1	1	3
13	0	0	1	1
14	0	1	0	1
15	0	1	1	2
16	1	1	1	3
Totals (C_j)	5	10	13	
Grand Total				28

3. Calculate the value for the test statistic χ^2 as

$$\chi^2_{test} = \frac{(C-1)\left[C\sum_{j=1}^{C}C_j^2 - \left(\sum_{j=1}^{C}C_j\right)^2\right]}{C\sum_{i=1}^{R}R_i - \sum_{i=1}^{R}R_i^2}$$

where C_j represents the total of entries in the jth column and R_i represents the total of entries in the ith row.

4. Compare the value of χ^2_{test} with that of $\chi^2_{critical}$ and state conclusions as below:

If $\chi^2_{test} \leq \chi^2_{critical}$, accept H_0.
If $\chi^2_{test} > \chi^2_{critical}$, accept H_1.

We apply the test to the hypothesis, $H_0: \pi_1 = \pi_2 = \pi_3$, and use data in Table 18.4. Choosing α at 0.05, we have $\chi^2_{critical}$ for 2 degrees of freedom at 5.991. For χ^2_{test} we have

$$\chi^2_{test} = \frac{(3-1)[3(25+100+169)-784]}{3(28)-60}$$

$$= 8.2$$

Consequently, we accept H_1: the dealer promotion seems to be effective.

Our test is called the **Cochran test,** after the statistician who developed it. It requires only one assumption, that R generally exceed 30. However, if $C \geq 3$, R may be as small as 16 and the test will still produce good results.[4]

TWO OR C INDEPENDENT SAMPLE DISTRIBUTIONS

Here we test the statistical significance of differences between frequency distributions obtained from two or more independent samples. The process parallels that discussed for testing differences between sample proportions—only now we test differences between every corresponding proportion or frequency in the two or more distributions. The test is commonly called a χ^2 **test of independence.** And, quite simply, it is our χ^2 test for independent sample proportions, without collapsing categories. Looking at data in Table 18.2, let us suppose that a researcher wishes to determine if the distributions of retailer type differ significantly across the five sales territories. Our test proceeds as follows.

1. State the null and alternate hypotheses as

H_0: Distributions of measurement values do not differ across the C populations

---

[4]W. G. Cochran, "The Comparison of Percentages in Matched Samples," *Biometrika* 37 (December 1950): 256–66.

H_1: Distributions of measurement values differ across the C populations

2. Choose a critical value of χ^2 from Table 4 in the Appendix for a desired α and $(R - 1)(C - 1)$ degrees of freedom.

3. Calculate the value for the test statistic χ^2 as

$$\chi^2_{test} = \sum_{i=1}^{R} \sum_{j=1}^{C} \frac{(O_{ij} - E_{ij})^2}{E_{ij}}$$

4. Compare the value of χ^2_{test} to that of $\chi^2_{critical}$ and state conclusions as below:

If $\chi^2_{test} \leq \chi^2_{critical}$, accept H_0.
If $\chi^2_{test} > \chi^2_{critical}$, accept H_1.

Let us state hypotheses as above and choose $\chi^2_{critical}$ for $\alpha = 0.01$ and 8 degrees of freedom at 20.090. We have

$$\chi^2_{test} = \frac{(50 - 50)^2}{50} + \frac{(40 - 50)^2}{50} + \frac{(45 - 50)^2}{50} + \frac{(60 - 50)^2}{50} + \frac{(55 - 50)^2}{50}$$

$$+ \frac{(30 - 35)^2}{35} + \frac{(45 - 35)^2}{35} + \frac{(35 - 35)^2}{35} + \frac{(30 - 35)^2}{35} + \frac{(35 - 35)^2}{35}$$

$$+ \frac{(20 - 15)^2}{15} + \frac{(15 - 15)^2}{15} + \frac{(20 - 15)^2}{15} + \frac{(10 - 15)^2}{15} + \frac{(10 - 15)^2}{15}$$

$$= 16.0$$

Thus, we conclude H_0: the distributions do not differ significantly more than expected by chance.

Ordinal Measurement Differences Between Groups

Let us now consider measurement values produced by an ordinal measurement process. Here measurement values indicate each sampling unit's possession of a greater or lesser quantity of the variable being measured. Thus, in addition to the equality or inequality of individual sampling units with respect to this variable, we may also determine their direction as either above or below each other.

The usual measure of typicalness with such data is the median value.[5] We simply order sampling units from least to most according to their possession of the variable of interest, locate the $n/2$ sampling unit from one end of the ordered sample, and designate its measurement value as the median.

---

[5]Of course, we may measure typicalness by the modal value. If we do, analysis methods discussed earlier apply.

To illustrate, let us return but expand our ski manufacturer example in Chapter 17. Suppose each year the manufacturer randomly selects ski testers of varying abilities who reside near Western, Midwestern, and Eastern ski areas. Each tester receives unidentified pairs of skis throughout the season, tries them for four days, returns them, and reports their experience via telephone. Included with their report is an overall evaluation of the ski on a scale of 1 to 20.

We said earlier that such ratings likely represent ordinal data because diverse testers will not rate skis using identical intervals between all evaluation scale rating points. Suppose data for two particular ski models reported by two groups of testers appear as in Table 18.5. At issue is whether median ratings differ between the two groups more than that expected by chance.

MEDIAN DIFFERENCES BETWEEN INDEPENDENT GROUPS

TABLE 18.5
Overall Performance Ratings and Combined Ranks for Ski Models X and Y

OVERALL PERFORMANCE RATINGS		COMBINED RANKS	
Model X Testers	Model Y Testers	Model X Testers	Model Y Testers
19	4	3.0	49.0
11	5	32.5	48.0
6	18	47.5	5.0
14	19	17.5	3.5
14	20	17.5	1.5
12	15	28.0	12.5
15	14	12.5	17.5
16	3	9.0	50.0
7	13	45.5	23.0
14	16	17.5	9.0
14	11	17.5	32.5
15	13	12.5	23.0
12	10	28.0	36.0
8	9	42.5	39.0
11	13	32.5	23.0
13	12	23.0	28.0
20	8	1.5	42.5
8	8	42.5	42.5
9	12	39.0	28.0
11	17	32.5	6.5
12	9	28.0	39.0
13	10	23.0	36.0
17	14	6.5	17.5
16	15	9.0	12.5
10	7	36.0	45.5
	Totals	604.5	670.5

Two Independent Groups.   Such an example describes an application for the test of median differences between two independent groups. The test is called a **Mann-Whitney U test.**

To begin, we combine the two samples into one large sample and rank each score. Tied scores receive the average of ranks that would have been assigned had their scores been slightly different. For example, two testers in the combined sample gave their skis scores of 20. They tie for top score and receive a rank of $(1 + 2)/2$ or 1.5 each. One tester provided the lowest score of 6 and receives the bottom rank of 50. These ranks and others for the combined sample also appear in Table 18.5.

Our test proceeds as follows.

1. State the null and alternate hypotheses as

$$H_0: \mu_{mdx} - \mu_{mdy} = 0 \qquad \text{(two-tail test)}$$

$$H_1: \mu_{mdx} - \mu_{mdy} \neq 0$$

2. Choose a critical value of Z from Table 2 in the Appendix for a desired α.

3. Calculate the value for the test statistic Z as

$$Z_{test} = \frac{U - (n_1 n_2/2)}{\sqrt{n_1 n_2 (n_1 + n_2 + 1)/12}}$$

4. Compare the value of Z_{test} to that of $Z_{critical}$ and state conclusions as below:
   If $-Z_{critical} \leq Z_{test} \leq +Z_{critical}$, accept H_0.
   Otherwise, accept H_1.

Our test lacks only a definition for U in step 3:

$$U = n_1 n_2 + \frac{n_1(n_1 + 1)}{2} - L_1$$

where L_1 is the sum of the ranks assigned to members of the first group, and n_1 and n_2 represent sample sizes for the two groups. For our data, we have $L_1 = 604.5$ and

$$U = (25)(25) + \frac{(25)(26)}{2} - 604.5$$

$$= 345.5$$

Let us state hypotheses as above, choose $Z_{critical}$ at 1.96 (allowing $\alpha = 0.05$), and apply the test to data in Table 18.5. We have

$$Z_{test} = \frac{345.5 - 312.5}{\sqrt{(25)(25)(25 + 25 + 1)/12}}$$

$$= 0.64$$

Because the interval ± 1.96 contains Z_{test}, we accept H_0. The median over-all performance rating is not significantly different between the two skis.

Beyond two independent samples, our test requires that both samples exceed 10 units in size.[6] Samples need not be of equal size. Our test is conservative by not adjusting for tied ranks. If the number of ties is quite large compared to sample size and Z_{test} lies close to either $+$ or $-Z_{critical}$, our test should be slightly modified.[7] Finally, our test may be further modified for the more powerful one-tail test.[8]

Three or C Independent Groups. Let us extend our example to now include a third sample that tests Model Z skis, as in Table 18.6. At issue here is whether median ratings differ between the three samples more than that expected by chance. For this inquiry, we need a slightly different test—the **Kruskal-Wallis one-way analysis of variance test.**

As we can see from Table 18.6, we again begin by combining our separate samples into one large sample and then rank each score. And, like before, tied scores receive the average of ranks for which they tied. Results of this ranking process also appear in Table 18.6.

Our test proceeds as follows.

1. State the null and alternate hypotheses as

$$H_0: \mu_{mdx} = \mu_{mdy} = \mu_{mdz}$$

H_1: Not all equalities in H_0 hold

2. Choose a critical value of χ^2 from Table 4 in the Appendix for a desired α and $C - 1$ degrees of freedom (C equals the number of independent groups).

3. Calculate the value for the test statistic χ^2 as

$$\chi^2_{test} = \frac{12}{N(N + 1)} \sum_{j=1}^{C} \frac{(L_j)^2}{n_j} - 3(N + 1)$$

4. Compare the value of χ^2_{test} to that of $\chi^2_{critical}$ and state conclusions as below:

If $\chi^2_{test} \leq \chi^2_{critical}$, accept H_0.
If $\chi^2_{test} > \chi^2_{critical}$, accept H_1.

For step 3, we define: N as the size of the combined sample; ΣL_j as the sum of the combined ranks of scores in the jth sample ($j = 1, 2, 3, \ldots, C$); and n_j as the size of the jth sample.

---

[6]Smaller samples use a slightly different test. See Sidney Siegel, *Nonparametric Statistics for the Behavioral Sciences* (New York: McGraw-Hill, 1956), pp. 116–20.

[7]Ibid., pp. 123–26.

[8]William Mendenhall and James E. Reinmuth, *Statistics for Management and Economics* (North Scituate, Mass: Duxbury Press, 1978), pp. 666–74.

TABLE 18.6
Overall Performance Ratings and Combined Ranks for Ski Models X, Y, and Z

OVERALL PERFORMANCE RATINGS			COMBINED RANKS		
Model X Testers	Model Y Testers	Model Z Testers	Model X Testers	Model Y Testers	Model Z Testers
19	4	18	3.5	69.5	6.0
11	5	18	43.5	68.0	6.0
6	18	9	67.0	6.0	54.0
14	19	8	24.0	3.5	59.5
14	20	15	24.0	1.5	17.5
12	15	4	37.0	17.5	69.5
15	14	3	17.5	24.0	72.0
16	3	7	12.0	72.0	64.5
7	13	2	64.5	30.5	74.0
14	16	16	24.0	12.0	12.0
14	11	15	24.0	43.5	17.5
15	13	12	17.5	30.5	37.0
12	10	10	37.0	49.0	49.0
8	9	11	59.5	54.0	43.5
11	13	3	43.5	30.5	72.0
13	12	14	30.5	37.0	24.0
20	8	16	1.5	59.5	12.0
8	8	8	59.5	59.5	59.5
9	12	7	54.0	37.0	64.5
11	17	13	43.5	8.5	30.5
12	9	1	37.0	54.0	75.0
13	10	10	30.5	49.0	49.0
17	14	11	8.5	24.0	43.5
16	15	9	12.0	17.5	54.0
10	7	12	49.0	64.5	37.0
		Totals (L_j)	824.5	922.5	1,103.0

We now can state hypotheses as above, then choose χ^2_{critical} for $\alpha = 0.05$ and 2 degrees of freedom at 5.991, and finally apply the test to data in Table 18.6. We have:

$$\chi^2_{\text{test}} = \frac{12}{(75)(76)} \left[\frac{(824.5)^2}{25} + \frac{(922.5)^2}{25} + \frac{(1,103.0)^2}{25} \right] - 3(76)$$

$$= 3.4$$

Because this value is less than that for χ^2_{critical}, we accept H_0. Sample data provide no evidence that unknown population median values differ from each other, when $\alpha = 0.05$.

Our test requires independent samples of at least size 5.[9] Samples

---

[9]Smaller samples use a slightly different test. See Siegel, *Nonparametric Statistics*, pp. 184–88.

need not be the same size. If the number of ties is large and χ^2_{test} is slightly less than $\chi^2_{critical}$, our test should be modified to correct for the attenuating effect of ties on the χ^2_{test}.[10] Finally, had our test accepted H_1, we would then investigate specific differences between pairs of medians for significant differences. The explanation of this contrasting procedure goes beyond our scope.[11]

Consider now the situation where samples are drawn dependently of one another. For example, suppose our ski manufacturer—instead of taking a separate random sample for each ski model tested—now matches testers of similar skiing abilities so that each sample now contains the same number of novice, intermediate, and advanced skiers. More precisely, suppose the researcher randomly chooses 3 novice, 15 intermediate, and 7 advanced skiers for each sample. Now if differences in median values between samples attain statistical significance, the researcher attaches more meaning: differences in skiing ability between samples could not have contributed to such results.

Of course, an even better control for skiing ability could be achieved by using only one sample of testers. Here each tester would receive all pairs of test skis (usually in a random sequence to prevent order bias) and report their ratings. Such is commonly called a **repeated measure design** and again illustrates dependent samples. Let us see how we test for significant median differences between such dependent groups.

MEDIAN DIFFERENCES BETWEEN DEPENDENT GROUPS

Two Dependent Groups. Consider two matched samples of 25 skiers each. Suppose that one member of each skier pair randomly receives a pair of Model X skis to test and that the other receives a pair of Model Y. We show data for the first two pairs of skiers below. How does analysis proceed?

Tester Pair	Model X Performance Rating	Model Y Performance Rating	Performance Rating Differences
A	19	13	6
B	11	13	−2

Actually, we answer the question quite easily with a test we already learned in Chapter 17—the **Wilcoxon signed-rank test.** There we applied

---

[10]See Siegel, *Nonparametric Statistics*, pp. 188–89 for a discussion of the procedure to correct for ties. Our data show ties occurring with 71 of the 75 sampling units, yet the application of this procedure increases the value for χ^2_{test} by only 0.5 percent.

[11]See Leonard A. Marascuilo and Maryellen McSweeney, "Nonparametric Post Hoc Comparisons for Trend," *Psychological Bulletin* 67 (December 1967): 401–12.

the test to data from a single sample appearing in Table 17.2. To indicate the parallel application here, notice that data above are identical to that in Table 17.2 for the first two sampling units.

As a more complete description, we first subtract the measurement value for each member of the second sample from that of its paired member in the first. Such differences are then treated exactly as the differences, $|X_i - \mu_{md}|$, in Table 17.2; we save space by not repeating the procedure here.

Three or C Dependent Groups. A different procedure applies to testing median differences between three or more dependent groups. The test is called the **Friedman two-way analysis of variance by ranks.** To illustrate its application, suppose our researcher now collects overall performance data on three ski models from three matched samples of 10 testers each. Results appear in Table 18.7.

Our first step in applying the test is to convert each raw score in Table 18.7 to a rank score within each group of sampling units. We do this in Table 18.8. As we can see, we merely assign ranks within each tester group based on original scores. Tied scores receive appropriate tied ranks. Our test continues as follows.

1. State null and alternate hypotheses as

    H_0: $\mu_{md_x} = \mu_{md_y} = \mu_{md_z}$

    H_1: Not all equalities in H_0 hold

2. Choose a critical value of χ^2 from Table 4 in the Appendix for a desired α and $C - 1$ degrees of freedom (C equals the number of dependent groups).

TABLE 18.7
Overall Performance Ratings for Ski Models X, Y, and Z

Tester Group	Model X Performance Rating	Model Y Performance Rating	Model Z Performance Rating
1	19	16	15
2	11	10	9
3	6	8	5
4	14	11	9
5	14	6	12
6	12	7	9
7	15	13	13
8	16	12	13
9	7	7	2
10	14	11	10

TABLE 18.8
Ranks of Performance Ratings for Ski Models X, Y, and Z

Tester Group	Model X Ranks	Model Y Ranks	Model Z Ranks
1	1	2	3
2	1	2	3
3	2	1	3
4	1	2	3
5	1	3	2
6	1	3	2
7	1	2.5	2.5
8	1	3	2
9	1.5	1.5	3
10	1	2	3
Totals (L_j)	11.5	22	26.5

3. Calculate the value of the test statistic χ^2 as

$$\chi_{test}^2 = \frac{12}{RC(C + 1)} \sum_{j=1}^{C} (L_j)^2 - 3R(C + 1)$$

4. Compare the value of χ_{test}^2 to that of $\chi_{critical}^2$ and state conclusions as below:

   If $\chi_{test}^2 \leq \chi_{critical}^2$, accept H_0.

   If $\chi_{test}^2 > \chi_{critical}^2$, accept H_1.

With knowledge that R in step 3 represents the number of rows in Table 18.8 and L_j the sum of each column ($j = 1, 2, 3, \ldots, C$), let us apply the test to our data.

We state hypotheses as above and choose χ^2 for $\alpha = 0.05$ and 2 degrees of freedom at 5.991. We have

$$\chi_{test}^2 = \frac{12}{(10)(3)(3 + 1)} [(11.5)^2 + (22.0)^2 + (26.5)^2] - 3(10)(3 + 1)$$

$$= 11.8$$

Consequently, we accept H_1: not all three population medians are equal. We cannot say which median exceeds which other, but it appears that ski Model X outperformed both Model Y and Model Z.[12]

Our test applies to dependent samples and to research designs such that $RC \geq 30$.[13] It is conservative because we do not adjust χ_{test}^2 for ties. If

---

[12]See Marascuilo and McSweeney, "Nonparametric Post Hoc Comparisons," for a discussion.

[13]E. L. Lehmann, *Nonparametrics: Statistical Methods Based on Ranks* (San Francisco: Holden-Day, 1975), p. 265.

the number of ties is large and χ^2_{test} is slightly less than $\chi^2_{critical}$, our test should be slightly modified.[14] It also may be modified to test more powerful directional hypotheses using inequalities instead of equal signs.[15]

Interval and Ratio Measurement Differences Between Groups

Our last major section in this chapter considers differences between measurement values produced by either interval or ratio measurement processes. Here measurement values indicate each sampling unit's possession of a greater or lesser quantity of the variable of interest, in terms of equal units of measurement. Thus, we may determine the equality, direction, and distance of individual sampling units with respect to this variable.

The usual measure of typicalness with such data is the mean.[16] Thus, our tests will examine mean differences between two samples and between C samples—in order to comment on the likelihood that differences represent true differences between unknown population means on a variable of interest. As with our earlier discussion in this chapter, the nature of such tests depends on the number of samples and on whether they are independent or dependent of each other.

MEAN DIFFERENCES BETWEEN TWO GROUPS   We introduce the test of mean differences between two groups with an example. Suppose a national chain of fast food restaurants shows concern for the cleanliness of customer areas in its several thousand franchises. Suppose it employs teams of inspectors, disguised as ordinary consumers, who visit and evaluate customer area hygiene. Each franchise's departure from company standards for customer areas outdoors and indoors is cited as a violation. Suppose data in Table 18.9 show results for two samples of restaurants in Pennsylvania and New York. A researcher wishes to know if the difference in mean violations between the two sales territories is statistically significant.

Two Independent Groups.   Such an example describes an application for the test of mean differences between two independent groups. Most readers can recall performing several such tests in an earlier statistics course. By way of review, then, our test proceeds as follows.

---

[14]Ibid., pp. 265–66.

[15]See James V. Bradley, *Distribution-Free Statistical Tests* (Englewood Cliffs, N.J.: Prentice-Hall, 1968), pp. 134–38 for a discussion.

[16]Of course, we may measure typicalness by either the median or modal values and apply earlier discussed methods of analysis.

TABLE 18.9
Mean Number of Cleanliness Violations for Pennsylvania and New York Territories

	TERRITORY (j)	
	Pennsylvania (1)	New York (2)
Sample Size (n_j)	50	70
Mean Number of Violations ($\overline{X}_j$)	4.4	4.9
Standard Deviation (s_j)	1.1	1.4

1. State null and alternate hypotheses as

$$H_0: \mu_1 - \mu_2 = 0$$

$$H_1: \mu_1 - \mu_2 \neq 0$$

2. Choose a critical value of Z from Table 2 in the Appendix for a desired α.

3. Calculate the value for the test statistic Z as

$$Z_{test} = \frac{(\overline{X}_1 - \overline{X}_2) - (\mu_1 - \mu_2)}{\sqrt{\dfrac{s_1^2}{n_1} + \dfrac{s_2^2}{n_2}}}$$

where s_j^2 and n_j represent the variance and the size of the jth sample.

4. Compare the value of Z_{test} to that of $Z_{critical}$ and state conclusions as below:

If $-Z_{critical} \leq Z_{test} \leq +Z_{critical}$, accept H_0.
Otherwise, accept H_1.

Stating hypotheses as above and choosing $Z_{critical}$ at 1.96, we apply the test to data in Table 18.9. We have under the null hypothesis:

$$Z_{test} = \frac{(4.4 - 4.9) - (0)}{\sqrt{\dfrac{(1.1)^2}{50} + \dfrac{(1.4)^2}{70}}} = -2.2$$

Thus, we accept H_1: at a 95 percent confidence level the two population means are not equal.

Notice that we do not conclude that significantly fewer cleanliness violations occurred in Pennsylvania than in New York. We did not test

500

this hypothesis. Rather, we tested the hypothesis of no difference and concluded that data failed to support only it. However, we may further state that it appears that fewer violations occurred in Pennsylvania.[17]

Two Dependent Groups. Let us modify our example slightly to test for significant differences between two dependent groups. Suppose our researcher would now like to see if cleanliness in customer areas improved for operations in New York during the most recent year. That is, suppose that teams of inspectors repeat their visits to the same 70 New York restaurants after a six-month interval. The two sets of sample data they produce are no longer independent (for example, a restaurant showing a large number of violations the first time might be expected to show a large number the second time) and our earlier discussion no longer applies.

Instead we use a different test with a much smaller standard error. It applies to differences in the number of violations between each matched pair in the sample (we have 70 such pairs because each restaurant is matched with itself). We obtain 70 differences by subtracting the number of violations noted at each second visit from the number of violations noted at each first visit. Suppose data for the first four restaurants in the study appear as follows:

Restaurant (i)	First Visit Number of Violations (X_{i1})	Second Visit Number of Violations (X_{i2})	Difference (d_i)
1	4	5	-1
2	8	6	2
3	7	5	2
4	1	2	-1

We denote the average of all differences as $\overline{X}_d$:

$$\overline{X}_d = \sum_{i=1}^{R} \frac{d_i}{R} \quad \text{where } d_i = X_{i1} - X_{i2}$$

and R is the number of rows or paired observations.

The statistic $\overline{X}_d$ estimates the unknown population difference μ_d. With this notation, our test proceeds as follows.

1. State null and alternate hypotheses as

$H_0: \mu_d = 0$

$H_1: \mu_d \neq 0$

[17]We could have instead tested this statement as a one-tail test; see any basic statistics text for details.

2. Choose a critical value of Z from Table 2 in the Appendix for a desired α.

3. Calculate the value for the test statistic Z as

$$Z_{\text{test}} = \frac{\overline{X}_d - \mu_d}{s_{\overline{X}_d}} \qquad \text{where } s_{\overline{X}_d} = \left[\sum_{i=1}^{R} \frac{(d_i - \overline{X}_d)^2}{R-1} \right]^{1/2} / \sqrt{R}$$

4. Compare the value of Z_{test} to that of Z_{critical} and state conclusions as below:

If $-Z_{\text{critical}} \leq Z_{\text{test}} \leq +Z_{\text{critical}}$, accept H_0.
Otherwise, accept H_1.

Only step 3 requires explanation. The symbol $s_{\overline{X}_d}$ estimates the standard error of the sampling distribution of the mean difference, exactly as $s_{\overline{X}}$ does for the sampling distribution of the mean. In fact, what we have here is a test identical to that for a single mean, discussed in Chapter 17, but where population and sample now consist of d_i instead of X_i values.

Suppose summary data for all $R = 70$ restaurants appear as below for an application of our test:

$$\overline{X}_d = -0.90, \qquad s_{\overline{X}_d} = 0.21$$

We state hypotheses as above, choose Z at 2.58, and have under the null hypothesis

$$Z_{\text{test}} = \frac{-0.90 - 0}{0.21} = -4.3$$

Consequently, we accept H_1. At a significance level of 0.01, differences in cleanliness exist between the two time periods. In particular, it appears that New York operations are becoming more clean.

Comments. Beyond interval or ratio data, our test of mean differences between two groups requires reasonably large samples. That is, when we have both sample sizes greatly exceeding thirty, then sampling distributions of Z_{test} closely approach normal distributions for all but very skewed populations. Yet often a researcher uses samples of thirty or less. In these instances, we require equal variances and normal distributions for the two populations under test and then resort to a slightly different t test.[18] If normality or these other requirements appear not to be met from an examination of the data, we would use instead a test of median differences between two groups.

---

[18]John Neter, William Wasserman, and G. A. Whitmore, *Applied Statistics* (Boston: Allyn and Bacon, 1978), pp. 311–27.

Finally, our tests describe procedures to test hypotheses of no mean difference between two groups. Other tests exist as simple modifications to test the more powerful hypothesis of a directional mean difference.[19]

MEAN DIFFERENCES BETWEEN THREE OR C GROUPS

Everything changes when a researcher wishes to examine three or more sample means for statistically significant differences. The general test procedure is called **analysis of variance,** usually abbreviated **ANOVA.** As an intuitive introduction,[20] consider data for our restaurant chain in Table 18.10, produced by independent samples of size $n_j = 3$ in each of the three states. At issue is whether differences between group means exceed those expected by chance.

Three or C Independent Groups.   Such a situation describes an ANOVA application for three independent groups. We begin by calculating $\overline{X}..$, the overall mean

$$\overline{X}.. = \sum_{j=1}^{C} \sum_{i=1}^{n_j} \frac{X_{ij}}{n_T}$$

where X_{ij} is the ith sample observation in the jth group, n_T the total sample size, n_j the sample size for the jth group, and C the number of groups. We now may express total variation or the *total* sum of squares as:

$$SSTO = \sum_{j=1}^{C} \sum_{i=1}^{n_j} (X_{ij} - \overline{X}..)^2$$

TABLE 18.10
Cleanliness Violations for Pennsylvania, New York, and Ohio Territories

OBSERVATION (i)	TERRITORY (j)		
	Pennsylvania (1)	New York (2)	Ohio (3)
1	4	7	11
2	5	8	10
3	6	9	12
Means ($\overline{X}_j$)	5	8	11

[19]Lawrence L. Lapin, *Statistics: Meaning and Method* (New York: Harcourt Brace Jovanovich, 1975), pp. 413–19.

[20]Statistics texts devote chapters or their entire contents to a discussion of ANOVA. An excellent introduction is Chapter 13 in Lapin, *Statistics: Meaning and Method.* Far more detail may be found in Chapters 13 through 20 of John Neter and William Wasserman, *Applied Linear Statistical Models* (Homewood, Ill.: Richard D. Irwin, 1974).

which for our data is:

$$SSTO = (4 - 8)^2 + (5 - 8)^2 + (6 - 8)^2 + \ldots + (12 - 8)^2$$

$$= 60$$

Such formulas and results appear as we might expect from our discussion of regression in Chapter 17.

Very easily we can calculate the variation or sum of squares *within* each group:

$$SSW = \sum_{j=1}^{C} \sum_{i=1}^{n_j} (X_{ij} - \overline{X}_{.j})^2$$

$$= (4 - 5)^2 + (5 - 5)^2 + (6 - 5)^2 + (7 - 8)^2 + \ldots + (12 - 11)^2$$

$$= 6$$

We define $\overline{X}_{.j}$ in the calculation for SSW as the average measurement value for the jth group and calculate it by

$$\overline{X}_{.j} = \sum_{i=1}^{n_j} \frac{X_{ij}}{n_j}$$

The SSW parallels SSE in regression analysis. In fact, some texts identify SSW as the error sum of squares—that is, the sum of squares due to sampling and other error.

Similarly, we can calculate the variation or sum of squares *between* each group as

$$SSB = \sum_{j=1}^{C} n_j (\overline{X}_{.j} - \overline{X}_{..})^2$$

$$= 3(5 - 8)^2 + 3(8 - 8)^2 + 3(11 - 8)^2$$

$$= 54$$

The SSB parallels SSR in regression analysis.

As our data show, and as we might have guessed,

$$SSTO = SSW + SSB$$

or

$$60 = 6 + 54$$

Thus, SSB accounts for almost all the total variation in the data. This seems reasonable from an inspection of Table 18.10. Group means differ by at least three units from each other while individual values within each group differ from each other only by at least one unit.

Now, what would sums of squares look like if the three group means differed not at all? Let us see from some new data in Table 18.11, where all the variation occurs within groups. We now have $SSTO$ equal to 54,

TABLE 18.11
Cleanliness Violations for Pennsylvania, New York, and Ohio

OBSERVATION (i)	TERRITORY (j)		
	Pennsylvania (1)	New York (2)	Ohio (3)
1	4	4	4
2	7	7	7
3	10	10	10
Means ($\overline{X}_j$)	7	7	7

SSW also equal to 54, and *SSB* equal to 0. Thus, when groups are exactly identical, *SSB* will equal 0. Or, as group means approach each other, *SSB* approaches 0.

Equally telling, we could ask what would sums of squares look like if individual values showed no variation at all within groups? Rearranging Table 18.11 to this situation as Table 18.12, we get *SSTO* equal again to 54 but now *SSW* equals 0 and *SSB* becomes 54. Thus, when groups contain no variation within them, *SSB* equals *SSTO*. Or, as variation within groups approaches 0, *SSB* approaches *SSTO*.

Thus, we might expect ANOVA to compare the sizes of *SSW* and *SSB* in analyzing differences between groups. Just so. However, to account for the different number of squares that make up *SSW* and *SSB* we must first compute average or mean squares after the fashion of regression. We define our mean squares as

$$MSW = \frac{SSW}{n_T - C} \quad \text{and} \quad MSB = \frac{SSB}{C - 1}$$

and have for our original data in Table 18.10

$$MSW = 6/6 = 1 \quad \text{and} \quad MSB = 54/2 = 27$$

TABLE 18.12
Cleanliness Violations for Pennsylvania, New York, and Ohio

OBSERVATION (i)	TERRITORY (j)		
	Pennsylvania (1)	New York (2)	Ohio (3)
1	4	7	10
2	4	7	10
3	4	7	10
Means ($\overline{X}_j$)	4	7	10

With this notation, we now may state our test for significant differences between means from C independent groups as follows.

1. State null and alternate hypotheses as

   H_0: $\mu_1 = \mu_2 = \mu_3 = \ldots = \mu_C$

   H_1: Not all equalities in H_0 hold

2. Choose a critical value of F from Table 5 in the Appendix for a desired α and $C - 1$ and $n_T - C$ degrees of freedom in the numerator and denominator, respectively.

3. Calculate the value of the test statistic F_{test} as

   $$F_{\text{test}} = \frac{MSB}{MSW}$$

4. Compare the value of F_{test} to the chosen value of F_{critical} and state conclusions as below:

   If $F_{\text{test}} \leq F_{\text{critical}}$, accept H_0.
   If $F_{\text{test}} > F_{\text{critical}}$, accept H_1.

We state hypotheses as above, choose α at 0.05, and determine the critical value of F for 2 and 6 degrees of freedom at 5.14. We have

$F_{\text{test}} = 27/1 = 27$

Consequently, we accept H_1: at a 95 percent confidence level, not all μ_j are equal.

Usually a researcher would summarize findings in a conventional **ANOVA table,** as in Table 18.13. Our data appear in Table 18.14. Notice that Table 18.13 applies to a "single-factor study." That is, our example considered the effect of one factor, which we call territory, on cleanliness

TABLE 18.13
General Form of the ANOVA Table for a Single-Factor Study

Source of Variation	Sum of Squares	Degrees of Freedom	MS	F_{test}	Probability
Between	$SSB = \sum\limits_{j=1}^{C} n_j (\overline{X}_j - \overline{X}_{..})^2$	$C - 1$	$MSB = \dfrac{SSB}{C - 1}$	MSB/MSW	α
Within	$SSW = \sum\limits_{j=1}^{C} \sum\limits_{i=1}^{n_j} (X_{ij} - \overline{X}_j)^2$	$n_T - C$	$MSW = \dfrac{SSW}{n_T - C}$		
Total	$SSTO = \sum\limits_{j=1}^{C} \sum\limits_{i=1}^{n_j} (X_{ij} - \overline{X}_{..})^2$	$n_T - 1$			

TABLE 18.14
ANOVA Table for Example of Cleanliness Violations of Restaurants

Source of Variation	Sum of Squares	Degrees of Freedom	MS	F_{test}	Probability
Between	54	2	27	27	0.0016
Within	6	6	1		
Total	60	8			

violations. In Chapter 19, we shall see how to extend ANOVA to two- and multifactor studies.

With results like those in Table 18.14, a researcher would usually proceed to examine factor level means for each territory—to see which ones differ significantly from which others. The examination departs slightly from our earlier discussed test of mean differences between two groups. Here we use a confidence interval of the form

$$\mu_j - \mu_{j'} = \overline{X}_j - \overline{X}_{j'} \pm t \left[\frac{MSW}{n_j} + \frac{MSW}{n_{j'}} \right]^{1/2}$$

where j and j' identify the two groups of interest. If the confidence interval contains 0, we conclude that the two unknown population means do not differ, at a $1 - \alpha$ confidence level.

An example illustrates. Suppose we are interested in the difference $\mu_2 - \mu_1$. That is, suppose we wonder if the mean number of cleanliness violations shown in Table 18.10 differs between Pennsylvania and New York. Our confidence interval is (using t from Table 3 in the Appendix with $n_T - C$ or 6 degrees of freedom and $\alpha = 0.05$):

$$\mu_2 - \mu_1 = 8 - 5 \pm 2.447 \sqrt{1/3 + 1/3}$$

or

$$1 \le \mu_2 - \mu_1 \le 5$$

and we conclude the two population means are not equal. It appears that restaurants in New York show between 1 and 5 more violations than restaurants in Pennsylvania.

Similar tests would examine differences between $\mu_3 - \mu_1$ and $\mu_3 - \mu_2$. We have

$$4 \le \mu_3 - \mu_1 \le 8$$
$$1 \le \mu_3 - \mu_2 \le 5$$

Because no confidence interval includes 0, each pair of mean comparisons $\mu_j - \mu_{j'}$ is statistically significant at $\alpha = 0.05$. However, we cannot simultaneously consider all three confidence intervals as a family and conclude that significantly more violations occurred in Ohio as compared to New York and Pennsylvania and that more occurred in New York than in Pennsylvania at an $\alpha = 0.05$. To make such a simultaneous multiple comparison requires procedures that produce slightly larger confidence intervals, the discussion of which goes beyond our scope.[21] Moreover, the majority of these procedures apply to all possible comparisons between population means, specified either before or after data have been collected and analyzed. Our preceding confidence interval procedure requires instead that the researcher *state in advance* those population mean differences to be tested.

Three or C Dependent Groups.   One major change occurs with three or more dependent samples. Here our procedure explicitly considers and removes from SSW a part of variation due to inherent differences between sampling units. Such practice reduces both MSW and its degrees of freedom compared to that obtained if we instead had had independent groups. To show this, see data in Table 18.15 for a sample of three restaurants in Ohio. Notice that data represent results of a repeated measure research design, because each restaurant provides three measurements at three different times.

We begin the analysis by calculating $SSTO$ and SSB from the two formulas given in Table 18.13, as if we had independent groups. It might be good practice to confirm that these values are

$$SSTO = 76.00 \quad \text{and} \quad SSB = 16.67$$

for data in Table 18.15. We now calculate a new sum of squares as the blocking sum of squares due to differences between rows in Table 18.15.

TABLE 18.15
Cleanliness Violations for a Sample of 3 Ohio Restaurants Over 18 Months

Sampling Unit (i)	Violations at Time j:			Mean Violations $(\overline{X}_{i.})$
	1	2	3	
1	4	1	4	3.00
2	7	5	9	7.00
3	8	8	11	9.00
Mean Violations $(\overline{X}_{.j})$	6.33	4.67	8.00	

[21] The three most commonly used are the Tukey, Scheffé, and Bonferroni methods. See Neter and Wasserman, *Applied Linear Statistical Models*, Chap. 14 for a discussion.

We denote this sum of squares as $SSBL$ and calculate it by

$$SSBL = C \sum_{i=1}^{n_j} (\overline{X}_{i.} - \overline{X}_{..})^2$$

For Table 18.15 we have

$$\overline{X}_{..} = \sum_{j=1}^{C} \sum_{i=1}^{n_j} \frac{X_{ij}}{n_T} = 6.33$$

and

$$SSBL = 3[(3 - 6.33)^2 + (7 - 6.33)^2 + (9 - 6.33)]^2 = 56$$

We finally calculate the within-group sum of squares, from a different formula than that given in Table 18.13:

$$SSW = \sum_{j=1}^{C} \sum_{i=1}^{n_j} (X_{ij} - \overline{X}_{i.} - \overline{X}_{.j} + \overline{X}_{..})^2$$

Or, rather than endure such lengthy arithmetic, we instead can calculate SSW as

$$SSW = SSTO - SSBL - SSB$$

which, for our data, is

$$SSW = 76 - 56 - 16.67 = 3.33$$

As we did in Table 18.13 for independent samples, we summarize these terms in a general ANOVA table (in Table 18.16) for a blocked single-factor study. With a dependent sample, each of the n sampling units is stitutes a block or row of C dependent measurements.

With this notation and degrees of freedom, our test for significant dif-

TABLE 18.16
General Form of the ANOVA Table for a Blocked Single-Factor Study

Source of Variation	Sum of Squares	Degrees of Freedom	MS	F_{test}	Probability
Blocks	SSBL	$n - 1$			
Between	SSB	$C - 1$	$MSB = \dfrac{SSB}{C - 1}$	$\dfrac{MSB}{MSW}$	α
Within	SSW	$(n - 1)(C - 1)$	$MSW = \dfrac{SSW}{(n - 1)(C - 1)}$		
Total	SSTO	$nC - 1$			

TABLE 18.17
ANOVA Table for the Blocked Cleanliness Violation Example

Source of Variation	Sum of Squares	Degrees of Freedom	MS	F_{test}	Probability
Blocks	56.00	2			
Between	16.67	2	8.33	10.00	0.03
Within	3.33	4	0.83		
Total	76.00	8			

ferences between three or more dependent sample means proceeds identically to that for independent sample means. To save space, we present only the results in Table 18.17. We see that we accept the alternate hypothesis at $\alpha \leq 0.03$: not all dependent sample means are equal. Again saving space, we only note that our next task would be to compare each pair of means from the three time periods for significant differences, exactly as we did for independent samples.

Had data for the three time periods instead represented data from three *independent samples* we could not calculate *SSBL*. Instead, we would have applied formulas from Table 18.13 and accepted the *null* hypothesis with an F_{test} of 0.84. Such results, showing the relatively greater efficiency of the dependent sample design over the independent sample design, are typical.

Comments. Forms of ANOVA for independent and dependent samples require interval or ratio level measurements of the dependent variable. Both forms of ANOVA generally require larger sample sizes than illustrated here, of sufficient size to protect against Type I and Type II errors.[22] Both possess computational formulas different than those given here to facilitate computing *SSTO*, *SSB*, *SSW*, and *SSBL* for these larger samples. Rather than discuss the application of computational formulas, we note simply that a researcher will usually use a computer to analyze data from larger samples anyway.

Most important, both forms of ANOVA require the *C* samples to be drawn from approximately normal populations having equal variances. Serious violations of this requirement may mean either the Kruskal-Wallis or Friedman tests should be applied instead.

---

[22]See Neter and Wasserman, *Applied Linear Statistical Models*, pp. 492–501 for a discussion of two approaches estimating sample sizes for ANOVA.

Chapter Summary

The choice of statistical methods to examine differences between groups depends on measurement level and on sampling procedures associated with the data. We summarize the possibilities in Table 18.18.

Our intent in discussing these dozen or so methods is not to transform the researcher into an applied statistics expert. Nor is she or he expected to memorize the four parallel steps, including unique test statistics, that apply to all methods. Rather, we now should be:

1. acquainted with the various tests and their procedures, interpretations, and requirements;

2. aware of their similarities in process despite their differences in content; and

3. impressed with the need to employ the proper test, given its requirements and the data's measurement level and sampling procedures.

In leaving, we note here as we have several times earlier: all such statistical tests of significance apply to sample data. If data instead come from a census, we need only inspect results to see if the two or more groups differ; such groups either do or do not.

TABLE 18.18
Measurement Level, Sampling Procedure, and Tests of Differences Between Groups

| MEASUREMENT LEVEL | SAMPLING PROCEDURE | | | |
| | Independent Samples | | Dependent Samples | |
	2	3 or More	2	3 or More
Nominal	Z-test of proportions, χ^2 test of collapsed proportions, χ^2 test of independence	χ^2 test of collapsed proportions, χ^2 test of independence	Cochran test	Cochran test
Ordinal	Mann-Whitney U test	Kruskal-Wallis test	Wilcoxon signed-rank test	Friedman test
Interval or Ratio	Z-test, t-test	ANOVA	Z-test or t-test for dependent samples	ANOVA for blocked data

Chapter Review

Independent sample	Friedman test
Dependent sample	SSTO
Cochran test	SSB
Mann-Whitney U test	SSW
Kruskal-Wallis test	SSBL
Wilcoxon test	

KEY TERMS

DISCUSSION QUESTIONS

1. Compare and contrast these two data analysis purposes: showing relationships between variables and showing differences between groups.

2. A repeated measure research design produces a dependent sample and a reduced value for sampling error, compared to an independent sample. What sorts of errors often increase with a repeated measure design?

3. Intuitively, why would you expect a smaller standard error with a repeated-measure design compared to an independent samples design—all sample sizes being equal?

4. Suppose one week you visit a random sample of 25 fast food restaurants between the hours of 11:00 A.M. and 1:00 P.M. You classify the service into three categories (slow, ok, and fast). Exactly six hours later, you return and reclassify each restaurant. Describe how you would test

   a) the statistical significance of an apparent decrease in the proportion of restaurants classified as fast in the two time periods.

   b) the statistical significance of differences between the distributions of service frequencies for the two time periods.

5. Suppose you collected gasoline mileage data from random samples of 50 owners each for 7 different subcompact automobiles. Instead of using ANOVA to see if average mileage differences are significantly different at $\alpha = 0.05$, you decide to use Z-tests for the 21 pair differences (subcompact A versus subcompact B, subcompact A versus subcompact C, etc.). Comment on this data analysis plan.

PROBLEMS

1. Complete the ANOVA table below for a research design using three independent samples of size 21. Are the unknown population means identical, using $\alpha = 0.05$?

Source	Sum of Squares	Degrees of Freedom	MS	F_{test}
Between	4812	_____	_____	_____
Within	1504	_____	_____	
Total	_____			

2. A loan officer in a bank compiles the following data from simple random samples of size 100 among used car loans made to residents in one of four neighborhoods.

Neighborhood:	A	B	C	D
Number of Loans Delinquent:	5	7	6	10

a) Do the neighborhoods show significantly different delinquency rates, using $\alpha = 0.05$?

b) Suppose instead of representing data from four neighborhoods, data represent results of four random samples taken in the same neighborhood at three-month intervals. Would your recommended test of significant differences change from question 2a? Explain.

3. In Table 18.4, suppose the researcher collected data for only month 1 and month 2. Using $\alpha = 0.05$, test whether the proportions of retailers showing drills at eye level changed for the two time periods.

4. A researcher collects the following data from two independent random samples of 60 beer drinking college students.

	Fraternity Affiliated	Not Fraternity Affiliated
Drink generic branded beer	10	15
Drink national branded beer	50	45

Test proportions of generic beer drinkers for significant differences, using $\alpha = 0.05$ and a

a) Z-test;

b) χ^2 test.

c) Compare values of the test statistics for the two tests.

5. Consider the last twelve testers in Table 18.5 for both Model X and Model Y skis.

a) Test their ratings for a significant median difference, using $\alpha = 0.05$, and state your conclusions.

b) Another researcher accepts these ratings as interval data. Test for a significant mean difference, using ANOVA with $\alpha = 0.05$, and state your conclusions.

6. Consider the last ten ski testers in Table 18.6 for ski Models X, Y, and Z.

a) Test their ratings for a significant median difference, using $\alpha = 0.05$, and state your conclusions.

b) Another researcher is willing to accept ratings as interval data. Test ratings for a significant mean difference, using $\alpha = 0.05$, and state your conclusions.

7. Apply the Wilcoxon signed-rank test to data in Table 18.5, making the assumption that a dependent sampling process produced the two sets of rankings. Use $\alpha = 0.05$ and state your conclusions.

8. Consider the following ordinal rating data for eight wine tasters:

Taster	Wine A	Wine B	Wine C	Wine D
1	15	12	7	11
2	16	13	5	12
3	18	14	10	15
4	16	12	8	12
5	12	10	6	11
6	14	13	7	12
7	15	13	7	14
8	14	13	8	13

Are differences between the four wines statistically significant, using $\alpha = 0.05$?

9. Suppose you consider data in problem 8 to be interval data. Are differences between the four means statistically significant, using $\alpha = 0.05$? Construct the ANOVA table as part of your answer.

10. Data below came from two independent simple random samples of consumers. Is there a significant difference between the two sample means, at $\alpha = 0.01$?

	Zip Code: 55414	Zip Code: 55413
Sample size (n_j)	500	250
Weekday hours watching TV $(\overline{X}_j)$	1.7	2.0
Standard deviation (s_j)	1.0	1.5

Additional Readings

Most tests identified in Table 18.18 are discussed in basic statistics texts. See either Neter, Wasserman, and Whitmore's *Applied Statistics* (identified more completely at the end of Chapter 12) or Mendenhall and Reinmuth's *Statistics for Management and Economics* (identified at the end of Chapter 17) for good treatments. For more detail on ANOVA, see Neter and Wasserman's *Applied Linear Statistical Models* (also noted at the end of Chapter 17). Finally, we list one new text as a more complete source for many of the nominal and ordinal level tests:

Conover, W. J. *Practical Nonparametric Statistics*. New York: John Wiley & Sons, 1971.

19

CAUSALITY: Experimental and Quasi-Experimental Designs

An experiment investigates the extent to which a change in one variable leads to a change in another for an identified population under controlled conditions.[1] As an example, consider a sales manager who raises the sales commission rate for a laundry detergent from 10 percent to 15 percent during the last quarter of 1981. During the quarter she makes no changes to the product's price or to its advertising budget. At the end of the quarter she notes a SAMI-based market share increase of two percentage points. As another example, consider a marketing researcher measuring consumer reaction to several versions of a new orange flavored cake mix. He assembles six different samples of consumers to taste one of six different formulations, based on two levels of sugar and three levels of flavor. The sweet, strong flavor formulation outperforms all others.

These and all marketing research experiments share four basic concepts:

Treatments—levels of intensity or forms of a single independent variable in a single-factor experiment (or combinations of levels or forms of two or more independent variables in a multifactor experiment). Experiments test the effects of treatments.

---

[1]This chapter draws heavily from two sources: Donald T. Campbell and Julian C. Stanley, *Experimental and Quasi-Experimental Designs for Research* (Chicago: Rand McNally, 1963, 1966); and John Neter and William Wasserman, *Applied Linear Statistical Models* (Homewood, Ill.: Richard D. Irwin, 1974).

Dependent variable—the variable on which the researcher obtains measurements to indicate the influence of the treatments.

Test units—the population elements providing dependent variable measurements. A test unit may consist of a group of population elements.

Extraneous variables—other than the treatments, all factors that also influence dependent variable measurements.

Researchers apply these concepts as experimental designs. An **experimental design** specifies treatments, the dependent variable, test units, and extraneous variables. It also describes rules and procedures to conduct the experiment—how to make random assignments of treatments to experimental units (or vice versa), when to measure the dependent variable, and how to control extraneous variables. We should be able to identify these concepts in the preceding examples with little difficulty.

Only extraneous variables may give a problem. Our definition implies that extraneous variables are the conditions under which researchers conduct experiments. Researchers can control some extraneous variables but not others. For our laundry detergent experiment, examples of controllable extraneous variables include the firm's advertising appeals, salesforce size, product design, and price. Examples of uncontrollable extraneous variables include economic conditions and competitive marketing tactics. Suppose all these extraneous variables changed along with the sales commission rate in the last quarter of 1981. How would we interpret the influence of the experimental treatment on market share? Quite simply, we could not. Some or all of these extraneous variables could have partly or entirely caused the increase of two percentage points.

In a well-designed experiment, researchers attempt to control extraneous variables. If they do not, changes in the extraneous variables will make it impossible to measure the influence of only the treatment. In such a situation, researchers say that extraneous variables *confound the influence of the treatments.*

Our two opening examples yield three more points:

1. Researchers conduct experiments in both field and laboratory settings. They find the latter much more controllable.

2. Some experiments are more formally designed and conducted than others. We emphasize these in our discussion.

3. Test units can consist of people, organizations, and other entities (primarily objects and events). Any experimental design will use only one type of test unit.

Our next section discusses experimental designs and experimental data analyses. We will see that many designs use analysis procedures identical to those discussed in Chapter 18 for groups identified through survey results. Here the procedures will apply to groups identified through random assignment of test units to experimental treatments. All procedures have as their objective the investigation of causality, our seventh and final purpose in analyzing data.

Experimental Designs

We discuss seven experimental designs and analysis of their results with the help of the following symbols:

$\overline{X}_i$—the ith measurement value (average) on the dependent variable

T_j—the jth treatment

EG_j—the experimental group receiving the jth treatment

CG—the control group

A before-after experimental design looks like this:

EG_1: $\overline{X}_1$ T_1 $\overline{X}_2$

BEFORE-AFTER DESIGN

In words, the researcher randomly selects an experimental group, measures the dependent variable, introduces a treatment, and measures the dependent variable again. The influence of T_1 is given by

$Y_{T_1} = \overline{X}_2 - \overline{X}_1$

This difference can be easily tested for statistical significance using $\overline{X}_d$ as discussed in Chapter 18.

However, a significant difference in this design means nothing because a host of unspecified, uncontrolled, and unmeasured extraneous variables confound the difference. In short, the design represents our laundry detergent experiment and the influence of only T_1 cannot be measured under such conditions. Avoid this design in favor of the next.

The before-after with control design removes the confounding effect of most extraneous variables:

EG_1: $\overline{X}_1$ T_1 $\overline{X}_2$

CG: $\overline{X}_3$ $\overline{X}_4$

BEFORE-AFTER WITH CONTROL DESIGN

Again and in all following experimental designs the researcher randomly assigns test units to either experimental or control groups. We assume for the time being that EG_1 and CG contain a large number of test units. Once assigned, all test units produce dependent variable measurements at the same two points in time. However, test units in the experimental group produce their second dependent variable measurement after exposure to the treatment, while test units in the control group do not. The influence of T_1 is given by

$$Y_{T_1} = (\overline{X}_2 - \overline{X}_1) - (\overline{X}_4 - \overline{X}_3)$$

This difference can again be easily tested for statistical significance using a test procedure from Chapter 18. That is, we would treat values for the two terms in parentheses as means for two independent groups and then undertake a Z-test between the two means.

Look carefully at the second term in the expression and ask what could have led to the difference, $(\overline{X}_4 - \overline{X}_3)$? We should conclude that only extraneous variables could be responsible. Thus, by subtracting the second term from the first, we remove the influence of all extraneous variables *except one* in estimating the influence of T_1. Researchers call the remaining extraneous variable the *before measurement interaction effect*.

Why the before measurement interaction effect remains is due to its nature. The effect reflects the possibility that test units in the experimental group may react to the treatment differently than they normally should because of the before measurement. That is, the before measurement may alert or sensitize test units to the treatment, thereby raising or lowering its influence. When this happens, the before measurement and the treatment *interact* (and confound the experiment). A before measurement interaction effect can occur primarily when people constitute test units, and then not in every instance.

Why no other extraneous variable effects remain follows from one assumption and one fact. The assumption is that all other extraneous variables but the before measurement interaction effect operate to an equal extent in both the experimental and control groups. Not an extreme assumption, it stems from the fact that the researcher randomly identifies both groups and then treats them *exactly equally* except on one consideration: the treatment variable.

Let us consider an example. Suppose a laboratory researcher asks a consumer to name as many brands of radial tires as he can. On completing the task, he watches a half-hour situation comedy on a laboratory television monitor, still somewhat aware of the request. Part way through the show a commercial appears for Michelin. At the end of the show, the researcher asks the same question. Any difference in Michelin brand awareness, $(\overline{X}_2 - \overline{X}_1)$, for all experimental group members comes partly from the influence of the commercial and partly from the sensitizing first measurement. Our next experimental design eliminates this confounding effect.

AFTER-ONLY
WITH CONTROL
DESIGN

Look carefully at the expression for the influence of T_1 in the last design $(\overline{X}_2 - \overline{X}_1) - (\overline{X}_4 - \overline{X}_3)$. We can quite easily rewrite this expression as $(\overline{X}_2 - \overline{X}_4) - (\overline{X}_1 - \overline{X}_3)$ and ask what should be true about the last term?

If the researcher performed the random assignment properly and used large samples for experimental and control groups, $\overline{X}_1$ should equal $\overline{X}_3$, and the term should equal zero. Random assignment, large samples, and this equality assumption underlie the after-only with control design:

EG$_1$: T_1 $\overline{X}_1$

CG: $\overline{X}_2$

Here a researcher randomly assigns test units to either experimental or control groups. The experimental group receives the treatment and then both groups provide dependent variable measurements at the same two points in time. The influence of T_1 is given by

$$Y_{T_1} = \overline{X}_1 - \overline{X}_2$$

exactly equivalent to the first rewritten term above. This difference can again be easily tested for statistical significance using a Z-test procedure for two independent groups.

Note that a researcher can execute this design more quickly and more cheaply than our before-after with control design because it uses only two dependent variable measurements. Note particularly that no before measurement interacts with T_1 to confound the after measurement, $\overline{X}_1$. This idea of using no before measurement forms the basis for our next four experimental designs.

Usually a researcher experiments with more than one treatment. More treatments in an experiment come either from additional levels of one factor or from more than one factor. We call the first a **single-factor design** and the second a **multifactor** or **factorial design.** **COMPLETELY RANDOMIZED DESIGNS**

Single-Factor Design. In symbols, a single-factor design appears in Table 19.1 (assume the factor has three levels). Notice that our symbolic representation has grown slightly. The basic entry is X_{ij}, which signifies the dependent variable measurement value for the ith test unit when exposed to the jth factor level or treatment. Thus, X_{21} stands for the measurement obtained from the second test unit after being given the first treatment. Dots indicate that calculations are performed over test units, treatments, or both—depending on their location. For example, $\overline{X}_{.1}$ is the average for all test units exposed to treatment 1, and $\overline{X}_{..}$ is the overall average or grand mean for all test units over all treatments.

The analysis issue is whether $\overline{X}_{.1}$, $\overline{X}_{.2}$, or $\overline{X}_{.3}$ differ significantly. We explain with an example. Consider a marketing researcher employed by a regional chain of pizza restaurants. He wishes to investigate the influence of three price increases—5, 8, and 10 percent—on the number of pizzas sold over a 60-day period. Thus, price levels constitute factor levels or treatments and pizzas sold are the dependent variable in the design. The researcher proceeds by randomly selecting 18 of the chain's restau-

TABLE 19.1
A Single-Factor Experimental Design

TEST UNITS (i)	FACTOR LEVEL (T_j)			
	T_1	T_2	T_3	Total
1	X_{11}	X_{12}	X_{13}	
2	X_{21}	X_{22}	X_{23}	
3	X_{31}	X_{32}	X_{33}	
4	X_{41}	X_{42}	X_{43}	
5	X_{51}	X_{52}	X_{53}	
6	X_{61}	X_{62}	X_{63}	
Total	$\Sigma X_{.1}$	$\Sigma X_{.2}$	$\Sigma X_{.3}$	$\Sigma\Sigma X_{..}$
Mean	$\overline{X}_{.1}$	$\overline{X}_{.2}$	$\overline{X}_{.3}$	$\overline{X}_{..}$
Number of test units (n_j)	n_1	n_2	n_3	n_T

rants of approximately the same seating capacity. He then randomly assigns 6 restaurants to each treatment. Thus, groups of 3 restaurants constitute test units in the design. He raises prices and measures sales.

At the end of the experiment, he computes $\overline{X}_{.1}$, $\overline{X}_{.2}$, and $\overline{X}_{.3}$. He tests for statistical significance using ANOVA for three independent groups (Chapter 18) and concludes that unit sales did not differ significantly between any of the treatments. The restaurant chain implements the 10 percent increase.

Notice the absence of a control group. The design investigates only the relative influence of the three price increases; it does not investigate their influence compared to sales without a price increase. Of course, the design could have done this had the researcher been so interested. Notice also that we have dropped our assumption that each group contains a large number of test units.[2]

Factorial Design.   In contrast to a single-factor design, a factorial design includes more than one factor or independent variable. Treatments consist of combinations of factor levels instead of levels of a single factor as in the preceding example. We explain by adding to the example.

Suppose the researcher wishes also to investigate the influence on pizza sales of ingredient costs. Specifically, suppose he is also considering either cutting ingredient costs by 10 percent, keeping costs the same, or increasing them by 5 percent. He could conduct another single-factor experiment, in which he would hold prices constant and vary the ingre-

---

[2]See Neter and Wasserman, *Applied Linear Statistical Models*, pp. 492–501 for a discussion of procedures to estimate sample sizes for single-factor experiments.

dient costs (the new independent variable). However, conducting two single-factor experiments doubles costs and, as we shall see, actually provides less information than would one factorial design.

In symbols, a factorial design for our example appears in Table 19.2. Like Table 19.1, the basic entry in Table 19.2 is X_{ij}, the dependent variance measurement result for the ith test unit on the jth treatment. A researcher would describe such an experiment as a 3×3 (three by three) factorial design. It contains 2 factors, price and quality, each having 3 levels for a total of 9 treatments. A $4 \times 6 \times 3$ design would contain 3 factors, the first having 4 levels, the second having 6, and the third having 3. This design would have 72 treatments. So many treatments might be very expensive or impossible to execute (perhaps there are only 36 test units, for example). In this case, the researcher could either eliminate a factor, eliminate a factor level, or conduct a *fractional factorial experiment* containing fewer than all 72 treatments.

Analysis of factorial designs proceeds with somewhat more difficulty than single-factor designs.[3] However, analysis issues are quite straightforward. To show this, we adopt the usual convention of designating the first factor as A, the second factor as B, and so on. For our 3×3 design the basic issues are:

- Does factor A influence the dependent variable?
- Does factor B influence the dependent variable?

TABLE 19.2
A 3 × 3 Factorial Design

	TREATMENTS (T_j)								
	Prices + 5%			Prices + 8%			Prices + 10%		
TEST UNITS (i)	T_1 Costs -10%	T_2 Costs Same	T_3 Costs $+5\%$	T_4 Costs -10%	T_5 Costs Same	T_6 Costs $+5\%$	T_7 Costs -10%	T_8 Costs Same	T_9 Costs $+5\%$
1	X_{11}	X_{12}	X_{13}	X_{14}	X_{15}	X_{16}	X_{17}	X_{18}	X_{19}
2	X_{21}	X_{22}	X_{23}	X_{24}	X_{25}	X_{26}	X_{27}	X_{28}	X_{29}
Total	$\Sigma X_{.1}$	$\Sigma X_{.2}$	$\Sigma X_{.3}$	$\Sigma X_{.4}$	$\Sigma X_{.5}$	$\Sigma X_{.6}$	$\Sigma X_{.7}$	$\Sigma X_{.8}$	$\Sigma X_{.9}$
Mean	$\overline{X}_{.1}$	$\overline{X}_{.2}$	$\overline{X}_{.3}$	$\overline{X}_{.4}$	$\overline{X}_{.5}$	$\overline{X}_{.6}$	$\overline{X}_{.7}$	$\overline{X}_{.8}$	$\overline{X}_{.9}$
Number of Test Units (n_j)	n_1	n_2	n_3	n_4	n_5	n_6	n_7	n_8	n_9

[3]See Neter and Wasserman, *Applied Linear Statistical Models*, Chaps. 17 and 18 for an extensive discussion on the analysis of factorial designs.

- Do factors A and B combine to influence the dependent variable more than the total of each factor's singular influence?
- Which factor level combination of A and B provides the greatest influence?

Researchers call the separate influence of A or B the *main effects* in a factorial design. They call the combined influence of A and B the *factor interaction effect*. Do not confuse this term with the before measurement interaction effect.

To explain the factor interaction effect we apply our example at a more personal level. Suppose our favorite pizza restaurant raises its prices 10 percent. Unit sales might decrease, say, 2 percent. Now suppose instead it cuts the cost of ingredients 10 percent. Unit sales might decrease by 1 percent. Finally, suppose it simultaneously raises prices and cuts ingredients' costs by these amounts. Unit sales might decrease by 10 percent (or by 50 percent)! That is, the effect of both actions taken together exceeds the sum of the effects of both actions taken separately. The two factors interact.

The usual method of analysis for data produced by a factorial experiment uses ANOVA. The test begins exactly as if we had a single factor design; that is, test procedures and formulas from Table 18.13 apply. If data support H_1, analysis proceeds to test whether the effects of factor A, factor B, and their interaction are statistically significant. To explain, we need symbols as below:

i $(i = 1, 2, \ldots, n)$	test unit identifications
j $(j = 1, 2, \ldots, t)$	treatment identifications
k $(k = 1, 2, \ldots, a)$	levels of factor A
l $(l = 1, 2, \ldots, b)$	levels of factor B
$\overline{X}..$	overall mean
$\overline{X}_{Ak}$	kth level mean for factor A
$\overline{X}_{Bl}$	lth level mean for factor B

For sums of squares, we have:

$$SSTO = \sum_{i=1}^{n} \sum_{j=1}^{t} (X_{ij} - \overline{X}..)^2 \qquad \text{total sum of squares}$$

$$SSTR = n \sum_{j=1}^{t} (\overline{X}_{\cdot j} - \overline{X}..)^2 \qquad \text{treatment sum of squares}$$

$$SSA = bn \sum_{k=1}^{a} (\overline{X}_{Ak} - \overline{X}..)^2 \qquad \text{factor } A \text{ sum of squares}$$

$$SSB = an \sum_{l=1}^{b} (\overline{X}_{Bl} - \overline{X}..)^2 \qquad \text{factor } B \text{ sum of squares}$$

$$SSAB = SSTR - SSA - SSB \qquad \text{interaction sum of squares}$$

$$SSE = SSTO - SSTR \qquad \text{error sum of squares}$$

Each sum of squares has an associated degrees of freedom value and mean square, summarized in Table 19.3.

The test begins, as we said, with an examination of F_{test} between treatments. If this F_{test} value exceeds a chosen critical value of F for $ab - 1$ and $ab(n - 1)$ degrees of freedom for the numerator and denominator, respectively, the test proceeds to examine the interaction effect. If the interaction effect is significant, based on F_{test} for interaction, the researcher returns to the data summary in Table 19.2 and identifies the best treatment combination, based on values for $\overline{X}_{.j}$. If the interaction effect is not significant, the researcher proceeds to test the significance of factor A and B main effects. Either one or both may be significant. If a factor produces a significant main effect, additional tests follow to determine which levels of the factor produce significantly greater effects than which other levels.[4]

Such an application is called *two-way* ANOVA to distinguish it from that applied to a single-factor experiment, called *one-way* ANOVA. As we might expect, when we have three factors present in an experimental design, we apply three-way ANOVA; N factors require N-way ANOVA. Widely available computer analysis packages can perform up to five-way ANOVA.

In summary, factorial designs find more use in marketing research than single-factor designs. Their efficiency and ability to supply information on factor interactions are distinct advantages. Both single-factor and factorial designs find more use than do before-after, before-after with control, and after-only with control designs. Both take their names from the completely random process used to assign test units to treatments. This leads to their major weakness.

TABLE 19.3
General Form of the ANOVA Table for a Two-Factor Experimental Design

Source of Variation	Sum of Squares	Degrees of Freedom	MS	F_{test}
Between treatments	SSTR	$ab-1$	$SSTR/ab-1$	$MSTR/MSE$
Factor A	SSA	$a-1$	$SSA/a-1$	MSA/MSE
Factor B	SSB	$b-1$	$SSB/b-1$	MSB/MSE
Interaction	SSAB	$(a-1)(b-1)$	$SSAB/(a-1)(b-1)$	$MSAB/MSE$
Error	SSE	$ab(n-1)$	$SSE/ab(n-1)$	
Total	SSTO	$nab-1$		

[4]See Neter and Wasserman, *Applied Linear Statistical Models*, Chap. 18 for the discussion.

To see this, look again at Table 19.1 (similar statements apply to Table 19.2 as well). Only 18 restaurants supply these measurements. What would happen if random assignment placed two restaurants with historically large unit sales in treatment 3, one in treatment 2, and none in treatment 1? The answer, of course, is that $\overline{X}_{.3}$ might be much greater than $\overline{X}_{.2}$ and $\overline{X}_{.1}$ even though the influence of price increases works in the opposite direction. Consider another extraneous variable—market area income. If one treatment contained a large number of wealthy or of poor consumers, results again would be confounded. In short, when test units differ with respect to extraneous variables, completely randomized designs should be modified to take this into account.[5] Because such conditions typify much marketing research, we discuss one such modification as our next experimental design.

RANDOMIZED BLOCK DESIGN

Suppose our researcher decides to allow for the effect of past unit sales. A randomized block design does this by "blocking" test units *before* randomly assigning them to treatments. Blocking is akin to the marketing management concept of segmentation. It means sorting test units into more homogeneous groups based on two types of blocking criteria: characteristics of the test unit and characteristics of the experimental setting.

Characteristics of the test unit include such concepts as age, sex, income, attitudes, purchase intention, past experience, and product usage rate if people are the test units. If organizations are test units, characteristics include their size, market area characteristics, and competitive environments. Characteristics of the experimental setting include experimenter identity, time of the experiment, and other attendant conditions.

In our example, the researcher might proceed by blocking on the basis of past unit sales as derived from company records. He would order the restaurants from highest to lowest unit sales, block them, and then make random assignments from each block to treatments. In our single-factor design, this means that restaurants with the 3 largest historic unit sales would form test unit or block 1, the next 3 largest would form block 2, and so on. In our factorial design, it means that the 9 larger restaurants would form block 1 and the 9 smaller would form block 2. Each block would contain test units much alike on the blocking variable but much different from test units in other blocks.

It is quite right to feel somewhat uncomfortable with both blocked designs, especially the blocked factorial design. Despite random assignment, restaurants in each of the 9 treatments may well not have equal unit sales at the start of the experiment. On the average they will be more alike

---

[5]Strictly speaking, the completely randomized design can be kept if the extraneous variable can be measured on an interval or ratio scale and an analysis of covariance performed. Neter and Wasserman, *Applied Linear Statistical Models*, p. 758 favor our next design over this approach.

than if blocking were not used, but having only 2 restaurants per treatment strongly suggests this problem. The solution, of course, requires a larger number of restaurants and a larger number of blocks. Such would be the case in actual practice. In general, the more blocks in the design, the more sensitive the experiment will be in detecting the effects of blocking and treatments. Each block must contain at least one test unit per treatment.

For analysis purposes, blocking largely turns our single-factor design into a two-factor design. In other words, we now have a 3×6 factorial design with the first factor as price and the second as restaurant size. Almost. The one important distinction is that a randomized block design assumes no interaction between the blocking factor and the treatments. Similar comments apply to blocked factorial designs. (We would have a $3 \times 3 \times 2$ factorial design but assume no interaction effects due to the last factor, restaurant size).

Analysis of a blocked single-factor experimental design proceeds exactly as discussed with ANOVA for three or more dependent groups in Chapter 18. Analysis of a blocked factorial design may be found elsewhere.[6]

Randomized block designs represent an extremely useful modification to completely randomized designs. Most marketing experiments face one or two extraneous variables based either on charactertistics of the test units or of the experimental setting. By blocking we can remove much of their effect and obtain more precise estimates of treatment effects. However, a randomized block experiment requires slightly more information as a basis for blocking.

More than one extraneous variable may define blocks. For example, blocks could be jointly determined by both historical unit sales and market area income as below:

| | Test Unit Characteristics |
Block	(Historic Unit Sales, Per Capita Market Income)
1	Below 10,000 pizzas, below $10,000
2	Below 10,000 pizzas, above $10,000
3	Above 10,000 pizzas, below $10,000
4	Above 10,000 pizzas, above $10,000

Blocks defined by more than one extraneous variable present no new problems in our designs. However, with jointly defined blocks we cannot determine the separate effects of each extraneous variable used to define the blocks. Such designs can measure only joint blocking effects. Recognize also that filling each treatment with an equal number of test units will now be more difficult or perhaps impossible.

To show the separate effects of more than one extraneous variable

---

[6]Neter and Wasserman, *Applied Linear Statistical Models*, pp. 731–33.

the researcher would quite simply treat each as a factor in a blocked factorial design. However, this can require a large number of test units. A 4 × 5 factorial design blocked by two 3-level blocking factors requires 180 test units.

LATIN SQUARE DESIGN   Alternatively, the researcher could use a latin square design to overcome this problem for a two-blocking variable situation. A latin square separately shows the effect of each blocking variable while using only the number of treatments as required by a completely randomized design (either single-factor or factorial). This occurs not without some costs:

1. The number of classes of the two blocking variables must exactly equal the number of treatments.

2. The design assumes no interactions between either blocking variable and the treatments, and none between either blocking variable.

3. The random assignment of test units to treatments is more complex.

See any good experimental design text for details.[7]

Quasi-Experimental Designs

All formal experimental designs we have discussed apply to either laboratory or field settings. Three less formal or **quasi-experimental designs** follow that apply almost exclusively to the field. All differ further from experimental designs in their nonrandom assignment of test units to experimental and control groups. The last two quasi-experimental designs we discuss also differ in that the researcher lacks full control over the timing of treatment exposure. Such differences generally imply greater potential for the influence of extraneous variables on the dependent variable.

NON-EQUIVALENT CONTROL GROUP DESIGN   In symbols, the nonequivalent control group design looks like this:

$$EG_1:\ \overline{X}_1\ T_1\ \overline{X}_2$$

$$CG:\ \overline{X}_3\quad \overline{X}_4$$

The dashed line separating experimental and control groups indicates nonrandom assignment or the nonequivalence of the two groups.

---

[7]Neter and Wasserman, *Applied Linear Statistical Models*, Chap. 24.

A researcher using this design often experiments with convenience samples as the test units, selecting samples such that they are as similar to each other as the availability of population elements permits. For example, the residents of two retirement institutions may become experimental and control groups not as randomly assigned individuals but as collectives. Residents at one institution become the experimental group and residents at the other become the control. Apart from this difference, which implies that no statistical test of significance be used to analyze data, the design is identical to our earlier before-after with control design.

The influence of T_1 derives from the same expression as given for the before-after with control design:

$$Y_{T_1} = (\overline{X}_2 - \overline{X}_1) - (\overline{X}_4 - \overline{X}_3)$$

Almost the same interpretation can be given. The primary extraneous variable remaining is the one we discussed previously: the before measurement interaction effect. However, because the design uses a nonequivalent control group, another before measurement interaction effect might also exist, peculiar only to the experimental group.[8] For example, residents of one retirement institution could be richer, smarter, younger, and so on. Such differences might lead to a different before measurement interaction effect from what might be obtained when random assignment determines experimental and control groups. Still, a nonequivalent control group design provides less confounded results than a simple before-after design.

TIME SERIES DESIGN

This design represents data sometimes taken from a consumer panel (discussed in Chapter 4). It looks like this:

$$EG_1: \overline{X}_1 \ \overline{X}_2 \ \overline{X}_3 \ T_1 \ \overline{X}_4 \ \overline{X}_5 \ \overline{X}_6$$

In words—a researcher receives reports of the dependent variable measurement for three periods, introduces the treatment variable, and receives reports for three more periods. Graphic presentation of results as in Figure 19.1 aids interpretation. The timing of T_1 occurs midway between periods 3 and 4 as indicated by the vertical dashed line.

Visual inspection of results indicates that patterns A and B show no influence of T_1. Past patterns of $\overline{X}_i$ continue as before. Notice, however, that we would make this conclusion from a time series design but not from a simple before-after design. A simple before-after design would involve only time periods 3 and 4 and lead to a conclusion of a positive T_1 influ-

---

[8]See James A. Caporaso, "Quasi-Experimental Approaches to Social Science: Perspectives and Problems," in *Quasi-Experimental Approaches: Testing Theory and Evaluating Policy*, ed. James A. Caporaso and Leslie L. Roos, Jr. (Evanston, Ill.: Northwestern University Press, 1973), pp. 13–14.

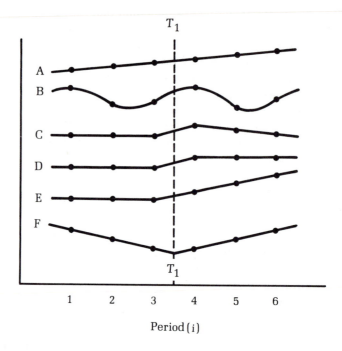

FIGURE 19.1
Six possible results of a time series design (adapted from James A. Caporaso and Leslie L. Roos, Jr., eds., *Quasi-Experimental Approaches: Testing Theory and Evaluating Policy* (Evanston, Ill.: Northwestern University Press, 1973), p. 20.

ence. Thus, panel data supply information about long term trends that all experimental and quasi-experimental designs discussed to here do not.

Patterns C, D, E, and F show a positive influence of T_1 (negative influences could also occur). Pattern C shows the weakest influence. Its $\overline{X}_4$ value (its intercept with line T_1) exceeds that for period 3. But the influence begins almost immediately to decline. Pattern D shows a stronger influence. Its intercept lies at the same level as Pattern C but values continue at a higher level indefinitely. Permanent change seems to have occurred. Patterns E and F show the strongest influence. Both the intercept and slope for pattern E show a change, while pattern F shows a stronger slope increase.

Beyond visual inspection, special statistical procedures measure the significance of intercept and slope changes.[9] Such procedures must be

---

[9]Ibid., pp. 26–31. See also Gilbert A. Churchill, Jr., *Marketing Research*, 2nd ed. (Hinsdale, Ill.: The Dryden Press, 1979), pp. 56–62 for a discussion of an alternate form of analysis often possible with time series data—called turnover analysis.

used with these designs. Conducting the usual test of differences between dependent group means $\overline{X}_4$ and $\overline{X}_3$ often leads to improper conclusions (see patterns A and B). Averaging $\overline{X}_i$ for several periods and then conducting a test of dependent group means is just as faulty (see patterns A and F).

Interpret these statements on the influence of T_1 in patterns A through F in the light of two cautions:

1. The time series design does not control for many extraneous variables.

2. The timing of T_1 can seldom be pinpointed with accuracy.

Concerning the first, we have no assurance that T_1 alone influences $\overline{X}_i$. Anything outside the quasi-experiment could have contributed.[10] So could have the before measurement interaction effect. These two confounding effects, coupled with a criticism that panel members often adopt a "guinea pig" orientation over time, make results difficult to generalize.

Concerning the second, we find it often difficult to know just when (and if) panel members are exposed to T_1. Suppose T_1 is a "buy 3, get 1 free" coupon for a brand of bar soap, distributed in an issue of *Better Homes and Gardens*. While the issue date is clear, exposure and usage is not. Some consumers receive the magazine through the mail, others buy it later at a newstand. Some read the issue promptly, others delay. Some use the coupon immediately, others wait. In fact, nearly 1 consumer in 7 will use the coupon two months after exposure or later.[11]

The time series with control design looks like this:

TIME SERIES WITH CONTROL DESIGN

$$EG_1: \overline{X}_1 \ \overline{X}_2 \ \overline{X}_3 \ T_1 \ \overline{X}_4 \ \overline{X}_5 \ \overline{X}_6$$

$$CG: \overline{X}_7 \ \overline{X}_8 \ \overline{X}_9 \qquad \overline{X}_{10} \ \overline{X}_{11} \ \overline{X}_{12}$$

The design merely adds a nonequivalent control group to our last design.

Of the three quasi-experimental designs, the time series with control design excels. It is vastly superior to a time series design without control; we can largely dismiss caution 1. That is, the time series with control design controls for all extraneous variables except the two before measurement interaction effects noted for the nonequivalent control group design. It surpasses this design by identifying trend patterns in $\overline{X}_i$. Caution 2 still applies, however.

---

[10]See B. C. Cotton and Emerson M. Babb, "Consumer Responses to Promotional Deals," *Journal of Marketing* 42 (July 1978): 109–13, for an elaboration on this point.

[11]*The Nielsen Researcher*, No. 1, 1976, A. C. Nielsen Co.

Further, the time series with control design is easier to analyze than the time series design without control. The same T_1 intercept and slope analysis procedure could be used but it will usually be simpler to work with just $(\overline{X}_4 - \overline{X}_3) - (\overline{X}_{10} - \overline{X}_9)$. Visual inspection of $\overline{X}_i$ patterns (before and after T_1) should support this practice whenever possible. To use the expression alone assumes identical trend patterns for experimental and control groups.

Design Decisions

To conduct an experiment or quasi-experiment, the researcher must have made a large number of design decisions. All divide into factor, dependent variable, test unit, extraneous variable, and procedure decisions.

FACTOR DECISIONS   Factor decisions identify factors and specify their treatment levels. To make these decisions requires that researchers be able to extract the essence of the marketing problem as no more than three or four contributing factors. These become factors and, consequently, treatments.

Experiments and quasi-experiments commonly use only two or three factors. Fewer than two provides limited information and saves little resources. More than three rapidly increases sample size and complicates analysis.

Limited as they are to two or three factors, researchers must select them carefully. We identify three useful criteria:

1. Factors must be manipulatable. Researchers must be able to alter intensities of factors at will in their designs. Decision makers must be able to alter these same factors in the real world.

2. Factors must be measurable. Only if factors meet this criterion can researchers executing the design and decision makers acting in the real world determine if the factor is present and at what levels.

3. Factors should be maximally different within the scope of the marketing problem. Such practice yields richer and more varied data.

Researchers must also specify the number of levels of each factor. This decision is important because the number of factor levels influences sample size more dramatically than the number of factors. The number of factor levels also dramatically influences the nature of potential conclusions. With a single-level factor, a design can conclude only the existence or nonexistence of the factor's effect on the dependent variable. With a two-level factor, a design can conclude this plus the extent of a linear relationship between the factor and the dependent variable. With a three- or more-level factor, a design can make the preceding conclusions plus decide the extent of a curvilinear relationship. Consequently, most marketing research experiments use two- or three-level factors.

Along with deciding on the number of levels, the researcher must choose their actual intensities. In our pizza example, price level intensities ranged from changes of $+5$ to $+10$ percent, while cost level intensities ranged from changes of -10 to $+5$ percent. In general, factor level intensities should be real world based and large enough to produce measurable variation in the dependent variable. The statement implies again a thorough understanding of the marketing problem and usually a pretest.

DEPENDENT VARIABLE MEASUREMENT DECISIONS

Dependent variable measurement decisions involve selecting the dependent variable from many alternatives and then specifying its measurement. The decision maker often aids selection by preferring results to be stated in terms of a certain dependent variable or performance parameter (a topic we discussed in Chapter 3). The researcher should accede if she or he can measure the variable, all by itself, with precision, on an interval or ratio scale. Chapters 7, 8, 9, 10, and 11 address this topic in depth. If she or he cannot use an interval or ratio scale, the researcher must employ other data analysis methods than Z-tests or ANOVA, methods we discussed in Chapter 18.

TEST UNIT DECISIONS

Most test unit decisions identify and select from populations of people, organizations, or objects. In other words, most test unit decisions reduce to sampling decisions, a topic we discussed in Chapters 12, 13, and 14. The one test unit decision we will discuss here relates to the number of dependent variable measurements taken from each test unit. A single measurement or a series of repeated measurements may be taken as we saw in our designs.

Repeated measure designs, where each test unit receives each treatment followed by a dependent variable measurement, interest us here. For example, a repeated measure design in our pizza experiment would require that each store randomly receive each treatment for 60 days while its sales record is measured. In effect, each store would form a test unit block all by itself. Such a design increases the power of the experiment for detecting treatment effects in comparison to single measure designs, as we showed in Chapter 18. However, achieving the increased power comes at a price, particularly when people constitute test units:

1. Many treatments must be applied to the same subject, which may be too time consuming or fatiguing for the subject.

2. There is a considerable possibility that *carry-over effects* may occur—that is, that the scores [measurements on the dependent variable] may be affected by preceding treatments as well as by the

current treatment. Carry-over effects may lead to misinterpretation of the results.[12]

The decision to use a repeated measure design should be made carefully.

EXTRANEOUS VARIABLE DECISIONS   Extraneous variable decisions identify and control those confounding factors (such as fatigue and carry-over effects) that jeopardize the design's internal and external validity. **Internal validity** refers to the degree that treatments in the design actually cause changes in the dependent variable. Internal validity addresses these questions:

- Did a treatment produce the dependent variable measurement?
- Did something other than a treatment also produce the dependent variable measurement?

We shall see that six types of extraneous variables can compromise internal validity.

External validity refers to the degree to which conclusions drawn about a treatment extend to the real world. Of course, results from an internally invalid design cannot be extended. Nor can results from an internally valid design, if conducted under sufficiently artificial circumstances. We shall see that two types of extraneous variables contribute to these circumstances; Box 19.1 provides details. Researchers commonly speak of these types of extraneous variables as *experimental biases.* Whether any or all present significant validity problems depends on design decisions.

If the design randomly assigns a large number of test units to each treatment group, uses good instructions and well-trained experimenters, treats each group identically except for the treatment, and compares results between treatments, internal validity biases should be adequately controlled. We should note why. Under these conditions, each treatment group suffers similarly from each internal validity bias. Therefore, testing differences between all $\overline{X}_j$ values removes the effect of these biases. These differences, if statistically significant, represent only the relative effect of one treatment against another.

If an internally valid design uses no before measurements and employs realistic procedures, external validity biases should be adequately controlled. We limit our comments to the last condition. Laboratory experiments tend to be unrealistic. Test units remove themselves to an unfamiliar location, receive instructions from a stranger, and, partly based on this knowledge, react. In contrast, field experiments tend to be much more realistic. However, random assignment and dependent vari-

---

[12] Wayne Lee, *Experimental Design and Analysis* (San Francisco: W. H. Freeman, 1975), p. 71.

BOX 19.1

Types of Extraneous Variables (Biases) in Experiments

Affecting Internal Validity

1. *History.* Specific events occurring during design execution, external to the test units, and beyond the researcher's control. Competitive actions in a field experiment and the loss of air conditioning in a laboratory typify history factors.

2. *Maturation.* Processes internal to the test units, occurring because of time passing. For examples, consumers becoming fatigued, bored, and smarter; stores becoming more efficient, cluttered, and older.

3. *Testing.* Effects on a later dependent variable measurement that are produced by an earlier measurement. Learning and memory typify testing effects.

4. *Instrumentation.* Changes in the dependent variable measurement process. An altered data collection form or a differently instructed interviewer midway through an experiment typify instrumentation effects.

5. *Selection.* Unequal experimental and control groups. Failure to assign a sufficiently large number of test units randomly to treatments typifies selection effects.

6. *Test Unit Mortality.* Differential loss from experimental and control groups of test units over time. Panel members dropping out and stores going bankrupt typify test unit mortality effects.

Affecting External Validity

1. *Lack of Internal Validity.*

2. *Before Measurement Interaction.* The sensitizing effect of a before measurement, alerting test units to a following treatment.

3. *Experimental Environment.* The guinea pig effect; test units reacting to treatments differently from the way they would otherwise. Panel consumers reporting smarter purchases and store clerks restocking faster than normal typify experimental environment effects.

able measurement can still contribute to external invalidity, especially when test units consist of consumers.

Researchers strive for realistic experiments as part of pretesting. They also measure the degree of realism perceived by actual test units as part of debriefing after the experiment. A question or two asked individually should suffice. Test units whose responses make the researcher suspect artificial behavior should be dropped from the main body of analysis.[13]

---

[13]See Richard P. Bagozzi, "Structural Equation Models in Experimental Research," *Journal of Marketing Research* 14 (May 1977): 209–26 for an alternate analysis procedure.

PROCEDURAL DECISIONS

Procedural decisions describe who will do what, to whom or which, when, and where in the execution of the design. One procedural decision the researcher must make is to determine when to take the dependent variable measurement. Taking it too soon or too late after the treatment constitutes another source of internal validity bias.[14]

Another procedural decision the researcher must make is to decide whether or not to include a control group in the design. Control groups consume research resources that may not be well spent. Only when the researcher knows little about expected treatment effects is a control group attractive. Under this condition, different treatments may produce quite different dependent variable measurements that mislead—for example, one may be superior to all others but inferior to no treatment at all. If used, the control group must be subjected to exactly the same procedures as the experimental group except for the treatment.

Yet another procedural decision for the researcher is to decide whether to execute the design in the laboratory or in the field. Laboratory designs tend to be faster, cheaper, and more internally valid than field designs. But, as we have seen, they tend to be less externally valid.

Chapter Summary

Experimental and quasi-experimental designs share four basic concepts: treatments, dependent variables, test units, and extraneous variables. Beyond this, their similarity ends. Experimental designs generally show more control over treatments, test units, and extraneous variable decisions. They generally show more internal and less external validity. They generally use some form of statistical analysis (discussed in Chapters 15 through 18).

Quasi-experimental designs find use when experimental designs are impossible. A large number exist beyond the three discussed here.[15] All generally employ nonprobability samples, field settings, and simple methods of analysis. Because of the first condition, results of their analyses lack a theory to generalize results to the population of interest.

One final point remains about experimental designs: in our discussion, we have assumed a *fixed effects model*, in which experimental treatments represent all possible treatments of interest. A fixed effects model contrasts with a *random effects model*, in which treatments represent a sample of all possible treatments of interest. If the latter model applies, analysis procedures differ, only slightly for a single-factor design but markedly for a factorial design.[16]

---

[14]Donald S. Tull and Del I. Hawkins, *Marketing Research: Meaning, Measurement, and Method* (New York: Macmillan, 1976), pp. 434–35.

[15]Caporaso and Roos, *Quasi-Experimental Approaches.*

[16]See Neter and Wasserman, *Applied Linear Statistical Models*, Chaps. 16, 19, and 20.

Chapter Review

DISCUSSION QUESTIONS

1. In the before-after with control design, why can't a before measurement interaction effect occur with both experimental and control groups?

2. What problems do small sample sizes present in experimental design?

3. What is so difficult about making factor decisions in experimental design?

4. Review our "buy 3, get 1 free" coupon example for a time series design. Will a researcher have a better idea of coupon exposure timing if the coupon is:

   a) enclosed in a shampoo package?

   b) printed in a newspaper?

   c) mailed to consumers?

5. Suppose a researcher wished to measure the effectiveness of a magazine advertisement in a field experiment. Instead of randomly assigning consumers to experimental and control groups, the researcher decides to let consumers "self-select" themselves into the two groups. That is, the first question asked in the study will be "Do you recall seeing this advertisement?" Depending on a consumer's answer, he or she will be placed in either the experimental or control group.

   a) What's wrong with this procedure?

   b) How would you improve the design?

PROBLEMS

1. Consider data below, which have been produced by large, independent probability samples in a laboratory experiment. Data represent mean values on the dependent variable.

   EG_1: 14.5 T_1 15.7

   EG_2: 14.7 T_2 18.5

   EG_3: 14.6 T_3 14.4

   CG: 14.7   14.9

   a) Estimate the effects of T_1, T_2, and T_3.

   b) What statistics are missing that would allow you more confidence in answering part a?

2. Consider the $\bar{p}_i$ values below, which represent proportions of consumers

who receive a score of 1 on the dependent variable in a laboratory experiment. Assume sample sizes of 100 for both groups and an α of .05. Estimate the effect of T_1.

EG_1:   0.20 T_1 0.30

CG: 0.22   0.26

3. Consider data below, produced by independent probability samples of size $n_j = 100$ in a laboratory experiment. Data represent sample proportions. Test values for statistical significance using $\alpha = .05$.

EG_1: T_1 0.32

EG_2: T_2 0.36

EG_3: T_3 0.41

CG: 0.32

4. Consider data below from a field experiment investigating the effects of two ingredients, present in high and low concentrations, in a new dishwashing liquid. Data represent interval scale values, measuring roughness of hands belonging to twenty-four dishwashing college students. Students used one of the four formulations exclusively for a ten-day period. Higher scores indicate smoother hands. Are either or both ingredients effective in preventing rough hands?

		Ingredient B Concentration	
		Low	High
Ingredient A Concentration	Low	20 22 25 24 28 26	18 19 24 26 27 26
	High	34 32 35 35 37 38	33 36 30 31 35 29

Additional Readings

Campbell, Donald T., and Stanley, Julian C. *Experimental and Quasi-Experimental Designs For Research*. Chicago: Rand McNally, 1966.

> *This paperback succinctly and clearly discusses experiments and quasi-experiments. For more detail on the latter designs, you may wish to see the treatment by Caporaso, James A., and Roos, Leslie L., Jr., eds.* Quasi-Experimental Approaches: Testing Theory and Evaluating Policy. *Evanston, Ill.: Northwestern University Press, 1973.*

Neter, John, and Wasserman, William. *Applied Linear Statistical Models*. Homewood, Ill.: Richard D. Irwin, 1974.

> *As we said at the end of our Chapter 6, Chapters 13 through 24 in this book discuss almost everything you will ever need to know about experiments. For an alternative discussion with similar rigor, clarity, and completeness, see Lee, Wayne.* Experimental Design and Analysis. *San Francisco: W. H. Freeman, 1975.*

14. State Hospital Association*

The State Hospital Association is a private organization representing all the hospitals in a large midwestern state. The Association provides a number of services to its members, including their representation in dealings with agencies of the state and federal government, industry, the medical profession, and the general public.

Early February of last year, Tom Broxton, one of the youngest members of the Association's management team, was complaining that "certain of our member hospitals and their employees develop efficient and improved methods, but there is no process for getting other hospitals to improve their operations by adopting these methods." He thought to himself, "Why not invite our members to submit these improvements to our headquarters, so we can evaluate and disseminate the best ones to all our hospitals? That way we can improve the operating efficiency of all our hospitals. We might even publicize the improved methods to hospitals in nearby states, once we get going." This thought furnished the basis for a "Best Methods Program" which Tom developed and proposed at the March meeting of the Association's Board of Directors.

After the meeting, Brandon Jones, one of the Board members, approached Broxton with some comments on his proposal. Jones, senior vice-president for marketing for a major hospital-supply manufacturer, said he thought the "Best Methods Program" was a good idea in theory, but that organizations in general, and hospitals in particular, were "inherently resistant to change." For this reason, he thought some marketing and promotional strategies should be created to get hospitals to adopt and implement the improved methods. A few other Board members from business joined the ensuing discussion in support of Jones' suggestion and, as a result of this and later discussions, Dr. Brien Sledge, Associate Professor of Marketing at a nearby university, was retained to develop a marketing plan for the "Best Methods Program."

While Dr. Sledge has been busy developing his plan, the Association staff has solicited and screened ideas for inclusion in the "Best Methods Program." The marketing plan finally developed consists of a direct-mail campaign to hospitals in the state, as well as to hospitals in nearby states. Pamphlets introducing the Program have been developed and are included in the mailings, along with a letter from the State Hospital Association's President and Chief Executive Officer.

Dr. Sledge, an expert in the area of consumer behavior, argues that

---

*Prepared by Grady D. Bruce, Jr., Professor of Marketing, California State University, Fullerton.

the campaign should be more successful in obtaining participation from members of the Association than from those in nearby states. He notes, that "Members of the Association should feel a commitment and loyalty to its programs which leads them to participate at a higher rate than non-members in neighboring states." Dr. Sledge has an opportunity to evaluate his contention, for results from a survey conducted by the Association have just been tabulated and forwarded to him. They are presented in Table C14.1.

The first thing Dr. Sledge saw in the table is that the percentages support his contention: there is a greater percentage of participation within the state than in nearby states. But he tells you, his research assistant, that the difference between in-state and out-of-state participation could be due to sampling error. He asks you to analyze the data and let him know the next morning.

You look at the table and strain to remember enough to decide on an appropriate statistical test. "Should I use the frequencies or the percentages? How do I incorporate those hospitals that are investigating a program, but have not yet adopted it (if I incorporate them at all)? Should I collapse all those categories that indicate non-utilization into one category? What do I do with the nonresponses, take them out of the totals?"

You feel a little overwhelmed by the number of questions that such a simple table can raise. After successfully fighting off the temptation to leave immediately for the nearest movie, you start work on Dr. Sledge's request.

TABLE C14.1
Tabulation of Survey Results

	IN-STATE HOSPITALS:		OUT-OF-STATE HOSPITALS:	
	No.	Percent	No.	Percent
Hospital has utilized or plans to utilize one or more Best Methods	76	61.8	27	57.4
Similar methods already in use	1	0.8	—	—
Hospital is investigating one or more Best Methods of possible interest	14	11.4	7	14.9
Hospital has not yet utilized Best Methods	25	20.3	10	21.3
No answer	7	5.7	3	6.4
TOTAL	123	100.0	47	100.0

15. Charismatics, Incorporated*

Charismatics, Incorporated, was formed in early 1977 to market a radically new system of managerial training. The system consisted of a series of cassette tapes on which were recorded the inspirational messages of Wadley Cantrell. Mr. Cantrell, who at one time served as a successful marketing vice-president for Kerin Soap Company, left that company to return to college to do graduate work in psychology. It was, in fact, while sitting in one of his graduate psychology courses reflecting on his marketing experience, that he developed the basic principle upon which Charismatics, Incorporated, was later founded. This principle—maintained as a personal secret for competitive reasons—served as a basis for construction of Mr. Cantrell's inspirational messages.

Chari-Matic, as the system finally developed, consists of a set of tapes arranged sequentially to have the effect of increasing—automatically—the charismatic power of any listener. The system of 12 tapes sells for $129.95 and is claimed to be as useful to a first-line supervisor as it is to a top-level executive, and to work for individuals supervising others in any kind of organization (profit or nonprofit, large or small). Even some housewives and mothers—not originally included in the target market—claimed to have benefited from listening to the tapes.

Owing to the widespread appeal of the system, it was introduced through a series of commercials shown on a late-night network "talk show." In order to measure the effectiveness of the commercials in creating awareness of the new system, Mr. Cantrell commissioned Morning-Call, a telephone polling and survey research firm, to do a study. Morning-Call is a national service specializing in WATS-line telephone surveys to random samples in different cities throughout the United States. These surveys are conducted each morning of the week and are designed to measure the impact of commercials shown the evening before. Different questions are included in the surveys for different clients.

For Mr. Cantrell, the following dichotomous question was included in the Saturday morning survey that followed the first week of television commercials: "Do you recall having seen or heard any television advertising for Chari-Matic in the preceding week?" Results for the five cities surveyed are shown below:

	Sample Size	Number Who Responded "Yes"
Seattle, Washington	625	125
Dallas, Texas	256	41

*Prepared by Grady D. Bruce, Jr., Professor of Marketing, California State University, Fullerton.

Atlanta, Georgia	400	80
Boston, Massachusetts	324	90
Detroit, Michigan	625	200

Mr. Cantrell wondered how he should analyze the data.

16. Teledyne Canada Limited*

In November 1975, the general manager of the Metal Products Division of Teledyne Canada Limited was faced with the problem of devising a marketing program for a household garbage-bag-handling system that might be added to the division's line of products.

Mr. Nutt, the division's general manager, had observed that plastic garbage bags were rapidly replacing the traditional garbage can, but storing these bags often posed a household problem. Plastic bags awaiting the weekly garbage pickup service gave off disagreeable odours, looked disorderly, were prey to animals, and provided a breeding place for flies.

To overcome this problem. Mr. Nutt had designed a special metal container. Despite the fact that the company's draftsmen had never developed a product similar to this, they were able to embody most of Mr. Nutt's ideas in a light, compact, and durable piece of household equipment (Exhibit C16.1). The container was made of rust-resistant heavy-gauge steel and the exterior faces had a green baked-enamel finish. It could be assembled in about five minutes with a slip-in corner system[1] that eliminated the need for tools and bolts to assemble the unit. The container had a bottom, a counter-balanced stay-open lid, and a bag support apparatus[2] that held the bag open for filling and sealed the bag when the lid was closed. There was enough storage area for at least four full bags.

THE COMPANY The division's primary line was cabs for off-highway equipment such as front-end loaders, crane carriers, road graders, and large open-pit-mining trucks. The second product line was fuel tanks, hydraulic oil tanks, and other fabricated parts for the same type of vehicles. A third line was job shop production of many different metal products for farm equipment. The plant was not at full capacity.

---

*This case was written by Professor Ken Hardy, University of Western Ontario. Used by permission.
[1] Patent applied for.
[2] Patent applied for.

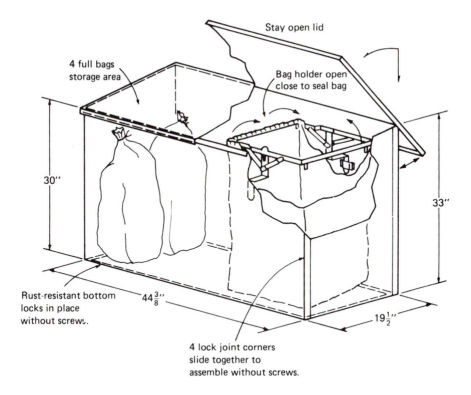

THE ALL NEW TELEDYNE HOUSEHOLD GARBAGE BAG HANDLING SYSTEM
The answer to every household's garbage bag handling and storage problem

1. A newly designed bag support which holds the bag open for filling and when closed, seals in odours and keeps flies out. (Patent applied for)
2. Extra storage area for a minimum of four full bags.
3. A self-stay-open lid.
4. Assembles in five minutes with the TELELOK corner system, eliminating the need for tools to bolt the assembly together. (Patent applied for)
5. Bottom locks in place to form support for bags.
6. Years of service through use of rust-resistant coated heavy gauge steel.
7. Will stay colour bright in outdoor use because all exterior faces have baked enamel finish.
8. Keeps animals and vermin out.
9. Can be used for storage of garbage cans.
10. Attractive design to enhance a usually messy disposal area.

TELEDYNE   CANADA   METAL   PRODUCTS
460 Industrial Ave. (1 block north of Timberjack)
Woodstock, Ontario   Phone 519–537–2355

EXHIBIT C16.1
Teledyne Garbage Bag Handling System

PRODUCTION Fabrication of the garbage-handling system was essentially a metalworking task. The component parts were stamped to shape, painted, and then packed unassembled into cardboard containers. The division's labour force was well acquainted with the necessary processes as a result of the division's experience in the production of its major lines.

The unit variable costs were $15 in materials and $6 in labour. Reducing the thickness of the steel would save $1 per gauge. At $10, the gauge would be equivalent to the steel found in their competitor's product. However, Mr. Nutt felt that this lighter-gauge steel appeared flimsy.

Manufacturing and administration overheads directly associated with the garbage-handling system would vary with unit volume, as shown below. The manufacturer's selling price would incorporate 12 percent federal sales tax.

Unit Volume	Estimated Total Overhead ($)
0– 1,000	5,000
1,001– 5,000	10,000
5,001–25,000	20,000

MARKETING Although no quantitative estimates of the market had been made by Mr. Nutt or his staff, they believed that the product met the needs of a large number of Canadian homeowners.

Because the division had never marketed a household consumer product, it was decided to make a trial production run of two hundred units. The trial run was to try out the tooling and various means of advertising in the Woodstock area in order to map future national marketing programs. Mr. Nutt believed it was wise to use a test market and thus avoid the possibility of investing a large amount in a new product that could have hidden defects or could not be developed into a profitable item. For the trial run he had purchased special tooling that cost $2700. The test market product was priced at $44.95 and sold directly to the consumer.

FIRST PROMOTION To decide on a name for the product, check consumer acceptance, and evaluate different advertising techniques, Mr. Nutt decided on a "Whatsit" contest. Anyone who had purchased a Teledyne Garbage Bag Handling System was eligible to enter the contest, and the prize was $100 for the best name.

To announce the contest and describe the product's features, one full-page ad (at a cost of $200) followed by a half-page ad (at a cost of $100) were placed in the *Oxford County Shopping Newspaper*, a free weekly tabloid. Orders were to be placed at the plant for free home delivery in Woodstock. A sample of the product and contest signs (the cost of the signs was $225) were placed at branches of the Royal Bank of

Canada and the Canadian Imperial Bank of Commerce in Woodstock as part of the bank's program of displaying local products of interest. In addition, company employees purchased the product and praised it to their friends.

Three days prior to the close of the contest, radio spot commercials at a total cost of $225 were used. These commercials ran for a minute each and were played twenty-eight times, evenly spaced throughout the three days. Sales of at least three units were directly attributable to the radio advertising.

Teledyne rented a booth at the Woodstock Fair for $40. The fair ran five days, and Mr. Nutt and his staff obtained a feel for consumer reaction to the new product. They learned that previous buyers were coming back to purchase a second container for uses Mr. Nutt had never thought of, such as a sail locker, tool storage bin, and oat bin for horses.

The winning name for the product was Garbage Geni. A picture of the winner receiving the cheque from Mr. Nutt was published in the local paper. In the announcement the winner said: "The product solved several garbage bag problems at my home. My wife can open the lid and operate the bag holder with one hand whereas before there was usually a mess because she did not have enough hands to hold the bag open and fill it at the same time".

The winner commented that he thought of the name because, like a geni, it made his garbage problems disappear. He suggested this as a slogan to Mr. Nutt.

The result of the promotion was 140 Garbage Genis sold in four months in the Woodstock area, which had a population in 1975 of approximately 26,500 persons. Mr. Nutt commented that a large part of the sales were the result of owners of Garbage Geni selling its merits to friends.

To Mr. Nutt's knowledge, there was only one competitive product on the market. It was called Garbage Can House and had been distributed through Home Hardware stores for two years. Although it sold to the consumer for $29.95, it did not have Garbage Geni's features. This garbage container was made of a lighter-gauge steel than the test market Garbage Geni, had no bottom, used screws and bolts, had no bag manager, and required the additional purchase of two garbage cans. Mr. Nutt felt that the superior features offered by Garbage Geni gave it a sales appeal not matched by its competitor. Mr. Nutt had heard rumors of a second competitor beginning production, but the details of the product were not known.

In November of 1975, Mr. Nutt was approached by three organizations seeking distribution rights to the Garbage Geni. During the initial test market period, a Garbage Geni had been displayed in the plant's reception area. Two manufacturers' agents saw the display and asked Mr.

FUTURE MARKETING

Nutt for exclusive rights to market the Garbage Geni in Canada. One agent was engaged in advertising for several products and the other agent had a liaison with six agents across Canada. Although Mr. Nutt did not talk price with these two men, both agents indicated that they would sell the product to retailers for a commission of 10 percent of the selling price to retailers. The retailers would take a markup of 50 percent of the selling price to their customers.

Mr. Nutt also had been invited to make a presentation to a large well-known chain of automotive stores. Although the direct factory price to the consumer in the test market had been $44.95, Mr. Nutt suggested that the automotive chain sell the Garbage Geni for $56.95 based on a factory-to-retailer price of $39.90. However, the automotive chain store buyer said that the Garbage Geni was too expensive at $56.95 and a 30 percent markup was inadequate for his chain. The buyer wanted a minimum markup of 50 percent on suggested list price, even though the chain probably would lower the consumer price slightly for competitive reasons.[3] Despite this discouraging view of an acceptable price, Mr. Nutt and his staff were of the opinion that the product could fill a real need for a large number of families in the middle and upper income levels.

During this time, Mr. Nutt had requested the estimating department to develop a new cost based on fully tooling the unit at an additional cost of $6000. The extra tooling could reduce labour costs by $1 per unit.

Mr. Nutt believed that the spring and summer of 1976 would produce good consumer acceptance for the product, but if he was to capitalize on that potential, he would have to make a decision soon on feasibility and marketing. Despite that pressure, Mr. Nutt did not feel that he was ready for full-scale negotiations with the chain store buyers, who he felt "would squeeze every last cent".

Mr. Nutt wondered whether he should use lighter-gauge steel and/or invest another $6000 in tooling in order to achieve a lower price. He could sell directly to consumers, sell through agents, or reopen talks with the automotive chain store buyers.

Mr. Nutt thought that building supply stores, lumber yards, hardware stores, discount stores, and catalogue operations would demand a 50 percent retail margin on their selling price. Point-of-purchase materials for retail stores would cost $5000, and he was told that $30,000 in cooperative advertising would help the acceptance of a new product. If he assembled his own sales force to sell Garbage Geni through hardware stores, building supply, and lumber yards, each salesman would cost $25,000 per year including travelling expenses.

Mr. Nutt had not discarded the idea of a door-to-door sales force,

---

[3]For example, if the manufacturer's selling price was $1, the retail organization would want to sell it for $2. This consumer price could be reduced to, say, $1.79 if the organization felt that it was necessary in order to give it a competitive edge.

perhaps employing students in the summer. The door-to-door salesmen might sell the Garbage Geni at $79.99 and take a 50 percent sales commission. Some recruiting and sales supervision would be necessary.

Mr. Nutt had considerable financial resources available from Teledyne Corporation provided he could foresee a reasonable financial contribution from the project. There were several combinations of options that he could visualize as alternative marketing strategies. He was enthusiastic about the prospects for the Garbage Geni, but he wondered what specific action he should take.

17. Samurai Pizza, Incorporated

"We're certainly going to have enough data," thought Sidney White as he held the questionnaire in his hands. "The trick will be in the analysis ... Bob and Ron may be sharp managers, but they're not statisticians!" With that, he turned to preparing a data analysis plan.

White's plan would be discussed at a meeting next week with his clients—Bob Smith, Operations Vice President of Samurai Pizza, Incorporated, and Ron Walton, manager of the San Diego restaurant. Both were quite interested in the upcoming research, particularly in the planned analysis of results, but for two different reasons. Smith was interested in the ability of the research to be applied to other Samurai restaurants as well as in the actual results for San Diego. Walton cared about only the actual results. If data made sense, both men would be satisfied, no matter whether it was good or bad news.

BACKGROUND

Samurai Pizza, Incorporated consisted of a chain of 32 pizza restaurants in southern California. The original restaurant in San Luis Obispo had opened in 1977. It and 5 others were owned by the corporation; the other 26 were franchised operations. Most restaurants were moderately profitable during 1981—a level of performance that was less than desirable and quite unexpected, considering the performance of a mere two years ago.

Samurai's history had once been described by Smith in these words: "Samurai began on a whim, limited capital, hard work, and some extraordinary good luck. That first restaurant seemed to grab the imagination of the pizza eating public, especially teenagers and college students." So much so, that the original partners had quickly expanded in 1978 to two other restaurants in Santa Barbara and Ventura. They incorporated and began to sell franchises late in 1978.

Everything seemed to go well until 1980, when friction developed among the original partners. The problem was partly due to operating results. Sales had failed to grow at the expected 16 percent rate and profits fell to less than 10 percent of sales. In addition, several of the franchisees had complained about untested new products (the pizza sandwich, in particular), quality control of corporate-supplied ingredients, and the lack of corporate managerial support. The rest of the problem seemed to come from differences of opinion between corporate officers over long-term strategy. One had wanted a "breathing spell," to take stock of the situation and plan direction for the future. Another (the Operations Vice President) had wanted to sell franchises at an accelerated pace, despite the flattened economy, before competition grew worse. The third had waffled both directions before casting her vote with the first. The result was the hiring of Bob Smith in late 1980 as the new Operations Vice President.

Smith's first action had been to acquaint himself with each corporate and franchise operation. What he had found was "shocking to someone even without restaurant experience." Some restaurants had looked exemplary: their employees were neatly dressed, courteous, and efficient; their kitchens, dining areas, and washrooms immaculate; and their product eye appealing, tasty, and hot. Unfortunately, more had looked average and some, too many in fact, had looked positively dangerous.

THE SAN DIEGO RESTAURANT

The worst was the San Diego restaurant—one of the corporate franchises. A number of factors seemed to Smith to be responsible, chief among them was the manager's incompetency. Proof appeared as poorly trained employees, high labor turnover, and low morale. The pizzas were nothing to shout about either: some were overcooked and served cold, while others were undercooked and served cold. Some contained too little cheese and meat but others contained near the proper quantities. One had actually contained a match, discarded by an employee who evidently had mistaken a pizza for an ashtray.

Ron Walton was hired to replace the manager soon after Smith's inspection. This had helped but some other problems still remained. Ingredient costs had continued to rise and the economy had continued to fall. Worse yet, other pizza restaurants in San Diego began promoting very aggressively with coupons and new products. Samurai could easily match the former tactic but had not, for fear of tarnishing its image. It had experienced some difficulty in matching the latter tactic—until now the firm was more interested in expansion through new outlets than through new products.

Smith and Walton also agreed that the location of the San Diego restaurant could have been better chosen. Parking was limited but the biggest problem was the lack of a nearby high school or college. Samurai customers in most markets seemed to be mostly under age 35 and without children. Relatively few families ate at a Samurai restaurant, a situation consistent with corporate strategy. Smith and Walton had concluded that the neighborhood surrounding the San Diego restaurant was just too mature.

All this had led them to request marketing research, beginning first with the San Diego market. If Samurai could gather good data, analyze and interpret it properly, and take appropriate action, perhaps the San Diego restaurant could be saved. Certainly anything Smith and Walton learned would improve performance and that would be a good first step. Further, if the research proved worthwhile, Smith would repeat the study for other restaurants in other market areas.

White had begun his assessment process by listening carefully to Smith and Walton as well as to other corporate officers, consumers, and pizza experts. The result of this preliminary research led him to design a study meeting four objectives:

THE RESEARCH DESIGN

1. Identify pizza consumers in demographic and usage rate terms for Samurai and competing restaurants.

2. Identify features consumers consider important in deciding among various pizza restaurants.

3. Compare Samurai and two competing pizza restaurants on features consumers consider important in deciding among various pizza restaurants.

4. Estimate the effect of several promotion plans designed to attract customers to a pizza restaurant.

He had designed a questionnaire to collect data meeting these objectives (Exhibit C17.1).

Actually, the questionnaire would appear in four versions, all identical except for the wording of question 5. Each version would test the potential impact of a different coupon: $2.00 off the regular price of any large Samurai pizza, $3.00 off, a free pitcher of soft drink, or a free spumoni-type dessert. Each version would be given to about one-fourth of the sample.

Plans were to station interviewers at separate public locations within a 3-mile radius of the Samurai restaurant. Interviewers would approach consumers and ask if they had eaten at any San Diego pizza restaurant within the past two weeks. If a consumer answered yes, the interviewer would question as to which restaurant or restaurants, and ask for the consumer's participation in a mail questionnaire marketing research study. Interviewers would explain that the questionnaire would require no more than 20 minutes to answer. They would not identify the survey sponsor. They would promise anonymity to consumers and a free

EXHIBIT C17.1
The Questionnaire

1. At what pizza restaurant have you eaten a pizza or other food item *in the past two weeks*? Write the name or names in the spaces below and also the number of times you ate there *in the past two weeks*.

Restaurant	Number of times
_____	_____ times
_____	_____ times
_____	_____ times
_____	_____ times

2. What things are important in deciding what pizza restaurant you ate at? Indicate the importance of *each* of the following features by circling the appropriate response to the right of each feature.

FEATURE	EXTREMELY IMPORTANT	MODERATELY IMPORTANT	IMPORTANT	LITTLE IMPORTANCE	NOT IMPORTANT
Cleanliness	EI	MI	I	LI	NI
Taste of the food	EI	MI	I	LI	NI
Fast service	EI	MI	I	LI	NI
Variety of the menu	EI	MI	I	LI	NI
Convenient location	EI	MI	I	LI	NI
Price	EI	MI	I	LI	NI
Familiarity with the restaurant	EI	MI	I	LI	NI
Identified manager on duty	EI	MI	I	LI	NI
Friendly employees	EI	MI	I	LI	NI
Comfortable atmosphere	EI	MI	I	LI	NI
Availability of wine or beer	EI	MI	I	LI	NI
Availability of entertainment	EI	MI	I	LI	NI
Availability of thick crust pizza	EI	MI	I	LI	NI
Availability of desserts	EI	MI	I	LI	NI

3. Now we would like your impression about several pizza restaurants in the San Diego area. Each restaurant on the next page has a group of words below it which can be used to describe it. Place an "X" on one of the spaces between *each pair* of words according to which word you think more closely describes the restaurant.

   For example, if you think the restaurant you are rating is extremely clean, has very good tasting food and extremely fast service, your responses would look like this:

	EXTREMELY	VERY	A LITTLE	A LITTLE	VERY	EXTREMELY	
Clean	X	—	—	—	—	—	Dirty
Bad tasting food	—	—	—	—	X	—	Good tasting food
Slow service	—	—	—	—	—	X	Fast service

Be sure to put an "X" for each pair of words.

Pizza Hut

	EXTREMELY	VERY	A LITTLE	A LITTLE	VERY	EXTREMELY	
Clean	—	—	—	—	—	—	Dirty
Bad tasting food	—	—	—	—	—	—	Good tasting food
Slow service	—	—	—	—	—	—	Fast service
Large menu variety	—	—	—	—	—	—	Small menu variety
Inconvenient location	—	—	—	—	—	—	Convenient location
Inexpensive	—	—	—	—	—	—	Expensive
Unfriendly employees	—	—	—	—	—	—	Friendly employees
Comfortable atmosphere	—	—	—	—	—	—	Uncomfortable atmosphere

Samurai Pizza

	EXTREMELY	VERY	A LITTLE	A LITTLE	VERY	EXTREMELY	
Clean	—	—	—	—	—	—	Dirty
Bad tasting food	—	—	—	—	—	—	Good tasting food
Slow service	—	—	—	—	—	—	Fast service
Large menu variety	—	—	—	—	—	—	Small menu variety
Inconvenient location	—	—	—	—	—	—	Convenient location
Inexpensive	—	—	—	—	—	—	Expensive
Unfriendly employees	—	—	—	—	—	—	Friendly employees
Comfortable atmosphere	—	—	—	—	—	—	Uncomfortable atmosphere

Square Pan Pizza

	EXTREMELY	VERY	A LITTLE	A LITTLE	VERY	EXTREMELY	
Clean	—	—	—	—	—	—	Dirty
Bad tasting food	—	—	—	—	—	—	Good tasting food
Slow service	—	—	—	—	—	—	Fast service
Large menu variety	—	—	—	—	—	—	Small menu variety

	EXTREMELY	VERY	A LITTLE	A LITTLE	VERY	EXTREMELY	
Inconvenient location	___	___	___	___	___	___	Convenient location
Inexpensive	___	___	___	___	___	___	Expensive
Unfriendly employees	___	___	___	___	___	___	Friendly employees
Comfortable atmosphere	___	___	___	___	___	___	Uncomfortable atmosphere

4. In the space below, please describe what you feel is missing from most pizza restaurants.

_____

_____

_____

5. Suppose you received a coupon good for $2.00 off the regular price of any large Samurai pizza. How likely is it that you would use it? Circle one below.

| Definitely would use it | Probably would use it | Might or might not use it | Probably would not use it | Definitely would not use it |

Finally, we would like some background information about you and your family. DO NOT put your name anywhere on this questionnaire—these questions are for statistical purposes only.

6. Age: (on your last birthday) _____ .
7. Sex: M   F
8. Marital Status: Not   Divorced or
                              Married   Married   Widowed   Separated
9. How large is your family, that is, how many people (parents, children, other relatives) live in your home? _____
10. What is your occupation? (Please be specific, e.g. self-employed electrician, owner of grocery store, clothing salesman at a big department store, primary school teacher, gasoline station attendant, etc.) If you are unemployed or retired, please write in *unemployed* or *retired*. (Please do *not* mention the name of the specific company or employer.)

_____

11. What was the last grade in school you completed?

____ no formal education   ____ some college

____ 6th grade or less   ____ completed (4 year) college

____ 7th or 8th grade   ____ some graduate work

____ some high school   ____ completed graduate work

____ completed high school   ____ other (write in) _____

12. What was your total family (household) gross (before taxes) *income* in 1981? Please include the income of all members of your household, from whatever sources this income (including welfare, unemployment compensation, etc.) came.

____ under $5000   ____ $12500 to $14999

____ $5000 to $7999   ____ $15000 to $19999

____ $8000 to $9999   ____ $20000 to $24999

____ $10000 to $12499   ____ $25000 and over

13. What newspaper do you have delivered to your home?

None ____   Evening Tribune ____

San Diego Union ____   _____
                          (other—write in)

14. What is your favorite radio station? _____

15. About how many hours a day do you listen to this station, on the average? _____ hrs.

As a thank you for completing this questionnaire, we would like you to receive a coupon good for one free pizza from a local restaurant. To receive this coupon, please write *only* your address on the label below. This label will be attached to a postcard coupon and promptly mailed back to you.

pizza from "a local pizza restaurant" in return for a completed questionnaire.

If a consumer agreed to participate, the interviewer would ask the consumer to write only his or her address on a mailing label. This label would be attached to an envelope containing the questionnaire and mailed the next day. White desired a sample of about 500 consumers, at least 180 of whom reported eating at Samurai.

THE DATA ANALYSIS PLAN

All that remained was for White to develop the data analysis plan. The plan would be the topic of a short, final meeting between Smith and Walton before White actually began data collection. "Probably the best way to proceed would be to decide on analyses for each research objective," White thought. "Also, I should be able to dummy up some tables to show Bob and Ron how results will look." He turned to his task.

18. Kramer Sportswear*

Earl Vernon, Western Regional Sales Manager for Kramer Sportswear, thought he had everything he needed. Earlier that day, his secretary had given him quarterly unit sales figures for the "Pro-Ball" jersey line for each calendar quarter beginning in 1970. "It ought to be easy," Vernon thought, "to come up with a forecast for the next five years. Let's see what we have here." And with that he turned to the data (Table C18.1).

BACKGROUND   Kramer Sportswear was one of the largest manufacturers of clothing for athletes age 11 to 25. The firm sold a complete line of team sport clothing through its own salesforce which called on:

1. elementary, junior high, senior high, and college coaches and athletic directors;

2. park and recreation league coaches and directors; and

3. owners and managers of better quality sporting goods stores and chains.

TABLE C18.1
"Pro-Ball" Jersey Sales by Quarter, 1970–1980 (000 units)

| Year | QUARTER | | | | |
	1	2	3	4	Total
1970	156.1	57.2	87.7	88.0	389.0
1971	168.1	57.4	86.1	102.5	414.1
1972	172.2	63.0	92.4	100.8	428.4
1973	223.6	90.3	94.6	100.4	508.9
1974	220.8	94.4	98.7	98.9	512.8
1975	243.5	112.5	157.6	184.2	697.8
1976	317.4	110.4	151.8	184.0	763.6
1977	380.7	145.7	206.8	216.2	949.4
1978	460.8	196.8	249.6	316.8	1,224.0
1979	499.8	205.8	274.4	323.4	1,303.0
1980	499.7	211.3	334.0	395.0	1,440.0

*Frank Lynch, graduate research assistant at the University of Minnesota, helped write this case.

The western region was Earl's responsibility and included the following states:

Alaska	Hawaii	New Mexico	Wyoming
Arizona	Idaho	Oregon	
California	Montana	Utah	
Colorado	Nevada	Washington	

Kramer sales varied in each state depending on the level of competition, number of people in the target segment, number of athletic teams, and other factors.

Several conditions placed a premium on accurate forecasting for the firm. For one, Kramer sales had shown a growth rate of about 14 percent per year for the period 1970 to 1980. Such rapid growth naturally meant problems in the operation of any firm. However, Kramer regularly operated "on the edge" and several departures from casual forecasts had in the past caused crises of rather serious degree. For another, sales of Kramer products tended to be quite seasonal—that is, light in the second, third, and fourth quarters and heavy in the first. Such seasonality affected the firm's need for cash, inventory, storage space, shipping help, and the like. For yet another, Vernon's allocation of advertising and

TABLE C18.2
State Data

State	Number of Public Secondary Schools, 1977	Number of Students in Public Secondary Schools, 1977 (000)	Number of Sporting Goods Stores (1977)	Sales (Units)
Alaska	298	27	132	4,170
Arizona	217	153	387	53,750
California	1,543	1,404	3,571	764,200
Colorado	418	184	657	62,650
Hawaii	52	56	157	5,800
Idaho	184	64	225	30,000
Montana	194	57	199	17,160
Nevada	80	48	134	24,130
New Mexico	175	92	178	21,890
Oregon	329	154	466	158,700
Utah	159	96	218	35,760
Washington	531	255	647	243,800
Wyoming	125	29	149	17,950

Sources: U.S. Statistical Abstract, U.S. Census of Retail Trade, and company records.

salesforce support to each state also depended on accurate state and total forecasts. Such decisions, if made poorly, would waste resources in some states and keep needed resources from others.

THE FIVE-YEAR AND 1981 STATE FORECASTS

Consequently, Kramer management had recently decided that a five-year forecast was crucial to the continued success of the firm. Vernon's forecast for the "Pro-Ball" jersey line, currently accounting for 28 percent of Kramer sales in the West, would be his first step in the process.

Vernon also felt it managerially and politically imperative that he prepare a "Pro-Ball" sales forecast for each state in his territory. However, rather than forecast each state's sales using its previous sales, he decided to forecast using some relevant measures of market potential. To this end, he had asked his secretary to assemble data on the number of public secondary schools in 1977, the number of students enrolled in public secondary schools in 1978, and the number of sporting goods stores operating in 1977 for each of the thirteen states (Table C18.2). With these data, Vernon felt, he should be able to develop a model to forecast state sales.

PART **VI**

Communicating Results and Research Ethics

20

Interpreting and Reporting Research Results

After data analysis, the researcher undertakes three activities to complete the marketing research process: interpreting results, reporting results, and evaluating the research design. Interpretation occurs as the researcher *attaches meaning* to results of completed data analyses. When satisfied that data can produce little additional understanding, the researcher assembles and reports results. The researcher concludes post-data analysis activities by appraising the entire research process. All three activities require attention to detail, skill, and energy, as we shall see.

Interpreting Results

Results of any data analysis seldom make sense at a glance. Instead, a researcher usually spends considerable time interpreting results, in order to describe to decision makers what the results actually mean. Compared to the rigorous analytical techniques discussed in the past five chapters, the process of interpreting results is much less structured. Still, we can identify two phases to the process—reviewing the data's background and explaining results.

573

DATA BACKGROUND   The first step in interpreting results involves the researcher reviewing the data's background. At a minimum, this means that the researcher must be familiar with the research design employed in the study:

- the marketing problem statement and research hypotheses,
- types of data sources,
- data collection methods and forms,
- sampling procedures, and
- analytical techniques.

Such a review will be especially important for results produced by large, lengthy, and complex studies as well as those based on all types of secondary data. The review must convince the researcher that the research design produced data sufficiently valid and reliable to warrant interpreting: the best data interpretation in the world cannot make sense of faulty data.

But beyond looking for an adequate research design, the researcher also reviews the data's background to reemphasize an awareness of the decision maker's key performance parameters. We discussed performance parameters in Chapter 3 as variables along which decision makers evaluate operations under their separate responsibilities. For example, a health and beauty aids department manager in a discount store may identify key performance parameters as sales per square foot and inventory turnover. With this knowledge, a researcher will focus interpretation efforts on explaining data variations on these variables rather than on, say, merchandise returns.

Finally, the researcher reviews the data's background looking specifically for statistical significance. We remember that the term indicates the likelihood that chance, as operating through the sampling process, could have produced results of the data analysis. Statistical significance depends on both data values and sample size. For example, suppose our health and beauty aids manager finds average inventory turnover rates for couponed and noncouponed products to be 20.6 and 11.4, respectively. Consider the interpretation of these values—based first on sample sizes of 2 products each and second on sample sizes of 200 products each. Obviously we would interpret results from the larger samples as more meaningful; this interpretation is an intuitive counterpart to a test of statistical significance using rigorous statistical theory.

Yet statistical significance does not equal managerial significance. To illustrate, suppose average turnover rates for couponed and noncouponed products were instead 20.6 and 20.4 and were based on samples of size 80 each. Further suppose that a test of mean differences showed results to be statistically significant. Our interpretation is that couponed products show higher turnover rates than noncouponed products but that this statistically significant difference is so slight as to be managerially nonexistent. The decision maker would consider the difference in turnover rates as inconsequential in making couponing decisions. We conclude from this discussion that statistically significant results may be interpreted as meaningful only if data values show managerially worthwhile information.

Statistically insignificant results may at best be interpreted as "interesting." That is, some statistically insignificant results may indicate sufficient potential that the researcher may pursue additional research, perhaps with a different research design using a larger sample. Most insignificant results will indicate no further effort be expended.

Finally, we note that even managerially significant results in our example leave a host of other interpretation questions unanswered:

- Do couponed products show higher turnover rates than uncouponed products because of the coupon?
- Did consumers actually increase their consumption of couponed products or did they merely stock up on them, postponing future purchases?
- After considering coupon processing costs, did the department realize more profit on couponed than on noncouponed products?
- Do some couponed products show higher turnover rates than other couponed products? Why?

Such questions (and their answers) really illustrate our topic matter for the next section, which is explaining research results.

EXPLAINING RESULTS

The second step in interpreting data consists in the researcher actually explaining results. Largely this is a process of developing insights into results through diligence, logic, intuition, and luck. To illustrate, consider a researcher interpreting some research results for a new accounts officer in a savings and loan association. Suppose the officer had requested research to aid in deciding whether or not to continue the firm's support for a Welcome Wagon service in its market area. The service called on newcomers to the area and presented them with, among other things, a savings account at the association with a starting balance of $10. Beyond this initial deposit, the firm also paid $10 to the Welcome Wagon service for each new account opened.

Research results from a sample of 200 new accounts showed an average balance of $420 over the twelve months following the Welcome Wagon visit. Because the savings firm netted 1.8 percent annually on savings accounts, the researcher initially interpreted the average balance as inadequate; that is, the firm was spending $20 to open new accounts that returned an average of only ($420) (0.018), or $7.56.

However, additional interpretation effort provided the researcher with more insight. Some further research showed that accounts remained with the firm for an average of 7 years and that their balances grew at about 14 percent each year. The firm netted 1.8 percent on these balances for each of these years and, thus, easily recouped its initial cost on most accounts. The researcher also found that only about 3 percent of all savings accounts were closed for purposes of the holder reopening the account at a competitor. Once a firm captured an account, it kept it. Moreover, the Welcome Wagon service operated on an exclusive basis, opening accounts only for the savings and loan firm and not for either of its two competitors. Finally, the researcher learned that the market area was currently growing at about 6.5 percent per year. Thus, newcomers constituted an opportunity for rapid growth.

All these insights led the researcher to recommend retaining the Welcome Wagon service. All had taken additional effort to develop, had relied on reason and intuition, and would henceforth appear more quickly because of the researcher's experience. All also followed from the application of these guidelines:

1. Follow up clues or hints as they surface during the early stages of data analysis. Sometimes support (or the lack of it) for an interpretation already exists in the form of other research results; more often clues or hints will indicate additional data analysis.

2. Attempt to see the "forest in spite of the trees." That is, freely examine research results in isolation but before concluding an interpretation, examine how the results fit together. Results that support each other produce recommendations that carry more influence with the decision maker.

3. Identify several alternative interpretations that also explain results. Then examine each alternative with respect to the data and to other data to learn which are likely, which are possible, and which are unlikely.

4. Prefer simple interpretations to the more elegant. Begin with an interpretation of results based on analyses of a single variable. Then proceed to results based on simultaneous analyses of several variables. Seldom will a variable show lackluster performance all by itself only to blossom into a powerful explanatory variable in the presence of other variables.

5. Remain open minded and fair.[1] That is, interpret and report *all* results relevant to the recommendations, even those that contradict them. Only if the researcher does this can the decision maker receive a true understanding of results.

Other guidelines will appear along with research experience.

---

[1]David J. Luck et al., *Marketing Research*, 5th ed. (Englewood Cliffs, N.J.: Prentice-Hall, 1978), p. 393.

Interpreting research results is every bit as important as deriving them in the first place. Casual and superficial interpretations reduce the worth of a research study as surely as do mistakes made in designing data collection forms, samples, and data analysis plans. Diligent and creative interpretations result in more meaningful recommendations to the decision maker. They lead to long-term relationships.

SUMMARY OF INTERPRETING RESULTS

Reporting Results

To introduce the reporting of research results, we borrow an observation from Cox: Decision makers tend to look not technically but practically at research results. On the other hand, researchers tend to avoid pragmatic in favor of scientific interpretations of results.[2] Thus, a basic communications gap about research results exists between decision makers and researchers, a gap bridged by formal and informal research reports.

Our interest lies with formal research reports made on paper and in person. Such reports appear with a variety of topic outlines, styles, and emphases. They do so because of the variety of research designs, standard company report formats, decision makers, and researchers. However, despite this diversity, we can discuss some common written and oral report sections in terms of their content and organization. We can also comment on their form.

Most research designs provide for a written report to the decision maker. The report evidences the design's completion, summarizes research activities, presents results, and allows for convenient storage. In accomplishing the second and third functions, a good report should:

WRITTEN REPORTS

1. continually reflect an understanding of its audiences;

2. emphasize results, interpretations of results, and recommendations based on results; and

3. like a research proposal, clarify rather than obscure.

Overall, the written report should "convey the impression of a thorough and professional marketing research effort" to increase the decision maker's faith in the results.[3] Let us look more closely.

Sections of the Written Report. Exhibit 20.1 outlines major research report sections. Complex research designs often have report sections that

---

[2]Eli P. Cox, III, *Marketing Research: Information for Decision Making* (New York: Harper & Row, 1979), p. 366–67.

[3]Robert W. Joselyn, *Designing the Marketing Research Project* (New York: Petrocelli/ Charter, 1977), p. 248.

EXHIBIT 20.1
Major Sections in a Marketing Research Report

   I. Title page

  II. Table of contents

 III. Decision maker summary
     A. Introduction
     B. Research objectives
     C. Principal results
     D. Interpretations and recommendations

 IV. Introduction

  V. Research objectives

 VI. Methodology

 VII. Results

VIII. Limitations

 IX. Interpretations and recommendations

  X. Appendix
     A. Sampling plan
     B. Data collection forms
     C. Analysis details

Source: Adapted from Eli P. Cox, III, *Marketing Research: Information for Decision Making* (New York: Harper & Row, 1979), p. 369.

average several pages of somewhat technical prose; simple designs usually possess similarly worded sections but in the form of short paragraphs. Some very simple research designs may not have certain sections at all. Thus, our following statements about report sections must necessarily generalize.

Title Page. This section of the research report identifies the nature of the study in ten words or less. Some examples:

- The Feasibility of an Electronics Parts Wholesaling Operation
- Test Market Results for X90 Shampoo
- Price Elasticities for Soft Drinks in the Phoenix Market
- Newspaper Coupon Usage in Chicago Supermarkets

The title page also identifies who performed the research and who wrote the report. It states for whom the research was conducted—that is, it identifies the decision maker and the decision maker's organization. Sometimes the title page will state the names of others allowed to read the report, if the report contains confidential material.

Table of Contents.   This part lists report headings and page numbers to allow readers rapid access. Sometimes a second table lists titles and locations of tables, figures, exhibits, or other illustrative matter, if many of one of these types of presentation devices are used. Each table of contents should be centered horizontally and vertically on a separate page.

Decision Maker Summary.   This section starts the actual report—by presenting in one or two pages those pieces of information most relevant to the decision maker. The summary section consists of an introduction followed by short statements of research objectives, research results, and interpretations and recommendations. Introductory comments usually occupy a paragraph—identifying the marketing problem, basic research approach, and managerial emphasis of the section. Research objectives usually take the next paragraph, telling readers exactly what the design intended to accomplish. Principal research results follow, taking several paragraphs and appearing in sentence, not tabular, form. Often such statements of research results appear in an order paralleling the sequence given earlier to research objectives. Interpretations and recommendations conclude the section, occupying space at least equal to that taken by results. Interpretations and recommendations receive much of the decision maker's attention.

In fact, many decision makers will read little beyond the summary section. Experienced decision makers, those in higher management positions, and all others who trust the researcher, often read further only to confirm a detail, answer a question, or understand a particular facet of the study. Others, however, will read every word at least once and expect the entire report to stand up to such close scrutiny.

Introduction.   This section continues the report, presenting details of the marketing problem as seen by the researcher. The introduction section contains a description of the problem in terms of its key symptoms. It identifies key marketing actions taken in the past that have influenced key symptoms, and it describes aspects of the organization's and decision maker's environments that presently influence and constrain these symptoms. It identifies potential marketing actions that might solve the problem, along with their estimated performance consequences. An introduction often repeats part of the marketing problem statement, which we discussed earlier in Chapter 3. In sum, an introduction section tells the reader exactly how the researcher views tentative causes, effects, and marketing actions as they occur in the various marketing environments. Statements further introduce research objectives, the next report section.

Research Objectives. This section tells readers exactly what the research design intended to accomplish. An example of the research objectives for a feasibility study of an electronics parts wholesaling operation might appear like this:

1. Estimate the size of the electronics parts market at wholesale (SIC code 5065) for Illinois, Indiana, and Ohio for 1982 through 1987.

2. Estimate a firm's fixed and variable costs of operation, assuming it attained 1, 5, and 10 percent shares of market for each year through 1987.

3. Estimate a firm's profitability at 1, 5, and 10 percent shares of market for each year through 1987.

4. Identify 100 potential customers in the market area and estimate their annual purchases of electronics parts through 1987.

5. Identify major competitors, their market areas, strengths, and weaknesses.

We see that research objectives quite narrowly identify the nature of the research study in terms of expected outputs. As with the introduction section, the researcher often can take this portion of the research report directly or with little modification from the earlier written problem statement.

Methodology. This part details the nature of the study in terms of research activities. Paragraphs in this section describe data sources, data collection methods, sample designs, data collection forms, and data analyses. Of necessity, descriptions must greatly summarize the many decisions taken to execute the research design. Thus, descriptions require large numbers of editorial decisions: to include too little detail will raise unnecessary questions; to include too much will bore and perhaps confuse. Like the rest of the research report, the methodology section communicates primarily with decision makers who find overly technical discussions irrelevant and, perhaps, incomprehensible; thus, descriptions use a minimum of technical terms. A useful rule of thumb is this—if a researcher thinks a part of the methodology discussion might contain too much detail or technical jargon, it does. If the part can be rewritten at a less esoteric level, it should be, and be kept in the section. If it cannot, it belongs in the report either as part of an appendix or not at all.

Results. This section summarizes the products of data analysis. That is, it presents not result after result after result but instead an overview of results. Usually results are organized into tables with summary comments used both to highlight major findings and to separate the tables. Often results appear in a sequence further governed by the order of research objectives. Those pertaining to the first objective appear first, those pertaining to the second follow, and so on. Results of analyses made apart from research objectives (for example, analyses to assess sample representativeness or to validate responses) often appear last or, better yet, in an appendix. Such an organization shows more logic to the decision maker than does an organization by unitary portion of the data collection form or by analytical technique.

Limitations. This part tells the reader about deficiencies in the methodology. Such deficiencies accompany all research designs and appear in the form of limits and errors. Limits exist because of sampling frames and time periods, for example. To illustrate, the sampling frame used may not have listed all elements in the population of interest once and only once. Or, the time period during which data were collected may not have represented all time periods. Errors exist either because of the inherent nature of the design or because of its improper execution. For example, all designs using samples produce sampling errors (as estimated for the mean by $Zs_{\bar{x}}$), just as all designs asking questions produce response errors (as stable and random departures from truth). Within any one design, errors further appear when members of the research team intentionally or unintentionally depart from proper research practice. All such deficiencies should be identified in the limitations section by a responsible researcher. More than this, a responsible researcher should estimate the effect of these errors in this section so that decision makers may estimate the extent to which results can be trusted.

Interpretations and Recommendations. Interpretations of results should appear much as we discussed earlier in this chapter. They should evidence an understanding of the data's background. They should explain results logically and completely, citing findings in support and in opposition. Usually the researcher would organize the presentation of interpretations parallel to that for the research objectives and results sections. Recommendations for decision maker action end the section. Here the researcher often will organize in a descending order of priority: stronger recommendations appear first, followed by those less well supported by results. Each recommendation should be followed immediately by a justification showing support in the data. Each should be within the decision maker's decision freedom in the organization. Often the researcher will further discuss implementation considerations for each recommendation in terms of who might do what by when.

Appendix. This section concludes the research report. Discussions about sampling, data collection forms, and data analyses too detailed or too technical for the body of the report appear here for the perusal of enthusiasts. Here is where they would find copies of interviewer instructions and the complete data collection form, complete calculations for sampling error, and technical discussions of data analyses. However, researchers should resist the temptation to put everything into the appendix for the appearance of substantiality. Like the rest of the research report, the appendix should include only treatment of topics relevant to an understanding of the research design. The decision maker does not pay for the research report on the basis of its weight.

Form of the Written Report. Equal with a concern for content of the written research report is a concern for form. Stated simply, even though research reports are technical business documents, they still must conform to the conventions of written English. Well-written reports reflect a number of guidelines:

1. Produce a grammatically correct report. This means spelling, punctuation, word choice, and other mechanics of English communication must be completed correctly. To do otherwise invites faulty interpretations of the report and an inference that the researcher's research ability might be as poor as his or her writing ability. Good research and correct recommendations that are poorly expressed will meet with doubt, lack of action, and occasionally ridicule.

2. Write from a suitable design. At a minimum this means following the content outline (as in Exhibit 20.1, or one similar) in writing the report. However, better written reports use more detailed outlines to guide writing within each report section. They use paragraphs to introduce each section and topic sentences to introduce most paragraphs. They limit each paragraph to one basic thought. They use no more than three levels of headings to separate groups of related thoughts, and they use at least one heading on every other page.

3. Write with nouns and verbs. This means writing sentences with a minimum of adjectives and adverbs. Such superfluous words generally qualify and usually weaken a competent researcher's true thoughts to a severe degree except in very, very rare and unusual circumstances. In contrast, nouns and verbs produce interesting prose.

4. Be clear and concise. To write clearly means using the proper word to express the intended thought. A large vocabulary, a dictionary, and a thesaurus aid good writing. To write clearly also means constructing simple sentences. Most sentences should consist of short strings of words in this order: noun, verb, and complement. To write clearly also means using parallel construction. Readers find it easier to understand related ideas when they appear in parallel form.

5. Revise and rewrite. This usually means writing the research report in more than one but less than four drafts. The first draft should rest undisturbed for several days, allowing the researcher to achieve some distance before the first revision. The researcher should then read the draft for accuracy, clarity, and consistency in tone and terms, then revise and rewrite. The second draft, too, should sit by itself before being read, revised, and rewritten. Before duplicating the final draft, the researcher should proofread everything for errors.

Most good writers follow these and other guidelines;[4] most good writers are made, not born.

On the last point, researchers should try to develop an interesting writing style. This does not mean researchers should be capable of turning a phrase as adeptly as a poet or a novelist. It does mean they should acquire the eyes and ears of a good technical writer. To begin this process, a researcher should select some of his recent work and read it critically, alone and aloud. If the writing is good, the words will make sense, rouse the interest, and produce a pleasant sound. If the writing is bad, the words won't.

Once convinced that his writing can be improved, a researcher should seek instruction. Most universities and similar institutions offer a technical writing course beyond elementary composition. Almost all sell writing reference books in their bookstores.[5] Either form of instruction can in a short time provide a wealth of good writing advice. The researcher should take it. That is, the researcher should practice and experiment to improve his writing skill just as he would to improve any other. The researcher should further seek out good writers, ask for their advice and constructive criticism, accept them, and then practice and experiment some more.

Finally, the researcher should read the works of good writers critically to learn how they wrote so well. He will find that good writers practice what the reference books preach: they write in the active voice, vary their sentence lengths, avoid short choppy paragraphs, and usually place important ideas at the ends of sentences. Let us look only at the first and last practices in more detail.

Sentences may appear either in the active or passive voice. A sentence in the active voice uses this sequence of words: actor, action, object. That is, some actor or noun takes some action with respect to some object.

---

[4]These and other guidelines appear in William Strunk, Jr., and E. B. White, *The Elements of Style,* 2nd ed. (New York: Macmillan, 1972).

[5]See Strunk and White, *The Elements of Style* or Wilson Follett, *Modern American Usage* (New York: Warner Books, 1977) or Hans P. Guth, *Concise English Handbook,* 4th ed. (Belmont, Cal.: Wadsworth, 1977).

A sentence in the passive voice rearranges the sequence: object, action, actor. Look at these examples:

Active Voice Sentences	Consumers hate the product.
	In 10 of the 15 territories, sales exceed quotas.
	The ad portrays women in a disparaging manner.
Passive Voice Sentences	The product is hated by consumers.
	In 10 of the 15 territories, quotas have been exceeded by sales.
	Women are portrayed by that ad in a disparaging manner.

Notice that sentences in the passive voice take more words to express the same thought. Notice also that they lack vigor and simplicity. In short, sentences in the passive voice take more effort to read.

A sentence should usually contain its important idea at its end. Such construction stresses the important idea and makes the sentence more interesting to the reader. Some good examples are:

> Good writing takes instruction, practice, and diligence.
> The advertisement must contain fewer than 50 words of copy.
> Slightly over half of the retailers surveyed last week said they would carry the product.

Some bad examples:

> Instruction, practice, and diligence are required by good writing.
> Copy of less than 50 words must appear in the advertisement.
> Retailers who said they would carry the product were slightly over half of those surveyed last week.

Placing the important idea at the end of the sentence arouses the reader's curiosity and gives the sentence an air of mystery—the sentence's meaning is not apparent until the very end. It adds emphasis to the important idea.

ORAL REPORTS   Oral reports of marketing research differ little from written reports in terms of their content and form. They still discuss research objectives, methodology, results, limitations, and interpretations and recommendations. Most still begin with a decision maker summary. All should be grammatically correct, follow an outline, depend on nouns and verbs, be clear and concise, and come from a carefully written set of notes. Thus, Exhibit 20.1 and our five written report guidelines still apply.

However, oral reports do differ in important ways. For one, oral reports require the researcher to be a good public speaker.[6] A good public speaker approaches the oral report feeling anxious rather than complacent (most researchers take this advice rather well). A good public speaker quickly establishes eye contact with listeners to gather feedback. She uses natural gestures to emphasize important points in the report. She uses notes and visual aids comfortably. She does not use "OK?" or "you know" to end every third sentence. She starts the report on time (even if not everyone has arrived, as a courtesy to those who have budgeted their time properly) and finishes similarly (or earlier). Having practiced the presentation at least once, she executes the oral report confidently.

Another difference is that oral reports are limited to ninety minutes or less. This means that the researcher emphasizes only major points from the written report. It means that oral reports often reduce to a presentation of the decision maker summary section plus a brief explanation of research methodology and limitations. Oral reports also appear in a much less technical and a much more managerial tone. They must—because of the audience's background and interest and the fact that oral reports proceed at a sequence and pace largely beyond the audience's control. Oral reports make simple, managerial statements.

Yet another difference is that oral reports require the researcher to be an expert in audio and visual aids. No researcher can expect to communicate a research report adequately using words and gestures alone. Rather, the researcher uses aids to explain things more easily, completely, and dramatically. Aids range from blackboards to simple flip charts to overhead transparencies to color slides to video tape recordings, all perhaps used in the same session. Aids consist of the several graphic presentation forms discussed in Chapters 15 through 19: frequency distribution tables, frequency polygons, histograms, ogives, pie charts, crosstab tables, scattergrams, regression lines, ANOVA tables, line charts, and other special tables and figures. To be most effective, the researcher should observe these requirements with visual aids:

1. Use slides, charts or handouts to convey no more than one thought at a time.

2. Suppress detail mercilessly. Additional information should be presented orally; visual material is usually best utilized to focus attention, to dramatize, to provide a frame of reference, to furnish a springboard for further presentation and discussion.

3. Be sure equipment is available and in working order. Be certain beforehand that adequate extension cords, screens, easels, and blackboards are on hand. Check the location of working electrical outlets.

---

[6]The following discussion comes from William C. Himstreet and Wayne Murlin Baty, *Business Communications: Principles and Methods*, 5th ed. (Belmont Cal.: Wadsworth, 1977), pp. 396-98.

4. Anticipate the risk of equipment breakdown by having spare bulbs or whatever else is needed in handy reserve. Better yet, know where a reserve piece of equipment could be obtained in a hurry.

5. Consider the nature and dimensions of the room to be sure that each aid is truly visible to all members of the audience.[7]

To this excellent advice, we add that the researcher must understand each aid completely and be prepared to answer all audience questions arising from it.

This questioning activity is the last major difference between written and oral reports. Oral reports allow, expect, and even encourage questions from the audience. Questions occur at some cost but provide a certain benefit. Costs come from the researcher's time spent preparing for the oral report. Costs come further from other members of the research team who must also prepare for and attend the oral report. Each must be ready to answer questions on her or his area of technical specialty. Costs come also from wasted time on the part of all present who lack interest in the question or answer. Benefits are the immediate two-way communication between researcher and audience.

We should recognize that not all (in fact, not a majority of) research designs end with oral reports of such formal structure. Formal oral reports take much preparation time and much execution time (in terms of the total of all the participants' time); they occur during normally busy work schedules. In consequence, formal oral reports are given only "when the problem is serious, when amplification and discussion of information are essential, or when there are conflicting points of view."[8]

However, we should further recognize that almost all research designs end with informal oral reports. That is, almost always the researcher meets with the decision maker after distributing the report, at a time convenient to both parties, and in a place where neither is likely to be disturbed. The researcher then takes the decision maker through the report, listens to questions and comments, and responds, clearly and candidly. Such a discussion, apart from good research in the first place, helps build a long-term relationship between researcher and decision maker.

Epilogue: Following Up the Research Report

The researcher completes a particular research design not with the final report but with some later follow-up activities. The first activity is the evaluation of the research design. Here the researcher identifies what

---

[7]Lee Adler and Charles S. Mayer, *Managing the Marketing Research Function* (Chicago: American Marketing Association, 1977), p. 53.

[8]Ibid, p. 51.

worked well and what worked poorly during the execution of the design. In particular, the researcher examines problem definition processes and those associated with measurement, sampling, data analysis, and research reporting—all for potential improvements. Improvements will appear as possibilities for cheaper, faster, more accurate, and more relevant data. Sources of this information will include other members of the research team, both inside and outside the firm, and the decision maker. In essence, evaluation activities reduce to this basic question: If we were to repeat the study tomorrow, what would we do differently?

The second follow-up activity centers on the decision maker—to learn which recommendations were taken and which were not. Such a feedback process really focuses on the acceptability of research recommendations.[9] Some recommendations, of course, are accepted; the researcher should attempt to find out why. For the most part, the decision maker should have accepted recommendations using the same reasoning as the researcher used in making them. Other recommendations, of course, are rejected; and again the researcher should attempt to learn why. For example, before rejecting a recommendation, the decision maker may interpret results creatively, logically, diligently, but differently from the way the researcher saw them. On the other hand, the decision maker may interpret results improperly or not at all before taking the same action. Either way, the researcher needs feedback on the acceptability of research recommendations to complete the research design professionally. The decision maker deserves the benefit of the researcher's questioning about accepted and rejected recommendations; the researcher deserves to know how the decision maker actually makes a decision. Insight into how each other thinks helps in the design of better research in the future.

The third follow-up activity compares anticipated research benefits with actual research costs. As we said earlier, of benefits and costs, the easier ones to measure are costs. Most accounting systems can provide a reasonably accurate estimate of research costs, especially after the study is complete or when an outside supplier performs the research. However, they can provide only crude estimates of research benefits under any circumstances, largely because of the numerous factors beyond marketing research recommendations that affect the firm's performance. Still, both researcher and decision maker need to examine the worth of marketing research as part of their follow-up activities. The decision maker tends to see marketing research as a staff operation—a net consumer of corporate resources. The researcher tends to see marketing research as a net producer. The two parties should share their views.

The fourth and last follow-up activity prepares for the possibility of further research. Such preparation should proceed in an ethical manner

---

[9]An alternate treatment of acceptability appears in Luck et al., *Marketing Research*, 5th ed., pp. 421–22.

to consider research that would solve new issues arising from the just-completed study. For example, a study may conclude that a hair drier manufacturer should increase prices by 8 percent because of volume and profit considerations. However, the researcher may have noticed that data also show that a certain segment very strongly associates price with product quality. These consumers might be more receptive to as much as a 40 percent price increase and, of course, a modified product. The wisdom of such an action forms a new research problem that might be attacked with a further analysis of existing data. Or, it might require a completely new research design. The researcher should recognize this and be ready to respond at least in general terms when the decision maker asks, "Where do we go from here?"

In sum, we recognize that marketing research is a discontinuous activity. It starts with a marketing problem and ends with activities that follow up the research report. However, this does not mean that researchers complete their studies, tip their hats, and scurry back to the secure confines of the research department. Rather, it means that researchers should develop long-term, continuous relationships with the decision maker in preparation for the next call to action. Researchers must enlarge their role from that of technician to that of one who attracts and keeps satisfied customers.

Chapter Summary

A marketing research design ends with the researcher interpreting research results, summarizing and reporting the design, and following up the report. Such activities differ from the rather objective, structured, and technical matters associated with most of the earlier stages of the research design. Here we expect the researcher to adopt a broader, more eclectic viewpoint. We expect the researcher to be creative, intuitive, and expressive. And we expect the researcher to like working with words and with people, as well as with numbers.

Chapter Review

KEY TERMS	Results interpretation	Limitations section
	Managerial significance	Research follow-up

DISCUSSION QUESTIONS

1. Why don't marketing research data ever "speak for themselves?"

2. Why does a researcher review the data's background before interpreting research results?

3. Compare and contrast statistical significance with managerial significance.

4. What types of discussions ought to be contained in the final research report? What types ought not?

5. What does the limitations section of the written research report discuss? Why even have such a section?

6. "It's not so much what you say in the marketing research report; it's how you say it." Comment.

7. Forms of the verb be (am, is, are, was, were) often appear in what type of sentence construction? Find two sentences using this construction in this chapter and rewrite them without using the verb form of be. Compare the rewritten and original sentences.

8. Describe how oral research reports differ from written research reports. Under what conditions should each type of report be used?

9. Why doesn't the marketing research process end with the delivery of the final research report?

10. "The first and last stages of the marketing research process are the most difficult for marketing researchers to execute well." Why might an experienced researcher say this?

Additional Readings

Britt, Steuart H., "The Writing of Readable Research Reports." *Journal of Marketing Research* 8 (May 1971):262–66.

> *This article describes an orientation toward writing from the viewpoints of the writer, the message, and the reader. Needless to say, the article is well written and worth reading.*

Guth, Hans P. *Concise English Handbook*. 4th ed. Belmont, Cal.: Wadsworth, 1977.

> *This short paperback contains everything you need to know about spoken and written English. Sections discuss grammar and usage, words, sentences, paragraphs, themes, mechanics and spelling, punctuation, and the research paper, among others. This book also contains good advice for writing various sorts of letters and answers to essay exam questions.*

Himstreet, William C., and Baty, Wayne Murlin. *Business Communications*. 6th ed. Boston: Kent, 1981.

> *This book overviews English usage and spends the bulk of its discussion on business letters, résumés, written reports, and oral reports.*

Tukey, John W. *Exploratory Data Analysis*. Reading, Mass.: Addison-Wesley, 1977.

> *Here is an alternative, exploratory way of interpreting research data. The book stresses initial investigations to help understand forces contributing to observed values. Such investigations require nothing more than paper and pencil and perhaps a pocket calculator.*

21

Ethics and Marketing Research

Perhaps the title of this chapter is somewhat puzzling.[1] Many students do not immediately recognize the relationship between ethics and marketing research: how can a profession that purports to be scientific in nature and objective in analysis relate at all to either ethical or unethical behavior? Questionnaire design, experimentation, tests of statistical significance, and so forth simply do not seem to be the stuff of which ethical issues are made.

Yet the relationship between ethics and marketing research does exist—as we see by considering the activities and orientation of this profession. First, except for those research studies relying solely on secondary data sources or on simulation models, marketing research requires continual and close contact with the general public. Any activity that so heavily uses the general public lies open to the possibility of misuse or abuse of those people.

Second, most applied marketing research is conducted either by or for enterprises oriented toward profits. With a bit of creativity, we can imagine a set of circumstances in which the desire for competitive advantage can force the scientific nature or objectivity of a marketing research study to be compromised. Consider, for example, an advertising manager who develops a new campaign around the theme that Brand X tastes bet-

---

[1]This chapter was written by Kenneth C. Schneider, Associate Professor of Marketing and Marketing Research at St. Cloud State University, St. Cloud, Minn.

ter than Brand Y, but who currently lacks data beyond his own personal perceptions to support this claim. Or, consider a researcher who knows that a prospective client will not be willing to fund a particular project if she proposes a statistically sound but expensive research design. Both of these situations, if not handled properly by the researcher, can result in ethical problems apart from those that arise in dealing with the general public.

Ethics and Corporate Social Responsibility

The issue of ethics in marketing research has received considerable attention within the research profession in recent years. We can best understand this increased interest by briefly examining the evolution of a larger issue, corporate social responsibility. Corporate social responsibility has passed through four distinct stages or eras, as described in Table 21.1.[2] In the first, the so-called Philanthropic Era, the social responsibility of business was defined solely in terms of charitable giving. The Awareness Era saw a more direct involvement in local and regional affairs on the part of business leaders who felt it important that their firms be viewed as "good corporate citizens." This period also saw a great deal of debate within the business community as to what the proper relationship between business and society ought to be.[3] The Issue Era was characterized by a plethora of social problems, including racial and sexual discrimination, the Vietnam war, pollution and other environmental problems, and so forth. During this era, much of the business community found itself reacting to one crisis after another.

The fourth stage of evolution, the Era of Corporate Social Responsiveness, began with the relative calm of the mid-1970s. Corporations started to respond with a positive, leadership role in areas of social responsibility. As noted in Table 21.1, one very important development during this current stage occurred as firms looked inward to evaluate the ethics of employee conduct. Undoubtedly, a major catalyst for this effort was the public outcry in 1976 at the discovery of large-scale domestic and international payoffs, bribes, and kickbacks.[4,5] One highly publicized

---

[2]For a comprehensive discussion of the evolution of corporate social responsibility, see Patrick E. Murphy, "An Evolution: Corporate Social Responsiveness," *University of Michigan Business Review* 30 (November 1978): 19–25.

[3]There was, of course, a controversy during this period over the issue of what the business community owed society. For two particularly divergent viewpoints, see Louis Finkelstein, "The Businessman's Moral Failure," *Fortune* (September 1958), pp. 116–17; and Theodore Levitt, "The Dangers of Social Responsibility," *Harvard Business Review* (September–October 1958), pp. 41–50.

[4]*Business Week*, "The Global Costs of Bribery" (March 15, 1976), pp. 22–23.

[5]James D. Snyder, "Bribery in Selling: The Scandal Comes Home," *Sales and Marketing Management* (May 10, 1976), pp. 35–38.

TABLE 21.1
Corporate Social Responsibility Eras

Era	Dates	Primary Characteristics
Philanthropic	To early 1950s	Concentration on charitable donations
Awareness	1953–1967	Recognition of overall responsibility Involvement in community affairs
Issue	1968–1973	Concern about urban decay Correction of racial discrimination Alleviation of pollution problems Assessment of the social impact of technology
Responsiveness	1974–present	Alteration of boards of directors Examination of ethics and corporate behavior Utilization of social performance disclosures

Source: Patrick E. Murphy, "An Evolution: Corporate Social Responsiveness," *University of Michigan Business Review* 30 (November 1978): p. 20. Reprinted with permission.

example of this was the Lockheed scandal, involving huge payoffs to foreign officials.[6] As a direct result of this and other such scandals, many corporations instituted a code of ethics, to serve as a guide for ethical sales operations at home and abroad.

A less direct but perhaps more far-reaching effect of these bribery scandals and the resultant concern over ethical sales behavior has been an increased discussion of ethics in other areas of corporate behavior. Thus, this concern about employee conduct fueled the debate over ethics in marketing research that had been occurring, though sporadically, since at least the early 1960s.[7] Today more than ever, individuals and organizations engaged in research, as well as various professional associations of researchers, are discussing methods to ensure that ethical standards are maintained throughout the research profession.

Ethical Issues, Researchers, and the Public

Let us turn our attention to marketing research activities that have been questioned on ethical grounds. Such questioning has produced numerous ethical issues of two fundamental types: those pertaining to the relationship between researchers and those pertaining to the general public. We discuss the latter in this section.

Table 21.2 lists research activities that apply directly to the use of peo-

[6] *Time*, "Payola, Golden Eggs and Greed" (February 23, 1976), pp. 34–38.
[7] Leo Bogart, "The Researcher's Dilemma," *Journal of Marketing* 26 (January 1962): 6–11.

TABLE 21.2
Ethical Concerns in the Relationship Between Researcher and Subject or Respondent

Deceptive Practices
   Unrealized Promise of Anonymity
   Falsified Sponsor Identification
   Selling Under the Guise of Research
   Lying About Research Procedures
      Questionnaire or Interview Length
      Possible Follow-up Contacts
      Purpose of Study
      Uses Made of Results
      Undelivered Compensation (premiums, summaries of results)

Invasion of Privacy
   Observation Studies Without Informed Consent
   Use of Qualitative Research Techniques
   Merging Data From Several Sources
   Questions Concerning Persons Other Than Respondent
   Overly Personal Questions and Topics

Lack of Concern for Subjects or Respondents
   Contacting Respondents at Inconvenient Times
   Incompetent or Insensitive Interviewers
   Failure to Debrief After Deception or Disguise
   Research Producing a Depressing Effect on Subjects or Respondents
   Too Frequent Use of Public in Research
   Nondisclosure of Research Procedures (length, follow-up, purpose, use)

ple as information sources in conducting marketing research. Each activity has been criticized at one time or another as being unethical. Each falls into one of three broadly defined categories: deceptive practices, invasion of privacy, and lack of concern for subjects or respondents. Let us overview the nature of these categories before looking at specific activities.

DECEPTIVE PRACTICES Deceptive practices occur whenever a researcher, *for whatever reason,* misrepresents:

- the purpose of the research,
- research procedures, or
- possible use of the research results.

Such misrepresentation could take any of a variety of forms; Table 21.2 shows the sorts of activities typically included under deceptive practices.

Deceptive (really, dishonest) practices are among the most serious ethical issues facing the research profession. Honesty in personal dealings has always been one of the highest ideals in the American culture. So, too, in business activity. In fact, the Federal Trade Commission, whose primary function is to prevent unfair methods of competition among businesses, has spent vast amounts of energy and money in ensuring instead that consumers are treated honestly in the marketplace. Further, an unwritten consumer protection policy operating in our culture holds that if a firm must lie to or otherwise deceive a potential buyer into a purchase decision, that transaction is very likely not in the consumer's best interest. Moreover, since it is very difficult for the consumer to detect such deception, he or she must be afforded protection against unscrupulous practices. This attitude, of course, is far removed from the principle of "buyer beware" which once governed the relationship between business and consumers.

An argument similar to this is often made in connection with the relationship between marketing researcher and subject (or respondent). The researcher certainly sells the idea of cooperating with a study, often without monetary compensation. If the researcher uses deception to make this sale, the question of whether it is in the respondent's or subject's best interest to participate is raised. And, whether or not the question is valid is not so important as the fact that it is raised—as a logical extension of the prevailing attitude of society toward its relationship with business. Researchers, therefore, ought to be very concerned that society not perceive the research industry as one plagued with a variety of deceptive practices.

The second type of ethical concern in the relationship between researcher and respondent includes a number of research practices related to the issue of invasion of privacy. These practices include: **INVASION OF PRIVACY**

- projective methods, depth interviews, and other qualitative research designed to study less conscious reasons why consumers behave the way they do,
- questions concerning persons other than the interviewee, and
- questions of a very personal nature.

In many of these situations, the research technique is specifically designed to obtain information the respondent otherwise would not, or perhaps could not, willingly provide. The most pervasive research practice of this type is probably the unobtrusive observation study, in which the person whose behavior is being measured has not consented to participate in the study.

There are a number of reasons for identifying research practices that may be construed as violating the respondent's right to individual privacy.

First, the concept of personal privacy is being addressed in a variety of other areas, including credit and employment applications, government data collection and storage operations, computerized data banks and retrieval systems, and so forth. Given this climate of concern for individual privacy, it is logical to anticipate that research practices must eventually come under similar scrutiny from those outside the business community. Second, these practices arise more frequently than much other research activity that involves questionable ethics. Indeed, qualitative research and observation studies are among the most basic research approaches and, hence, find continual use in the industry. Third, and perhaps most important, the very nature of these techniques makes it impossible for consumers to reach fully informed decisions regarding participation. In fact, if a qualitative research study has been adequately disguised, the participant has no way of knowing either the true purpose of the investigation or the nature of the information sought. And, as we just said, in many observation studies, the participant is unaware that his or her actions are even being researched.

LACK OF CONCERN FOR SUBJECTS OR RESPONDENTS Practices criticized as demonstrating a lack of concern for the persons participating in the study range from contacting respondents at inconvenient hours to overuse of the general public in surveys and other research. These types of practices generally do not raise the same degree of social concern as deception or invasion of privacy. For example, sending interviewers into the field without proper training will certainly frustrate respondents, who agree to participate only to discover that the interviewer is incompetent or, worse yet, rude and insensitive. However, it is unlikely that respondents' experiences would ever lead to public outcry against the ethics of research.

On the other hand, there are two quite important reasons for including issues concerned with the general treatment of subjects and respondents in our discussion. First, a lack of demonstrable public anger with any particular activity does not imply it is not an ethical issue. The topic of ethics deals with more than well-recognized social issues; it relates to the determination of proper and improper conduct in everyday affairs. Moreover, we will later address a whole set of ethical issues about which the general public would not be expected to be the least bit concerned. Second, public outcry is just one form of reaction to perceived injustice. As we will also see later, individuals could react very quietly but still very forcefully to unethical behavior.

PARTICULAR ETHICAL ISSUES The issue of ethics in the relationship between researcher and the general public is not nearly so "cut and dried" as the previous discussion may have made it seem. Many in the research industry differ greatly as to whether or not any given situation even poses an ethical problem to be addressed, much less which of the research activities cited in Table 21.2

are, in fact, unethical. Quite simply, the issues themselves are not black and white. Circumstances surrounding any one activity can make it highly unethical in one instance but perfectly acceptable in another. To illustrate all of this better, let us discuss in detail a number of activities from Table 21.2.

Unrealized Promise of Anonymity.   People are usually promised anonymity as an attempt to increase the response rate in survey research, although available evidence suggests that respondent identification does not necessarily have a negative effect on response rates.[8] Anonymity is also promised when it is felt that respondents will provide more honest answers.

Failure to honor such a promise of anonymity arises for a number of reasons. Most often the promise is broken in order to send a reminder note to those respondents who have not returned the questionnaire in the allotted time period. Consider the following example:

> Recently, a research firm was found carefully marking identification numbers on questionnaires in invisible ink. The purpose was to identify those on the mailing list who sent back questionnaires, to enable a second mailing to nonrespondents. In the accompanying letter, the recipient was told that no identification was necessary, and it certainly wasn't; it was already there, but without his knowledge.[9]

Of course, there are other, less defensible reasons for failing to honor a promise of anonymity. Suppose a bank designed a mail questionnaire (including a promise of anonymity) to measure customer attitudes toward various new banking services that it had recently instituted. Now, suppose further that the bank wished to examine customer attitudes by size of account. One way to accomplish this would be to ask each respondent in the survey to indicate their current account balance. However, if the bank suspected that customers would be unable to recall their specific balance, or unwilling to check personal records for an accurate response, or, even more likely, unwilling to share this information on a questionnaire, the bank could instead precode the questionnaires to identify individual respondents. Later, upon receipt of the completed questionnaire, a researcher could cross-reference bank records to add the necessary information on account balances.

This example illustrates quite clearly how well-intentioned research efforts sometimes become entangled in ethical problems. The researcher

---

[8]See A. S. Linsky, "Stimulating Responses to Mailed Questionnaires: A Literature Review," *Public Opinion Quarterly* 39 (Spring 1975): 82–101; and L. Kanuk and C. Berenson, "Mail Surveys and Response Rates: A Literature Review," *Journal of Marketing Research* 12 (November 1975): 440–53.

[9]A. B. Blankenship, "Point of View: Consumerism and Consumer Research," *Journal of Advertising* 11 (August 1971):45.

in this example quite likely had no intention of misusing or otherwise harming respondents. However, even if no other use was made of the information provided, respondents were, in fact, deceived when they were promised anonymity but not given it.

On the other hand, not all ethical issues arise as the result of good intentions gone awry. To continue the same scenario, suppose the bank attitude questionnaire contained a number of questions concerning the use of traveller's checks when on vacation. Responses to these sorts of questions logically serve to identify prospects for a bank card. Suppose, then, that names of these prospects were sold to a company in the bank card business. And, suppose at some later date, these respondents receive promotional literature or, perhaps, a telephone solicitation from the bank card company. Again, the promise of anonymity was violated, but this time with additional consequences for the respondent.

Note further that our continued example also illustrates the merging of data from several sources, which raises the additional issue of invasion of privacy. It further illustrates the issue of misrepresenting the possible use of the results of a research study. Thus, we begin to see how complex, important, and pervasive the issue of ethics is in marketing research.

Falsified Sponsor Identification. This research practice is typically used in situations in which the researcher suspects that respondent or subject knowledge of the identity of the sponsor could bias results of the study. To illustrate the ethical issue that is raised when the sponsor's identity is concealed, consider the following hypothetical but plausible situation:

> An insurance company designed a research study to investigate the consumer decision process that precedes the purchase of individual life insurance. Their research staff drafted a questionnaire to obtain this information and made plans to conduct telephone interviews with a random sample of consumers who had recently purchased an individual life insurance policy from the company. As final plans were being made, concern was raised that respondents might be more frank in their answers if they were unaware that the study was commissioned by the insurance company from which they had just purchased a policy. Accordingly, the researchers instructed telephone interviewers to present themselves as employees of "Market Information and Data, Inc."

Now, before we decide whether or not it is ethical to conceal a sponsor's identity in this manner, we should take into account the fact that the example has at least two possible endings. Read each, and then decide on the ethical stature of this practice.

1. The name "Market Information and Data, Inc." is the legal name of the research agency that had been contracted to complete the telephone interviews.

2. The name "Market Information and Data, Inc." is a ficticious name that was used to conceal the identity of the insurance company, which had hired part-time workers to complete the telephone interviews.

Conducting a marketing research study under the auspices of the consulting firm or research agency hired to collect the required data commonly occurs. The practice occurs so frequently, in fact, that it is very rarely questioned as unethical. (But is it?) However, when a company conducts a research study without an outside agency and conceals its corporate identity by creating a fictitious name (or, perhaps, by incorporating a wholly owned subsidiary solely for this purpose), doubt is more frequently raised about the ethics of the company involved.

We have some interesting empirical evidence bearing on this practice. In a national probability sample of marketing managers and research directors, a researcher found that the overwhelming majority approved the use of ficticious names to conceal a sponsor's identity. According to one typical response, "Most marketing research studies hide the identity of the sponsor. Why should a corporation have to purchase outside services for this privilege? Respondents generally know that research has a commercial purpose and is intended for a sponsor."[10] Even among the fifteen percent who disapproved, concern more often centered on procedural issues than on the ethics of concealment.

Consumers, on the other hand, seem to distinguish more clearly between the act of concealment and the use of a fictitious name to effect that concealment. In a regionally based sample of households, respondents perceived the use of a fictitious name as less honest than using an agency's real name.[11] The public seems to feel the organization collecting data in a study should identify itself, even though that organization might not be paying for or benefiting from the results. However, to be acceptable, the identified organization should be a real entity involved in the study, not merely a ficticious one created solely for the purpose of concealing the identity of the true sponsor.

Selling Under Guise of Research. Selling under the guise of research was probably the earliest practice criticized as unethical. On the basis of a review of published criticism, we would conclude that everyone is

---

[10]C. Merle Crawford, "Attitudes of Marketing Executives Toward Ethics in Marketing Research," *Journal of Marketing* 34 (April 1970): 48.

[11]Kenneth C. Schneider and James C. Johnson, "Consumers' Perception of the Honesty of Marketing Research Practices" (paper delivered at the Southwestern American Marketing Association, Spring Meeting, San Antonio, March 1980).

opposed to it (everyone, that is, except those who continue to employ it). Upon further reflection, we would also conclude that selling under the guise of marketing research is really not an ethical issue in research at all. Rather, it is an ethical issue concerned with selling techniques. Consider, for example, the following reconstructed telephone conversation that actually took place between the author (respondent, R) and a so-called interviewer (I) several years ago.

I. Hello. My name is _____. I am representing the _____ Agency. We are currently conducting a survey on physical fitness. I would like just a few minutes of your time to respond to these questions.

R. Certainly.

I. Would you say that you are now in excellent physical condition?

R. Not really. Probably not even average.

I. Are you currently on a regular exercise program?

R. No. I do play golf and tennis on occasion but nothing in the line of regular exercise.

I. Well, are you physically active on the job?

R. (Getting a bit suspicious of the unstructured format of the interview.) No. I mostly just sit all day.

I. Have you ever been a member of a health club?

R. (Irritably.) No.

I. Well, I would like to take a minute or two to introduce you to the _____. We are currently offering a special introductory rate for new members. . . . (etc., etc.).

The experience is not an isolated instance of the misuse of research methodology. On the basis of a number of somewhat dated studies, it appears that from one-fourth to one-third of the general population has been personally exposed to at least one sales solicitation disguised as a survey, either in person or by telephone.[12] While neither researchers nor the research industry can be criticized for the existence of this ethical problem, they are rightly concerned over its consequences on future consumer attitudes toward and participation in legitimate research efforts. That is, exposure to a sales presentation disguised as a survey might well make consumers suspicious of future attempts at interviewing.[13] Such exposure has been shown to decrease willingness to participate in later, legitimate research studies (see Box 21.1).

---

[12] See Irving L. Allen and J. David Colfax, "Respondents' Attitudes Toward Legitimate Surveys in Four Cities," *Journal of Marketing Research* 5 (November 1968): 431–33; and Richard Baxter, "An Inquiry Into the Misuse of the Survey Technique by Sales Soliciters," *Public Opinion Quarterly* 28 (Spring 1964): 124–34.

[13] Allen and Colfax, "Respondents' Attitudes," p. 431.

BOX 21.1

Sales Solicitation and Future Research Studies

One of the most interesting experimental studies of the effect of exposure to sales solicitation under the guise of marketing research on willingness to participate in future research studies was published in *Public Opinion Quarterly* by three University of Toledo undergraduate students and their instructor in a marketing research class. In this study, experimental and control groups of middle-income, suburban residents were defined as follows.

Experimental Group (*n* = 104) — Each respondent in this group was asked to participate in a market research study. Those who consented were exposed to a fake survey ending in a sales solicitation for a fictitious product. Two to four days later, each respondent who consented to the fake survey was again asked to participate in a market research study.

Control Group (*n* = 70) — Each respondent in this group was asked to participate only in the second market research study.

Consent and refusal rates for this study are as shown in the table above.

As these results indicate, participation in a

Condition	Experimental Group	Control Group
First Interview (Fake Survey)		
Refused	48.1% (*n* = 50)	—
Consented	51.9% (*n* = 54)	—
Total	100.0% (*n* = 104)	
Second Interview (Legitimate Survey)		
Refused	75.5% (*n* = 37)	48.6% (*n* = 34)
Consented	24.5% (*n* = 12)	51.4% (*n* = 36)
Total	100.0% (*n* = 49[a])	100.0% (*n* = 70)

[a]Five of the original 54 respondents who had consented to the fake survey were not available for the second survey.

fake survey dramatically reduces cooperation in later research studies, at least in the short run. Participation rates were slightly more than 50 percent for the first exposure in both the experimental and control groups. However, after exposure to a fake survey, the experimental group showed a participation rate for the second interview of less than 25 percent.

Source: Thomas Sheets et al., "Deceived Respondents: Once Bitten, Twice Shy," *Public Opinion Quarterly* 36 (Summer 1974): 261–63.

Observation Studies Without Informed Consent. Unlike many other research practices that have been questioned as unethical, observation studies do not arise as sporadic attempts either to increase response rates or to enhance the quality of responses. Rather, observation studies represent a *basic research approach*, accounting for thousands of research projects each year. They constitute an important and sensitive area in the discussion of research ethics.

To see this, we will find it useful to distinguish between consumer actions that occur in full public view and those that take place in semi-private or private environments. Consumer behavior that fits into the fully public category includes, for example, taking one route as opposed to another to the supermarket, patronizing one supermarket over another, and following one of many possible "shopping paths" through the store. Such consumer behavior is almost always specifically excluded in discussions of ethics in research. In these instances, consumers willingly place themselves on public display, recognizing beforehand that their activities are open to scrutiny by anyone at any time. As such, it really does not matter if observation is formalized as in a research study or performed casually by a friend, relative, neighbor, or stranger.

Consumer behavior that arises under the second category, in private or semiprivate settings, however, is a totally different matter. Here, potential for ethical issues abounds: Should the video camera that monitors customer flow in a supermarket be similarly used to follow shoppers into the dressing room of a department store for purposes of researching consumer behavior when trying on garments? Would it make a difference if customers have already been warned that such a device is used anyway to maintain store security? Or—a less emotional issue—can a researcher ethically record an interview if respondents have agreed to participate but are unaware of the tape recorder? Similar questions can even be raised in terms of behavior at home. Should researchers use radar vans to monitor television viewing habits without the consent of those whose sets are being monitored? Can researchers ethically sort through collected trash to measure liquor consumption?

As if these questions weren't difficult enough, a case can be made that the extent to which a setting is public or private is more properly defined in the mind of the consumer than in the mind of the researcher. While most consumers would likely not object to being followed through a supermarket, have they then also implicitly consented to having planted "shoppers" record and analyze their childrens' attempts to influence product or brand choices? After all, such attempts occur in full public view. Similarly, have they implicitly consented to allow conversations with sales clerks to be recorded so the store can study customer-salesperson interaction? Most consumers would probably respond with a resounding NO!

The majority of marketing research professionals and consumers alike agree that, except for very public actions of consumers, observation studies should not be conducted without each consumer's informed consent.[14] Fortunately, researchers may make a small additional step in an observation study to remove most negative reactions. Consumers are usually not asked to cooperate prior to observing behavior since researchers

---

[14]See, for example, Crawford, "Attitudes of Marketing Executives," p. 47; and Kenneth C. Schneider, "Observation Studies and Invasion of Privacy: What the Consumer Has to Say" (Working Paper, Office of Research, Development and Community Service, St. Cloud State University, St. Cloud, Minn.).

correctly feel that such a request, in and of itself, could significantly alter the behavior to be measured. However, there is no possible way behavior could be altered if researchers asked after measurement had been completed—except for the usual problem of response rate: if a consumer in the study objects after having been fully informed of the research procedure, the record of that person's behavior could be immediately destroyed or, if possible, handed to her or him. Preliminary studies have shown that consumers find this approach much more palatable than not being asked.[15]

Our discussion leads to another important point: Researchers generally face a larger choice than either using unethical practices or abandoning the study. The entire research industry should be devoting effort to identifying these *more* ethical alternatives to questionable research practices and urging their immediate adoption.

DEFENDING CRITICIZED PRACTICES

It is also important to recognize that use of questionable research practices in no way implies a conscious attempt to subvert the best interests of consumers. Quite the contrary, the ultimate goal of any research activity is indirectly to serve those best interests by providing decision makers with the most reliable, valid, and relevant information possible. Consumer interests are subsequently served with better, more functional, and more aesthetically pleasing products from which to choose, more information upon which to base purchase decisions, wider or more convenient availability of products, and so forth. All research practices have been originally developed with this ultimate end; the issue of their ethical stature has arisen as an unfortunate byproduct.

Once the issue of ethics has been raised, however, criticized research practices become somewhat difficult to defend. Most attempts to do so focus on the purported absence of any harmful impact on subjects and respondents. In fact, some researchers often claim that the whole issue of ethics in this regard is irrelevant because they observe no real physical or emotional damage to subjects or respondents. For example, one research practitioner, in responding to the charge that certain disguised procedures may reveal facts about a beer drinker's behavior that he might find disturbing or stressful, said, "[To] speak of anxiety being induced in the average beer drinker by the revelation of his lack of taste discrimination is to demonstrate an extraordinary ignorance of the ways in which beer drinkers behave and talk among themselves."[16]

This defense is inappropriate for three reasons. First, it invokes the orientation of the marketing researcher as searcher for the aggregated, average response. While such aggregation is common in analyzing market

---

[15]Schneider, "Observation Studies," p. 9.

[16]Robert L. Day, "A Comment on 'Ethics in Marketing Research'," *Journal of Marketing Research* 12 (May 1975): 232.

or consumer data, it is inappropriate as a defense to criticisms of unethical practice. Ethical concerns center not on what happens to respondents on the average, but on what happens to each individual involved in the study.

Second, the argument is simply unfounded. While probably true of many uncriticized marketing research techniques, no research supports the claim that some techniques do not adversely affect many subjects or respondents in the study. In fact, available empirical evidence from other social sciences suggests that, for example, most psychological research can produce small amounts of stress and anxiety among most of those involved.[17] In the absence of any direct research results, the old adage that cautions one to proceed slowly in strange waters would suggest that the problem cannot be solved by simply assuming it away.

Third, the defense is invalid because it misses the whole point of the criticism. At issue is the question of deception and invasion of privacy, and not the presence or absence of consequences thereof. As an experienced researcher has said: "Too often, we have taken the position that if our efforts don't really damage the consumer [respondent], they aren't really all that bad. . . . Let's be honest with ourselves; that is merely saying that the end justifies the means."[18] To paraphrase, questions of the ethical stature of research practices must be evaluated on their own merits and not on some higher purpose of research activity.

Legal Developments Concerning Research Practices

Unlike many other areas of business, marketing research has so far experienced relatively little external regulation. However, a few largely separate legal developments indicate the trend such regulations might take should they become more extensive. Constitutional, tort, and legislative law have addressed the issue of invasion of privacy. Administrative law has focused on deceptive practices. Neither has addressed the lack of concern for subjects or respondents.

THE LAW AND INVASION OF PRIVACY

Constitutional and Tort Law.   In 1965, the United States Supreme Court concluded that the U.S. Constitution provides not only for a specific right to privacy (for example, against unreasonable search and seizure) but for a general right to privacy.[19] To what extent this constitutional right to privacy might constrain research activity, however, has not to date been tested. An examination of trends in tort law, on the other hand, is more enlightening. In one excellent discussion of this issue, two researchers

---

[17]Alice M. Tybout and Gerald Zaltman, "Ethics in Marketing Research: Their Practical Relevance," *Journal of Marketing Research* 11 (November 1974): 357–68.

[18]Blankenship, "Point of View," p. 45.

[19] *Griswold* v. *Connecticut*, 381, U.S. 479, 1965.

argue that courts are becoming increasingly willing to include psychological intrusion (for example, intrusion on one's mental solitude or seclusion) as a breach of privacy and, hence, a civil wrong. They imply the trend for marketing research is clear:

> Psychological intrusion would provide a clear outside boundary of legitimacy for marketing research in that disguised or projective questioning would be illegal. The initiation of the judicial process would be left to the intruded-upon respondent. Such a lawsuit might be a long time coming. Psychological intrusion might, however, prove to be an invitation to legal scrutiny if disguised or projective questioning is continued despite the evolution of the new tort.[20]

Legislative Law. Legislative trends with respect to invasion of privacy are more difficult to track, because of both the rapid rate at which new legislation is being enacted and the differences across legislative jurisdictions. For example, by 1963 over 250 local communities in thirty-four states had placed some restrictions on interviewing activity.[21] Since then, other communities have undoubtedly added to this number. Such local regulations range from simply requiring the researcher to register with an appropriate local office to outright banning of any door-to-door or telephone activity.

Recent experience indicates that federal and state legislatures have been at least as concerned as local communities over individual rights to privacy. Probably the most comprehensive bill so far enacted is the *U.S. Privacy Act of 1974*, designed to protect individual privacy in data collection and storage activities of federal agencies.[22] Main provisions of this Act, as contained in Section 2(b), permit an individual to:

1. determine what records pertaining to him are collected, maintained, used or disseminated by such agencies;

2. prevent records pertaining to him obtained by such agencies for a particular purpose from being used or made available for another purpose without his consent; and

3. gain access to information pertaining to him in Federal agency records, to have a copy made of all or any portion thereof, and to correct or amend such records.

There is also evidence that legislative interest in personal privacy extends beyond the *Privacy Act of 1974*. For example, in 1975, no less than four-

---

[20]Charles S. Mayer and Charles H. White, Jr., "The Law of Privacy and Marketing Research," *Journal of Marketing* 33 (April 1969): 4.

[21]Rome G. Arnold, "The Interview in Jeopardy: A Problem in Public Relations," *Public Opinion Quarterly* 28 (Spring 1964): 119–23.

[22]*Data Management*, "The Privacy Act of 1974" (June 1975), pp. 36–43.

teen bills dealing with various aspects of individual privacy were introduced into the United States Congress. And, more than forty privacy-related bills were heard in various state legislatures in 1977.[23]

Federal and state legislation so far enacted in the area of personal privacy affects only government data-gathering activities; it does not extend to the private sector. However, this in no way implies that legislative bodies lack either the concern for citizens' rights to privacy or the will to protect those rights in the private sector. In fact, the *Privacy Act of 1974* established the *Privacy Protection Study Commission (PPSC)* which, according to Section 5(b), Paragraph (2), was to "report on such other legislative recommendations as it may determine to be necessary to protect the privacy of individuals while meeting the legitimate needs of government *and society* for information" (emphasis added). In its final report in 1977, the PPSC recommended a number of proposals for legislation and for voluntary industry policies, some of which directly or indirectly affect marketing research.[24] For example, the PPSC proposed a ban on all disguised or "pretext" interviews in insurance and pre-employment investigations. While this does not, per se, include marketing research activities, it does lay the legal foundation for extending coverage to them, should lawmakers ever perceive such a need. Similarly, the PPSC recommended that organizations in the private sector fully disclose the purpose and potential use of personal data prior to its collection and, further, that no other use be made of such data without the individual's consent. Again, if this is construed to include market research data, severe constraints will have been placed on data collection and storage practices.

THE LAW AND DECEPTIVE PRACTICES

Most federal regulatory activity that directly affects the research industry has taken place through the Federal Trade Commission (FTC). Although the FTC has not given top priority to deceptive research practices, it has become at least cognizant of the relevant issues. Specifically, it has devoted considerable effort to controlling the practice of selling under the guise of research by issuing numerous cease and desist orders against a variety of firms.[25] It has also ruled that "researchers who purport to obtain information from consumers under a grant of anonymity, but who actually code questionnaires with invisible ink so as to identify respondents commit an unfair or deceptive trade practice."[26] It has also examined other practices, such as the misleading use of the word "research" in company names and advertising; the misrepresentation of the statistical accuracy of

---

[23]Jerome Lobel, "Computer Privacy States' Side: Seeking Cooperation Amid Confusion," *Data Management* (April 1977), pp. 12–17.

[24]J. T. Westermeier and Kenneth D. Polin, "Privacy Report to Alter Relation of Business to the Individual," *Data Management* (July 1977), pp. 21–24.

[25]Cynthia J. Frey and Thomas C. Kinnear, "Legal Constraints and Marketing Research: Review and Call to Action," *Journal of Marketing Research* 16 (August 1979): 295–302.

[26]*Journal of Marketing* 43 (Spring 1979): 114.

research results; and the use of automated telephone dialing for purposes of solicitation and interviewing.[27] On the last issue, for example, the FTC spent three years studying the impact and effects of the recent explosion in unsolicited telephone contact on consumers before concluding, in early 1980, that FTC action to restrict this practice was not warranted.

Future FTC activity in the area of regulating research practices depends on a number of factors. Most important is the extent of public criticism of research tactics. If the issue of ethics in marketing research should become as visible, as, say, deceptive advertising, further FTC investigations and rules are almost guaranteed. However, future FTC movements into this and other areas is also a function of actions taken by Congress and the executive branch designed to limit FTC power.

Our discussion of the legal status of marketing research practices that have been criticized as unethical is important for several reasons. First, it shows that some of these practices (namely, projective techniques and other devices to probe beyond a respondent's psychological defense mechanisms) may already be a civil wrong, at least as interpreted through emerging case law. Whether or not they are tested in court depends on (a) whether an "injured" party can ever detect and prove their use in a specified situation (which may in itself be very difficult), and (b) whether that party feels sufficiently injured to pursue the matter in court. Second, it demonstrates that political and other law-making units are most definitely aware of these issues. Further, it demonstrates that such units are in a mood to provide legislation to protect citizens within their respective jurisdictions against perceived injustices. Third, it points out that the practicing researcher, research agency, and corporate research department has even more at stake here than personal or organizational decisions regarding appropriate research conduct. In the long run, all researchers may find that continued use of particular techniques could involve legal as well as ethical decisions.

IMPLICATIONS OF LEGAL TRENDS

Ethical Issues, Researchers, and Decision Makers

Earlier in this chapter we noted that ethical issues arise from each of two fundamental relationships that exist in marketing research. We have already discussed issues that pertain to the relationship between researcher and the respondent or subject; now we will turn to the relationship between researcher and the decision maker. In this discussion we emphasize the relationship between researchers and decision makers employed outside the researcher's organization, that is, between researchers and clients.

---

[27]Frey and Kenner, "Legal Constraints".

TABLE 21.3
Ethical Concerns in the Relationship Between Researcher and Client

Abuse of Research Design or Methodology or Results
    Conducting Unnecessary Research
    Researching Wrong or Irrelevant Problems
    Use of Unwarranted Shortcuts to Secure Contract or Save Expenses
    Misrepresenting Limitations of Research Design
    Inappropriate Analytical Techniques
    Lack of Sufficient Expertise to Conduct Required Research
    Overly Technical Language in Research Report
    Overstating Validity or Reliability of Conclusions
    Espionage (Spying) Under the Guise of Research

Researcher Abuse of Researcher-Client Relationship
    Overbilling the Project
    Failure to Maintain Client Confidentiality
    Failure to Avoid Possible Conflict of Interest

Client Abuse of Researcher-Client Relationship
    Inappropriate Use of Research Proposals
    Disclosure or Use of the Researcher's Specialized Techniques and Models
    Cancellation of Project (or Refusal to Pay) Without Cause
    Conducting Research Solely to Support *a priori* Conclusions
    Failure to Act upon Dangerous or Damaging Findings

Table 21.3 presents a list of practices that have been called unethical. The practices fall into three categories: abuse of research design, methodology, and results; abuse of the researcher-client relationship by researchers; and abuse by clients. The first two categories address both the protection of clients and the integrity of the profession from unethical research and researchers. The third category addresses the protection of researchers from unethical practices by clients.

ABUSE OF RESEARCH DESIGN OR METHODOLOGY OR RESULTS

As indicated in Table 21.3, possibilities for abuse exist in all research design phases, from defining the problem incorrectly to reporting results improperly. For example, a researcher might define a problem as a complex brand image deficiency when it is instead a simple imbalance in media budgeting. Of course, all researchers cannot be expected to define every problem perfectly; every practicing researcher has in good faith erred in the problem definition phase of a project at least once in his or her career. However, an opportunity does exist during problem definition for researchers to lead prospective clients to conduct research where none is required, or to unnecessarily enlarge the scope (and budget) of the study. Near the other end of the research process, a researcher might perform a complex, multiple regression analysis, which, though it impresses the client with the researcher's technical skill, may nevertheless be inappropriate if assumptions of the regression model are not met in that particular application.

Design and methodological abuses of all sorts are not only unethical but also constitute poor business policy in the long run. However, they often offer the chance of increased economic gain in the short run and, hence, occur all too often in the research industry.

While these examples deal with problems of the researcher who tries to do more than the decision maker's needs indicate, there is also the problem of doing too little. Two especially troublesome issues appear in this regard. First: the researcher may propose a study commensurate with the needs of the client, but the client balks at the size of the budget required to complete the research. Rather than try to convince the client that the expenditure is justified, thereby risking losing the contract altogether, the researcher often takes the path of least resistance and scales down the proposal. The resulting study, albeit funded and conducted, may be so severely limited in design as to be worthless. Second: every researcher and research agency has a certain scope of acquired expertise. When situations arise that lie outside that area of expertise, it is very difficult to do the ethical thing, which is to admit that the client would be better off dealing with a competitor.

This discussion does not suggest that every design and methodological shortcut or overkill is unethical. To a large extent, researchers and decision makers are free to conduct any study, however good or bad, long or short, expensive or inexpensive, to which they agree. On the other hand, clients are less technically trained and less skilled in marketing research and, consequently, can be taken advantage of by unscrupulous or incompetent researchers. Indeed, clients very often rely on the researcher to tell them what research is required in a given situation. It is at this point that the issue of ethics and professional integrity must be raised, to ensure that users of research get what they pay for (but no more than they need) and that they receive full disclosure of specifics of the research design (including limitations), so that they are able to reach fully informed decisions.

Table 21.3 also indicates that industrial espionage or spying is many times included as an unethical abuse of the marketing research methodology. Although these subversive, often illegal, practices are sometimes conducted under the name of marketing research, they are in fact totally outside its scope. However, like selling under the guise of research, these practices can have a decidedly detrimental impact on the image of the research profession. As such, they ought to be resisted by practicing researchers whenever encountered.[28]

---

[28]For a more complete discussion of corporate espionage, see Jim Montgomery, "A Secret Life," *Wall Street Journal* 60 (January 21, 1980): 1; John Perham, "The Great Game of Corporate Espionage," *Dun's Review* (October 1970): 30–33, 93–96; and Jerry L. Wall, "What the Competition is Doing: Your Need to Know," *Harvard Business Review* 52 (November/December 1974): 22–38, 162–66.

A number of ethical issues in addition to misusing research procedures should be addressed. Some entail researcher abuse of the trust relationship necessary between researcher and client while others entail just the opposite.

Abuse by Researchers. One abuse by researchers is overbilling or charging a fee that greatly exceeds the value of services rendered. It is important to recognize that there is a difference between cost-plus pricing, market-oriented pricing, and overbilling. Most research agencies practice a form of cost-plus pricing, in which fees are based on the cost of the study plus a markup to cover administrative overhead and profit. Some, but fewer, agencies practice a form of market-oriented pricing whenever possible. In such cases, proposed fees reflect not only the cost structure of the agency but the market value of the research to the client. Thus, critical or major research efforts may be priced disproportionately higher than other studies. In essence, this pricing strategy is tied at least in part to the client's anticipated payoff from having the information available. Overbilling is tied to neither research costs nor anticipated payoffs. Rather it is set on the basis of client ability or willingness to pay. This pricing strategy, when used by manufacturing firms, is often referred to as charging what the market will bear or, in extreme cases, as gouging. Though usually legal, extreme overbilling raises serious ethical questions.

Beyond fair billing procedures, researchers have a responsibility to maintain as confidential any information relating to the clients' study and operations as well as to avoid potential conflicts of interest. The latter point usually implies that a researcher will not work for two competitors at the same time unless prior arrangements have been made among all three parties.

Abuse by Clients. Clients also have certain responsibilities to the research agency. One ethical problem involving the client's breach of the trust relationship centers on inappropriate uses of research proposals. Suppose, for example, that a firm requests proposals from several different research agencies—as is frequently done. However, suppose the purpose in this case is not to secure the most competitive bid but to generate free advice from a variety of experts, combine this advice, and then conduct the study in-house. Alternatively, the firm might already have selected a research agency on the basis of satisfaction with service provided in the past but, nevertheless, requests proposals from several others to satisfy corporate purchasing policy. It is clearly unfair to ask researchers to prepare proposals, a task that can easily account for a substantial percentage of the total research effort, when the proposal has no chance of being accepted. Unfortunately, these and other misuses of research proposals do occur.[29]

Another ethical problem occurs occasionally when research agencies

---

[29]Robert Bezilla, Joel B. Haynes, and Clifford Elliot, "Ethics in Marketing Research," *Business Horizons* (April 1976), pp. 83–86.

develop specialized research techniques and models that are used repeatedly in conducting similar studies for a number of clients. Often these techniques and models take extreme amounts of resources to develop. So, just as it is important for the researcher to keep client information confidential, clients must also refrain from using or disclosing information about the agency's techniques and models.

Finally, research agencies occasionally encounter difficulty because the client doesn't pay on schedule or, similarly, because the client cancels a research project after it has been initiated. Both actions are serious improprieties. Nevertheless, they occur, especially if major changes are made in the scope or environment of the project after an initial agreement has been reached. Project cancellation is most often caused by a shift in the environment of the client, which sometimes dramatically alters information needs or even completely negates the need for research. Refusal to pay follows from a variety of situations—including additions to the research design (and, hence, expenses that were not reflected in the original budget), second thoughts about the value of the research, market opportunities that disappear due to factors beyond the client's control and, sometimes, financial inability to pay.

There is substantial agreement within the research industry that the practices cited in Table 21.3 are, in fact, unethical and ought to be prevented. **POTENTIAL SOLUTIONS** Perhaps the best solution to many of these problems lies in the development of quite specific written contracts entered into at the time a research proposal is accepted. However, it is surprising how many studies are undertaken with no contract, much less one that identifies in considerable detail the complete research design and methodology as well as obligations and responsibilities of both researcher and client. Although such an approach would not entirely solve the problem of unethical conduct, it would simplify legal recourse should abuses arise.

Abuses of the researcher-client relationship are not highly visible. Therefore, it is unlikely that either legislative or administrative action of any consequence will be taken soon on these matters.

Resolving Ethical Issues

The last topic we consider concerns the response of researchers as a profession to ethical problems that now confront them. It is extremely important that researchers address, discuss, and resolve these issues to avoid negative consequences. Doing nothing—whether because of apathy, lack of consensus, or inability to implement—would almost surely lead to:

1. reduced public confidence in the integrity of marketing research;

2. reduced public cooperation, including both quantity and quality of participation in research studies;

3. decline in morale of research personnel, from interviewers to project directors;

4. increased legal constraints and government regulations concerning research activity;

5. greatly increased research costs coupled with decreased data quality; and

6. reduced use of research-based decision making by marketing managers.[30]

The last possibility is particularly disturbing.

SETTING ETHICAL STANDARDS   Yet researchers have done next to nothing. Perhaps the major reason why is that researchers as a profession have not yet agreed on *whose* standards of ethics they should meet. At least three possibilities exist: those of individual researchers, of the research profession as a whole, or of consumers.

Standards of Individual Researchers.   Certainly, the integrity of individual researchers and research organizations must be maintained. No researcher should ever engage in activities that violate his or her personal ethical standards. Nor should individual researchers allow such activities to go unquestioned if engaged in by others.

There are, however, two deficiencies to being wholly satisfied with individual definitions of ethical conduct. First, given the subordinate position of most researchers, coupled with increasing decision maker demands for maximum data quality at minimum cost, researchers often find it difficult to balance ethical concerns with other, more immediate needs. That is, while the issue of ethics is somewhat removed, the issue of satisfying the often-conflicting demands of the decision maker is very near. Second, it is highly doubtful that researchers ever would or ever could reach a consensus as to what is and is not ethical. Given the sheer number of practicing researchers, it is likely that some, acting in good conscience, would adopt the position that whatever is legal is ethical, while others would adopt a much more conservative stance.

Standards of the Research Profession.   It would appear that if the industry ever is to have a singular set of ethical rules by which the research game ought to be played, it must come from within the research profession as a whole. Unfortunately, the profession is, for the most part, not a whole but rather a loosely knit group of entrepreneurs, academicians, and corporate employees. Moreover, they belong to one or more of several

---

[30]Kenneth C. Schneider, "Subject and Respondent Abuse in Marketing Research," *MSU Business Topics* 25 (Spring 1977): 13–19.

professional associations, including the American Marketing Association, Marketing Research Association, American Association for Public Opinion Research, and Council of American Survey Research Organizations. Participation is entirely voluntary.

To be truly effective in addressing the issue of ethical standards in marketing research, one professional association must attain a leadership position. That is, one professional association must attain a relationship to its members like that now characterizing the American Bar Association, the American Medical Association, and the American Accounting Association. Were this to come about, a number of important changes probably would occur within the research industry.

First, a transformation from industry to profession would probably take place. This would afford researchers the proper image with the general public. Research organizations would then be seen as something more than commercial enterprises, perhaps as entities possessing a degree of objectivity apart from advocacy of any client's products. Second, this profession probably would require minimum standards of expertise, similar in scope and design to the bar exam or CPA exam, before granting

---

BOX 21.2

Code of Marketing Research Ethics for the American Marketing Association

The American Marketing Association in furtherance of its central objective of the advancement of science in marketing and in recognition of its obligation to the public, has established these principles of ethical practice of marketing research for the guidance of its members. In an increasingly complex society, marketing management is more and more dependent upon marketing information intelligently and systematically obtained. The consumer is the source of much of this information. Seeking the cooperation of the consumer in the development of information, marketing management must acknowledge its obligation to protect the public from misrepresentation and exploitation under the guise of research.

Similarly the research practitioner has an obligation to the discipline he practices and to those who provide support for his practice—an obligation to adhere to basic and commonly accepted standards of scientific investigation as they apply to the domain of marketing research.

It is the intent of this code to define ethical standards required of marketing research in satisfying these obligations.

Adherence to this code will assure the users of marketing research that the research was done in accordance with acceptable ethical practices. Those engaged in research will find in this code an affirmation of sound and honest basic principles which have developed over the years as the profession has grown. The field interviewers who are the point of contact between the profession and the consumer will also find guidance in fulfilling their vitally important role.

For Research Users, Practitioners and Interviewers

1. No individual or organization will undertake any activity which is directly or indirectly represented to be marketing research, but which has as its real purpose the attempted sale of merchandise or services to some or all of the respondents interviewed in the course of the research.

2. If a respondent has been led to believe, directly or indirectly that he is participating in a marketing research survey and that his anonymity will be protected, his name shall not be made known to anyone outside the research organization or research department, or used for other than research purposes.

For Research Practitioners

1. There will be no intentional or deliberate misrepresentation of research methods or results. An adequate description of methods employed will be made available upon request to the sponsor of the research. Evidence that field work has been completed according to specifications will, upon request, be made available to buyers of research.

2. The identity of the survey sponsor and/or the ultimate client for whom a survey is being done will be held in confidence at all times, unless this identity is to be revealed as part of the research design. Research information shall be held in confidence by the research organization or department and not used for personal gain or made available to any outside party unless the client specifically authorizes such release.

3. A research organization shall not undertake marketing studies for competitive clients when such studies would jeopardize the confidential nature of client-agency relationships.

For Users of Marketing Research

1. A user of research shall not knowingly disseminate conclusions from a given research project or service that are inconsistent with or not warranted by the data.

2. To the extent that there is involved in a research project a unique design involving techniques, approaches or concepts not commonly available to research practitioners, the prospective user of research shall not solicit such a design from one practitioner and deliver it to another for execution without the approval of the design originator.

For Field Interviewers

1. Research assignments and materials received, as well as information obtained from respondents, shall be held in confidence by the interviewer and revealed to no one except the research organization conducting the marketing study.

2. No information gained through a marketing research activity shall be used directly or indirectly, for the personal gain or advantage of the interviewer.

3. Interviews shall be conducted in strict accordance with specifications and instructions received.

4. An interviewer shall not carry out two or more interviewing assignments simultaneously unless authorized by all contractors or employers concerned.

Members of the American Marketing Association will be expected to conduct themselves in accordance with the provisions of this Code in all of their marketing research activities.

Source: American Marketing Association. Reprinted with permission.

membership to researchers. Though there has been considerable talk of the need for such a certification program, relatively little progress has been made to date.[31] Third, the profession probably would evolve accepted procedural and ethical standards for the conduct of research activity as well as sanctions against members who violate those standards (for example, censure, disbarment). The research industry currently has available a number of *Codes of Ethics* through the various professional associations, one of which is reproduced in Box 21.2.

Standards of Consumers.   A last issue that should be addressed is, given a strong centralized organization with the power to develop and enforce a comprehensive *Code of Ethics for Research Professionals*, from whom should that organization seek input in determining appropriate ethical conduct? From its membership and clients, certainly. However, it would be erroneous to exclude consumers from this process, especially as their input relates to issues involving the general public.

In fact, we have evidence that the general public currently is not satisfied with ethical standards in the industry. In one recent national survey, 31 percent of the respondents felt that "polls or research surveys are an invasion of privacy" while 42 percent felt that "some questions asked in polls or research surveys are too personal."[32] We also have evidence that this dissatisfaction has already decreased the public's willingness to participate in research studies.[33] Yet, if there is one thing that researchers need to survive, it is consumer willingness to serve as experimental subjects and as survey respondents.

It would seem equally apparent that one way to help ensure their continued service would be through the adoption of ethical standards commensurate with consumers' perceptions regarding acceptable research practices. Such consumer input could be obtained either through consumer representation in whatever decision-making bodies evolve, or preferably, through a program of research designed to measure consumer perceptions of ethics and invasion of privacy in marketing research.

The Iron Law of Responsibility, which states that those who do not take responsibility for their power will ultimately lose it, can be adapted to the relationship between business and society.[34] In adapted form, the Iron Law implies that, in the long run, the amount of social power enjoyed by

EPILOGUE ON ETHICAL ISSUES

---

[31]Philip Daugherty, "Researcher Certification Sought," *New York Times* (March 24, 1976), p. 67.

[32]Frank D. Walker, "'Privacy,' 'Sales Pitches' Irk Some, But Surveys' Image Better," *Marketing News* 12 (January 12, 1979): 1, 12.

[33]*Advertising Age*, "Public Resistance Imperils Research: Carl W. Nichols," 47 (May 10, 1976): 42.

[34]K. David, "Understanding the Social Responsibility Puzzle," *Business Horizons* (Winter 1967), pp. 45–50.

business must balance with the amount of social responsibility assumed by business. On numerous occasions throughout our history, business leaders have found themselves in positions of imbalance—operating with more social power than social responsibility. On each occasion, one of two things happened: either social responsibility increased or social power declined.

Too often, American business has allowed its social power to decline. The consumer movement of the late 1960s provides an excellent illustration: between 1966 and 1970, the movement led to no less than nineteen major consumer protection bills passed by the U.S. Congress, adding federal regulations in such diverse areas of business activity as product safety, packaging, labeling, credit, and insurance.[35] In essence, business lost a great deal of social power during this period by failing to react more positively to perceived injustices toward consumers.

In contrast, marketing researchers have practiced their trade relatively unencumbered by the number of federal regulations that constrain other industries. The general public, by and large, has accepted marketing research as a legitimate function and has cooperated with data collection activities. At the same time, the industry has not exactly been eager to accept its social responsibility, including that of assuring society that it operates within acceptable ethical standards regarding protection of consumers.

Thus, today the research industry retains the option of choosing which route it prefers in balancing social power and responsibility; either accepting more responsibility or losing its power and freedom of operation. As mentioned earlier in this chapter, corporate concern over ethics in other business operations provides an internal climate favoring the former approach. Further, current public and governmental opinion seem to allow for this approach. But action must occur soon. As with most problems that arise in the relationship between business and society, a critical level exists beyond which credibility of the research industry likely will become so tarnished that only external action reducing social power will prove acceptable to consumers.

Chapter Summary

Regardless of whether our career paths lead to marketing research, sales, retailing, brand management, or some other position in business or government, every one of us will be involved with market research studies, perhaps as a researcher and certainly as a decision maker. As either, we must encounter ethical issues.

---

[35]Burson-Marsteller, "Consumer Protection Laws Now in Effect," in *The Social Dynamics of Marketing*, ed. Conrad Berenson and Henry Eilbirt (New York: Random House, 1973), pp. 114–16.

As we have discussed, ethical issues relate both to subjects and respondents and to decision makers. With regard to subjects and respondents, research practices that deceive, invade privacy, or simply demonstrate a lack of concern for people raise ethical issues. They raise also the possibility of legal action, taken by government units or by injured subjects or respondents. With regard to researchers and decision makers, research practices that abuse research designs or either of the two parties also raise ethical issues. Such issues may lead to civil law suits but probably not to regulatory action. Finally, we ended the chapter urging that the profession actively resolve all ethical issues.

The purpose of the chapter was not to insist upon any one set of ethical standards. Until professional standards are agreed upon and implemented, each of us must follow her or his own conscience. However, we now have been exposed to the existence of these issues and, hopefully, have acquired the knowledge necessary to stand up to unethical research practices we may encounter.

Chapter Review

DISCUSSION QUESTIONS

1. What ethical issues accompany the practice of marketing research?

2. Why have ethical issues arisen in connection with marketing research?

3. A researcher remarks that he constantly "reinvents the wheel for clients. For example, I no sooner finish predicting county population trends for one client than another requests the same data. Ethically, I have to repeat my entire design." Does he?

4. What does a promise of anonymity mean to a researcher? To a respondent? To you?

5. The test of whether or not a marketing research practice is ethical depends on whether respondents are injured. Discuss.

6. The test of whether or not a marketing research practice is ethical depends on the researcher's intentions during research design and execution. Discuss.

7. What are the strengths and weaknesses of requiring marketing researchers to pass a test of competency (like the CPA exam) before being allowed to practice?

8. Only doers (and not users) of marketing research can behave unethically. Discuss.

Cases for Part VI

19. Pioneer Federal Savings and Loan Association

"What I have to do," thought Albert Cummings, "is to free up at least four hours before Friday. Unless I get some time, I'm dead as far as being able to justify any changes to the operation is concerned. Let's see, today's Wednesday . . . maybe tomorrow morning I can shut my door and get something done. Actually, there's no choice, I'll have to do it tomorrow!"

Changes to the operation of course, would come from his interpretations of Dvorak and Associates' final research report on Pioneer Federal's two operations. The report had been lying on Albert's desk for about a week now and Albert knew most of the Pioneer Federal officers had already read it. It would be up to him as marketing manager to propose any changes for the officers' consideration.

With this partly out of his mind, Albert went about the rest of his business. "Here we are again," he thought, "running a savings ad in Pearson and a loan ad in New Landon. That's not too serious . . . but what's this? Did we actually run a savings ad in the Pearson Gazette while the Pearson radio stations were playing home improvement loan commercials? Brother!" It certainly looked that way. Invoices, tear sheets, and radio affidavits all pointed toward a confused advertising schedule last month. He would have to talk to Harry Irle, the Pearson branch manager, about this. "It certainly wasn't the first time this had happened but it better be the last," Albert thought. "I'll have to call Harry . . . but not today."

PIONEER FEDERAL Pioneer Federal was a federally chartered savings and loan association with its original office in New Landon, Maine, a town of 12,000 residents having a largely agricultural economic base. The New Landon operation employed fifteen persons, had been in continuous operation since 1921, and had assets of nearly $32 million at the end of 1976.

The Association's other operation was located in Pearson, a community of 45,000 residents approximately 40 miles from New Landon. Pearson was also an agricultural community but enjoyed the presence of one of the state's branch universities, annually enrolling nearly 12,000 students in a variety of undergraduate and graduate programs. In many respects, Pearson was a typical "college town" and was experiencing rapid growth in contrast to New Landon (Exhibit C19.1 presents selected demographic and economic statistics for the two communities). The Pearson operation employed eleven persons, had been in continuous operation since 1955, and had assets of nearly $22 million. Organization charts for the two operations appear in Exhibit C19.2.

EXHIBIT C19.1
Selected Characteristics of the Pearson and New Landon Markets

Age (Years)	Pearson	New Landon
Under 18	8,748	2,754
18—24	8,930	729
25—34	4,155	784
35—49	4,013	1,578
50—64	3,281	1,593
65–and over	2,850	1,565
Total	31,977	9,003
Median Age (years)	22.8	37.8
Median Years of School Completed	13.4	12.0
Persons Per Household	2.8	2.9
Median 1969 Household Income ($)	8,980	7,724
Unemployment Rate 1970 (%)	5.1	7.0
Total Bank Assets 1970 ($000)	127,412 $(N = 4)$	47,318 $(N = 2)$
Saving and Loan Assets 1970 ($000)	11,458	18,450

Source: Government Publications (1970).

NEXT MORNING

Next morning Albert shut his door and settled down to review the Dvorak report. His mind went back to a meeting between Calvin Dvorak and himself some ten weeks ago, when the subject had been the research.

Albert had expressed concern over the Pearson branch, concern that was shared by the other New Landon officers, saying that "they just have not done as well as expected in the Pearson market." There was no one activity in the Pearson office suspected of being the cause, so Dvorak and Associates had been called in to evaluate the problem. Dvorak's reaction was to refer to some preliminary notes he had already made on financial institutions in Pearson and to promise a research proposal for the next week.

Dvorak had noted that all financial institutions in both markets were, in his mind, recent, modern facilities. In addition, all "full-service" banks appeared to have good parking areas, drive-up windows, an abundance of tellers, similar interest rates, and similar hours. "In short," he had said, "my comparison of available financial services between competing banks in either market shows little difference."

The only contrast to the competing banks was that Pioneer Federal's two offices offered higher interest rates on savings deposits and fewer financial services. By law and tradition, savings and loan associations cannot provide such services as a checking account, personal and most other installment loans, and most types of business loans to its customers. Thus, while offering modern facilities, ample parking, and a drive-up window, Pioneer Federal's offices were smaller than competing

New Landon office:

Pearson office:

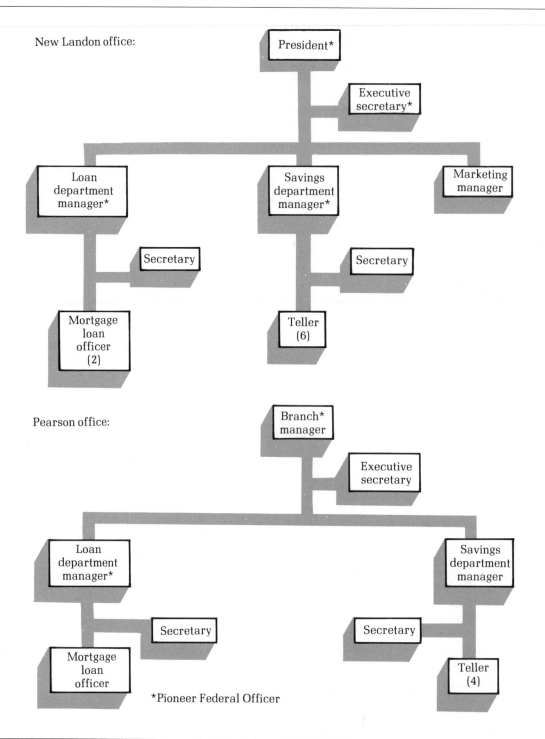

*Pioneer Federal Officer

banks. A summary of Dvorak's notes on selected financial services of competing Pearson financial institutions is presented in Exhibit C19.3; data for New Landon were quite similar.

Albert recalled that Dvorak had cautioned him that his suspicion of lackluster performance in the Pearson market may be an illusion. "Do you know for sure a problem exists?" he had asked. "That is, maybe there should be some research here first before we search for solutions." Albert had dismissed the idea of "problem-existence" research, relied instead on his and the New Landon officers' intuition, and next week approved the research proposal.

Now, Dvorak's caution troubled him and Albert thought the first thing he should do is review Pioneer Federal's performance for the two locations. His secretary had done just that by preparing a table of deposit and loan volumes for each Pioneer Federal operation and competing banks (Exhibit C19.4). Albert thought that some time spent on this question would perhaps strengthen his position (whatever it might be) in tomorrow's meeting with Pioneer Federal officers.

THE DVORAK REPORT

The real issue, however, was interpreting the Dvorak report. "It *looks* to be worth the $5000," Albert thought, "but let's just see what it says." He noted that data had been collected in three areas:

1. a comparison of "tangibles" or selected actual services, qualities, and costs between competing financial institutions in the Pearson market;

2. a description of consumers' knowledge and awareness of Pearson financial institutions including their knowledge of differences in service availability, interest rates, and recent advertisements; and

3. a description of consumers' subjective feelings regarding the importance of financial services in deciding where savings accounts are kept and the image they hold of each competing financial institution in both markets.

EXHIBIT C19.3
Dvorak's Notes on Competing Financial Institutions in the Pearson Market

Bank C
Bank and FHA home mortgage loans available, but down payment requirement on bank loans now 30–35 percent due to a shortage of loan money. FHA: 10 percent down, 6 points, 1 percent loan fee to bank, $40 appraisal fee, $30 credit report, $60 title insurance, 9½ + ½ FHA ins. = 10 percent loan. Bank: 30–35 percent down, 3–4 points, $75 appraisal, $30 credit report, $60 title insurance, 9¾ percent loan, 90-day prepayment interest penalty.

Passbook: 5 percent, $5 minimum, daily interest
CDs: 1 year, 6 percent, $500 minimum
    2½ year, 6½ percent, $500 minimum
    4 year, 7¼ percent, $1,000 minimum

Home Improvement Loan: approximately 13 percent.

EXHIBIT C19.3 *(continued)*

Bank D
Hasn't written bank home mortgage loan in over four weeks. They get money at
10½ to 10¾ now so with a 9¾ loan rate they make up difference by discounting loan
heavily with points (but refused to estimate how many points). Loans are now
FHA at 9½ and 6 points, plus bank closing costs. Last bank loans required
minimum of 20 percent down. No prepayment penalty in effect at present.

Passbook: 5 percent, $5 minimum, daily interest
CDs: 90 day, 5½ percent, $100 minimum
    1 year, 6 percent, $100 minimum
    2½ year, 6½ percent, $100 minimum
    4 year, "negotiable," $1000 minimum

Home Improvement Loan:
must have account here;
12.8 percent approximately.

Bank E
No home mortgage money available for 6 months to 1 year. Bank loan with ⅛ to ¼
down. 2-3 points closing, 1 percent origination fee, ½ percent insurance + "other
fees." Prepayment penalty 2-6 months interest when they get loan money plus
closing costs, but none in effect now. Didn't mention FHA.

Passbook: 5 percent, no minimum, daily interest
CDs: 90 day, 5½ percent, no minimum
    1 year, 6 percent, no minimum
    2½ year, 6½ percent, no minimum
    4 year, 7½ percent, $1,000 minimum

Home Improvement Loan:
need account here; 12.8
percent approximately.

Bank F
Has no loan money for houses and doesn't foresee any for at least six months.
Also said that FHA loans were unavailable in town, though other banks were
willing to provide them. He looked and acted more like a used car salesman than
a bank officer.

Passbook: 5 percent, no minimum, daily interest
CDs: 4 year, 7¼ percent, $1,000 minimum
    30 month, 6½ percent, $100 minimum
    1 year, 6 percent, $100 minimum
    3 month, 5½ percent, $100 minimum

Home Improvement Loan:
no information gathered
because officer responsible
was unavailable.

Safety Deposit boxes: 3 × 5 $7.50
                       3 × 10 $12
                       5 × 10 $18
                   10 × 10 $24, unavailable

Pioneer Federal
"A limited number of loans available." They write on old and new homes, but he
apparently didn't know the criteria, 25 percent down, 9¾ percent, for 25 years, 1½
percent closing. Didn't mention FHA.

Passbook: 5¼ percent, no minimum, daily interest
CDs: 4 year, 7½ percent, $15,000 minimum
    4 year, 7¼ percent, $10,000 minimum
    4 year, 7 percent, $5,000 minimum
    2½ or 3 year, 6¾ percent, $1000 minimum
    1 or 2 year, 6½ percent, $1000 minimum
    6 month, 5¾ percent, $1000 minimum

Home Improvement Loan:
9.06 percent; not necessary
to have account here but
"nice gesture."

Sufficient demographic data were also collected to identify who was responding in commonly used demographic terms and to allow comments on sample representativeness.

The "Procedures" section of the report seemed overly long and complex. "Maybe they were trying to impress us," Albert thought. "If they were, they succeeded!" As he sifted through the technical jargon,

EXHIBIT C19.4
Deposit and Loan Volumes for New Landon and Pearson Financial Institutions ($000) 1960–1976

Financial Institution	New Landon Deposits								
	1960	1962	1964	1966	1968	1970	1972	1974	1976
PIONEER FEDERAL	9001	10214	11641	12223	12990	13527	16634	19844	26789
Bank A	4332	5082	6560	8481	11100	13276	16622	20467	27930
Bank B	1754	2768	3922	5704	8277	10104	13784	16456	22216
Total	15087	18064	22123	26408	32367	36907	47040	56767	76935

	New Landon Loans								
	1960	1962	1964	1966	1968	1970	1972	1974	1976
PIONEER FEDERAL	8250	9694	11293	11401	12134	13666	16304	19109	25415
Bank A	2034	1809	2613	2762	2849	3115	3877	3220	4186
Bank B	246	302	322	330	352	242	1061	2692	4307
Total	10530	11805	14228	14493	15335	17023	21242	25021	33908

	Pearson Deposits								
	1960	1962	1964	1966	1968	1970	1972	1974	1976
PIONEER FEDERAL	2379	3501	5320	5688	6484	7080	10115	12945	17110
Bank C	6691	8146	9818	14202	19547	22763	29197	37976	51647
Bank D	1913	2544	2921	3273	4006	4949	7170	9841	12596
Bank E	5454	7076	9125	12388	15533	19011	26829	32905	43118
Bank F	—	—	—	—	—	54	2825	5115	9121
Total	16437	21267	27184	35551	45570	53857	76136	98782	133592

	Pearson Loans								
	1960	1962	1964	1966	1968	1970	1972	1974	1976
PIONEER FEDERAL	2800	3100	4558	5704	6541	7844	11595	13069	17251
Bank C	3144	4272	4876	6093	8098	9495	16214	23522	31931
Bank D	1796	1548	1276	1742	1354	1656	3349	4914	5897
Bank E	1653	1765	2861	3931	4759	4889	11143	15783	20833
Bank F	—	—	—	—	—	24	670	1581	2371
Total	9393	10685	13571	17470	20752	23908	42971	58869	78283

Notes: Data are for the end of the calendar year indicated. Deposits are Time Deposits only; loans consist of Real Estate Loans, Mobile Home Loans, and Home Improvement Loans.

Albert saw that, to compare tangibles, three researchers had separately "shopped" each Pearson financial institution. Apparently the researchers were all interested in (1) the availability, interest rates, and down payment requirements of a home mortgage needed "in about a year;" (2) present passbook and certificate of deposit interest rates; (3) availability and interest rates of a presently needed home improvement loan; and (4) costs of a presently needed safety deposit box. One researcher had identified himself as an auto mechanic, moving to the Pearson area, another as a new sales engineer for a local manufacturing firm, and the other as a university professor. After each visit, the interviewer had evaluated his experience and summarized his notes (Exhibit C19.5).

To measure consumer knowledge and awareness of Pearson financial services, a telephone survey of a random sample of 190 Pearson and surrounding area residents was taken. Before asking any questions, the telephone interviewer first determined that the respondent was the person in the family who "usually decided about money matters." Results of this portion of the research study are summarized in Exhibit C19.6.

Finally, pertaining to consumers' subjective feelings, a door-to-door, two-stage random area sample of 410 Pearson residents and 145 New Landon residents was completed. At each household where the resident agreed to cooperate, a paper and pencil questionnaire was left for the "money matter decider" to complete and return by mail. Results are reproduced as Exhibit C19.7 and C19.8.

The "Procedures" section concluded this way:

> Performing this research were experienced personnel from Dvorak and Associates. Based on various considerations, the data can be considered valid and reliable.

Albert tended to agree or at least feel he was in a poor position to disagree. Some things puzzled him though. "I wonder why they had to use such a variety of methods," he thought, "couldn't just a mail survey have been used? And why did the researchers inquire about safety deposit boxes when we don't even offer them? I'd better call Calvin Dvorak for an explanation this afternoon."

THE REPORT'S LAST SECTION   Albert pressed on to the "Recommendations" section; here at last was the part of the report in which he was most interested. He settled down with a cup of coffee, noted that it was now 10:30, and began to read:

> Based on findings outlined earlier in this report, several strategic recommendations are in order. Presentation order of the following recommendations is not meant to indicate priority or relative importance; justifications appear with each recommendation.

EXHIBIT C19.5
Summary of Interviewers, Impressions of Pearson Financial Institutions

Variable	Pioneer Federal	Bank C	Bank D	Bank E	Bank F
Average Finding Out Time (mins.)	1.0	1.0	2.7	1.7	1.3
Average Waiting Time (mins.)	0	3	7	5	16
Total Number of Transfers	0	4	4	4	4
Total Number of Sales Attempts	0	1	3	1	0
Greeting	3.0	2.7	2.3	2.7	4.7
Appearance, Mannerisms	2.7	2.3	1.7	2.0	3.0
Technical Competence	3.0	3.0	1.3	1.7	2.5
Interest in Customer	3.3	3.0	1.3	2.7	4.7
Courtesy	2.3	2.7	2.0	2.0	4.3
Parking Facilities	2.3	1.7	2.0	2.7	2.7
Exterior Appearance	1.3	2.0	2.3	2.0	2.0
Interior Appearance	2.0	2.3	1.7	1.0	1.7
Short Teller Lines	2.7	2.0	3.0	1.0	1.0
Drive-Up Facilities	2.7	2.0	3.7	1.3	1.7

Note: For all variables except Total Number of Sales Attempts, a low value is desirable. All variables following Total Number of Sales Attempts were rated on a 5-point scale.

Bank C: *Ms. X.*   Nothing great . . . no attempt to find out who I was. Seemed to know what she was talking about but no great wealth of helpful information. Cool reception from her, then found out I wasn't a student and was moving here and warmed up. This bank seemed the most efficient. Each person knew his job and also knew who else did what. However, they lacked some of the personal care and service. August 28, 2:15 P.M.

  Mr. Y.   Had to transfer to customer service for CD pamphlet and then to vault area for box information. Safety deposit box information was weak, perhaps a stand-in on duty. August 30, 12:00 A.M.

  Ms. Z.   First I was to talk to Mr. Y, but he was busy so I was asked to talk to Ms. Z. She "had very little experience" with home improvement loans and twice had to check with others during the interview. Pleasant but extremely unsure of herself. September 5, 10:20 A.M.

Bank D: *Mr. A.*   Warm introduction by everyone. Mr. A very helpful about investments—where is the best place to buy land, mortgage, etc. Very impressive fellow, by far the most helpful. Very courteous, soft sell. Had to run around and see too many people for different things. A little disorganized—didn't really know other employee's jobs well enough to direct a customer to the right place. August 28, 1:43 P.M.

  Mr. A   Had to go to teller for CD information (got pamphlet, to safety deposit box desk for that information. Professional—good knowledge. August 30, 1:30 P.M.

EXHIBIT 19.5   *(continued)*

> Mr. B.　Smiled, sense of humor. Asked questions about me. Gave card, soft sell on checking program, seemed eager to get account. Overall rating was only satisfactory because of a 20-minute wait. September 5, 11:20 A.M.

Bank E:　Mr. C.　Was supposed to talk to someone else who hadn't returned from lunch. Very friendly, competent, soft sell. No particular person to answer or to take care of new people coming in. Different questions handled by different people. August 28 and 29, 2:40 P.M. and 1:06 P.M.

> Mr. D.　Was sent to information desk and then across bank to CD desk and across bank and downstairs to safety box desk—very confusing and no central information station. Had no loan money, so fairly uninterested. Cluttered inside. August 30, 11:30 A.M.

> Mr. E.　Seemed ill at ease at start—kind of blah, monotone, knowledgeable on all topics. Since I wasn't a present customer, I couldn't get a home improvement loan. Rates competitive, September 5, 10:40 A.M.

Bank F:　Mr. F.　The first day I interviewed a lady about CDs, but Mr. F out. Second day I got to talk to Mr. F. No introduction, not very friendly at all, apathy, got the feeling I was taking up his "valuable" time, very little interest or courtesy. None of the employees displayed any interest in me. August 28 and 29, 1:28 P.M. and 11:31 A.M.

> Mr. F.　Receptionist (?) at unlabeled desk—asked about CDs and she knew rates but not minimums, had to go downstairs for safety deposit box information. Mr. F received phone call and secretary for signing papers without excusing the interruption—ignored me completely to talk with others. August 30, 2:00 P.M.

> Mr. F.　Was directed to Mr. F, but he didn't handle home improvement loans so I waited for Mr. G who did. Mr. F received one phone call and no "excuse me" and ignored me as I sat and waited for Mr. G. September 10, 9:15 A.M.

Pioneer Federal:　Mr. H.　Listened, not overly aggressive, stared through me a lot of the time as in a daze. He gave "canned" answers on mortgage—no additional information, even after pumping him. Didn't get into personal relationships, asked me no questions. I had to ask to get the information. Polite but not overly friendly. Nothing dynamic in the total interview. August 28, 3:00 P.M.

> Mr. H.　Looked a little scared, seemed green and unsure. Didn't expend much effort checking figures, had to use calculator to find ¼ of $40,000. August 30, 11:10 A.M.

> Mr. H.　Seemed a bit uncomfortable, handled escrow, CD questions well. Did end the conversation with a smile. September 5, 11:00 A.M.

Note: The order of interviewer comments and interviewer identity is constant across the institutions above.

Recommendation 1: Increase the advertising budget from $38,000 to $50,000 for the Pearson market.

Justification: Telephone survey results showed 8 in 10 consumers were aware of Pioneer Federal but near half did not know Pioneer

Federal savings interest rates were higher than competing banks. Only 1 consumer in 7 could recall a Pioneer Federal ad and less than 1 in 9 could identify Pioneer Federal's slogan in an aided-recall situation. These percentages are significantly under similar data for competing banks.

Recommendation 2: Reduce the minimum investment amount requirements for certificates of deposit to competitive levels.

Justification: Pioneer Federal's minimums are several times higher than competing banks.

Recommendation 3: Add a 24-hour cash machine to the Pearson office.

Justification: While only two competing banks in the Pearson market have a 24-hour cash machine, 32 percent of the telephone respondents reported using one. Further, mail survey respondents view the machine as almost as important as several Pioneer Federal

EXHIBIT C19.6
Telephone Survey Results (n = 190)

Question 1: Awareness of Pearson financial institution (% naming):

Bank C	100	Bank F	69
Bank D	78	PIONEER FEDERAL	81
Bank E	87	Pearson Federal Credit Union	11

Question 2: Institution paying highest interest rate on regular savings account (% naming):

PIONEER FEDERAL	53
Bank C	4
Bank E	4
Don't know	39

Question 3: Respondents' estimate of highest interest rate paid in Pearson (%):

Average value 6.1 (n = 145)
Don't know   (n = 45)
Maximum   8.0, Minimum   4.0

Question 4: Respondents' estimate of the availability of daily interest at Pearson financial institutions (% naming):

Bank C	26	Bank F	20
Bank D	22	PIONEER FEDERAL	24
Bank E	26	Pearson Federal Credit Union	7

Question 5: Respondents' knowledge of service availability at banks or at savings and loan institutions (% correctly responding):

*Savings Account	91
*Mortgage Loan	73
Personal Loan	36
*Home Improvement Loan	52

EXHIBIT C19.6   *(continued)*

Business Loan	36
*Traveler's Checks	21
*Money Orders	18
*Certificates of Deposit	48
*Christmas Club	39
Safety Deposit Boxes	61
24-Hour Cash Machine	52
*Financial Counseling	66
*Drive-Up Window	69

*Note: Services available at Pioneer Federal.

Question 6: Advertising recall(%)

Bank C	14	Bank F	38
Bank D	11	PIONEER FEDERAL	14
Bank E	9	Pearson Federal Credit Union	0

Question 7: Slogan knowledge:

	% of All Respondents Correctly Identifying Slogan User	% of Heavy Users of Financial Services Correctly Identifying Slogan User*
PIONEER FEDERAL	11	17
Bank C	49	48
Bank E	26	26
Bank D	6	9

*Note: Heavy users were defined as respondents who had used four or more of the services in Question 8 in the preceding 6 months.

Question 8: Usage of financial services in the past six months (%):

Drive-Up Window	80
Late Friday Banking	64
Money Orders	37
Bank-by-Mail	34
Safety Deposit Boxes	32
24-Hour Cash Machine	32
Traveler's Checks	30
Insurance Agent Service	21
Mortgage Loan	19
Certificates of Deposit	19
Financial Counseling	17
Christmas Club	8
Business Loan	8
Home Improvement Loan	6

Question 9: Respondents switching the location of one or more savings accounts in the past six months (n):

Bank C	1
Bank E	1

EXHIBIT C19.7
Relative Importance of Financial Features and Services for Pearson (n = 410)
and New Landon (n = 145) Markets

Feature	Pearson Importance Score	New Landon Importance Score
Good parking facilities	2.95	2.93
Friendly, courteous employees	2.07	2.21
Convenient location	2.67	2.88
Fast service	2.30	2.25
Capable employees	1.90	1.83
Open on Saturday	3.88	3.95
Open Friday evenings	3.61	3.88
Open late afternoons	3.06	3.28
Personal service	2.35	2.50
Low interest rates on loans	1.88	2.00
Modern facilities	3.24	3.60
Income tax preparation servie	4.09	4.22
Financial counselling service	3.34	3.54
Insurance agency service	4.10	4.18
Daily interest on savings	2.24	2.17
Drive-up window	2.70	2.73
Walk-up window	3.44	3.49
High interest rate on savings	1.80	1.88
Gifts for opening or adding to accounts	4.22	4.20
Bank-by-mail service	3.01	3.15
Privacy in talking to loan officer	2.25	2.19
Privacy in talking to savings officer	2.51	2.54
Christmas club	4.24	4.15
Safety deposit boxes	2.69	2.93
An ID card to cash checks more easily	2.98	3.37
24-hour cash machine	2.89	3.45
Coffee, soft-drink vending machines	4.71	4.85
Trust services	3.06	3.58
Business loans	2.72	3.27
Money orders	3.22	3.51
Traveler's checks	2.73	3.00
Place to sit and talk in the lobby	4.22	4.32
The same place as where the mortgage is	3.63	3.62
Bank is active in community affairs	3.15	3.00

Key: Extremely Important = 1, Very Important = 2, Important = 3, Little Important = 4, Unimportant = 5.

features which are presently available (drive-up windows and traveler's checks, for example). The addition of a 24-hour cash machine before remaining banks add one would enhance Pioneer Federal's image as a modern, progressive institution.

Recommendation 4: Management at both Pioneer Federal offices should become more active in the community by sponsoring some visible, socially responsible activity.

EXHIBIT C19.8
Image Scores of Three New Landon and an Ideal Financial Institution

	Pioneer Federal	Bank A	Bank B	Ideal	
Friendly	2.26	2.43	2.09	1.92	Unfriendly
Old-Fashioned	4.80	4.94	4.86	4.69	Modern
High Interest Rates on Savings	2.48	3.40	2.67	1.80	Low Interest Rates on Savings
Fast Service	2.30	2.81	2.34	1.74	Slow Service
Honest Employees	2.06	1.76	2.00	1.46	Dishonest Employees
Good Parking	3.45	3.28	1.80	1.87	Poor Parking
Inconvenient Location	4.84	5.00	4.83	5.00	Convenient Location
Inconvenient Hours	4.27	4.34	4.52	5.17	Convenient Hours
Unattractive Inside	5.36	5.40	5.00	5.06	Attractive Inside
Capable Employees	2.66	2.90	2.42	1.92	Incapable Employees
Informative Advertising	2.48	2.48	1.27	1.87	Uninformative Advertising
Inactive in Community	3.88	4.52	4.75	4.85	Active in Community
Reserved and Conservative	3.44	3.22	4.62	4.56	Liberal and Outgoing
Small	4.30	4.37	3.96	4.32	Large
Easy to Get Mortgage Loans	3.92	3.35	3.25	2.50	Hard to Get Mortgage Loans

Note: Image scores above represent average values for consumer responses to a six-step semantic differential scale. Responses were coded 1 through 6 from left to right for each adjective pair. Respondents who marked "Neither" or "Don't Know" were dropped from the analysis on that item.

Justification: Mail survey respondents rate such activities as important in financial institution selection but perceive Pioneer Federal as less active in the community than all competing banks.

Recommendation 5: Advertisements should stress Pioneer Federal's advantage in interest rates on savings in both markets.

Justification: Mail survey results show consumers feel high interest rates on savings are the most important consideration in deciding where their money is kept (Exhibit C19.8). Pioneer Federal has a quarter percent advantage here but consumers apparently are not aware of it (Exhibit C19.6). Further, mail survey respondents view Pioneer Federal's advertising as the least "informative" relative to competing banks in each market.

Recommendation 6: Eliminate the Christmas Club as a customer service at both banks.

Justification: Mail survey respondents see this service as of little importance in deciding where their money is kept. The Pearson

EXHIBIT C19.8 *(continued)*
Image Scores of Five Pearson and an Ideal Financial Institution

	Pioneer Federal	Bank C	Bank D	Bank E	Bank F	Ideal	
Friendly	2.58	2.75	2.64	2.41	2.17	1.75	Unfriendly
Old-Fashioned	4.26	4.78	4.27	4.84	4.86	4.44	Modern
High Interest Rates on Savings	3.03	3.23	3.04	3.01	2.86	1.70	Low Interest Rates on Savings
Fast Service	2.67	2.65	2.99	2.46	2.23	1.62	Slow Service
Honest Employees	2.11	2.14	2.26	2.05	1.83	1.30	Dishonest Employees
Good Parking	2.58	2.10	2.34	2.16	2.12	1.71	Poor Parking
Inconvenient Location	4.53	4.65	4.36	4.74	3.78	5.07	Convenient Location
Inconvenient Hours	4.34	4.38	4.62	4.62	4.55	5.33	Convenient Hours
Unattractive Inside	4.92	4.96	4.69	5.08	5.01	4.96	Attractive Inside
Capable Employees	3.10	3.07	3.28	2.72	2.56	1.68	Incapable Employees
Informative Advertising	3.16	2.99	2.68	2.59	3.10	1.85	Uninformative Advertising
Inactive in Community	4.00	4.60	4.20	4.56	4.07	4.76	Active in Community
Reserved and Conservative	3.08	2.91	3.28	3.56	3.50	3.99	Liberal and Outgoing
Small	3.49	4.80	3.10	4.51	2.85	4.19	Large
Easy to Get Mortgage Loans	2.86	3.46	3.20	3.10	3.53	2.38	Hard to Get Mortgage Loans

Note: Image scores above represent average values for consumer responses to a six-step semantic differential scale. Responses were coded 1 through 6 from left to right for each adjective pair. Respondents who marked "Neither" or "Don't Know" were dropped from the analysis on that item.

office has only 28 such accounts (of approximately 3800 total) and Pioneer Federal employees could spend their time more profitably elsewhere.

Recommendation 7: Reconsider the role that gifts or premiums play in savings account promotion activities at both offices.

Justification: Gifts or premiums for opening or adding to savings accounts are not viewed as important by mail survey respondents.

Recommendation 8: Repeat the study in three years.

Justification: Management should make the above recommended changes and evaluate their effectiveness by measuring consumer change.

Dvorak and Associates realizes some recommendations can be effected more easily than others. Further, some recommendations may appear to be extreme, given the data; and Pioneer Federal may wish to examine each recommendation and its implications in more detail.

Finally, other recommendations may emerge from an examination of research results by Pioneer Federal personnel. This is expected and encouraged. If more information is needed to examine any recommendations, Dvorak and Associates will certainly provide assistance.

Albert was impressed. The recommendations were clearly action oriented and, in his mind, justifiable from the data. "Would the officers agree?" he wondered. "Maybe I should examine some cost implications to show them the feasibility. There should be enough time for that this afternoon." So thinking, Albert turned to some files he had made up earlier on the advertising budget, 24-hour cash machines, Christmas Club accounts, and last month's premium promotion. Lunch would have to wait.

20. Ethical Problems in Marketing Research*

Marketing managers and marketing researchers in businesses, nonprofit organizations and government agencies are frequently confronted by ethical problems and dilemmas. Gathering, analyzing, and presenting information all are procedures that raise a number of important ethical questions in which the manager's need to know and understand the market in order to develop effective marketing programs must be balanced against an individual's right to privacy. The interpretation and use of data can also raise ethical questions.

The following pages present a set of ethical dilemmas that might arise in marketing research. Your assignment is to decide what action to take in each instance. You should be prepared to justify your decision. Bear in mind that there are no *right* or *wrong* answers; reasonable people may choose different courses of action.

1. As market research director of a pharmaceutical company, you are given the suggestion by the executive director that physicians be telephoned by company interviewers under the name of a fictitious market research agency. The purpose of the survey is to help assess the per-

---

*These ethical problems have been generated from a number of sources, including C. Merle Crawford, "Attitudes of Marketing Executives Toward Ethics in Marketing Research," *Journal of Marketing* 34 (April 1970): 46–52. They were prepared by Professor Charles B. Weinberg, Faculty of Commerce and Business Administration, University of British Columbia. Reprinted from *Stanford Business Cases 1977* with permission of the publisher, Stanford University Graduate School of Business. © 1977 by the Board of Trustees of the Leland Stanford Junior University.

ceived quality of the company's products, and it is felt that the suggested procedure will result in more objective responses.

What action would you take?

2. Your company is supervising a study of restaurants conducted for an agency of the federal government. The data, which have already been collected, include specific buying information and prices paid. Respondent organizations have been promised confidentiality. The federal agency demands that all responses be identified by business name. Their rationale is that they plan to repeat the study and wish to limit sampling error by returning to the same respondents. Open bidding requires that the government maintain control of the sample.

What action would you take?

3. You are the market research director in a manufacturing company. The project director requests permission to use ultraviolet ink in precoding questionnaires on a mail survey. He points out that the accompanying letter refers to a confidential survey, but he needs to be able to identify respondents to permit adequate cross-tabulation of the data and to save on postage costs if a second mailing is required.

What action would you take?

4. Your company, along with several other well-known market research companies, has been asked to prepare a research proposal to study the trial and repeat rates of buyers of state lottery tickets. The lottery proceeds, which help to support the state's welfare program, have fallen short of the original goals. The director of the lottery is unsure if this is because too few people have ever bought tickets or because not enough of those who try the lottery repeat their purchases on a regular basis. In particular, the director wants to relate geographic and socioeconomic factors to lottery ticket purchases. The director claims that the lottery takes revenue away from illegal numbers rackets; others claim that it induces participation from those who can least afford to gamble. Because the state takes at least 40 percent of the total receipts for social welfare programs, many illegal numbers games return more to the bettors than does the state lottery.

As president of the company, what do you do?

5. You are employed by a marketing research firm and have conducted an attitude study for a client. Your data indicate that the product is not being marketed properly. This finding is ill received by the client's product management team. They request that you omit that data from your formal report—which you know will be widely distributed—on the grounds that the verbal presentation was adequate for their needs.

What do you do?

6. You are a project director on a study funded by a somewhat unpopular federal agency. The study is on marijuana use among young people in a community and its relationship, if any, to crime. You will be using a structured questionnaire to gather data for the agency on marijuana use and criminal activities. You believe that if you reveal the name of the funding agency and/or the actual purposes of the study to respondents, you will seriously depress response rates and thereby increase nonresponse bias.

What information would you disclose to respondents?

7. You are employed by a market research company. A clothing manufacturer has retained your firm to conduct a study for them. The manufacturer wants to know something about how women choose clothing, such as blouses and sweaters. The manufacturer wants to conduct group interviews, supplemented by a session which would be devoted to observing the women trying on clothing, in order to discover which types of garments are chosen first, how thoroughly they touch and examine the clothing, and whether they look for and read a label or price tag. The client suggests that the observation be performed unobtrusively by female observers at a local department store, via a one-way mirror. One of your associates argues that this would constitute an invasion of privacy.

What action would you take?

8. You are a study director for a research company undertaking a project for a regular client of your company. A study you are working on is about to go into the field when the questionnaire you sent to the client for the final approval comes back drastically modified. The client has rewritten it, introducing leading questions and biased scales. An accompanying letter indicates that the questionnaire must be sent out as revised. You do not believe that valid information can be gathered using the revised instrument.

What action would you take?

9. A well-respected public figure is going to face trial on a conspiracy charge brought by the U.S. Justice Department. The defense lawyers have asked you, as a market research specialist, to do a research study to determine the characteristics of people most likely to sympathize with the defendant and hence to vote for acquittal. The defense lawyers have read newspaper accounts of how this approach has been used in a number of instances (for example, in the 1974 criminal conspiracy trial of John N. Mitchell and Maurice H. Stans, and the 1976 trial of JoAnn Little, a black woman accused of murdering a jailer who allegedly attacked her).

What do you do?

10. You are the market research director for a large chemical company. Recent research indicates that many customers of your company are misusing one of its principal products. There is no danger resulting from this misuse, though the customers are wasting money by using too much of the product at one time. You are shown the new advertising campaign by the advertising agency. The ads not only ignore this problem of misuse, but actually seem to encourage it.

What action would you take?

Appendix
Tables

TABLE 1
2,500 Random Numbers

50384	85138	50423	99653	99634	99469	06147	79389	56031	32784
45446	21985	92691	82222	04716	71069	99283	93902	79840	78768
82817	28617	60943	91751	53122	84003	23977	15847	99863	45697
95029	65201	68302	47132	35191	93920	01462	41251	30530	68324
97288	46456	18600	87075	27563	37146	13616	37816	01301	96232
49247	86161	39665	07642	82510	05142	29779	78284	49613	78059
14537	67342	43019	58647	62375	34485	15155	71344	17330	56304
23278	17916	43274	41386	60709	43007	74870	59634	27826	15880
64717	04117	31951	36419	43437	29325	37161	74701	27515	26832
26763	77539	35411	03525	92335	77480	23169	44641	38202	79443
13543	02008	67206	92136	13164	91382	44794	40309	89437	55900
90830	19471	49841	07676	04022	46793	06601	71951	32297	05342
73312	72642	19307	40996	55535	86078	85232	10841	63898	46210
03348	15094	78330	02479	02368	79372	77140	09051	94062	50386
91310	28918	95858	32861	40482	40281	62468	64111	90656	81837
94390	87875	74118	41338	68749	95125	42232	67329	43431	90882
41815	09913	91111	13032	38778	34917	66416	34106	62274	63401
50222	64057	95081	92939	78864	39811	73793	00839	93186	21525
07772	69782	84817	08418	39206	14419	10551	11832	20611	39221
06265	78969	98329	50734	01814	88935	95866	04626	33536	09212
98068	03532	16355	36259	37501	74580	12075	97459	79209	58582
26718	86935	01361	34346	20663	18291	34368	12553	48627	10849
53690	62562	63124	70007	57664	41684	30771	58016	11177	19068
90319	80880	86384	14087	20431	38026	64323	18995	70717	81751
50485	37028	93309	53839	71247	18470	66960	05119	75119	29088
11363	91479	68259	59812	41275	65118	22925	20692	11221	62541
26866	03114	95241	35622	63067	99767	53623	56851	53857	85544
20536	90545	79192	48657	52126	09961	28603	91649	72907	90465
75899	63319	52743	23558	15608	49089	48424	32966	22027	20687
09600	09198	17034	78646	04959	92237	66182	14194	73665	17599
03985	25593	54991	29602	44277	10983	57464	93459	40050	96359
94752	47444	33575	78080	75399	31543	20491	04181	88253	38853
43789	38797	24531	98985	87911	39385	16455	47868	48264	49642
03124	98417	70412	74476	33457	83122	78514	11300	68931	68475
13959	85567	56353	64626	69669	19117	89275	39294	16478	61819
64957	86587	16738	83468	83536	01068	78923	25834	05492	74330
59221	54716	71479	35122	06666	07998	55727	04467	97981	57769
95233	87652	61470	12733	88273	76819	70794	86935	09729	88615
67644	16683	99041	61690	77416	18003	72410	86383	96835	91406
68690	79225	71625	04859	50011	98882	71933	94552	32095	48784
20478	62525	98481	10511	98528	88951	75130	22239	57977	34546
83557	07315	81820	51138	43900	49072	36493	40352	77397	84647
50106	44769	22064	04943	79304	23440	05667	45032	07122	87887
08611	20434	47615	68550	90670	17948	00551	68995	22452	70189
14078	26664	90599	70403	44291	88886	52363	44399	98895	99946
58775	95672	28974	77707	26967	81569	81356	16411	08935	60588
15704	16371	65841	38968	08756	21519	14924	51467	59967	00638
26043	68366	37371	54661	41287	10260	52004	90992	73520	42621
94834	02497	09060	31510	11761	14032	05177	82248	16444	74515
15434	87504	40004	39532	16039	69272	62712	58679	58027	00254

TABLE 2
Areas Under the Standard Normal Curve
Entry is the area under the standard normal curve from O to Z.

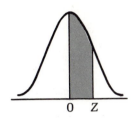

Z	0.00	0.01	0.02	0.03	0.04	0.05	0.06	0.07	0.08	0.09
0.0	0.0000	0.0040	0.0080	0.0120	0.0160	0.0199	0.0239	0.0279	0.0319	0.0359
0.1	.0398	.0438	.0478	.0517	.0557	.0596	.0636	.0675	.0714	.0753
0.2	.0793	.0832	.0871	.0910	.0948	.0987	.1026	.1064	.1103	.1141
0.3	.1179	.1217	.1255	.1293	.1331	.1368	.1406	.1443	.1480	.1517
0.4	.1554	.1591	.1628	.1664	.1700	.1736	.1772	.1808	.1844	.1879
0.5	.1915	.1950	.1985	.2019	.2054	.2088	.2123	.2157	.2190	.2224
0.6	.2257	.2291	.2324	.2357	.2389	.2422	.2454	.2486	.2517	.2549
0.7	.2580	.2611	.2642	.2673	.2704	.2734	.2764	.2794	.2823	.2852
0.8	.2881	.2910	.2939	.2967	.2995	.3023	.3051	.3078	.3106	.3133
0.9	.3159	.3186	.3212	.3238	.3264	.3289	.3315	.3340	.3365	.3389
1.0	.3413	.3438	.3461	.3485	.3508	.3531	.3554	.3577	.3599	.3621
1.1	.3643	.3665	.3686	.3708	.3729	.3749	.3770	.3790	.3810	.3830
1.2	.3849	.3869	.3888	.3907	.3925	.3944	.3962	.3980	.3997	.4015
1.3	.4032	.4049	.4066	.4082	.4099	.4115	.4131	.4147	.4162	.4177
1.4	.4192	.4207	.4222	.4236	.4251	.4265	.4279	.4292	.4306	.4319
1.5	.4332	.4345	.4357	.4370	.4382	.4394	.4406	.4418	.4429	.4441
1.6	.4452	.4463	.4474	.4484	.4495	.4505	.4515	.4525	.4535	.4545
1.7	.4554	.4564	.4573	.4582	.4591	.4599	.4608	.4616	.4625	.4633
1.8	.4641	.4649	.4656	.4664	.4671	.4678	.4686	.4693	.4699	.4706
1.9	.4713	.4719	.4726	.4732	.4738	.4744	.4750	.4756	.4761	.4767
2.0	.4772	.4778	.4783	.4788	.4793	.4798	.4803	.4808	.4812	.4817
2.1	.4821	.4826	.4830	.4834	.4838	.4842	.4846	.4850	.4854	.4857
2.2	.4861	.4864	.4868	.4871	.4875	.4878	.4881	.4884	.4887	.4890
2.3	.4893	.4896	.4898	.4901	.4904	.4906	.4909	.4911	.4913	.4916
2.4	.4918	.4920	.4922	.4925	.4927	.4929	.4931	.4932	.4934	.4936
2.5	.4938	.4940	.4941	.4943	.4945	.4946	.4948	.4949	.4951	.4952
2.6	.4953	.4955	.4956	.4957	.4959	.4960	.4961	.4962	.4963	.4964
2.7	.4965	.4966	.4967	.4968	.4969	.4970	.4971	.4972	.4973	.4974
2.8	.4974	.4975	.4976	.4977	.4977	.4978	.4979	.4979	.4980	.4981
2.9	.4981	.4982	.4982	.4983	.4984	.4984	.4985	.4985	.4986	.4986
3.0	.4987	.4987	.4987	.4988	.4988	.4989	.4989	.4989	.4990	.4990
3.1	.4990	.4991	.4991	.4991	.4992	.4992	.4992	.4992	.4993	.4993
3.2	.4993	.4993	.4994	.4994	.4994	.4994	.4994	.4995	.4995	.4995
3.3	.4995	.4995	.4995	.4996	.4996	.4996	.4996	.4996	.4996	.4997
3.4	.4997	.4997	.4997	.4997	.4997	.4997	.4997	.4997	.4997	.4998
3.6	.4998	.4998	.4999	.4999	.4999	.4999	.4999	.4999	.4999	.4999
3.9	.5000									

Source: Reprinted by permission from *Statistical Methods* by George W. Snedecor and William G. Cochran, 7th ed. Copyright 1980 by Iowa State University Press, Ames, Iowa, 50010.

TABLE 3
Critical Values of *t*
Entry is the value of *t* at $1 - \alpha$ and n degrees of freedom.

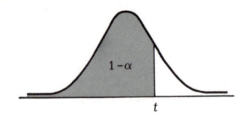

					$1-\alpha$				
n	.75	.80	.85	.90	.95	.975	.99	.995	.9995
1	1.000	1.376	1.963	3.078	6.314	12.706	31.821	63.657	636.619
2	.816	1.061	1.386	1.886	2.920	4.303	6.965	9.925	31.598
3	.765	.978	1.250	1.638	2.353	3.182	4.541	5.841	12.924
4	.741	.941	1.190	1.533	2.132	2.776	3.747	4.604	8.610
5	.727	.920	1.156	1.476	2.015	2.571	3.365	4.032	6.869
6	.718	.906	1.134	1.440	1.943	2.447	3.143	3.707	5.959
7	.711	.896	1.119	1.415	1.895	2.365	2.998	3.499	5.408
8	.706	.889	1.108	1.397	1.860	2.306	2.896	3.355	5.041
9	.703	.883	1.100	1.383	1.833	2.262	2.821	3.250	4.781
10	.700	.879	1.093	1.372	1.812	2.228	2.764	3.169	4.587
11	.697	.876	1.088	1.363	1.796	2.201	2.718	3.106	4.437
12	.695	.873	1.083	1.356	1.782	2.179	2.681	3.055	4.318
13	.694	.870	1.079	1.350	1.771	2.160	2.650	3.012	4.221
14	.692	.868	1.076	1.345	1.761	2.145	2.624	2.977	4.140
15	.691	.866	1.074	1.341	1.753	2.131	2.602	2.947	4.073
16	.690	.865	1.071	1.337	1.746	2.120	2.583	2.921	4.015
17	.689	.863	1.069	1.333	1.740	2.110	2.567	2.898	3.965
18	.688	.862	1.067	1.330	1.734	2.101	2.552	2.878	3.922
19	.688	.861	1.066	1.328	1.729	2.093	2.539	2.861	3.883
20	.687	.860	1.064	1.325	1.725	2.086	2.528	2.845	3.850
21	.686	.859	1.063	1.323	1.721	2.080	2.518	2.831	3.819
22	.686	.858	1.061	1.321	1.717	2.074	2.508	2.819	3.792
23	.685	.858	1.060	1.319	1.714	2.069	2.500	2.807	3.767
24	.685	.857	1.059	1.318	1.711	2.064	2.492	2.797	3.745
25	.684	.856	1.058	1.316	1.708	2.060	2.485	2.787	3.725
26	.684	.856	1.058	1.315	1.706	2.056	2.479	2.779	3.707
27	.684	.855	1.057	1.314	1.703	2.052	2.473	2.771	3.690
28	.683	.855	1.056	1.313	1.701	2.048	2.467	2.763	3.674
29	.683	.854	1.055	1.311	1.699	2.045	2.462	2.756	3.659
30	.683	.854	1.055	1.310	1.697	2.042	2.457	2.750	3.646
40	.681	.851	1.050	1.303	1.684	2.021	2.423	2.704	3.551
60	.679	.848	1.046	1.296	1.671	2.000	2.390	2.660	3.460
120	.677	.845	1.041	1.289	1.658	1.980	2.358	2.617	3.373
∞	.674	.842	1.036	1.282	1.645	1.960	2.326	2.576	3.291

Source: Taken from Table III of Fisher and Yates: *Statistical Tables for Biological, Agricultural and Medical Research,* published by Longman Group Ltd. London (previously published by Oliver & Boyd Ltd. Edinburgh); used by permission of the authors and publishers.

TABLE 4
Critical Values of χ^2
Entry is the value of χ^2 at $1 - \alpha$ and n degrees of freedom.

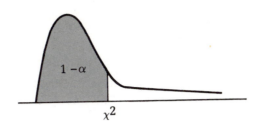

n	$1-\alpha$						
	.01	.05	.10	.90	.95	.99	.999
1	.003157	.00393	.0158	2.706	3.841	6.635	10.827
2	.0201	.103	.211	4.605	5.991	9.210	13.815
3	.115	.352	.584	6.251	7.815	11.345	16.266
4	.297	.711	1.064	7.779	9.488	13.277	18.467
5	.554	1.145	1.610	9.236	11.070	15.086	20.515
6	.872	1.635	2.204	10.645	12.592	16.812	22.457
7	1.239	2.167	2.833	12.017	14.067	18.475	24.322
8	1.646	2.733	3.490	13.362	15.507	20.090	26.125
9	2.088	3.325	4.168	14.684	16.919	21.666	27.877
10	2.558	3.940	4.865	15.987	18.307	23.209	29.588
11	3.053	4.575	5.578	17.275	19.675	24.725	31.264
12	3.571	5.226	6.304	18.549	21.026	26.217	32.909
13	4.107	5.892	7.042	19.812	22.362	27.688	34.528
14	4.660	6.571	7.790	21.064	23.685	29.141	36.123
15	5.229	7.261	8.547	22.307	24.996	30.578	37.697
16	5.812	7.962	9.312	23.542	26.296	32.000	39.252
17	6.408	8.672	10.085	24.769	27.587	33.409	40.790
18	7.015	9.390	10.865	25.989	28.869	34.805	42.312
19	7.633	10.117	11.651	27.204	30.144	36.191	43.820
20	8.260	10.851	12.443	28.412	31.410	37.566	45.315
21	8.897	11.591	13.240	29.615	32.671	38.932	46.797
22	9.542	12.338	14.041	30.813	33.924	40.289	48.268
23	10.196	13.091	14.848	32.007	35.172	41.638	49.728
24	10.856	13.848	15.659	33.196	36.415	42.980	51.179
25	11.524	14.611	16.473	34.382	37.652	44.314	52.620
26	12.198	15.379	17.292	35.563	38.885	45.642	54.052
27	12.879	16.151	18.114	36.741	40.113	46.963	55.476
28	13.565	16.928	18.939	37.916	41.337	48.278	56.893
29	14.256	17.708	19.768	39.087	42.557	49.588	58.302
30	14.953	18.493	20.599	40.256	43.773	50.892	59.703
40	22.164	26.509	29.051	51.805	55.759	63.691	73.402
50	29.707	34.764	37.689	63.167	67.505	76.154	86.661
60	37.485	43.188	46.459	74.397	79.082	88.379	99.607
70	45.442	51.739	55.329	85.527	90.531	100.425	112.317

Source: Taken from Table IV of Fisher and Yates: *Statistical Tables for Biological, Agricultural and Medical Research*, published by Longman Group Ltd. London (previously published by Oliver & Boyd Ltd. Edinburgh); used by permission of the authors and publishers.

TABLE 5A
Critical Values of F for $1 - \alpha = .95$
Entry is the value of F for $1 - \alpha$, numerator df, and denominator df.

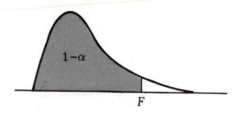

Denominator df	\multicolumn{10}{c}{Numerator df}
	1	2	3	4	5	6	8	12	24	∞
1	161.4	199.5	215.7	224.6	230.2	234.0	238.9	243.9	249.0	254.3
2	18.51	19.00	19.16	19.25	19.30	19.33	19.37	19.41	19.45	19.50
3	10.13	9.55	9.28	9.12	9.01	8.94	8.84	8.74	8.64	8.53
4	7.71	6.94	6.59	6.39	6.26	6.16	6.04	5.91	5.77	5.63
5	6.61	5.79	5.41	5.19	5.05	4.95	4.82	4.68	4.53	4.36
6	5.99	5.14	4.76	4.53	4.39	4.28	4.15	4.00	3.84	3.67
7	5.59	4.74	4.35	4.12	3.97	3.87	3.73	3.57	3.41	3.23
8	5.32	4.46	4.07	3.84	3.69	3.58	3.44	3.28	3.12	2.93
9	5.12	4.26	3.86	3.63	3.48	3.37	3.23	3.07	2.90	2.71
10	4.96	4.10	3.71	3.48	3.33	3.22	3.07	2.91	2.74	2.54
11	4.84	3.98	3.59	3.36	3.20	3.09	2.95	2.79	2.61	2.40
12	4.75	3.88	3.49	3.26	3.11	3.00	2.85	2.69	2.50	2.30
13	4.67	3.80	3.41	3.18	3.02	2.92	2.77	2.60	2.42	2.21
14	4.60	3.74	3.34	3.11	2.96	2.85	2.70	2.53	2.35	2.13
15	4.54	3.68	3.29	3.06	2.90	2.79	2.64	2.48	2.29	2.07
16	4.49	3.63	3.24	3.01	2.85	2.74	2.59	2.42	2.24	2.01
17	4.45	3.59	3.20	2.96	2.81	2.70	2.55	2.38	2.19	1.96
18	4.41	3.55	3.16	2.93	2.77	2.66	2.51	2.34	2.15	1.92
19	4.38	3.52	3.13	2.90	2.74	2.63	2.48	2.31	2.11	1.88
20	4.35	3.49	3.10	2.87	2.71	2.60	2.45	2.28	2.08	1.84
21	4.32	3.47	3.07	2.84	2.68	2.57	2.42	2.25	2.05	1.81
22	4.30	3.44	3.05	2.82	2.66	2.55	2.40	2.23	2.03	1.78
23	4.28	3.42	3.03	2.80	2.64	2.53	2.38	2.20	2.00	1.76
24	4.26	3.40	3.01	2.78	2.62	2.51	2.36	2.18	1.98	1.73
25	4.24	3.38	2.99	2.76	2.60	2.49	2.34	2.16	1.96	1.71
26	4.22	3.37	2.98	2.74	2.59	2.47	2.32	2.15	1.95	1.69
27	4.21	3.35	2.96	2.73	2.57	2.46	2.30	2.13	1.93	1.67
28	4.20	3.34	2.95	2.71	2.56	2.44	2.29	2.12	1.91	1.65
29	4.18	3.33	2.93	2.70	2.54	2.43	2.28	2.10	1.90	1.64
30	4.17	3.32	2.92	2.69	2.53	2.42	2.27	2.09	1.89	1.62
40	4.08	3.23	2.84	2.61	2.45	2.34	2.18	2.00	1.79	1.51
60	4.00	3.15	2.76	2.52	2.37	2.25	2.10	1.92	1.70	1.39
120	3.92	3.07	2.68	2.45	2.29	2.17	2.02	1.83	1.61	1.25
∞	3.84	2.99	2.60	2.37	2.21	2.10	1.94	1.75	1.52	1.00

Source: Taken from Table V of Fisher and Yates: *Statistical Tables for Biological, Agricultural and Medical Research*, published by Longman Group Ltd. London (previously published by Oliver & Boyd Ltd. Edinburgh); used by permission of the authors and publishers.

TABLE 5B
Critical Values of F for $1 - \alpha = .99$
Entry is the value of F for $1 - \alpha$, numerator df, and denominator df.

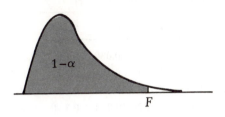

Denominator df	Numerator df									
	1	2	3	4	5	6	8	12	24	∞
1	4052	4999	5403	5625	5764	5859	5982	6106	6234	6366
2	98.50	99.00	99.17	99.25	99.30	99.33	99.37	99.42	99.46	99.50
3	34.12	30.82	29.46	28.71	28.24	27.91	27.49	27.05	26.60	26.12
4	21.20	18.00	16.69	15.98	15.52	15.21	14.80	14.37	13.93	13.46
5	16.26	13.27	12.06	11.39	10.97	10.67	10.29	9.89	9.47	9.02
6	13.74	10.92	9.78	9.15	8.75	8.47	8.10	7.72	7.31	6.88
7	12.25	9.55	8.45	7.85	7.46	7.19	6.84	6.47	6.07	5.65
8	11.26	8.65	7.59	7.01	6.63	6.37	6.03	5.67	5.28	4.86
9	10.56	8.02	6.99	6.42	6.06	5.80	5.47	5.11	4.73	4.31
10	10.04	7.56	6.55	5.99	5.64	5.39	5.06	4.71	4.33	3.91
11	9.65	7.20	6.22	5.67	5.32	5.07	4.74	4.40	4.02	3.60
12	9.33	6.93	5.95	5.41	5.06	4.82	4.50	4.16	3.78	3.36
13	9.07	6.70	5.74	5.20	4.86	4.62	4.30	3.96	3.59	3.16
14	8.86	6.51	5.56	5.03	4.69	4.46	4.14	3.80	3.43	3.00
15	8.68	6.36	5.42	4.89	4.56	4.32	4.00	3.67	3.29	2.87
16	8.53	6.23	5.29	4.77	4.44	4.20	3.89	3.55	3.18	2.75
17	8.40	6.11	5.18	4.67	4.34	4.10	3.79	3.45	3.08	2.65
18	8.28	6.01	5.09	4.58	4.25	4.01	3.71	3.37	3.00	2.57
19	8.18	5.93	5.01	4.50	4.17	3.94	3.63	3.30	2.92	2.49
20	8.10	5.85	4.94	4.43	4.10	3.87	3.56	3.23	2.86	2.42
21	8.02	5.78	4.87	4.37	4.04	3.81	3.51	3.17	2.80	2.36
22	7.94	5.72	4.82	4.31	3.99	3.76	3.45	3.12	2.75	2.31
23	7.88	5.66	4.76	4.26	3.94	3.71	3.41	3.07	2.70	2.26
24	7.82	5.61	4.72	4.22	3.90	3.67	3.36	3.03	2.66	2.21
25	7.77	5.57	4.68	4.18	3.86	3.63	3.32	2.99	2.62	2.17
26	7.72	5.53	4.64	4.14	3.82	3.59	3.29	2.96	2.58	2.13
27	7.68	5.49	4.60	4.11	3.78	3.56	3.26	2.93	2.55	2.10
28	7.64	5.45	4.57	4.07	3.75	3.53	3.23	2.90	2.52	2.06
29	7.60	5.42	4.54	4.04	3.73	3.50	3.20	2.87	2.49	2.03
30	7.56	5.39	4.51	4.02	3.70	3.47	3.17	2.84	2.47	2.01
40	7.31	5.18	4.31	3.83	3.51	3.29	2.99	2.66	2.29	1.80
60	7.08	4.98	4.13	3.65	3.34	3.12	2.82	2.50	2.12	1.60
120	6.85	4.79	3.95	3.48	3.17	2.96	2.66	2.34	1.95	1.38
∞	6.64	4.60	3.78	3.32	3.02	2.80	2.51	2.18	1.79	1.00

Source: Taken from Table V of Fisher and Yates: *Statistical Tables for Biological, Agricultural and Medical Research*, published by Longman Group Ltd. London (previously published by Oliver & Boyd Ltd. Edinburgh); used by permission of the authors and publishers.

TABLE 6
Values for $1.1513 \log_{10} (1 + r)/(1 - r)$

r	0.00	0.01	0.02	0.03	0.04	0.05	0.06	0.07	0.08	0.09
0.0	0.000	0.010	0.020	0.030	0.040	0.050	0.060	0.070	0.080	0.090
0.1	0.100	0.110	0.121	0.131	0.141	0.151	0.161	0.172	0.182	0.192
0.2	0.203	0.213	0.224	0.234	0.245	0.255	0.266	0.277	0.288	0.299
0.3	0.310	0.321	0.332	0.343	0.354	0.365	0.377	0.388	0.400	0.412
0.4	0.424	0.436	0.448	0.460	0.472	0.485	0.497	0.510	0.523	0.536
0.5	0.549	0.563	0.576	0.590	0.604	0.618	0.633	0.648	0.662	0.678
0.6	0.693	0.709	0.725	0.741	0.758	0.775	0.793	0.811	0.829	0.848
0.7	0.867	0.887	0.908	0.929	0.950	0.973	0.996	1.020	1.045	1.071
0.8	1.099	1.127	1.157	1.188	1.221	1.256	1.293	1.333	1.376	1.422
0.9	1.472	1.528	1.589	1.658	1.738	1.832	1.946	2.092	2.298	2.647

Glossary

Absolute zero point a measurement position that indicates the complete absence of a variable of interest.

Advance notification communication prior to a survey that alerts sample members to the study.

Alternate form reliability a procedure for assessing reliability using two (or more) parallel versions of the items under investigation which are given to a sample of respondents on two (or more) occasions.

Analysis of variance (ANOVA) a statistical procedure that tests the null hypothesis of equal means in two or more populations.

Applied marketing research investigations that help marketing decision makers achieve specific organizational goals.

Attitude scale a set of belief items on a data collection form that indicates the respondent's overall like or dislike of a consumption related alternative.

Autocorrelation the relationship between error or residual values in a regression analysis of data values that represent different time periods.

Autoregressive forecast a forecast using simple linear or multiple regression applied directly to sales data from past time periods.

Average the arithmetic mean; the sum of all data values in a set divided by the number of values.

Balanced loadings the practice of phrasing Likert statements in positive and negative terms in approximately equal numbers on the data collection form.

Basic marketing research investigations that increase theoretical knowledge about marketing.

Behavior question   an item on a data collection form that measures past or present action.

Belief question   an item on a data collection form that measures a respondent's view about a consumption related alternative's performance on a choice criterion.

Bivariate relationship   a relationship between two variables.

Blocked design   an experiment in which test units are grouped into homogeneous groups before being exposed to treatments.

Break off   a refusal in a telephone survey, typically occurring in the first 15 seconds of the interview.

Callbacks   in telephone and personal interview surveys, repeated attempts to obtain responses from not-at-homes.

Causal model   a forecast based on values for variables other than past sales.

Causal research   investigations showing that a change in one variable produces a change in another.

Census   a process that attempts to take measurements from all members in the population of interest.

Central limit theorem   the sampling distribution of $\overline{X}$ approximates a normal probability distribution if all possible sample combinations have an equal chance of being selected and sample size is large.

Chi-square test of independence   a statistical procedure testing the hypothesis of independence between two nominal variables.

Choice criterion question   an item on a data collection form that measures the importance of an attribute in making a consumption related decision.

Clerical error   measurement or response error of a data entry or data manipulation nature.

Cluster   a group of population elements or a unit of area that contains a group of population elements.

Cluster sampling   a probability sampling procedure where sampling units consist either of groups of population elements or units of area that contain a group of population elements.

Cochran test   a statistical procedure testing the hypothesis of equal proportions when samples are dependent.

Codebook   coding instructions that describe the location of variables on the data collection form, coding procedures, and computer card columns where coded values will be keypunched.

Coding   the assigning of numbers to responses on a data collection form in order to allow data analysis.

Complex sample   a stratified or cluster sample.

Confidence coefficient   the probability, $1 - \alpha$, associated with a confidence interval.

Confidence interval   a range of values that contains the unknown population mean or proportion $100(1 - \alpha)$ percent of the time in a large number of probability samples.

Consumer life style question   an item on a data collection form that measures consumer activities, interests, opinions, needs, or values.

Content validity   the ability of a measurement item or process to measure using items contained in a specified universe of all possible items.

Control group   test units in an experiment that are exposed to no experimental treatment.

Construct validity   the ability of a measurement item or process to measure an abstract, unobservable characteristic.

Continuous variable   a variable that takes on an infinite number of values.

Convenience sampling   a nonprobability sampling procedure where population elements are chosen on the basis of ease to the researcher.

Cover letter   the letter accompanying the questionnaire in a mail survey.

Critical region   values for a test statistic that lead to a rejection of the null hypothesis.

Critical value   the value of a test statistic that separates the acceptance from the critical region in a test of the null hypothesis.

Crosstab table (cross classification table)   a table showing the joint frequency distribution of two or more variables in a sample or population.

Data   numbers or words capable of yielding information about people, things, events, concepts, or organizations.

Data analysis   the manipulation of numbers, words, or other symbols to facilitate data interpretation.

Data analysis plan   a document that describes data analysis procedures for major research variables.

Data collection control   a research method's potential for gathering information according to procedures established by the researcher.

Data interpretation   the attachment of meaning to numbers, words, or other symbols.

Data reduction   analysis procedures that describe the central tendency, variability, and distribution of data.

Data source   some person, object, or organization that provides information.

Debriefing   after formal data collection activities are completed, the efforts to answer respondents' questions and reduce their anxieties.

Deceptive research practice   a misrepresentation of either the purpose of research, research procedures, or use of research results.

Decision maker   a person who takes management action; a person who funds marketing research.

Delphi method   a rigorous subjective forecast employing a number of isolated forecasters and several forecasting rounds to achieve a consensus.

Dependent sample   a probability sample whose members are selected with regard for members in one or more other probability samples.

Dependent variable   a research variable whose changing data values are interpreted by the researcher as caused by changes in one or more independent variables.

Depth interview   a qualitative research technique that measures psychological characteristics by a lengthy, unstructured interview between a researcher and a respondent.

Descriptive research   investigations that explain details about consumers, organizations, objects, concepts, or events.

Design effect   the square of the standard error of a complex sample divided by the square of the standard error of a simple random sample of the same size.

Dichotomous question   an item on a data collection form having a structured response format with only two possible responses.

Dichotomous variable   a discrete variable that takes on only two values.

Discrete variable   a variable that takes on only certain values, usually integers.

Disguise question   an item included on the data collection form to conceal from respondents either the purpose or the sponsor of the research.

Disproportionate sample   a probability sample whose size in a stratum bears no relationship to the stratum's population size.

Dual-recording   a research practice used in telephone interviewing where a supervisor simultaneously records responses along with a telephone interviewer.

Editing   the examining of data for errors and the taking of remedial action when an error is discovered.

Estimate   an expected typical value for a variable based on other values for that variable.

Ethics   a code of morals or standards of conduct.

Experiment   a primary data collection method that investigates the extent that a change in one or more variables leads to a change in another for an identified population under controlled conditions.

Experimental group   test units in an experiment that are exposed to one or more experimental treatments.

Experimenter expectancy effect   the influence on experimental results due to the experimenter's anticipation of results.

Exploratory research   investigations that help a decision maker and researcher understand marketing problems more completely by identifying both potential causes and potential solutions.

External validity   the degree to which conclusions drawn about a treatment in an experiment apply in the real world.

Extraneous variable   a factor other than a treatment that influences a dependent variable measurement in an experiment.

Factor   an independent variable in an experiment.

Factor analysis   a procedure that explains the underlying structure of relationships among a large set of variables by identifying a smaller number of mathematically derived variables called factors.

Factorial design   a multifactor design.

Field experiment   an experiment taking place in a real world environment.

Filtering question   an item on the data collection form that qualifies a respondent for later questions that would otherwise be meaningless.

First-order relationship   a relationship between two variables considering or controlling for the effects of a third variable.

Fixed costs of sampling   sampling related expenses whose total stays constant while sample size changes.

Focus group interview   a qualitative research technique that measures psychological characteristics by a lengthy, weakly structured interview between a researcher and a group of respondents.

Follow-up request   a second or later invitation to respond to a mail survey.

Forecast   expected typical values for sales data.

Frequency distribution   a tabular presentation of counts of variable values falling within specified ranges or classes.

Friedman two-way analysis of variance   a statistical procedure testing the hypothesis of equal medians using three or more dependent samples.

Gamma   a measure of relationship between two ordinal variables.

Halo effect   the tendency of respondents to respond to a belief item based on their general feelings and not on their reaction to the item itself.

Histogram   a bar chart or pictorial presentation of a frequency distribution.

Hypothesis test   a statistical procedure that examines the potential falsity of a statement phrased in quantitative terms.

Independent sample   a probability sample whose members are selected separately from and without regard for members in any other probability sample.

Independent variable   a concept whose changing data values are viewed by the researcher as influencing data values for a dependent variable.

Internal consistency reliability   a procedure for assessing reliability of a multiple item scale or similar measurement process using one group of respondents and one occasion.

Internal validity   the degree to which treatments and not extraneous variables in an experiment cause changes in values of the dependent variable.

Interval data   numbers that indicate equality and inequality, direction, and distance of measurement objects on some variable of interest.

Interval estimate   a range of values as an estimate.

Item nonresponse   a failure to respond to any item on a data collection form.

Item to total score correlation coefficient   an expression of the relationship between a rating scale item's responses and the total scores obtained by summing responses to all rating scale items.

Judgment or purposive sampling   a nonprobability sampling procedure where population elements are selected on the basis of an expert's judgment that elements satisfy a stated purpose.

Knowledge question   an item on a data collection form that measures the respondent's awareness and understanding of consumption related experiences.

Kruskal-Wallis one-way analysis of variance test   a statistical procedure testing the hypothesis of equal medians in three or more populations using three independent samples.

Laboratory experiment   an experiment taking place in an isolated, controlled environment.

Lambda   a measure of relationship between two nominal variables.

Likert scale   a rating scale consisting of a set of belief statements placed next to a set of response categories using agree/disagree steps as anchors.

Mall intercept survey   a data collection method executed partly or entirely at one or more shopping areas.

Managerial significance   the import of research results on a decision.

Mann-Whitney U test   a statistical procedure testing the hypothesis of equal medians in two populations using two independent samples.

Marketing information system (MKIS) an integrated activity in an organization that collects, structures, and transmits marketing data to decision makers on a regular, orderly basis.

Marketing research the systematic, impartial, and complete design, execution, and reporting of investigations to help solve product, price, distribution, and promotion problems.

Marketing researcher a person who performs marketing research.

Marketing research design a set of plans to execute a specific marketing research project.

Marketing research process a sequence of interrelated activities common to all marketing research projects.

Marketing research proposal a document summarizing intended research and submitted to the decision maker for approval before research begins.

Measurement process rules to assign numbers to objects to indicate their possession of some variable of interest.

Median the measurement value possessed by the middle ($n/2$) observation when all n values have been ordered from least to most or most to least.

Mini-market (forced-distribution test market) a test market employing a private service to obtain distribution in retail stores.

Mode the measurement value occurring most frequently in a set of values.

Multiple-choice question an item on a data collection form that has a structured response format with more than two responses.

Multicollinearity when two or more predictor variables in a multiple regression analysis correlate highly with each other.

Multifactor design an experiment testing the effect of more than one independent variable on the same group of test units at the same time.

Multiple regression a procedure using values of two or more interval or ratio variables to predict or forecast values for one interval or ratio variable through an equation expressing a straight line.

Multivariate relationship a relationship between three or more variables or a relationship between two variables while controlling for one or more other variables.

Nominal data words, numbers, or other symbols that indicate only equality or inequality of measurement objects on some variable of interest.

Nonordered variable a variable whose values do not allow expression of ordered relationship.

Nonprobability sample a sampling procedure where each sampling unit has an unknown chance of being selected.

Nonrespondents members of a population of interest who refuse to participate in a survey or who are not-at-home.

Nonresponse error difference between an obtained data value and the value found if all designated sample members had responded.

Nonresponse rate the quantity obtained by subtracting the response rate from 1.0.

Normal distribution a bell-shaped, symmetrical probability distribution.

Not-at-home error part of nonresponse error caused by sample members who are outside their residences during the time(s) of survey contact.

Null hypothesis a statement assumed to be true and tested in an hypothesis test.

Objective forecast   a prediction for sales based on explicit rules that manipulate quantitative data.

Observation   a data collection method employing perception and little or no interaction between researcher and data sources.

Obtrusive measurement   a data collection method requiring the sample member's cooperation before he or she responds.

On-line interview   a data collection method where a computer displays questions and immediately accepts responses, usually used with telephone and personal interviews.

Ordered variable   a variable whose values allow expression of ordered relationship.

Ordinal data   numbers that indicate equality and inequality and direction of measurement objects on some variable of interest.

Outlier   an extreme data value.

Partial relationship   a relationship between two variables controlling for one or more other variables.

Pearson product-moment correlation   a measure of relationship between two interval variables, two ratio variables, or one interval and one ratio variable.

Percentile   a variable value such that a specified proportion of data values lies below it.

Performance variance analysis   an analysis of differences between planned and actual values for revenues, costs, and other marketing related performance parameters.

Phi correlation   a measure of relationship between two dichotomous variables.

Plants   persons employed by the surveying firm to act as a respondent and check and evaluate interviewer behavior.

Point estimate   a single value estimate.

Population element   one individual data source in the population of interest.

Population of interest   a description of a set of data sources that in theory are desired to provide measurements.

Population parameter   a descriptive measure of a population of interest.

Poststratification   the practice of stratifying population elements after sample selection and not before.

Precision   half of the width of a confidence interval; the value $Zs_{\bar{x}}$.

Prediction   an expected typical value for a variable based on values of another or several other variables.

Predictive validity   the ability of a measurement item or process to forecast future behavior.

Premium   an incentive, often monetary, used as an inducement to reduce refusal errors in a survey.

Pretest   trial of the data collection form on a representative sample of respondents for the purpose of evaluating aspects of the research design.

Primary cluster   a first level cluster in a multi-stage cluster sample.

Primary data source   People, objects, or organizations that provide information specifically to solve the marketing problem under investigation.

Probability proportional to size sampling (PPS)   a probability sampling procedure where primary clusters are selected in proportion to their size and equal sample sizes then taken in each primary cluster.

Probability sample a sampling procedure where each sampling unit has a known chance of being selected.

Probability statement a statement about the value for a population parameter that holds true with a $1 - \alpha$ likelihood.

Profile analysis a plot of average belief scores for several consumption related alternatives as obtained from applying a rating scale to one or more samples of respondents.

Projective methods (techniques) qualitative research that measures psychological characteristics with respect to sensitive or threatening research topics; includes word association, sentence completion, and construction techniques.

Proportion the number of objects in a set that possess a specified measurement value divided by the number of objects.

Psychological characteristic question an item on a data collection form that measures abstract qualities or features of human behavior.

Purchase intention question an item on a data collection form that measures the respondent's subjective probability of purchase during some specified time period.

Qualitative psychological research data collection techniques that measure psychological characteristics in words (not numbers).

Quantitative psychological research data collection techniques that measure psychological characteristics in numbers (not words).

Quasi-experimental design a research design similar to an experiment but using nonrandom assignment of test units to experimental and control groups.

Question sequence the order of items in a data collection form.

Quota sampling a nonprobability sampling procedure where population elements are selected based on their possession of selected socioeconomic characteristics.

Random digit dialing a procedure used in telephone surveys to generate a probability sample of telephone numbers often without using a telephone directory.

Random error a nonrepeatable research inaccuracy.

Randomized block design a blocked design.

Random numbers numbers that are independent of each other and have the same probability distribution.

Random selection a choice among alternatives based solely on chance.

Randomized response technique a method of obtaining answers to a sensitive question from one part of a sample by asking an innocuous question of another part.

Range the difference between the largest and smallest values for a variable in a set of data.

Rating scale a set of multiple choice questions or statements that measures a psychological characteristic.

Ratio data numbers that indicate equality and inequality, direction, distance, and absolute amounts with respect to some variable of interest as possessed by measurement objects.

Raw data matrix an array in n rows and m columns showing responses to all m items on a data collection form by each of n respondents.

Refusal error part of nonresponse error caused by identified sample members who decide not to respond to an item or to the entire data collection form.

Relationship between variables when measurement values for two or more variables as obtained from a group of sampling units at a point in time either occur jointly or vary together.

Relationship direction whether a relationship is positive or negative.

Relationship strength the degree of shared variation between two or more variables.

Reliability the ability of any measurement item or process to measure a concept with a minimum of random error.

Repeated measure design a research design where data sources provide a series of responses over time.

Research accuracy the absence of stable and random departures in the data from usually unknown, true values.

Research hypotheses statements in a form that allow statistical testing.

Research variable a concept that takes on different values.

Response anchors words that describe response categories in a rating scale.

Response error difference between an obtained data value and a true, unknown data value for respondents, caused by the measurement process.

Response format the procedure used to indicate answers to an item on a data collection form, may be unstructured or structured.

Response rate the number of completed data collection forms divided by the number of sample members contacted.

Response sequence error (position bias) a response error caused by the order of response categories or alternatives in a structured response format.

Sample a subset of the population of interest.

Sample statistic a descriptive measure of a sample; an estimate of a population parameter.

Sampling control a survey method's potential for gathering information only from designated members of the population of interest.

Sampling distribution of $\overline{X}$ a description of the relative frequency of all values for $\overline{X}$ possible when taking samples of size n in a population of size N.

Sampling error the difference between a data value obtained from a sample and the true, unknown data value for the population, caused by the random sampling process.

Sampling fraction the ratio of sample size, n, divided by population size, N.

Sampling frame a list of population elements or groups of population elements actually available for selection as a sample.

Sampling plan a written summary that describes the population of interest, sampling frame, sampling procedures, and sample size for a marketing research project.

Sampling unit a population element or group of population elements listed on the sampling frame.

Satisfaction question an item on a data collection form that measures the respondent's comparison of beliefs about a product before and after purchase.

Scatter diagram (scattergram) a pictorial display of the joint distribution of measurement values for two variables as obtained from one group of sampling units.

Secondary data source some person, object, or organization that provides information originally collected for some other purpose than to solve the marketing problem under investigation.

Segment contribution analysis an analysis of contributions to profit and uncontrollable fixed expenses for identified marketing units.

Semantic differential scale a rating scale consisting of a set of opposite terms or phrases each separated by a stepped set of response categories.

Significant digits numbers that have meaning (rather than numbers that are artifacts of an arithmetic operation).

Simple linear regression a procedure using values for one interval or ratio variable to predict or forecast values for one other interval or ratio variable through an equation expressing a straight line.

Simple random sampling (SRS) a probability sampling procedure where each combination of population elements of sample size n has an equal chance of being selected.

Simulation a data collection method using an abstract model as its data source.

Single factor design an experimental design investigating the effects of one independent variable.

Situation analysis part of the problem definition process, an examination of circumstances surrounding the research request and the marketing problem's potential solutions.

Skip instructions statements on a data collection form that guide respondents past meaningless questions.

Social desirability a tendency for respondents to answer questions in a manner consistent with core-cultural values.

Socioeconomic characteristic question an item on a data collection form that measures demographic, social, or economic features of people.

Spearman's rho a measure of relationship between two sets of ranks.

Spurious relation a noncausal relationship between two variables that is explained by the variables' common relationship with a third variable.

Stable error a repeatable research inaccuracy.

Standard consolidated statistical area (SCSA) an area containing one standard metropolitan statistical area of at least 1,000,000 inhabitants plus other, adjacent standard metropolitan statistical areas.

Standard deviation the positive square root of the variance.

Standard error the standard deviation divided by the square root of sample size; the standard deviation of the sampling distribution of $\overline{X}$.

Standard industrial classification (SIC) a code containing 2 or more digits to identify the nature of industrial activities.

Standard market a test market using regular distribution channels.

Standard metropolitan statistical area (SMSA) a one or more county area containing a city with 50,000 or more inhabitants.

Standard normal variable Z, a variable whose probability distribution is normal, with mean 0 and variance 1.

Stapel scale a rating scale consisting of a set of terms, each term placed between a stepped set of numeric response categories.

Statistical significance the probability in an hypothesis test of making a Type I error.

Stratification variable a variable used to separate population elements into homogeneous strata or groups.

Stratified sampling a probability sampling procedure where a separate probability sample is taken in each group or stratum in a population of interest.

Stratum   a homogeneous group of population elements on some variable.

Subjective forecast   a prediction for sales based on a person's intuition, experience, and judgment.

Subsample   part of a sample that receives special treatment or measurement.

Suppressor variable   a control variable that produces a strong relationship between two other variables when their zero-order relationship is weak.

Survey   a data collection method that systematically questions members of the population of interest.

Systematic sampling   a probability sampling procedure where every kth population element listed on the sampling frame is selected after a random start within the first k elements.

Test market   a field experiment, usually for a new product, that investigates the effects of different price, distribution, and promotion strategies on consumers, retailers, and wholesalers.

Times series forecast   a forecast that explicitly considers trend, cyclical, seasonal, and irregular influences on sales.

Treatment   a level of intensity or form of a single independent variable in a single factor experiment or combinations of levels or forms of two or more independent variables in a multifactor experiment.

Type I error   the probability of rejecting H_0 in an hypothesis test when it is in fact correct.

Type II error   the probability of accepting H_0 in an hypothesis test when it is in fact false.

Unitary portion   part of a data collection form that contains items measuring similar variables and using a similar response format.

Unobtrusive measurement   a data collection method where researchers observe behavior or artifacts of behavior without the knowledge of members of the sample.

Validation procedures   editing activities to confirm selected answers to selected data collection forms (usually 10 to 15%).

Validity   the ability of any measurement item or process to measure the concept it is meant to measure.

Variable   a concept or property of a measurement object that takes on different values.

Variable costs of sampling   sampling related expenses whose total varies directly with sample size.

Variance   a measure of dispersion; the sum of squared deviations of a set of measurements about their mean divided either by population size (population variance) or by sample size minus 1 (sample variance).

Versatility   a survey method's potential to apply to a variety of marketing problems.

Wilcoxon signed-rank test   a statistical procedure to test hypotheses about values for the median in one population or to test the hypothesis of equal medians in two dependent populations.

Zero-order relationship   a relationship between two variables without considering or controlling for the effects of another variable.

Author Index

Subject Index